Cooking Light®

ANNUAL RECIPES 2015

Oxmoor House®

A Year at *Cooking Light*

2014 was an exceptional year at *Cooking Light*. Fresh produce from home gardens (including our own *Cooking Light* Garden) and farmers markets alike were a fixture in our Test Kitchen and on the pages of our magazine as locally sourced food continues to thrive. We tapped various experts to share their knowledge on topics ranging from canning to vegan cuisine to grilling and myriad topics in between.

It was a year filled with progress and new culinary discoveries as we forged new ground for healthy food that's easy and delicious. We remain constant in our commitments to developing recipes that are achievable for the busy home cook.

Carrot Cake Sandwich Cookies *(page 92)*
All the pleasures of traditional carrot cake in a fun-to-eat package. Fluffy cream cheese frosting serves as the delightful sandwich "filling."

Here are some of the highlights from 2014:

• In January, we encouraged readers to start the year off light by offering healthier versions of classic comfort foods. Our Test Kitchen created versions of six recipes for foods like spaghetti, lasagna, and meatloaf—dishes notorious for derailing healthy eating resolutions—that contain half their traditional calorie counts (page 21).

• "High Praise for the Lowly Tilapia" (page 82) in April showcased ways to prepare this simple, easy-to-love fish. Tilapia is one of the most widely consumed fish species in the country and a food that our readers most often ask us how to cook. This selection of delicious and healthy recipes and our shopping and preparation tips are sure to make tilapia one of your most-requested and easiest-to-make dishes.

• We debuted our "Fast Issue" in May, delivering on our promise that every recipe be made in less than 25 minutes. Our collection of "25 Mains in 25 Minutes or Less" (page 104) was one of our most tasty and practical features yet. Sorted by cuisine—everything from Asian to Italian—these dishes will satisfy cravings and leave you with time to spare.

• In June, we shared our annual "Summer Cookbook" (page 137) that highlights the best the season has to offer. Deborah Madison, writer of *Vegetable Literacy*—an instant classic on cooking with garden-grown goodness—shared her wisdom and a fresh crop of recipes for fruits and vegetables.

• The topic of grilling has never been hotter. In August, the *Cooking Light* Test Kitchen fired up the grill to come up with our most flavorful and satisfying grilled dishes yet. Not only does the grill add that special hint of charcoal and smoke to a sundry of foods, but also it is the healthy-eater's favorite tool for low-fat feasting (page 193).

• This year we introduced Keith Schroeder as a new columnist for our regular "Cooking Class" feature. Each month Keith teaches us a new lesson for the kitchen, making recipes approachable and fun by explaining why each ingredient is used to make food taste delicious. In October, Keith made our mouths water with his recipe for "Slow Baked Chicken Thighs with Tomato, Fennel and Lemon" (page 293).

• And as always, in November we compiled our most festive, healthy, and filling recipes to create our reader-favorite "Holiday Cookbook" (page 307). The holidays are a time to serve traditional and well-loved meals; however, they are also the perfect opportunity to cook new favorites for friends and family. We are confident that this year's selection of drinks, entrées, sides, and desserts will please any crowd.

At *Cooking Light*, we thrive on the input we receive from you, our faithful readers. We deeply appreciate your feedback whether it is through Instagram, Facebook, e-mail, snail mail, and beyond. May this compilation bring you delicious meals for years to come.

—the editors of *Cooking Light*

Hazelnut Lace *(page 126)*
A cross between your favorite crispy cookie, caramel candy, and nut brittle, ready in just 20 minutes. Drizzle with warm hazelnut-chocolate spread for a dazzling dessert.

Our Favorite Recipes

Not all recipes are created equal.

At *Cooking Light*, only those that have received a passing grade from our Test Kitchen staff and food editors—a group with very high standards—make it onto the pages of our magazine. We test each recipe rigorously, often two or three times, to ensure that it's healthy, reliable, and tastes as good as it possibly can. So which of our recipes are our favorites? They're the dishes that we can't forget: The ones readers write or call us about, the ones our staff regularly make for their own families and friends.

▶ **Crab and Heirloom Tomato Salad** *(page 195)*
This fresh, no-cook salad is a staff favorite. Multicolored heirloom tomatoes and mini sweet bell peppers make this a gorgeous 20-minute main.

▼ **Lemon-Caper-Parmesan Potato Salad Bites** *(page 162)*
Parmesan potato poppers are creamy, cheesy, and irresistible, with a briny bite from finely chopped capers. Friends will beg for the recipe.

Farro, Cherry, and Walnut Salad *(page 141)*
We take this summer fruit out of dessert territory. Sweet-tart cherries, crisp celery, and walnuts enhance whole-grain farro.

Chicken Stew and Dumplings *(page 286)*
It'll be tough to keep your hands off the mini drop biscuits as the stew cooks, but the wait is worth the reward.
Hearty vegetables absorb the rich, chicken-y flavor.

Classic Lasagna with Meat Sauce *(page 279)*
We lose half the saturated fat and sodium, yet
keep all the cheesy, meaty, saucy goodness of
a classic lasagna.

Pan-Charred Green Beans with Tarragon
(page 89)
A quick, high heat sauté concentrates flavor, and a butter-tarragon sauce makes for a divine side dish.

Isan-Inspired Larb
(page 148)
Fresh herbs, lime, and chiles create a symphony of bold flavors in a refreshing, authentically Thai salad, full of color and texture.

Slow-Baked Chicken Thighs
(page 293)
Throw conventional cook times out the window and braise the chicken low and slow. Fennel, garlic, and tomato form a cohesive sauce; thigh meat becomes almost buttery.

Braised Oxtail and Short Rib Stew
(page 288)
Short ribs and oxtail yield meltingly tender results in the Dutch oven. The sauce is dark and rich, almost gravy-like. Serve up a bowl on cold winter nights.

BLT Pizza with White Sauce *(page 162)*
America's favorite sandwich takes to slice form. Even the signature mayo spread morphs into a garlicky white sauce drizzle.

Sweet and Sour Chicken *(page 108)*
A vibrant, flavor-packed sauce coats tender chicken pieces—faster, healthier, and more delicious than any neighborhood take out.

Carne Asada Pizza *(page 251)*
Mexico and Italy come together in one ingenious pie: charred steak, poblanos, cool queso fresco, and adobo-spiked marinara top fresh pizza dough.

Mesquite-Smoked Beer Can Chicken *(page 192)*
Five ingredients, one stunning entrée. The beer slowly evaporates inside the chicken on the grill, so the bird absorbs smoke and stays wonderfully juicy.

Coconut Curry Halibut *(page 25)*
Light coconut milk, steeped with red curry, lime, fresh mint, and basil, reduces to a beautiful sauce. A pile of gingery stir-fried vegetables rounds out the meal.

Chicken Tetrazzini *(page 29)*
Keep everything you love about this comforting chicken casserole—creamy sauce, pasta, vegetables, and a crunchy crumb topping—and lose the fat. Our version saves 15 grams of saturated fat and 500mg sodium per serving.

Watermelon-Lime Soda *(page 163)*
Incredibly refreshing and spiked with fresh ginger, this cool drink leaves all sugary alternatives behind.

Mom's Creamy Chicken and Broccoli Casserole *(page 33)*
Classic chicken casserole gets a total makeover, with less than half the calories of the original and all the cheesy, creamy goodness. Did we mention it's ready in 20 minutes?

Chicken Cutlets with Mushrooms and Pearl Onions *(page 48)*
A touch of butter gets the rich mushroom sauce gorgeously glossy. Pair with simply steamed haricots verts for a French-inspired meal.

Individual White Chicken Pizzas *(page 55)*
Pack your freezer full with cheesy pies, individually wrapped for convenience. Quick, homemade ricotta cheese takes a weeknight favorite over the top.

Tahini Swirl Brownies *(page 73)*
Think sesame seed paste is just for hummus? Think again. A swirl of tahini compliments bittersweet chocolate brownies, adding nutty depth of flavor.

Salmon Salad on Arugula *(page 78)*
A beautiful salad designed to give you maximum energy, from omega-3-rich salmon to iron-rich greens, plus an added hit of vitamin C from a squeeze of citrus.

Spicy Bean and Quinoa Salad with Mole *(page 78)*
We pack those smoky, citrusy, earthy flavors into a quick vinaigrette, perfect for a hearty vegetarian quinoa salad.

Fennel Soup with Almond-Mint Topping *(page 113)*
Fennel is gently sautéed until tender, and then pureed with cannellini beans for a silky smooth finish.

Spaghetti with Toasty Garlic Tomato Sauce *(page 147)*
Thinly sliced garlic and grape tomatoes melt into a fresh, simple sauce, ready in just 19 minutes.

Tomatillo Braised Chicken Thighs *(page 112)*
Chicken thighs braise in fresh tomatillo sauce, brightened with jalapeño and cilantro, and finished with tangy crema.

Quick Pickled Peaches *(page 198)*
Slightly spicy and tangy-sweet, pickled peaches perk up any dessert and make simply roasted pork or chicken sing.

Caprese Mac and Cheese *(page 268)*
Caprese salad and mac and cheese come together in one weeknight favorite. Creamy pasta combined with fresh tomatoes, mozzarella, and basil take a classic to new heights.

Slow Cooker Red Beans and Rice *(page 253)*
The slow cooker transforms humble dried beans, aromatics, and andouille sausage into a pot-licking good meal with big, rich New Orleans flavor.

Deep Dish Mushroom and Onion Pizza *(page 252)*
This lighter, ultimate Chicago-style pie has all the hallmarks of the original: a chewy, slightly crisp crust and plenty of saucy, cheesy filling.

Golden Beet Soup with Toasted Grains *(page 369)*
You could say this soup borrows its whimsy from Dr. Seuss. Earthy gold beets and fennel form a velvety soup base. A pickled striped beet slaw cuts through the earthiness.

Rustic Chard, Potato, and Goat Cheese Tart *(page 336)*
The piecrust is tender (and low in saturated fat, thanks to olive oil), yet sturdy enough to hold plenty of vegetable filling. Carnivores won't miss the meat, and vegetarians will have a hearty winter main worth bragging about.

Thyme-Crusted Tenderloin with Cognac Butter *(page 325)*
Start with a beautifully cooked, naturally lean tenderloin and splurge on a cognac-spiked butter topper. Skip the spuds and balance the plate with a creamy carrot mash and Brussels sprouts topped with crispy shallots.

Cranberry Hoisin Turkey Buns *(page 317)*
Thanksgiving leftovers have never looked so colorful or been so fun to eat. Top pillowy steamed buns with fresh pickled cucumber, shredded turkey tossed in hoisin sauce, and tart-sweet cranberry sauce.

Fudge Brownie Pops *(page 327)*
Cake pops have nothing on super fudgy brownie pops. Bittersweet chocolate and unsweetened cocoa deliver a dark chocolate wallop in the brownie, which is crumbled, rolled, and dipped into melted chocolate. Delicious straight out of the fridge or freezer.

Risotto-Style Pasta with Caramelized Onions *(page 312)*
Give short, acini di pepe pasta the risotto treatment for rich, cheesy, creamy results. This dish received top marks by our Test Kitchen staff.

CONTENTS

ISBN-13: 978-0-8487-4362-8
ISBN-10: 0-8487-4362-8

Printed in the United States of America
First Printing 2014

Be sure to check with your health-care provider before making any changes in your diet.

Oxmoor House
Editorial Director: Leah McLaughlin
Creative Director: Felicity Keane
Art Director: Christopher Rhoads
Executive Photo Director: Iain Bagwell
Executive Food Director: Grace Parisi
Managing Editor: Elizabeth Tyler Austin
Assistant Managing Editor: Jeanne de Lathouder

Cooking Light Annual Recipes 2015
Senior Editor: Betty Wong
Editor: Rachel Quinlivan West, R.D.
Editorial Assistant: April Smitherman
Food Stylist: Victoria E. Cox
Senior Photo Stylist: Mindi Shapiro
Associate Production Manager: Kimberly Marshall
Assistant Production Manager: Diane Rose Keener

Contributors
Assistant Project Editors: Megan Brown, Laura Medlin
Designer: Carol Damsky
Copy Editor: Jacqueline Giovanelli
Proofreader: Adrienne Davis
Indexer: Mary Ann Laurens
Fellows: Kylie Dazzo, Nicole Fisher, Amanda Widis

Time Home Entertainment Inc.
Vice President and Associate Publisher: Margot Schupf
Vice President, Finance: Vandana Patel
Executive Director, Marketing Services: Carol Pittard
Publishing Director: Megan Pearlman
Assistant General Counsel: Simone Procas

Cooking Light
Editor: Scott Mowbray
Creative Director: Dimity Jones
Executive Editor, Food: Ann Taylor Pittman
Executive Editor, Digital: Allison Long Lowery
Senior Food Editors: Timothy Q. Cebula, Cheryl Slocum
Senior Editor: Cindy Hatcher
Nutrition Editor: Sidney Fry, M.S., R.D.
Associate Editor: Hannah Klinger
Assistant Editor: Kimberly Holland
Assistant Food Editor: Darcy Lenz
Recipe Testers and Developers: Robin Bashinsky, Adam Hickman, Deb Wise
Art Directors: Rachel Cardina Lasserre, Sheri Wilson
Senior Designer: Hagen Stegall Baker
Designer: Nicole Gerrity
Tablet Designer: Daniel Boone
Photo Editor: Amy Delaune
Senior Photographer: Randy Mayor
Assistant Prop Stylists: Lindsey Lower, Claire Spollen
Chief Food Stylist: Kellie Gerber Kelley
Food Styling Assistant: Blakeslee Wright Giles
Production Director: Liz Rhoades
Production Editor: Hazel Reynolds Eddins
Production Coordinator: Christina Harrison
Copy Director: Susan Roberts McWilliams
Copy Editor: Kate Johnson
Office Manager: Alice Summerville
CookingLight.com Editor: Mallory Daughtery Brasseale
CookingLight.com Assistant Editor/Producer: Michelle Klug
Produce Guru: Robert Schueller
Garden Gurus: Mary Beth and David Shaddix

To order additional publications, call 1-800-765-6400 or 1-800-491-0551.

For more books to enrich your life, visit **oxmoorhouse.com**

To search, savor, and share thousands of recipes, visit **myrecipes.com**

Cover: *Chicken Parmesan with Spaghetti (page 24)*
Back Cover (left to right): *Creamy Asparagus, Herb, and Pea Pasta (page 93), Chicken Cutlets with Mushrooms and Pearl Onions (page 48), No-Bake Peach Pie (page 206)*
Page 1: *Quick Pickled Peaches (page 205)*

START YOUR YEAR OFF LIGHT

Morning-to-midnight recipes and tips for loving every bite of food you eat in the new year!

THE MORNING GRAINS SOLUTION

These bowls of hot cereal and nourishing toppings get you to 75% of your daily whole-grains goal before you walk out the door.

Creamy Wheat with Pear and Ginger
This whole-grain hot cereal loads 42g whole grains into each packet and is ready in just 1 minute.

Toss ½ cup sliced fresh pear with 1½ teaspoons brown sugar and a dash of cinnamon. Prepare 1 packet *Cream of Wheat Healthy Grain* according to package directions. Top with pear mixture, 1 tablespoon chopped toasted walnuts, and 1 crushed gingersnap.

CALORIES 325; **FAT** 7.1g (sat 0.7g); **PROTEIN** 7.9g; **CARB** 60.6g; **FIBER** 8.2g; **SODIUM** 258mg

SWEET DESSERT COMFORT IN A HEALTHY BREAKFAST BOWL.

Steel Cut Oats with Warm Berry Compote
These steel cut oats pack in 41g whole grains per serving.

Melt 1 teaspoon butter in a saucepan over medium heat. Add 2 tablespoons honey, 2 teaspoons fresh lemon juice, a dash of ground cinnamon, and 1 (12-ounce) bag frozen mixed berries; bring to a boil. Reduce heat; simmer 5 minutes. Spoon ⅓ cup compote over 1 serving prepared *McCann's Quick & Easy Steel Cut Irish Oatmeal*; top with chopped fresh basil. Refrigerate remaining compote; reheat as needed.

CALORIES 218; **FAT** 3.8g (sat 1.1g); **PROTEIN** 6.7g; **CARB** 46.2g; **FIBER** 6.5g; **SODIUM** 1mg

Rolled Oats with Carrot and Apple
A mix of oats, wheat, barley, and rye with a robust 37g whole grains per serving.

Combine ⅔ cup 1% low-fat milk, 2 tablespoons grated carrot, 2 tablespoons grated apple, 1 tablespoon golden raisins, 1½ teaspoons brown sugar, and a dash each of nutmeg, ground ginger, and cinnamon in a microwave-safe bowl. Add 1 packet *365 Everyday Value Organic Multigrain with Flax Hot Cereal*. Microwave at HIGH 45 to 60 seconds or until thick. Top with 1 tablespoon ⅓-less-fat cream cheese mixed with 1 teaspoon powdered sugar.

CALORIES 252; **FAT** 6.1g (sat 1.8g); **PROTEIN** 6.5g; **CARB** 48g; **FIBER** 5.1g; **SODIUM** 83mg

Quinoa with Strawberries and Buttermilk
Cook quinoa for dinner, save leftovers for breakfast, and start the day with 46g whole grains per serving.

Combine ¾ cup cooked quinoa *(such as Ancient Harvest Traditional Organic)* and ¼ cup low-fat buttermilk in a microwave-safe bowl. Microwave at HIGH 45 seconds. Stir; let stand 1 minute. Top with ½ cup sliced strawberries, 2 tablespoons toasted sliced almonds, and 1 teaspoon honey.

CALORIES 301; **FAT** 9.1g (sat 0.8g); **PROTEIN** 11.1g; **CARB** 45.8g; **FIBER** 6.9g; **SODIUM** 76mg

Spiced Warm Muesli with Honeyed Ricotta
With grains, nuts, and a touch of brown sugar, this muesli gives you 38g whole grains per ⅔ cup.

Combine ⅔ cup *Alpen Original All Natural Muesli* and ½ cup 1% low-fat milk in a microwave-safe bowl. Microwave at HIGH 1 minute. Combine ½ cup part-skim ricotta, 1½ teaspoons honey, and ½ teaspoon grated lemon rind. Dollop 2 tablespoons over each serving of warm muesli, and top with chopped fresh mint. Save remaining ricotta mixture for the rest of the week's breakfast grains.

CALORIES 309; **FAT** 6.6g (sat 2.3g); **PROTEIN** 13.7g; **CARB** 49.1g; **FIBER** 5g; **SODIUM** 108mg

Crunchy Peanut Butter Bulgur with Berries

This grain sets up while you sleep—a no-cook cereal with 40g whole grains per serving.

Combine 1 cup uncooked *Bob's Red Mill Bulgur* and 1½ cups 1% low-fat milk in a small bowl. Cover and refrigerate overnight. Fluff in the morning. Place ¾ cup soaked grains in a small microwave-safe bowl. Microwave at HIGH 1 minute. Stir in 1 tablespoon peanut butter. Top with ½ cup raspberries, 1 tablespoon plain fat-free Greek yogurt, and 2 teaspoons chopped peanuts.

CALORIES 327; **FAT** 12.8g (sat 2.8g); **PROTEIN** 14.8g; **CARB** 43.5g; **FIBER** 11.9g; **SODIUM** 126mg

Coconut-Banana Grape-Nuts with Lime

These crunchy wheat-and-barley nuggets are packed with 49g whole grains per serving.

Combine ½ cup *Grape-Nuts cereal* and ⅓ cup 1% low-fat milk in a microwave-safe bowl. Microwave at HIGH for 1 minute (less for more crunch). Top with ⅓ cup sliced banana, 1 tablespoon toasted unsweetened flaked coconut, 1½ teaspoons chopped macadamia nuts, a dash of cinnamon, and a squeeze of lime, if desired.

CALORIES 351; **FAT** 8.3g (sat 3.9g); **PROTEIN** 11.9g; **CARB** 61.2g; **FIBER** 9.4g; **SODIUM** 328mg

JAZZED UP MICROWAVE LUNCHES

6 ways to turn up the nutrition—and flavor—on frozen take-to-work meals

Kashi Lemongrass Coconut Chicken + ½ cup diced mango (either fresh or frozen, thawed) + 1 tablespoon slivered toasted almonds

This dish has a very strong lemongrass flavor. The mango softens that a bit and goes well with the coconut flakes; plus it pumps up the fiber. The almonds add a nice crunch to the other tender components—juicy chicken, veggies, and whole grains.

CALORIES 384; **FAT** 11.4g (sat 4.3g); **PROTEIN** 20g; **CARB** 51g; **FIBER** 11g; **SODIUM** 680mg

Gardenburger Black Bean Chipotle Burger + ¼ cup sliced cucumber + 2 tablespoons hummus + ½ whole-wheat pita

We sauced up this flavorful vegan burger with a generous dollop of hummus and added cucumber slices for crunch. The pita helps boost fiber without the higher sodium tally of a burger bun.

CALORIES 234; **FAT** 6.5g (sat 0.9g); **PROTEIN** 10.4g; **CARB** 39g; **FIBER** 8.8g; **SODIUM** 671mg

> IT'S ALL HERE: FRUIT, VEGGIES, WHOLE GRAINS, PROTEIN, AND HEART-HEALTHY NUTS.

Amy's Light & Lean Italian Vegetable Pizza + 2 tablespoons chopped toasted walnuts

Walnuts add richness, crunch, and healthy fat to this multigrain thin-crust pizza that's topped with spinach, artichoke hearts, mushrooms, and part-skim mozzarella. The best part: You get to eat the whole thing!

CALORIES 378; **FAT** 16g (sat 3g); **PROTEIN** 15g; **CARB** 38g; **FIBER** 5g; **SODIUM** 560mg

> GET YOUR GREEN ON! SPINACH AND AVOCADO PACK IN FLAVOR AND NUTRIENTS.

Lean Cuisine Salad Additions Southwest-Style Chicken + 2 cups baby spinach + ½ avocado

This kit contains everything but the greens. Inside you'll find tender grilled chicken strips and a hearty mix of black beans, corn, and roasted peppers—plus a separate package of crunchy tortilla strips and a kicky chipotle ranch. Adding the spinach instead of romaine ups the iron ante, and the avocado pairs perfectly with the southwestern flavors.

CALORIES 388; **FAT** 19.5g (sat 3g); **PROTEIN** 21g; **CARB** 34g; **FIBER** 10g; **SODIUM** 642mg

Annie Chun's Sprouted Brown Sticky Rice + 1 cup Cascadian Farm Chinese-Style Stirfry Blend + 2 teaspoons Annie Chun's Gochujang Korean Sweet & Spicy Sauce

When paired with a delicious blend of Asian-inspired vegetables and a spicy-sweet sauce, a simple bowl of sticky rice makes for a satisfying lunch. It's plenty tasty and takes just minutes to prepare.

CALORIES 325; **FAT** 1.4g (sat 0g); **PROTEIN** 7g; **CARB** 71g; **FIBER** 5g; **SODIUM** 249mg

Weight Watchers Smart Ones Chicken Fajitas + ¼ avocado + 2 tablespoons salsa

Two fajitas + rice and beans = one hearty meal. Seasoned peppers and onions add a pop of flavor to chicken strips, and the rice and beans that come with the meal have the welcome addition of zucchini and green chiles. We add sliced avocado for freshness and richness, and salsa kicks up the spice level.

CALORIES 357; FAT 10g (sat 2.3g); PROTEIN 17g; CARB 49g; FIBER 7g; SODIUM 673mg

LIGHTER FAST FOOD LUNCHES

1. Panera Bread
Power Mediterranean Chicken Salad + Açai Berry Green Tea (regular size)

You won't find Panera's Power Mediterranean Chicken on the menu board. It's on the chain's "hidden" menu, which anyone can order from. Silly marketing gimmick? Maybe. But the nutrition is serious: The salad is a mix of baby spinach, romaine, lemon pepper chicken, tomatoes, smoky bacon, and chopped eggs, all dressed simply with fresh lemon juice and olive oil.

CALORIES 360; FAT 20g (sat 4g); PROTEIN 35g; CARB 8g; FIBER 3g; SODIUM 590mg

2. Wendy's
Apple Pecan Chicken Salad (half size) + Strawberry Tea (small)

Garden Sensations Salads are a relatively new addition to Wendy's tried-and-true menu. Order the half-size salad to keep the sodium in check (the regular size has 1,350mg sodium—yikes!). It includes pomegranate vinaigrette dressing, grilled chicken, roasted pecans, blue cheese, apple chunks, dried cranberries, and a mix of iceberg, romaine, and spring mix. Naturally sweet Strawberry Tea contains no artificial colors or flavors—pretty great for fast food.

CALORIES 390; FAT 18g (sat 4.5g); PROTEIN 19g; CARB 28g; FIBER 4g; SODIUM 710mg

3. Au Bon Pain
Caesar Asiago Salad + Tomato Basil Bisque (small)

Order an Italianized salad and soup combo.

CALORIES 340; FAT 15g (sat 7.5g); PROTEIN 14g; CARB 39g; FIBER 5g; SODIUM 620mg

4. Starbucks
Hearty Veggie & Brown Rice Salad Bowl + Evolution Fresh Essential Greens with Lime Juice Blend

Hardly your standard premade salad. A rainbow of veggies (broccoli, beets, kale, red cabbage, peas, and roasted butternut squash) is tossed with rice and lemon-tahini dressing. Keep a good-for-you thing going with Evolution Fresh's Essential Greens with Lime blend. It's a lively combo of celery, cucumber, spinach, romaine, kale, lime, parsley, wheatgrass, and clover sprouts (bottle contains 2 servings; nutrition listed here is for 1).

CALORIES 475; FAT 22g (sat 3g); PROTEIN 12g; CARB 57g; FIBER 8g; SODIUM 800mg

5. California Pizza Kitchen
Grilled Chicken Chimichurri

You get plenty of food with this selection from the Lite Adventures menu. It features 6 ounces of grilled chicken, pan-roasted vegetables (zucchini, cauliflower, eggplant, carrots, Broccolini, mushrooms, and spinach), and a garlicky chimichurri sauce. Pair it with water or unsweetened iced tea.

CALORIES 460; FAT 27g (sat 4g); PROTEIN 41g; CARB 19g; FIBER 8g; SODIUM 820mg

FULL PLATE/ HALF THE CALORIES!

Each of these heaping servings of healthy comfort food cuts 50% or more calories from the traditional recipe.

Kid Friendly • Make Ahead

Cremini Mushroom Meat Loaf

with Cauliflower Mash and Browned Butter Peas and Carrots

***Hands-on: 55 min. Total: 55 min.** Cube any leftover meat loaf, brown it in a skillet, and make spaghetti and meat loaf.*

1 pound cremini mushrooms
1 tablespoon canola oil
1¼ cups finely chopped onion
6 garlic cloves, minced
2 tablespoons dry sherry
2 teaspoons chopped fresh thyme
½ cup panko breadcrumbs
⅝ teaspoon kosher salt
½ teaspoon black pepper
8 ounces ground sirloin (90% lean)
1 large egg, lightly beaten
Cooking spray
¼ cup lower-sodium ketchup, divided

1. Preheat oven to 375°.
2. Place half of mushrooms in a food processor; process until minced. Placed minced mushrooms in a bowl. Repeat procedure with remaining mushrooms.
3. Heat a large skillet over medium-high heat. Add oil to pan; swirl to coat. Add onion; sauté 3 minutes. Add garlic; sauté 1 minute. Add mushrooms; cook 7 minutes or until liquid evaporates and mushrooms

continued

begin to brown. Add sherry; cook 1 minute, stirring frequently. Remove from heat; stir in thyme. Cool slightly.
4. Combine mushroom mixture, panko, and next 4 ingredients, mixing until well combined. Shape mixture into a 7 x 3–inch free-form loaf on a foil-lined baking sheet coated with cooking spray. Bake at 375° for 20 minutes. Remove from oven; brush with half of ketchup. Bake an additional 10 to 15 minutes or until a thermometer registers 160°. Remove from oven; brush with remaining ketchup. Cut into 8 slices. Serves 4 (serving size: 2 slices)

CALORIES 253; **FAT** 10.9g (sat 3g, mono 5.2g, poly 1.5g); **PROTEIN** 17.9g; **CARB** 20.2g; **FIBER** 2.1g; **CHOL** 83mg; **IRON** 2.3mg; **SODIUM** 389mg; **CALC** 59mg

Cauliflower Mash

Place 3 cups chopped cauliflower florets and 1 (8-ounce) chopped peeled baking potato in a saucepan; cover with water. Bring to a boil; reduce heat, and simmer 14 minutes or until very tender. Drain; place in food processor. Add ¼ cup heavy cream, ½ teaspoon kosher salt, and ¼ teaspoon black pepper; process until smooth (about 1 minute). Serves 4 (serving size: about ¾ cup)

CALORIES 118; **FAT** 5.8g (sat 3.5g); **SODIUM** 272mg

Browned Butter Peas and Carrots

Place 1 pound sugar snap peas and ¼ cup water in a large microwave-safe bowl. Cover with plastic wrap; pierce plastic wrap to vent. Microwave at HIGH 3 minutes. Melt 1 tablespoon butter in a medium skillet over medium heat; cook 2 minutes or until browned and very fragrant. Drain peas; add to butter in pan, tossing to coat. Add 1 large carrot, shaved into ribbons with a vegetable peeler; cook 30 seconds or just until carrot starts to wilt, tossing well. Sprinkle evenly with ⅛ teaspoon kosher salt and ⅛ teaspoon black pepper; toss to combine. Serves 4 (serving size: about ¾ cup)

CALORIES 80; **FAT** 2.9g (sat 1.8g); **SODIUM** 98mg

Kid Friendly • *Make Ahead*

Kale and Mushroom Lasagna

with Fresh Orange Salad

Hands-on: 1 hr. 20 min. Total: 2 hr. 10 min. *A small amount of pancetta adds richness and depth to the mushroom mixture; feel free to omit it—and swap in vegetable stock for beef—for a vegetarian version.*

1 tablespoon extra-virgin olive oil
1 cup chopped onion
10 garlic cloves, minced and divided
2 tablespoons unsalted tomato paste
¼ cup dry red wine
1 cup chopped fresh basil
3 tablespoons chopped fresh oregano
1 (14.5-ounce) can unsalted fire-roasted diced tomatoes
1 (14-ounce) can unsalted crushed tomatoes
1 bay leaf
½ teaspoon kosher salt, divided
1 ounce pancetta
1 pound cremini mushrooms
¾ cup unsalted beef stock, divided
2 tablespoons half-and-half
8 cups chopped kale
1 teaspoon red wine vinegar
Cooking spray
6 uncooked no-boil lasagna noodles
½ cup part-skim ricotta cheese
1 ounce Parmesan cheese, grated (about ¼ cup)
1 ounce part-skim mozzarella cheese, shredded (about ¼ cup)
1 tablespoon chopped fresh parsley
¼ teaspoon black pepper

1. Heat a large saucepan over medium heat. Add oil to pan; swirl to coat. Add onion; cook 5 minutes or until tender, stirring occasionally. Add 8 garlic cloves; cook 1 minute. Add tomato paste, and cook 2 minutes, stirring to combine. Add wine; cook 1 minute. Add basil and next 4 ingredients (through bay leaf). Stir in ¼ teaspoon salt. Bring to a boil; reduce heat, and simmer 15 minutes, stirring occasionally. Discard bay leaf.
2. Place pancetta in a food processor; process until finely ground. Remove pancetta. Place mushrooms in food processor; process until finely ground.
3. Heat a large skillet over medium-low heat. Add pancetta; cook 6 minutes or until crisp, stirring to crumble. Add ¼ teaspoon salt, mushrooms, and ¼ cup stock. Increase heat to medium. Cook 10 minutes or until almost dry. Remove from heat; stir in half-and-half.
4. Heat a medium saucepan over medium-high heat. Add ½ cup stock and 2 garlic cloves; bring to a boil. Add kale; cook 10 minutes or until kale wilts, stirring occasionally. Stir in vinegar.
5. Preheat oven to 350°.
6. Spread 1 cup sauce in bottom of an 8-inch square broiler-safe glass or ceramic baking dish coated with cooking spray. Arrange 2 noodles over sauce; top noodles with all of kale and ¾ cup sauce. Arrange 2 noodles over kale and sauce; top with mushroom mixture and ricotta. Top with remaining 2 noodles. Spread remaining sauce over noodles; sprinkle with Parmesan. Cover and bake at 350° for 45 minutes.
7. Turn on broiler (do not remove dish from oven). Uncover; sprinkle with mozzarella. Broil 2 minutes or until cheese melts. Let stand 5

minutes; sprinkle with parsley and pepper. Serves 4 (serving size: 1 piece)

CALORIES 454; **FAT** 13.5g (sat 5.3g, mono 4.5g, poly 1.1g); **PROTEIN** 24.1g; **CARB** 61.2g; **FIBER** 8.3g; **CHOL** 26mg; **IRON** 5.6mg; **SODIUM** 654mg; **CALC** 479mg

Fresh Orange Salad

Combine 1 tablespoon extra-virgin olive oil, 2 teaspoons red wine vinegar, ½ teaspoon Dijon mustard, ¼ teaspoon kosher salt, and ⅛ teaspoon sugar in a large bowl; whisk until sugar dissolves. Add 5 cups baby lettuce and spinach salad mix; toss. Arrange 1½ cups salad on each of 4 plates; divide ¾ cup orange sections and ¼ cup slivered red onion over salads. Serves 4

HOW WE HALF IT

Most vegetable-based **lasagnas** lean heavily on cream sauces. Go with tomato sauce instead, as we do here, and loads of fat and calories fall away. That rewards the cook with a large but light portion. We also use fewer noodles—only 2 layers—and add heft with earthy kale and mushrooms. The side salad is lightly dressed and uses juicy oranges—not an oil slick—to keep the leaves moist.

CALORIES 56; **FAT** 3.4g (sat 0.5g); **SODIUM** 146mg

Kid Friendly • Quick & Easy

Shorty Shrimp Po'boys

with Baked Pickle Chips and Garlicky Sautéed Kale

Hands-on: 25 min. Total: 25 min. Grab a shorty! Our smaller-scale sandwich is truly satisfying, especially with pickle chips and kale.

2 tablespoons low-fat buttermilk, divided
1 tablespoon canola mayonnaise

1 tablespoon water
2 teaspoons fresh lemon juice
1½ teaspoons whole-grain mustard
½ teaspoon ground red pepper
16 medium shrimp, peeled and deveined (about ¾ pound)
¼ cup yellow cornmeal
Cooking spray
1 (12-ounce) French bread baguette, cut crosswise into 4 pieces
2 cups thinly sliced green leaf lettuce
8 (¼-inch-thick) slices tomato

1. Place a baking sheet in oven. Preheat oven to 450° (leave pan in oven).
2. Combine 1 tablespoon buttermilk, mayonnaise, and next 4 ingredients, stirring with a whisk. Set aside.
3. Combine 1 tablespoon buttermilk and shrimp in a bowl; toss to coat. Sprinkle with cornmeal; toss to coat. Carefully remove preheated pan from oven. Arrange shrimp in a single layer on pan. Lightly coat shrimp with cooking spray. Bake at 450° for 8 minutes or until done.
4. Cut bread pieces through the top, cutting to, but not through, the bottom. Hollow out bread, leaving a ½-inch-thick shell. Combine 2 tablespoons mayonnaise mixture and lettuce; toss to coat. Divide lettuce mixture, tomatoes, shrimp, and remaining mayonnaise mixture among bread pieces. Serves 4 (serving size: 1 sandwich)

CALORIES 304; **FAT** 4.9g (sat 0.6g, mono 2.2g, poly 1.6g); **PROTEIN** 13.4g; **CARB** 51.6g; **FIBER** 3g; **CHOL** 32mg; **IRON** 3.2mg; **SODIUM** 435mg; **CALC** 66mg

Baked Pickle Chips

Preheat oven to 450°. Heat a skillet over medium-high heat. Add ½ cup panko; cook 2 minutes or until golden, shaking pan frequently. Place panko in a shallow dish. Place 2 tablespoons all-purpose flour in another shallow dish; place 2 lightly beaten egg whites in another shallow dish. Pat 32 low-sodium kosher dill pickle chips dry with paper towels. Dredge pickles in flour; dip in

egg whites, and dredge in panko. Arrange pickles in a single layer on a baking sheet. Bake at 450° for 8 minutes on each side or until crisp. Serves 4 (serving size: 8 pickle chips)

CALORIES 59; **FAT** 0.4g (sat 0g); **SODIUM** 58mg

Garlicky Sautéed Kale

Heat a large skillet over medium-high heat. Add 2 teaspoons olive oil to pan; swirl to coat. Add 1 tablespoon sliced garlic; cook 2 minutes or just until garlic begins to brown. Add 8 packed cups chopped Lacinato kale; sauté 2 minutes, tossing frequently. Stir in ¼ cup unsalted chicken stock, ¼ teaspoon salt, and ¼ teaspoon freshly ground black pepper; cover and cook 3 minutes on medium heat or just until kale wilts. Serves 4 (serving size: about 1 cup)

CALORIES 93; **FAT** 3.3g (sat 0.5g); **SODIUM** 214mg

HOW WE HALF IT

This dramatic **po'boy** makeover results from two strategies: a reasonable portion approach and oven-frying. Our sandwich is a wonderfully messy handful, just nowhere near a foot-long monster that in a traditional recipe can deliver an entire day's worth of calories and more than a day's worth of fat. Calorie cutting begins with keeping the shrimp and pickles away from the deep fryer, yet there's still the required crunch and yum because high-heat baking crisps things up mighty fine. You get a heap of garlicky kale on the side.

Chicken Parmesan with Spaghetti

with Sautéed Broccoli Rabe
(pictured on page 211)

Hands-on: 45 min. Total: 45 min.
To save time and effort, boil the broccoli rabe first, scoop it out with a slotted spoon, and cook the pasta in the same pot of boiling water.

4 ounces uncooked spaghetti
2 (14.5-ounce) cans unsalted petite-diced tomatoes, drained
1½ tablespoons olive oil, divided
¼ teaspoon crushed red pepper
6 garlic cloves, thinly sliced
½ teaspoon kosher salt, divided
3 tablespoons finely chopped fresh basil
2 (8-ounce) skinless, boneless chicken breast halves
2 tablespoons all-purpose flour
1 teaspoon garlic powder
1 large egg, lightly beaten
½ cup panko (Japanese breadcrumbs)
1 ounce Parmigiano-Reggiano cheese, grated (about ¼ cup)
1 teaspoon butter
2 ounces part-skim mozzarella cheese, thinly sliced
Torn basil leaves (optional)

1. Preheat broiler to high.
2. Cook pasta according to package directions, omitting salt and fat; drain.
3. While pasta cooks, place tomatoes in a food processor; process until almost smooth. Heat a saucepan over medium-low heat. Add 1½ teaspoons oil to pan; swirl to coat. Add pepper and garlic; cook 1 minute or until fragrant, stirring occasionally. Add tomatoes and ⅜ teaspoon salt; cook 15 minutes or until slightly thick-ened, stirring occasionally. Stir in chopped basil. Toss 1 cup sauce with pasta; keep warm.
4. While sauce cooks, split each chicken breast half horizontally to form 2 cutlets (4 total). Combine flour, garlic powder, and ⅛ teaspoon salt. Sprinkle tops of cutlets with half of flour mixture; pat evenly onto cutlets. Turn cutlets over. Sprinkle with remaining flour mixture; pat onto cutlets. Shake off any excess flour. Place egg in a shallow dish. Combine panko and Parmigiano-Reggiano in another shallow dish. Dip cutlets in egg; dredge in panko mixture.
5. Heat a large nonstick skillet over medium-high heat. Add 1 tablespoon oil and butter to pan; swirl until butter melts. Add chicken to pan; cook 4 minutes on each side or until browned and done. Place chicken on a baking sheet; top evenly with mozzarella. Broil 2 minutes or until cheese melts.
6. Arrange about ½ cup pasta mixture on each of 4 plates; top each with 1 cutlet and about 3 tablespoons remaining sauce. Sprinkle with torn basil, if desired. Serves 4

CALORIES 460; **FAT** 14.8g (sat 5g, mono 6.5g, poly 1.6g); **PROTEIN** 38.3g; **CARB** 40.7g; **FIBER** 2.5g; **CHOL** 136mg; **IRON** 2.8mg; **SODIUM** 634mg; **CALC** 247mg

Sautéed Broccoli Rabe

Cook 1 pound trimmed broccoli rabe in boiling water 3 minutes or until crisp-tender. Remove from pan; rinse with cold water. Drain. Set aside until ready to serve. Heat 1½ teaspoons olive oil in a skillet over medium-high heat. Add broccoli rabe; sauté 2 minutes. Drizzle with 1 tablespoon red wine vinegar, and sprinkle with ¼ teaspoon kosher salt. Serves 4

CALORIES 43; **FAT** 1.7g (sat 0.2g); **SODIUM** 147mg

Kid Friendly • Quick & Easy

Savory Pan-Fried Chicken with Hot Sauce

with Creamed Corn and Stewed Collards

Hands-on: 20 min. Total: 20 min. *This simple recipe is a revelation: It tastes as good as the old-school, supersavory chicken you'd get in a bucket.*

8 (3-ounce) skinless, boneless chicken thighs
1 large egg, lightly beaten
1.5 ounces all-purpose flour (about ⅓ cup)
½ teaspoon kosher salt, divided
1 teaspoon garlic powder
1 teaspoon onion powder
1 teaspoon freshly ground black pepper
½ teaspoon ground red pepper
1½ tablespoons canola oil
1½ tablespoons hot sauce

1. Combine chicken and egg in a shallow dish; toss to coat. Combine flour, ¼ teaspoon salt, garlic powder, and next 3 ingredients in a shal-

low dish; dredge chicken in flour mixture. Heat a large nonstick skillet over medium-high heat. Add oil to pan; swirl to coat. Add chicken; cook 5 minutes on each side or until browned and done. Drain chicken on a plate lined with paper towels. Sprinkle with ¼ teaspoon salt; top with hot sauce. Serves 4 (serving size: 2 thighs)

CALORIES 312; FAT 13.6g (sat 2.6g, mono 6.2g, poly 3.4g); PROTEIN 35.8g; CARB 9.6g; FIBER 0.7g; CHOL 208mg; IRON 2.3mg; SODIUM 444mg; CALC 30mg

Creamed Corn

Melt 1 tablespoon butter in a medium saucepan over medium-high heat; swirl until butter foams. Add ½ cup chopped red bell pepper and 1 tablespoon chopped fresh thyme; sauté 3 minutes. Add 2 cups frozen whole-kernel corn, thawed; sauté 2 minutes. Add 1 cup 2% reduced-fat milk, 1 tablespoon all-purpose flour, and ¼ teaspoon kosher salt, stirring with a whisk. Cover; bring to a boil. Reduce heat to low, and simmer 15 minutes, stirring occasionally. Place ½ cup corn mixture in a mini food processor; process until smooth. Return to pan; stir well. Serves 4 (serving size: ½ cup)

CALORIES 129; FAT 4.7g (sat 2.7g); SODIUM 152mg

Stewed Collards

Heat a Dutch oven over medium-high heat. Coat pan with cooking spray. Add 1 cup vertically sliced onion; sauté 3 minutes. Add 8 cups chopped collard greens, 2 cups unsalted chicken stock, 1 teaspoon sugar, and ¼ teaspoon salt. Cover; bring to a boil. Reduce heat to low; simmer 20 minutes or until very tender. Stir in 2 teaspoons cider vinegar. Serves 4 (serving size: ⅔ cup)

CALORIES 52; FAT 0.5g (sat 0.1g); SODIUM 201mg

Coconut-Curry Halibut

with Cashew Rice and Stir-Fried Vegetables
(pictured on page 211)

Hands-on: 45 min. Total: 45 min.
Pacific halibut (often labeled Alaskan halibut) is a good choice for sustainability. Less-expensive options include most U.S.-farmed tilapia and Atlantic/Icelandic cod.

1½ tablespoons brown sugar
2 tablespoons red curry paste
1 tablespoon lower-sodium soy sauce
1 tablespoon rice vinegar
1 (14-ounce) can light coconut milk
1 tablespoon fresh lime juice
3 mint sprigs
3 basil sprigs
1 tablespoon canola oil
4 (6-ounce) halibut fillets
¼ teaspoon freshly ground black pepper
⅛ teaspoon kosher salt

1. Combine first 5 ingredients in a medium saucepan over high heat, whisking until smooth. Bring to a boil; reduce heat, and simmer until reduced to ¾ cup (about 25 minutes). Remove from heat. Stir in lime juice, mint, and basil; let stand 5 minutes. Strain into a measuring cup; discard solids. Keep sauce warm.
2. Heat a large nonstick skillet over medium-high heat. Add oil; swirl to coat. Sprinkle fish evenly with pepper and salt. Add fish to pan; cook 4 minutes on each side or until desired degree of doneness. Serve fish with sauce. Serves 4 (serving size: 1 fillet and 3 tablespoons sauce)

CALORIES 274; FAT 11.1g (sat 5.7g, mono 3g, poly 1.5g); PROTEIN 33.2g; CARB 10.7g; FIBER 0.1g; CHOL 83mg; IRON 0.8mg; SODIUM 482mg; CALC 17mg

Cashew Rice

Place 1 cup uncooked sushi rice in a fine-mesh sieve. Rinse under cold water, stirring rice until water runs clear (about 30 seconds). Combine rice, 1¼ cups water, and ¼ teaspoon kosher salt in a small saucepan. Bring to a boil; cover, reduce heat, and simmer 15 minutes. Remove from heat; let stand 10 minutes. Uncover and fluff rice. Stir in ⅓ cup chopped unsalted dry-roasted cashews, ¼ cup thinly sliced green onions, ¼ cup chopped fresh cilantro, 2 tablespoons thinly sliced serrano pepper, and 1 tablespoon rice vinegar. Serves 4 (serving size: about ½ cup)

CALORIES 138; FAT 5.4g (sat 1.1g); SODIUM 204mg

Stir-Fried Vegetables

Heat a large skillet over medium-high heat. Add 1 tablespoon dark sesame oil to pan; swirl to coat. Add 1 tablespoon minced peeled fresh ginger and 5 minced garlic cloves; cook 2 minutes or until garlic just begins to brown. Add 1 cup sliced red bell pepper and 8 ounces sliced shiitake mushroom caps; stir-fry 4 minutes. Add 2 vertically sliced baby bok choy and ¼ cup water; cook 2 minutes or until bok choy is crisp-tender and water evaporates. Remove from heat; stir in 1 tablespoon lower-sodium soy sauce. Serves 4 (serving size: about ½ cup)

CALORIES 71; FAT 3.9g (sat 0.5g); SODIUM 170mg

continued

SWEET LITTLE BITES!

Carla Hall's approach to treats is just right for right now: big flavor, wee portions.

In this time of New Year's resolutions, don't make the mistake of denying yourself dessert; just make the end-of-meal serving smaller. And make the food taste really good. "If I take everything that I would have in a big dessert and make it smaller, I am perfectly satisfied with the sweetness and the richness and don't need any more," says Hall. That's the philosophy behind these adorable whoopie pies and cheesecakes—full satisfaction in a just-so package. "It's not going to really get any better after those first couple of bites anyway," says Hall. We've set the portion size at two pieces, but you may find yourself happy after only one. The cheesecakes freeze beautifully, which has an added benefit: They're not all in eat-right-now mode, "which is great for discipline," says Hall.

Kid Friendly • Freezable
Make Ahead

Mini Blueberry Cheesecakes

Hands-on: 47 min. Total: 3 hr. 19 min. These are great because you can make them ahead and freeze them (without the jam).

Crust:
1/2 cup slivered almonds, finely ground
1/2 cup graham cracker crumbs (about 3 cookie sheets)
1 tablespoon sugar
Dash of salt
2 tablespoons unsalted butter, melted
Filling:
1/2 cup sugar
2 teaspoons cornstarch
2 teaspoons vanilla extract
Dash of salt
14 ounces 1/3-less-fat cream cheese, softened
2 large eggs
3 tablespoons sour cream
48 blueberries
Jam:
2 cups blueberries
2 tablespoons sugar
1 tablespoon grated lemon rind
3 tablespoons fresh lemon juice

1. Preheat oven to 350°.
2. To prepare crust, combine first 4 ingredients in a bowl, stirring with a whisk. Add butter, and toss until well combined. Place 48 paper mini muffin cup liners in mini muffin cups. Spoon 1 rounded teaspoon crust mixture into each. Lightly press into bottom. Bake at 350° for 5 minutes. Cool completely on wire racks (leave oven on).
3. To prepare filling, place 1/2 cup sugar and next 4 ingredients in a medium bowl. Beat with a mixer at medium speed 3 minutes or until well combined. Add eggs, 1 at a time, beating well after each addition. Add sour cream; beat 1 minute or until combined. Scoop about 1 tablespoon filling into each muffin cup. Place 1 blueberry on top of each cheesecake. Bake at 350° for 12 minutes or until set. Cool cheesecakes completely on a wire rack. Chill at least 2 hours.
4. To prepare jam, combine 2 cups blueberries and remaining ingredients in a small saucepan. Bring to a boil. Mash mixture with a potato masher. Simmer 12 minutes or until thick and syrupy. Cool to room temperature. Top each cheesecake with about 2 teaspoons jam. Serves 24 (serving size: 2 cheesecakes)

CALORIES 113; FAT 6.7g (sat 3.1g, mono 2.1g, poly 0.6g); PROTEIN 2.9g; CARB 11g; FIBER 0.7g; CHOL 31mg; IRON 0.3mg; SODIUM 83mg; CALC 33mg

Kid Friendly • Make Ahead

Zucchini Bread Whoopie Pies

Hands-on: 1 hr. 17 min. Total: 1 hr. 27 min. These little bites combine sweet zucchini spice cake with a rich chocolate-cream cheese filling.

Cakes:
1/2 cup granulated sugar
1/4 cup packed brown sugar
1/4 cup canola oil
1/2 teaspoon vanilla extract
2 large eggs
1 cup grated zucchini
6.75 ounces all-purpose flour (about 1 1/2 cups)
1/2 cup old-fashioned rolled oats
1 teaspoon ground cinnamon
1/2 teaspoon baking soda
1/2 teaspoon baking powder
1/2 teaspoon salt
Filling:
2 tablespoons unsalted butter, softened
6 ounces 1/3-less-fat cream cheese, softened
2/3 cup powdered sugar
1 cup semisweet chocolate chips, melted and cooled

1. Preheat oven to 350°.

2. To prepare cakes, cover 2 baking sheets with parchment paper. Draw 25 (1-inch) circles on each paper. Turn paper over; secure with masking tape. Set aside.

3. Place first 5 ingredients in a large bowl. Beat with a mixer at medium speed 3 minutes or until well combined. Add zucchini; beat at low speed 1 minute or just until combined.

4. Weigh or lightly spoon flour into dry measuring cups; level with a knife. Combine flour and next 5 ingredients in a bowl; stir with a whisk. Add flour mixture to sugar mixture; beat at low speed just until combined. Spoon mixture into a large heavy-duty zip-top plastic bag; seal. Snip a small hole in 1 bottom corner of bag. Pipe 50 (1-inch) mounds onto prepared papers. Bake at 350° for 11 minutes or until lightly browned on edges. Remove pans from oven; cool completely. Remove cakes from paper, and place on a wire rack. Repeat procedure with remaining batter to yield 100 cakes, reusing prepared parchment paper.

5. To prepare filling, place butter and cream cheese in a bowl. Beat with a mixer at medium speed 2 minutes or until well combined. Add powdered sugar; beat at low speed 1 minute or until smooth. Add chocolate; beat at low speed 1 minute or until well combined. Spoon filling into a heavy-duty zip-top plastic bag; seal. Snip a small hole in 1 corner of bag. Pipe about 1 tablespoon filling onto flat sides of 50 cakes; top with remaining cakes. Serves 25 (serving size: 2 pies)

CALORIES 155; FAT 7.3g (sat 3g, mono 2.9g, poly 1g); PROTEIN 2.5g; CARB 21.2g; FIBER 0.9g; CHOL 22mg; IRON 0.8mg; SODIUM 113mg; CALC 23mg

PRACTICAL SNACKS

This year, banish the boring or too-big snack. These protein- and fiber-packed bites will satisfy without blowing your calorie budget. The focus is on fruits, veggies, and whole grains.

On the Go

Fruit and Nut Bar
We adore the KIND Cranberry Almond + Antioxidants bar.

CALORIES 190; FAT 13g (sat 1.5g); PROTEIN 4g; CARB 20g; FIBER 3g; SODIUM 25mg

Kid Friendly • Quick & Easy Vegetarian
Mini Pita Sammy
Cut 1 mini whole-wheat pita in half. Spread 1½ teaspoons hummus over each half; top each half with 2 basil leaves and 1 plum tomato slice.

CALORIES 100; FAT 1.5g (sat 0.2g); PROTEIN 4.4g; CARB 19.1g; FIBER 2.3g; SODIUM 123mg

Kid Friendly • Quick & Easy Gluten Free • Make Ahead Vegetarian
Mozza Fruit Skewers
Cut 1 part-skim mozzarella cheese stick into 4 pieces. Thread cheese, 4 pineapple chunks, 4 strawberry halves, and 8 grapes onto 2 skewers.

CALORIES 99; FAT 2.6g (sat 1.5g); PROTEIN 6.6g; CARB 13.6g; FIBER 1.4g; SODIUM 181mg

Kid Friendly • Quick & Easy Make Ahead • Vegetarian
Apple-Cinnamon Bagel
Toast 1 whole-wheat thin bagel (such as Thomas' Bagel Thins). Spread 1 wedge ⅓-less-fat cinnamon cream cheese over bottom half. Top with ¼ cup sliced apple and top half of bagel.

CALORIES 169; FAT 5.6g (sat 2.5g); PROTEIN 8.1g; CARB 29.8g; FIBER 5.7g; SODIUM 300mg

Kid Friendly • Quick & Easy Make Ahead • Vegetarian
Nuts and Bolts Trail Mix
Combine ½ cup unsalted mixed nuts, 2½ cups multigrain toasted oat cereal, ½ cup dried cherries, ½ cup M&M's, 1 cup mini pretzel twists, and 1 cup whole-grain cheddar Goldfish crackers. Portion into ½-cup servings.

CALORIES 146; FAT 5.5g (sat 1.6g); PROTEIN 2.7g; CARB 21.3g; FIBER 2.4g; SODIUM 127mg

Staff Fave

A Stash o' Pistachios
Shell and enjoy 1 (1.5-ounce) bag Roasted and Salted Wonderful pistachios.

CALORIES 130; FAT 11g (sat 1.5g); PROTEIN 5g; CARB 6g; FIBER 2g; SODIUM 125mg

At Your Desk

Kid Friendly • Quick & Easy Vegetarian
Strawberry-Hazelnut Graham
Smear 2 teaspoons chocolate-hazelnut spread (such as Nutella) over 1 whole-wheat graham cracker sheet. Top with ¼ cup sliced strawberries.

CALORIES 135; FAT 5.2g (sat 1.4g); PROTEIN 2.3g; CARB 21.1g; FIBER 1.6g; SODIUM 72mg

Kid Friendly • Quick & Easy Vegetarian
Raspberry-Ricotta Waffle
Toast 1 frozen whole-wheat waffle (such as Van's). Dollop with 1 tablespoon part-skim ricotta cheese and 2 teaspoons raspberry preserves.

CALORIES 134; FAT 4.2g (sat 0.8g); PROTEIN 3.3g; CARB 23.5g; FIBER 3g; SODIUM 134mg

continued

Kid Friendly • Quick & Easy
Make Ahead • Vegetarian
Cucumber-Feta Bites

Mix 3 tablespoons nonfat Greek yogurt, 2 teaspoons ⅓-less-fat cream cheese, and 1 tablespoon feta. Spoon into 1 small cucumber, halved lengthwise and seeded; top with 2 teaspoons walnuts.

CALORIES 122; FAT 7.5g (sat 2.9g); PROTEIN 7.4g; CARB 6.9g; FIBER 1.4g; SODIUM 170mg

Quick & Easy • Make Ahead
Vegetarian
Salsa Guac and Pita Chips

Stir 1 tablespoon fresh salsa into 1½ tablespoons prepared guacamole. Enjoy with 10 whole-grain pita chips (such as Stacy's).

CALORIES 136; FAT 6.6g (sat 0.8g); PROTEIN 2.9g; CARB 15.6g; FIBER 2.9g; SODIUM 287mg

Quick & Easy • Make Ahead
Vegetarian
Egg with a Kick

Drizzle ½ teaspoon Sriracha over 1 hard-cooked large egg.

CALORIES 80; FAT 5.3g (sat 1.6g); PROTEIN 6.3g; CARB 1.1g; FIBER 0g; SODIUM 112mg

Fig-Filled Wheat Bars

Pack 2 Barbara's Whole-Wheat Fig Bars in a snack baggie; tote to work.

CALORIES 110; FAT 0.5g (sat 0g); PROTEIN 1g; CARB 25g; FIBER 2g; SODIUM 50mg

Late-night munchies

Frozen Blueberries

Pour 1 cup frozen blueberries into a small bowl. For a refreshing, slushy-like crunch, do not thaw.

CALORIES 80; FAT 1g (sat 0g); PROTEIN 0.7g; CARB 18.9g; FIBER 4.2g; SODIUM 2mg

Kid Friendly • Quick & Easy
Vegetarian
Banana Fluffer Nutters

Cut 1 small banana in half lengthwise. Combine 1½ tablespoons marshmallow creme and 1 teaspoon peanut butter in a small bowl. Spread peanut butter mixture over 1 half of banana; top with remaining half.

CALORIES 151; FAT 3g (sat 0.7g); PROTEIN 2.4g; CARB 31.6g; FIBER 3g; SODIUM 33mg

Kid Friendly • Quick & Easy
Gingery Lemon Curd Sundae

Top ⅓ cup frozen nonfat vanilla Greek yogurt with 2 teaspoons prepared lemon curd. Sprinkle with 1 crushed gingersnap.

CALORIES 140; FAT 1.3g (sat 0.4g); PROTEIN 4.3g; CARB 28.2g; FIBER 1.6g; SODIUM 6mg

Kid Friendly • Quick & Easy
Gluten Free • Make Ahead
Vegetarian
Edamame Crunch

Boil ½ cup shelled edamame until crisp-tender. Sprinkle with 1 teaspoon toasted sesame seeds and a dash of kosher salt.

CALORIES 115; FAT 4.3g (sat 0.2g); PROTEIN 8.5g; CARB 9.7g; FIBER 4.5g; SODIUM 150mg

Quick & Easy • Vegetarian
Smashed Avocado on Toast

Mash ¼ cup diced avocado onto 1 (1-ounce) slice toasted whole-grain bread. Sprinkle with black pepper and a dash of kosher salt.

CALORIES 130; FAT 6.5g (sat 1g); PROTEIN 4.5g; CARB 14.9g; FIBER 4.4g; SODIUM 257mg

RECIPE MAKEOVER

TAKING BACK TETRAZZINI

Up the veg, cut the cream, and drop 234 calories with our light version.

Tetrazzini is one of those dishes that practical cooks love: It makes delicious use of leftover chicken or turkey and is bound to please your crowd. The traditional dish is a cozy casserole for sure, but with a rich cast of characters—cream, butter, cheese, pasta—that packs 670 calories and a day's worth of sat fat into just one helping. The New Year calls for a new casserole. How about the same comfort-filled yum for just 435 calories?

We start by lightening the béchamel sauce, using less butter while keeping it ultracreamy with evaporated low-fat milk instead of heavy cream. Light cream cheese and savory Parmesan thicken the sauce with cheesy goodness. We toss cooked chicken breast into the sauce to moisten it up—a great way to revive those leftovers. And we trim the calorie-dense pasta and add bulk with lots of veggies—more than 8 cups, to be precise.

Crusty baguette crumbs create a crunchy finishing touch for this creamy casserole. It's a hearty, stick-to-your-ribs kind of meal that will leave you feeling lighter, just in time for the New Year.

Chicken Tetrazzini

Hands-on: 35 min. Total: 65 min.

10 ounces uncooked linguine
2 tablespoons butter
1/4 cup all-purpose flour
2 1/2 cups unsalted chicken stock
1 (12-ounce) can evaporated
    low-fat milk
2.5 ounces grated Parmigiano-
    Reggiano cheese, divided
1 ounce 1/3-less-fat cream cheese
1 teaspoon kosher salt
1/2 teaspoon black pepper
4 teaspoons olive oil, divided
2 (8-ounce) packages sliced
    mushrooms
1 cup chopped onion
1 1/2 tablespoons minced garlic (about
    6 cloves)
2 teaspoons chopped fresh thyme
1/2 cup dry white wine
3 cups shredded cooked chicken
    breast
1 cup frozen green peas
Cooking spray
1 1/2 ounces French bread baguette,
    torn into pieces
1/4 cup chopped fresh flat-leaf parsley

1. Preheat oven to 375°.
2. Cook pasta according to package directions, omitting salt and fat; drain.
3. Melt butter in a medium saucepan over medium heat. Stir in flour; cook 2 minutes, stirring constantly with a whisk. Gradually add stock and milk; bring to a boil. Reduce heat, and simmer 5 minutes. Remove from heat; stir in 2 ounces Parmigiano-

Reggiano cheese, cream cheese, salt, and pepper.
4. Heat a large skillet over medium-high heat. Add 1 tablespoon oil to pan; swirl to coat. Add mushrooms; sauté 3 minutes, stirring occasionally. Add onion, garlic, and thyme; sauté 3 minutes. Add wine; cook 1 minute. Combine milk mixture, mushroom mixture, pasta, chicken, and peas; toss to combine. Spoon pasta mixture into a 13 x 9–inch glass or ceramic baking dish coated with cooking spray.
5. Place bread in a food processor; drizzle with 1 teaspoon oil. Process until coarse crumbs form. Combine breadcrumbs and remaining Parmigiano-Reggiano; sprinkle evenly over pasta. Bake at 375° for 30 minutes or until browned and bubbly. Top with parsley. Serves 8 (serving size: about 1¼ cups)

CALORIES 435; FAT 12.2g (sat 4.9g, mono 4.1g, poly 1.3g); PROTEIN 33.2g; CARB 45g; FIBER 3.6g; CHOL 69mg; IRON 3mg; SODIUM 573mg; CALC 249mg

TETRAZZINI TRANSFORMATION

EVAPORATED LOW-FAT MILK replaces whipping cream and whole milk to save 145 calories and 9.2g sat fat per serving. Unsalted chicken stock and wine enrich the sauce with savory and acidic notes.

8 CUPS OF FRESH MUSHROOMS, GREEN PEAS, AND ONIONS sub in for 25% of the calorie-heavy pasta to add maximum flavor with minimum salt and fat, shaving another 82 calories per serving.

PARMIGIANO-REGGIANO + 1/3-LESS-FAT CREAM CHEESE replace the traditional stick of butter and add a rich, creamy cheesiness to our light béchamel sauce—saving 68 calories and 6.2g sat fat per serving.

6 SUPER KALE SALADS

Fresh takes with America's favorite green! Curly and Lacinato leaves are hearty, baby ones tender.

Tahini-Lemon
Combine 1 tablespoon water, 1 tablespoon fresh lemon juice, 1 tablespoon olive oil, 1 tablespoon tahini, 2 teaspoons lower-sodium soy sauce, and ¼ teaspoon pepper in a large bowl, stirring with a whisk. Add 6 cups thinly sliced stemmed Lacinato kale and ¾ cup cooked quinoa; toss. Serves 4 (serving size: 1½ cups)

CALORIES 147; FAT 6.8g (sat 0.8g); SODIUM 136mg

Apple & Cheddar
Combine 1 tablespoon cider vinegar, 1 tablespoon olive oil, 1 teaspoon Dijon mustard, ¼ teaspoon sugar, ¼ teaspoon pepper, and ⅛ teaspoon salt in a large bowl, stirring with a whisk. Add 6 cups chopped stemmed Lacinato kale and 1 small, thinly sliced sweet apple; toss. Top with 1 ounce shredded extra-sharp white cheddar cheese. Serves 6 (serving size: 1 cup)

CALORIES 85; FAT 4.3g (sat 1.4g); SODIUM 129mg

Mango & Coconut
Combine 1 tablespoon olive oil, 2 teaspoons fresh lime juice, 1 teaspoon honey, ½ teaspoon crushed red pepper, and ¼ teaspoon kosher salt in a large bowl, stirring with a whisk. Add 6 cups chopped stemmed curly kale, ½ cup diced peeled avocado, ¼ cup toasted unsweetened flaked coconut, and 1 diced peeled ripe mango; toss. Serves 6 (serving size: 1⅓ cups)

CALORIES 133; FAT 6.9g (sat 2.6g); SODIUM 112mg

continued

Garden

Combine 1 tablespoon olive oil, 2 teaspoons sherry vinegar, 1 teaspoon chopped fresh thyme, 1 teaspoon Dijon mustard, ¼ teaspoon kosher salt, and 1 minced garlic clove in a large bowl, stirring with a whisk. Add 6 cups chopped stemmed curly kale, ½ cup matchstick-cut carrots, ¼ cup thinly sliced radishes, 1 thinly sliced peeled golden beet (uncooked), and 2 ounces grated Asiago cheese (about ½ cup); toss. Serves 6 (serving size: 2 cups)

CALORIES 104; **FAT** 5.8g (sat 2.1g); **SODIUM** 240mg

Cherry & Sunflower Seed

Combine 1½ tablespoons cider vinegar, 1 tablespoon olive oil, 1 teaspoon Dijon mustard, 1 teaspoon honey, ¼ teaspoon kosher salt, and ¼ teaspoon pepper in a large bowl. Add 5 ounces baby kale, ¼ cup dried cherries, ¼ cup sliced red onion, and 2 tablespoons sunflower seeds; toss. Serves 4 (serving size: 1½ cups)

CALORIES 117; **FAT** 5.6g (sat 0.7g); **SODIUM** 184mg

Caesar

Combine 2 tablespoons hot water, 2 tablespoons canola mayo, 1 tablespoon olive oil, 1 tablespoon fresh lemon juice, ½ teaspoon anchovy paste, ¼ teaspoon pepper, and 1 grated garlic clove in a bowl. Stir in 2 tablespoons grated Parmesan cheese. Add 5 ounces baby kale; toss. Top with 2 ounces toasted cubed baguette. Serves 4 (serving size: 1¼ cups)

CALORIES 118; **FAT** 6.3g (sat 1g); **SODIUM** 238mg

THE LESSON: CREAM-FREE CREAMY PASTA

Cook like a genius with tips from chef and teacher Keith Schroeder.

Here's a great new way to cook pasta. It borrows from rice pilaf and risotto recipes, in that we sauté uncooked pasta in hot oil, provoking the Maillard reaction (the process responsible for making things taste roasty-toasty). We then gradually add stock rather than put the pasta in a boiling bath. The toasted starches slough off into the simmering liquid, creating a creamy sauce that elevates rather than masks the flavor of the pasta. Through this slow, gradual cooking process, the pasta achieves a perfectly even al dente texture without the unpleasant snap that sometimes accompanies not-quite-cooked-enough boiled pastas. It's a flexible method. Play with other short pastas and liquids, like fresh tomato juice or a wine-water mix.

Kid Friendly

Skillet-Toasted Penne with Chicken Sausage

Hands-on: 55 min. Total: 55 min.
Here's a saucy, creamy pasta dish without a lick of cream or milk and only a wee bit of cheese. The trick is to cook the pasta like risotto, which releases starch into the liquid that becomes the sauce. The toasting step adds nutty, rich character and is a step we don't advise skipping.

6 cups unsalted chicken stock (such as Swanson)
2 tablespoons olive oil, divided
8 ounces uncooked penne pasta
1 cup sliced sweet onion

13 ounces Italian chicken sausage, casings removed
2 tablespoons fresh lemon juice
1 tablespoon minced Calabrian chiles or hot red chiles
¼ teaspoon kosher salt
0.5 ounce grated Parmigiano-Reggiano cheese (about 2 tablespoons)
Oregano leaves (optional)

1. Bring stock to a simmer in a saucepan (do not boil). Keep warm over low heat.
2. Heat a large skillet over medium heat. Add 1 tablespoon oil to pan; swirl to coat. Add pasta; cook 5 minutes or until toasted, stirring frequently. Remove pasta from pan.
3. Add 1 tablespoon oil, onion, and sausage to pan; cook 4 minutes or until browned, stirring to crumble.

Remove sausage mixture from pan. Reduce heat to medium-low. Return pasta to pan. Add stock, 1 cup at a time, stirring constantly until each portion of stock is nearly absorbed before adding the next (about 35 minutes total), stirring frequently. Stir in sausage mixture, juice, chiles, salt, and cheese. Garnish with oregano, if desired. Serves 4 (serving size: 1 cup)

CALORIES 411; **FAT** 14.6g (sat 3.1g, mono 8.4g, poly 1.3g); **PROTEIN** 22.3g; **CARB** 46.1g; **FIBER** 2.4g; **CHOL** 63mg; **IRON** 6.4mg; **SODIUM** 620mg; **CALC** 74mg

Variation: Skillet-Toasted Penne with Bacon and Spinach
Follow steps 1 and 2. Substitute 4 chopped center-cut bacon slices for the sausage, and ½ cup sliced shallots and 8 sliced garlic cloves for the onion. Substitute 1 tablespoon fresh lemon juice and ½ teaspoon grated lemon rind for the 2 tablespoons lemon juice. Substitute 6 ounces baby spinach for the chiles. Serves 4 (serving size: 1 cup)

CALORIES 394; **FAT** 11.8g (sat 3.1g); **SODIUM** 601mg

STEPS TO CREAMY PASTA

TOAST THE PASTA
Cook dry penne in heated oil until it's a nutty brown color; this adds great flavor.

PRETEND IT'S RISOTTO
Stir in a little stock until absorbed; repeat until sauce clings.

TRADITIONAL METHODS ARE NOT MANDATES. TRY A NEW APPROACH.

SUPERFAST 20-MINUTE COOKING

Quick & Easy • Gluten Free Vegetarian

Sautéed Cabbage and Apples

A quick sauté keeps the cabbage slightly crisp as the apples begin to soften.

1 tablespoon unsalted butter
2 teaspoons canola oil
8 cups sliced green cabbage
2 cups sliced apple
1 teaspoon caraway seeds
½ teaspoon salt

1. Heat a large skillet over medium-high heat. Add butter and oil to pan; swirl until butter melts. Add cabbage, apple, caraway seeds, and salt; cover and cook 5 minutes. Uncover and cook 5 minutes or until cabbage and apples are tender, stirring occasionally. Serves 6 (serving size: 1 cup)

CALORIES 73; **FAT** 3.7g (sat 1.4g, mono 1.5g, poly 0.6g); **PROTEIN** 1.4g; **CARB** 10.3g; **FIBER** 2.9g; **CHOL** 5mg; **IRON** 0.5mg; **SODIUM** 214mg; **CALC** 42mg

Quick & Easy • Vegetarian

Cider-Braised
Heat a large skillet over medium-high heat. Add 1 tablespoon canola oil; swirl to coat. Add 2 cups sliced onion; sauté 2 minutes. Add 8 cups sliced green cabbage, 1 cup hard cider or regular cider, 2 tablespoons whole-grain mustard, and ¼ teaspoon salt, tossing to combine. Cook, covered, 5 minutes. Uncover and cook 8 minutes or until cabbage wilts, stirring occasionally. Stir in 1 tablespoon cider vinegar. Serves 6 (serving size: 1 cup)

CALORIES 85; **FAT** 2.5g (sat 0.2g); **SODIUM** 237mg

Mango Vinaigrette

Place ½ cup chopped mango,
1 tablespoon canola oil, 1 tablespoon
fresh lime juice, and ¼ teaspoon salt
in a mini food processor; process
until smooth. Place 5 cups thinly
sliced green cabbage, ½ cup diced
mango, and ¼ cup thinly sliced green
onions in a large bowl, tossing to
combine. Drizzle cabbage mixture
with pureed mango mixture; toss to
coat. Sprinkle with 3 tablespoons
chopped toasted cashews. Serves 6
(serving size: about ¾ cup)

CALORIES 78; FAT 4.5g (sat 0.6g); SODIUM 111mg

Quick & Easy

Chile-Garlic

Combine 4 teaspoons fresh lime
juice, 4 teaspoons brown sugar,
2 teaspoons fish sauce, and 1 teaspoon sambal oelek in a small bowl.
Heat a large skillet over medium-
high heat. Add 1 tablespoon dark
sesame oil; swirl to coat. Add 8 cups
sliced green cabbage to pan; cook
7 minutes or until lightly browned.
Stir in brown sugar mixture; cook
4 minutes, stirring occasionally. Stir
in ¼ cup chopped fresh cilantro
leaves. Serves 6 (serving size: ⅔ cup)

CALORIES 57; FAT 2.4g (sat 0.4g); SODIUM 193mg

FAST TIP:
USE THE SLICING
BLADE OF YOUR
FOOD PROCESSOR
TO SHORTEN
CABBAGE PREP TIME.

Kid Friendly • Quick & Easy

Shrimp and Broccoli Scampi

8 ounces uncooked thin spaghetti
12 ounces broccoli florets
Cooking spray
**1 pound medium shrimp, peeled and
deveined**
1 tablespoon butter
2 teaspoons canola oil
10 garlic cloves, minced
¾ cup unsalted chicken stock
1 tablespoon water
2 teaspoons cornstarch
¼ cup finely chopped fresh parsley
1 tablespoon grated lemon rind
2 tablespoons fresh lemon juice
¼ teaspoon kosher salt
**1 ounce Parmesan cheese, shaved or
grated (about ¼ cup)**

1. Cook pasta according to package directions, omitting salt and fat.
Add broccoli in the last 2 minutes of
cooking. Drain.
2. Heat a large skillet over high heat.
Coat pan with cooking spray. Add
shrimp; cook 2 minutes on each side.
Remove shrimp from pan.
3. Heat pan over medium-low heat.
Add butter and oil; swirl to coat. Add
garlic; sauté 1 minute. Add stock;
bring to a boil, scraping pan to
loosen browned bits. Combine 1
tablespoon water and cornstarch in a
small bowl. Stir cornstarch mixture
into stock mixture; cook 1 minute.
Stir in shrimp, pasta mixture, parsley,
rind, juice, and salt; cook 1 minute, tossing to coat. Sprinkle with
Parmesan cheese. Serve immediately.
Serves 4 (serving size: 2 cups)

CALORIES 417; FAT 9.8g (sat 3.6g, mono 3g, poly 1.5g);
PROTEIN 29.7g; CARB 53g; FIBER 4.8g; CHOL 157mg;
IRON 3.4mg; SODIUM 476mg; CALC 219mg

Quick & Easy

Seared Steaks with Red Wine, Mushrooms, and Onions

*Serve with blue cheese mashed potatoes
and broccoli.*

**2 (8-ounce) New York strip steaks,
trimmed**
¾ teaspoon kosher salt, divided
¾ teaspoon black pepper, divided
4 teaspoons canola oil, divided
½ cup prechopped onion
½ teaspoon chopped fresh rosemary
**1 (8-ounce) package sliced cremini
mushrooms**
2 teaspoons all-purpose flour
¾ cup red wine
1 tablespoon unsalted butter

1. Sprinkle steaks with ½ teaspoon
salt and ½ teaspoon pepper. Heat
a large heavy skillet over medium-
high heat. Add 1 tablespoon oil to
pan; swirl to coat. Add steaks to pan;
cook 4 minutes on each side or until
desired degree of doneness. Remove
steaks from pan, and keep warm.
Add 1 teaspoon oil to pan; swirl
to coat. Add onion, rosemary, and
mushrooms; cook 5 minutes or until
mushrooms begin to brown. Sprinkle
mushroom mixture with flour; cook
30 seconds. Add wine; bring to a
boil. Cook 1 minute, scraping pan to
loosen browned bits. Add ¼ teaspoon
salt, ¼ teaspoon pepper, and butter
to pan, stirring until butter melts.
Cut steaks across the grain into
thin slices. Serve with sauce. Serves
4 (serving size: 3 ounces steak and
about 5 tablespoons sauce)

CALORIES 363; FAT 18.2g (sat 6.3g, mono 8g, poly 1.9g);
PROTEIN 24.5g; CARB 6.1g; FIBER 1.1g; CHOL 103mg;
IRON 2.8mg; SODIUM 429mg; CALC 33mg

Mom's Creamy Chicken and Broccoli Casserole

A traditional creamy chicken casserole can have more than 800 calories per serving!

1 (12-ounce) package steam-in-bag broccoli florets
1 tablespoon canola oil
1 cup prechopped onion
2 (8-ounce) packages presliced mushrooms
3 tablespoons all-purpose flour
1 1/2 cups fat-free milk
12 ounces chopped skinless, boneless rotisserie chicken breast (about 3 cups)
1/2 cup plain fat-free Greek yogurt
1/4 cup canola mayonnaise
1/2 teaspoon freshly ground black pepper
1/4 teaspoon salt
2 ounces sharp cheddar cheese, shredded (about 1/2 cup)
1 ounce Parmesan cheese, grated (about 1/4 cup)

1. Preheat broiler.
2. Prepare broccoli in microwave according to package directions.
3. Heat a large ovenproof skillet over medium-high heat. Add oil to pan; swirl to coat. Add onion and mushrooms; cook 12 minutes or until mushrooms brown and liquid evaporates, stirring occasionally. Sprinkle mushroom mixture with flour; cook 1 minute, stirring constantly. Stir in milk. Bring to a boil; cook 3 minutes or until thick and bubbly. Stir in broccoli and chicken; cook 1 minute. Remove pan from heat. Stir in yogurt, mayonnaise, pepper, and salt. Top evenly with cheeses; broil 2 minutes. Serves 6 (serving size: 1 1/2 cups)

CALORIES 277; FAT 11.9g (sat 3.6g, mono 5.1g, poly 2.2g); PROTEIN 29.1g; CARB 15.2g; FIBER 3.1g; CHOL 66mg; IRON 1.5mg; SODIUM 547mg; CALC 253mg

Mu Shu Chicken Lettuce Wraps

(pictured on page 211)

Lettuce wraps are a fresh alternative to pancakes or tortillas. If you can't find Bibb lettuce, iceberg will work.

2 tablespoons lower-sodium soy sauce
1 tablespoon dry sherry
1 tablespoon hoisin sauce
1 teaspoon rice vinegar
1 tablespoon dark sesame oil
1 tablespoon minced fresh garlic
1 tablespoon minced peeled fresh ginger
1 (14-ounce) package coleslaw (about 4 cups)
6 ounces shredded skinless, boneless rotisserie chicken breast (about 1 1/2 cups)
1/2 cup sliced green onions, divided
12 Bibb lettuce leaves
1/4 cup chopped cashews

1. Combine first 4 ingredients in a small bowl, stirring with a whisk.
2. Heat a large skillet over medium-high heat. Add oil to pan; swirl to coat. Add garlic and ginger; sauté 30 seconds. Add soy sauce mixture and coleslaw; cook 1 minute, stirring frequently. Add chicken and 1/4 cup onions; cook 1 minute or until coleslaw just begins to wilt. Divide chicken mixture evenly among lettuce leaves; sprinkle evenly with 1/4 cup onions and cashews. Serves 4 (serving size: 3 wraps)

CALORIES 193; FAT 8.5g (sat 1.6g, mono 4.1g, poly 2.4g); PROTEIN 15.9g; CARB 13.2g; FIBER 3.4g; CHOL 38mg; IRON 1.3mg; SODIUM 534mg; CALC 79mg

Poached Fruit over Vanilla Frozen Yogurt

Any unsweetened juice (such as apple or cherry) will work. We love a mix of dried plum, pear, and apple. Dried figs, apricots, and cherries would also be delicious.

1 1/2 cups no-sugar-added cranberry juice
1/8 teaspoon salt
2 (3 x 1-inch) orange rind strips
1 (8-ounce) package mixed dried fruit, coarsely chopped (about 1 1/2 cups)
1 cinnamon stick
3 cups vanilla frozen Greek yogurt
1/4 cup slivered almonds, toasted

1. Bring juice, salt, orange rind, fruit, and cinnamon stick to a boil in a small saucepan. Reduce heat to low, and simmer 10 minutes. Cool slightly. Scoop 1/2 cup frozen yogurt into each of 6 bowls, and top each serving with about 1/4 cup fruit mixture and about 2 teaspoons toasted almonds. Serve immediately. Serves 6

CALORIES 280; FAT 2.5g (sat 0.2g, mono 1.5g, poly 0.6g); PROTEIN 11.2g; CARB 56.9g; FIBER 4.2g; CHOL 5mg; IRON 3.7mg; SODIUM 118mg; CALC 33mg

A SUNNY SPLASH OF CITRUS

Sugary oranges and tangerines, bittersweet grapefruit, tangy lemons, zingy limes: These juicy, fragrant fruits are at their best midwinter, right when you need their bright flavors the most. Here they add pop to simple salads, succulent roasted meats, and easy but dazzling desserts.

Grapefruit and Hearts of Palm Salad
(pictured on page 211)

Hands-on: 22 min. Total: 22 min.

Grapefruit adds a perfect sweet-tart zing to this salad. Hearts of palm have a semifirm texture and nutty flavor similar to that of artichoke hearts, which you could sub in a pinch. If you like the pungency of black pepper, finish with an additional sprinkle.

2 tablespoons canola oil
½ teaspoon grated lime rind
1 tablespoon fresh lime juice
1 tablespoon canola mayonnaise
1 teaspoon honey
⅛ teaspoon black pepper
4 cups baby kale

1½ cups ruby red grapefruit sections (about 2 large grapefruit)
½ cup thinly sliced red onion
2 (14-ounce) cans hearts of palm, rinsed, drained, and cut diagonally into ¼-inch slices
1 small red chile, seeded and thinly sliced
1 ripe peeled avocado, cut into thin wedges

1. Combine first 6 ingredients in a small bowl; stir with a whisk until smooth.
2. Place ⅔ cup kale on each of 6 plates. Arrange grapefruit sections, onion, hearts of palm, chile, and avocado evenly over kale. Drizzle with dressing. Serves 6 (serving size: about 1 cup salad and about 2 teaspoons dressing)

CALORIES 183; FAT 11.1g (sat 1.2g, mono 6.7g, poly 2.5g); PROTEIN 4.8g; CARB 20.4g; FIBER 6.2g; CHOL 0mg; IRON 3.5mg; SODIUM 240mg; CALC 122mg

Orange-Mustard Glazed Pork Chops
(pictured on page 210)

Hands-on: 30 min. Total: 40 min.
Marmalade provides pectin to give the glaze syrupy body and balances the sweet orange juice with a touch of pleasant bitterness.

½ cup fresh orange juice (about 2 oranges)
2 tablespoons orange marmalade
1 tablespoon whole-grain mustard
1 tablespoon canola oil
4 (6-ounce) bone-in pork loin chops (1 inch thick)
¼ teaspoon kosher salt
¼ teaspoon black pepper
2 rosemary sprigs
1 medium red onion, cut into ½-inch wedges
2 tablespoons fresh lime juice

1. Preheat oven to 425°.
2. Combine juice, marmalade, and mustard in a saucepan over medium-high heat. Bring to a boil, reduce heat, and simmer 15 minutes or until syrupy.
3. Heat a large ovenproof skillet over medium-high heat. Add oil; swirl to coat. Sprinkle pork with salt and pepper. Add to pan; cook 5 minutes or until browned. Turn pork; add rosemary and onion to pan. Pour juice mixture over pork; bake at 425° for 10 minutes or until a thermometer registers 140°. Place onion and rosemary on a platter. Return pan to medium-high heat; add lime juice. Cook 4 minutes or until liquid is syrupy. Add pork to platter; drizzle with sauce. Serves 4 (serving size: 1 chop, about 3 onion wedges, and about 3 tablespoons sauce)

CALORIES 303; FAT 9.9g (sat 2.2g, mono 4.5g, poly 1.7g); PROTEIN 38g; CARB 14g; FIBER 0.7g; CHOL 117mg; IRON 1.3mg; SODIUM 316mg; CALC 47mg

Four Citrus–Herb Chicken

Hands-on: 40 min. Total: 5 hr. 30 min.

Citrus zest perfumes the chicken while it marinates. A fresh salsa of citrus segments and herbs doubles down on fruit flavor.

2 large limes
1 large ruby red grapefruit
1 large tangerine
1 large navel orange
¼ cup extra-virgin olive oil, divided
1 tablespoon minced garlic
1 tablespoon minced serrano chile
1 (3½-pound) whole chicken
¾ teaspoon kosher salt, divided
⅜ teaspoon freshly ground black pepper, divided
1 cup vertically sliced red onion
¼ cup chopped fresh mint
2 tablespoons chopped fresh cilantro

1. Grate 1 teaspoon rind and squeeze 5 tablespoons juice from limes. Place rind and 4 tablespoons juice in a medium bowl; place 1 tablespoon juice in a separate medium bowl. Grate 1 teaspoon grapefruit rind; section grapefruit. Grate 1 teaspoon tangerine rind; section tangerine. Grate 1 teaspoon orange rind; section orange. Add citrus sections to 1 tablespoon lime juice in bowl; set aside. Add rinds to lime rind mixture. Add 2 tablespoons oil, garlic, and chile to rind mixture; stir with a whisk.

2. Place chicken, breast side down, on a cutting board. Using poultry shears, cut along both sides of backbone, and open chicken like a book. Turn chicken breast side up; using the heel of your hand, press firmly against the breastbone until it cracks. Lift wing tips up and over back; tuck under chicken. Discard backbone and skin. Place chicken on a rimmed baking sheet. Spread citrus rind mixture evenly over chicken. Cover and refrigerate at least 4 hours.

3. Position oven rack in lower third of oven. Preheat broiler to high.

4. Sprinkle chicken with ½ teaspoon salt and ¼ teaspoon black pepper. Broil chicken, breast side down, 20 minutes. Turn chicken over; broil an additional 20 minutes or until done, turning pan occasionally. Let stand 10 minutes.

5. Combine reserved citrus section mixture, 2 tablespoons oil, ¼ teaspoon salt, ⅛ teaspoon pepper, red onion, mint, and cilantro; toss to combine. Serve with chicken. Serves 4 (serving size: one-fourth of chicken and ½ cup salsa)

CALORIES 369; **FAT** 17.6g (sat 2.9g, mono 11.1g, poly 2.4g); **PROTEIN** 30.7g; **CARB** 24.2g; **FIBER** 6.5g; **CHOL** 92mg; **IRON** 2.5mg; **SODIUM** 473mg; **CALC** 76mg

HEALTHY DASHES OF CITRUS BOOST WINTER ENTRÉE APPEAL BY BALANCING AND ENHANCING THE WARMING UMAMI FLAVORS OF MEAT.

THE GINGER
HEAT AND THE
CITRUS ZING
MAKE THE ORANGE
GRATIN TASTY.
GROWN-UP
ADDITION: A
BOURBON
DRIZZLE.

Orange Gratin

Hands-on: 25 min. Total: 35 min.

Serve this simple dessert to wow dinner guests—present it in a gratin dish, and serve individually at the table. Peppery ginger is a natural partner for sweet citrus.

2 large navel oranges
1 small ruby red grapefruit
1 large Minneola orange (tangelo)
3 clementines
2 tablespoons sugar
1 tablespoon minced candied ginger
1/2 cup plain 2% reduced-fat Greek yogurt
1 tablespoon orange marmalade
2 tablespoons sliced almonds, toasted

1. Peel oranges, grapefruit, and Minneola orange; cut crosswise into 1/2-inch slices. Peel clementines; cut in half crosswise. Arrange citrus in a single layer on a jelly-roll pan. Sprinkle with sugar and candied ginger.
2. Preheat broiler to high.
3. Broil citrus 15 minutes or until lightly charred, rotating pan occasionally. Combine yogurt and marmalade in a small bowl. Divide citrus evenly among 4 shallow bowls. Drizzle evenly with pan juices. Top each serving with 2 tablespoons yogurt mixture and 1½ teaspoons almonds. Serves 4

CALORIES 187; FAT 2.3g (sat 0.6g, mono 0.9g, poly 0.4g); PROTEIN 5.3g; CARB 40.1g; FIBER 4.3g; CHOL 2mg; IRON 0.4mg; SODIUM 16mg; CALC 108mg

Chewy Meringues with Tangerine-Lemon Curd

(pictured on page 212)

Hands-on: 48 min. Total: 4 hr. 48 min.

The meringues and curd can be made up to a day ahead for convenience. Store meringues at room temperature in an airtight container, and keep curd chilled with plastic wrap directly on the surface so it doesn't form a skin.

Meringues:
3 large egg whites
Dash of salt
3/4 cup superfine sugar
1½ teaspoons cornstarch
1/2 teaspoon grated lemon rind
1½ teaspoons fresh lemon juice
Curd:
6 tablespoons granulated sugar
1/2 teaspoon grated lemon rind
1/3 cup fresh lemon juice
1/3 cup fresh tangerine juice
1 tablespoon cornstarch
3 large egg yolks
1 tablespoon unsalted butter
3 tangerines

1. Preheat oven to 325°.
2. To prepare meringues, line a baking sheet with parchment paper. Draw 6 (3-inch) circles on paper. Turn paper over; secure paper with masking tape onto baking sheet.
3. Place egg whites and salt in a large bowl; beat with a mixer at medium speed until foamy. Increase mixer speed to medium-high. Gradually add sugar, 1 tablespoon at a time, beating until stiff peaks form. Add 1½ teaspoons cornstarch, 1/2 teaspoon lemon rind, and 1½ teaspoons lemon juice; beat 1 minute or until mixture is well combined.
4. Divide egg white mixture among 6 drawn circles on parchment paper. Shape meringues into nests with 1-inch sides using the back of a spoon. Place baking sheet in oven; immediately reduce oven temperature to 225°. Bake meringues at 225° for 1 hour or until dry to the touch. Turn oven off (leave pan in oven); partially open oven door. Cool meringues in oven 1 hour. Remove pan from oven; carefully remove meringues from paper. (Meringues will be crisp on the outside and soft on the inside.)
5. To prepare curd, combine granulated sugar and next 5 ingredients in a medium saucepan; bring to a boil, stirring constantly. Reduce heat, and cook 1 minute or until thick and bubbly, stirring constantly. Remove pan from heat; add butter, stirring until butter melts. Pour mixture through a sieve into a bowl. Place plastic wrap on surface of curd, and chill.
6. Peel and section tangerines; discard membranes. Spoon about 2½ tablespoons curd into each meringue. Top each meringue with about 3 tangerine sections. Serves 6 (serving size: 1 filled meringue)

CALORIES 239; FAT 4.4g (sat 2.1g, mono 1.5g, poly 0.5g); PROTEIN 3.7g; CARB 48.4g; FIBER 0.9g; CHOL 97mg; IRON 0.4mg; SODIUM 58mg; CALC 33mg

CHICKEN WITH POM SAUCE

From chef Graham Elliot of Primary Food & Drink in Greenwich, CT

There's something mysterious about a pomegranate.

It looks like an oversized Christmas tree ornament, the pulp is inedible, and the seeds (also called arils) play hard-to-get. But once you've savored the juicy-crunchy fruit and sipped the complex juice with its perfect balance of sweetness and tannic acidity, the appeal is obvious, and you're hooked.

Graham Elliot, celebrated chef/ restaurateur of Graham Elliot Bistro in Chicago and the just-opened Primary Food & Drink in Greenwich, Connecticut, knows full well the appeal of the ancient red fruit.

"The arils are jewel-like," Elliot says. "They have that great texture: soft on the outside, and crunchy in the middle. And there's a ton of flavor that comes out of something that small."

Elliot likes to use the fruit as a gleaming garnish for salads, and the crimson juice brightens up flavor in a vinaigrette. The juice and arils also combine for a killer sauce for chicken, as in the dish featured here.

"I came up with this dish by thinking of what I'd want to eat on a cold winter night. It's a comforting dish, and you can be blindfolded and taste it and know exactly what season it is." The roasted chicken, earthy rice, and peppery turnips are indeed classic comforts, but the sauce—registering on the palate as the pure sweet-tart essence of pomegranate—makes the dish sing.

Try Elliot's original dish this month at Primary Food & Drink.

Gluten Free

Chicken with Turnips and Pomegranate Sauce

Hands-on: 40 min. Total: 1 hr. 15 min.

3 cups unsalted chicken stock (such as Swanson), divided
1 cup uncooked wild rice
1 tablespoon chopped fresh thyme leaves
1¼ teaspoons black pepper, divided
¾ teaspoon kosher salt, divided
1 cup pomegranate juice
½ cup pomegranate arils
2 large turnips, peeled and cut into ¼-inch slices
2 tablespoons olive oil, divided
4 (6-ounce) skinless, boneless chicken breast halves

1. Preheat oven to 400°.
2. Combine 2 cups stock, rice, and thyme in a medium saucepan. Bring to a boil. Cover, reduce heat, and simmer 50 minutes. Drain. Stir in ½ teaspoon pepper and ¼ teaspoon salt.
3. Combine 1 cup stock and juice in a small saucepan. Bring to a boil; reduce heat, and cook 20 minutes or until mixture is reduced to ⅓ cup. Remove from heat; stir in arils.
4. Combine turnips, ¼ teaspoon salt, ½ teaspoon pepper, and 1 tablespoon oil in a bowl; toss to coat. Arrange turnip mixture on a baking sheet. Bake at 400° for 20 minutes or until browned and tender, turning once.
5. Sprinkle ¼ teaspoon salt and ¼ teaspoon pepper over chicken. Heat a large skillet over medium-high heat. Add 1 tablespoon oil to pan; swirl to coat. Add chicken; cook 4 minutes. Turn chicken, and place pan in oven. Bake at 400° for 8 minutes or until chicken is done.
6. Spoon about ½ cup rice onto each of 4 plates. Top evenly with about ⅓ cup turnips and 1 chicken breast half. Drizzle each serving with about 4 teaspoons pomegranate sauce. Serves 4

CALORIES 489; FAT 11.7g (sat 2g, mono 6.3g, poly 1.7g); PROTEIN 45.1g; CARB 50.6g; FIBER 4.4g; CHOL 109mg; IRON 2.1mg; SODIUM 678mg; CALC 68mg

DINNER TONIGHT

One week, five fast meals

Pork Tenderloin Paprikash + Egg Noodles + Apple Salad

6 ounces uncooked egg noodles
1 (1-pound) pork tenderloin, trimmed and cut into 1-inch pieces
½ teaspoon salt, divided
½ teaspoon freshly ground black pepper, divided
5 teaspoons olive oil, divided
1½ cups chopped onion
1 cup chopped green bell pepper
2 teaspoons chopped fresh garlic
2 tablespoons all-purpose flour
2 tablespoons tomato paste
1 teaspoon chopped fresh thyme
1 teaspoon hot paprika
½ cup dry white wine
1 cup unsalted chicken stock (such as Swanson)
1 tablespoon cider vinegar
3 tablespoons reduced-fat sour cream

1. Cook noodles according to package directions, omitting salt and fat; drain.

continued

2. Sprinkle pork with ¼ teaspoon salt and ¼ teaspoon black pepper. Heat a large skillet over medium-high heat. Add 2 teaspoons oil; swirl to coat. Add pork; cook 4 minutes, browning on all sides. Remove pork from pan. Reduce heat to medium. Add 1 tablespoon oil to pan; swirl to coat. Add onion, bell pepper, garlic, ¼ teaspoon salt, and ¼ teaspoon black pepper; sauté 4 minutes or until vegetables are tender. Add flour, tomato paste, thyme, and paprika; sauté 30 seconds. Add wine; cook 1 minute, scraping pan to loosen browned bits. Add stock and vinegar; bring to a boil. Add pork; reduce heat, and simmer 5 minutes or until pork is tender. Remove pan from heat; stir in sour cream. Serve over noodles. Serves 4 (serving size: about ½ cup noodles and 1 cup pork mixture)

CALORIES 441; FAT 11.9g (sat 3.2g, mono 5.4g, poly 1.1g); PROTEIN 33.3g; CARB 44.4g; FIBER 3.7g; CHOL 128mg; IRON 3.5mg; SODIUM 479mg; CALC 66mg

Apple Salad with Mustard Dressing
Combine 1½ tablespoons extra-virgin olive oil, 1½ tablespoons cider vinegar, 1 tablespoon minced shallot, 2 teaspoons whole-grain Dijon mustard, 2 teaspoons honey, ¼ teaspoon salt, and ¼ teaspoon freshly ground black pepper in a large bowl, stirring with a whisk. Add 2 cups thinly sliced Fuji apple and 1 (5-ounce) package mixed spring greens; toss to coat. Serves 4 (serving size: about 1½ cups salad)

CALORIES 93; FAT 5.1g (sat 0.7g); SODIUM 221mg

PREPARE THE PORK MIXTURE, WITHOUT THE SOUR CREAM, UP TO A WEEK IN ADVANCE. TO SERVE, COOK NOODLES, REHEAT PORK MIXTURE, AND STIR IN SOUR CREAM.

READY IN
35
MINUTES

SHOPPING LIST

Pork Tenderloin Paprikash with Egg Noodles
Green bell pepper
Onion
Garlic
Fresh thyme
Hot paprika
All-purpose flour
Tomato paste
Olive oil
Cider vinegar
Unsalted chicken stock (such as Swanson)
Dry white wine
Uncooked egg noodles
Reduced-fat sour cream
1 pound pork tenderloin

Apple Salad with Mustard Dressing
Fuji apples
Shallot
1 (5-ounce) container spring mix greens
Cider vinegar
Extra-virgin olive oil
Whole-grain Dijon mustard
Honey

GAME PLAN

While noodles cook:
■ Prepare pork mixture.
While pork simmers:
■ Prepare apple salad.

Stuffed Chicken & Herb Gravy + Polenta + Green Beans

Chicken and gravy:
4 (6-ounce) skinless, boneless chicken breast halves
2 very thin prosciutto slices (about ½ ounce), halved
4 (⅔-ounce) slices reduced-fat provolone cheese
1 tablespoon canola oil
¼ teaspoon freshly ground black pepper
2 tablespoons minced shallots
1 tablespoon chopped fresh thyme
1½ cups unsalted chicken stock (such as Swanson), divided
1 tablespoon all-purpose flour
1½ tablespoons unsalted butter
1 tablespoon chopped fresh flat-leaf parsley
1½ teaspoons chopped fresh tarragon
Polenta:
2 cups 1% low-fat milk
⅓ cup water
½ cup uncooked polenta
¼ teaspoon kosher salt

1. To prepare chicken, cut each breast horizontally to, but not through, the other side to create a pocket. Lift top flap of chicken pocket; arrange ½ prosciutto slice in each pocket. Top each prosciutto slice with 1 cheese slice; press top flap of pocket down over filling. Heat a large skillet over medium-high heat. Add oil; swirl to coat. Sprinkle chicken with pepper. Add chicken to pan, top side down; sauté 5 minutes or until deeply browned. Turn and cook 4 minutes or until done. Remove from pan; keep warm.

2. Add shallots and thyme to pan; sauté 30 seconds, stirring constantly. Combine 2 tablespoons stock and flour in a small bowl, stirring with a whisk. Add flour mixture and remaining stock to pan. Bring to a boil; cook 3 minutes or until reduced to ¾ cup, scraping pan to loosen browned bits. Remove from heat; stir in butter, parsley, and tarragon.

3. To prepare polenta, bring milk and ⅓ cup water to a simmer. Gradually add polenta, stirring constantly with a whisk. Cook 3 minutes or until thick, stirring constantly. Stir in ¼ teaspoon salt. Serve polenta with chicken and gravy. Serves 4 (serving size: 1 stuffed breast half, 3 tablespoons gravy, and ½ cup polenta)

CALORIES 449; **FAT** 17.9g (sat 6.9g, mono 6.1g, poly 2.2g); **PROTEIN** 49.8g; **CARB** 21g; **FIBER** 1.5g; **CHOL** 139mg; **IRON** 1.7mg; **SODIUM** 662mg; **CALC** 328mg

Bacon Green Beans

Cook 2 chopped center-cut bacon slices in a large skillet over medium-high heat until done. Remove bacon from pan with a slotted spoon. Add 12 ounces trimmed haricots verts to drippings in pan; toss to combine. Sauté 2 minutes. Add 3 tablespoons water; cover and cook 2 minutes or until crisp-tender. Sprinkle with bacon and ⅛ teaspoon black pepper. Serves 4 (serving size: about ½ cup)

CALORIES 39; **FAT** 1.2g (sat 0.5g); **SODIUM** 73mg

INSTEAD OF TARRAGON, YOU CAN USE FRESH SAGE OR MORE THYME.

READY IN 40 MINUTES

SHOPPING LIST

Stuffed Chicken and Herb Gravy with Polenta
Shallot
Fresh flat-leaf parsley
Fresh thyme
Fresh tarragon
Canola oil
All-purpose flour
Uncooked polenta
Unsalted chicken stock
1% low-fat milk
Reduced-fat provolone cheese slices
Unsalted butter
Prosciutto slices
4 skinless, boneless chicken breast halves

Bacon Green Beans
Haricots verts
Center-cut bacon

GAME PLAN

While chicken cooks:
- Mince shallots.
- Chop thyme, parsley, and tarragon.

While polenta cooks:
- Prepare green beans.

Hearty Beef and Stout Stew + Kale Mashed Potatoes

12 ounces boneless beef chuck, trimmed and thinly sliced
¼ teaspoon salt
¼ teaspoon black pepper
5 teaspoons olive oil, divided
2 cups finely chopped onion
1½ cups (¼-inch-thick) diagonally cut carrot
6 ounces presliced cremini mushrooms (about 2 cups)
3 thyme sprigs
1 tablespoon tomato paste
2 teaspoons minced fresh garlic
¾ cup stout beer (such as Guinness)
1½ cups unsalted beef stock (such as Swanson)
1 tablespoon all-purpose flour
1½ teaspoons lower-sodium soy sauce

1. Sprinkle beef with salt and pepper. Heat a large skillet over medium-high heat. Add 1 tablespoon olive oil to pan, and swirl to coat. Add beef to pan, and cook 3 minutes, browning on all sides. Remove beef from pan. Add remaining 2 teaspoons oil to pan, and swirl to coat. Add chopped onion, carrot, mushrooms, and thyme sprigs; sauté for 4 minutes. Add tomato paste and minced garlic; sauté 1 minute. Add beer; cook 1 minute, scraping pan to loosen browned bits. Combine beef stock and flour in a small bowl, stirring with a whisk. Add stock mixture to pan. Cover, reduce heat, and simmer 15 minutes. Stir in beef, and cook 1 minute or until thoroughly heated. Stir in soy sauce. Discard thyme. Serves 4 (serving size: 1 cup)

CALORIES 318; **FAT** 16.7g (sat 5.1g, mono 8.7g, poly 1.2g); **PROTEIN** 20.8g; **CARB** 18.9g; **FIBER** 3.5g; **CHOL** 66mg; **IRON** 2.3mg; **SODIUM** 370mg; **CALC** 51mg

continued

Kale Mashed Potatoes

Cook 2 cups frozen mashed potatoes
(such as Ore-Ida Steam 'n' Mash)
according to package directions. Melt
1 tablespoon butter in a large skillet
over medium heat. Add 2 cups sliced
Lacinato kale and ¼ cup sliced green
onions; sauté 1 minute. Stir in ½ cup
2% milk and ½ teaspoon pepper. Add
kale to potatoes; stir to combine.
Serves 4 (serving size: about ½ cup)

CALORIES 114; **FAT** 3.7g (sat 2.2g); **SODIUM** 229mg

READY IN **40** MINUTES

SHOPPING LIST

Hearty Beef and Stout Stew
Onion
Carrots
1 (8-ounce) package presliced cremini
  mushrooms
Garlic
Fresh thyme
All-purpose flour
Tomato paste
Lower-sodium soy sauce
Unsalted beef stock
1 (12-ounce) can stout beer
12 ounces boneless beef chuck
Olive oil

Kale Mashed Potatoes
Lacinato kale
Green onions
2% reduced-fat milk
Butter
1 (24-ounce) package frozen diced potatoes

GAME PLAN

While beef cooks:
- Cut carrots.
While stew simmers:
- Prepare mashed potatoes.

Browned Butter Flounder + Snap Peas + Brown Rice Pilaf

4 (6-ounce) flounder fillets
½ teaspoon freshly ground black
  pepper
⅛ teaspoon kosher salt
3 tablespoons all-purpose flour
4 teaspoons canola oil, divided
2 tablespoons unsalted butter, diced
1 tablespoon chopped fresh flat-leaf
  parsley
5 teaspoons fresh lemon juice, divided
8 ounces sugar snap peas, trimmed
1½ tablespoons chopped fresh mint
1 teaspoon grated lemon rind

1. Sprinkle fish evenly with pepper
and salt. Place flour in a shallow
dish; dredge fish in flour. Heat a
large nonstick skillet over medium-
high heat. Add 1 tablespoon oil to
pan; swirl to coat. Add fish to pan;
cook 3 minutes on each side or
until fish flakes easily with a fork.
Remove fish from pan; keep warm.
2. Return pan to medium heat.
Add butter; cook 45 seconds or until
butter begins to brown. Remove
pan from heat; stir in parsley and
1 tablespoon lemon juice. Place
butter mixture in a small bowl.
3. Return pan to medium-high heat.
Add 1 teaspoon oil to pan; swirl to
coat. Add snap peas; sauté 3 minutes
or just until crisp-tender. Stir in
2 teaspoons lemon juice, mint, and
rind. Serves 4 (serving size: 1 fillet,
2 teaspoons sauce, and about ⅔ cup
snap peas)

CALORIES 260; **FAT** 13.9g (sat 4.8g, mono 5.4g, poly 2.3g);
PROTEIN 23.5g; **CARB** 9.6g; **FIBER** 1.9g; **CHOL** 92mg;
IRON 1.9mg; **SODIUM** 202mg; **CALC** 68mg

Brown Rice Pilaf with Pecans
Heat 1 (8.8-ounce) package
precooked whole-grain brown rice
blend (such as Uncle Ben's) according to the package directions. Heat a
large skillet over medium heat. Add
2 teaspoons olive oil to pan; swirl to
coat. Add 1 thinly sliced leek (white
and light green parts only) and
2 cups sliced shiitake mushroom
caps, and sauté 4 minutes or until
tender, stirring occasionally. Add
¼ cup water, scraping pan to loosen
browned bits. Stir in cooked rice,
3 tablespoons chopped toasted pecans,
¼ teaspoon salt, and ¼ teaspoon
freshly ground black pepper. Serves
4 (serving size: ½ cup)

CALORIES 162; **FAT** 7.5g (sat 0.7g); **SODIUM** 160mg

READY IN **35** MINUTES

SHOPPING LIST

**Browned Butter Flounder with
  Lemon Snap Peas**
Lemon
Fresh sugar snap peas
Fresh flat-leaf parsley
Mint
All-purpose flour
Unsalted butter
Canola oil
4 (6-ounce) flounder fillets

Brown Rice Pilaf with Pecans
Leek
Shiitake mushroom caps (about 8
  ounces)
Pecans
Olive oil
1 (8.8-ounce) package precooked
  whole-grain brown rice blend

GAME PLAN

While Fish Cooks:
- Toast pecans.
While Rice Cooks:
- Prepare snap peas.

Picadillo Sloppy Joes + Spinach and Parmesan Salad

1 teaspoon olive oil
¾ cup chopped onion
2 teaspoons minced fresh garlic
1 pound 90% lean ground sirloin
2 teaspoons dried oregano
2 teaspoons ground cumin
1 teaspoon ground cinnamon
½ cup water
3 tablespoons dried currants
1 tablespoon capers, rinsed and
    drained
2¼ ounces pitted green olives,
    chopped (about 12)
1 (15-ounce) can unsalted crushed
    tomatoes, undrained
½ cup chopped fresh cilantro
2 tablespoons red wine vinegar
1 tablespoon minced pickled jalapeño
    pepper
Cooking spray
1 medium red onion, cut into 6
    (½-inch-thick) slices
6 (1½-ounce) hamburger buns with
    sesame seeds
6 small green leaf lettuce leaves

1. Heat a large saucepan over medium heat. Add oil; swirl to coat. Add chopped onion and garlic; sauté 4 minutes. Add beef to pan; cook 5 minutes or until browned, stirring to crumble. Stir in oregano, cumin, and cinnamon; cook 1 minute. Add ½ cup water and next 4 ingredients. Cover, reduce heat to low, and simmer 20 minutes, stirring occasionally. Stir in cilantro, vinegar, and jalapeño.
2. Heat a grill pan over medium-high heat. Coat with cooking spray. Add onion slices to pan; grill 4 minutes on each side. Remove onion from pan. Place buns, cut sides down, on grill pan; grill 1 minute or until toasted.

3. Place 1 lettuce leaf on bottom half of each bun; top each with ½ cup beef mixture. Divide onion slices evenly among servings; top with top halves of buns. Serves 6 (serving size: 1 sandwich)

CALORIES 323; **FAT** 10.7g (sat 3g, mono 4.9g, poly 1.4g); **PROTEIN** 20.8g; **CARB** 34.5g; **FIBER** 4g; **CHOL** 46mg; **IRON** 4.6mg; **SODIUM** 498mg; **CALC** 142mg

Spinach and Parmesan Salad
Combine 1 tablespoon fresh lemon juice, 1 tablespoon olive oil, 1½ teaspoons Worcestershire sauce, and ¼ teaspoon freshly ground black pepper in a large bowl, stirring with a whisk. Add 4 cups baby spinach and 4 cups baby arugula; toss to coat. Sprinkle with 1 ounce shaved Parmesan cheese. Serves 6 (serving size: 1 cup)

CALORIES 52; **FAT** 3.7g (sat 1.1g); **SODIUM** 116mg

CAPERS AND OLIVES ADD GREAT BRINY FLAVOR TO THE SLOPPY JOE MIXTURE, BUT FEEL FREE TO OMIT THEM.

READY IN
35
MINUTES

SHOPPING LIST

Picadillo Sloppy Joes
Green leaf lettuce
White onion
Red onion
Garlic
Fresh cilantro
Dried oregano
Ground cumin
Ground cinnamon
Red wine vinegar
Dried currants
Capers
Pitted green olives
1 (15-ounce) can unsalted crushed
    tomatoes
Pickled jalapeño pepper
6 (1½-ounce) hamburger buns with
    sesame seeds
1 pound 90% lean ground sirloin
Olive oil

Spinach and Parmesan Salad
Lemon
Baby spinach
Baby arugula
Worcestershire sauce
Olive oil
Parmesan cheese

GAME PLAN

While beef mixture cooks:
■ Grill onions.
■ Toast hamburger buns.
■ Prepare salad.

DELICATA SQUASH

It's thin-skinned. It's beautiful. Time to try this squash.

If you love winter squash but find yourself in a butternut rut, branch out and try delicata. It's less assertively sweet than butternut, which makes it more versatile. And while butternut isn't the easiest veg to prep—peeling and chopping the bigger ones requires heavy-duty blades and Popeye's forearm—delicata skin is so thin and tender you can leave it on and eat it: It adds subtle snap to the buttery flesh.

Kid Friendly • Gluten Free Vegetarian

Roasted Delicata with Cranberries and Pumpkinseeds

Hands-on: 10 min. Total: 45 min. This impressive yet simple side dish is great for company. And remember: You can eat the skin.

2 (12-ounce) delicata squashes
4 teaspoons canola oil, divided
½ teaspoon kosher salt, divided
¼ teaspoon freshly ground black
  pepper, divided
Cooking spray
4 thyme sprigs
3 tablespoons dried sweetened
  cranberries
2 teaspoons butter
1 teaspoon fresh lemon juice
2 tablespoons pumpkinseed kernels,
  toasted

1. Preheat oven to 425°.
2. Cut each squash in half lengthwise; scoop out and discard seeds and membranes. Brush flesh with 2 teaspoons oil; sprinkle evenly with ¼ teaspoon salt and ⅛ teaspoon pepper. Place squash halves, cut sides down, in a 13 x 9–inch glass or ceramic baking dish coated with cooking spray. Bake at 425° for 15 minutes. Turn over (cut sides up); place 1 thyme sprig in each. Bake an additional 17 minutes or until tender. Sprinkle with ¼ teaspoon salt and ⅛ teaspoon pepper.
3. Preheat broiler to high.
4. Broil squash 2 minutes or until lightly browned.
5. Place cranberries in a small bowl; cover with water. Microwave at HIGH 45 seconds; drain.
6. Melt butter in a small skillet over medium heat; cook 3 minutes or until browned. Stir in 2 teaspoons oil and lemon juice. Drizzle butter mixture over squash. Divide cranberries and pumpkinseeds among squash halves. Serves 4 (serving size: 1 squash half)

CALORIES 160; FAT 8.6g (sat 1.9g, mono 4.1g, poly 2.2g); PROTEIN 3.3g; CARB 19.4g; FIBER 2.3g; CHOL 5.1mg; IRON 1.1mg; SODIUM 257mg; CALC 44mg

DELICATA LIVES UP TO ITS NAME: IT'S A SUBTLE SQUASH THAT WORKS WELL WITH BOLD, BRIGHT FLAVORS LIKE CRANBERRY.

RISOTTO

Matisse stirs up a classic, with a little help from her friends.

"You'll want to make this with a friend, as four hands are better than two with risotto. One person can pour in the stock while the other one stirs. You can eat this dish as a side or throw in some shrimp or sliced cooked chicken to make it a main dish. If you're a vegetarian, use vegetable stock and omit the bacon. I loved the creaminess and texture of the rice. I ate it cold for lunch the next day and it was delicious, so I recommend you make extra. Follow the directions carefully, and you will end up with a yummy dish the whole family will love."

Bacon and Leek Risotto

Hands-on: 50 min. Total: 50 min.

5 cups unsalted chicken stock (such
  as Swanson)
2 cups water
4 bacon slices
1 tablespoon olive oil
4 cups thinly sliced leek (about 4 large)
½ cup sliced shallots
1½ tablespoons chopped fresh thyme
2 garlic cloves, minced
2 cups uncooked Arborio rice
2 tablespoons fresh lemon juice
1½ tablespoons unsalted butter
1 teaspoon freshly ground black pepper
½ teaspoon kosher salt
2 ounces Parmigiano-Reggiano
  cheese, grated (about ½ cup)
2 tablespoons chopped fresh flat-leaf
  parsley

1. Bring stock and 2 cups water to a simmer in a medium saucepan (do not boil). Keep warm over low heat. **2.** Cook bacon in a large nonstick skillet over medium heat until crisp. Remove bacon from pan; crumble. Add oil to pan; swirl to coat. Add leek, shallots, thyme, and garlic to pan; sauté 4 minutes or until tender. Stir in rice; cook 2 minutes. Stir in ½ cup stock mixture; cook 5 minutes or until liquid is nearly absorbed, stirring constantly. Reserve ⅓ cup stock mixture. Add remaining stock mixture, ¼ cup at a time, stirring constantly until liquid is absorbed before adding more (about 25 minutes total). Stir in lemon juice, butter, pepper, salt, and Parmigiano-Reggiano. Remove pan from heat. Stir in reserved ⅓ cup stock mixture. Sprinkle with reserved bacon and chopped parsley. Serve immediately. Serves 8 (serving size: about ⅔ cup)

CALORIES 305; FAT 7.9g (sat 3.3g, mono 3g, poly 0.6g); PROTEIN 12.1g; CARB 47.8g; FIBER 3.3g; CHOL 15mg; IRON 1.8mg; SODIUM 394mg; CALC 128mg

THE VERDICT

ANGELA (AGE 11)
She loved all the flavors and will definitely eat this again. **10/10**

IAN (AGE 12)
He was a little skeptical because he doesn't usually eat rice. He loved the flavor and texture. **9/10**

MATISSE (AGE 13)
I loved how creamy the rice was, having absorbed all the yummy stock. **10/10**

12 HEALTHY HABITS

EAT 3 MORE SERVINGS OF VEGGIES EACH DAY

Kick-start the journey to a healthier you with new ways to enjoy vegetables.

Tara Duggan didn't spend her college summers on beaches or partying with friends. She wasn't taking classes or buried in books, either. Instead, she used that time to explore food on a global scale. Duggan's military father transferred to Italy when she was in college, so she spent a lot of time exploring international cuisines during summer visits. "My parents really love to eat and travel, and we ate out a lot. I'd then go buy local ingredients and try to re-create the dishes at home," she says. The family ate plenty of pizza and pasta, of course, but Duggan says she also discovered an entirely new world: vegetables.

"Italy, especially southern Italy, puts a lot of focus on vegetables and using all the different vegetable parts," she says. Previously, in Duggan's eyes, "vegetables were kind of a side thought, something you were duty-bound to eat. But all of a sudden, I realized vegetables could be really delicious and have unique qualities and flavors."

After graduating from the University of California at Berkeley in 1994, Duggan settled in San Francisco and started a career in travel journalism. Eventually, however, she felt the lure of the food world again, so she went to culinary school and soon landed at the *San Francisco Chronicle* as a food writer and recipe developer. She also covered farms and farmers' markets, which were quickly growing in popularity in

California and around the country. Spending time on farms, she says, lets you see how uniquely wonderful each vegetable or fruit is. "When you see how much work goes into them, you don't want to waste them," she says. We asked Duggan to share her favorite ways for making the most out of fresh vegetables.

TARA'S 3 TIPS FOR GETTING MORE FROM VEGGIES

1. TAKE IT FROM THE TOP. "You can use beet tops instead of Swiss chard. They're very similar. And carrot tops taste a lot like parsley, so I use them in a delicious riff on salsa verde. It's great on roasted veggies in the winter."

2. ROAST 'EM. Roasting veggies is pretty low-maintenance. "Throw them in the oven, and let them cook. I find that with boiling you can quickly overdo it. But with roasted vegetables, even slightly overdone is still delicious."

3. FORGET THE PEEL. "Try leaving the peel in place when you roast squash. The skins get dehydrated in the oven, so they turn crispy and are perfectly edible. Younger butternut squash is great for this. The smaller ones are more of a cylinder; they don't have a bulb yet. You can slice the squash into rounds and roast at high heat."

Shaved Broccoli Stalk Salad with Lime

"One of the few vegetables my kids will eat is broccoli," Duggan says, "so I found new ways to use it." Sodium reflects ⅛ teaspoon kosher salt.

Leaves and stalks from 1 bunch broccoli (about 3 stalks), cut into batons
1 tablespoon extra-virgin olive oil
1½ teaspoons fresh lime juice
Kosher salt and black pepper
¼ cup crumbled cotija or feta cheese

1. Place broccoli batons flat on a cutting board, and then use a sharp vegetable peeler to shave the broccoli into paper-thin strips.
2. Place shaved broccoli and leaves in a medium bowl, and toss with olive oil, lime juice, and salt and pepper to taste. Gently fold in cheese, and serve immediately. Serves 2 (serving size: 1 cup)

CALORIES 143; **FAT** 11.2g (sat 3.8g, mono 5.8g, poly 1g); **PROTEIN** 6.1g; **CARB** 7.2g; **FIBER** 3.5g; **CHOL** 17mg; **IRON** 1.2mg; **SODIUM** 360mg; **CALC** 149mg

Reprinted with permission from Root-to-Stalk Cooking: The Art of Using the Whole Vegetable, by Tara Duggan, copyright 2013. Published by Ten Speed Press, a division of Random House, Inc.

MEATLESS MONDAYS

COZY ONE-DISH DINNERS

Nutty whole grains make a perfect bed for a bowl of saucy winter veggies.

Make Ahead • Vegetarian

Winter Squash and Tofu Panang Curry

Hands-on: 45 min. Total: 60 min.

1¾ cups water
1 cup uncooked brown jasmine rice
1 teaspoon minced peeled fresh ginger
¼ teaspoon kosher salt
½ cup chopped fresh cilantro
1 (14-ounce) block extra-firm tofu, drained and cut into 1-inch cubes
5 teaspoons canola oil, divided
2 tablespoons creamy peanut butter
1½ tablespoons Thai red curry paste
1 teaspoon ground cumin
1 teaspoon ground coriander
1 (14-ounce) can light coconut milk
3 tablespoons lower-sodium soy sauce
1 tablespoon brown sugar
3 cups cubed peeled kabocha squash
1 cup chopped red bell pepper
⅓ cup sliced shallots
1½ teaspoons grated lime rind
2 tablespoons fresh lime juice
½ cup fresh basil leaves

1. Combine first 4 ingredients in a saucepan. Bring to a boil; cover, reduce heat, and simmer 35 minutes. Let stand 10 minutes. Add cilantro; fluff rice mixture.
2. Place tofu on several layers of paper towels. Cover with additional paper towels. Let stand for 30 minutes, pressing down occasionally.
3. Heat a wok or large skillet over medium-high heat. Add 1 tablespoon oil to pan; swirl to coat. Add tofu; sauté 8 minutes or until golden brown, stirring occasionally. Remove tofu from pan; keep warm.
4. Return pan to medium heat. Add 2 teaspoons oil to pan; swirl to coat. Add peanut butter, curry paste, cumin, and coriander; cook 15 seconds. Add coconut milk, soy sauce, and sugar, stirring with a whisk until smooth. Add squash, bell pepper, and shallots. Bring to a boil; reduce heat, and simmer 15 minutes or until squash is tender. Gently stir in tofu, rind, and juice. Cook 1 minute. Sprinkle evenly with basil; serve over rice. Serves 6 (serving size: about 1 cup curry and ⅔ cup rice)

CALORIES 341; **FAT** 14.7g (sat 4.3g, mono 7g, poly 2.6g); **PROTEIN** 12.9g; **CARB** 44.3g; **FIBER** 4.2g; **CHOL** 0mg; **IRON** 3.3mg; **SODIUM** 467mg; **CALC** 182mg

IF YOU HAVE TROUBLE FINDING KABOCHA SQUASH, AN ACORN OR BUTTERNUT VARIETY IS AN EASY, JUST-AS-DELICIOUS SUBSTITUTE.

Stewed Bulgur and Broccoli Rabe with Poached Eggs

Hands-on: 20 min. Total: 40 min.
For less cleanup, poach the eggs directly in the stew once the broccoli rabe is tender.

2 teaspoons extra-virgin olive oil
1½ cups chopped onion
½ teaspoon crushed red pepper
4 garlic cloves, minced
3 cups organic vegetable broth
1 cup water
¾ cup uncooked bulgur
¼ teaspoon salt
1 bunch broccoli rabe (rapini), cut into 2-inch-long pieces (about 1 pound)
1 tablespoon fresh lemon juice
1 tablespoon white vinegar
6 large eggs
1.5 ounces vegetarian Parmesan cheese, shaved (about 6 tablespoons)
¼ teaspoon black pepper

1. Heat a large Dutch oven over medium heat. Add oil to pan; swirl to coat. Add onion; sauté 10 minutes. Stir in red pepper and garlic; cook 1 minute. Add broth and 1 cup water; bring to a boil. Stir in bulgur and salt. Cover and simmer 10 minutes. Add broccoli rabe. Cover and simmer 12 minutes or until broccoli rabe is tender; stir in lemon juice. Ladle stew evenly into 6 shallow bowls.
2. Add water to a large skillet, filling two-thirds full; bring to a boil. Reduce heat; simmer. Add vinegar. Break each egg into a custard cup, and pour each gently into pan; cook 3 minutes or until desired degree of doneness. Carefully remove eggs from pan using a slotted spoon; place 1 poached egg on each serving of stew. Sprinkle evenly with cheese and black pepper. Serves 6 (serving size: about 1 cup stew, 1 egg, and 1 tablespoon cheese)

CALORIES 226; FAT 8.6g (sat 3.1g, mono 3.6g, poly 1.3g); PROTEIN 14.4g; CARB 23.7g; FIBER 4g; CHOL 192mg; IRON 2.2mg; SODIUM 579mg; CALC 162mg

SLOW COOKER

OSSO BUCO: STILL SLOW, NOW EASIER

We sub less expensive beef for traditional veal in this rich, slow cooker classic.

Kid Friendly • Make Ahead Freezable

Easy Beef Osso Buco

Hands-on: 30 min. Total: 8 hr. 30 min.

1¾ teaspoons kosher salt, divided
3 pounds cross-cut bone-in beef shanks
1 tablespoon canola oil, divided
Cooking spray
2 cups sliced onion
¾ cup chopped celery
¾ cup chopped carrot
2 tablespoons tomato paste
8 garlic cloves, crushed
1 cup unsalted beef stock
¼ ounce dried porcini mushrooms, chopped
½ cup dry red wine
2 teaspoons cornstarch
¾ teaspoon black pepper
1 bay leaf
8 plum tomatoes
6 tablespoons chopped fresh flat-leaf parsley
1 tablespoon grated lemon rind
1 tablespoon minced fresh garlic

1. Preheat broiler.
2. Sprinkle ½ teaspoon salt over beef. Heat a large skillet over medium-high heat. Add 1½ teaspoons oil; swirl to coat. Add beef; cook 4 minutes on each side or until browned. Add beef to a 6-quart electric slow cooker coated with cooking spray. Add 1½ teaspoons oil to skillet; swirl. Add onion, celery, carrot, tomato paste, and garlic; sauté 4 minutes. Add stock and mushrooms. Bring to a boil; cook 1 minute, scraping pan to loosen browned bits. Add stock mixture, wine, cornstarch, pepper, and bay leaf to slow cooker.
3. Place tomatoes on a jelly-roll pan. Broil 8 minutes or until blackened. Place tomatoes on beef, pressing lightly to crush.
4. Cover and cook on LOW 8 hours or until beef is tender. Remove beef from cooker. Remove meat from bones; discard bones. Stir meat and 1¼ teaspoons salt into cooker. Discard bay leaf.
5. Combine parsley, rind, and garlic. Sprinkle on top. Serves 8 (serving size: about 1 cup beef mixture and 2 teaspoons gremolata)

CALORIES 207; FAT 6g (sat 1.5g, mono 2.9g, poly 0.8g); PROTEIN 24.3g; CARB 10.8g; FIBER 2.4g; CHOL 40mg; IRON 3.3mg; SODIUM 557mg; CALC 57mg

FEED 4 FOR LESS THAN $10

Two comforting family favorites get delicious modern updates.

Kid Friendly • Quick & Easy

Cheddar BLT Panini

$2.48 PER SERVING

Hands-on: 25 min. Total: 25 min.
If you can't find French bread rolls, halve an 8-ounce baguette lengthwise, and cut into fourths. Serve with carrot sticks.

3 center-cut bacon slices
2 (6-ounce) skinless, boneless chicken breast halves, halved lengthwise
4 cups baby spinach leaves
2 teaspoons balsamic vinegar
3 ounces reduced-fat white cheddar cheese, shredded (about ¾ cup)
2 tablespoons ⅓-less-fat cream cheese
4 (2-ounce) French bread rolls, halved lengthwise
8 tomato slices
Cooking spray

1. Heat a large skillet over medium heat. Add bacon; cook until crisp. Remove bacon from pan using a slotted spoon; crumble. Add chicken to drippings in pan; cook 2 minutes on each side or until done. Remove chicken from pan. Add baby spinach to pan; cook 30 seconds or until spinach begins to wilt, stirring constantly. Stir in balsamic vinegar.
2. Combine cheddar cheese and cream cheese in a small microwave-safe bowl. Microwave at HIGH 30 seconds or until melted; stir with a whisk until smooth. Stir in bacon. Spread cheese mixture evenly over cut sides of rolls. Divide tomatoes evenly over bottom halves of rolls; top with chicken and spinach mixture. Top sandwiches with top halves of rolls. Return pan to medium heat. Coat both sides of sandwiches with cooking spray. Add sandwiches to pan. Place a cast-iron skillet on top of sandwiches; press gently to flatten. Cook sandwiches 3 minutes on each side or until bread is toasted (leave skillet on sandwiches as they cook). Cut each sandwich in half diagonally. Serves 4 (serving size: 1 sandwich)

CALORIES 375; FAT 12.5g (sat 5.9g, mono 3g, poly 1.3g); PROTEIN 31.4g; CARB 32.5g; FIBER 2.8g; CHOL 80mg; IRON 2.8mg; SODIUM 723mg; CALC 246mg

THE HUMBLE BLT GETS FANCY WITH CHICKEN AND SAUTÉED SPINACH.

Kid Friendly • Make Ahead

Braised Beef with Onion, Sweet Potato, and Parsnip

$2.33 PER SERVING

Hands-on: 15 min. Total: 2 hr. 10 min.

2 tablespoons olive oil, divided
1 (1-pound) boneless chuck roast, trimmed
½ teaspoon kosher salt, divided
½ teaspoon black pepper, divided
1 medium onion, chopped
1 tablespoon tomato paste
3 garlic cloves, minced
2 cups fat-free, lower-sodium beef broth
1 (½-inch-thick) diagonally cut parsnip
1 (¾-inch-thick) diagonally cut carrot
12 ounces diced peeled sweet potato

1. Preheat oven to 325°.
2. Heat a Dutch oven over medium-high heat. Add 1 tablespoon oil; swirl. Sprinkle beef with ¼ teaspoon salt and ¼ teaspoon pepper; cook 10 minutes, browning on all sides. Remove from pan. Add onion; sauté 4 minutes. Add tomato paste and garlic; sauté 1 minute. Add beef and broth; bring to a boil. Cover and bake at 325° for 2 hours.
3. Combine remaining 1 tablespoon oil, parsnip, carrot, sweet potato, ¼ teaspoon salt, and ¼ teaspoon pepper on a foil-lined jelly-roll pan; toss to coat. Place pan on bottom rack in oven; bake at 325° for 50 minutes, stirring once.
4. Cut beef across grain into slices. Return Dutch oven to medium-high heat; cook sauce 5 minutes. Place ½ cup vegetables in each of 4 shallow bowls; top with 3 ounces beef and ¼ cup sauce. Serves 4

CALORIES 369; FAT 14.4g (sat 3.5g, mono 8.6g, poly 1.4g); PROTEIN 28.5g; CARB 31g; FIBER 5.8g; CHOL 65mg; IRON 4mg; SODIUM 440mg; CALC 68mg

WHAT IS BUDGET COOKING?

Prices are derived from midsized-city supermarkets. Side dishes mentioned in recipe notes are included in the cost of the meal. For specialty or highly perishable ingredients, like some Asian sauces or fresh herbs, we account for the entire cost of the ingredient. For staples and other ingredients, we include the cost for only the amount used. Salt, pepper, and cooking spray are freebies.

THE PERFECT CHICKEN COLLECTION!

Twelve delectable dishes that feature your favorite chicken cuts, whether you like your meat light, dark, or rotisserie-style

Kid Friendly • Quick & Easy

Chicken Breast with Pancetta Cream and Peas

Hands-on: 37 min. Total: 37 min. *You can substitute bacon for pancetta, and cream cheese for mascarpone.*

1 tablespoon olive oil
4 garlic cloves, thinly sliced
1¹/₂ ounces pancetta, chopped
4 (6-ounce) skinless, boneless chicken breast halves
³/₈ teaspoon kosher salt
¹/₄ teaspoon freshly ground black pepper
¹/₂ cup dry white wine
1 cup unsalted chicken stock (such as Swanson)
2 tablespoons mascarpone cheese
2 tablespoons water
2 teaspoons all-purpose flour
1 cup frozen green peas, thawed

1. Heat a large skillet over medium heat. Add oil to pan; swirl to coat. Add garlic; cook 2 minutes, stirring frequently. Remove garlic from pan using a slotted spoon; reserve garlic. Increase heat to medium-high. Add pancetta; sauté 4 minutes or until crisp. Remove pancetta from pan using a slotted spoon; reserve pancetta. **2.** Sprinkle chicken with salt and pepper; sauté 4 minutes on each side. Remove chicken from pan. Add wine; bring to a boil, scraping pan to loosen browned bits. Cook until liquid almost evaporates (about 3 minutes). Return chicken to pan. Add stock; bring to a boil. Reduce heat to medium, cover, and cook 6 minutes or until chicken is done. Remove chicken from pan. **3.** Add mascarpone to pan, stirring with a whisk until smooth. Combine water and flour, stirring with a whisk. Add flour mixture to pan; bring to a boil. Cook 2 minutes; stir in pancetta, garlic, and peas. Cook 1 minute. Serve sauce over chicken. Serves 4 (serving size: 1 breast half and about 2 tablespoons sauce)

CALORIES 387; FAT 17.9g (sat 6.4g, mono 6.8g, poly 3.1g); PROTEIN 42g; CARB 7.7g; FIBER 1.6g; CHOL 134mg; IRON 1.5mg; SODIUM 630mg; CALC 50mg

FOOLPROOF, QUICK, EASY RECIPES FOR THOSE WITH A PASSION FOR POULTRY

Quick & Easy

Sautéed Chicken with Roasted Pepper Pasta

Hands-on: 35 min. Total: 35 min. *If you can't find mozzarella pearls, dice a block of mozzarella.*

6 ounces uncooked rotini
12 baby bell peppers
3 ounces fresh mozzarella pearls (about ³/₄ cup)
2 tablespoons olive oil
2 teaspoons white wine vinegar
2 garlic cloves, minced
¹/₂ cup chopped fresh parsley
¹/₂ teaspoon salt, divided
Cooking spray
4 (6-ounce) skinless, boneless chicken breast halves
¹/₂ teaspoon black pepper

1. Preheat broiler to high. **2.** Cook pasta; drain. Place in a large bowl; keep warm. **3.** Cut bell peppers in half lengthwise; discard seeds and membranes. Place peppers, skin sides up, on a foil-lined baking sheet; flatten. Broil 6 minutes or until blackened. Let stand 5 minutes. Peel; cut into strips. Add peppers and cheese to pasta. Combine oil, vinegar, and garlic; stir into pasta mixture. Stir in parsley and ¼ teaspoon salt. **4.** Heat a large skillet over medium-high heat. Coat pan with cooking spray. Sprinkle chicken with remaining salt and pepper; sauté 6 minutes on each side or until done. Slice chicken. Serve over pasta mixture. Serves 4 (serving size: 1 breast half and about 1 cup pasta mixture)

CALORIES 503; FAT 16.8g (sat 5.1g, mono 6.3g, poly 1.7g); PROTEIN 46.8g; CARB 38.4g; FIBER 3.7g; CHOL 124mg; IRON 3mg; SODIUM 564mg; CALC 158mg

Chicken Cutlets with Mushrooms and Pearl Onions

(pictured on page 214)

Hands-on: 38 min. Total: 43 min. *The brandy-spiked sauce adds an elegant touch to this simple supper; you can sub wine.*

4 (6-ounce) skinless, boneless chicken breast halves
½ teaspoon kosher salt, divided
¼ teaspoon freshly ground black pepper
2 tablespoons all-purpose flour
3 tablespoons olive oil, divided
¾ cup frozen pearl onions, thawed and drained
8 ounces quartered button mushrooms
⅔ cup brandy
1 cup unsalted chicken stock
2 teaspoons cornstarch
1 tablespoon butter
1 teaspoon thyme leaves

1. Cut each chicken breast half in half horizontally to form 8 cutlets. Heat a large skillet over medium-high heat. Sprinkle chicken evenly with ¼ teaspoon salt and pepper. Place flour in a shallow dish; dredge chicken in flour, shaking off excess.
2. Add 1 tablespoon olive oil to pan; swirl to coat. Add 4 cutlets to pan; cook 2 minutes on each side or until done. Remove chicken from pan, and keep warm. Repeat procedure with 1 tablespoon olive oil and remaining 4 cutlets.
3. Add 1 tablespoon oil to pan; swirl to coat. Add pearl onions and mushrooms; sauté 6 minutes or until browned. Remove pan from heat. Carefully add brandy to pan; return pan to medium-high heat, and bring mixture to a boil. Cook until liquid almost evaporates (about 2 minutes). Combine stock and cornstarch, stirring with a whisk until smooth. Add stock mixture to pan, stirring with a whisk; cook 2 minutes, stirring occasionally. Return chicken to pan; cook 1 minute. Remove from heat; stir in ¼ teaspoon salt, butter, and thyme. Serves 4 (serving size: 2 cutlets and about ¾ cup mushroom mixture)

CALORIES 402; FAT 17.7g (sat 4.2g, mono 9.4g, poly 2g); PROTEIN 39.9g; CARB 9.2g; FIBER 1.3g; CHOL 116mg; IRON 1.4mg; SODIUM 500mg; CALC 25mg

CASUAL AND COMFORTING CHICKEN DINNERS ARE A WEEKNIGHT FAVORITE.

Kid Friendly • Quick & Easy

Parmesan and Pine Nut-Crusted Oven-Fried Chicken

Hands-on: 15 min. Total: 25 min.
The crust gets golden and crisp in the skillet and helps insulate the chicken to keep it supremely juicy.

3 tablespoons pine nuts, toasted
1 tablespoon finely ground yellow cornmeal
½ teaspoon onion powder
½ teaspoon baking soda
½ teaspoon finely chopped rosemary leaves
2.25 ounces all-purpose flour (about ½ cup)
1 ounce Parmesan cheese, grated (about ¼ cup)
½ cup nonfat buttermilk
1 large egg white
4 (6-ounce) skinless, boneless chicken breast halves
½ teaspoon kosher salt
¼ teaspoon freshly ground black pepper
2 tablespoons canola oil

1. Preheat oven to 425°.
2. Combine first 3 ingredients in a mini chopper. Pulse until finely ground. Combine nut mixture, baking soda, and next 3 ingredients (through cheese) in a shallow dish. Combine buttermilk and egg white in a shallow dish. Dip chicken in buttermilk mixture; sprinkle evenly with salt and pepper. Dredge in flour mixture.
3. Heat a large ovenproof skillet over medium-high heat. Add oil; swirl. Add chicken; sauté 3 minutes or until browned. Turn chicken over. Place pan in oven; bake at 425° for 10 minutes or until chicken is done. Serves 4 (serving size: 1 breast half)

CALORIES 390; FAT 17.5g (sat 3.2g, mono 7.6g, poly 5.1g); PROTEIN 41.5g; CARB 14.9g; FIBER 0.7g; CHOL 101mg; IRON 2.3mg; SODIUM 632mg; CALC 137mg

THE PERFECT CHICKEN BREASTS

For many cooks, breast meat is the favorite chicken cut, but skinless, boneless breasts need a little love to keep them juicy and flavorful. To that end, we sauté them hot and fast to get them golden brown outside and moist within. Then, for maximum deliciousness, we coat them in savory crusts and dress them with light but zingy sauces.

Stacked Chicken Enchiladas

Hands-on: 45 min. Total: 60 min.
Because you layer this Tex-Mex dish, lasagna-style, instead of rolling each enchilada individually, you save time in the kitchen. Plus, the results are ultimately healthier because the tortillas don't have to be fried or softened in oil before you assemble the casserole. Look for Mexican crema at Latin food markets or with the Mexican cheeses in the supermarket.

2 tablespoons canola oil
8 skinless, boneless chicken thighs (about 2 pounds)
1 teaspoon ground cumin
$1/2$ teaspoon kosher salt
$1/4$ teaspoon ground red pepper
2 cups chopped white onion
8 garlic cloves, minced
1 (15-ounce) can organic whole peeled tomatoes, undrained and crushed
1 cup chopped fresh cilantro, divided
3 tablespoons fresh lime juice
1 (7-ounce) can salsa verde
Cooking spray
12 (6-inch) corn tortillas
3 ounces shredded pepper-Jack cheese (about $3/4$ cup)
6 tablespoons Mexican crema

1. Place a small roasting pan in oven. Preheat oven to 425° (leave roasting pan in oven as it preheats).
2. Heat a large skillet over medium-high heat. Add oil to pan; swirl to coat. Sprinkle both sides of chicken evenly with cumin, salt, and pepper. Add chicken to pan; sauté 3 minutes. Turn chicken over, and place in preheated roasting pan. Add onion, garlic, and tomatoes to pan; bake at 425° for 15 minutes or until chicken is done. Cool. Shred chicken; toss with tomato mixture.
3. Combine ¾ cup cilantro, juice, and salsa verde; spread ¼ cup salsa mixture in the bottom of an 11 x 7–inch glass or ceramic baking dish coated with cooking spray. Top with 4 overlapping tortillas, half of chicken mixture, and ¼ cup salsa mixture. Repeat layers. Top with remaining 4 tortillas and remaining salsa mixture; sprinkle evenly with cheese. Bake at 425° for 15 minutes or until golden; sprinkle with ¼ cup cilantro. Top each serving with 1 tablespoon crema. Serves 6 (serving size: about 1¼ cups)

CALORIES 385; **FAT** 17.3g (sat 4.9g, mono 7.3g, poly 3.7g); **PROTEIN** 25.4g; **CARB** 32.2g; **FIBER** 4.3g; **CHOL** 111mg; **IRON** 1.9mg; **SODIUM** 645mg; **CALC** 151mg

Chicken with Mustard-White Wine Sauce and Spring Vegetables

Hands-on: 60 min. Total: 60 min. *This dish pairs early spring produce with cold-weather comfort.*

4 large shallots, peeled and quartered
12 baby carrots, peeled
1 pound small red potatoes, halved lengthwise
$2^1/2$ tablespoons olive oil, divided
$3/4$ teaspoon kosher salt, divided
$1/2$ teaspoon freshly ground black pepper, divided
$1^1/2$ pounds (about 8) skinless, boneless chicken thighs
1 cup white wine
2 thyme sprigs
1 rosemary sprig
1 tablespoon all-purpose flour
$1^1/2$ cups unsalted chicken stock (such as Swanson), divided
1 tablespoon Dijon mustard
2 tablespoons chopped fresh flat-leaf parsley
2 teaspoons chopped thyme leaves

1. Place a jelly-roll pan in oven. Preheat oven to 425° (leave jelly-roll pan in oven as it preheats).
2. Combine first 3 ingredients in a bowl; drizzle with 1½ tablespoons oil. Sprinkle with ¼ teaspoon salt and ¼ teaspoon pepper; toss well to coat. Add vegetable mixture to preheated pan. Bake at 425° for 30 minutes or until golden and almost tender, stirring once.
3. Heat a large ovenproof skillet over medium-high heat. Add 1 tablespoon oil to pan; swirl to coat. Sprinkle ½ teaspoon salt and ¼ teaspoon pepper evenly over both sides of chicken. Add chicken to pan; cook 3 minutes. Turn chicken over. Place pan in oven; bake chicken at 425° for 10 minutes or until done. Remove from pan, and let stand 10 minutes.
4. Return skillet to stovetop over medium-high heat. Add wine, thyme sprigs, and rosemary sprig; bring to a boil, scraping pan to loosen browned bits. Cook until liquid is reduced to 3 tablespoons (about 10 minutes). Place flour in a small bowl. Stir in ½ cup stock and mustard; add to pan. Cook 1 minute, stirring constantly with a whisk. Add 1 cup stock and vegetable mixture to pan. Bring to a simmer; cook 2 minutes. Remove from heat; discard thyme and rosemary sprigs. Stir in chopped parsley and chopped thyme. Serve chicken with sauce and vegetables. Serves 4 (serving size: 2 thighs and about 1 cup vegetable mixture)

CALORIES 445; **FAT** 15.8g (sat 3g, mono 8.6g, poly 2.6g); **PROTEIN** 38.6g; **CARB** 32g; **FIBER** 3.8g; **CHOL** 162mg; **IRON** 3.3mg; **SODIUM** 709mg; **CALC** 60mg

Quick & Easy

Chicken Thighs with Cilantro Sauce

Hands-on: 20 min. Total: 20 min. *As a variation, you could grill the chicken thighs—a little charring would complement the sauce. No mortar and pestle? Process the paste base in a mini chopper.*

Cooking spray
8 skinless, boneless chicken thighs (about 2 pounds)
1/2 teaspoon kosher salt, divided
2 tablespoons finely chopped shallots
1 large garlic clove, minced
1/3 cup finely chopped fresh cilantro
1 1/2 tablespoons dark sesame oil
1 tablespoon lower-sodium soy sauce
1/2 teaspoon Sriracha (hot chile sauce)
1/2 teaspoon grated lime rind

1. Heat a large skillet over medium-high heat. Coat pan with cooking spray. Sprinkle chicken evenly with 1/4 teaspoon salt. Add chicken to pan; sauté 6 minutes or until browned. Turn; sauté 4 minutes or until chicken is done. Place chicken on a platter.
2. Combine 1/4 teaspoon salt, shallots, and garlic in a mortar and pestle; smash mixture to a paste. Combine garlic mixture, cilantro, and remaining ingredients. Spread 1 1/2 teaspoons cilantro mixture over each chicken thigh. Serves 4 (serving size: 2 thighs and 1 tablespoon sauce)

CALORIES 260; FAT 14.8g (sat 3.4g, mono 6g, poly 4.1g); PROTEIN 28.5g; CARB 1.6g; FIBER 0.2g; CHOL 159mg; IRON 1.4mg; SODIUM 489mg; CALC 16mg

Quick & Easy

Balsamic Chicken with Olives and Walnuts

Hands-on: 33 min. Total: 33 min.

4 teaspoons olive oil, divided
12 skinless, boneless chicken thighs (about 3 pounds)
1/2 teaspoon kosher salt
1/2 teaspoon black pepper
5 medium shallots, quartered (about 2 cups)
1/3 cup balsamic vinegar
1/4 cup unsalted chicken stock (such as Swanson)
1 tablespoon lower-sodium soy sauce
1 1/2 teaspoons brown sugar
3 thyme sprigs
1/3 cup halved pitted Castelvetrano olives
3 tablespoons chopped walnuts, toasted
1 tablespoon chopped fresh chives
2 teaspoons chopped fresh thyme

1. Heat a Dutch oven over medium-high heat. Add 2 teaspoons oil to pan; swirl to coat. Sprinkle chicken with salt and pepper. Add 6 chicken thighs to pan; cook 6 minutes or until browned. Turn chicken over; cook 1 minute. Remove chicken from pan. Repeat procedure with remaining chicken. Remove chicken from pan.
2. Add 2 teaspoons oil to pan; swirl to coat. Add shallots to pan; cook 3 minutes or until browned, stirring occasionally. Remove shallots from pan. Add vinegar to pan; cook 10 seconds, scraping pan to loosen browned bits. Add stock, soy sauce, sugar, and thyme; cook 30 seconds, stirring constantly. Return chicken and shallots to pan; toss to coat. Reduce heat to low; cook 5 minutes or until chicken is done. Discard thyme. Sprinkle with olives and remaining ingredients. Serves 6 (serving size: 2 thighs, about 2 teaspoons olives, and 2 teaspoons walnuts)

CALORIES 395; FAT 19.1g (sat 4.2g, mono 8.6g, poly 4.3g); PROTEIN 40.4g; CARB 13.9g; FIBER 2.4g; CHOL 211mg; IRON 3mg; SODIUM 460mg; CALC 54mg

DRESS THE BIRD BOLDLY WITH BRINY OLIVES AND TANGY-SWEET VINEGAR.

Quick & Easy

Chicken Taco Salad

Hands-on: 25 min. Total: 25 min.
Using rotisserie chicken helps you pull this convenient dish together in a flash.

6 (6-inch) corn tortillas
Cooking spray
3/8 teaspoon ground chipotle chile pepper
1 cup salsa verde
3 ounces 1/3-less-fat cream cheese (about 1/3 cup)
1 1/2 cups shredded skinless, boneless rotisserie chicken breast
1 1/2 cups chopped skinless, boneless rotisserie chicken thigh or drumstick
1/2 cup sliced green onions
2 tablespoons fresh lime juice, divided
5 teaspoons extra-virgin olive oil, divided
2/3 cup organic black beans, rinsed and drained
2/3 cup frozen corn kernels, thawed

2/3 cup chopped red bell pepper
1/4 cup chopped fresh cilantro
6 cups chopped romaine lettuce
3 radishes, very thinly sliced

1. Preheat oven to 450°.
2. Cut tortillas into 1/4-inch-thick strips. Place tortillas on a jelly-roll pan. Lightly coat tortillas with cooking spray; sprinkle with chipotle pepper. Bake at 450° for 10 minutes, stirring after 5 minutes. Cool.
3. Heat a medium skillet over medium heat. Add salsa and cheese to pan; cook 4 minutes or until cheese melts, stirring to combine. Stir in chicken; cook 1 minute. Stir in onions and 1 tablespoon lime juice. Remove chicken mixture from pan; keep warm. Rinse pan with water. Return pan to medium-high heat. Add 2 teaspoons oil to pan; swirl to coat. Add beans, corn, and red bell pepper to pan; sauté 2 minutes. Stir in cilantro.
4. Combine 1 tablespoon lime juice and 1 tablespoon oil in a large bowl; stir with a whisk. Add lettuce to bowl; toss to coat. Place about 1 cup lettuce mixture on each of 6 plates; top each serving with about 3/4 cup chicken mixture and 1/3 cup corn mixture. Sprinkle with tortilla strips and radishes. Serves 6

CALORIES 295; FAT 13.4g (sat 3.6g, mono 5.9g, poly 1.6g); PROTEIN 23g; CARB 23.2g; FIBER 4.5g; CHOL 82mg; IRON 1.7mg; SODIUM 665mg; CALC 73mg

THE PERFECT ROTISSERIE CHICKEN

What's not to love about roast chicken conveniently packaged and ready to go? The only work required on your end is pulling the juicy, seasoned meat off the bone. We use it as a shortcut for salads, soups, and potpies to help you get delicious dinners to the table in a hurry. These reliable recipes take just 40 minutes or less.

Kid Friendly • Quick & Easy

Crisp-Crust Chicken Potpie

Hands-on: 35 min. Total: 35 min.

2 sheets frozen puff pastry dough, thawed
Cooking spray
1 tablespoon canola oil
1 cup chopped onion
1 cup chopped carrot
1/2 cup chopped celery
2 teaspoons all-purpose flour
2 cups unsalted chicken stock (such as Swanson)
1 1/2 cups chopped skinless, boneless rotisserie chicken breast
1 1/2 cups chopped skinless, boneless rotisserie chicken thigh or drumstick
2 ounces 1/3-less-fat cream cheese
2 tablespoons chopped fresh flat-leaf parsley
2 teaspoons chopped fresh thyme
1/2 teaspoon kosher salt
1/2 teaspoon freshly ground black pepper

1. Preheat oven to 400°.
2. Place 1 sheet of pastry dough on a work surface lightly dusted with flour. Cut dough with a 4-inch round cutter into 3 rounds (about 1 1/4 ounces each). Gently roll each round into a 6-inch circle. Place dough on a baking sheet coated with cooking spray. Bake at 400° for 15 minutes or until golden brown; set aside. Repeat procedure with remaining puff pastry.
3. Heat a large skillet over medium-high heat. Add oil to pan; swirl to coat. Add onion, carrot, and celery; sauté 4 minutes or until lightly browned. Stir in flour, and sauté 1 minute. Stir in chicken stock; bring to a boil, stirring frequently. Reduce heat to medium; simmer 10 minutes or until carrot is tender. Stir in chicken; cook 1 minute. Remove pan from heat. Add cream

cheese, stirring until cheese melts. Stir in parsley and remaining ingredients. Serve with pastry. Serves 6 (serving size: 1 pastry round and about 3/4 cup chicken mixture)

CALORIES 389; FAT 22.7g (sat 4.7g, mono 6.6g, poly 9.3g); PROTEIN 23.6g; CARB 22.9g; FIBER 1.9g; CHOL 78mg; IRON 1.8mg; SODIUM 580mg; CALC 46mg

Quick & Easy

Spicy-Sweet Chicken Lettuce Cups

Hands-on: 25 min. Total: 40 min.

2 cups cider vinegar
1 cup water
1/2 cup sugar
2 tablespoons sliced serrano chile
3/4 teaspoon kosher salt
1 small garlic clove, crushed
1 cup matchstick-cut carrot
1 1/2 cups shredded skinless, boneless rotisserie chicken breast
1 1/2 cups shredded skinless, boneless rotisserie chicken thigh or drumstick
12 butter lettuce leaves
24 English cucumber slices
6 tablespoons dry-roasted peanuts, chopped
1/4 cup torn fresh mint

1. Combine first 6 ingredients in a medium saucepan. Bring mixture to a boil; cook 20 minutes. Remove from heat. Stir in carrot; let stand 10 minutes to soften. Add chicken to carrot mixture; let stand 5 minutes. Drain and discard liquid.
2. Place about 1/4 cup chicken mixture in each lettuce leaf, and top each lettuce leaf with 2 cucumber slices, 1 1/2 teaspoons peanuts, and 1 teaspoon mint. Serves 6 (serving size: 2 lettuce cups)

CALORIES 147; FAT 7g (sat 1.4g, mono 3.2g, poly 1.6g); PROTEIN 17.5g; CARB 4.7g; FIBER 1g; CHOL 58mg; IRON 1mg; SODIUM 265mg; CALC 25mg

Curried Coconut Soup with Chicken

Hands-on: 30 min. Total: 30 min. *For a lighter meal, you can omit the rice noodles.*

- 2 teaspoons canola oil
- ½ cup thinly sliced shallots
- 4 teaspoons Thai red curry paste
- 1 tablespoon minced fresh garlic
- 4 cups unsalted chicken stock (such as Swanson)
- 1 cup light coconut milk
- 2 cups chopped skinless, boneless rotisserie chicken breast
- ⅔ cup thinly sliced cucumber
- ½ cup torn fresh basil
- 2 teaspoons sambal oelek (ground fresh chile paste)
- 1 teaspoon dark sesame oil
- 2 cups cooked rice noodles
- 4 lime wedges

1. Heat a large saucepan over medium-high heat. Add canola oil to pan; swirl to coat. Add shallots; sauté 2 minutes. Add curry paste and garlic; sauté 1 minute. Add stock and coconut milk; bring to a boil. Reduce heat; simmer 20 minutes.
2. Combine chicken, cucumber, basil, sambal oelek, and sesame oil in a medium bowl; toss to coat. Place ½ cup chicken mixture and ½ cup noodles in each of 4 bowls. Pour about 1¼ cups stock mixture into each bowl. Serve with lime. Serves 4

CALORIES 330; **FAT** 9.4g (sat 3.8g, mono 3.1g, poly 1.6g); **PROTEIN** 29.2g; **CARB** 33.5g; **FIBER** 2.3g; **CHOL** 66mg; **IRON** 1.6mg; **SODIUM** 564mg; **CALC** 60mg

FREEZE IT!

Eat a batch tonight and freeze one for later: New tricks for quick-thawing perfection.

You can freeze pretty much any food, but the devil is in the thaw. Some dishes become mushy, pale versions of their former selves: zombie food. Others take so long to properly thaw and reheat that you might as well cook from scratch. We set out to develop recipes that address these problems head-on and will turn your freezer into more than a way station for leftovers.

And we set the bar high: no more than one hour to thaw and reheat a dish. That meant using freezer-friendly ingredients and properly portioned dishes, and it meant that thawing in the fridge was out of the question. The one-hour rule required a lot of testing to yield the outstanding recipes here—the hot new stars of our deep freeze. The final bonus: Each recipe is a twofer; it makes enough for a meal the day you cook, plus a second full serving to freeze for another day.

Some dishes require microwave thawing. Others can be popped directly into the oven.

Kid Friendly • Freezable
Make Ahead
Pork and Shiitake Pot Stickers
(pictured on page 215)

Hands-on: 30 min. Total: 60 min. *It's never a bad idea to have a good supply of dumplings on hand. Ours taste way better and are much lower in sodium than what you'll find at the store. Plus, they go from freezer to plate in only 10 minutes—what could be easier?*

- 2 tablespoons dark sesame oil
- ¾ cup thinly sliced green onions, divided
- 1 tablespoon minced fresh garlic
- 1 tablespoon grated peeled fresh ginger
- 4 ounces thinly sliced shiitake mushroom caps
- 5 tablespoons lower-sodium soy sauce, divided
- 1 tablespoon hoisin sauce
- ½ teaspoon freshly ground black pepper
- 14 ounces lean ground pork
- 40 gyoza skins or round wonton wrappers
- Cornstarch
- ¼ cup hot water
- 2 tablespoons brown sugar
- 2 tablespoons rice wine vinegar
- 1½ tablespoons sambal oelek (ground fresh chile paste)
- Cooking spray

1. Heat a large skillet over high heat. Add oil to pan; swirl to coat. Add ½ cup onions, garlic, ginger, and mushrooms; stir-fry 3 minutes. Remove from pan; cool slightly. Combine mushroom mixture, 1 tablespoon soy sauce, hoisin sauce, pepper, and pork in a medium bowl.
2. Arrange 8 gyoza skins on a clean work surface; cover remaining skins with a damp towel to keep

them from drying. Spoon about 1½ teaspoons pork mixture in the center of each skin. Moisten edges of skin with water. Fold in half; press edges together with fingertips to seal. Place on a baking sheet sprinkled with cornstarch; cover to prevent drying. Repeat procedure with remaining gyoza skins and pork mixture.

3. Combine ¼ cup hot water and brown sugar in a small bowl, stirring until sugar dissolves. Add ¼ cup green onions, ¼ cup soy sauce, vinegar, and sambal, stirring with a whisk until well combined.

4. Heat a large heavy skillet over high heat. Generously coat pan with cooking spray. Add 10 pot stickers to pan; cook 30 seconds or until browned on one side. Turn pot stickers over; carefully add ⅓ cup water to pan. Cover tightly; steam 4 minutes. Repeat procedure in batches with remaining pot stickers and more water, or follow freezing instructions. After cooking, serve pot stickers immediately with dipping sauce. Serves 8 (serving size: 5 pot stickers and 1 tablespoon sauce)

CALORIES 221; FAT 8.1g (sat 2.3g, mono 3.7g, poly 1.8g); PROTEIN 11g; CARB 23g; FIBER 0.7g; CHOL 37mg; IRON 0.3mg; SODIUM 609mg; CALC 13mg

---

TO FREEZE
Freeze dumplings flat on a baking sheet sprinkled with cornstarch 10 minutes or until firm. Place in a large zip-top plastic freezer bag with 1 teaspoon cornstarch; toss. Freeze sauce in a small zip-top plastic freezer bag. Freeze up to 2 months.

TO THAW
Thaw sauce in the microwave at HIGH in 30-second increments. No need to thaw pot stickers.

TO REHEAT
Follow recipe instructions for cooking, placing frozen dumplings in pan and increasing steaming time by 2 minutes.

Freezable • Gluten Free
Make Ahead

Stuffed Poblano Peppers

Hands-on: 40 min. Total: 60 min.
Poblano peppers range in heat level from quite spicy to rather mild, and there's no way to know what you're getting until you take a bite. If your peppers are too hot, cool off with a dollop of sour cream.

8 large poblano peppers
4 dried ancho chiles
2 tablespoons canola oil
3 cups chopped onion
10 garlic cloves, minced
1 teaspoon kosher salt, divided
1 teaspoon black pepper
12 ounces 90% lean ground sirloin
4 ounces ⅓-less-fat cream cheese, softened
1½ cups precooked brown rice (such as Uncle Ben's Ready Rice)
6 ounces queso fresco, crumbled and divided (about 1½ cups)
¼ cup fresh lime juice
1 tablespoon ground cumin
2 teaspoons sugar
2 (14.5-ounce) cans unsalted diced tomatoes, undrained
Cooking spray
¼ cup cilantro leaves

1. Preheat broiler.
2. Place poblanos on a foil-lined baking sheet; broil 3 inches from heat 12 minutes or until blackened, turning after 6 minutes. Place in a paper bag; fold to close tightly. Let stand 15 minutes. Peel and discard skins. Cut a lengthwise slit in each pepper; discard seeds and membranes. Set aside.
3. While poblanos broil, place ancho chiles in a bowl. Cover with boiling water; let stand 10 minutes. Drain.

---

4. Reduce oven temperature to 400°.
5. Heat a large skillet over medium heat. Add oil to pan; swirl to coat. Add onion and garlic; cook 4 minutes or until crisp-tender. Reserve half of onion mixture. Add ½ teaspoon salt, black pepper, and beef; cook 8 minutes or until beef is done, stirring to crumble. Remove from heat. Add cream cheese, stirring until well combined. Stir in rice and half of queso fresco.
6. Place ancho chiles, reserved onion mixture, juice, cumin, sugar, tomatoes, and ½ teaspoon salt in a blender; process until smooth. Pour 1 cup sauce into each of 2 (8-inch) square glass or ceramic baking dishes coated with cooking spray. Open each poblano chile; flatten slightly with hand. Divide beef mixture evenly among chiles (chiles will be very full). Arrange 4 chiles in each dish; top evenly with remaining sauce and queso. Bake at 400° for 20 minutes or until bubbly, or follow freezing instructions. Sprinkle with cilantro after cooking. Serves 8 (serving size: 1 stuffed chile and about ⅔ cup sauce)

CALORIES 334; FAT 14.8g (sat 5.2g, mono 5.5g, poly 1.8g); PROTEIN 17.6g; CARB 35g; FIBER 7.2g; CHOL 45mg; IRON 3.7mg; SODIUM 369mg; CALC 148mg

---

TO FREEZE
These do best in a shallow vessel, so follow the recipe instructions to use a standard 8-inch square dish. Cover tightly with heavy-duty foil; freeze up to 2 months.

TO REHEAT
No thawing step is necessary. Remove foil, and cover dish tightly with plastic wrap. Pierce plastic wrap 4 or 5 times. Microwave at HIGH 14 to 15 minutes or until thoroughly heated. (We tried oven reheating and don't recommend it.)

Chili Mac

Hands-on: 40 min. Total: 55 min. Talk about old-school comfort: This is a hearty, filling, family-friendly classic. Slightly under- cook the pasta to ensure it doesn't end up too mushy. Reduce the amount of ground red pepper for sensitive palates, or crank it up for hotheads. You can brighten the look with a sprinkling of fresh parsley.

12 ounces uncooked rotini, spiral macaroni, or wagon wheel pasta
2 cups canned red kidney beans, rinsed and drained
2 tablespoons olive oil
2 cups chopped onion
2 tablespoons minced fresh garlic
1 pound cremini mushrooms, finely chopped
20 ounces ground turkey breast
2 cups chopped green bell pepper
4 teaspoons ground cumin
2 teaspoons dried oregano
1 teaspoon kosher salt
1 teaspoon smoked paprika
1 teaspoon ancho chile powder
1 teaspoon freshly ground black pepper
¼ to 1 teaspoon ground red pepper
4 cups lower-sodium marinara sauce
Cooking spray
4 ounces extra-sharp cheddar cheese, shredded (about 1 cup)

1. Preheat oven to 350°.
2. Cook pasta in boiling water until almost al dente. Drain. Combine pasta and beans in a large bowl.
3. Heat a large skillet over medium heat. Add oil to pan; swirl to coat. Add onion, garlic, and mushrooms to pan; cook 11 minutes or until liquid almost evaporates. Add turkey; cook 5 minutes or until done, stirring to crumble. Add bell pepper and next 7 ingredients; cook 1 minute. Stir in marinara sauce; bring to a boil. Add marinara mixture to pasta mixture; toss to coat. Divide mixture evenly between 2 (2-quart) glass baking dishes coated with cooking spray. Top evenly with cheese. Bake at 350° for 10 minutes or until cheese melts, or follow freezing instructions. Serves 8 (serving size: about 1½ cups)

CALORIES 497; FAT 14.5g (sat 5.2g, mono 6.7g, poly 0.9g); PROTEIN 33.8g; CARB 60.1g; FIBER 10.6g; CHOL 44mg; IRON 3.5mg; SODIUM 650mg; CALC 174mg

---

TO FREEZE
Spoon half of unbaked mixture into a 2-quart glass baking dish (such as a Ziploc VersaGlass large square container). Cover with lid; freeze up to 2 months.

TO THAW
Remove lid; place casserole in microwave. Microwave at 30% power 30 to 40 min- utes (or on defrost setting for 3.75 pounds).

TO REHEAT
Cover casserole with foil; bake at 400° for 20 minutes or until a thermometer in- serted in center registers 160°.

White Bean, Sage, and Sausage Soup
(pictured on page 215)

Hands-on: 16 min. Total: 35 min. This soup gets a double hit of fennel essence from chopped fennel bulb and the fennel seeds that flavor the sausage. Enjoy half for dinner tonight, and spoon half into a freezer bag to make life easier another night.

Cooking spray
2 cups chopped onion
1 cup chopped fennel bulb
½ to 1 teaspoon crushed red pepper
20 ounces hot Italian sausage links, casings removed
8 garlic cloves, minced
¼ cup chopped fresh sage
1 tablespoon tomato paste
1 cup dry white wine
6 cups unsalted chicken stock (such as Swanson)
2 cups chopped plum tomato
4 (14.5-ounce) cans organic cannellini beans, rinsed and drained
¼ cup chopped fresh flat-leaf parsley

1. Heat a large Dutch oven over medium heat. Coat pan with cook- ing spray. Add onion and next 4 ingredients (through garlic); cook 3 minutes. Reduce heat; cook 10 minutes or until sausage is browned and vegetables are tender, stirring to crumble sausage. Add sage and tomato paste; cook 1 minute, stirring constantly. Add wine; cook 3 min- utes or until liquid is reduced by half. Add stock; bring to a boil, reduce heat, and simmer 5 minutes. Add to- mato and beans, and cook 2 minutes. Sprinkle with chopped parsley, or follow freezing instructions. Serves 8 (serving size: 1½ cups)

CALORIES 282; FAT 7.9g (sat 2.2g, mono 2.6g, poly 2.1g); PROTEIN 23.9g; CARB 26.4g; FIBER 6.9g; CHOL 60mg; IRON 3.6mg; SODIUM 591mg; CALC 90mg

---

TO FREEZE
Cool soup to room temperature; seal in a large zip-top plastic freezer bag. Lay bag flat in freezer; freeze up to 2 months.

TO THAW
Microwave soup in bag at MEDIUM (50% power) for 4 minutes or until pliable.

TO REHEAT
Pour soup into a Dutch oven. Cover and cook over medium heat until thoroughly heated (about 20 minutes).

Kid Friendly • Freezable
Make Ahead

Individual White Chicken Pizzas

(pictured on page 215)

Hands-on: 57 min. Total: 57 min. *Cook up as many pizzas as you want tonight, and freeze the rest. The key to the deliciousness (and believe us, these cheesy pizzas are amazing) is to make fresh ricotta cheese, which is more moist and creamy than store-bought. It's fast and easy to do in the microwave.*

30 ounces refrigerated fresh pizza dough, divided
1/2 cup olive oil
1/4 cup chopped fresh basil
1 teaspoon crushed red pepper
8 garlic cloves, crushed
4 thyme sprigs
4 cups 2% reduced-fat milk
1 cup plain fat-free Greek yogurt
4 teaspoons cider vinegar
1/2 teaspoon kosher salt
12 ounces shredded cooked chicken breast
6.5 ounces preshredded reduced-fat 4-cheese Italian-blend cheese (about 1²/₃ cups)
3 ounces fresh part-skim mozzarella cheese, torn into small pieces
2 tablespoons thyme leaves
1¹/₂ teaspoons black pepper
1/2 cup small basil leaves

1. Place a pizza stone or heavy baking sheet in oven. Preheat oven to 450° (keep pizza stone or baking sheet in oven as it preheats).
2. Let pizza dough rest, covered, at room temperature as oven preheats.
3. Combine oil and next 4 ingredients (through thyme sprigs) in a small saucepan over medium heat. Cook 4 minutes or until garlic begins to brown, stirring frequently. Remove from heat; let stand 5 minutes. Strain mixture through a fine sieve over a small bowl; discard solids.

4. Combine milk, yogurt, and vinegar in a large microwave-safe bowl. Microwave at HIGH 6 minutes. Gently stir to form small curds. Strain curds through a fine sieve; let stand 5 minutes. Discard liquid. Combine oil mixture, cheese curds, and salt, stirring gently.
5. Divide dough into 12 equal pieces (about 2.5 ounces each). Roll each piece into a 6-inch circle on a lightly floured surface (keep dough covered with a damp towel to prevent drying). Spread about 1½ tablespoons oil mixture over each pizza, leaving a ½-inch border. Divide chicken, Italian-blend cheese, and mozzarella cheese evenly among pizzas; sprinkle evenly with thyme leaves and black pepper. Carefully remove pizza stone from oven. Arrange 3 to 4 pizzas on pizza stone. Bake at 450° for 8 minutes or until dough is golden and cheese browns. Repeat procedure with remaining pizzas, or follow freezing instructions. Sprinkle pizzas evenly with fresh basil leaves. Serves 12 (serving size: 1 pizza)

CALORIES 410; **FAT** 16.7g (sat 4.9g, mono 8.1g, poly 1.9g); **PROTEIN** 23.4g; **CARB** 39.5g; **FIBER** 5.3g; **CHOL** 37mg; **IRON** 1.2mg; **SODIUM** 646mg; **CALC** 282mg

---

TO FREEZE
Bake pizzas on preheated stone for only 5 minutes. Cool; wrap individually in heavy-duty foil, stack, and freeze up to 2 months.

TO REHEAT
No thawing: Place frozen pizzas on a baking sheet that's not preheated; bake at 450° for 13 minutes or until cheese browns.

---

5 TIPS FOR BETTER FREEZING

1. WHAT FREEZES WELL
The most freezer-friendly foods are saucy dishes, soups and stews, and individual food items like our dumplings and pizzas. Pasta and rice can be trickier because they have a tendency to mush out.

2. CONSIDER THE CONTAINER
Make sure the container fits in both the freezer and what you'll be using for reheating. We sought out casserole dishes without handles so they wouldn't hog space in the freezer or microwave; we loved Ziploc VersaGlass square containers. (We also avoided disposable aluminum foil pans because we did a lot of microwave thawing.) If you freeze soup flat in a zip-top plastic bag—as you should so it stacks nicely—it may be too large to fit in a Dutch oven for thawing and reheating. For that reason, we thaw these in the microwave until they're pliable, and then proceed to the pot.

3. LABEL CLEARLY, AND USE FAIRLY SOON
Unlabeled food is remarkably hard to recognize in its icy state. We recommend freezing our recipes for no more than 2 months; longer than that risks freezer burn.

4. THAW SAFELY
The USDA recognizes three methods of safe thawing: refrigeration, cold-water submersion, and microwave defrosting/immediate reheating, the latter of which we used in our recipes to save time. Common practices like setting frozen foods on the counter or immersing them in hot water are not safe because they allow bacteria that were present before freezing to multiply.

5. FINISH WITH A FLOURISH
Liven up reheated dishes with fresh herbs or a brief stint under the broiler for a kiss of yummy browning.

Chicken Tikka Masala

Hands-on: 45 min. Total: 45 min.

2 tablespoons olive oil, divided
3 pounds skinless, boneless chicken
  thighs, cut into 1½-inch cubes
2 teaspoons kosher salt, divided
2 teaspoons ground cumin
2 teaspoons ground cinnamon
1 cup finely chopped onion
3 tablespoons minced fresh garlic
2 tablespoons minced peeled fresh
  ginger
2 serrano chiles, minced
2 teaspoons garam masala
¾ teaspoon ground red pepper
½ cup unsalted chicken stock (such
  as Swanson)
½ cup half-and-half
2 (26.5-ounce) boxes chopped
  tomatoes (such as Pomì), undrained
¼ cup butter
6 cups hot cooked basmati rice
½ cup chopped fresh cilantro

1. Heat a large Dutch oven over medium-high heat. Add 1 tablespoon oil to pan; swirl to coat. Sprinkle chicken with 1 teaspoon salt, cumin, and cinnamon. Add half of chicken to pan; cook 5 minutes or until browned, stirring once. Remove chicken from pan. Repeat procedure with remaining chicken; remove from pan.
2. Add 1 tablespoon oil, onion, garlic, ginger, and serrano to pan; sauté 1 minute. Reduce heat to low; cook 5 minutes or until softened, stirring frequently. Add garam masala and red pepper; cook 1 minute, stirring constantly. Add 1 teaspoon salt, stock, half-and-half, and tomatoes, scraping pan to loosen browned bits. Bring to a boil over high heat. Reduce heat to low; stir in chicken. Simmer 6 minutes or until chicken is done. Remove from heat; stir in

butter until butter melts. Serve over rice, or follow freezing instructions. Sprinkle with cilantro. Serves 12 (serving size: ½ cup rice and about 1 cup chicken mixture)

CALORIES 343; FAT 12.3g (sat 4.7g, mono 4.3g, poly 1.4g); PROTEIN 25.9g; CARB 31.4g; FIBER 3g; CHOL 122mg; IRON 2.5mg; SODIUM 516mg; CALC 61mg

---

TO FREEZE
Cool chicken mixture and rice to room temperature; seal in separate large zip-top plastic freezer bags. Lay bags flat in freezer; freeze up to 2 months.

TO THAW
Microwave chicken mixture in bag at MEDIUM (50% power) for 4 minutes or until pliable. No need to thaw rice.

TO REHEAT
Place sealed bag of chicken mixture in a large pot of boiling water; cook 10 minutes or until heated. Pour rice into a microwave-safe bowl; microwave at HIGH 3 minutes.

NUTRITION MADE EASY

GRILLED CHEESE TRICK

Cheesy and golden-crisp with half the sat fat. How'd we do it?

Making an iconic grilled cheese—complete with gooey, melty goodness and golden-crisp bread—is no small feat for a nutrition-minded cook. An impeccably creamy interior is easy to achieve with several ounces of hearty cheddar, and even easier with American. Fry it in a chunk of butter, and you're in 400-plus-calorie territory, double-digit sat fat, and nearly 1,000 milligrams of sodium for a three-ingredient meal.

To duplicate the irresistible texture of the original, we used a combination of reduced-fat shredded cheddar with light cream cheese and canola mayo for a mixture that has 40% less saturated fat than regular

cheddar. When slathered on whole-grain bread and sautéed in olive oil, the mixture melts into the gloriously silky, ultracheesy filling you see here.

The Formula
Combine ½ ounce ⅓-less-fat cream cheese and 1 teaspoon canola mayo. Add 1 ounce 2% reduced-fat shredded cheddar cheese. Spread between 2 (1-ounce) slices whole-grain bread. Heat a small skillet over medium heat; sear each side in ¼ teaspoon olive oil until bread is browned and crisp.

CALORIES 288; FAT 13.8g (sat 5.8g); SODIUM 556mg

RECIPE MAKEOVER

CREAM SCONES, SLIMMED DOWN

Fruity, whole-grain, buttery goodness with 60% less fat.

Scones fall into one of two traditions: The English version is very dry and crumbly, a platform on which to slather jam and clotted cream (a thicker take on the whipped variety). The Americanized scone folds the cream directly into the batter, along with a hefty dose of butter and sugar. Either way, you've got a start to the day that can approach 500 calories.

Here, we lighten the scone while nodding to both traditions. The key is part-skim ricotta cheese. It has a richness similar to that of whipping cream with a fraction of the fat. Half gets stirred into the batter, lending a tender crumb to our scones, while the remainder is whipped with vanilla and citrus and dolloped over the freshly baked pastry—a healthier alternative to clotted cream. We work in some whole-wheat pastry flour and replace some of the butter with heart-healthy canola oil for a more nutrient-dense goodie that still bakes up fluffy. Dried cherries plump in orange juice to soak up flavor, and toasted almonds add nutty crunch. These delicate treats are a proper, healthy way to start your day.

OURS SAVES
214 calories, 7.4g saturated fat, and 7.3g total fat over classic cherry cream scones

Cherry Almond Ricotta Drop Scones

Hands-on: 36 min. Total: 51 min.

½ cup dried tart cherries
¼ cup fresh orange juice
1 cup part-skim ricotta cheese (such as Calabro)
¼ cup packed brown sugar, divided
1 teaspoon grated orange rind
1 teaspoon vanilla extract
⅓ cup plus 1 tablespoon nonfat buttermilk, divided
2 tablespoons canola oil
4.5 ounces whole-grain pastry flour (about 1 cup)
3.4 ounces unbleached all-purpose flour (about ¾ cup)
1 tablespoon baking powder
½ teaspoon salt
4 tablespoons cold unsalted butter, diced
⅓ cup sliced almonds, toasted
1 large egg, lightly beaten

1. Preheat oven to 425°.
2. Combine cherries and juice in a small microwave-safe bowl. Microwave at HIGH 1 minute; let stand 5 minutes. Drain; discard liquid. Finely chop cherries.
3. Combine ricotta cheese, 1 tablespoon sugar, rind, and vanilla in a medium bowl. Reserve ½ cup of the ricotta mixture. Add ⅓ cup buttermilk and canola oil to remaining ricotta mixture, stirring until smooth.
4. Weigh or lightly spoon flours into dry measuring cups; level with a knife. Combine flours, 3 tablespoons sugar, baking powder, and salt in a large bowl; cut in butter with a pastry blender or 2 knives until mixture resembles coarse meal. Add cherries and almonds; toss. Add buttermilk mixture; stir just until combined.
5. Drop dough by ¼ cupfuls 3 inches apart onto a baking sheet lined with parchment paper. Combine egg and remaining 1 tablespoon buttermilk, stirring with a whisk. Gently brush top and sides of dough with egg mixture. Bake at 425° for 15 to 16 minutes or until golden. Remove from pan; cool slightly on a wire rack.
6. Beat reserved ricotta mixture at medium speed 3 minutes or until fluffy. Serve with warm scones. Serves 10 (serving size: 1 scone and about 2 teaspoons ricotta mixture)

CALORIES 261; FAT 11.7g (sat 4.6g, mono 4.7g, poly 1.5g); PROTEIN 7g; CARB 31.7g; FIBER 3.2g; CHOL 39mg; IRON 1.6mg; SODIUM 287mg; CALC 187mg

SECRETS TO LIGHTER SCONES

PART-SKIM RICOTTA CHEESE
Replaces heavy cream to save 50 calories and 4.5g sat fat per scone. Vanilla and orange zest add sweet and floral notes.

FREE-FORM DROP METHOD
Instead of rolling the dough (which is very wet), we scoop and drop it, making prep easier and allowing for crisp browned edges.

DRIED CHERRIES + FRESH OJ
Plumping dried fruit in juice adds more vivid flavor. Fresh fruit would add too much moisture and dilute the buttery batter.

SUPERFAST 20-MINUTE COOKING

Kid Friendly • Quick & Easy Make Ahead • Vegetarian

Crisp Cauliflower Fritters

1 (10-ounce) package steam-in-bag fresh cauliflower florets
½ cup prechopped onion
2 tablespoons whole-wheat flour
2 teaspoons minced fresh garlic
⅝ teaspoon kosher salt, divided
½ teaspoon black pepper
¼ teaspoon grated lemon rind
¾ cup refrigerated shredded hash brown potatoes
2 ounces white cheddar cheese, shredded (about ½ cup)
2 large eggs, lightly beaten
2 teaspoons olive oil
¼ cup plain 2% Greek yogurt
2 tablespoons minced green onions
2 tablespoons canola mayonnaise
2 teaspoons fresh lemon juice

1. Prepare cauliflower according to directions. Place in a bowl; mash with a potato masher. Stir in onion, flour, garlic, ½ teaspoon salt, pepper, rind, potatoes, cheese, and eggs. Form into 8 patties. Heat a large nonstick skillet over medium-high heat. Add oil; swirl. Cook patties 4 minutes on each side. Combine ⅛ teaspoon salt, yogurt, and remaining ingredients; serve sauce with fritters. Serves 4 (serving size: 2 fritters and 1 tablespoon sauce)

CALORIES 212; FAT 11.9g (sat 3.9g, mono 3.8g, poly 1.6g); PROTEIN 10.9g; CARB 16.7g; FIBER 2.9g; CHOL 109mg; IRON 1.4mg; SODIUM 521mg; CALC 156mg

Mexican Chorizo Hash

2 ounces raw Mexican chorizo
1 cup prechopped onion
¼ cup coarsely chopped bottled roasted red bell peppers
½ teaspoon kosher salt
½ teaspoon freshly ground black pepper
1 (6-ounce) package baby spinach
2 teaspoons olive oil
2½ cups refrigerated shredded hash brown potatoes (such as Simply Potatoes)
4 large eggs

1. Heat a large skillet over medium-high heat. Add chorizo to pan; cook 3 minutes or until browned, stirring to crumble. Add onion, bell peppers, salt, and black pepper; cook 3 minutes, stirring occasionally. Add spinach; stir until spinach wilts. Remove sausage mixture from pan. Add oil to pan; swirl to coat. Add potatoes; cook 8 minutes or until bottom is crisp. Stir in sausage mixture. Make 4 egg-size spaces in pan with a spoon. Crack 1 egg into each space. Cover and cook 4 minutes or until egg yolks are slightly set. Serves 4 (serving size: 1 egg and about 1 cup potato mixture)

CALORIES 279; FAT 11.1g (sat 3.9g, mono 3.5g, poly 1.2g); PROTEIN 12.7g; CARB 33.1g; FIBER 4.7g; CHOL 206mg; IRON 2.3mg; SODIUM 616mg; CALC 68mg

Grape Tomato, Olive, and Spinach Pasta

We love small, sweet grape tomatoes in this quick meatless pasta dish, but you can sub cherry tomatoes or larger tomatoes that have been seeded and diced.

8 ounces uncooked penne (about 2 cups)
2 teaspoons olive oil
¼ teaspoon crushed red pepper
1 large garlic clove, thinly sliced
2 cups grape tomatoes, halved
½ cup organic vegetable broth (such as Swanson)
¼ teaspoon kosher salt
¼ teaspoon freshly ground black pepper
10 kalamata olives, pitted and coarsely chopped
4 cups baby spinach
¼ cup torn basil leaves
1 ounce Parmesan cheese, grated (about ¼ cup)

1. Bring a large saucepan of water to a boil. Add pasta; cook 8 minutes or until al dente, omitting salt and fat. Drain in a colander over a bowl, reserving ½ cup cooking liquid.
2. Heat a large skillet over medium heat. Add oil to pan; swirl to coat. Add red pepper and garlic; sauté 30 seconds. Add tomatoes, broth, salt, black pepper, and olives; cook 6 minutes or until tomatoes begin to break down, stirring occasionally. Add pasta and ½ cup reserved cooking liquid to pan; simmer 2 minutes. Stir in spinach and basil; cook 2 minutes or until greens wilt. Divide pasta mixture evenly among 4 bowls; top evenly with Parmesan cheese. Serve immediately. Serves 4 (serving size: 1¼ cups)

CALORIES 305; FAT 7.1g (sat 2g, mono 3.7g, poly 0.6g); PROTEIN 11.9g; CARB 49.5g; FIBER 4g; CHOL 6mg; IRON 3mg; SODIUM 458mg; CALC 123mg

Spice-Roasted Salmon

Garam masala, a warm Indian spice blend, makes a simple rub for fish, chicken, pork, or lamb. Serve the salmon with steamed snow peas and precooked jasmine rice (such as Uncle Ben's).

1½ tablespoons olive oil, divided
4 (6-ounce) sustainable salmon fillets
¾ teaspoon garam masala
⅝ teaspoon kosher salt, divided
⅓ cup plain 2% reduced-fat Greek yogurt
2 tablespoons thinly sliced green onions
2 tablespoons crème fraîche or sour cream
1 teaspoon fresh lime juice
1 lemon, cut into wedges

1. Heat a large skillet over medium-high heat. Add 2 teaspoons oil to pan; swirl to coat. Sprinkle fillets evenly with garam masala and ½ teaspoon salt. Add fillets to pan, skin side down. Cook 7 minutes; turn over, and cook 1 minute or until desired degree of doneness.
2. Combine 2½ teaspoons oil, ⅛ teaspoon salt, yogurt, green onions, crème fraîche, and lime juice in a small bowl, stirring with a whisk. Serve yogurt mixture with fillets. Serve with lemon wedges. Serves 4 (serving size: 1 fillet, about 2 tablespoons yogurt mixture, and 1 lemon wedge)

CALORIES 326; FAT 17.6g (sat 4.6g, mono 6.9g, poly 3.8g); PROTEIN 38.1g; CARB 1.1g; FIBER 0.1g; CHOL 98mg; IRON 0.8mg; SODIUM 389mg; CALC 32mg

Nutty Almond-Sesame Red Quinoa

We love the color and texture of red quinoa, but regular quinoa also works well.

1²/₃ cups water
1 cup red quinoa
¼ cup sliced almonds, toasted
2 tablespoons fresh lemon juice
2 teaspoons olive oil
2 teaspoons dark sesame oil
¼ teaspoon kosher salt
3 green onions, thinly sliced

1. Bring 1⅔ cups water and quinoa to a boil in a medium saucepan. Reduce heat to low, and simmer 12 minutes or until quinoa is tender; drain. Stir in almonds, juice, oils, salt, and onions. Serves 4 (serving size: about ½ cup)

CALORIES 238; FAT 10g (sat 0.9g, mono 4.4g, poly 1.9g); PROTEIN 7.5g; CARB 31.6g; FIBER 3g; CHOL 0mg; IRON 3.1mg; SODIUM 132mg; CALC 44mg

Balsamic and Grape Quinoa
Prepare quinoa as directed in main recipe; drain. Place quinoa in a bowl. Add 2 tablespoons chopped fresh flat-leaf parsley, 1 tablespoon white balsamic vinegar, 2 teaspoons extra-virgin olive oil, ¼ teaspoon kosher salt, and 20 halved seedless red grapes, stirring to combine. Serves 4 (serving size: about ¾ cup)

CALORIES 201; FAT 4.8g (sat 0.3g); SODIUM 133mg

Lemon–Snap Pea Quinoa
Prepare quinoa as directed in main recipe; drain. Add 1 cup diagonally halved sugar snap peas, ¼ cup fresh lemon juice, 1 tablespoon extra-virgin olive oil, 1 teaspoon chopped fresh thyme, ¼ teaspoon kosher salt, and ¼ teaspoon freshly ground black pepper, stirring to combine. Serves 4 (serving size: about ⅔ cup)

CALORIES 201; FAT 6g (sat 0.5g); SODIUM 131mg

Bean Salad Quinoa
Prepare quinoa as directed in main recipe; drain. Add ¼ cup minced red onion; 4 teaspoons red wine vinegar; 1 tablespoon extra-virgin olive oil; ¼ teaspoon kosher salt; 1 (15-ounce) can unsalted cannellini beans, rinsed and drained; and 2 diced plum tomatoes, stirring to combine. Serves 4 (serving size: about 1 cup)

CALORIES 243; FAT 6.4g (sat 0.5g); SODIUM 150mg

QUINOA IS DONE WHEN LIQUID IS ABSORBED AND TINY CURLY TAILS EMERGE FROM THE SEEDS.

Tortilla Soup

with Chorizo & Turkey Meatballs
(pictured on page 215)

2 teaspoons olive oil
1 cup prechopped onion
³/₄ cup chopped seeded poblano pepper
1 ounce smoked Spanish chorizo, finely chopped
4 cups unsalted chicken stock (such as Swanson)
1 (14.5-ounce) can unsalted diced tomatoes, drained
2 corn tortillas, chopped
¹/₂ teaspoon kosher salt, divided
¹/₂ teaspoon garlic powder
¹/₂ teaspoon ground cumin
¹/₂ teaspoon ground coriander
12 ounces 93% lean ground turkey
1 large egg
Cooking spray
³/₄ cup frozen corn kernels
¹/₄ cup chopped fresh cilantro

1. Heat a large saucepan over medium-high heat. Add oil; swirl to coat. Add onion, poblano, and chorizo; sauté 2 minutes. Add stock and tomatoes; bring to a simmer. Stir in tortillas.
2. Combine ¼ teaspoon salt, garlic powder, and next 4 ingredients (through egg). Shape turkey mixture into 12 meatballs. Heat a large skillet over medium-high heat. Coat pan with cooking spray. Add meatballs; cook 4 minutes, browning on all sides. Add meatballs, ¼ teaspoon salt, and corn to stock mixture, and simmer 5 minutes. Top with cilantro. Serves 4 (serving size: about 1½ cups)

CALORIES 288; FAT 11.1g (sat 2.9g, mono 4.8g, poly 2.6g); PROTEIN 27.4g; CARB 21.2g; FIBER 2.9g; CHOL 95mg; IRON 2.8mg; SODIUM 466mg; CALC 61mg

Mini Philly Cheeseburgers

2 teaspoons extra-virgin olive oil
1 cup finely chopped sweet onion
½ cup chopped red bell pepper
½ cup chopped green bell pepper
½ cup chopped cremini mushrooms
1 teaspoon Worcestershire sauce
¼ teaspoon minced fresh thyme
¼ teaspoon kosher salt
¼ teaspoon black pepper
12 ounces 90% lean ground sirloin
Cooking spray
1 ounce reduced-fat provolone
   cheese, shredded (about ¼ cup)
8 (1-ounce) slider buns

1. Preheat broiler.
2. Heat a large skillet over medium-high heat. Add oil to pan; swirl to coat. Add onion, bell peppers, and mushrooms; sauté 5 minutes. Combine onion mixture and next 5 ingredients in a bowl. Shape beef mixture into 8 (⅓-inch-thick) patties.
3. Heat a grill pan over high heat; coat with cooking spray. Cook patties 3 minutes; turn, top with cheese, and cook 2 minutes.
4. Arrange buns, cut sides up, on a baking sheet; broil 30 seconds. Assemble sandwiches. Serves 4 (serving size: 2 sliders)

CALORIES 400; **FAT** 15.8g (sat 5.1g, mono 6.2g, poly 0.7g); **PROTEIN** 29g; **CARB** 32.6g; **FIBER** 3.5g; **CHOL** 76mg; **IRON** 2.7mg; **SODIUM** 529mg; **CALC** 80mg

Quick BBQ Chicken Pizzas

Baking the pizzas directly on the oven rack gives you a crisp crust in less time. You can substitute shredded part-skim mozzarella cheese for fresh.

Cooking spray
¾ cup chopped red onion
1½ cups shredded skinless, boneless
   rotisserie chicken breast
   (about 6 ounces)
¼ cup unsalted chicken stock (such
   as Swanson)
¼ cup lower-sodium marinara sauce
   (such as Dell'Amore)
¼ cup barbecue sauce (such as
   Stubb's)
3 (7-inch) thin pizza crusts (such as
   Mama Mary's)
2 ounces fresh mozzarella cheese,
   sliced
⅓ cup chopped green onions
½ teaspoon freshly ground black
   pepper

1. Preheat oven to 450°.
2. Heat a saucepan over medium heat. Coat pan with cooking spray. Add onion; sauté 2 minutes or until translucent. Stir in chicken, stock, marinara, and barbecue sauce; cook 3 minutes or until thoroughly heated. Remove pan from heat.
3. Spread about ½ cup chicken mixture over each crust; top evenly with mozzarella cheese. Place pizzas directly on oven rack; bake at 450° for 9 minutes or until cheese melts. Top with green onions and pepper. Cut each pizza into 4 wedges. Serves 4 (serving size: 3 wedges)

CALORIES 337; **FAT** 11g (sat 3.3g, mono 2.5g, poly 2.9g); **PROTEIN** 21.3g; **CARB** 37.4g; **FIBER** 2.6g; **CHOL** 52mg; **IRON** 2.6mg; **SODIUM** 538mg; **CALC** 136mg

QUICK TRICKS

6 EASY ASPARAGUS SIDES

Start with a pound of trimmed asparagus, and then choose any variation below.

Tomato & Feta
Preheat oven to 425°. Place 1½ cups halved grape tomatoes and 1 tablespoon olive oil on a jelly-roll pan; toss. Bake at 425° for 4 minutes. Add asparagus; bake 9 minutes. Top with 1 tablespoon white balsamic vinegar, ¼ teaspoon kosher salt, ¼ teaspoon pepper, and 1 ounce crumbled feta cheese. Serves 4

CALORIES 75; **FAT** 5.1g (sat 1.6g); **SODIUM** 204mg

Olive Tapenade
Place 2 tablespoons minced fresh basil, 1 tablespoon fresh lemon juice, 1 tablespoon olive oil, ½ teaspoon fresh thyme leaves, ¾ ounce Castelvetrano olives, ¾ ounce pitted kalamata olives, 1 anchovy fillet, and 1 garlic clove in a mini food processor; pulse to combine. Heat a large skillet over medium-high heat. Add 1 tablespoon olive oil to pan; swirl to coat. Add asparagus; sauté 6 minutes. Sprinkle with ⅛ teaspoon pepper. Top with olive mixture. Serves 4

CALORIES 107; **FAT** 9.7g (sat 1.2g); **SODIUM** 230mg

Balsamic Onion & Blue Cheese
Preheat oven to 425°. Combine asparagus, 2 teaspoons olive oil, ⅛ teaspoon kosher salt, and ⅛ teaspoon pepper on a baking sheet. Bake at 425° for 9 minutes. Heat a large skillet over medium heat. Add 1½ teaspoons olive oil; swirl to coat. Add 1½ cups vertically sliced sweet onion

to pan; sauté 6 minutes. Stir in 1 tablespoon balsamic vinegar, 1 teaspoon thyme, and ⅛ teaspoon kosher salt. Top asparagus with onion mixture and 1 ounce crumbled blue cheese. Serves 4

CALORIES 104; **FAT** 6.2g (sat 1.9g); **SODIUM** 224mg

Red Pepper & Manchego

Heat a large skillet over medium-high heat. Add 2 teaspoons canola oil; swirl to coat. Add asparagus; cook 5 minutes, stirring occasionally. Add 1 cup thinly sliced red bell pepper, ¼ teaspoon hot smoked paprika, ¼ teaspoon black pepper, and ⅛ teaspoon kosher salt; cook 2 minutes. Top with 1 ounce shaved Manchego cheese. Serves 4

CALORIES 82; **FAT** 5.1g (sat 2g); **SODIUM** 106mg

Pea & Prosciutto

Preheat oven to 425°. Bake asparagus and 1 very thin prosciutto slice at 425° for 9 minutes. Microwave 1 cup frozen green peas, ⅓ cup unsalted chicken stock, and 1 teaspoon butter at HIGH 2 minutes. Pulse pea mixture and 1½ tablespoons chopped fresh mint in a mini processor. Top asparagus with pea mixture. Crumble prosciutto over top. Serves 4

CALORIES 75; **FAT** 2g (sat 0.9g); **SODIUM** 248mg

Chanterelle & Hazelnut

Preheat oven to 425°. Combine asparagus, 2 teaspoons olive oil, ¼ teaspoon pepper, and ¼ teaspoon kosher salt on a baking sheet; bake at 425° for 9 minutes. Melt 1 teaspoon butter in a skillet over medium-high heat. Add 1½ ounces sliced chanterelle mushrooms; sauté 3 minutes. Stir in 2 tablespoons chopped toasted hazelnuts, 2 tablespoons dry white wine, and ½ teaspoon fresh thyme; cook 1 minute. Stir in 1 tablespoon crème fraîche. Top asparagus with mushroom mixture. Serves 4

CALORIES 92; **FAT** 6.9g (sat 1.9g); **SODIUM** 133mg

ME: VEGAN

Tim Cebula, omnivore, switched to an all-plant diet with the expert help of our favorite vegan chefs, Richard Landau and Kate Jacoby of Vedge in Philadelphia. He went in growling, came out crowing.

Whole Roasted Carrots with Black Lentils and Green Harissa

Hands-on: 20 min. Total: 50 min.
The green harissa, Landau and Jacoby's take on classic Tunisian hot sauce, adds balancing tang.

5 tablespoons olive oil, divided
1½ cups chopped onion, divided
1 tablespoon minced fresh garlic
3 cups Vedge-Style Vegetable Stock (page 62) or unsalted vegetable stock
2 cups uncooked black lentils, rinsed
2 tablespoons plus 2 teaspoons Cajun seasoning, divided
2 pounds large carrots
2 cups cilantro leaves
2 tablespoons rice wine vinegar
1 teaspoon salt
1 teaspoon sugar
1 teaspoon ground cumin
1 teaspoon ground coriander
1 teaspoon freshly ground black pepper
2 garlic cloves
2 jalapeño peppers, seeded

1. Heat a medium saucepan over medium-high heat. Add 1 tablespoon olive oil to pan; swirl to coat. Add ½ cup onion and minced garlic; sauté 5 minutes or until golden. Add stock, lentils, and 2 teaspoons Cajun seasoning; bring to a boil. Cover, reduce heat, and simmer 45 minutes or until lentils are tender.
2. Preheat oven to 400°.
3. Combine carrots, 2 tablespoons oil, and 2 tablespoons Cajun seasoning, tossing well to coat. Arrange carrot mixture in a single layer on a baking sheet. Bake at 400° for 30 minutes or until tender.
4. Place 1 cup onion, 2 tablespoons oil, cilantro, and remaining ingredients in a blender; process until smooth.
5. Place lentils on a serving dish; arrange carrots on top. Serve with harissa. Serves 6 (serving size: about 5 ounces carrots, about 1 cup lentils, and about 3 tablespoons harissa)

CALORIES 427; **FAT** 12.1g (sat 1.7g, mono 8.4g, poly 1.5g); **PROTEIN** 21.4g; **CARB** 63.6g; **FIBER** 14.1g; **CHOL** 0mg; **IRON** 6.6mg; **SODIUM** 504mg; **CALC** 72mg

continued

Portobello Frites

Hands-on: 42 min. Total: 42 min.
This spin on the bistro staple steak frites offers plenty of umami satisfaction in the form of juicy, meaty portobello mushrooms and a savory wine sauce. Finishing the sauce with a touch of vegan butter gives it luxurious and velvety consistency.

1 tablespoon olive oil
1 teaspoon minced fresh garlic
1 teaspoon minced shallots
½ teaspoon salt, divided
½ teaspoon freshly ground black
    pepper, divided
4 portobello mushrooms, stems
    removed
½ cup dry red wine
¼ cup Vedge-Style Vegetable Stock
    (at right) or unsalted vegetable
    stock
1 teaspoon Dijon mustard
1 teaspoon water
¼ teaspoon cornstarch
1 tablespoon vegan butter
1 tablespoon chopped tarragon
2 tablespoons canola oil
2 baked baking potatoes, cooled and
    cut lengthwise into 8 wedges each

1. Preheat oven to 400°.
2. Combine first 3 ingredients, ¼ teaspoon salt, and ¼ teaspoon pepper in a large bowl. Add mushrooms; toss gently to coat. Arrange mushrooms, cap sides down, on a jelly-roll pan. Bake at 400° for 12 minutes or until tender. Remove from oven. Place 1 mushroom on each of 4 plates. Add wine, stock, and mustard to jelly-roll pan; stir with a whisk to mix with mushroom juices. Pour wine mixture into a small saucepan over medium heat. Bring to a boil; cook until wine mixture is reduced to ¼ cup (about 15 minutes). Combine 1 teaspoon water and cornstarch, stirring with a whisk. Stir cornstarch mixture into wine mixture; boil 1 minute or until mixture begins to thicken, stirring constantly with a whisk. Remove

from heat. Add vegan butter and tarragon, stirring until butter melts.
3. Heat a large skillet over medium-high heat. Add canola oil to pan; swirl to coat. Add potato wedges; cook 3 minutes on each side or until wedges are browned. Sprinkle with ¼ teaspoon salt and ¼ teaspoon pepper. Serve with mushrooms and wine sauce. Serves 4 (serving size: 1 mushroom cap, about 4 teaspoons sauce, and 4 potato wedges)

CALORIES 297; FAT 14.4g (sat 1.3g, mono 9.2g, poly 3.5g); PROTEIN 5.4g; CARB 34g; FIBER 3.3g; CHOL 0mg; IRON 1.9mg; SODIUM 343mg; CALC 32mg

Can't-Believe-It's-Vegan Chili

Hands-on: 25 min. Total: 35 min.
This dish is sure to make it into your regular rotation: completely satisfying chili that cooks in a fraction of the time it takes to make traditional meat chili. Vegan sausage varies widely in taste and texture; we liked the meatiness and mild heat of the Field Roast brand, Mexican Chipotle flavor.

2 tablespoons olive oil
1 cup chopped onion
1 cup chopped red bell pepper
1 tablespoon chopped fresh garlic
1 (12.95-ounce) package vegan
    sausage, chopped (such as Field
    Roast Mexican Chipotle)
2 cups chopped tomato
½ cup white wine
2 teaspoons black pepper
1 teaspoon salt
1 teaspoon dried ground sage
1 teaspoon crushed red pepper
6 cups Vedge-Style Vegetable
    Stock (at right) or unsalted
    vegetable stock
3 (15-ounce) cans unsalted cannellini
    beans, rinsed, drained, and divided
2 (15-ounce) cans unsalted kidney
    beans, rinsed, drained, and divided
2 cups chopped kale
2 tablespoons chopped fresh oregano

1. Heat a large Dutch oven over medium-high heat. Add oil to pan; swirl to coat. Add onion and next 3 ingredients (through sausage); sauté 4 minutes. Add tomato and next 5 ingredients (through red pepper). Bring to a boil; cook until liquid is reduced by half (about 1 minute). Stir in stock. Combine 2 cans cannellini beans and 1 can kidney beans in a medium bowl; mash with a potato masher. Add bean mixture and remaining beans to pan. Bring to a simmer; cook 5 minutes. Add kale; cover and simmer 5 minutes. Sprinkle with oregano. Serves 10 (serving size: 1½ cups)

CALORIES 192; FAT 6.1g (sat 0.7g, mono 3.7g, poly 1.6g); PROTEIN 9.1g; CARB 24.8g; FIBER 6.9g; CHOL 0mg; IRON 2.8mg; SODIUM 378mg; CALC 86mg

Vedge-Style Vegetable Stock
Hands-on: 10 min. Total: 45 min.
Searing some of the veggies over high heat until lightly charred gives the stock alluringly complex flavor and a hint of smokiness. Simmering the mixture no longer than 25 minutes keeps the vegetable flavor fresh and vibrant.

Heat a large stockpot over high heat. Add 2 teaspoons canola oil to pan; swirl to coat. Add 6 chopped carrots, 3 chopped celery stalks with leaves, 2 rinsed and chopped leeks, 2 chopped onions with skins, and 1 chopped turnip to pan; cook, stirring occasionally, 3 minutes or until browned and slightly charred. Add 6 quarts water; bring to a boil. Reduce heat to low. Add 3 green cabbage leaves, 3 cups broccoli stems, and 2 cups kale stems; simmer 25 minutes. Strain; cool. Yield 5 quarts (serving size: ½ cup)

CALORIES 5; FAT 0.3g (sat 0g); SODIUM 3mg

Quick & Easy • Gluten Free Vegetarian

Spicy Grilled Mango with Chiles and Crema

Hands-on: 15 min. Total: 15 min. *This quick dish is a study in balance: Sweet, spicy, sour, and salty flavors come together harmoniously and for maximum effect.*

3 tablespoons fresh lime juice, divided
1 thinly sliced green jalapeño pepper
1 thinly sliced red jalapeño pepper
2 ripe peeled mangoes, cut into ⅓-inch-thick slices
Cooking spray
¼ teaspoon kosher salt
¼ teaspoon freshly ground black pepper
⅛ teaspoon ground red pepper
3 tablespoons Mexican crema
¼ cup cilantro leaves

1. Combine 2 tablespoons juice and jalapeños in a small bowl.
2. Coat mango slices with cooking spray; sprinkle with salt, black pepper, and ground red pepper. Heat a grill pan over high heat until smoking hot. Coat pan with cooking spray. Add mango to pan. Cook, without moving, 4 minutes or until well marked. Turn and cook 2 minutes; place on a platter.
3. Combine 1 tablespoon juice and crema in a small bowl, stirring with a whisk until smooth. Spoon jalapeños over mango. Drizzle with crema mixture; sprinkle with cilantro leaves. Serves 4 (serving size: ½ mango and 1 tablespoon sauce)

CALORIES 128; **FAT** 2.6g (sat 1.8g, mono 0.2g, poly 0.1g); **PROTEIN** 1.9g; **CARB** 27.5g; **FIBER** 2.9g; **CHOL** 6mg; **IRON** 0.3mg; **SODIUM** 172mg; **CALC** 22mg

THIS MONTH'S LESSON: THE BEST DELI-STYLE ROAST BEEF

Cook like a genius with tips from chef and teacher Keith Schroeder.

Deli-counter roast beef is often laden with salt, and the flavor of the meat gets lost in briny translation. In the main recipe here, bold ingredients blanket the exterior of a lean but flavorful cut—eye of round. You'll get a spice-rubbed, almost charred flavor that highlights rather than overwhelms the sandwich. The variation is a spruced-up beef tenderloin for ritzy, open-faced presentations—ideal for parties. A high-temperature start forms a good-looking crust, while the lower temperature taper allows an edge-to-edge, rosy eye that will delight fans of a straight-ahead roast beef on rye. Be sure to use a probe thermometer rather than relying on time references alone, which are merely guidelines. The flatter the roast, the quicker it will cook. Find one with a consistent diameter for the most even result.

Kid Friendly • Gluten Free Make Ahead

Chili and Coffee-Rubbed Eye of Round

Hands-on: 15 min. Total: 10 hr. *Chilling the meat overnight and slicing it thinly the next day for sandwiches gives the spice rub more time to flavor the meat. The beef tenderloin variation, with its overnight chill, is a great make-ahead dish for parties; serve on toasted baguette with horseradish sauce and arugula.*

¼ cup grated yellow onion
2 tablespoons instant coffee granules
2 teaspoons grated orange rind
2 tablespoons fresh orange juice
1½ tablespoons chili powder
1½ teaspoons kosher salt
4 garlic cloves, grated
1 (2-pound) eye-of-round roast, trimmed

1. Preheat oven to 475°.
2. Combine first 7 ingredients; massage mixture evenly onto roast. Place roast in a small roasting pan; bake at 475° for 20 minutes, turning after 10 minutes.

continued

3. Reduce oven temperature to 300° (do not remove roast from oven); bake an additional 30 minutes or until a thermometer registers 120°. Remove roast from oven, and place on a cutting board or work surface. Let rest at room temperature 30 minutes.

4. Wrap roast in parchment paper, then in plastic wrap; refrigerate 8 hours or overnight. Cut into very thin slices for sandwiches. Serves 8 (serving size: about 3 ounces)

CALORIES 148; **FAT** 3.6g (sat 1.2g, mono 1.5g, poly 0.1g); **PROTEIN** 25.6g; **CARB** 1.8g; **FIBER** 0.2g; **CHOL** 64mg; **IRON** 2.2mg; **SODIUM** 439mg; **CALC** 11mg

Kid Friendly • Gluten Free Make Ahead Mustard-Tarragon Beef Tenderloin: Replace the coffee with 2 tablespoons dry mustard, and the chili powder with 1½ tablespoons brown sugar. Omit orange juice; decrease salt to 1 teaspoon. Replace eye-of-round roast with a 2-pound beef tenderloin roast, rimmed. After beef cooks and rests for 30 minutes, roll it in ¼ cup chopped fresh tarragon. After refrigerating, cut into very thin slices for hors d'oeuvres. Serves 12 (serving size: about 2 ounces)

CALORIES 111; **FAT** 4.3g (sat 1.6g); **SODIUM** 190mg

GO BOLD WITH THE RUB–YOU'LL BE SLICING THE MEAT THINLY.

COOK MORE OFTEN

A desire to grow her own food inspired this month's hero to flee the corporate coop and rediscover her inner chef.

Getting a homemade meal on the table when you're a young, single professional can be a tall order. For Mary Beth Shaddix, a decade of traveling for her business development job meant dinners out entertaining clients, yielding a full suitcase and an empty fridge. "I lived like a dude," she jokes. "I had Champagne, beer, and Chinese takeout. The cooking fell off, as anyone can relate, whether you're running kids to soccer or working past 7 o'clock at your desk."

By the time she reached her early 30s, Mary Beth was ready to put down roots. She quit her job and began seeking out her life's mission, which, literally involved putting down roots: "I thought, 'I want to garden,' which was weird because I had never done it before. But I looked at schools, consulted friends, and decided to work at a nursery to get the largest breadth of experience," she says.

There she met David Shaddix, the manager of the garden center. The two married three years later, and today she helps David at their wholesale nursery, Maple Valley, while managing the *Cooking Light* Garden. A love for the foods she grows and a rural reality—the nearest restaurant and grocery store are 15 miles away—mean she spends a lot of time in the kitchen. "Growing your own food creates curiosity, and it opens your palate a little bit," she says.

Mealtimes for Mary Beth now involve creatively use the bounty from the garden. "Sometimes it's just about staring at three bell peppers, some tomatoes, and some cilantro and inventing a meal around it," she says.

Vegetable and Greens Hash with Poached Egg

Hands-on: 40 min. Total: 40 min.

2 tablespoons olive oil
1 medium red onion, vertically sliced
1 tablespoon chopped fresh thyme
4 garlic cloves, chopped
2½ cups cubed peeled sweet potato
2½ cups cubed peeled red or Yukon gold potato
¼ cup water
4 ounces Lacinato kale, stemmed and chopped (about 2 packed cups)
3 ounces fresh spinach (about 3 cups)
½ teaspoon salt
½ teaspoon black pepper
1 tablespoon white vinegar
4 large eggs

1. Heat a large nonstick skillet over medium heat. Add olive oil to pan; swirl to coat. Add onion; cook 5 minutes or until tender and lightly browned. Add thyme and garlic, and cook 1 minute, stirring constantly. Add potatoes and ¼ cup water; cover and cook over medium-low heat for 15 minutes or until potatoes are tender, stirring every 5 minutes. Stir in kale, spinach, salt, and pepper; cook, covered, 3 minutes or until greens wilt. Remove pan from heat; keep warm.

2. Add water to a large skillet, filling two-thirds full, and bring to a boil. Reduce heat; simmer. Add vinegar. Break each egg into a custard cup, and pour each gently into pan; cook for 3 minutes or until desired degree of doneness. Carefully remove eggs from pan using a slotted spoon. Place about 1¼ cups hash on each of 4 plates, and top each serving with 1 poached egg. Serves 4

CALORIES 326; **FAT** 11.9g (sat 2.6g, mono 6.8g, poly 1.8g); **PROTEIN** 12.2g; **CARB** 43.4g; **FIBER** 5.5g; **CHOL** 186mg; **IRON** 3.6mg; **SODIUM** 511mg; **CALC** 128mg

LET'S GET COOKING

TODAY'S SPECIAL: KALE SALAD WITH GRILLED ARTICHOKES

From chef Wolfgang Puck of the café at Spago in Las Vegas

In the world of winter greens, kale is king. It's become a shining star among veggies in general, thanks to its reputation as a healthy superfood. "Nowadays, it seems like everyone in the world knows that kale is good for you," says Wolfgang Puck—himself a king among chefs and garnering some of the best restaurant reviews of his amazing career. "It's incredibly healthful, rich in vitamins A, C, and K, and packed with calcium, iron, and other nutrients." Kale also offers the earthy flavor and chewy texture that make for supremely satisfying salads. Puck developed the salad here—a variation of which will be served at the Governor's Ball following the Academy Awards—because he loves strong flavors. "Both kale and artichokes have strong flavors, so I thought, why not mix them together?" A pressure cooker speeds the artichoke prep time. Pine nuts add crunch; plumped raisins balance the zingy Dijon-spiked dressing. Try his version this month at the café at Spago in Las Vegas.

Gluten Free • Vegetarian

Kale Salad with Grilled Artichokes

Hands-on: 40 min. Total: 1 hr. 15 min.
If you don't have a pressure cooker, simmer the artichoke mixture in a Dutch oven for 40 minutes or until tender.

2 lemons, halved crosswise
2 cups dry white wine
2 cups water
1 bay leaf
1 thyme sprig
4 large artichokes
Cooking spray
3 tablespoons extra-virgin olive oil, divided
1/2 teaspoon black pepper, divided
1/4 teaspoon salt, divided
1/4 cup golden raisins
1/2 cup hot water
2 tablespoons fresh lemon juice
1 tablespoon minced shallots
1/2 teaspoon Dijon mustard
1/4 teaspoon sugar
6 cups chopped Lacinato kale
1/4 cup pine nuts, toasted

1. Squeeze juice from lemon halves into a 6- or 8-quart pressure cooker. Add lemon halves, wine, 2 cups water, bay leaf, and thyme to cooker. Cut off stem of each artichoke to within 1 inch of base; peel stem. Remove bottom leaves and tough outer leaves, leaving tender heart and bottom. Add artichokes to pressure cooker. Close lid securely; bring to high pressure over high heat. Reduce heat to medium or level needed to maintain high pressure; cook 10 minutes. Remove from heat; release pressure through steam vent, or place cooker under cold water to release pressure. Remove lid; let stand 30 minutes. Remove artichokes from cooking liquid. Cut each artichoke in half lengthwise. Remove fuzzy thistle from bottom with a spoon.
2. Heat a grill pan over medium-high heat; coat pan with cooking spray. Combine 1 tablespoon oil, artichokes, 1/4 teaspoon pepper, and 1/8 teaspoon salt in a medium bowl. Add artichokes to pan; cook 3 minutes on each side or until grill marks appear. Cut each artichoke half in half lengthwise.
3. Combine raisins and 1/2 cup hot water; let stand 10 minutes. Drain.
4. Combine 1/4 teaspoon pepper, 1/8 teaspoon salt, 2 tablespoons oil, 2 tablespoons juice, and next 3 ingredients in a medium bowl, stirring with a whisk. Add kale; toss to coat. Place 1 cup kale mixture on each of 4 plates; top each serving with 4 artichoke pieces, 1 tablespoon raisins, and 1 tablespoon nuts. Serves 4

CALORIES 315; FAT 16.9g (sat 2g, mono 9g, poly 4.4g); PROTEIN 10.2g; CARB 37.1g; FIBER 11.6g; CHOL 0mg; IRON 4.6mg; SODIUM 360mg; CALC 217mg

DINNER TONIGHT

Seared Salmon Fillets + Orzo Pilaf + Garlic Broccolini

5 teaspoons olive oil, divided
3/4 cup uncooked orzo
1 1/2 cups unsalted chicken stock
1/2 teaspoon salt, divided
1/4 cup bottled roasted red bell peppers, thinly sliced
2 tablespoons chopped fresh dill
2 tablespoons fresh lemon juice
1 ounce chopped pitted kalamata olives
4 (6-ounce) salmon fillets
1/2 teaspoon freshly ground black pepper

1. Heat a medium saucepan over medium-high heat. Add 2 teaspoons oil to pan; swirl to coat. Add orzo; sauté 2 minutes or until toasted. Add stock and 1/4 teaspoon salt; bring to a boil. Cover, reduce heat, and simmer 15 minutes. Stir in bell peppers, dill, juice, and olives; keep warm.
2. Heat a large nonstick skillet over medium-high heat. Add 1 tablespoon oil to pan; swirl. Sprinkle filets with 1/4 teaspoon salt and black pepper. Cook 3 minutes on each side or until desired degree of doneness. Serve with orzo mixture. Serves 4 (serving size: 1 fillet and about 2/3 cup orzo mixture)

CALORIES 475; **FAT** 17.8g (sat 3g, mono 8.7g, poly 4.1g); **PROTEIN** 43.6g; **CARB** 32.9g; **FIBER** 1.7g; **CHOL** 90mg; **IRON** 2.3mg; **SODIUM** 566mg; **CALC** 29mg

Garlic Broccolini

Heat a large skillet over medium-high heat. Add 1 tablespoon olive oil; swirl to coat. Add 1 pound Broccolini, trimmed and cut into 1-inch pieces; sauté 2 minutes. Add 4 thinly sliced garlic cloves; sauté 2 minutes. Add 1/4 cup water to pan; cover and cook 2 minutes or until Broccolini is crisp-tender. Sprinkle with 1/4 teaspoon salt. Serves 4 (serving size: about 3/4 cup)

CALORIES 81; **FAT** 3.4g (sat 0.5g); **SODIUM** 181mg

READY IN
30
MINUTES

SHOPPING LIST

Seared Salmon Fillets with Orzo Pilaf
Uncooked orzo
Unsalted chicken stock
Bottled roasted red bell peppers
Fresh dill
Lemon
Kalamata olives
4 (6-ounce) salmon fillets

Garlic Broccolini
Broccolini
Garlic cloves

GAME PLAN

While orzo cooks:
▪ Chop dill and olives.
▪ Slice peppers.
While fish cooks:
▪ Cook Broccolini.

Flank Steak Tacos + Slaw + Sweet Potato-Black Bean Salad

Cooking spray
2 teaspoons chili powder
1 teaspoon brown sugar
1/2 teaspoon ground cumin
1/2 teaspoon unsweetened cocoa
1/2 teaspoon salt, divided
1 (12-ounce) flank steak, trimmed
1 red bell pepper
1 yellow bell pepper
1 tablespoon cider vinegar
1 tablespoon extra-virgin olive oil
1 teaspoon honey mustard
1 cup julienne-cut jicama
1 cup thinly sliced radicchio
1/4 cup cilantro leaves
8 corn tortillas
1 small lime, cut into 8 wedges

1. Heat a grill pan over medium-high heat. Coat pan with cooking spray. Combine chili powder, sugar, cumin, cocoa, and 3/8 teaspoon salt; rub spice mixture evenly over steak. Add steak to pan; cook 5 minutes on each side. Let stand 10 minutes; cut across the grain into thin slices. Cut bell peppers into quarters; discard seeds and membranes. Add bell peppers to pan; cook 4 minutes on each side. Cut into thin slices.
2. Combine 1/8 teaspoon salt, vinegar, oil, and mustard in a medium bowl; stir with a whisk. Add jicama, radicchio, and cilantro; toss to coat.
3. Heat tortillas in grill pan coated with cooking spray 30 seconds or until lightly charred. Divide beef, bell peppers, and jicama mixture evenly among tortillas; serve with lime wedges. Serves 4 (serving size: 2 tacos)

CALORIES 281; **FAT** 9.8g (sat 2.3g, mono 4.2g, poly 1.2g); **PROTEIN** 21.6g; **CARB** 29g; **FIBER** 5.9g; **CHOL** 53mg; **IRON** 2.2mg; **SODIUM** 391mg; **CALC** 58mg

READY IN 40 MINUTES

SHOPPING LIST

Flank Steak Tacos with Slaw

Chili powder
Brown sugar
Ground cumin
Unsweetened cocoa
12-ounce flank steak
Red bell pepper
Yellow bell pepper
Cider vinegar
Extra-virgin olive oil
Honey mustard
Jicama
Radicchio
Cilantro leaves
Corn tortillas
Lime

Warm Sweet Potato-Black Bean Salad

Sweet potato
Unsalted chicken stock
1 can unsalted black beans
Fresh oregano
Lime

GAME PLAN

While steak cooks:
▪ Prepare black bean mixture for salad.
While steak rests:
▪ Prepare slaw.

Warm Sweet Potato-Black Bean Salad

Combine 1 cup diced peeled sweet potato and ¼ cup unsalted chicken stock in a saucepan; bring to a boil. Cover, reduce heat, and simmer 10 minutes. Stir in 1 (15-ounce) can unsalted black beans, rinsed and drained; 1 tablespoon chopped fresh oregano; 1 tablespoon fresh lime juice; ¼ teaspoon salt; and ¼ teaspoon black pepper. Cook 2 minutes or until thoroughly heated. Serves 4 (serving size: ½ cup)

CALORIES 83; **FAT** 0.1g (sat 0g); **SODIUM** 182mg

Chicken Kebabs + Cucumber Noodles + Sesame-Carrot Salad

7 ounces uncooked soba noodles
3 tablespoons rice vinegar, divided
2 tablespoons dark sesame oil
2 tablespoons honey, divided
¼ teaspoon sugar
¼ cup thinly sliced green onions
1 medium cucumber, seeded and thinly sliced
2 tablespoons lower-sodium soy sauce, divided
1 tablespoon minced peeled fresh ginger
1 tablespoon peanut oil
1 pound skinless, boneless chicken breast, cut into 1½-inch pieces
Cooking spray
¼ cup creamy peanut butter
2 tablespoons water
2 teaspoons sambal oelek (ground fresh chile paste) or chile garlic paste
Chopped fresh cilantro

1. Cook noodles according to package directions, omitting salt and fat; drain and rinse with cold water. Drain. Combine 2 tablespoons vinegar, sesame oil, 1 tablespoon honey, and sugar in a large bowl, stirring with a whisk. Add noodles, onions, and cucumber; toss to combine.
2. Combine 1 tablespoon honey, 1 tablespoon soy sauce, ginger, and peanut oil in a medium bowl, stirring with a whisk. Add chicken to bowl; toss to coat. Thread chicken evenly onto 4 (10-inch) skewers.
3. Heat a grill pan over medium-high heat. Coat with cooking spray. Add kebabs to pan; cook 12 minutes or until done, turning to brown all sides.
4. Combine 1 tablespoon vinegar, 1 tablespoon soy sauce, peanut butter, 2 tablespoons water, and sambal oelek in a medium bowl, stirring with a whisk. Drizzle mixture over chicken. Garnish with cilantro. Serve with noodles. Serves 4 (serving size: 1 kebab, ¾ cup noodles, and 2½ tablespoons sauce)

CALORIES 414; **FAT** 21.6g (sat 3.9g, mono 9.3g, poly 6.8g); **PROTEIN** 32g; **CARB** 26.1g; **FIBER** 2g; **CHOL** 73mg; **IRON** 1.5mg; **SODIUM** 558mg; **CALC** 37mg

Sesame-Carrot Salad

Combine 3 cups matchstick-cut carrots, 1½ tablespoons toasted sesame seeds, 1½ tablespoons rice vinegar, 1 tablespoon dark sesame oil, 1 teaspoon lower-sodium soy sauce, and ½ teaspoon freshly ground black pepper in a large bowl; toss well to coat. Serves 4 (serving size: ¾ cup)

CALORIES 89; **FAT** 5.4g (sat 0.8g); **SODIUM** 108mg

continued

**READY IN
40
MINUTES**

SHOPPING LIST

Chicken Kebabs and Cucumber Noodles

Uncooked soba noodles
Rice vinegar
Dark sesame oil
Honey
Green onions
Cucumber
Lower-sodium soy sauce
Fresh ginger
Peanut oil
1 pound skinless, boneless chicken breasts
Creamy peanut butter
Sugar
Sambal oelek
Fresh cilantro

Sesame-Carrot Salad

Carrots
Sesame seeds
Rice vinegar
Dark sesame oil
Lower-sodium soy sauce

GAME PLAN

While noodles cook:
■ Prepare cucumber mixture.
While chicken cooks:
■ Prepare peanut sauce.
■ Prepare carrot salad.

Hazelnut Chicken + Roasted Squash + Wilted Spinach

Cooking spray
2 teaspoons Dijon mustard
1 large egg
½ cup panko (Japanese breadcrumbs)
⅓ cup finely chopped hazelnuts
1½ teaspoons dried rubbed sage
4 (6-ounce) skinless, boneless chicken breast halves
½ teaspoon freshly ground black pepper, divided
¼ teaspoon kosher salt
4 teaspoons olive oil, divided
2 tablespoons chopped shallots
¾ cup unsalted chicken stock
½ cup ruby port or other sweet red wine
¼ cup dried cranberries
2 teaspoons balsamic vinegar
2 teaspoons unsalted butter

1. Preheat oven to 425°.
2. Place a wire rack on a baking sheet; coat with cooking spray. Combine mustard and egg in a shallow dish, stirring with a whisk. Combine panko, hazelnuts, and sage in a shallow dish. Sprinkle chicken evenly with ¼ teaspoon pepper and salt. Dip chicken in egg mixture; dredge in panko mixture, pressing to adhere.
3. Heat a large nonstick skillet over medium-high heat. Add 1 tablespoon olive oil to pan, and swirl to coat. Add chicken, and cook 2 minutes on each side or until browned. Place chicken on prepared rack, and bake at 425° for 12 to 15 minutes or until done.

4. Wipe skillet with a paper towel; heat over medium heat. Add 1 teaspoon oil to pan; swirl to coat. Add shallots; cook 1 minute or until tender. Add ¼ teaspoon pepper, chicken stock, port, and cranberries; bring to a boil. Reduce heat to low; simmer 4 minutes or until liquid is reduced by half. Remove pan from heat. Add balsamic vinegar and butter to pan, stirring until butter melts. Spoon port mixture over chicken. Serves 4 (serving size: 1 breast half and about 3 tablespoons sauce)

CALORIES 419; FAT 18.4g (sat 3.7g, mono 9.9g, poly 2.3g); PROTEIN 41.3g; CARB 17.3g; FIBER 2g; CHOL 161mg; IRON 1.7mg; SODIUM 444mg; CALC 41mg

Garlic and Thyme Roasted Butternut Squash

Preheat oven to 425°. Combine 1 tablespoon chopped fresh thyme, 1 tablespoon olive oil, ½ teaspoon kosher salt, 1 (12-ounce) package fresh cubed butternut squash, and 8 peeled garlic cloves on a baking sheet; toss. Bake at 425° for 30 minutes; stir after 15 minutes. Mash garlic with a fork; toss with squash. Serves 4 (serving size: 1 cup)

CALORIES 78; FAT 3.5g (sat 0.5g); SODIUM 245mg

Wilted Spinach

Heat 2 tablespoons unsalted chicken stock in a skillet over medium heat. Add 1 (9-ounce) package baby spinach; toss until spinach wilts. Serves 4 (serving size: about ⅓ cup)

CALORIES 27; FAT 0g; SODIUM 105mg

SHOPPING LIST

Hazelnut Chicken

Dijon mustard
Egg
Panko
Hazelnuts
Dried sage
Skinless, boneless chicken breasts
Kosher salt
Shallots
Unsalted chicken stock
Ruby port or other sweet red wine
Dried cranberries
Balsamic vinegar
Unsalted butter

Garlic and Thyme Roasted Butternut Squash

Fresh thyme
Kosher salt
1 (12-ounce) package fresh cubed butternut squash
Garlic cloves

Wilted Spinach

Unsalted chicken stock
1 (9-ounce) package baby spinach

GAME PLAN

While squash cooks:
- Prepare chicken.

While chicken cooks:
- Prepare port mixture.
- Prepare spinach.

Turkey Meatball Subs + Skillet-Blistered Green Beans

4 (2½-ounce) hoagie rolls with sesame seeds, split
3 tablespoons fat-free milk
½ teaspoon dried oregano
¼ teaspoon salt
12 ounces ground turkey breast
1 large egg white
4 teaspoons olive oil, divided
¾ cup chopped yellow onion
1 teaspoon minced fresh garlic
¼ cup dry white wine
1¾ cups lower-sodium marinara sauce
¼ cup chopped fresh basil
1 tablespoon balsamic vinegar
5 teaspoons grated Parmigiano-Reggiano cheese

1. Preheat broiler.
2. Hollow out top and bottom halves of bread, leaving a ½-inch-thick shell. Place torn bread in a large bowl. Add milk, stirring with a fork until smooth. Add oregano, salt, turkey, and egg white to bread mixture, stirring just until combined. Working with damp hands, shape turkey mixture into 12 meatballs.
3. Heat a large nonstick skillet over medium heat. Add 1 tablespoon oil to pan; swirl to coat. Add meatballs; cook 5 minutes, turning to brown on all sides. Remove meatballs from pan. Add 1 teaspoon oil to pan; swirl to coat. Add onion and garlic to pan; sauté 4 minutes or until tender. Add wine; cook 1 minute, scraping pan to loosen browned bits. Stir in marinara, basil, and vinegar; bring to a boil. Return meatballs to pan. Cover, reduce heat, and simmer 15 minutes or until meatballs are done.
4. Arrange rolls, cut sides up, on a baking sheet; broil 1 minute or until

toasted. Top bottom half of each roll with 3 meatballs, about ⅓ cup sauce, and top half of roll. Sprinkle evenly with Parmigiano-Reggiano. Serves 4 (serving size: 1 sandwich)

CALORIES 386; **FAT** 9.7g (sat 2.4g, mono 4.2g, poly 1.8g); **PROTEIN** 30.2g; **CARB** 46.8g; **FIBER** 3.5g; **CHOL** 36mg; **IRON** 4.8mg; **SODIUM** 688mg; **CALC** 132mg

SHOPPING LIST

Turkey Meatball Subs

Hoagie rolls
Fat-free milk
Dried oregano
12 ounces ground turkey breast
Egg
Yellow onion
Garlic cloves
Dry white wine
Lower-sodium marinara sauce
Fresh basil
Balsamic vinegar
Parmigiano-Reggiano cheese

Skillet-Blistered Green Beans

Crushed red pepper
Green beans
Dry white wine
Kosher salt

GAME PLAN

While meatballs cook:
- Chop onion and basil.
- Mince garlic.

While sauce simmers:
- Prepare green beans.
- Toast rolls.

continued

Skillet-Blistered Green Beans
Heat a skillet over medium-high heat. Add 2 teaspoons olive oil; swirl. Add ¼ teaspoon crushed red pepper and 12 ounces trimmed green beans; cook 3 minutes or until blistered. Add ¼ cup dry white wine; cook 2 minutes or until liquid evaporates, stirring often. Sprinkle with ¼ teaspoon kosher salt. Serves 4 (serving size: about ½ cup)

CALORIES 53; **FAT** 2.5g (sat 0.4g); **SODIUM** 126mg

BUDGET COOKING

FEED 4 FOR LESS THAN $10

Three simple, delicious dinners geared to impress. Bonus: They're weeknight-fast, too!

Kid Friendly • Make Ahead

Root Vegetable Minestrone with Bacon

$2.45 PER SERVING

Hands-on: 30 min. Total: 60 min.
For a simple salad, combine 1 tablespoon fresh lemon juice, 2 teaspoons olive oil, ¼ teaspoon kosher salt, and ¼ teaspoon pepper. Add 6 cups chopped romaine, 2 ounces walnuts, and 1 ounce shaved Parmesan. Toss.

- **5 center-cut bacon slices, chopped**
- **1⅓ cups chopped peeled butternut squash**
- **1 cup chopped onion**
- **⅔ cup chopped carrot**
- **½ cup chopped parsnip**
- **½ cup chopped celery**

- **4 teaspoons unsalted tomato paste**
- **½ teaspoon dried basil**
- **½ teaspoon dried thyme**
- **3 garlic cloves, minced**
- **2⅔ cups unsalted chicken stock**
- **¼ cup uncooked ditalini pasta**
- **¾ cup unsalted cannellini beans, rinsed and drained**
- **¼ teaspoon kosher salt**
- **¼ teaspoon black pepper**

1. Cook bacon in a large Dutch oven over medium heat until crisp. Remove bacon from pan; reserve 1 tablespoon drippings in pan. Increase heat to medium-high. Add butternut squash and next 8 ingredients (through garlic) to drippings in pan; sauté 8 minutes, stirring occasionally. Add chicken stock, scraping pan to loosen browned bits. Bring to a boil; cover, reduce heat, and simmer 15 minutes. Stir in uncooked pasta; cook 10 minutes. Stir in cannellini beans, salt, and pepper; cook 2 minutes or until vegetables and pasta are tender. Divide soup evenly among 4 bowls; top evenly with bacon. Serves 4 (serving size: 1½ cups)

CALORIES 202; **FAT** 3.3g (sat 1.4g, mono 0.1g, poly 0.1g); **PROTEIN** 11.5g; **CARB** 33.7g; **FIBER** 6.4g; **CHOL** 9mg; **IRON** 2.4mg; **SODIUM** 426mg; **CALC** 97mg

Kid Friendly • Quick & Easy

Chicken and Basil Rice Bowl with Cashews

$2.41 PER SERVING

Hands-on: 17 min. Total: 25 min.

- **1 cup uncooked long-grain white rice**
- **½ teaspoon grated lime rind**
- **1 tablespoon canola oil, divided**
- **1 teaspoon dark sesame oil**
- **1 pound skinless, boneless chicken thighs, cut into 1-inch pieces**

- **2 tablespoons lower-sodium soy sauce, divided**
- **1 tablespoon minced fresh garlic**
- **1 tablespoon minced peeled fresh ginger**
- **½ teaspoon crushed red pepper**
- **2 cups broccoli florets**
- **1 medium red bell pepper, cut into 1-inch pieces**
- **⅔ cup fat-free, lower-sodium chicken broth**
- **2 teaspoons cornstarch**
- **¾ cup torn basil leaves, divided**
- **2 tablespoons fresh lime juice**
- **2 tablespoons unsalted cashews, chopped**

1. Cook rice according to package directions, omitting salt and fat. Fluff rice. Stir in lime rind.
2. Heat a large nonstick skillet over medium-high heat. Add 1½ teaspoons canola oil and sesame oil to pan; swirl to coat. Combine chicken, 1 tablespoon soy sauce, garlic, ginger, and crushed red pepper in a bowl; toss to coat. Add chicken mixture to pan; cook 6 minutes or until chicken begins to brown, stirring frequently. Remove chicken from pan. Add remaining 1½ teaspoons canola oil to pan; swirl to coat. Add broccoli and bell pepper to pan; cook 3 minutes or until crisp-tender, stirring occasionally.
3. Combine remaining 1 tablespoon soy sauce, chicken broth, and cornstarch in a bowl. Add chicken mixture and broth mixture to pan. Bring to a boil; cook 2 minutes or until sauce begins to thicken, stirring occasionally. Add ½ cup basil to pan, stirring until basil wilts. Remove pan from heat; stir in lime juice. Spoon ½ cup rice mixture into each of 4 bowls; top each serving with about 1½ cups chicken mixture. Sprinkle evenly with remaining ¼ cup basil and chopped cashews. Serves 4

CALORIES 413; **FAT** 13.7g (sat 2.7g, mono 6.6g, poly 3.3g); **PROTEIN** 25.5g; **CARB** 46g; **FIBER** 2.8g; **CHOL** 106mg; **IRON** 4mg; **SODIUM** 445mg; **CALC** 63mg

Pork Cutlets with Orange Gremolata

$2.31 PER SERVING

***Hands-on: 19 min. Total: 19 min.** Make sure to grate the rind before juicing the orange. For a quick side, combine 1½ cups cooked orzo with 2 teaspoons olive oil, 1 teaspoon lemon juice, 2 sliced green onions, and 2 ounces dried cranberries.*

2 tablespoons all-purpose flour
1 (1-pound) pork tenderloin, trimmed and cut into 12 thin slices
³⁄₄ teaspoon kosher salt, divided
4 teaspoons extra-virgin olive oil, divided
²⁄₃ cup fresh orange juice (about 2 medium oranges)
¹⁄₃ cup water
2 tablespoons orange marmalade
2 teaspoons balsamic vinegar
¹⁄₄ teaspoon black pepper
2 tablespoons finely chopped fresh flat-leaf parsley
1 teaspoon grated orange rind
¹⁄₂ teaspoon minced fresh garlic

1. Heat a large nonstick skillet over medium-high heat. Place flour in a shallow dish. Sprinkle pork with ½ teaspoon salt; dredge pork in flour. Add 2 teaspoons oil to pan; swirl to coat. Add 6 pork slices to pan; cook 2 minutes on each side or until browned and done. Place cooked pork on a platter; keep warm. Repeat procedure with 2 teaspoons oil and remaining 6 pork slices.
2. Add orange juice, ⅓ cup water, marmalade, and vinegar to pan, scraping pan to loosen browned bits. Bring to a boil; cook 3 minutes or until liquid is reduced to ½ cup. Stir in ¼ teaspoon salt and pepper.
3. Place parsley, orange rind, and garlic in a small bowl; stir with a fork to combine. Spoon orange juice mixture over pork; sprinkle evenly with orange rind mixture. Serves 4 (serving size: 3 ounces pork and 2 tablespoons sauce)

CALORIES 238; FAT 8.7g (sat 2g, mono 4.8g, poly 1.2g); PROTEIN 24.3g; CARB 14.8g; FIBER 0.4g; CHOL 74mg; IRON 1.6mg; SODIUM 427mg; CALC 21mg

MEATLESS MONDAYS

LAYERED, LIGHTENED GREEK CASSEROLE

We swap the typical butter-based béchamel for creamy Greek yogurt and feta.

Make Ahead • Vegetarian

Cheesy Vegetable Moussaka

***Hands-on: 40 min. Total: 1 hr. 30 min.** Broiling the eggplant coaxes out a deeper, more complex flavor.*

2 tablespoons olive oil, divided
2 cups finely chopped onion
6 garlic cloves, chopped
1 cup water
¹⁄₂ cup uncooked quinoa
2 tablespoons unsalted tomato paste
³⁄₈ teaspoon kosher salt
¹⁄₄ teaspoon freshly ground black pepper
1 (28-ounce) can unsalted diced tomatoes, undrained
2 tablespoons chopped fresh basil
2 large eggplants, cut into ½-inch-thick slices (about 2½ pounds)
Cooking spray
3 (8-ounce) packages presliced mushrooms
¹⁄₂ cup dry white wine
2 tablespoons lower-sodium soy sauce
2 tablespoons chopped fresh dill
1¹⁄₂ cups plain fat-free Greek yogurt
2.5 ounces feta cheese, crumbled (about ²⁄₃ cup)
2 large eggs
1 large egg white
1 ounce vegetarian Parmesan cheese, grated (about ¹⁄₄ cup)

1. Heat a medium saucepan over medium-high heat. Add 1 tablespoon oil to pan; swirl to coat. Add onion; cook 6 minutes or until onion is tender. Add garlic; cook 1 minute. Add 1 cup water, quinoa, tomato paste, salt, pepper, and tomatoes. Bring to a boil; reduce heat, and simmer 20 minutes. Remove from heat; stir in basil.
2. Preheat broiler to high.
3. Place half of eggplant slices on a foil-lined baking sheet coated with cooking spray; lightly coat both sides of eggplant slices with cooking spray. Broil 5 inches from heat for 5 minutes on each side or until browned. Repeat procedure with remaining eggplant. Set eggplant aside.
4. Reduce oven temperature to 350°.
5. Heat a large skillet over medium-high heat. Add 1 tablespoon oil to pan; swirl to coat. Add mushrooms; cook 8 minutes. Add wine and soy sauce; simmer 4 minutes. Remove from heat; stir in dill.
6. Combine yogurt, feta cheese, eggs, and egg white in a bowl, stirring well with a whisk until smooth.
7. Spread half of the tomato sauce in bottom of a 13 x 9–inch glass or ceramic baking dish coated with cooking spray. Arrange half of eggplant slices over sauce. Spread mushroom mixture over eggplant; sprinkle with Parmesan cheese. Spoon remaining tomato sauce over cheese; top with remaining eggplant slices. Spoon yogurt mixture evenly over eggplant. Bake at 350° for 45 minutes or until topping is lightly browned. Serves 6

CALORIES 335; FAT 11.9g (sat 4g, mono 5.1g, poly 1.8g); PROTEIN 20.6g; CARB 38g; FIBER 9.9g; CHOL 77mg; IRON 3.8mg; SODIUM 586mg; CALC 247mg

FLIPPING FOR A TORTILLA

Matisse gets cracking with a quick, easy Spanish-style omelet.

"Today I made a really nice omelet-style dish that feeds the whole family without having to make individual omelets for each person. I thought there would be lots of stirring and standing over the pan, but I was wrong. This dish was simple and really quick to make. You could cook this for any meal, not just breakfast! If you don't have sherry vinegar, you can cook the onions with balsamic vinegar; it's just as delicious. You could also add other ingredients like ham, bacon, or other vegetables—anything you like to make it your own. I thought this dish was very flavorful. The tortilla tasted good warm or cold, so you could take it on a spring picnic or have leftovers for lunch the next day (that is, if there's any tortilla left over!)."

THE VERDICT

MONICA (AGE 12)
She thought the dish was amazing. There was nothing she didn't like about it. **10/10**

SADE (AGE 12)
She said, "Yum! This is delicious. I like it warm—I'm not sure about having it cold." **9/10**

MATISSE (AGE 13)
The creaminess of the egg with the crunch of the bell pepper made a nice balance of texture. **10/10**

Kid Friendly • Quick & Easy
Gluten Free • Make Ahead
Vegetarian

Tortilla Española

Hands-on: 10 min. Total: 35 min.
Unlike a fluffy French omelet, this Spanish classic traditionally includes olive oil and cooked potato with some egg. Shaking the pan helps prevent the omelet from sticking while allowing the egg and potato mixture to cook together.

1 pound Yukon gold or small red potatoes, cut into ¼-inch-thick slices
1 large red bell pepper
2 tablespoons extra-virgin olive oil, divided
2½ cups thinly vertically sliced onion (about 1 large)
1 tablespoon sherry vinegar
¼ cup chopped fresh flat-leaf parsley
¼ cup 2% reduced-fat milk
1 tablespoon chopped fresh oregano
¾ teaspoon salt
½ teaspoon black pepper
6 large eggs, lightly beaten
3 large egg whites, lightly beaten

1. Preheat broiler.
2. Place potatoes in a medium saucepan; cover with water. Bring to a boil. Reduce heat, and simmer 10 minutes or until potatoes are crisp-tender; drain.
3. Cut bell pepper in half lengthwise, and discard seeds and membranes. Place pepper halves, skin sides up, on a foil-lined baking sheet; flatten with hand. Broil 10 minutes or until blackened. Place pepper halves in a paper bag; fold to close tightly. Let stand 10 minutes. Peel and chop.
4. Reduce oven temperature to 425°.
5. Heat a 10-inch nonstick oven-proof skillet over medium-high heat. Add 1 tablespoon oil to pan; swirl to coat. Add onion; cook 5 minutes or until golden and tender, stirring frequently. Add vinegar; cook 1 minute, stirring constantly. Remove pan from heat.
6. Combine parsley, milk, oregano, salt, black pepper, eggs, and egg whites in a large bowl, stirring with a whisk. Gently stir in bell peppers, potatoes, and onion mixture.
7. Return pan to medium-high heat. Add 1 tablespoon oil; swirl to coat. Add egg mixture to pan; cook 2 minutes, shaking pan occasionally. Place pan in oven. Bake at 425° for 10 minutes or until eggs are thoroughly cooked and top is lightly browned. Invert tortilla onto a serving platter. Cool slightly. Cut into 6 wedges. Serves 6 (serving size: 1 wedge)

CALORIES 209; FAT 9.8g (sat 2.4g, mono 5.2g, poly 1.5g); PROTEIN 10.8g; CARB 19.5g; FIBER 2.8g; CHOL 187mg; IRON 1.9mg; SODIUM 416mg; CALC 69mg

---

GLOBAL PANTRY

NUTTY TAHINI BROWNIES

By Naomi Duguid

Delicious new ideas take sesame butter way beyond hummus.

After making a batch of hummus, you might wonder what else you can do with that jar of sesame seed paste. Don't let it languish in the fridge (which is where you should store it, as it is high in fats that keep best chilled). For everyday use, you can blend tahini with honey and use it in place of peanut butter.

It's also delicious as a silky dressing for grilled vegetables or Asian noodles. For grilled vegetables, whisk together ¼ cup each tahini and lukewarm water, and then add 3 tablespoons freshly squeezed lemon juice, a bit of salt, and, if you wish, some fresh mint. For noodles, whisk the tahini with an equal volume of hot water, add soy sauce and cider vinegar to taste, and toss in a generous pinch of ground red pepper, if desired.

Tahini can also be a wonderful addition to sweets, just as peanut butter is, and the recipe below is a great example.

Tahini Swirl Brownies

(pictured on page 213)

Hands-on: 15 min. Total: 50 min.
You start with brownies, and then top them with a swirl of sweetened tahini that gives a delightful nutty depth of flavor and richness. Be sure to use untoasted sesame oil in the batter; the dark, toasted kind would be too strong.

Cooking spray
1/4 cup untoasted sesame oil
3 tablespoons butter, coarsely chopped
4 ounces bittersweet chocolate, coarsely chopped
3/4 cup granulated sugar
3 large eggs, divided
1 teaspoon vanilla extract
1/2 teaspoon salt
3 ounces all-purpose flour (about 2/3 cup)
1/4 cup tahini (sesame seed paste), at room temperature
1 tablespoon brown sugar

1. Place an oven rack in the upper third of oven. Preheat oven to 350°.
2. Line an 8-inch square metal baking pan (not dark nonstick) with parchment paper; lightly coat parchment paper with cooking spray.
3. Combine sesame oil, butter, and chocolate in the top of a double boiler. Cook over simmering water until chocolate almost fully melts, stirring gently with a spatula. Remove top of double boiler; stir until chocolate fully melts. Pour chocolate mixture

into a large bowl; add granulated sugar, stirring with a whisk until well combined. Add 2 eggs, stirring with a whisk. Stir in vanilla and salt. Fold in flour in two or three batches. Pour mixture into prepared pan. Combine tahini, brown sugar, and 1 egg in a small bowl. Drop spoonfuls of tahini mixture onto brownie batter; swirl with the tip of a knife.
4. Bake at 350° for 30 minutes or until a wooden pick inserted in center comes out with moist crumbs clinging. Cool in pan on a wire rack at least 15 minutes before serving. Serves 16 (serving size: 1 brownie)

CALORIES 181; FAT 11.7g (sat 4g, mono 4g, poly 2.7g); PROTEIN 2.9g; CARB 18.7g; FIBER 0.8g; CHOL 41mg; IRON 0.8mg; SODIUM 108mg; CALC 13mg

ST. PAT'S TWIST

Roasted Cabbage Steaks
Preheat oven to 425°. Cut 4 (1-inch) vertical slices from a head of cabbage. Heat 2 teaspoons canola oil and 1/2 teaspoon butter in a cast-iron skillet over medium-high heat. Add 1 cabbage steak; cook 4 minutes. Place, seared side up, on a baking sheet coated with cooking spray. Repeat with more oil and butter and remaining cabbage. Bake cabbage steaks at 425° for 15 to 20 minutes. Serves 4 (serving size: 1 steak)

CALORIES 160; FAT 11.5g (sat 2g); SODIUM 238mg

SLOW COOKER

Great for a weekend, this recipe reaches slow-cooked, saucy perfection in just four hours.

Make Ahead

Spicy Chicken Cacciatore

Hands-on: 25 min. Total: 4 hr. 25 min.

1/2 cup all-purpose flour
8 skinless, boneless chicken thighs (about 2 pounds)
1 tablespoon olive oil
3 cups chopped onion
2 cups chopped red bell pepper
6 garlic cloves, minced
1/2 cup dry red wine
1/2 cup tomato puree
2 tablespoons capers
1 1/2 teaspoons crushed red pepper
1 teaspoon dried oregano
1 teaspoon black pepper
3/4 teaspoon salt
1 (14.5-ounce) can unsalted petite diced tomatoes, undrained
1/4 cup chopped fresh parsley

1. Place flour in a shallow dish; dredge chicken in flour, shaking off excess.
2. Heat a large skillet over medium-high heat. Add oil; swirl. Add half of chicken; cook 4 minutes on each side or until browned. Place chicken in a 6-quart electric slow cooker. Repeat procedure with remaining chicken. Reduce heat to medium. Add onion, bell pepper, and garlic; sauté 4 minutes. Add wine; bring to a boil. Simmer 2 minutes. Add bell pepper mixture, tomato puree, and next 6 ingredients to slow cooker. Cover and cook on LOW for 4 hours or until chicken is tender. Sprinkle with parsley. Serves 8 (serving size: 1 thigh and about 1/2 cup sauce)

CALORIES 307; FAT 11.4g (sat 2.9g, mono 5.1g, poly 2.1g); PROTEIN 29.8g; CARB 17.4g; FIBER 3g; CHOL 153mg; IRON 2.7mg; SODIUM 458mg; CALC 52mg

THE ZING OF SPRING

After this year's roaring bear of a winter, it's a welcome joy to see the arrival of crisp asparagus, tangy-grassy rhubarb, delicate baby artichokes, sweet new beets, and fragrant strawberries.

Gluten Free • Vegetarian

Roasted Baby Beets with Creamy Goat Cheese Dip

Hands-on: 15 min. Total: 1 hr. 40 min.
If using multiple colors of beets, roast the red ones separately to keep their color from bleeding into the others.

1½ pounds baby beets (about 12)
¼ cup water
2 unpeeled garlic cloves
4 thyme sprigs
¾ cup low-fat buttermilk
1 tablespoon chopped fresh dill
2 tablespoons prepared horseradish
½ teaspoon finely grated lemon rind
¼ teaspoon kosher salt
¼ teaspoon freshly ground black pepper
3 ounces soft goat cheese (about ⅓ cup)
Dill sprigs (optional)

1. Preheat oven to 400°.
2. Rinse beets thoroughly. Leave 1-inch stem on beets; reserve greens for another use. Arrange the beets, ¼ cup water, garlic, and thyme in a 13 x 9–inch glass or ceramic baking dish. Cover with foil; bake at 400° for 1 hour or until tender. Uncover dish; cool completely. Reserve garlic and pan juices; discard thyme. Peel beets, keeping stems intact. Cut beets lengthwise into quarters.
3. Squeeze garlic pulp into a mini chopper; discard peels. Add buttermilk and next 6 ingredients; process until smooth. Spoon 3 tablespoons sauce onto each of 6 plates; arrange 8 beet quarters over sauce. Drizzle ½ teaspoon pan juices over each serving; garnish with dill sprigs, if desired. Serves 6

CALORIES 101; FAT 3.8g (sat 2.5g, mono 0.9g, poly 0.2g); PROTEIN 6g; CARB 12g; FIBER 3g; CHOL 9mg; IRON 1mg; SODIUM 254mg; CALC 86mg

Quick & Easy • Gluten Free
Vegetarian

Shaved Asparagus Salad with Manchego and Almonds

Hands-on: 23 min. Total: 23 min.
To shave the asparagus, hold the tough stem in your fingers and start at the green tender part. Peel toward the head with a sharp peeler to make thin ribbons. Medium or thick asparagus works best for shaving. If walnut oil isn't available, substitute 1½ teaspoons extra-virgin olive oil. This dish makes for a quick and delicious light lunch. Round out the meal with toasted or grilled crusty whole-grain bread.

1½ tablespoons extra-virgin olive oil
2 teaspoons sherry vinegar
1½ teaspoons walnut oil
1 teaspoon minced fresh garlic
¼ teaspoon salt
¼ teaspoon freshly ground black pepper
1 pound large asparagus
1 tablespoon chopped fresh flat-leaf parsley
8 cups water
2 tablespoons white vinegar
4 large eggs
2 tablespoons slivered almonds, toasted
1 ounce Manchego cheese, shaved (about ¼ cup)

1. Combine first 6 ingredients in a large bowl, stirring with a whisk. Using a sharp peeler, thinly peel asparagus to equal 3 cups asparagus ribbons. Add asparagus and parsley to bowl; toss gently to coat.
2. Combine 8 cups water and white vinegar in a large skillet; bring to a simmer. Break each egg into a custard cup, and pour each gently

into pan. Cook 3 minutes or until desired degree of doneness. Remove eggs from pan using a slotted spoon. **3.** Place about ⅔ cup asparagus mixture on each of 4 plates. Sprinkle each serving with 1½ teaspoons almonds; top each serving with 1 egg. Sprinkle evenly with Manchego cheese. Serves 4

CALORIES 207; **FAT** 16.4g (sat 4.4g, mono 8.7g, poly 2.5g); **PROTEIN** 11g; **CARB** 5g; **FIBER** 2g; **CHOL** 194mg; **IRON** 3mg; **SODIUM** 279mg; **CALC** 154mg

Gluten Free • Make Ahead

Grilled Chicken with Spicy Rhubarb-BQ Sauce

Hands-on: 45 min. Total: 45 min.
Barbecue sauce is hardly an expected place to find rhubarb, and that's part of what we love about this addictive, tangy-sweet sauce tinged with smoky chipotle heat. Extra sauce can be refrigerated for up to one month. Also try it on pork and burgers.

1 tablespoon canola oil
8 bone-in chicken thighs, skinned (about 2½ pounds)
¼ teaspoon freshly ground black pepper
⅛ teaspoon salt
Cooking spray
1 cup Spicy Rhubarb-BQ Sauce

1. Preheat grill to high heat.
2. Combine oil and chicken; toss to coat. Sprinkle chicken with pepper and salt. Place chicken on grill rack coated with cooking spray, and grill 6 minutes or until well-marked. Place 1 cup Rhubarb-BQ Sauce in a large bowl. Add chicken to bowl, tossing to coat chicken. Return chicken to grill; cook, turning and brushing with sauce from the bowl

until glossy and caramelized, about 12 minutes. Serves 4 (serving size: 2 chicken thighs).

CALORIES 255; **FAT** 10.7g (sat 2.6g, mono 4.6g, poly 2.3g); **PROTEIN** 27g; **CARB** 12g; **FIBER** 1g; **CHOL** 135mg; **IRON** 1mg; **SODIUM** 351mg; **CALC** 46mg

Spicy Rhubarb-BQ Sauce
Hands-on: 22 min. Total: 29 min.

1 tablespoon butter
½ cup finely chopped onion
1 garlic clove, minced
2¼ cups (½-inch) slices rhubarb
½ cup water
⅓ cup sugar
¼ cup ketchup
2 tablespoons white vinegar
½ teaspoon chipotle chile powder
1 teaspoon Dijon mustard
⅛ teaspoon salt

1. Melt butter in a large saucepan over medium heat. Add onion and garlic; cook 5 minutes or until onion is tender, stirring occasionally. Add rhubarb; cook 3 minutes or until rhubarb is translucent, stirring occasionally. Add ½ cup water, sugar, ketchup, vinegar, and chipotle; bring to a boil. Reduce heat, and simmer 6 minutes or until rhubarb is tender.
2. Place half of rhubarb mixture in a blender. Remove center piece of blender lid (to allow steam to escape); secure blender lid on blender. Place a clean towel over opening in blender lid (to avoid splatters). Blend rhubarb mixture until smooth. Pour into a large bowl. Repeat procedure with remaining rhubarb mixture.
3. Return rhubarb mixture to saucepan. Bring to a simmer; cook 1 minute or until hot. Stir in mustard and salt. Makes 2 cups (serving size: 2 tablespoons)

CALORIES 26; **FAT** 0.8g (sat 0.5g, mono 0.2g, poly 0.1g); **PROTEIN** 0g; **CARB** 5g; **FIBER** 0g; **CHOL** 2mg; **IRON** 0mg; **SODIUM** 83mg; **CALC** 16mg

Gluten Free • Vegetarian

Pan-Roasted Artichokes with Lemon and Garlic

Hands-on: 25 min. Total: 45 min.

6 cups water
3 tablespoons fresh lemon juice
18 baby artichokes (about 1¾ pounds)
3 tablespoons olive oil
¼ teaspoon salt
¼ teaspoon freshly ground black pepper
4 large garlic cloves, halved
½ lemon, thinly sliced
1 (6-inch) rosemary sprig
2 teaspoons fresh lemon juice

1. Preheat oven to 425°.
2. Combine water and 3 tablespoons juice in a bowl. Cut off top ½ inch of artichokes. Cut stems to within 1 inch of bases; peel stems. Remove tough outer leaves, leaving tender cores. Halve each lengthwise; add to water.
3. Drain artichokes; pat dry. Combine artichokes, oil, salt, pepper, and garlic in a bowl; toss to coat. Heat a large ovenproof skillet over high heat. Add half of artichoke mixture to pan; cook 1 minute on each side or until lightly browned. Remove from pan. Repeat procedure with remaining artichoke mixture. Return artichokes to pan; add lemon slices and rosemary. Bake at 425° for 20 minutes, stirring once. Remove rosemary leaves, and sprinkle over artichoke mixture; discard stem and any blackened lemon. Sprinkle with 2 teaspoons lemon juice. Serves 6 (serving size: 6 artichoke halves)

CALORIES 128; **FAT** 7g (sat 1g, mono 4.9g, poly 0.8g); **PROTEIN** 4g; **CARB** 16g; **FIBER** 8g; **CHOL** 0mg; **IRON** 2mg; **SODIUM** 223mg; **CALC** 66mg

Layered Strawberry-Coconut Panna Cotta

Hands-on: 35 min. Total: 2 hr. 35 min.
If you'd prefer to use all light coconut milk in the panna cotta, you certainly can, but we were amazed at how much more flavor and silky consistency we got from mixing in a little full-fat coconut milk, while still keeping the dish's overall fat content in check.

Strawberry gelatin:
1 teaspoon gelatin
1 tablespoon water
¾ cup sliced strawberries
3 tablespoons granulated sugar
1 teaspoon fresh lemon juice
¾ cup coconut water

Panna cotta:
¾ teaspoon gelatin
1 tablespoon water
½ cup coconut milk
¼ cup light coconut milk
2½ tablespoons granulated sugar
1 teaspoon fresh lemon juice

Strawberries:
2 cups sliced strawberries
2 tablespoons powdered sugar
1 teaspoon chopped fresh thyme
1 teaspoon fresh lemon juice

1. To prepare strawberry gelatin, sprinkle 1 teaspoon gelatin over 1 tablespoon water in a small bowl. Combine ¾ cup strawberries, 3 tablespoons granulated sugar, and 1 teaspoon juice in a small saucepan; let stand 5 minutes. Mash mixture with a fork or potato masher. Place pan over medium-high heat. Bring to a simmer; cook 2 minutes or until sugar dissolves. Add coconut water; return to a simmer. Remove pan from heat. Add gelatin mixture, stirring until gelatin dissolves. Strain mixture through a fine sieve into a measuring cup, pressing on solids to extract as much liquid as possible. Discard solids. Divide strawberry mixture evenly among 4 wineglasses. Chill 1 hour or until set.
2. To prepare panna cotta, sprinkle ¾ teaspoon gelatin over 1 tablespoon water in a small bowl. Combine coconut milks, 2½ tablespoons granulated sugar, and 1 teaspoon juice in a saucepan; bring to a simmer. Remove pan from heat. Add gelatin mixture, stirring until gelatin dissolves. Cool to room temperature. Carefully pour one-fourth of coconut milk mixture on top of each strawberry gelatin. Chill 1 hour or until set.
3. To prepare strawberries, combine strawberries and remaining ingredients in a bowl; toss gently. Let stand 5 minutes. Divide strawberry mixture evenly among glasses. Serves 4

CALORIES 178; **FAT** 5g (sat 4.7g, mono 0.1g, poly 0.2g); **PROTEIN** 2g; **CARB** 33g; **FIBER** 2g; **CHOL** 0mg; **IRON** 1mg; **SODIUM** 20mg; **CALC** 26mg

FROM THE CL GARDEN

LEEKS, ONIONS & CHIVES

It's finally here—the first happy harvest from this year's Cooking Light Garden: fragrant bundles of alliums.

There is more to the onion family than round roots. Peel back the layers to discover the delicate flavors of leeks, chives, and young green onions.

You can start these alliums from seed, but get a head start with young seedlings or onion sets. Planting your own can save you green at the grocery store and up your garden game. For leeks, simply press the handle of a garden rake or a dibble into the soil to make uniform, 6-inch-deep holes; then drop in seedlings for soldier-straight rows. For fat, milky-white stalks, let rain fill in holes over time. With onions, leave a 6-inch space between plants so bulbs can form. Or space closely and harvest alternating plants as a midseason treat: tender green onions. Chives are almost carefree; they will live happily season to season with regular harvesting.

Let a few plants send up blooms. The globes of white or lavender star-shaped flowers are just one more reason why alliums are so stinking beautiful.

Grilled Leek and Radicchio Salad with Citrus-Walnut Vinaigrette

Hands-on: 20 min. Total: 30 min.
Bitter meets sweet in this warm salad.

1 tablespoon grated orange rind
5 tablespoons fresh orange juice
½ teaspoon honey
3 tablespoons toasted walnut oil
3 heads radicchio, quartered (about 1½ pounds)
3 leeks, washed, trimmed, and halved lengthwise
Cooking spray
½ teaspoon kosher salt
¾ teaspoon freshly ground black pepper
1 ounce pecorino Romano cheese, shaved (about ¼ cup)
¼ cup chopped walnuts, toasted

1. Preheat grill to high.

2. Combine rind, juice, and honey in a large bowl. Gradually add oil, stirring constantly with a whisk.
3. Coat radicchio and leeks with cooking spray. Place on grill rack coated with cooking spray. Grill 7 minutes, turning to brown on all sides. Remove to a cutting board; cool slightly. Coarsely chop vegetables.
4. Add chopped vegetables, salt, and pepper to dressing; toss to coat. Top with pecorino Romano and walnuts; serve immediately. Serves 8 (serving size: ¾ cup)

CALORIES 112; **FAT** 8.8g (sat 1.6g, mono 1.5g, poly 5g); **PROTEIN** 2g; **CARB** 7g; **FIBER** 1g; **CHOL** 4mg; **IRON** 1mg; **SODIUM** 197mg; **CALC** 59mg

Gluten Free • Make Ahead

Braised Chicken with Honey-Lemon Leeks

Hands-on: 25 min. Total: 43 min.
Lemon is a bright partner for the caramelized leeks, which cook twice.

4 teaspoons olive oil, divided
8 bone-in, skinless chicken thighs (about 2 pounds)
¾ teaspoon kosher salt, divided
½ teaspoon freshly ground black pepper
1 tablespoon grated lemon rind
4 cups thinly sliced leek (about 3 large)
3 tablespoons fresh lemon juice
2 teaspoons honey
2 tablespoons chopped fresh parsley or chives (optional)

1. Preheat oven to 400°.
2. Heat a large ovenproof skillet over medium heat. Add 2 teaspoons oil to pan; swirl to coat. Sprinkle chicken evenly with ½ teaspoon salt and pepper. Massage lemon rind into chicken. Place chicken in pan; cook 4 minutes on each side or until browned. Remove chicken from pan; keep warm.
3. Add 2 teaspoons oil to pan; swirl to coat. Add leek and ¼ teaspoon salt; cook 15 minutes or until leek begins to brown, scraping pan to loosen browned bits. Remove pan from heat; stir in lemon juice and honey. Return chicken to pan. Mound leeks on top of chicken thighs. Bake chicken at 400° for 15 minutes or until a thermometer registers 165°. Top with fresh parsley or chives, if desired. Serves 4 (serving size: 2 thighs and about ¼ cup leek mixture)

CALORIES 339; **FAT** 15.6g (sat 3.6g, mono 7.7g, poly 2.8g); **PROTEIN** 33g; **CARB** 17g; **FIBER** 2g; **CHOL** 175mg; **IRON** 4mg; **SODIUM** 492mg; **CALC** 72mg

Gluten Free • Make Ahead
Vegetarian

Refrigerator Scallion Pickles

Hands-on: 20 min. Total: 24 hr. 20 min. *These delicious pickles make great stirrers for Bloody Marys, add bright flavor to a crudité platter, or become a tangy garnish for fish or grilled meats.*

2 quarts water
1 tablespoon kosher salt
70 green onions (about 8 bunches)
4 (2-inch) lemon rind strips
4 thyme sprigs
1½ cups white vinegar
⅓ cup sugar
1 teaspoon black peppercorns
1 teaspoon yellow mustard seeds
1 teaspoon coriander seeds
¼ teaspoon fennel seeds

1. Combine 2 quarts water and salt in a large saucepan or Dutch oven; bring to a boil. Cut bottom halves of green onions into 4-inch pieces; reserve tops for another use. Add green onions to water; cook 30 seconds. Plunge into ice water; drain. Divide green onions equally among 2 (1-pint) mason jars. Divide rind and thyme evenly among jars.
2. Combine vinegar and remaining ingredients in a saucepan; bring to a boil. Reduce heat; simmer 5 minutes, stirring to dissolve sugar. Divide vinegar mixture evenly between jars; cool. Cover and chill at least 24 hours. Serves 23 (serving size: about 3 pieces).

CALORIES 23; **FAT** 0.1g (sat 0g, mono 0g, poly 0g); **PROTEIN** 1g; **CARB** 5g; **FIBER** 1g; **CHOL** 0mg; **IRON** 0mg; **SODIUM** 87mg; **CALC** 21mg

ONION CHIVES
A perennial plant in zones 3 to 10, chives belong in every kitchen garden. The thin leaves have a mild onion flavor, as do the flowers.

AMERICAN FLAG LEEKS
A long-loved heirloom, these produce stocky, pearl-white shanks. They are especially cold-tolerant.

ALL-DAY-ENERGY EATING

If your energy levels rise and fall like a roller coaster throughout the day, use these strategies and recipes to help smooth out the highs and lows.

Our bodies need calories to create the energy we need to experience that vim, zip, and get-up-and-go. But it matters how those calories are packaged—whether they're bundled with protein, fiber, and healthy fats or delivered as refined carbs and sugars. Refined, simple carbs, found in many snacks, cause a spike in blood sugar followed by the notorious crash. Complex foods mediate blood sugar levels, yielding a steady supply of energy. They also keep you feeling full longer. When it comes to eating on an ordinary day (as opposed to, say, fueling up on a long bike ride), you want foods that burn slow, not fast. Here we've identified eight energy-boosting sources and incorporated them into balanced recipes designed to keep energy levels steady.

Quick & Easy • Gluten Free
Make Ahead • Vegetarian

Spicy Bean and Quinoa Salad with "Mole" Vinaigrette

(pictured on page 217)

Hands-on: 15 min. Total: 15 min.

1 teaspoon grated orange rind
¾ teaspoon unsweetened cocoa
½ teaspoon ground cumin
½ teaspoon ground cinnamon
2 tablespoons fresh orange juice
1½ tablespoons red wine vinegar
1 tablespoon adobo sauce from canned chipotle chiles in adobo sauce
2 tablespoons olive oil
3 cups cooked quinoa, at room temperature
½ cup unsalted pumpkinseed kernels (pepitas), toasted
¼ cup chopped fresh cilantro
½ teaspoon kosher salt
2 green onions, thinly sliced
1 Fresno chile or jalapeño pepper, very thinly sliced
1 (15-ounce) can black beans, rinsed and drained
4 cups baby spinach leaves

1. Combine first 7 ingredients in a small bowl; gradually add oil, stirring well with a whisk.
2. Combine quinoa and next 6 ingredients through black beans in a large bowl. Add vinaigrette; toss to coat. Add spinach; toss to combine. Serves 6 (serving size: 1⅔ cups)

CALORIES 258; FAT 11.6g (sat 1.5g, mono 5.2g, poly 2.4g); PROTEIN 10g; CARB 31g; FIBER 7g; CHOL 0mg; IRON 4mg; SODIUM 377mg; CALC 55mg

Gluten Free

Salmon Salad on Arugula

Hands-on: 15 min. Total: 1 hr. 15 min.
Keep this salad refrigerated in an airtight container up to two days.

4 (6-ounce) salmon fillets, skinned
¼ teaspoon kosher salt
¼ teaspoon black pepper
2 tablespoons olive oil, divided
2 tablespoons fresh lemon juice, divided
2 tablespoons plain fat-free Greek yogurt
2 tablespoons crème fraîche or sour cream
2 tablespoons thinly sliced fresh basil
4 teaspoons capers, rinsed, drained, and chopped
4 cups baby arugula leaves
1 cup very thinly vertically sliced red onion

1. Sprinkle salmon evenly with salt and pepper. Heat a medium nonstick skillet over medium-high heat. Add 1 tablespoon oil to pan; swirl to coat. Add salmon; cook 6 minutes on each side or until desired degree of doneness. Cool to room temperature; flake with a fork.

2. Combine salmon, 1 tablespoon juice, yogurt, and next 3 ingredients in a medium bowl. Refrigerate 30 minutes or up to 3 hours.

3. Combine 1 tablespoon oil, 1 tablespoon juice, arugula, and onion in a bowl. Toss gently to coat. Divide arugula mixture among 4 plates. Top with salmon mixture. Serves 4 (serving size: 1 cup arugula and ⅔ cup salmon mixture)

CALORIES 354; FAT 19.4g (sat 4.6g, mono 8.6g, poly 4g); PROTEIN 38g; CARB 5g; FIBER 1g; CHOL 97mg; IRON 1mg; SODIUM 297mg; CALC 65mg

---

BOOST YOUR MENTAL GAME AT LUNCH

This plate is filled with omega-3-rich salmon and iron-packed dark greens. Studies show that too little of either may cause signs of fatigue. Salmon is a top source of omega-3 fats, packing a day's worth in just 4 ounces. Here it's drizzled with citrus, whose vitamin C will boost your body's ability to absorb iron from the greens. Greek yogurt adds a gram of protein to the dressing and has 85% fewer calories than mayo.

Kid Friendly • Make Ahead Vegetarian

Cranberry-Pistachio Energy Bars

(pictured on page 209)

Hands-on: 10 min. Total: 35 min. *Store in an airtight container up to three days.*

1 cup uncooked old-fashioned rolled oats
¾ cup uncooked quinoa
¾ cup sweetened dried cranberries, coarsely chopped
½ cup salted, dry-roasted pistachios, chopped
⅓ cup flaked unsweetened coconut
2 tablespoons flaxseed meal
1 ounce bittersweet chocolate, finely chopped
½ cup unsalted creamy almond butter
6 tablespoons agave nectar
1 tablespoon canola oil
¼ teaspoon salt
Cooking spray

1. Preheat oven to 350°.

2. Spread oats and quinoa on a baking sheet. Bake at 350° for 8 minutes or until lightly browned. Cool. Place oat mixture in a large bowl, and stir in cranberries, pistachios, coconut, flaxseed meal, and chocolate.

3. Combine almond butter, agave, oil, and salt in a saucepan over medium heat; bring to a boil. Cook 1 minute, stirring constantly. Pour almond butter mixture over oat mixture; toss well to coat. Press mixture into an 8-inch square glass or ceramic baking dish coated with cooking spray. Bake at 350° for 13 minutes or until lightly browned. Cool completely in dish. Cut into (1 x 4–inch) bars. Serves 16 (serving size: 1 bar)

CALORIES 193; FAT 10.1g (sat 2.1g, mono 4.6g, poly 2.6g); PROTEIN 5g; CARB 23g; FIBER 3g; CHOL 0mg; IRON 1mg; SODIUM 72mg; CALC 43mg

---

PACK A SNACK WITH PROTEIN AND FIBER, NOT SUGAR.

When nuts meet dried fruit, chocolate, and crunchy whole grains, you get a hearty snack with 5g protein and 3g fiber. We sweeten the bars with honey or agave because these sources have a lower glycemic index to better control blood sugar spikes. Dark chocolate provides a natural caffeine buzz that's mild enough to prevent the subsequent crash (and often excessive sugar) you get with highly caffeinated beverages.

Cherry-Almond Energy Bars
Substitute coarsely chopped tart dried cherries for the cranberries, and chopped salted, dry-roasted almonds for the pistachios. Substitute honey for the agave nectar. Serves 16 (serving size: 1 bar)

CALORIES 205; FAT 10.6g (sat 2.1g, mono 5.1g, poly 2.6g); PROTEIN 5g; CARB 25g; FIBER 3g; CHOL 0mg; IRON 1mg; SODIUM 54mg; CALC 47mg

Peanut Butter Oatmeal-Raisin Energy Bars
Substitute golden raisins for the cranberries and chopped salted, dry-roasted peanuts for the pistachios. Omit the coconut and chocolate. Add ½ teaspoon ground cinnamon to the oat mixture in step 2. Substitute creamy peanut butter for the almond butter and honey for the agave nectar. Serves 16 (serving size: 1 bar)

CALORIES 179; FAT 8.6g (sat 1.2g, mono 2.8g, poly 2g); PROTEIN 6g; CARB 23g; FIBER 2g; CHOL 0mg; IRON 1mg; SODIUM 94mg; CALC 18mg

JUMP-START YOUR DAY WITH A DOSE OF WHOLE GRAINS, CITRUS, AND PROTEIN-PACKED YOGURT.

Breakfast is the time of day to fire up both mental and physical engines. Choose foods filled with fiber and protein for a quick boost that has a lasting effect. We thicken this smoothie with whole-grain oats (all forms are whole: rolled, steel-cut, even instant), full of complex carbohydrates that the body absorbs more slowly than refined carbs so you feel fuller longer. Just the scent of citrus in this smoothie can increase your alertness and may boost feel-good serotonin levels. Greek yogurt packs full protein punch: One cup has 20g to keep you full for hours—along with 20% of your daily calcium needs. Added bonus: Our recipe has about half the sugar of those from a smoothie shop.

Kid Friendly • Quick & Easy

Citrusy Banana-Oat Smoothie

Hands-on: 5 min. Total: 30 min.

²/₃ cup fresh orange juice
½ cup prepared quick-cooking oats
½ cup plain 2% reduced-fat Greek yogurt
1 tablespoon flaxseed meal
1 tablespoon honey
½ teaspoon grated orange rind
1 large banana, sliced and frozen
1 cup ice cubes

1. Place first 7 ingredients in a blender; pulse to combine. Add ice; process until smooth. Serves 2 (serving size: 1½ cups)

CALORIES 228; FAT 3.9g (sat 1.2g, mono 0.6g, poly 1.4g); PROTEIN 8g; CARB 43g; FIBER 4g; CHOL 4mg; IRON 1mg; SODIUM 24mg; CALC 66mg

Quick & Easy • Gluten Free
Make Ahead • Vegetarian

Nutty Edamame Spread

Hands-on: 14 min. Total: 14 min.

2 cups frozen shelled edamame
2 garlic cloves, peeled
½ cup packed basil leaves
2 tablespoons pine nuts, toasted
2 tablespoons plain 2% reduced-fat Greek yogurt
¼ cup water
2 tablespoons extra-virgin olive oil
2 tablespoons fresh lemon juice
¾ teaspoon kosher salt
½ teaspoon grated lemon rind
¼ teaspoon ground black pepper

1. Combine edamame and garlic in a small saucepan; cover with water to 2 inches above edamame. Bring to a boil; cook 2 minutes or until edamame is tender. Remove from heat; drain well.
2. Place edamame, garlic, basil, pine nuts, and yogurt in a food processor; pulse 10 times or until coarsely ground. Add ¼ cup water and remaining ingredients; process until almost smooth. Serves 8 (serving size: about ¼ cup)

CALORIES 99; FAT 6.7g (sat 0.6g, mono 2.9g, poly 1.1g); PROTEIN 6g; CARB 5g; FIBER 2g; CHOL 0mg; IRON 2mg; SODIUM 184mg; CALC 29mg

EMBRACE THE BEAN, A PLANT-BASED, FIBER-PACKED PROTEIN.

Beans are a starchy mix of protein and fiber—a powerful combination that triggers satiety early and keeps you from overeating into a slump. Just ½ cup edamame has more than 4g fiber and 8g protein. This recipe yields a deliciously versatile spread.

LIGHTER SPINACH-BACON QUICHE

Flaky olive oil pastry and cheesy, veggie-filled custard for only 317 calories.

We've never quite understood how a cream, bacon, and cheese–filled custard surrounded by rich, buttery pastry found its way onto the "lighter side" of the brunch menu. Quiche is certainly delicious, but it's far from dainty: That little wedge hovers around 600 calories and a day's worth of sat fat. With spring being the season of Easter and brunch, we felt it our duty to deliver a deliciously lighter French pastry.

We could have easily removed the crust to shave calories and fat, but we couldn't bear the thought of a crustless quiche—the pastry is one of the defining pleasures of this savory pie. Instead, we trade the traditional butter and shortening–packed dough for one made with heart-healthy olive oil, which lends a green, earthy flavor to the crust. Spinach and mushrooms bulk up the filling with few calories and serve as the perfect complement to nutty aged Gruyère cheese. A splash of half-and-half adds richness to 1% low-fat milk in our custard, a lighter but still luscious stand-in for heavy cream. We finish with a sprinkle of crispy center-cut bacon, which hits the palate first to maximize the savory goodness in every bite. It's a 317-calorie slice of heaven that's worthy of a starring role on your spring brunch menu.

Kid Friendly • Make Ahead

Mushroom, Gruyère, and Spinach Quiche

Hands-on: 39 min. Total: 1 hr. 30 min.

5.6 ounces unbleached all-purpose flour (about 1 cup plus 2 tablespoons)
¾ teaspoon kosher salt, divided
½ teaspoon freshly ground black pepper, divided
¼ teaspoon baking powder
¼ cup extra-virgin olive oil
3 tablespoons ice water
Cooking spray
3 center-cut bacon slices
¼ cup chopped shallots
1 (8-ounce) package presliced mushrooms
2 teaspoons fresh thyme
2 cups packed baby spinach
1 cup 1% low-fat milk
⅓ cup half-and-half
3 large eggs
1 large egg white
2 ounces cave-aged Gruyère cheese, grated

1. Preheat oven to 425°.
2. Weigh or lightly spoon flour into dry measuring cups; level with a knife. Place flour, ¼ teaspoon salt, ¼ teaspoon pepper, and baking powder in a food processor; pulse 2 times to combine. Combine oil and 3 tablespoons water. With processor on, slowly add oil mixture through food chute; process until dough comes together. Turn dough out onto a lightly floured surface. Knead 1 minute. Press dough into a 5-inch disk; wrap in plastic wrap, and chill 20 minutes.
3. Roll dough into a 12-inch circle. Fit dough into a 9-inch deep-dish pie plate coated with cooking spray. Line dough with foil; arrange pie weights or dried beans on foil. Bake at 425° for 12 minutes or until edges are golden. Remove weights and foil; bake an additional 2 minutes. Cool on a wire rack.
4. Reduce oven temperature to 350°.
5. Cook bacon in a large skillet over medium-high heat until crisp. Remove bacon from pan, reserving drippings; crumble. Return pan to medium-high heat. Add shallots to drippings in pan; sauté 2 minutes. Add mushrooms and thyme; cook 10 minutes, stirring occasionally. Stir in spinach; cook 2 minutes or until spinach wilts. Remove from heat; let stand 10 minutes. Drain any excess liquid.
6. Place milk, half-and-half, eggs, egg white, ½ teaspoon salt, and ¼ teaspoon pepper in a blender; process until smooth.
7. Arrange half of cheese over bottom of crust; top with spinach mixture and remaining half of cheese. Carefully pour milk mixture over cheese. Sprinkle with bacon. Bake at 350° for 45 minutes or until filling is set. Let stand 10 minutes. Serves 6 (serving size: 1 wedge)

CALORIES 317; FAT 17.5g (sat 5.6g, mono 8.1g, poly 1.7g); PROTEIN 13g; CARB 26g; FIBER 2g; CHOL 111mg; IRON 2mg; SODIUM 435mg; CALC 217mg

HIGH PRAISE FOR THE LOWLY TILAPIA

Turns out this mild white fish is one of the easiest, most versatile ingredients to cook with.

Tilapia is one of the most searched terms on CookingLight.com and one of the most consumed fish species in America. In the high-end restaurant world, where—and this may surprise some readers—tilapia is disdained with a strangely passionate fervor by many chefs and foodies. Tilapia is flavorless, they claim, and irresponsibly farmed, and generally a sign of, if not the apocalypse, at least of the blandness of the American palate. Turns out the chefs are wrong on this one. Tilapia has a lot going for it. It's cheap, and it's everywhere—both highly compelling reasons to give it a try. Sustainably farmed versions are easy to find, an important consideration, with wild fish species under such threat around the world. Flavor-wise, tilapia is admittedly the mildest of the mild flaky white fish, but that can be turned into a virtue: It's a great starter fish for kids or anyone wary of seafood that is too "fishy." For cooks, the neutral flavor can be exploited, too: It makes tilapia a versatile base for a multitude of flavor approaches, evidenced here by recipes ranging from Southern American to Mediterranean to Southeast Asian to Eastern European. Tilapia's firm flesh holds up to sautéing, breading, poaching, steaming, or whatever you can think to do with it. Unlike more expensive varieties, it's not going to fall apart on you in the pan. And there are proper ways to use the frozen stuff, too.

Quick & Easy
Tilapia with Lemon-Garlic Sauce

Hands-on: 15 min. Total: 15 min.
This is an entrée that's elegant enough for entertaining and fast enough to brighten weeknight dinner doldrums.

4 (6-ounce) tilapia fillets
¼ teaspoon salt
¼ teaspoon freshly ground black pepper
3 tablespoons quick-mixing flour (such as Wondra)
2 tablespoons unsalted butter, divided
1 tablespoon olive oil
1 tablespoon minced fresh garlic
⅓ cup dry white wine
⅓ cup unsalted chicken stock
2 tablespoons chopped fresh parsley
1 tablespoon fresh lemon juice

1. Sprinkle fish with salt and pepper. Place flour in a shallow dish. Dredge both sides of fish in flour; reserve unused flour. Heat a large skillet over medium-high heat. Add 1 tablespoon butter and oil to pan; swirl to coat. Add fish to pan; cook 2 minutes on each side or until fish flakes easily when tested with a fork. Remove from pan; keep warm.
2. Add reserved flour and garlic to pan; cook 90 seconds or until lightly browned, stirring constantly. Add wine and stock, stirring with a whisk; bring to a boil. Cook 2 minutes or until slightly thickened. Remove pan from heat; stir in 1 tablespoon butter, parsley, and lemon juice. Serve fish with sauce. Serves 4 (serving size: 1 fillet and about 2 tablespoons sauce)

CALORIES 295; **FAT** 12.4g (sat 5.1g, mono 4.8g, poly 1.2g); **PROTEIN** 35g; **CARB** 6g; **FIBER** 0g; **CHOL** 100mg; **IRON** 1mg; **SODIUM** 248mg; **CALC** 26mg

TILAPIA TIPS

SUSTAINABILITY AND SAFETY
Although there is controversy over the quality of tilapia imported from China, as of this printing, Monterey Bay Aquarium's Seafood Watch gives farmed tilapia from China and Taiwan the "good alternative" stamp, while Ecuadorean-, Canadian-, and U.S.-farmed tilapia are listed as "best choice." In general, seek out tilapia from North and South America.

NUTRITION
Tilapia is a lean, low-calorie source of protein that's low in saturated fat, so it's a good choice for healthy eating. Although it's not an omega-3 powerhouse like heart-healthy salmon, a 3-ounce portion of cooked tilapia still has 10% of your daily omega-3 needs.

FRESH VS. FROZEN
If you plan to serve whole tilapia fillets, go to the fish counter, where the fillets tend to be bigger and prettier than what you'll find in the freezer case. Frozen fillets are smaller, usually around 4 ounces each, and are ideal for recipes that call for the fish to be cut into pieces.

THAWING
Consult the package directions for the manufacturer's recommendations. In testing, we found it best to quick-thaw by running cold water over frozen tilapia fillets in a colander for about 10 minutes; we then patted the fish dry with paper towels before proceeding with a recipe.

Spicy Hungarian Tilapia Stew

***Hands-on: 30 min. Total: 40 min.** Talk about packing some heat: This stew is fiery-fantastic, and we absolutely love it. You can alter the spiciness by using a milder pepper (such as banana pepper or Anaheim chile).*

3 Hungarian wax chiles
1/3 cup chopped tomato
2 teaspoons cider vinegar
2 tablespoons butter
1 cup thinly sliced leek (white and light green parts only)
1 tablespoon chopped fresh thyme
1/2 teaspoon kosher salt, divided
1 tablespoon tomato paste
1 tablespoon Hungarian sweet paprika
2 teaspoons Hungarian hot paprika
1 cup clam juice
1 cup unsalted chicken stock (such as Swanson)
3/4 cup dry white wine
1 1/2 pounds tilapia fillets, cut into (3-inch) pieces
1/4 cup dill fronds

1. Thinly slice chiles; discard stems. Combine 1/2 cup sliced chiles, tomato, and vinegar in a small bowl; set aside.
2. Melt butter in a Dutch oven over medium-high heat; swirl until butter foams. Add remaining sliced chiles, leek, thyme, and 1/4 teaspoon salt; sauté 3 minutes or until softened. Add tomato paste and sweet and hot paprikas; cook 30 seconds, stirring constantly. Add 1/4 teaspoon salt, clam juice, stock, and wine. Bring to a boil; cover, reduce heat, and simmer 10 minutes. Add fish; cover and simmer 5 minutes or until fish flakes easily when tested with a fork. Ladle soup into shallow bowls; top with tomato mixture. Sprinkle evenly with dill. Serves 4 (serving size: about 1 1/3 cups soup, 3 tablespoons tomato mixture, and 1 tablespoon dill)

CALORIES 263; FAT 8.9g (sat 4.7g, mono 2.4g, poly 1g); PROTEIN 37g; CARB 7g; FIBER 1g; CHOL 102mg; IRON 2mg; SODIUM 580mg; CALC 55mg

Vietnamese Tilapia with Turmeric and Dill

***Hands-on: 30 min. Total: 2 hr. 30 min.** A killer savory marinade of shallots, fish sauce, toasted sesame oil, garlic, and turmeric permeates the fish and gives it a beautiful golden color.*

1/4 cup sliced shallots
1 tablespoon chopped fresh dill
1 tablespoon minced fresh garlic
1 tablespoon grated peeled fresh ginger
2 tablespoons fish sauce
1 tablespoon dark sesame oil
1 teaspoon ground turmeric
1/2 teaspoon freshly ground black pepper
4 (6-ounce) tilapia fillets, each cut into 4 pieces
2 tablespoons peanut oil
Cooking spray
4 cups vertically sliced sweet onion
1/2 cup torn fresh dill, divided
4 green onions, cut into (2-inch) pieces
1 tablespoon lower-sodium soy sauce
2 teaspoons sugar
1/4 cup unsalted, dry-roasted peanuts, crushed
8 lemon wedges

1. Combine first 8 ingredients in a large bowl, stirring with a whisk until smooth. Add fish; toss to coat. Cover and chill 2 hours.
2. Remove fish from marinade; discard marinade and solids. Combine fish and peanut oil in a bowl; toss to coat.
3. Heat a large heavy skillet over high heat. Coat pan with cooking spray. Add onion, 1/4 cup dill, and green onions; stir-fry 3 minutes. Add soy sauce and sugar; stir-fry 1 minute. Arrange onion mixture on a platter. Return pan to high heat. Add half of fish to pan; cook 3 minutes. Turn fish over, and cook 1 minute or until fish flakes easily when tested with a fork. Place fish on platter over onion mixture. Repeat procedure with remaining fish. Sprinkle with 1/4 cup dill and peanuts. Serve with lemon wedges. Serves 4 (serving size: about 2/3 cup onion mixture, 4 fish pieces, and 2 lemon wedges)

CALORIES 368; FAT 15.3g (sat 3g, mono 6.6g, poly 4.6g); PROTEIN 39g; CARB 21g; FIBER 4g; CHOL 85mg; IRON 2mg; SODIUM 419mg; CALC 75mg

TILAPIA CAN STAND WHATEVER HEAT YOUR KITCHEN CAN DISH OUT.

Tilapia Cakes with Mango-Coconut Curry Sauce

Hands-on: 40 min. Total: 40 min.
Boasting big, bold global flavors, these crunchy cakes are a fun alternative to salmon croquettes or crab cakes.

1¼ cups light coconut milk, divided
½ cup chopped mango
1 tablespoon brown sugar
1 tablespoon red curry paste
2 teaspoons rice vinegar
2 teaspoons lower-sodium soy sauce
1 tablespoon fresh lime juice
12 ounces tilapia, finely chopped
¾ cup panko (Japanese breadcrumbs), divided
¼ cup dry-roasted peanuts, finely chopped
3 tablespoons minced green onions
3 tablespoons chopped fresh cilantro
1 tablespoon fish sauce
2 teaspoons minced fresh garlic
2 teaspoons minced serrano chile
2 teaspoons minced peeled fresh ginger
2 large eggs, lightly beaten
1 tablespoon butter
1 tablespoon olive oil
3 cups hot cooked rice

1. Place ¼ cup coconut milk, mango, and next 4 ingredients in a mini food processor; process until smooth. Combine mango mixture and 1 cup coconut milk in a small saucepan over high heat; bring to a boil. Cook until reduced to 1 cup (about 10 minutes). Stir in lime juice.
2. Combine tilapia, ⅓ cup panko, and next 8 ingredients in a large bowl; toss gently to combine. Using damp hands, shape mixture into 6 equal balls. Place remaining panko in a shallow dish. Coat balls in panko; gently press each ball into a (3-inch) patty.
3. Heat a large skillet over medium heat. Add butter and oil to pan; swirl to coat. Add patties; cook 4 minutes on each side or until browned. Serve with sauce and rice. Serves 6 (serving size: 1 patty, ½ cup rice, and about 2½ tablespoons sauce)

CALORIES 345; FAT 13.5g (sat 5.3g, mono 4.9g, poly 2.1g); PROTEIN 19g; CARB 37g; FIBER 2g; CHOL 96mg; IRON 2mg; SODIUM 503mg; CALC 35mg

Saffron Rice with Tilapia and Shrimp

Hands-on: 35 min. Total: 55 min.
This paella-inspired dish starts by infusing purchased chicken stock with shrimpy goodness; it's an easy step that makes full use of shrimp shells that would otherwise be discarded.

8 ounces unpeeled large shrimp
3⅓ cups unsalted chicken stock (such as Swanson)
⅔ cup water
⅛ teaspoon saffron threads, crushed
1 cup chopped ripe tomato
1 cup chopped onion
1⅛ teaspoons salt, divided
½ teaspoon sugar
4 garlic cloves
3 tablespoons olive oil
1¼ cups uncooked short-grain rice
12 ounces tilapia, cut into 1-inch pieces
½ cup frozen green peas
¼ cup chopped fresh flat-leaf parsley
6 lemon wedges

1. Preheat oven to 450°.
2. Peel shrimp, reserving shells; set shrimp aside. Combine shrimp shells, chicken stock, ⅔ cup water, and saffron in a medium saucepan. Bring to a boil; reduce heat, and keep warm.
3. Place chopped tomato, onion, ½ teaspoon salt, sugar, and garlic in a food processor; process until smooth.
4. Heat a large ovenproof skillet over medium-high heat. Add oil to pan; swirl to coat. Add tomato mixture to pan; cook 6 minutes or until liquid almost evaporates, stirring occasionally. Add uncooked rice to pan; cook 3 minutes, stirring frequently. Drain stock mixture over a bowl; discard solids. Add stock mixture to pan; bring to a boil. Cook over medium heat 12 minutes or until rice is tender and liquid is absorbed (do not stir). Top with reserved shrimp, tilapia, and peas. Sprinkle with ⅝ teaspoon salt. Cover and bake at 450° for 15 minutes or until fish flakes easily when tested with a fork. Sprinkle with parsley; serve with lemon wedges. Serves 6 (serving size: about 1½ cups rice mixture and 1 lemon wedge)

CALORIES 338; FAT 8.8g (sat 1.5g, mono 5.4g, poly 1.4g); PROTEIN 24g; CARB 41g; FIBER 3g; CHOL 76mg; IRON 3mg; SODIUM 600mg; CALC 60mg

SUBTLER PREPARATIONS WORK BEAUTIFULLY. TILAPIA PAIRS SEAMLESSLY WITH SWEET PEAS AND SAFFRON-SCENTED RICE.

Cornmeal-Crusted Tilapia with Squash Salad

Hands-on: 18 min. Total: 18 min. *You just can't beat a crisp breaded fish fillet; this one, with its cornmeal crust, is reminiscent of Southern-fried catfish (but with a sweeter fish at the center).*

Salad:
1 medium zucchini (about 8 ounces)
1 large yellow squash (about 8 ounces)
1 tablespoon fresh lime juice
1 tablespoon olive oil
1 teaspoon minced fresh garlic
¼ teaspoon kosher salt
⅛ teaspoon cumin seeds, toasted and crushed
Dash of sugar
1 ounce queso fresco, crumbled (about ¼ cup)
Tilapia:
4 (6-ounce) tilapia fillets
½ teaspoon kosher salt
¼ teaspoon freshly ground black pepper
1 large egg white, lightly beaten
⅓ cup yellow cornmeal
1 tablespoon all-purpose flour
2 tablespoons canola oil

1. To prepare salad, shave zucchini and yellow squash thinly with a vegetable peeler to equal 2 cups each. Combine lime juice and next 5 ingredients in a medium bowl, stirring with a whisk. Add zucchini mixture, tossing to coat vegetables. Sprinkle with cheese. Set salad aside.
2. To prepare tilapia, pat fish dry with a paper towel. Sprinkle fillets evenly with ½ teaspoon salt and pepper. Place egg white in a shallow dish. Combine cornmeal and flour in another shallow dish. Dip each fillet in egg white, and dredge in cornmeal mixture, shaking off excess.
3. Heat a large nonstick skillet over medium-high heat. Add canola oil to pan; swirl to coat. Add fillets to pan; cook 3 minutes on each side or until fish flakes easily when tested with a fork. Top fillets with salad. Serves 4 (serving size: 1 fillet and about ¾ cup salad)

CALORIES 348; **FAT** 14.5g (sat 2.5g, mono 8g, poly 3.2g); **PROTEIN** 38g; **CARB** 17g; **FIBER** 2g; **CHOL** 87mg; **IRON** 2mg; **SODIUM** 478mg; **CALC** 62mg

MEATLESS MONDAYS

CREAMY, SPRINGY VEGGIE MAINS

A sparkling risotto, artichoke-asparagus lasagna, and cheesy crepes truly satisfy.

Champagne Risotto with Peppers and Asparagus

Hands-on: 55 min. Total: 55 min. *If you don't want to open a full bottle of bubbly, buy a four-pack of minis. A mini is about 1 cup.*

2 large red bell peppers
1 pound asparagus, trimmed and cut into ¾-inch pieces
2 tablespoons extra-virgin olive oil, divided
½ teaspoon grated lemon rind
2 cups organic vegetable broth
2 cups water
1 cup chopped onion
1½ tablespoons chopped fresh garlic
1 tablespoon chopped shallots
½ teaspoon freshly ground black pepper
¼ teaspoon salt
1 cup uncooked Arborio rice
1 cup Champagne or sparkling wine
2 ounces goat cheese (about ¼ cup)

1. Preheat broiler to high.
2. Cut bell peppers in half lengthwise; discard seeds and membranes. Place pepper halves, skin sides up, on a foil-lined baking sheet; flatten with hand. Combine asparagus and 1 tablespoon oil in a medium bowl; add to baking sheet. Broil 5 minutes. Remove asparagus from pan; set aside. Broil peppers an additional 5 minutes or until blackened. Place peppers in a paper bag; fold to close tightly. Let stand 10 minutes. Peel and chop peppers. Combine asparagus, peppers, and rind in a medium bowl; toss to combine.
3. Bring broth and 2 cups water to a simmer in a medium saucepan (do not boil). Keep warm over low heat.
4. Heat a large saucepan over medium heat. Add 1 tablespoon oil to pan; swirl to coat. Add onion; cook 4 minutes, stirring frequently. Add garlic, shallots, black pepper, and salt; cook 2 minutes, stirring frequently. Add rice; cook 1 minute, stirring frequently. Stir in Champagne; cook until liquid is absorbed (about 2 minutes), stirring constantly. Stir in ½ cup broth mixture; cook 4 minutes or until liquid is nearly absorbed, stirring constantly. Reserve ¼ cup broth mixture. Add remaining broth mixture, ½ cup at a time, stirring constantly until each portion is absorbed before adding the next (about 22 minutes total). Stir in asparagus mixture; cook 1 minute or until thoroughly heated. Remove from heat; stir in reserved ¼ cup broth mixture and cheese. Serves 4 (serving size: about 1¼ cups)

CALORIES 379; **FAT** 10.6g (sat 3.1g, mono 5.6g, poly 0.9g); **PROTEIN** 10g; **CARB** 53g; **FIBER** 6g; **CHOL** 7mg; **IRON** 2mg; **SODIUM** 482mg; **CALC** 57mg

Make Ahead • Vegetarian

Creamy Artichoke and Asparagus Lasagna

Hands-on: 35 min. Total: 1 hr. 10 min.

1 tablespoon olive oil
2 cups thinly sliced leek (about 2 large)
1 pound asparagus, trimmed and cut into 1-inch pieces
2 teaspoons minced fresh garlic
2 teaspoons chopped fresh thyme
7 ounces frozen artichokes, thawed and coarsely chopped (about 2 cups)
1½ cups 1% low-fat milk, divided
3 tablespoons all-purpose flour
1 cup organic vegetable broth
1½ teaspoons grated lemon rind
½ teaspoon kosher salt
½ teaspoon black pepper
⅛ teaspoon nutmeg
Dash of ground red pepper
4 ounces part-skim mozzarella cheese, shredded (about 1 cup)
2 ounces vegetarian Parmesan cheese, grated (about ½ cup)
Cooking spray
6 cooked lasagna noodles

1. Preheat oven to 375°.
2. Heat a large skillet over medium heat. Add oil to pan; swirl to coat. Add leek; cook 3 minutes, stirring occasionally. Add asparagus, and cook 3 minutes, stirring occasionally. Add garlic and thyme; cook 1 minute. Stir in artichokes; remove from heat.
3. Combine ½ cup milk and flour in a saucepan, stirring with a whisk until smooth. Stir in remaining 1 cup milk and broth. Bring to a simmer over medium heat, stirring frequently. Simmer 1 minute or until thickened. Add rind and next 4 ingredients.
4. Combine cheeses in a small bowl. Spread ½ cup milk mixture in bottom of an 8-inch square glass or ceramic baking dish coated with cooking spray. Cut bottom third off each noodle to form 6 large and 6 small noodles. In a single layer, arrange 2 large and 2 small noodles over milk mixture to fit pan; top with one-third of vegetable mixture, one-third of remaining milk mixture, and one-third of cheese mixture. Repeat layers twice, ending with cheese. Cover with foil coated with cooking spray. Bake at 375° for 25 minutes.
5. Preheat broiler to high.
6. Uncover lasagna; broil on middle rack of oven 2 minutes or until cheese is browned. Let stand 5 minutes before serving. Serves 6

CALORIES 276; **FAT** 10.4g (sat 4.4g, mono 3.5g, poly 0.7g); **PROTEIN** 16g; **CARB** 31g; **FIBER** 4g; **CHOL** 22mg; **IRON** 3mg; **SODIUM** 575mg; **CALC** 367mg

Vegetarian

Chard, Caramelized Onion, and Gruyère Crepes

Hands-on: 45 min. Total: 45 min.
Nutty whole-wheat pastry flour keeps these crepes light as air. Get ahead: Make crepes, stack between paper towels, and store in the fridge for a couple of days or in the freezer for a few weeks.

Crepes:
3.4 ounces whole-wheat pastry flour (about ¾ cup)
¾ cup plus 2 tablespoons 1% low-fat milk
½ teaspoon chopped fresh rosemary
¼ teaspoon salt
2 large eggs
2 tablespoons olive oil, divided
2 teaspoons butter, melted
Filling:
1 teaspoon olive oil
1 large onion, halved and thinly sliced
2 tablespoons water
1½ teaspoons minced fresh garlic
1 pound Swiss chard, trimmed and thinly sliced (about 8 cups)
2 tablespoons pine nuts, toasted
½ teaspoon freshly ground black pepper
¼ teaspoon salt
1 ounce ⅓-less-fat cream cheese
Cooking spray
1 ounce Gruyère cheese, finely grated (about ¼ cup)

1. To prepare crepes, weigh or lightly spoon flour into dry measuring cups; level with a knife. Place milk, rosemary, ¼ teaspoon salt, and eggs in a blender; process until smooth. Add flour; process until smooth, scraping sides. With blender on, add 1 tablespoon oil and butter. Pour batter into a medium bowl. Refrigerate 15 minutes.

2. Heat an 8-inch crepe pan or non-stick skillet over medium-high heat. Place 1 tablespoon oil in a small bowl. Brush a thin layer of oil to coat bottom of pan. Pour ¼ cup batter into center of pan; quickly tilt pan in all directions so batter covers pan with a thin film. Cook about 1 minute. Carefully lift edge of crepe with a spatula to test for doneness. Turn crepe over when it can be shaken loose from the pan and the underside is lightly browned; cook 30 seconds. Place crepe on a clean towel; keep warm. Repeat procedure 7 times with remaining batter and oil. Stack crepes between single layers of paper towels to prevent sticking.

3. To prepare filling, heat a large nonstick skillet over medium-high heat. Add 1 teaspoon oil to pan; swirl to coat. Add onion; cook 3 minutes. Reduce heat to low; cook 15 minutes or until browned, stirring occasionally. Add 2 table-spoons water, garlic, and Swiss chard; cook 5 minutes or until chard wilts. Add pine nuts, pepper, ¼ teaspoon salt, and cream cheese, stirring until cream cheese melts. Remove from heat.

4. Preheat broiler to high. Place oven rack 6 inches below broiler.

5. Spoon ¼ cup chard mixture in center of each crepe; roll up. Arrange filled crepes, seam sides down, in an 8-inch square glass or ceramic baking dish coated with cooking spray. Sprinkle evenly with Gruyère cheese. Broil 3 minutes or until cheese is bubbly. Serve immediately. Serves 4 (serving size: 2 crepes)

CALORIES 315; **FAT** 20g (sat 5.9g, mono 9.3g, poly 3.1g); **PROTEIN** 12g; **CARB** 24g; **FIBER** 4g; **CHOL** 114mg; **IRON** 2mg; **SODIUM** 553mg; **CALC** 222mg

A DOZEN DEVILED EGGS

Start with 12 hard-cooked eggs, and mash the yolks. Then stir in your favorite flavor combo.

**Kid Friendly • Quick & Easy
Gluten Free • Make Ahead
Vegetarian
Mushroom**
Sauté ¾ cup chopped cremini mushrooms, 2 teaspoons minced shallots, 2 teaspoons fresh chopped thyme, ¼ teaspoon kosher salt, and ¼ teaspoon pepper in 1 teaspoon butter for 4 minutes. Stir mushroom mixture, 3 tablespoons canola mayo, and 3 tablespoons 2% Greek yogurt into yolks. Divide among whites; top with ½ ounce shaved Manchego. Serves 12

CALORIES 93; **FAT** 6.5g (sat 2.1g); **SODIUM** 149mg

**Quick & Easy • Gluten Free
Make Ahead • Vegetarian
Curried**
Stir ⅓ cup minced green onions, ¼ cup canola mayo, 3 tablespoons 2% Greek yogurt, 1 teaspoon fresh lem-on juice, 1 teaspoon Dijon mustard, ¾ teaspoon curry powder, ½ teaspoon ground cumin, ¼ teaspoon kosher salt, and ⅛ teaspoon ground red pepper into yolks. Divide among whites; sprinkle with minced green onions and red pepper. Serves 12

CALORIES 89; **FAT** 6.1g (sat 1.6g); **SODIUM** 159mg

**Quick & Easy • Gluten Free
Make Ahead • Vegetarian
Pickle & Jalapeño**
Stir 3 tablespoons canola mayo, 3 tablespoons 2% Greek yogurt, 1½ tablespoons minced gherkins, 1 tablespoon minced pickled jala-peño, 1 tablespoon cider vinegar, ¼ teaspoon kosher salt, and ¼ taspoon black pepper into yolks. Divide among whites; top each egg with 2 thinly sliced gherkin pieces. Serves 12

CALORIES 87; **FAT** 5.8g (sat 1.6g); **SODIUM** 166mg

**Kid Friendly • Quick & Easy
Gluten Free • Make Ahead
Green Eggs & Ham**
Stir ¾ cup diced avocado, 2 tablespoons grated red onion, 1½ tablespoons canola mayo, 1 tablespoon lemon juice, ¾ teaspoon garlic powder, ½ teaspoon crushed red pepper, ¼ teaspoon black pepper, and ¼ teaspoon kosher salt into yolks. Divide among whites; top with 1 ounce prosciutto slices, crisped and crumbled. Serves 12

CALORIES 98; **FAT** 6.9g (sat 1.9g); **SODIUM** 189mg

**Quick & Easy • Gluten Free
Make Ahead
Mediterranean**
Stir 6 tablespoons finely chopped sun-dried tomatoes, 6 tablespoons 2% Greek yogurt, 2 tablespoons chopped fresh chives, 4 teaspoons fresh lemon juice, and 6 finely chopped anchovy fillets into yolks. Divide among whites; top each egg with 1 oregano leaf. Sprinkle with ¼ teaspoon crushed red pepper, if desired. Serves 12

CALORIES 85; **FAT** 5.2g (sat 1.7g); **SODIUM** 151mg

continued

FOR PERFECTLY COOKED EGGS THAT SLIP OUT OF THEIR SHELLS, STEAM EGGS IN A VEGETABLE STEAMER 16 MINUTES; COOL SLIGHTLY, AND PEEL.

Kid Friendly • Quick & Easy
Make Ahead
Pimiento Cheese
Stir ¼ cup finely chopped bottled roasted red bell peppers (about 2 ounces), ¼ cup canola mayo, ½ teaspoon hot sauce, ½ teaspoon Worcestershire sauce, ¼ teaspoon kosher salt, ¼ teaspoon pepper, and ¾ ounce shredded aged white cheddar into yolks. Divide among whites; top with 2 tablespoons chopped toasted pecans. Serves 12

CALORIES 100; **FAT** 7.4g (sat 2g); **SODIUM** 175mg

Kid Friendly • Quick & Easy
Gluten Free • Make Ahead
Vegetarian
Rémoulade
Stir ¼ cup diced celery, ¼ cup canola mayo, 3 tablespoons 2% Greek yogurt, 2 tablespoons minced celery leaves, 1 tablespoon chopped capers, 1 tablespoon Creole mustard, 2 teaspoons lemon juice, ¼ teaspoon fresh black pepper, ⅛ teaspoon kosher salt, and ⅛ teaspoon ground red pepper into yolks. Divide among whites; top with sliced celery. Serves 12

CALORIES 90; **FAT** 6.2g (sat 1.6g); **SODIUM** 189mg

Kid Friendly • Quick & Easy
Make Ahead • Vegetarian
Herb & Crumb
Sauté 2 tablespoons panko in 1 teaspoon butter 2 minutes. Stir ¼ cup canola mayo, 3 tablespoons light sour cream, 3 tablespoons chopped green onions, 1 tablespoon chopped fresh parsley, 1 teaspoon chopped fresh tarragon, 1 teaspoon Dijon mustard, 1 teaspoon fresh lemon juice, ¼ teaspoon kosher salt, and ¼ teaspoon pepper into yolks. Divide among whites; top with panko. Serves 12

CALORIES 96; **FAT** 6.8g (sat 2g); **SODIUM** 164mg

Quick & Easy • Gluten Free
Make Ahead •Vegetarian
Romesco
Process 1 bottled roasted red bell pepper, 2 tablespoons chopped blanched toasted almonds, 2 teaspoons sherry vinegar, ⅛ teaspoon smoked paprika, ⅛ teaspoon ground red pepper, and 2 garlic cloves in a food processor until smooth. Stir bell pepper mixture, 1 tablespoon canola mayo, and ½ teaspoon kosher salt into yolks. Divide among whites; top with 1 tablespoon sliced toasted almonds. Serves 12

CALORIES 90; **FAT** 6.3g (sat 1.7g); **SODIUM** 174mg

Quick & Easy • Gluten Free
Make Ahead • Vegetarian
Wasabi-Ginger
Stir ¼ cup canola mayo, 2 tablespoons chopped cilantro, 4 teaspoons grated peeled fresh ginger, 4 teaspoons wasabi paste, and 4 teaspoons fresh lime juice into yolks. Divide among whites; top with ¼ sheet nori, cut into slivers, and ⅛ teaspoon coarsely ground Korean chile (gochugaru) or black sesame seeds. Serves 12

CALORIES 90; **FAT** 6.2g (sat 1.6g); **SODIUM** 138mg

Kid Friendly • Quick & Easy
Make Ahead • Vegetarian
Triple Onion
Stir ¼ cup finely chopped green onions, ¼ cup canola mayo, ¼ cup plain 2% reduced-fat Greek yogurt, 1 teaspoon Dijon mustard, ½ teaspoon freshly ground black pepper, ¼ teaspoon kosher salt, and 5 pickled cocktail onions, finely chopped, into yolks. Divide among whites; top evenly with 1 ounce (about ½ cup) French-fried onions (such as French's). Serves 12

CALORIES 103; **FAT** 7.1g (sat 1.9g); **SODIUM** 185mg

Kid Friendly • Quick & Easy
Gluten Free • Make Ahead
Bacon & Blue Cheese
Stir 1 tablespoon cooked chopped bacon, 3 tablespoons canola mayo, 3 tablespoons 2% Greek yogurt, 4 teaspoons crumbled blue cheese, 1 teaspoon Dijon mustard, ¼ teaspoon pepper, and ⅛ teaspoon kosher salt into yolks. Divide among whites; top with 2 teaspoons bacon and ¼ teaspoon pepper. Serves 12

CALORIES 91; **FAT** 6.3g (sat 1.9g); **SODIUM** 156mg

MAKE AHEAD: STORE FILLING IN A ZIP-TOP BAG. SNIP OFF A CORNER AND PIPE INTO WHITES BEFORE SERVING.

THE LESSON: PAN-CHARRED GREEN VEGGIES

Cook like a genius with tips from chef and teacher Keith Schroeder.

It turns out that many of the foods we eat are mostly water, and cooks take advantage of that one way or another through the physics of cooking. In the case of green vegetables, such as beans and asparagus, we often lightly boil or steam them to prevent drying out or overcooking. But there's another approach: manipulate the water content through dry-heat cooking, which concentrates the flavors as some of the water inside the vegetables evaporates. Bonus: This is even easier and faster than boiling and shocking in ice water.

KEITH'S RECIPE BREAKDOWN
PAN-CHARRED GREEN BEANS WITH TARRAGON
Hands-on: 11 min. Total: 11 min.

INGREDIENT	AMOUNT	WHY
cooking spray		To facilitate blistering of the beans. It's a fry/char instead of a burn/char. You'll see.
fresh green beans	8 ounces, washed and trimmed	They can handle the heat, and they become gloriously wilted while retaining a perfect snap.
butter	1½ teaspoons	The finishing "sauce" is a riff on béarnaise, and that requires butter—though here we're using much less.
cider vinegar	1 tablespoon	A balanced sauce needs a little acid. This vinegar is sweeter and milder than others, so it doesn't overwhelm the beans.
fresh tarragon	2 teaspoons chopped	Béarnaise is typically finished with this herb, so I'm going with it here. That distinct anise flavor is a must.
kosher salt	¼ teaspoon	A little is all you need to enhance the taste of everything, even the butter.

Follow These Steps:

• Heat a medium, heavy skillet (not nonstick) over high heat for 2 minutes.
• Coat pan with cooking spray. Immediately add green beans to pan, shaking them into a single layer; cook, without stirring, 2 minutes or until beans are very lightly charred. Cook beans 5 more minutes or until crisp-tender and evenly charred, tossing occasionally.
• Remove pan from heat. Let beans rest 1 minute. Add butter; toss until butter melts and coats beans. Add vinegar; toss. Turn on heat if necessary to evaporate most of liquid. Sprinkle beans with tarragon and salt; toss. Serve immediately. Serves 4 (serving size: 2 ounces)

CALORIES 33; FAT 1.8g (sat 0.9g, mono 0.4g, poly 0.1g); PROTEIN 1g; CARB 4g; FIBER 2g; CHOL 4mg; IRON 1mg; SODIUM 136mg; CALC 23mg

YOU WON'T BELIEVE HOW GOOD THESE GREEN BEANS ARE—AND THEY TAKE ONLY 11 MINUTES.

Pan-Charred Asparagus
In place of green beans, use 8 ounces (2½-inch) pieces of trimmed asparagus. Use 1½ teaspoons toasted walnut oil in place of butter and 2 teaspoons fresh lemon juice in place of vinegar. After tossing asparagus with tarragon and salt, sprinkle with 1 tablespoon chopped, toasted walnuts and 2 tablespoons shaved Parmigiano-Reggiano. Serves 4 (serving size: about ⅔ cup)

CALORIES 52; FAT 4g (sat 0.7g); SODIUM 160mg

EASY PASSOVER BRISKET

Kid Friendly • Freezable
Gluten Free • Make Ahead

Sweet and Tangy Slow Cooker Brisket

Hands-on: 30 min. Total: 8 hr. 30 min.
Start the brisket at the beginning of your Passover seder preparations—it will have rested and will be ready to slice by the meal portion of the evening.

1 (4½-pound) flat-cut brisket roast, fat cap trimmed to ⅛-inch thickness
1¼ teaspoons kosher salt, divided
½ teaspoon freshly ground black pepper
1 tablespoon canola oil
1½ teaspoons garlic powder
1 teaspoon paprika
3 medium carrots, peeled and cut into thirds
3 celery stalks, cut into thirds
Cooking spray
2 large onions, halved and vertically sliced
4 garlic cloves, chopped
1 cup unsalted beef stock (such as Swanson)
1 (15-ounce) can crushed tomatoes
2 tablespoons brown sugar
2 tablespoons cider vinegar
5 thyme sprigs
2 bay leaves
Flat-leaf parsley leaves (optional)

1. Sprinkle brisket evenly with 1 teaspoon salt and pepper. Heat a large skillet over medium-high heat. Add oil; swirl to coat. Add brisket; cook 5 minutes, turning to brown on all sides. Rub brisket with garlic powder and paprika. Arrange carrots and celery in a 6-quart electric slow cooker coated with cooking spray; top with brisket, fat cap side up.
2. Return skillet to medium heat. Add onions to pan; cover and cook 10 minutes, stirring occasionally. Uncover. Stir in garlic; cook 5 minutes or until onions are tender and golden. Arrange onion mixture over brisket.
3. Combine ¼ teaspoon salt, stock, tomatoes, brown sugar, and vinegar in hot skillet, stirring with a whisk to loosen browned bits. Pour tomato mixture around brisket. Place thyme and bay leaves in slow cooker, pressing into tomato mixture. Cover and cook on LOW 7 hours or until brisket is tender when sliced. Cool slightly in cooker, about 1 hour.
4. Place brisket on a cutting board. Trim fat cap; discard fat. Cut brisket across the grain into thin slices. Pour sauce through a sieve over a bowl; discard carrots, celery, thyme, and bay leaves. Return onions to sauce. Serve brisket with sauce. Garnish with fresh parsley, if desired. Serves 12 (serving size: about 3 ounces beef and about ⅔ cup sauce)

CALORIES 307; FAT 15.1g (sat 5g, mono 7.1g, poly 0.8g); PROTEIN 33g; CARB 8g; FIBER 1g; CHOL 100mg; IRON 4mg; SODIUM 338mg; CALC 31mg

THANKS TO THE SLOW COOKER, THIS CLASSIC SEDER DISH CAN SLOWLY SIMMER TO PERFECTION.

FEED 4 FOR LESS THAN $10

Pizza, pasta, rice bowl: Three favorite dinners get delicious new flavor twists.

Kid Friendly

$2.44
PER SERVING

Pear, Blue Cheese, and Bacon Focaccia-Style Pizza

Hands-on: 35 min. Total: 2 hr. 30 min.
If you don't own a pizza pan, you can find inexpensive, disposable rimmed pizza pans at the supermarket. For a quick side, combine 1 tablespoon olive oil, 1 tablespoon lemon juice, and 1 teaspoon Dijon mustard in a bowl. Add ½ cup halved grape tomatoes, 5 cups mixed greens, ½ cup toasted walnuts, and ¼ cup chopped pitted dates; toss to coat.

½ cup warm water (100° to 110°)
2 tablespoons extra-virgin olive oil, divided
1 package dry yeast (about 2¼ teaspoons)
1 teaspoon sugar
7.9 ounces all-purpose flour (about 1¾ cups)
½ teaspoon kosher salt
Cooking spray
1 tablespoon cornmeal
3 center-cut bacon slices, chopped
1 cup chopped red onion
½ cup part-skim ricotta cheese
⅛ teaspoon ground nutmeg
1 ounce blue cheese, crumbled (about ¼ cup)
2 cups baby arugula
1 Bosc pear, thinly sliced
¾ teaspoon freshly ground black pepper

1. Combine ½ cup warm water, 5 teaspoons oil, yeast, and sugar in a large bowl; let stand 5 minutes or until bubbly. Weigh or lightly spoon flour into dry measuring cups; level with a knife. Add flour and salt to yeast mixture; stir until a soft dough forms. Knead dough on a lightly floured surface until smooth and elastic.

2. Place dough in a large bowl coated with cooking spray, turning to coat top. Cover and let rise in a warm place (85°), free from drafts, 1½ hours or until doubled in size.

3. Preheat oven to 450°.

4. Punch dough down; cover and let rest 5 minutes. Roll dough into a 12-inch circle on a lightly floured surface. Place dough on a 12-inch rimmed pizza pan sprinkled with cornmeal. Let stand 5 minutes. Pierce entire surface liberally with a fork. Bake at 450° for 10 minutes.

5. Cook bacon in a nonstick skillet over medium heat until crisp. Remove bacon from pan with a slotted spoon. Return pan to medium heat. Add onion to drippings; cook 4 minutes or until tender, stirring occasionally.

6. Combine ricotta and nutmeg in a small bowl. Spread ricotta mixture over dough, leaving a ½-inch border; top evenly with bacon, onion mixture, and blue cheese. Brush edges of dough with 1 teaspoon oil. Bake at 450° for 12 minutes or until edges are golden. Top pizza evenly with arugula and pear; sprinkle with pepper. Cut into 8 wedges. Serves 4 (serving size: 2 wedges)

CALORIES 417; FAT 13.8g (sat 4.7g, mono 6.4g, poly 1.2g); PROTEIN 14g; CARB 60g; FIBER 4g; CHOL 21mg; IRON 3mg; SODIUM 486mg; CALC 162mg

HOW CONVENIENT: EVERYTHING COOKS IN THE SAME POT—INCLUDING THE RICE, WHICH SOAKS UP ALL KINDS OF FLAVOR FROM THE BRAISE.

Kid Friendly • Make Ahead

Soy-Braised Pork and Rice

$2.43 PER SERVING

Hands-on: 18 min. Total: 1 hr. 28 min.
Braising the pork in soy sauce and chile paste infuses it with flavor and keeps it tender. Serve with sesame-soy cucumbers: Combine 1 tablespoon rice vinegar, 2 teaspoons lower-sodium soy sauce, 1 teaspoon dark sesame oil, and 2 sliced English cucumbers.

4 teaspoons dark sesame oil, divided
12 ounces pork shoulder, trimmed and cut into ½-inch pieces
2 tablespoons minced fresh garlic
1¾ cups water, divided
2 tablespoons lower-sodium soy sauce
1½ tablespoons rice vinegar
2 teaspoons sambal oelek (ground fresh chile paste)
1 cup finely chopped onion
⅔ cup sliced carrot
1 cup long-grain white rice
1¾ cups unsalted chicken stock (such as Swanson)
1 cup frozen green peas
¼ cup thinly sliced green onions

1. Heat a large saucepan over medium-high heat. Add 2 teaspoons sesame oil to pan; swirl to coat. Add pork to pan; cook 5 minutes, turning to brown on all sides. Add garlic to pan; cook 1 minute, stirring constantly. Stir in 1 cup water and next 3 ingredients; bring mixture to a boil. Reduce heat; simmer 45 minutes or until liquid evaporates, stirring occasionally. Remove pork from pan; keep warm.

2. Return pan to medium-high heat. Add 2 teaspoons sesame oil to pan; swirl to coat. Add onion and carrot; sauté 3 minutes. Add rice, and cook 1 minute, stirring frequently. Stir in pork, ¾ cup water, and chicken stock; bring to a boil. Cover, reduce heat, and cook 20 minutes or until liquid is absorbed and rice is tender. Stir in peas; cook 1 minute or until thoroughly heated. Sprinkle with green onions. Serves 4 (serving size: 1¼ cups)

CALORIES 427; FAT 11.3g (sat 2.9g, mono 4.7g, poly 2.8g); PROTEIN 26g; CARB 54g; FIBER 4g; CHOL 57mg; IRON 4mg; SODIUM 499mg; CALC 72mg

Pasta with Shrimp and Tomato-Caper Sauce

$2.48
PER
SERVING

(pictured on page 216)

Hands-on: 23 min. Total: 28 min.

8 ounces uncooked linguine
2¹/₂ teaspoons olive oil, divided
12 ounces medium shrimp, peeled
  and deveined
1 cup chopped zucchini
¹/₂ cup chopped onion
3 garlic cloves, minced
¹/₄ teaspoon kosher salt
¹/₄ teaspoon crushed red pepper
1 (28-ounce) can whole plum
  tomatoes, rinsed and drained
¹/₄ cup fat-free, lower-sodium chicken
  broth
1 tablespoon capers, drained and
  chopped
¹/₄ cup small basil leaves

1. Cook pasta according to package directions, omitting salt and fat; drain.
2. Heat a large nonstick skillet over medium-high heat. Add 1½ teaspoons oil; swirl to coat. Add shrimp; cook 3 minutes or until done. Remove shrimp from pan.
3. Wipe out pan with a paper towel. Return pan to medium-high heat. Add 1 teaspoon oil; swirl to coat. Add zucchini and onion; sauté 3 minutes. Add garlic; sauté 30 seconds. Add salt, red pepper, and tomatoes; lightly mash tomatoes with a potato masher. Reduce heat to medium; simmer 8 minutes. Stir in broth; return to a simmer. Stir in pasta, shrimp, and capers; toss. Remove pan from heat; top with basil. Serve immediately. Serves 4 (serving size: 1½ cups)

CALORIES 340; **FAT** 4.7g (sat 0.8g, mono 2.1g, poly 0.5g); **PROTEIN** 22g; **CARB** 53g; **FIBER** 4g; **CHOL** 107mg; **IRON** 3mg; **SODIUM** 654mg; **CALC** 99mg

---

BAKE A SECOND BATCH

SWEET EASTER TREATS

Give some, keep some: Carrot cake cookies are surefire smile-makers.

Based on the classic whoopie pie, these soft sandwich cookies provide all the pleasures of traditional carrot cake in a fun-to-eat package, including the thick, tangy cream cheese frosting—especially the cream cheese frosting. They pack up easily; just stack between wax paper so they won't stick together. Give a batch to your neighbor, your kid's teacher, or the person hosting Easter brunch. And don't forget to make a batch of your own; it would be a shame not to enjoy them yourself.

Carrot Cake Sandwich Cookies

Hands-on: 30 min. Total: 50 min.
To bake a second batch, mix up and bake two separate batches of cookie batter instead of one large batch. You can make just one big double-batch of the cream cheese filling, though.

2 cups shredded carrot
²/₃ cup packed brown sugar, divided
¹/₄ cup unsalted butter, divided
2 tablespoons canola oil
1 teaspoon grated orange rind
³/₄ teaspoon vanilla extract, divided
1 large egg
4.5 ounces unbleached all-purpose
  flour (about 1 cup)
1 teaspoon ground cinnamon
³/₈ teaspoon salt, divided
¹/₄ teaspoon baking soda
4 ounces ¹/₃-less-fat cream cheese,
  softened
1 cup powdered sugar

1. Preheat oven to 350°. Cover 2 baking sheets with parchment paper; set aside.
2. Combine carrot and 3 tablespoons brown sugar in a bowl; toss to coat. Place carrot mixture in a fine mesh sieve; let stand to drain 10 minutes. Discard liquid.
3. Place 2 tablespoons butter in a medium microwave-safe bowl. Microwave at HIGH 45 seconds or until melted. Add oil, rind, ½ teaspoon vanilla extract, and egg; stir with a whisk until well combined.
4. Weigh or lightly spoon flour into a dry measuring cup; level with a knife. Combine flour, remaining brown sugar (about ½ cup), cinnamon, ¼ teaspoon salt, and baking soda in a large bowl; stir well with a whisk. Add carrot mixture and butter mixture; stir until just combined. Drop dough by tablespoonfuls 2 inches apart onto prepared baking sheets for a total of 28 cookies (14 per baking sheet); gently pat dough down to form 2-inch circles. Bake at 350° for 11 minutes or until set.

Remove pans from oven; let stand 3 minutes. Remove cookies from pans; cool completely on a wire rack.

5. Combine cream cheese, 2 tablespoons butter, ¼ teaspoon vanilla extract, and ⅛ teaspoon salt in a medium bowl; beat with a mixer at medium speed 3 minutes or until fluffy. Add powdered sugar; beat at low speed 1 minute or until well combined (do not overbeat). Spread about 1 tablespoon icing on flat side of 1 cookie; top with another cookie, flat side down. Repeat procedure with remaining cookies and filling. Serves 14 (serving size: 1 cookie sandwich)

CALORIES 186; FAT 7.5g (sat 3.5g, mono 2.3g, poly 0.8g); PROTEIN 2g; CARB 28g; FIBER 1g; CHOL 8mg; IRON 1mg; SODIUM 137mg; CALC 26mg

FOR GIVING, STACK BETWEEN LAYERS OF WAX PAPER IN A BOX. IF THEY'RE AN EASTER GIFT, ARRANGE IN THE BOX ON A BED OF EASTER-BASKET GRASS.

CARROT CAKE SANDWICH COOKIES TIPS

1. Macerating the carrot with sugar helps to break down the carrot's tough fibers, ensuring that it will be tender after the short cook time.

2. After scooping dough onto baking sheets, gently pat it down so that cookies bake generally flat; aim for 2-inch circles.

3. When assembling the cookie sandwiches, press together gently so filling flattens and spreads all the way out to the edges.

SUPERFAST 20-MINUTE COOKING

Kid Friendly • Quick & Easy

Creamy Asparagus, Herb, and Pea Pasta

(pictured on page 218)

2 thin pancetta slices (about ⅝ ounce)
1 large garlic clove, thinly sliced
⅔ cup unsalted chicken stock
3 ounces ⅓-less-fat cream cheese
3 tablespoons mascarpone cheese
8 ounces uncooked pappardelle (wide ribbon pasta)
1½ cups (1-inch) asparagus pieces
½ cup frozen green peas
½ teaspoon kosher salt
¼ teaspoon black pepper
1 tablespoon chopped fresh flat-leaf parsley
1 tablespoon thinly sliced fresh chives

1. Place pancetta in a large skillet over medium heat; cook 6 minutes or until pancetta begins to crisp, stirring occasionally. Add garlic; cook 30 seconds, stirring constantly. Add stock; bring to a boil. Reduce heat; simmer 4 minutes. Add cream cheese and mascarpone, stirring with a whisk until smooth. Strain sauce through a fine sieve over a large bowl. Discard solids.

2. Cook pasta according to package directions; omitting salt and fat. Add asparagus and peas during last 2 minutes of cooking; cook 2 minutes. Drain. Add pasta mixture, salt, and pepper to sauce in bowl; toss well. Sprinkle with parsley and chives. Serves 4 (serving size: about 1½ cups)

CALORIES 388; FAT 12.3g (sat 5.8g, mono 3g, poly 1.3g); PROTEIN 17g; CARB 53g; FIBER 7g; CHOL 61mg; IRON 7mg; SODIUM 407mg; CALC 118mg

Quick & Easy • Gluten Free
Vegetarian

Radish Salad with Orange Vinaigrette

Fresh radishes add peppery heat and crunch to spring salads.

2 tablespoons extra-virgin olive oil
2 tablespoons fresh orange juice
1 tablespoon white wine vinegar
¼ teaspoon salt
¼ teaspoon freshly ground
 black pepper
1 cup thinly sliced radishes
½ cup shredded carrot
1 (5-ounce) package mixed
 baby greens

1. Combine first 5 ingredients in a large bowl, stirring with a whisk. Add radishes, carrot, and mixed baby greens just before serving; toss. Serves 6 (serving size: about 1 cup)

CALORIES 55; **FAT** 4.7g (sat 0.4g, mono 3g, poly 1.3g); **PROTEIN** 1g; **CARB** 3g; **FIBER** 1g; **CHOL** 0mg; **IRON** 0mg; **SODIUM** 121mg; **CALC** 9mg

Avocado Dressing

Place ½ cup diced avocado, ¼ cup cilantro leaves, 1 tablespoon fresh lime juice, 1 tablespoon olive oil, ¼ teaspoon salt, and ¼ teaspoon hot sauce in a blender; blend until smooth. Combine 1 cup sliced radishes, ½ cup halved grape tomatoes, and 5 ounces mixed greens; drizzle with dressing. Top with ¼ cup pumpkin seeds. Serves 6 (serving size: about 1½ cups)

CALORIES 80; **FAT** 6.7g (sat 1.1g); **SODIUM** 121mg

Buttermilk-Herb Dressing

Combine 3 tablespoons buttermilk, 2 tablespoons light sour cream, 1 tablespoon chopped fresh dill, ¼ teaspoon salt, and ⅛ teaspoon pepper. Combine 1 cup thinly sliced radishes, ½ cup diagonally sliced sugar snap peas, and 5 ounces mixed greens; drizzle with dressing. Top with ¼ cup toasted sliced almonds. Serves 6 (serving size: about 1½ cups)

CALORIES 44; **FAT** 2.7g (sat 0.7g); **SODIUM** 127mg

Sesame-Honey Vinaigrette

Combine 1 tablespoon rice vinegar, 1 tablespoon dark sesame oil, 1 tablespoon lower-sodium soy sauce, and 1 teaspoon honey in a large bowl, stirring with a whisk. Add 1 cup thinly sliced radishes, ½ cup thinly sliced yellow bell pepper, and 5 ounces mixed greens; toss. Sprinkle with 2 tablespoons chopped toasted cashews. Serves 6 (serving size: about 1 cup)

CALORIES 51; **FAT** 3.6g (sat 0.6g); **SODIUM** 106mg

Kid Friendly • Quick & Easy
Make Ahead

Peanut Butter Granola Crunch Parfaits

1 cup old-fashioned rolled oats
2 tablespoons sliced almonds
1 tablespoon dark brown sugar
1 tablespoon toasted wheat germ
½ teaspoon ground cinnamon
¼ teaspoon salt
¼ cup maple syrup
2 tablespoons reduced-fat creamy
 peanut butter
2 teaspoons canola oil
1 teaspoon vanilla extract
3 cups vanilla frozen Greek yogurt

1. Preheat oven to 450°.
2. Combine first 6 ingredients in a large bowl. Heat syrup, peanut butter, oil, and vanilla in a saucepan over high heat, stirring until smooth. Add to oat mixture; toss to coat.
3. Spread oat mixture on a foil-lined baking sheet. Bake 9 minutes, stirring after 5 minutes. Divide yogurt among 6 parfait glasses; top each serving with ⅓ cup granola. Serves 6

CALORIES 286; **FAT** 5.7g (sat 0.7g, mono 2.9g, poly 1.6g); **PROTEIN** 13g; **CARB** 47g; **FIBER** 2g; **CHOL** 5mg; **IRON** 1mg; **SODIUM** 193mg; **CALC** 26mg

Quick & Easy • Vegetarian

Linguine with Garlicky Kale and White Beans

This dish gets its flavor from loads of chopped fresh garlic. We recommend serving it with toasted baguette slices and a glass of white wine.

8 ounces uncooked linguine
3 tablespoons extra-virgin olive oil
¼ cup chopped fresh garlic
½ cup water
1 (8-ounce) package prechopped
 kale
1 (15-ounce) can unsalted cannellini
 beans, rinsed and drained
¾ teaspoon black pepper, divided
½ teaspoon salt

1. Cook pasta according to package directions, omitting salt and fat.

Drain in a colander over a bowl, reserving ¼ cup cooking liquid. **2.** Heat a large skillet over medium heat. Add oil to pan; swirl to coat. Add garlic to pan. When garlic begins to sizzle, add ½ cup water and kale; cover and cook 5 minutes or until kale is tender, stirring occasionally. Add beans, ½ teaspoon pepper, and salt; cook 1 minute or until thoroughly heated, stirring occasionally. Add pasta and reserved ¼ cup cooking liquid to pan; toss to coat. Sprinkle remaining ¼ teaspoon pepper over pasta. Serve immediately. Serves 4 (serving size: about 1¾ cups)

CALORIES 381; **FAT** 11.8g (sat 1.7g, mono 7.4g, poly 1.3g); **PROTEIN** 13g; **CARB** 58g; **FIBER** 5g; **CHOL** 0mg; **IRON** 4mg; **SODIUM** 341mg; **CALC** 121mg

**Kid Friendly • Quick & Easy
Gluten Free**

Chicken, Rice, and Parmesan Skillet

**2 teaspoons olive oil
5 skinless, boneless chicken thighs, cut into bite-sized pieces (about 1¼ pounds)
1 cup chopped red bell pepper
¾ cup uncooked quick-cooking basmati rice (such as Uncle Ben's)
1½ cups water
½ teaspoon freshly ground black pepper
¼ teaspoon salt
3 cups broccoli florets
2 ounces Parmesan cheese, shaved (about ½ cup)**

1. Heat a large skillet over medium-high heat. Add oil to pan; swirl to coat. Add chicken; cook 5 minutes or until browned, stirring occasionally. Add bell pepper and rice; cook 2 minutes, stirring occasionally. Add 1½ cups water, black pepper, and salt to pan; bring to a boil. Cover, reduce heat, and simmer 5 minutes.

Add broccoli; cook 5 minutes or until broccoli is crisp-tender and rice is done. Sprinkle with Parmesan. Serves 4 (serving size: 1¼ cups)

CALORIES 412; **FAT** 12.4g (sat 4.3g, mono 4.9g, poly 1.8g); **PROTEIN** 37g; **CARB** 40g; **FIBER** 3g; **CHOL** 147mg; **IRON** 3mg; **SODIUM** 506mg; **CALC** 199mg

Kid Friendly • Quick & Easy

Garlicky Grilled Cheese

with Bacon & Spinach

**½ teaspoon olive oil
2 large garlic cloves, thinly sliced
4 cups baby spinach leaves
4 cups baby arugula leaves
4 center-cut bacon slices, halved
8 (1-ounce) rustic Italian bread slices
2 ounces part-skim mozzarella cheese, shredded (about ½ cup)
2 ounces fontina cheese, shredded (about ½ cup)**

1. Heat a large skillet over medium-high heat. Add oil; swirl to coat. Add garlic to pan; sauté 1 minute. Add spinach and arugula; stir until wilted. Remove spinach mixture from pan. Return pan to medium-high heat. Add bacon; cook until crisp. Remove bacon.
2. Top 4 bread slices evenly with cheeses, bacon pieces, spinach mixture, and remaining 4 bread slices.
3. Heat pan over medium heat. Add sandwiches to drippings in pan; weigh down with a plate. Cook 2 minutes on each side. Serves 4 (serving size: 1 sandwich)

CALORIES 300; **FAT** 11.9g (sat 5.8g, mono 2.8g, poly 1.2g); **PROTEIN** 16g; **CARB** 33g; **FIBER** 3g; **CHOL** 32mg; **IRON** 3mg; **SODIUM** 716mg; **CALC** 279mg

LET'S GET COOKING

FAVA BEAN SALAD WITH FENNEL AND RADISH

This salad comes from chef Mike Lata of FIG in Charleston, South Carolina.

The first produce of spring gets chefs all excited. Mike Lata, chef-owner of highly acclaimed restaurants FIG and The Ordinary in Charleston, South Carolina, considers fava beans to be the ultimate signal of the mild new season. "They're inspiring, from a chef's perspective, after working with the same turnips and hardy winter greens for the last several months," he says. "They're tender and sweet. They completely symbolize spring."

Favas are not in every market—farmers' markets and gourmet grocers are your best bets—and they take a little extra work to prep (pulling them from their big green pods, and then peeling the individual beans). But they're worth the effort. "It's a labor of love for the home cook," Lata says. In his restaurants, Lata and his staff sometimes prepare them as a puree with a little olive oil, garlic, and lemon for a bright-flavored crostini topping. If he can spare enough hands, his staff might make a pureed fava bean soup. But sprinkling favas into a salad is one of the simplest ways to showcase their nutty, slightly sweet flavor and tender, creamy texture.

Favas are blanched very briefly for this salad. Cook time depends
continued

on how young the raw favas are—if they're tender enough, Lata says, they don't need to be cooked at all. He pairs the beans in traditional Italian fashion with salty sheep's-milk cheese and fresh lemon juice, and then adds a little more of spring's bounty with peppery radish slices. Shaved fennel adds fragrant crunch, while the walnuts "give the salad a little weightiness, making it that much more satisfying." Try Lata's original version of the fava bean salad this month at his FIG restaurant in Charleston.

FAVAS TAKE A LITTLE EXTRA WORK TO PREP, BUT THEY'RE WORTH THE EFFORT.

Quick & Easy • Gluten Free Vegetarian

Fava Bean Salad with Fennel and Radish

Hands-on: 30 min. Total: 30 min.
Lata uses Singing Brook cheese, an artisanal aged sheep's-milk cheese produced by Blackberry Farm in Tennessee. Order it at blackberryfarm.com, or use pecorino Romano. To best gauge the doneness of the beans, Lata removes the tough outer skins with a paring knife first, before blanching. This can be tricky for cooks new to favas, so instead we remove the skins after blanching, which makes the job a little easier. If fava beans aren't available, substitute English peas. Or use edamame, as we did.

1½ **pounds unshelled whole fava beans (about 1 cup shelled)**
1½ **tablespoons fresh lemon juice**
1½ **teaspoons extra-virgin olive oil**
¼ **teaspoon freshly ground black pepper**
⅛ **teaspoon salt**
2 **cups very thinly sliced fennel bulb**
2 **cups arugula leaves**
¼ **cup thinly sliced radish**
¼ **cup walnuts, toasted and chopped**
1.5 **ounces Singing Brook or pecorino Romano cheese, crumbled (about ⅓ cup)**

1. Remove shells from beans. Place beans in a large pot of boiling water; cook 20 seconds. Drain; rinse with cold water. Drain well. Remove and discard tough outer skins from beans. **2.** Combine juice, oil, pepper, and salt in a large bowl, stirring with a whisk. Add beans, fennel, and arugula; toss to coat. Place about ¾ cup fennel mixture on each of 6 plates. Sprinkle evenly with radish, walnuts, and cheese. Serves 6

CALORIES 98; **FAT** 6.8g (sat 2.3g, mono 1.3g, poly 2.5g); **PROTEIN** 4g; **CARB** 6g; **FIBER** 2g; **CHOL** 8mg; **IRON** 1mg; **SODIUM** 220mg; **CALC** 103mg

KID IN THE KITCHEN

DUMPLINGS FOR DIPPING

Matisse and friends have fun filling, sealing, dunking, and eating.

"Today I made shrimp and edamame dumplings that were very tasty. This recipe was a little fiddly to make but well worth the effort. It might be a little bit hard for smaller kids, but older kids will like it, especially with an extra set of hands or two to help speed up the process of wrapping. I loved the combination of fresh ginger and lime—it was really refreshing. Fresh ginger and garlic are much better than what you get in the store-bought jars. You can peel and freeze fresh ginger and simply grate the amount you need. For the garlic, press on the clove with the back of a butter knife to remove the skin, and then crush with a fork to release the aroma. Blended together, these flavors will just explode and will make you want to go back for more!"

DON'T LET THE WRAPPERS DRY OUT: COVER WITH A DAMP PAPER TOWEL WHILE NOT IN USE.

Shrimp and Edamame Dumplings

Hands-on: 30 min. Total: 45 min.
Having multiple sets of hands makes dumpling assembly easy and fun. To make ahead, dust the uncooked dumplings with cornstarch. Freeze in a single layer on a baking sheet. Store frozen dumplings in a large zip-top plastic bag in the freezer up to one month.

1/2 cup frozen shelled edamame (green soybeans)
1 teaspoon cornstarch
2 teaspoons lower-sodium soy sauce
1 teaspoon grated peeled fresh ginger
1 teaspoon minced fresh garlic
1 teaspoon rice vinegar
1/2 teaspoon sugar
1/2 teaspoon dark sesame oil
18 medium shrimp, peeled and deveined (about 8 ounces)
1 large egg white
1/2 cup finely chopped napa (Chinese) cabbage
1 tablespoon hot water
2 teaspoons brown sugar
2 tablespoons fresh lime juice
1 teaspoon chili garlic sauce
1/2 teaspoon fish sauce
24 round wonton wrappers or gyoza skins
Cooking spray
1/2 cup water, divided

1. Cook edamame according to package directions; drain. Rinse under cold water; drain.
2. Place cornstarch and next 8 ingredients in the bowl of a food processor; pulse until finely chopped. Combine edamame, shrimp mixture, and cabbage in a bowl. Refrigerate mixture 10 minutes.
3. Combine 1 tablespoon hot water and brown sugar in a bowl, stirring until brown sugar dissolves. Stir in lime juice, chili garlic sauce, and fish sauce.
4. Working with 1 wonton wrapper at a time (cover remaining wrappers to keep them from drying), moisten outside edge of wrapper with water. Spoon about 1½ teaspoons shrimp mixture into center of circle. Fold wrapper over filling; pinch edges together to seal. Repeat procedure with remaining wrappers and shrimp mixture (cover formed dumplings to keep them from drying).
5. Heat a large skillet over high heat. Coat pan with cooking spray. Arrange 12 dumplings in pan; cook 1 minute. Turn dumplings over. Carefully add ¼ cup water to pan; cover immediately. Cook 2 minutes; place cooked dumplings on a platter. Wipe pan with a paper towel. Repeat procedure with cooking spray, remaining 12 dumplings, and ¼ cup water. Serve immediately with sauce. Serves 4 (serving size: 6 dumplings and 1½ tablespoons sauce)

CALORIES 211; **FAT** 2.6g (sat 0.3g, mono 0.4g, poly 0.6g); **PROTEIN** 12g; **CARB** 35g; **FIBER** 2g; **CHOL** 44mg; **IRON** 2mg; **SODIUM** 504mg; **CALC** 58mg

THE VERDICT

CHLOE (AGE 11)
She thought the ginger was a little overwhelming. That didn't stop her from eating them, though! **9 out of 10**

SARAH (AGE 12)
She thought the dumplings were tasty and liked that they weren't spicy. **10 out of 10**

MATISSE (AGE 13)
The flavors and textures worked really well together. I love seafood, so I thought the shrimp in the wonton was a great alternative to pork. **9 out of 10**

GLOBAL PANTRY

FRAGRANT FISH CURRY

In this Indian-inflected African dish, halibut stews in a lick-the-bowl-good coconut sauce.

Gluten Free

Fish in Coconut Curry

Hands-on: 20 min. Total: 47 min.
Coconut milk enriches the sauce, giving it a tropical flavor. Serve over boiled yucca, potatoes, or rice.

1 (1¼-pound) skinless halibut or other firm white fish fillet
1½ teaspoons Madras curry powder, divided
3/4 teaspoon salt, divided
1/4 teaspoon freshly ground black pepper, divided
1 tablespoon canola oil
1 cup finely chopped onion
1 cup finely chopped red bell pepper
2 teaspoons minced peeled fresh ginger
3 garlic cloves, minced
2¾ cups chopped tomato
2 tablespoons fresh lemon juice
3/4 cup light coconut milk
4 lemon wedges
Chopped fresh cilantro (optional)

1. Sprinkle fish with ¾ teaspoon curry powder, ⅜ teaspoon salt, and ⅛ teaspoon black pepper.
2. Heat a large nonstick skillet over medium-high heat. Add oil to pan; swirl to coat. Add fish to pan; cook 4 minutes or until fish is deeply browned on bottom but undercooked on top (fish will finish cooking later in sauce). Remove fish

continued

from pan; set aside.

3. Add onion and bell pepper to pan; sauté 4 minutes or until tender. Add ginger and garlic; sauté 1 minute. Add ¾ teaspoon curry powder, ⅜ teaspoon salt, ⅛ teaspoon black pepper, tomato, and lemon juice. Reduce heat to medium-low, and cook 10 minutes or until tomato breaks down, stirring occasionally. Mash tomato with a wooden spoon.

4. Stir in coconut milk. Return fish along with accumulated juices to pan, browned side up. Reduce heat to low; cover and cook 8 minutes or until fish flakes easily when tested with a fork. Cut fish into 4 equal portions. Spoon sauce into shallow bowls; top with fish. Serve with lemon wedges and cilantro, if desired. Serves 4 (serving size: ½ cup sauce, 5 ounces fish, and 1 lemon wedge)

CALORIES 265; FAT 10.1g (sat 3g, mono 3g, poly 1.6g); PROTEIN 29g; CARB 15g; FIBER 3g; CHOL 70mg; IRON 1mg; SODIUM 549mg; CALC 51mg

12 HEALTHY HABITS

EAT MORE WHOLE GRAINS

Sure, they're good for you, but that's just one reason we love them. This month's hero shows us how to get excited about the many fast, flavorful options out there.

There are plenty of whole-grain choices, ranging from "ancient" and heritage grains to good old oats. Whole grains may help lower the risk of heart disease and diabetes, and they have a positive role in weight control. They also stave off hunger better than processed grains and simply taste delicious.

Many whole grains can be prepared quickly. "So many grains are actually done in less than 30 minutes, some as quick as 10 minutes," says Megan Gordon, this month's hero and author of *Whole-Grain Mornings*. Her fast favorites include bulgur, millet, and amaranth. "If you become familiar with fast-cooking grains, you're going to have a side dish or the beginning of a meal in a matter of minutes."

Gordon, who's also a cooking instructor, food writer, and owner of Seattle-based Marge Granola, is happy to share her love with the grain-curious, especially when it comes to baking.

"A really great starter flour, beyond whole-wheat, is spelt flour. It acts like white all-purpose flour in recipes, so you can actually substitute it 100% in many recipes, and it'll work just fine," she says. "Or choose a whole-grain flour you might not be familiar with, and start slowly experimenting, using a quarter of the amount in the recipe."

Zucchini-Farro Cakes with Herbed Goat Cheese and Slow-Roasted Tomatoes

Hands-on: 45 min. Total: 3 hr. 10 min.
For a more time-friendly topper, use fresh grape tomatoes, halved and sprinkled with salt and pepper.

Tomatoes:
1½ pounds grape tomatoes
2 tablespoons extra-virgin olive oil
¼ teaspoon kosher salt
¼ teaspoon freshly ground black pepper
Cakes:
3½ cups shredded zucchini (about 1 pound)
1 teaspoon kosher salt, divided

2 cups cooked farro
1 cup fresh breadcrumbs
3 tablespoons finely chopped green onions
3 tablespoons chopped fresh flat-leaf parsley
2 tablespoons whole-wheat flour
1 tablespoon chopped fresh thyme
3 large eggs, lightly beaten
2 garlic cloves, minced
2 tablespoons extra-virgin olive oil, divided
Cheese:
2.5 ounces goat cheese (at room temperature)
1½ tablespoons 1% low-fat milk
1 teaspoon chopped fresh chives
½ teaspoon chopped fresh dill
½ teaspoon chopped fresh tarragon
¼ teaspoon freshly ground pepper

1. To prepare tomatoes, preheat oven to 250°.

2. Combine tomatoes, 2 tablespoons olive oil, ¼ teaspoon salt, and ¼ teaspoon pepper in a large bowl; toss to coat. Arrange tomatoes in a single layer on a foil-lined baking sheet. Bake at 250° for 3 hours or until very tender, stirring every hour.

3. To prepare cakes: While tomatoes roast, combine zucchini and ½ teaspoon salt in a cheesecloth-lined bowl. Let stand 10 minutes. Gather edges of cheesecloth; squeeze zucchini in cloth until barely moist. Combine zucchini, ½ teaspoon salt, farro, and next 7 ingredients in a large bowl. Let stand 5 minutes. Shape mixture into 12 (3-inch) patties, about ¾ inch thick.

4. Heat a large skillet over medium heat. Add 2 teaspoons oil to pan; swirl to coat. Add 4 patties; cook 4 minutes on each side or until golden. Repeat in two more batches with remaining oil and patties. Keep warm.

5. To prepare cheese, combine cheese and remaining ingredients in a small bowl, stirring until well combined.

6. Arrange 2 zucchini cakes on each of 6 plates. Top with 1 tablespoon cheese mixture and ¼ cup tomatoes. Serves 6

CALORIES 289; FAT 15.3g (sat 3.9g, mono 8.2g, poly 1.8g); PROTEIN 12g; CARB 33g; FIBER 5g; CHOL 99mg; IRON 2mg; SODIUM 463mg; CALC 73mg

Adapted with permission from Whole-Grain Mornings: New Breakfast Recipes to Span the Seasons *by Megan Gordon (Ten Speed Press, © 2013)*

DINNER TONIGHT

Kid Friendly • Make Ahead Freezable

Chicken Posole + Corn Bread Muffins + Avocado Salad

⅓ cup 1% low-fat milk
1 teaspoon chili powder
1 minced seeded jalapeño pepper, divided
1 large egg
1 (6.5-ounce) package corn bread and muffin mix
Cooking spray
5 canned tomatillos
½ cup chopped fresh cilantro
1 teaspoon ground cumin
1 teaspoon dried oregano
½ teaspoon black pepper
1 tablespoon olive oil
1 cup chopped onion
2 garlic cloves, minced
2 cups unsalted chicken stock (such as Swanson)
1 cup canned white hominy, drained
2 (6-ounce) skinless, boneless chicken breast halves
1 tablespoon fresh lime juice
¼ cup thinly sliced radishes

1. Preheat oven to 400°.
2. Combine milk, chili powder, 1 tablespoon minced jalapeño, and egg in a bowl, stirring with a whisk. Add muffin mix; stir just until combined. Divide batter among 4 (8-ounce) ramekins coated with cooking spray. Place ramekins on a baking sheet. Bake at 400° for 15 minutes or until a wooden pick inserted in center comes out clean. Cool on a wire rack for 5 minutes; remove muffins from ramekins.
3. Place remaining minced jalapeño, tomatillos, and next 4 ingredients in a food processor; process until almost smooth.
4. Heat a Dutch oven over medium-high heat. Add oil to pan; swirl to coat. Add onion; cook 4 minutes, stirring occasionally. Add garlic; sauté 30 seconds. Stir in tomatillo mixture, stock, and hominy; bring to a boil. Add chicken to pan; simmer, covered, 5 minutes. Turn chicken over; simmer, covered, 5 minutes or until chicken is done. Place chicken on a cutting board; cut into bite-sized pieces. Return chicken to pan. Stir in lime juice. Divide soup evenly among 4 bowls; top with radishes. Serve with corn muffins. Serves 4 (serving size: 1½ cups soup, 1 tablespoon radishes, and 1 muffin)

CALORIES 399; FAT 10g (sat 1.6g, mono 3.8g, poly 1.2g); PROTEIN 28g; CARB 49g; FIBER 4g; CHOL 102mg; IRON 2mg; SODIUM 687mg; CALC 83mg

Tangerine and Avocado Salad with Pumpkin Seeds

Cut 2 peeled tangerines into rounds. Combine tangerines, 1 small sliced peeled avocado, 1 tablespoon fresh lime juice, and 1 teaspoon extra-virgin olive oil; toss gently to coat. Sprinkle with 3 tablespoons toasted pumpkin seeds, ¼ teaspoon chili powder, and a dash of kosher salt. Serves 4 (serving size: about ½ cup)

CALORIES 149; FAT 11.6g (sat 1.8g); SODIUM 38mg

READY IN
40
MINUTES

SHOPPING LIST

Chicken Posole with Corn Bread Muffins

1% low-fat milk
Chili powder
Jalapeño pepper
Egg
1 (6.5-ounce) package corn bread and muffin mix
Canned tomatillos
Fresh cilantro
Ground cumin
Dried oregano
Olive oil
Onion
Unsalted chicken stock
Canned white hominy
2 (6-ounce) skinless, boneless chicken breast halves
Lime
Radishes

Tangerine and Avocado Salad with Pumpkin Seeds

Tangerines
Avocado
Lime juice
Extra-virgin olive oil
Pumpkin seeds
Chili powder
Kosher salt

GAME PLAN

While muffins bake:
■ Prepare soup.
While soup simmers:
■ Prepare salad.

SHOPPING LIST

**Pork Tenderloin with Cannellini
Beans**

Fresh rosemary
Fennel seeds
Kosher salt
Pork tenderloin
Olive oil
Garlic cloves
Tomato
Fresh sage
Unsalted chicken stock
Crushed red pepper
1 can unsalted cannellini beans
Fresh flat-leaf parsley

**Arugula Salad with Parmesan
Vinaigrette**

Lemon
Olive oil
Parmesan cheese
Green onion
Arugula
Fennel bulb

GAME PLAN

While pork browns:
■ Chop sage and parsley.
■ Chop onion and slice garlic.
While pork roasts:
■ Prepare salad.

Pork Tenderloin + Cannellini Beans + Arugula Salad

1 teaspoon chopped fresh rosemary
½ teaspoon fennel seeds, lightly
 crushed
¾ teaspoon kosher salt, divided
¾ teaspoon freshly ground black
 pepper, divided
1 (1-pound) pork tenderloin,
 trimmed
1 tablespoon olive oil
½ cup chopped onion
4 large garlic cloves, thinly sliced
1 cup chopped tomato
1 teaspoon chopped fresh sage
1 cup unsalted chicken stock (such as
 Swanson)
¼ teaspoon crushed red pepper
1 (15-ounce) can unsalted cannellini
 beans, rinsed and drained
2 tablespoons chopped fresh flat-leaf
 parsley

1. Preheat oven to 425°.
2. Combine rosemary, fennel seeds,
½ teaspoon salt, and ½ teaspoon
black pepper in a small bowl. Rub
spice mixture evenly over pork.
3. Heat a large ovenproof skillet over
medium-high heat. Add oil; swirl
to coat. Add pork; cook 9 minutes,
browning on all sides. Remove pork
from pan. Add onion and garlic;
sauté 2 minutes. Add tomato and
sage; cook 1 minute, scraping pan to
loosen browned bits. Add ¼ teaspoon salt, ¼ teaspoon black pepper, chicken stock, red pepper, and
cannellini beans, and bring to a boil.
Return pork to pan, and place pan in
oven. Bake at 425° for 12 minutes or
until a thermometer registers 140°.
4. Place pork on a cutting board;
let stand 5 minutes. Heat pan over
medium heat; cook bean mixture 2
minutes or until slightly thickened.

Sprinkle with parsley. Thinly slice
pork; serve with bean mixture. Serves
4 (serving size: about 3 ounces pork
and ½ cup bean mixture)

CALORIES 227; FAT 6.5g (sat 1.3g, mono 3.4g, poly 0.8g);
PROTEIN 30g; CARB 13g; FIBER 3g; CHOL 74mg;
IRON 2mg; SODIUM 475mg; CALC 51mg

**Arugula Salad with Parmesan
Vinaigrette**
Combine 4 teaspoons fresh lemon
juice, 4 teaspoons olive oil, 3 tablespoons grated fresh Parmesan, and 1
chopped green onion in a large bowl,
stirring with a whisk. Add 4 cups
arugula, ½ cup thinly sliced fennel
bulb, ⅛ teaspoon kosher salt, and ⅛
teaspoon pepper; toss gently to coat.
Serves 4 (serving size: about 1 cup)

CALORIES 67; FAT 5.8g (sat 1.3g); SODIUM 129mg

Crab Cakes + Buttermilk Ranch Dressing + Orzo Salad

Crab cakes:
¼ cup chopped fresh chives
1 tablespoon canola mayonnaise
1 teaspoon grated lemon rind
1 tablespoon fresh lemon juice
¼ teaspoon freshly ground black
 pepper
1 large egg, lightly beaten
⅔ cup panko (Japanese
 breadcrumbs)
1 pound lump crabmeat, shell pieces
 removed
3 tablespoons canola oil, divided
Dressing:
⅓ cup whole buttermilk
1 tablespoon canola mayonnaise
1 teaspoon fresh lemon juice
¼ teaspoon black pepper
1 small garlic clove, grated
1 tablespoon chopped fresh chives,
 divided

1½ teaspoons minced fresh parsley, divided
1 teaspoon minced fresh dill, divided
Bibb lettuce leaves

1. To prepare crab cakes, combine first 6 ingredients in a bowl, stirring well with a whisk. Stir in panko. Add crabmeat; stir gently to combine. Let mixture stand 10 minutes.
2. Divide crab mixture into 8 equal portions; gently shape each portion into a ¾-inch-thick patty. Heat a large nonstick skillet over medium-high heat. Add 1½ tablespoons canola oil to pan; swirl to coat. Add 4 patties to pan; cook 3 to 4 minutes on each side or until golden. Remove patties from pan; keep warm. Repeat procedure with 1½ tablespoons canola oil and remaining 4 patties.
3. To prepare dressing, combine buttermilk and next 4 ingredients, stirring with a whisk. Stir in 1½ teaspoons chives, ¾ teaspoon parsley, and ½ teaspoon dill. Arrange lettuce leaves on a platter; top with crab cakes. Spoon dressing over crab cakes; sprinkle with 1½ teaspoons chives, ¾ teaspoon parsley, and ½ teaspoon dill. Serves 4. (serving size: 2 crab cakes and 2 tablespoons dressing)

CALORIES 318; **FAT** 16g (sat 1.6g, mono 8.4g, poly 4g); **PROTEIN** 31g; **CARB** 9g; **FIBER** 1g; **CHOL** 169mg; **IRON** 2mg; **SODIUM** 549mg; **CALC** 150mg

Greek Orzo Salad

Cook ¾ cup orzo according to package directions, omitting salt and fat; drain. Combine 1 tablespoon olive oil, 1 tablespoon red wine vinegar, ¼ teaspoon sugar, ¼ teaspoon kosher salt, and ¼ teaspoon black pepper in a large bowl, stirring with a whisk until sugar dissolves. Add orzo, ¾ cup diced seeded tomato, ½ cup chopped green bell pepper, ¼ cup chopped red onion, 3 tablespoons chopped fresh parsley, and 4 sliced Castelvetrano olives; stir to combine. Serves 4 (serving size: about ¾ cup)

CALORIES 202; **FAT** 4.7g (sat 0.6g); **SODIUM** 157mg

READY IN 35 MINUTES

SHOPPING LIST

Crab Cakes and Buttermilk Ranch Dressing
Fresh chives
Canola mayonnaise
Lemon
Egg
Panko
1 pound lump crabmeat
Canola oil
Buttermilk
Garlic
Fresh parsley
Fresh dill
Bibb lettuce

Greek Orzo Salad
Orzo
Olive oil
Red wine vinegar
Sugar
Kosher salt
Tomato
Green bell pepper
Red onion
Castelvetrano olives

GAME PLAN

While orzo cooks:
■ Make crab mixture.
While crab mixture stands:
■ Make dressing.

Quick & Easy • Gluten Free

Shrimp-Mango Stir-Fry + Rice Noodles + Cucumber Salad

5 ounces uncooked rice noodles
3 tablespoons water
4 teaspoons fresh lime juice
2 teaspoons brown sugar
2 teaspoons fish sauce
½ teaspoon cornstarch
¼ teaspoon crushed red pepper
¼ teaspoon freshly ground black pepper
12 ounces large shrimp, peeled and deveined
1 tablespoon canola oil, divided
1 cup sliced yellow onion
1 cup sliced red bell pepper
1 tablespoon minced peeled fresh ginger
1 cup cubed peeled ripe mango
½ cup torn basil leaves

1. Prepare noodles according to package directions. Drain.
2. Combine 3 tablespoons water and next 4 ingredients in a bowl. Set aside.
3. Combine red pepper, black pepper, and shrimp in a bowl; toss to coat.
4. Heat a wok or a large skillet over high heat. Add 1½ teaspoons oil; swirl. Add shrimp mixture; cook 3 minutes or until shrimp are almost done, turning once. Remove shrimp mixture from pan. Add 1½ teaspoons oil to pan; swirl. Add onion, bell pepper, and ginger; cook 2 minutes. Return shrimp mixture and juice mixture to pan. Add mango; cook 1 minute or until liquid thickens slightly and shrimp are done. Sprinkle with basil. Serve over noodles. Serves 4 (serving size: about ⅔ cup noodles and 1 cup shrimp mixture)

CALORIES 275; **FAT** 4.7g (sat 0.4g, mono 2.4g, poly 1.2g); **PROTEIN** 13g; **CARB** 45g; **FIBER** 2g; **CHOL** 107mg; **IRON** 1mg; **SODIUM** 369mg; **CALC** 82mg

continued

Shaved Cucumber and Red Onion Salad

Combine 3 tablespoons rice vinegar, 1 tablespoon dark sesame oil, 1 teaspoon sugar, ¼ teaspoon freshly ground black pepper, and a dash of salt in a medium bowl, stirring with a whisk. Add 2 cups thinly sliced English cucumber and 1 cup very thinly sliced red onion; toss to coat. Serves 4 (serving size: about ⅔ cup)

CALORIES 53; FAT 3.5g (sat 0.5g); SODIUM 32mg

SHOPPING LIST

Shrimp-Mango Stir-Fry with Rice Noodles

Rice noodles
Lime
Brown sugar
Fish sauce
Cornstarch
Crushed red pepper
12 ounces shrimp
Canola Oil
Yellow onion
Red bell pepper
Ginger
Mango
Fresh basil

Shaved Cucumber and Red Onion Salad

Rice vinegar
Dark sesame oil
Sugar
English cucumber
Red onion

GAME PLAN

While noodles cook:
■ Prepare juice mixture.
■ Prepare cucumber salad.
■ Cook stir-fry.

Kid Friendly • Quick & Easy

Coconut Chicken Strips + Basmati Rice + Broccolini

¾ cup brown basmati rice
1 cup unsalted chicken stock (such as Swanson)
2 tablespoons chopped fresh cilantro
1 tablespoon fresh lime juice
⅓ cup all-purpose flour
2 large egg whites, lightly beaten
¾ cup panko (Japanese breadcrumbs)
½ cup finely shredded unsweetened coconut
1 pound skinless, boneless chicken breast, cut lengthwise into 12 (½-inch-thick) strips
¼ teaspoon freshly ground black pepper
⅛ teaspoon kosher salt
Cooking spray
3 tablespoons canola mayonnaise
2 teaspoons rice vinegar
2 teaspoons Sriracha (hot chile sauce)
2 teaspoons lower-sodium soy sauce

1. Preheat oven to 450°. Place a foil-lined baking sheet in oven as it preheats.
2. Bring rice and stock to a boil in a small saucepan; cover, reduce heat to low, and simmer 25 minutes. Remove from heat; cover and let stand 5 minutes. Stir in cilantro and lime juice.
3. Place flour in a shallow dish. Place egg whites in a shallow dish. Combine panko and coconut in a shallow dish. Sprinkle chicken with pepper and salt. Dredge half of chicken in flour; dip in egg whites. Dredge in panko mixture, pressing to adhere. Place chicken on prepared baking sheet; coat chicken with cooking spray. Repeat procedure with remaining chicken. Bake at 450° for 6 minutes on each side or until done. Combine mayonnaise and remaining ingredients in a small bowl. Serve chicken with

---

dipping sauce and rice. Serves 4 (serving size: about 3 chicken strips, ½ cup rice, and about 1 tablespoon sauce)

CALORIES 452; FAT 13.8g (sat 6.6g, mono 3.3g, poly 2g); PROTEIN 33g; CARB 46g; FIBER 4g; CHOL 73mg; IRON 2mg; SODIUM 509mg; CALC 26mg

SHOPPING LIST

Coconut Chicken Strips with Basmati Rice

Brown basmati rice
Unsalted chicken stock
Fresh cilantro
Lime
All-purpose flour
Eggs
Panko
Coconut
1 pound skinless, boneless chicken breasts
Kosher salt
Canola mayonnaise
Rice vinegar
Sriracha
Lower-sodium soy sauce

Sesame Broccolini

Broccolini
Sesame seeds
Dark sesame oil

GAME PLAN

While rice cooks:
■ Prepare chicken strips.
While chicken cooks:
■ Make dipping sauce.
■ Cook Broccolini.

Sesame Broccolini

Bring a large saucepan of water to a boil over high heat. Add 1 pound trimmed Broccolini; cook 3½ minutes or until crisp-tender. Drain. Combine 1½ tablespoons lightly toasted sesame seeds, 1 teaspoon dark sesame oil, and ¼ teaspoon kosher salt in a large bowl. Add Broccolini to bowl; toss gently to coat. Serves 4 (serving size: 4 ounces)

CALORIES 76; **FAT** 2.8g (sat 0.4g); **SODIUM** 154mg

FRESH RIGHT NOW

MAGICAL MUSHROOMS

Morels evoke springtime in the woods.

Morel madness sets in with seasonal-food fiends this time of year. If you haven't had a fresh morel, the $30-a-pound price might seem insane. But you don't need many to get that morel essence, and they're not heavy. What you get is this: a delightfully chewy texture and woodsy, almost smoky flavor in a mushroom that has a pleasing honeycomb texture. If you need to economize, you can use half cremini or button mushrooms. The bold woodsy taste will suffuse the dish, and you'll now be a morel fiend.

CLEAN FRESH MORELS WITH A QUICK DUNK-AND-SWISH IN A BOWL OF WATER, AS WOODLAND DEBRIS COLLECTS IN THE HONEYCOMBS. PAT DRY.

Spring Pasta with Morels

Hands-on: 24 min. Total: 24 min. *If you substitute dried morels for fresh, a 2.5-ounce package will work.*

1 tablespoon butter
¼ cup minced shallots
1 tablespoon chopped fresh thyme
½ teaspoon kosher salt
6 ounces fresh morel mushrooms, cleaned and trimmed
¾ cup unsalted chicken stock (such as Swanson)
12 cups water
12 ounces asparagus, trimmed
1 (12-ounce) package fresh fettuccine
¼ cup half-and-half
1 teaspoon grated lemon rind
3 ounces ⅓-less-fat cream cheese, softened
½ teaspoon freshly ground black pepper
2 tablespoons tarragon leaves

1. Melt butter in a large skillet over medium-high heat. Add shallots, thyme, salt, and mushrooms; sauté 4 minutes. Add stock. Bring to a boil; reduce heat, and simmer until liquid is reduced by half (about 2 minutes). Remove from heat.

2. Bring 12 cups water to a boil in a Dutch oven. Shave asparagus into thin strips using a vegetable peeler. Add pasta to pan; cook 2 minutes. Add asparagus; cook 2 minutes. Drain.

3. Return mushroom mixture to medium-high heat; add half-and-half and lemon rind. Add cream cheese and pepper, stirring with a whisk until smooth. Add mushroom mixture to pasta mixture in Dutch oven; toss to combine. Top with tarragon. Serves 6 (serving size: 1½ cups)

CALORIES 359; **FAT** 8.1g (sat 5.3g, mono 1.7g, poly 0.6g); **PROTEIN** 18g; **CARB** 49g; **FIBER** 3g; **CHOL** 64mg; **IRON** 3mg; **SODIUM** 313mg; **CALC** 72mg

PASTA PERFECT, LIKE MANY OF THEIR FELLOW FUNGI, MORELS ARE RIGHT AT HOME WITH NOODLES AND CREAMY SAUCE.

25 MAINS IN 25 MINUTES OR LESS

From the heat of the kitchen to the fun of the table *lickety-split*

QUICKER COMFORTS

All the pleasures of slow-cooked, family-friendly classics are here, served up in far less time.

Kid Friendly • Quick & Easy

Chicken-Broccoli Mac and Cheese with Bacon
(pictured on page 220)

Hands-on: 25 min. Total: 25 min.

6 ounces uncooked large or regular elbow macaroni
3 cups prechopped broccoli florets
3 bacon slices, coarsely chopped
12 ounces skinless, boneless chicken breast, cut into 1/2-inch pieces
1 teaspoon kosher salt, divided
1 tablespoon minced fresh garlic
1/8 teaspoon ground turmeric
1 1/4 cups 1% low-fat milk
1 cup unsalted chicken stock (such as Swanson)
1/4 cup plus 1 teaspoon all-purpose flour
5 ounces sharp cheddar cheese, shredded (about 1 1/4 cups)

1. Preheat broiler to high.
2. Cook pasta according to package directions, omitting salt and fat. Add broccoli to pan during last 2 minutes of cooking. Drain.
3. While pasta cooks, place bacon in a large ovenproof skillet over medium-high heat; cook 4 minutes or until browned, stirring occasionally. Remove bacon from pan with a slotted spoon; reserve 1 1/2 teaspoons drippings in pan. Sprinkle chicken with 1/4 teaspoon salt. Add chicken to drippings in pan; cook 4 minutes. Sprinkle with garlic; cook 2 minutes, stirring occasionally. Sprinkle with turmeric; cook 30 seconds, stirring frequently.
4. Combine 3/4 teaspoon salt, milk, stock, and flour, stirring with a whisk. Add milk mixture to pan; bring to a boil, stirring frequently. Cook 2 minutes or until thickened. Add pasta mixture and 2 ounces cheese; toss to coat. Sprinkle with 3 ounces cheese and bacon. Broil 2 minutes or until cheese melts and just begins to brown. Serves 6 (serving size: about 1 1/3 cups)

CALORIES 343; FAT 12.2g (sat 6.5g, mono 3.7g, poly 0.9g); PROTEIN 26g; CARB 31g; FIBER 2g; CHOL 64mg; IRON 2mg; SODIUM 647mg; CALC 265mg

Kid Friendly • Quick & Easy

Chicken with Mashed Potatoes and Gravy

Hands-on: 24 min. Total: 24 min.
The gravy is the standout, perfect for stirring into mashed potatoes. Serve with quick-cooking greens like spinach or kale for an easy, family-friendly meal.

4 (6-ounce) skinless, boneless chicken breast halves
1 teaspoon freshly ground black pepper, divided
1/4 teaspoon salt, divided
1/4 cup quick-mixing flour (such as Wondra), divided
2 tablespoons canola oil, divided
2 tablespoons unsalted butter, divided
1 1/2 cups unsalted chicken stock (such as Swanson)
12 ounces frozen mashed potatoes (such as Ore-Ida Steam n' Mash)
1/3 cup whole milk
2 tablespoons chopped fresh flat-leaf parsley

1. Sprinkle chicken with 1/2 teaspoon pepper and 1/8 teaspoon salt. Place 2 tablespoons flour in a shallow dish. Dredge chicken in flour. Heat a large skillet over medium-high heat. Add 1 tablespoon oil and 1 tablespoon butter to pan; swirl to coat. Add chicken to pan; cook 5 minutes on each side or until done. Remove chicken from pan; keep warm.
2. Add 1 tablespoon oil to pan; swirl to coat. Add 2 tablespoons flour to pan; cook 30 seconds, stirring occasionally. Add stock to pan; bring to a boil, stirring with a whisk until smooth. Reduce heat; simmer 2 minutes. Stir in 1/4 teaspoon pepper and 1/8 teaspoon salt.
3. Cook potatoes according to package directions. Combine potatoes, 1/4 teaspoon pepper, 1 tablespoon

butter, and milk in a medium bowl; mash to desired consistency. Serve with chicken and gravy. Sprinkle with parsley. Serves 4 (serving size: 1 chicken breast half, about ½ cup potatoes, and about ¼ cup gravy)

CALORIES 428; FAT 17.9g (sat 5.5g, mono 7.4g, poly 2.9g); PROTEIN 41g; CARB 23g; FIBER 2g; CHOL 126mg; IRON 2mg; SODIUM 635mg; CALC 81mg

Kid Friendly • Quick & Easy
Make Ahead

Louisiana-Style Chicken Soup

Hands-on: 16 min. Total: 25 min.
OK, so technically we can't call this a gumbo because there is no roux. But it certainly tastes like a gumbo, right down to the Cajun trinity of onion, celery, and green bell pepper. Serve with a crusty baguette for mopping up every last delicious drop.

1 teaspoon canola oil
12 ounces skinless, boneless chicken thighs, cut into bite-sized pieces
½ teaspoon kosher salt
2 tablespoons unsalted tomato paste
1½ teaspoons salt-free Cajun seasoning
¼ teaspoon crushed red pepper
1 (8-ounce) container prechopped fresh onion, celery, and green bell pepper mix
1 (3-ounce) andouille sausage link, diced
1 bay leaf
1 (28-ounce) container unsalted chicken stock
1 cup frozen cut okra, thawed
1 cup water
⅔ cup precooked brown basmati rice (such as Uncle Ben's Ready Rice)
3 tablespoons chopped fresh flat-leaf parsley

1. Heat a medium saucepan over high heat. Add oil to pan; swirl to coat. Sprinkle chicken with salt. Add chicken to pan; cook 3 minutes, stirring once. Remove chicken from pan with a slotted spoon; set aside. Add tomato paste and next 5 ingredients; cook 6 minutes or until vegetables are tender, stirring frequently. Add stock, okra, and 1 cup water; bring to a boil. Return chicken to pan; stir in rice. Reduce heat, and simmer 9 minutes. Remove pan from heat; stir in parsley. Remove and discard bay leaf. Serves 4 (serving size: 2 cups)

CALORIES 240; FAT 8.3g (sat 2.1g, mono 3.5g, poly 1.4g); PROTEIN 26g; CARB 15g; FIBER 2g; CHOL 93mg; IRON 2mg; SODIUM 598mg; CALC 64mg

Kid Friendly • Quick & Easy

Rustic Tomato Soup with Cheesy Toasts

Hands-on: 23 min. Total: 23 min. The food processor speeds prep by finely chopping the veggies, in turn giving the soup a rustic, crisp-tender texture. If you want a smoother texture, process longer.

½ cup coarsely chopped carrot
½ cup coarsely chopped onion
½ cup coarsely chopped fennel bulb
1 celery stalk, coarsely chopped
1 tablespoon olive oil
1 (26.46-ounce) box unsalted chopped tomatoes (such as Pomì), undrained
1 cup unsalted chicken stock
¾ teaspoon freshly ground black pepper, divided
⅝ teaspoon salt
1 tablespoon butter
8 celery leaves
4 (1.5-ounce) slices diagonally cut whole-grain bread
3 ounces Gruyère cheese, shredded (about ¾ cup)

1. Preheat broiler to high.
2. Place first 4 ingredients in a food processor; process until finely chopped. Heat a large saucepan over medium-high heat. Add oil to pan; swirl to coat. Add vegetable mixture to pan; cook 5 minutes or until crisp-tender, stirring occasionally. Add tomatoes to food processor; pulse until finely chopped. Add tomatoes, stock, ½ teaspoon pepper, and salt to pan; bring to a simmer. Reduce heat to low; simmer 10 minutes. Stir in butter; sprinkle with celery leaves.
3. Place bread on a baking sheet. Broil 2 minutes. Turn bread slices over; sprinkle evenly with cheese. Broil 2 minutes or until cheese is lightly browned. Sprinkle with remaining ¼ teaspoon black pepper. Serve with soup. Serves 4 (serving size: about 1 cup soup and 1 cheese toast)

CALORIES 297; FAT 13.9g (sat 6.3g, mono 5.4g, poly 0.9g); PROTEIN 12g; CARB 34g; FIBER 11g; CHOL 31mg; IRON 2mg; SODIUM 644mg; CALC 375mg

Speedy Cincy Chili

Hands-on: 25 min. Total: 25 min.
Cincinnati chili is a unique style that includes sweet seasonings like cinnamon and chocolate and is served over spaghetti. If you like pungent touches, you can sprinkle some chopped raw onion on top.

6 ounces uncooked spaghetti
2 teaspoons olive oil
½ cup chopped onion
2 teaspoons minced fresh garlic
8 ounces ground sirloin
1 tablespoon chili powder
1 teaspoon ground cumin
1 teaspoon unsweetened cocoa
½ teaspoon salt
½ teaspoon freshly ground black pepper
¼ teaspoon ground cinnamon
¾ cup unsalted chicken stock (such as Swanson)
1 (14.5-ounce) can unsalted diced tomatoes, undrained
1 (15-ounce) can red kidney beans, rinsed and drained
2 teaspoons red wine vinegar
2 ounces cheddar cheese, shredded (about ½ cup)

1. Cook spaghetti according to package directions, omitting salt and fat. Drain.
2. While spaghetti cooks, heat a large skillet over medium-high heat. Add oil to pan; swirl to coat. Add onion and garlic to pan; cook 2 minutes, stirring frequently. Add beef; cook 4 minutes or until browned, stirring to crumble. Add chili powder and next 5 ingredients; sauté 30 seconds. Add stock and tomatoes; bring to a boil. Cover, reduce heat, and simmer 10 minutes. Stir in beans; cook 1 minute or until thoroughly heated. Stir in vinegar. Arrange about ⅔ cup spaghetti on each of 4 plates; top each serving with 1 cup chili and 2 tablespoons cheese. Serves 4

CALORIES 502; **FAT** 13.9g (sat 5.8g, mono 5.5g, poly 0.8g); **PROTEIN** 30g; **CARB** 63g; **FIBER** 12g; **CHOL** 52mg; **IRON** 4mg; **SODIUM** 457mg; **CALC** 151mg

THE FAST PANTRY FOR SPEEDING UP SLOW RECIPES

UNSALTED CHICKEN STOCK: The perfect base for sauces and soups. Choose unsalted so you get rich, roasted-chicken flavor, not a salt bomb.

BUTTER: You don't need a lot. Just a touch adds richness and creamy texture.

GARLIC: Don't underestimate the power of sautéed garlic; it's umami-rich and concentrated so a little permeates the entire dish.

QUICK-MIXING FLOUR: Its superfine texture is great for lightly breading chicken or pork chops and makes for silky-smooth gravy.

CHEDDAR CHEESE: The orange stuff! It instantly conveys gooey goodness and makes food seem more indulgent.

ACCELERATED ASIAN

Takeout favorites made weeknight-fast and anytime-healthy: Sweet and sour chicken, curried noodles, orange beef, and more.

Mushroom Ramen Bowl

Hands-on: 25 min. Total: 25 min.
In place of the normally time-consuming enriched broth, we infuse water with bacon for smoky richness, a trick we learned from chef David Chang.

7 cups water, divided
5 ounces center-cut bacon (about 8 slices)
1 ounce dried shiitake mushrooms
2 tablespoons lower-sodium soy sauce
4 large eggs
2 heads baby bok choy, thinly vertically sliced (about 2 cups)
8 ounces fresh Chinese egg noodles
1 bunch enoki mushrooms, trimmed (about 5 ounces)
1 (8-ounce) can sliced bamboo shoots, drained
4 nori sheets, halved
¼ cup thinly sliced green onions

1. Combine 5 cups water, bacon, and shiitake mushrooms in a saucepan; cover. Bring to a boil; remove from heat. Let stand, covered, 15 minutes. Strain through a fine-mesh sieve over a bowl; discard solids. Return broth to saucepan; stir in soy sauce. Keep warm.
2. Bring 2 cups water to a simmer in a Dutch oven. Place eggs in a vegetable steamer. Place steamer in pan over water; cover. Reduce heat to medium-low. Steam eggs, covered,

6 minutes. Add bok choy to steamer; steam 2 minutes. Set bok choy aside; place eggs in a bowl of ice water. Let eggs stand 1 minute or until slightly cool. Peel and halve eggs.

3. Divide noodles evenly among 4 deep bowls. Top evenly with bok choy, enoki mushrooms, and bamboo shoots. Ladle 1 cup warm broth into each bowl. Arrange nori around edges of bowls. Place 2 egg halves in center of each bowl; top evenly with green onions. Serve immediately. Serves 4

CALORIES 314; FAT 8.3g (sat 2.7g, mono 3.2g, poly 0.9g); PROTEIN 21g; CARB 40g; FIBER 4g; CHOL 194mg; IRON 2mg; SODIUM 642mg; CALC 78mg

Kid Friendly • Quick & Easy

Five-Spice Orange Beef and Broccoli

Hands-on: 20 min. Total: 20 min.
Orange rind and five-spice powder perfume the dish with sweet notes that are countered by a hit of red pepper heat. Decrease the pepper for kids or folks who prefer to walk on the mild side.

1 (1-pound) flank steak, trimmed
3/4 teaspoon five-spice powder
3/4 teaspoon black pepper
1/4 teaspoon kosher salt
2 tablespoons peanut oil, divided
2 cups small broccoli florets
1 1/2 cups vertically sliced onion
8 (1-inch) strips orange rind
4 garlic cloves, thinly sliced
1/2 cup unsalted beef stock
3 tablespoons orange juice
3 tablespoons hoisin sauce
1 tablespoon lower-sodium soy sauce
2 teaspoons rice vinegar
1 teaspoon cornstarch
3/4 teaspoon crushed red pepper
1 (8.8-ounce) package precooked white rice

1/2 cup sliced green onions
2 tablespoons toasted sesame seeds

1. Sprinkle steak evenly with five-spice powder, black pepper, and salt. Heat a large wok or skillet over high heat. Add 1 tablespoon oil to pan; swirl to coat. Add steak; cook 4 minutes on each side or until browned. Remove steak from pan; let stand 5 minutes. Cut steak across grain into thin slices.

2. Return pan to high heat. Add 1 tablespoon oil; swirl. Add broccoli, onion, rind, and garlic; stir-fry 3 minutes or until lightly browned. Combine stock and next 6 ingredients in a bowl, stirring with a whisk. Add stock mixture to pan; cook 1 minute or until slightly thickened.

3. Spoon 1/2 cup rice onto each of 4 plates; top each serving with 3/4 cup broccoli mixture and 3 ounces beef. Sprinkle evenly with green onions and sesame seeds. Serves 4

CALORIES 439; FAT 17.6g (sat 4.2g, mono 6.1g, poly 3.4g); PROTEIN 30g; CARB 39g; FIBER 4g; CHOL 70mg; IRON 4mg; SODIUM 532mg; CALC 91mg

Quick & Easy

Thai Shrimp Curry

Hands-on: 25 min. Total: 25 min.
For a vegetarian version, swap in cubes of drained, pressed tofu for shrimp, and use soy sauce in place of fish sauce.

4 ounces uncooked wide rice sticks (pad Thai noodles)
2 tablespoons peanut oil, divided
1 1/2 pounds large shrimp, peeled and deveined
1 cup vertically sliced onion
1 cup (1/8-inch-thick) diagonally sliced celery
2 tablespoons finely minced lemongrass
1 tablespoon grated peeled fresh ginger
1 cup light coconut milk
2 tablespoons Thai red curry paste

1 1/2 tablespoons brown sugar
2 teaspoons rice vinegar
1 1/2 teaspoons fish sauce
1 cup mung bean sprouts
2 tablespoons thinly sliced fresh basil
2 tablespoons thinly sliced fresh mint
1/4 cup chopped unsalted, dry-roasted cashews
1/4 cup celery leaves
8 lime wedges

1. Cook noodles according to package directions; drain.

2. Heat a large wok or skillet over high heat. Add 1 tablespoon oil to pan; swirl to coat. Add shrimp; stir-fry 4 minutes. Remove shrimp from pan. Return pan to high heat. Add 1 tablespoon oil; swirl to coat. Add onion, celery, lemongrass, and ginger; stir-fry 1 minute. Combine coconut milk and next 4 ingredients in a bowl, stirring with a whisk until sugar dissolves. Add coconut milk mixture to pan; cook 3 minutes or until sauce is slightly thickened.

3. Add noodles, shrimp, bean sprouts, basil, and mint to pan; toss to coat. Divide noodle mixture among 4 shallow bowls; sprinkle with cashews and celery leaves. Serve with lime wedges. Serves 4 (serving size: about 1 1/2 cups noodle mixture, 1 tablespoon cashews, 1 tablespoon celery leaves, and 2 lime wedges)

CALORIES 437; FAT 15.6g (sat 5g, mono 5.6g, poly 3.1g); PROTEIN 28g; CARB 47g; FIBER 3g; CHOL 214mg; IRON 3mg; SODIUM 676mg; CALC 126mg

NO WOK?

No problem! A stainless steel skillet or well-seasoned cast-iron skillet works well in its place. You just need a pan you can get screaming hot so the food gets that delicious stir-fried char.

Kid Friendly • Quick & Easy

Vietnamese Caramel Pork

Hands-on: 20 min. Total: 20 min.
Instead of making caramel from scratch, we use brown sugar, which is much quicker.

1 tablespoon dark sesame oil
1 (1-pound) pork tenderloin, trimmed and cut into 1-inch pieces
1 cup chopped onion
1 cup chopped carrot
1 tablespoon minced peeled fresh ginger
5 garlic cloves, thinly sliced
1 cup unsalted chicken stock (such as Swanson)
3 tablespoons dark brown sugar
1 tablespoon fish sauce
1 tablespoon lower-sodium soy sauce
2 teaspoons cornstarch
2 teaspoons rice vinegar
1/2 teaspoon crushed red pepper
1 (8.8-ounce) package precooked white rice
1 cup thinly sliced napa (Chinese) cabbage
1/4 cup chopped unsalted roasted peanuts
1/4 cup cilantro leaves
4 lime wedges

1. Heat a wok or large skillet over high heat. Add oil to pan; swirl to coat. Add pork; stir-fry 6 minutes, browning on all sides. Remove pork from pan. Add onion, carrot, ginger, and garlic to pan; stir-fry 2 minutes. Combine stock and next 6 ingredients in a bowl, stirring with a whisk. Add stock mixture to pan; bring to a boil. Reduce heat; simmer 4 minutes or until sauce is thick and bubbly. Return pork to pan; cook 1 minute, stirring to coat.
2. Spoon 1/2 cup rice onto each of 4 plates; top each serving with 3/4 cup pork mixture and 1/4 cup cabbage. Sprinkle each serving with 1 tablespoon peanuts and 1 tablespoon cilantro. Serve with lime wedges. Serves 4

CALORIES 402; **FAT** 10.8g (sat 2g, mono 4.6g, poly 3.4g); **PROTEIN** 31g; **CARB** 45g; **FIBER** 3g; **CHOL** 74mg; **IRON** 3mg; **SODIUM** 618mg; **CALC** 68mg

Kid Friendly • Quick & Easy

Sweet and Sour Chicken

Hands-on: 23 min. Total: 23 min.
Powdered peanut butter (which you'll find on the nut butters aisle) adds richness here; if you'd rather not use it, sub more flour. Find plum sauce in the Asian foods section.

1/4 cup mirin (sweet rice wine) or 1/4 cup dry sherry mixed with 2 teaspoons sugar
1 large egg, lightly beaten
1 pound skinless, boneless chicken breast tenders, cut into (2-inch) pieces
1/4 cup powdered peanut butter
3 tablespoons quick-mixing flour (such as Wondra)
3 tablespoons cornstarch
1 tablespoon sugar
3 tablespoons canola oil
3/4 cup sliced green onions
1 red bell pepper, chopped
5 tablespoons water
3 tablespoons ketchup
2 tablespoons Sriracha
1 tablespoon plum sauce
1 teaspoon Worcestershire sauce
1 (8.8-ounce) package precooked white rice
1/4 cup cilantro leaves
2 tablespoons toasted sesame seeds

1. Combine mirin and egg in a medium bowl, stirring with a whisk. Add chicken; toss to coat. Let stand 5 minutes; drain well.
2. Combine powdered peanut butter and next 3 ingredients in a bowl, stirring with a whisk. Add chicken; toss well to coat. Heat a large skillet over medium-high heat. Add oil to pan; swirl to coat. Add chicken; cook 3 minutes on each side or until done. Remove chicken from pan; keep warm.
3. Heat pan over high heat. Add onions and bell pepper; stir-fry 1 minute. Combine 5 tablespoons water and next 4 ingredients in a bowl, stirring with a whisk. Add chicken and ketchup mixture to pan; cook 1 minute, tossing to coat.
4. Place rice on each of 4 plates; top with chicken mixture. Sprinkle evenly with cilantro leaves and sesame seeds. Serves 4 (serving size: 1/2 cup rice, about 1 cup chicken mixture, 1 tablespoon cilantro, and 1 1/2 teaspoons sesame seeds)

CALORIES 474; **FAT** 16.6g (sat 1.8g, mono 8.4g, poly 4.4g); **PROTEIN** 31g; **CARB** 50g; **FIBER** 3g; **CHOL** 77mg; **IRON** 2mg; **SODIUM** 523mg; **CALC** 34mg

THE ESSENTIAL PANTRY FOR SALTY, SWEET, SOUR, AND SPICY FLAVORS

SRIRACHA: A squirt is all you need, saving you the time of working with fresh chiles.

BROWN SUGAR: An easy way to add instant caramel notes

LOWER-SODIUM SOY SAUCE: Deep umami notes with a faint hint of sweetness

DARK SESAME OIL: An intensely toasty oil that coats food with savory richness

RICE VINEGAR: More mellow than most vinegars; a splash brings flavors into equilibrium.

SUPER SPEEDY ITALIAN

Smart techniques allow you to enjoy the old-world dishes you crave—any night of the week.

Kid Friendly • Quick & Easy

Spinach and Pancetta Fake-Out Risotto

Hands-on: 23 min. Total: 23 min.
Precooked rice simmers in slightly thickened chicken stock to mimic the creamy texture of risotto. If you'd like to use your own leftover cooked rice, use 4 cups.

2 ounces prechopped pancetta
2 cups chopped leek (about 2 large)
3 garlic cloves, minced
2 cups unsalted chicken stock (such as Swanson)
1 tablespoon all-purpose flour
1 ounce 1/3-less-fat cream cheese
1 tablespoon thyme leaves
2 (8.8-ounce) pouches precooked white rice (such as Uncle Ben's Original Ready Rice)
1/2 teaspoon kosher salt
1/4 teaspoon freshly ground black pepper
1 (5-ounce) package fresh baby spinach
1 ounce Parmigiano-Reggiano cheese, grated (about 1/4 cup)

1. Heat a large nonstick skillet over medium heat. Add pancetta to pan; cook 4 minutes or until browned, stirring occasionally. Remove pancetta with a slotted spoon, reserving drippings in pan.
2. Add leek and garlic to drippings in pan; cook 5 minutes, stirring occasionally. Combine stock and flour, stirring with a whisk. Add stock mixture to pan; bring to a boil. Add cream cheese and thyme; stir until cheese melts.
3. Knead rice pouches to separate grains. Stir rice, salt, and pepper into pan; simmer 8 minutes or until sauce is thickened and creamy. Gradually add spinach, stirring until spinach wilts. Remove from heat; stir in Parmigiano-Reggiano. Sprinkle with pancetta. Serves 4 (serving size: about 1 1/4 cups risotto and 1 tablespoon pancetta)

CALORIES 337; FAT 11.1g (sat 5.4g, mono 2.6g, poly 1.2g); PROTEIN 13g; CARB 47g; FIBER 3g; CHOL 18mg; IRON 4mg; SODIUM 607mg; CALC 195mg

Quick & Easy

Chicken Scaloppine with Peperonata

Hands-on: 22 min. Total: 22 min.
Thin chicken cutlets cook in butter for a rich, savory flavor, while bell peppers stew in fruity olive oil.

2 tablespoons extra-virgin olive oil
1 large red bell pepper, cut into 1/2-inch-wide strips
1 large yellow bell pepper, cut into 1/2-inch-wide strips
1 cup vertically sliced yellow onion
3 garlic cloves, thinly sliced
1 cup halved grape tomatoes
2 tablespoons thinly sliced fresh basil
2 teaspoons balsamic vinegar
3/4 teaspoon kosher salt, divided
2 (8-ounce) skinless, boneless chicken breast halves
1/2 teaspoon freshly ground black pepper
3 tablespoons all-purpose flour
1 1/2 tablespoons butter

1. Heat a large skillet over medium heat. Add oil to pan; swirl to coat. Add bell peppers; cook 3 minutes, stirring occasionally. Add onion and garlic; cook 10 minutes, stirring occasionally. Add tomatoes; cook 1 minute or until tomatoes wilt. Remove from heat; stir in basil, vinegar, and 1/4 teaspoon salt.
2. While pepper mixture cooks, cut each breast half in half horizontally to form 4 cutlets. Cover cutlets with plastic wrap; pound to 1/3-inch thickness with a meat mallet or small heavy skillet. Discard plastic wrap; sprinkle chicken evenly with 1/2 teaspoon salt and black pepper. Dredge in flour; shake off excess. Melt butter in a large skillet over medium-high heat. Add chicken; cook 2 minutes on each side or until golden and done. Serve chicken with bell pepper mixture. Serves 4 (serving size: 1 cutlet and 3/4 cup peperonata)

CALORIES 300; FAT 14.3g (sat 4.4g, mono 6.9g, poly 1.4g); PROTEIN 26g; CARB 16g; FIBER 3g; CHOL 84mg; IRON 1mg; SODIUM 537mg; CALC 32mg

CUTLETS ARE QUICKER

Because chicken breasts have ballooned in size, we often split them in half to form cutlets—more reasonable portions that cook twice as fast as whole breasts.

Linguine with Ricotta Meatballs

Hands-on: 25 min. Total: 25 min.

Fresh pasta takes only 2 to 3 minutes to cook. Bring your pot of water to a boil early, and drop the pasta in just before the meatballs are finished so that everything is done at the same time. Ricotta cheese makes the meatballs light and tender and not too dense; they're a bit too fragile to toss with the pasta, so they're scooped out of the sauce, and then placed on top at the end. If you can't find fresh linguine, use fresh fettuccine.

1 (9-ounce) package refrigerated fresh linguine
1 ounce pecorino Romano cheese, grated and divided (about ¼ cup)
½ cup panko
⅓ cup part-skim ricotta cheese
8 ounces ground sirloin (90% lean)
1 large egg, lightly beaten
1 garlic clove, grated
Cooking spray
2 cups lower-sodium marinara sauce (such as Dell'Amore)
Small basil leaves (optional)

1. Cook pasta according to package directions, omitting salt and fat; drain and keep pasta warm.
2. While water for pasta comes to a boil, combine 2 tablespoons pecorino Romano, panko, and next 4 ingredients in a medium bowl. Shape mixture into 16 (1-inch) meatballs. Heat a large skillet over medium-high heat. Coat pan with cooking spray. Add meatballs to pan; cook 6 minutes, turning to brown on all sides. Add marinara; bring to a boil. Cover, reduce heat to medium, and cook 5 minutes or until meatballs are done. Remove pan from heat; remove meatballs from pan with a slotted spoon. Add pasta to pan; toss to coat. Top with meatballs and

2 tablespoons pecorino Romano. Garnish with basil, if desired. Serves 4 (serving size: about 1 cup pasta mixture, 4 meatballs, and 1½ teaspoons cheese)

CALORIES 459; **FAT** 15g (sat 5.3g, mono 6.9g, poly 1.1g); **PROTEIN** 26g; **CARB** 50g; **FIBER** 5g; **CHOL** 129mg; **IRON** 2mg; **SODIUM** 623mg; **CALC** 134mg

Prosciutto-Arugula Pizza

Hands-on: 20 min. Total: 20 min.

We love the thin crust of this pizza, which cooks up fast and as crisp as a cracker. After tasting many lower-sodium marinara sauces, we named Dell'Amore the winner for taste; the numbers are good, too, with sodium counts far lower than average.

½ cup lower-sodium marinara sauce (such as Dell'Amore)
1 (8-ounce) thin pizza crust (such as Mama Mary's Thin & Crispy)
4 ounces fresh mozzarella cheese, thinly sliced
2 ounces very thinly sliced prosciutto, torn into ½-inch-wide strips
1½ teaspoons canola oil
1 teaspoon fresh lemon juice
⅛ teaspoon kosher salt
⅛ teaspoon freshly ground black pepper
1⅓ cups baby arugula

1. Preheat oven to 450°.
2. Spread sauce over crust, leaving a ½-inch border; top evenly with mozzarella. Place pizza directly on middle oven rack. Bake at 450° for 10 minutes or until bottom of crust is browned and cheese melts. Remove pizza from oven; blot away any liquid from cheese using a paper towel. Top pizza with prosciutto.
3. Combine oil, juice, salt, and pepper in a medium bowl. Add arugula; toss well to coat. Arrange arugula

mixture over pizza. Cut pizza into 8 slices. Serves 4 (serving size: 2 slices)

CALORIES 322; **FAT** 15.9g (sat 5.3g, mono 8.1g, poly 1.8g); **PROTEIN** 13g; **CARB** 31g; **FIBER** 2g; **CHOL** 31mg; **IRON** 2mg; **SODIUM** 556mg; **CALC** 47mg

Eggplant Parmesan with Parsley Orzo

Hands-on: 25 min. Total: 25 min.

Removing intermittent strips of eggplant skin not only makes this dish easier to cut and eat but also retains some of the great flavor that's in the peel.

1 cup uncooked orzo pasta
¼ cup chopped fresh flat-leaf parsley
1 tablespoon extra-virgin olive oil
½ teaspoon kosher salt, divided
1 medium eggplant
3 tablespoons all-purpose flour
1 teaspoon water
1 large egg
¾ cup panko
½ teaspoon dried oregano
1 ounce Parmigiano-Reggiano cheese, grated (about ¼ cup)
Cooking spray
4 ounces fresh mozzarella cheese, thinly sliced
1⅓ cups lower-sodium marinara sauce
½ teaspoon black pepper

1. Arrange oven rack 10 inches below broiler element. Preheat broiler to high.
2. Cook orzo according to package directions, omitting salt and fat. Drain and return to pan. Add parsley, oil, and ¼ teaspoon salt; toss.
3. While orzo cooks, cut top and bottom off eggplant. Partially peel eggplant lengthwise with a vegetable peeler, leaving long purple stripes. Cut eggplant crosswise into 8 (½-inch-thick) slices; sprinkle with ¼

teaspoon salt. Place flour in a shallow dish. Combine 1 teaspoon water and egg in another shallow dish, stirring with a whisk. Combine panko, oregano, and Parmigiano-Reggiano in another shallow dish.

4. Dredge eggplant in flour, dip in egg mixture, and dredge in panko mixture, gently pressing mixture to adhere. Arrange on a baking sheet coated with cooking spray. Coat tops of eggplant slices with cooking spray. Broil 3 minutes on each side or until browned and tender but firm. Top evenly with mozzarella; broil 1 minute or until cheese melts.

5. Heat marinara in microwave at HIGH 1 minute or until thoroughly heated. Arrange ½ cup orzo mixture on each of 4 plates; top each serving with 2 eggplant slices and ⅓ cup marinara. Sprinkle evenly with pepper. Serves 4

CALORIES 464; **FAT** 17g (sat 6g, mono 7.3g, poly 1.5g); **PROTEIN** 19g; **CARB** 59g; **FIBER** 8g; **CHOL** 74mg; **IRON** 2mg; **SODIUM** 591mg; **CALC** 125mg

FRESH, SUN-KISSED FLAVORS

FRESH BASIL: An instant way to Italian-up a dish. If pressed for time, skip chopping and roughly tear leaves over the dish.

MARINARA SAUCE: A good brand offers fresh tomato flavor without tons of salt. (We like Dell'Amore marinara.)

BALSAMIC VINEGAR: Sweet and tangy, with winelike complexity

GRATING CHEESES: Reach for Parmigiano-Reggiano or pecorino Romano—grate finely so the intense flavor reaches further.

TOMATOES: Speed up the essence of rich tomatoey goodness by stirring a tablespoon of tomato paste into your marinara. Or for juicy bursts of freshness, add halved grape tomatoes.

ZIPPY MEXICAN

These five dinners emerge from the kitchen in a flash. Then, slow things right down at the table, and savor the bold flavors in each bite.

Kid Friendly • Quick & Easy Gluten Free

Chicken Verde Enchiladas

Hands-on: 25 min. Total: 25 min.
How do you shred chicken superfast? Insert two forks into the meat while it's still warm. Then pull apart to shred.

³/₄ cup prechopped onion
³/₄ cup unsalted chicken stock
½ cup salsa verde
⅓ cup finely chopped cilantro stems
2 tablespoons sliced pickled jalapeño pepper
5 teaspoons all-purpose flour
½ teaspoon ground cumin
2 garlic cloves, thinly sliced
8 ounces shredded skinless, boneless rotisserie chicken breast (about 2 cups)
³/₄ cup chopped tomato
3 tablespoons reduced-fat sour cream
1 ripe peeled avocado, coarsely mashed
8 (6-inch) corn tortillas
4 ounces reduced-fat sharp cheddar cheese, shaved
2 tablespoons cilantro leaves

1. Place oven rack in lower third of oven, and preheat broiler to high.
2. Combine first 8 ingredients in a medium saucepan, stirring with a whisk. Bring to a boil; reduce heat, and simmer 4 minutes. Stir in chicken; cook 1 minute or until

heated. Remove from heat. Stir in tomato, sour cream, and avocado.
3. Stack tortillas; wrap stack in damp paper towels, and microwave at HIGH 45 seconds. Spoon 1 cup chicken mixture into an 11 x 7–inch glass or ceramic baking dish. Spoon ⅓ cup chicken mixture in center of each tortilla; roll up. Arrange tortillas, seam sides down, in baking dish. Top with cheese. Broil 3 minutes or until cheese melts. Sprinkle with cilantro leaves. Serves 4 (serving size: 2 enchiladas)

CALORIES 400; **FAT** 18g (sat 6.5g, mono 7.9g, poly 2g); **PROTEIN** 29g; **CARB** 33g; **FIBER** 7g; **CHOL** 75mg; **IRON** 1mg; **SODIUM** 620mg; **CALC** 267mg

RICH, BOLD, LATIN FLAVORS

CUMIN: Earthy and supersavory. Toast to bring out more flavor.

JALAPEÑOS: Mild when you seed, fierce when you don't.

CREMA: A silky, rich finishing sauce. Quick sub: ¼ cup full-fat sour cream mixed with 1 teaspoon lime juice.

LIMES: A bright, zippy splash is as easy as squeezing a wedge over any dish.

CILANTRO: Has a pungent herbal fragrance. Stems are tender and have more robust flavor than leaves; chop or puree into sauces.

Tomatillo-Braised Chicken Thighs

Hands-on: 25 min. Total: 25 min.
The tomatillos in this sauce offer a tangy contrast to the rich chicken flavor. Select firm (but not hard) fruit that feels heavy in your hand and with the papery husk intact.

12 ounces tomatillos (about
   5 medium), husks removed
6 garlic cloves
1 medium jalapeño pepper, halved
   and seeded
1 cup chopped fresh cilantro
1/2 cup unsalted chicken stock (such
   as Swanson)
1 1/2 teaspoons all-purpose flour
8 bone-in chicken thighs (about
   1 3/4 pounds), skinned
1/2 teaspoon salt
1/2 teaspoon freshly ground black
   pepper
2 teaspoons olive oil
1/2 cup grape tomatoes, quartered
3 tablespoons Mexican crema

1. Preheat broiler to high.
2. Place first 3 ingredients on a jelly-roll pan; broil 9 minutes, turning after 5 minutes. Place tomatillo mixture, cilantro, stock, and flour in a blender; process until smooth.
3. Sprinkle chicken with salt and pepper. Heat a large skillet over medium-high heat. Add oil to pan; swirl to coat. Add chicken to pan, meaty side down; cook 5 minutes or until browned. Turn chicken over; top with tomatillo mixture. Partially cover pan; reduce heat to medium-low, and simmer 9 minutes or until chicken is done. Sprinkle with tomatoes; top with crema. Serves 4 (serving size: 2 chicken thighs, about 1/3 cup tomatillo sauce, 2 tablespoons tomatoes, and 2 1/4 teaspoons crema)

CALORIES 302; FAT 16g (sat 3.4g, mono 6g, poly 3.1g); PROTEIN 30g; CARB 9g; FIBER 2g; CHOL 105mg; IRON 2mg; SODIUM 446mg; CALC 34mg

Quick Pork Posole

Hands-on: 22 min. Total: 25 min.
Shave minutes off your prep and cleanup time by asking the butcher in the meat department to cut up the ribs for you.

4 garlic cloves, crushed
2 dried guajillo chiles, stemmed and
   seeded
3 cups unsalted chicken stock (such
   as Swanson), divided
1 (29-ounce) can hominy, drained and
   divided
2 teaspoons canola oil
12 ounces boneless country-style
   pork ribs, cut into bite-sized pieces
1 cup prechopped onion
2 tablespoons oregano leaves
2 teaspoons ground cumin
3/4 teaspoon salt
1/2 teaspoon sugar
1/4 teaspoon crushed red pepper
1 cup dark lager (such as Negra
   Modelo)
1 bay leaf
1/4 cup diced peeled avocado
1/4 cup diced tomato
1/4 cup cilantro leaves
6 lime wedges

1. Heat a medium skillet over high heat. Add garlic and chiles to pan; cook 1 minute, pressing down on chiles to flatten. Add 1 1/2 cups stock to pan; bring to a boil. Remove from heat; let stand 5 minutes. Place chile mixture and 1 cup hominy in a blender, and process until smooth.
2. Heat a large Dutch oven over high heat. Add oil to pan; swirl to coat. Add pork; cook 4 minutes or until browned on all sides. Remove pork from pan; set aside. Add onion and next 5 ingredients to pan; cook 1 minute, stirring. Add beer; cook 30 seconds. Stir in 1 1/2 cups stock, chile mixture, remaining hominy, and bay leaf. Bring to a boil. Cover, reduce heat, and simmer 6 minutes. Stir in

pork; simmer, uncovered, 5 minutes. Discard bay leaf. Serve with avocado, tomato, cilantro, and lime. Serves 6 (serving size: 1 1/4 cups soup; 2 teaspoons each avocado, tomato, and cilantro; and 1 lime wedge)

CALORIES 289; FAT 9.9g (sat 2.7g, mono 4.6g, poly 1.7g); PROTEIN 16g; CARB 28g; FIBER 4g; CHOL 37mg; IRON 3mg; SODIUM 588mg; CALC 74mg

Crispy Vegetable Quesadillas

Hands-on: 21 min. Total: 21 min.
A sparing amount of cooking spray is key to perfectly crisp quesadillas—too much and the fat absorbs into the tortilla. Plus, spreading mashed beans onto each tortilla forms a protective layer that keeps the veggie juices contained (and the tortillas crisp).

1 teaspoon canola oil
1 cup coarsely chopped poblano
   chile
1/2 cup frozen whole-kernel corn
3/4 cup packaged precooked quinoa
   and brown rice (such as Seeds of
   Change)
1/4 teaspoon salt
5 ounces fresh spinach (about 8 3/4
   cups)
3 ounces sharp cheddar cheese,
   shredded (about 3/4 cup)
1 cup canned unsalted black beans,
   rinsed and drained
2 teaspoons Mexican hot sauce
   (such as Cholula)
8 (6-inch) flour tortillas
Cooking spray
6 tablespoons light sour cream
6 lime wedges

1. Place oven rack in middle of oven. Preheat broiler to high. Place a baking sheet on rack in oven (keep pan in oven as it preheats).
2. Heat a large skillet over medium-high heat. Add oil to pan; swirl to

coat. Add poblano and corn; cook 5 minutes, stirring once. Add quinoa, salt, and spinach; sauté 2 minutes or until spinach wilts. Remove from heat; stir in cheese.

3. Combine beans and hot sauce in a small bowl; mash with fork until smooth. Spread 2½ tablespoons bean mixture on each of 4 tortillas; top each with ½ cup spinach mixture and 1 tortilla. Lightly coat quesadillas with cooking spray. Arrange quesadillas on preheated pan in oven; broil 3 minutes or until lightly browned, turning once.

4. Cut each quesadilla into 6 wedges. Serve with sour cream and lime. Serves 6 (serving size: 4 quesadilla wedges, 1 tablespoon sour cream, and 1 lime wedge)

CALORIES 300; **FAT** 10.4g (sat 4.9g, mono 3.3g, poly 0.9g); **PROTEIN** 12g; **CARB** 41g; **FIBER** 6g; **CHOL** 13mg; **IRON** 3mg; **SODIUM** 611mg; **CALC** 187mg

Kid Friendly • Quick & Easy
Gluten Free

Roasted Pork Tenderloin Tacos

Hands-on: 19 min. Total: 24 min.

1 (1-pound) pork tenderloin, trimmed
½ teaspoon freshly ground black pepper
¼ teaspoon salt
1 tablespoon canola oil
2 tablespoons mojo marinade (such as Goya)
½ cup white wine vinegar
3 tablespoons water
1½ tablespoons sugar
1 cup thinly vertically sliced red onion
8 (6-inch) corn tortillas
1 jalapeño pepper, cut into 16 slices
1 ripe avocado, cut into 16 wedges
¼ cup Mexican crema

1. Preheat oven to 425°.
2. Sprinkle pork with pepper and salt.

Heat a large ovenproof skillet over medium-high heat. Add oil to pan; swirl to coat. Add pork; cook 5 minutes, turning to brown on all sides. Place pan in oven. Bake at 425° for 8 minutes or until a thermometer registers 145° (slightly pink); let stand 5 minutes. Cut crosswise into 16 slices. Combine pork and mojo marinade in a medium bowl; toss to coat pork.

3. Combine vinegar, 3 tablespoons water, and sugar in a small saucepan; bring to a boil. Remove from heat; add onion. Let stand 10 minutes; drain.

4. Working with 1 tortilla at a time, toast in a pan or over a flame of a gas burner until tender and blackened in spots. Arrange 2 pork slices in center of each tortilla; top with about 2 tablespoons onion, 2 jalapeño slices, 2 avocado wedges, and 1½ teaspoons crema. Serves 4 (serving size: 2 tacos)

CALORIES 362; **FAT** 16.9g (sat 2.1g, mono 8g, poly 2.8g); **PROTEIN** 28g; **CARB** 27g; **FIBER** 6g; **CHOL** 82mg; **IRON** 2mg; **SODIUM** 423mg; **CALC** 55mg

HIGH-VELOCITY VEGETARIAN

Bring on a variety of fresh farmers' market produce for easy, colorful, truly satisfying meatless meals.

Quick & Easy • Gluten Free
Make Ahead • Vegetarian

Fennel Soup with Almond-Mint Topping

Hands-on: 20 min. Total: 20 min.
Fennel gently cooks until it has a faint lick of licorice, and then gets pureed with white beans for a silky texture.

5 teaspoons olive oil, divided
3 cups sliced fennel bulb
1 cup chopped onion
3 garlic cloves, minced
½ teaspoon kosher salt, divided
2½ cups water
½ teaspoon white wine vinegar
1 (15-ounce) can cannellini beans, rinsed and drained
½ cup sliced almonds, toasted
3 tablespoons small mint leaves
1 teaspoon lemon rind strips
1 ounce vegetarian Parmesan cheese, finely shredded (about ¼ cup)

1. Heat a Dutch oven over medium heat. Add 1 tablespoon oil; swirl to coat. Add fennel, onion, garlic, and ¼ teaspoon salt; cook 1 minute. Reduce heat to medium-low, cover, and cook 6 minutes or until crisp-tender (do not brown), stirring occasionally.

2. Add ¼ teaspoon salt, 2½ cups water, vinegar, and beans. Bring to a boil; cover, reduce heat, and simmer 10 minutes. Place half of mixture in a blender. Remove center piece of blender lid (to allow steam to escape); secure blender lid on blender. Place a clean towel over opening in blender lid (to avoid splatters). Blend until smooth. Pour into a large bowl. Repeat procedure with remaining mixture.

3. Combine almonds, mint, rind, and cheese. Ladle soup into each of 4 bowls; top with almond mixture. Drizzle with 2 teaspoons oil. Serves 4 (serving size: 1⅓ cups soup, 2 tablespoons nut mixture, and ½ teaspoon oil)

CALORIES 237; **FAT** 13.7g (sat 2.5g, mono 8.7g, poly 2g); **PROTEIN** 10g; **CARB** 21g; **FIBER** 7g; **CHOL** 5mg; **IRON** 2mg; **SODIUM** 549mg; **CALC** 205mg

Corn, Squash, and Green Onion Flatbreads

Hands-on: 15 min. Total: 23 min.
If you can't find naan, use four pitas instead.

Cooking spray
1 (8.8-ounce) package whole-wheat tandoori naan bread
8 green onions, cut into 3-inch pieces
1 garlic clove, halved
4 teaspoons extra-virgin olive oil, divided
1 (7-ounce) yellow squash, thinly sliced (about 1 1/3 cups)
1 cup fresh corn kernels
1/2 teaspoon freshly ground black pepper, divided
1/4 teaspoon kosher salt
2.5 ounces vegetarian part-skim mozzarella cheese, shredded (about 2/3 cup)
2 ounces vegetarian fontina cheese, shredded (about 1/2 cup)
2 teaspoons thyme leaves

1. Place rack in upper third of oven. Preheat oven to 400°.
2. Heat a grill pan over high heat. Lightly coat pan with cooking spray. Add naan; grill 1 minute on each side or until grill marks appear. Place naan on a baking sheet. Add onions to pan; grill 2 minutes, turning once.
3. Rub cut sides of garlic over top side of naan. Drizzle with 2 teaspoons oil. Layer squash over naan, leaving a 1/2-inch border. Sprinkle corn over squash; top with onions. Sprinkle with 1/4 teaspoon pepper and salt; top with cheeses. Bake at 400° for 8 minutes. Turn broiler on (do not remove flatbreads from oven); broil 2 minutes or until lightly browned. Sprinkle with 2 teaspoons oil, 1/4 teaspoon pepper, and thyme. Cut each flatbread in half. Serves 4 (serving size: 1/2 flatbread)

CALORIES 397; FAT 16g (sat 5.8g, mono 7.2g, poly 1.4g); PROTEIN 18g; CARB 47g; FIBER 9g; CHOL 26mg; IRON 3mg; SODIUM 607mg; CALC 274mg

Shiitake-Stuffed Butternut with Quinoa Streusel

Hands-on: 15 min. Total: 25 min.
Look for quinoa flakes on the hot cereals aisle. If you can't find them, use all panko for the topping.

1 (2-pound) butternut squash, halved lengthwise and seeded
1 cup hot water
5 teaspoons canola oil, divided
12 ounces sliced shiitake mushroom caps
2 teaspoons grated peeled fresh ginger
4 garlic cloves, minced
3/4 teaspoon kosher salt, divided
1/2 teaspoon freshly ground black pepper, divided
6 ounces baby spinach
3 tablespoons butter, cut into pieces
1/2 cup quinoa flakes
1/4 cup panko
12 ounces Broccolini, trimmed
2 tablespoons water
1 1/2 teaspoons grated lime rind

1. Arrange squash halves, cut sides down, in a microwave-safe baking dish. Add 1 cup hot water; cover with plastic wrap. Microwave at HIGH 15 minutes or until squash is tender. Let stand 3 minutes.
2. While squash cooks, heat a large skillet over medium-high heat. Add 1 tablespoon oil; swirl. Add mushrooms, ginger, and garlic; cook 4 minutes or until mushrooms begin to release their liquid. Add 1/2 teaspoon salt, 1/4 teaspoon black pepper, and spinach, stirring until spinach wilts. Spoon flesh from squash into skillet; stir to combine. Sauté 2 minutes or until liquid evaporates. Spoon mixture into squash halves. Wipe pan clean.
3. Melt butter in a medium skillet over medium heat. Add quinoa flakes and panko, and sauté 2 minutes or until toasted, stirring constantly. Stir in 1/8 teaspoon salt and 1/8 teaspoon pepper.
4. Heat large skillet over medium-high heat. Add 2 teaspoons oil; swirl. Add Broccolini and 2 tablespoons water; cook 4 minutes or until crisp-tender. Add 1/8 teaspoon salt, 1/8 teaspoon pepper, and rind, tossing to coat. Cut each squash half in half. Top evenly with quinoa mixture. Serve with Broccolini. Serves 4 (1 stuffed squash piece and 3 ounces Broccolini)

CALORIES 364; FAT 16g (sat 6g, mono 6g, poly 2.1g); PROTEIN 10g; CARB 51g; FIBER 10g; CHOL 23mg; IRON 5mg; SODIUM 556mg; CALC 192mg

HEARTY MAINLESS MEALS

CANNED BEANS: Incredibly versatile and filling. Puree for an alternative to mashed potatoes, blend into creamy soups, or mash for bean cakes.

MUSHROOMS: Meaty flavors and textures combine in this quick-cooking vegetable.

QUINOA FLAKES: Rolled quinoa grains (similar to rolled oats) cook in a fraction of the time needed for regular quinoa and can be used for stuffings or streusel toppings. Look for them near the hot cereals.

NUTS: A handful bulks up a dish with filling protein. Toast in a skillet for more flavor and crunch.

Black Bean Cakes with Ginger-Cilantro Cream

Hands-on: 23 min. Total: 23 min.
The black bean mixture is delicate. Turn the cakes gently, as they may fall apart. If they do, don't worry—you can press them back together. Serve with a simple salad of lettuce, sliced cucumbers and radishes, and carrot ribbons.

2 tablespoons butter, divided
¹/₂ cup finely chopped onion
1 tablespoon minced fresh garlic
³/₄ teaspoon ground cumin
³/₄ teaspoon kosher salt, divided
¹/₂ teaspoon ground coriander
¹/₂ teaspoon crushed red pepper
¹/₂ teaspoon freshly ground black pepper, divided
¹/₄ cup panko
1 tablespoon fresh lime juice
1 (14.5-ounce) can unsalted black beans, rinsed and drained
2 large eggs, lightly beaten
¹/₄ cup reduced-fat sour cream
2 tablespoons finely chopped fresh cilantro
1 teaspoon grated peeled fresh ginger

1. Heat a medium skillet over medium heat. Add 1 tablespoon butter; swirl until butter melts. Add onion and garlic; cook 4 minutes, stirring occasionally. Stir in cumin, ¹/₂ teaspoon salt, coriander, red pepper, and ¹/₄ teaspoon black pepper; cook 30 seconds, stirring. Remove from heat. Stir in panko and lime juice.
2. Place beans in a bowl; coarsely mash with a fork. Stir in eggs. Stir in onion mixture. Divide bean mixture into 4 portions, gently shaping each into a ¹/₂-inch-thick patty. Heat

pan over medium-high heat. Add 1 tablespoon butter to pan; swirl until butter melts. Add patties to pan; cook 3 minutes on each side or until browned.
3. Combine ¹/₄ teaspoon salt, ¹/₄ teaspoon black pepper, sour cream, cilantro, and ginger. Serve with cakes. Serves 4 (serving size: 1 cake and about ¹/₄ cup sauce)

CALORIES 192; FAT 10.3g (sat 5.6g, mono 2.4g, poly 0.7g); PROTEIN 9g; CARB 16g; FIBER 4g; CHOL 116mg; IRON 2mg; SODIUM 476mg; CALC 86mg

Roasted Mushrooms on White Bean Puree

Hands-on: 23 min. Total: 23 min.

4 large portobello mushroom caps, stemmed
1 cup thin zucchini slices
2 tablespoons extra-virgin olive oil, divided
¹/₂ teaspoon salt, divided
4 garlic cloves, minced and divided
4 ounces fresh mozzarella cheese, thinly sliced
2 teaspoons chopped fresh oregano
2 plum tomatoes, seeded and chopped
¹/₂ cup fat-free milk
¹/₄ teaspoon black pepper
¹/₈ teaspoon white pepper
2 (14.5-ounce) cans unsalted Great Northern beans, rinsed and drained
1 tablespoon chopped fresh flat-leaf parsley
2 teaspoons chopped fresh thyme

1. Preheat oven to 425°.
2. Combine mushrooms, zucchini, and 1 tablespoon oil. Set zucchini aside. Arrange mushrooms, gill sides down, in a single layer on a jelly-roll pan. Bake at 425° for 4 minutes. Turn mushrooms over; sprinkle with ¹/₈ teaspoon salt and 2 garlic cloves. Carefully layer zucchini slices over mushrooms. Bake at 425° for 6 minutes. Top evenly with cheese. Bake 2 minutes or until cheese melts.
3. Combine 1 tablespoon oil, ¹/₈ teaspoon salt, oregano, and tomatoes.
4. Combine ¹/₄ teaspoon salt, 2 garlic cloves, milk, peppers, and beans in a saucepan. Bring to a boil; reduce heat, and simmer 3 minutes. Place mixture in a blender. Remove center piece of blender lid (to allow steam to escape); secure lid on blender. Place a towel over opening in lid (to avoid splatters). Blend until smooth. Add parsley and thyme; pulse 5 times or until well combined. Place puree on each of 4 plates. Arrange mushrooms over puree; top with tomato mixture. Serves 4 (serving size: ¹/₂ cup puree, 1 topped mushroom, and ¹/₄ cup tomato mixture)

CALORIES 305; FAT 16.3g (sat 6.1g, mono 7.3g, poly 1.4g); PROTEIN 12g; CARB 27g; FIBER 9g; CHOL 21mg; IRON 2mg; SODIUM 434mg; CALC 128mg

SHORT ORDER SIDES

28 fresh, fuss-free sides to complement any fast weeknight meal.

1. Asparagus with Dill Vinaigrette

Steam 1 pound pencil-thin asparagus 2 to 3 minutes. Combine 2 tablespoons chopped fresh dill, 2 tablespoons olive oil, 2 tablespoons white wine vinegar, ¼ teaspoon salt, ¼ teaspoon freshly ground black pepper, and 1 minced shallot; toss with cooked asparagus. Serves 4 (serving size: 4 ounces)

CALORIES 88; FAT 6.9g (sat 1g); SODIUM 151mg

2. Citrusy Carrots with Parsley

Cut 1 pound peeled carrots into 1-inch pieces. Bring to a boil in a large skillet with ¼ cup water, ¼ cup fresh orange juice, and 1 tablespoon honey; reduce heat to medium, cover, and cook 8 minutes or until crisp-tender. Drain and toss with 1 tablespoon butter, ¼ cup chopped fresh parsley, ¼ teaspoon kosher salt, and ¼ teaspoon freshly ground black pepper. Serves 4 (serving size: about ½ cup)

CALORIES 97; FAT 3.2g (sat 1.9g); SODIUM 226mg

3. Wilted Kale with Toasted Shallots

Heat 1 tablespoon olive oil in a large skillet over medium-high heat. Add 2 very thinly sliced shallots; sauté 2 minutes or until golden brown. Add 1 pound stemmed chopped Lacinato kale; cook 3 minutes or until kale wilts. Stir in ¼ teaspoon kosher salt and ¼ teaspoon freshly ground black pepper. Serves 4 (serving size: about 1 cup)

CALORIES 97; FAT 4.2g (sat 0.6g); SODIUM 171mg

4. Tarragon-Tomato Salad

Combine 1 minced shallot, 1 tablespoon chopped fresh tarragon, 1½ tablespoons white wine vinegar, ¼ teaspoon kosher salt, and ⅛ teaspoon freshly ground black pepper in a jar; let stand 10 minutes. Add 3 tablespoons olive oil; cover jar tightly, and shake. Arrange 4 medium ripe tomatoes, sliced, on a platter; drizzle with dressing. Serves 4 (serving size: 1 tomato and about 1 tablespoon dressing)

CALORIES 118; FAT 10.4g (sat 1.4g); SODIUM 127mg

5. Corn with Chile-Cheese Mayo

Cook 6 ears shucked corn in boiling water 6 minutes; drain and dry thoroughly. Spread 1 tablespoon canola mayonnaise evenly over each cob. Combine 2 tablespoons chopped fresh cilantro, 1 tablespoon finely grated Parmesan cheese, and ¼ teaspoon chili powder in a small bowl; sprinkle over corn cobs. Serves 6 (serving size: 1 cob)

CALORIES 129; FAT 5.3g (sat 0.5g); SODIUM 135mg

6. Cider Vinegar–Spiked Steamed Baby Spinach

Place 1 (16-ounce) container baby spinach and 1 tablespoon water in a large microwave-safe bowl covered with plastic wrap. Microwave at HIGH 3 minutes or until spinach wilts. Drain well. Toss with 2 tablespoons cider vinegar, ¼ teaspoon crushed red pepper, and ⅛ teaspoon kosher salt. Serves 4 (serving size: ¾ cup)

CALORIES 49; FAT 0g; SODIUM 241mg

7. Cucumber, Black Olive & Mint Salad

Combine 2 cups thinly sliced English cucumber, ¼ cup chopped pitted kalamata olives, 3 tablespoons chopped fresh mint, 2 tablespoons fresh lemon juice, 1 tablespoon olive oil, and ½ teaspoon black pepper. Serves 4 (serving size: about ½ cup)

CALORIES 70; FAT 6.1g (sat 0.8g); SODIUM 164mg

8. Green Beans with Lime

Steam 2 (8-ounce) bags fresh ready-to-cook haricots verts in microwave according to package directions. Toss with 1½ teaspoons olive oil, 1 teaspoon grated lime rind, 1 tablespoon fresh lime juice, ½ teaspoon kosher salt, and ¼ teaspoon crushed red pepper. Serves 4 (serving size: about ⅔ cup)

CALORIES 46; FAT 1.7g (sat 0.2g); SODIUM 240mg

9. Smashed Yukon Gold Potatoes with Gorgonzola & Sage

Place 2 pounds unpeeled Yukon gold potatoes in a saucepan; cover with water. Bring to a boil. Cook 20 minutes or until tender; drain. Place in a large bowl with 1½ tablespoons butter, ½ cup 1% low-fat milk, ½ teaspoon kosher salt, and ½ teaspoon freshly ground black pepper. Mash coarsely with a potato masher. Fold in ¼ cup crumbled Gorgonzola or other blue cheese and 1 tablespoon chopped fresh sage. Serves 6 (serving size: about ¾ cup)

CALORIES 192; FAT 4.6g (sat 3g); SODIUM 185mg

10. Green Bean, Arugula & Clementine Toss

Steam 2 (8-ounce) packages ready-to-cook fresh haricot verts in the microwave according to package directions; halve beans crosswise. Cool 5 minutes; toss with 3 cups arugula, the segments of 2 clementines, 2 tablespoons olive oil, 4 teaspoons rice vinegar, and ¼ teaspoon salt. Serves 4 (serving size: about 1 cup)

CALORIES 108; FAT 6.9g (sat 0.9g); SODIUM 152mg

11. Gingered Sweet Potatoes

Pierce 4 sweet potatoes with a fork. Microwave at HIGH 10 to 12 minutes or until tender, turning over halfway through. Peel, cut into large chunks, and process in a food processor with ⅓ cup fresh orange juice, 1½ tablespoons grated peeled fresh ginger, and 1 teaspoon grated orange rind until smooth. Stir in ½ teaspoon kosher salt and ½ teaspoon freshly ground black pepper. Serves 4 (serving size: about ⅔ cup)

CALORIES 115; **FAT** 0.2g (sat 0.1g); **SODIUM** 282mg

12. Edamame with Lime-Sesame Salt

Combine 2 tablespoons toasted sesame seeds, 2 tablespoons grated lime rind, and ⅜ teaspoon kosher salt on a cutting board; rock knife over mixture to crush some of the sesame seeds. Toss sesame mixture with 2 cups cooked shelled edamame. Serves 4 (serving size: ½ cup)

CALORIES 127; **FAT** 5.2g (sat 0.3g); **SODIUM** 211mg

13. Sesame Broccoli

Toast 3 tablespoons sesame seeds in a skillet over medium heat 2 to 3 minutes, until fragrant. Combine 2 tablespoons toasted sesame seeds, 2 tablespoons rice vinegar, 1 tablespoon dark sesame oil, and 1 tablespoon lower-sodium soy sauce. Toss with 1 (12-ounce) package fresh broccoli florets, steamed according to package directions. Garnish with 1 tablespoon toasted sesame seeds, if desired. Serves 4 (serving size: about ¾ cup)

CALORIES 95; **FAT** 7.1g (sat 1g); **SODIUM** 167mg

14. Shaved Fennel with Orange & Olives

Peel and section 2 oranges over a bowl, reserving juices. Shave 1 trimmed fennel bulb on a mandoline; toss with orange sections, juices, 12 pitted and coarsely chopped kalamata olives, and ¼ teaspoon freshly ground black pepper.

Garnish with chopped fennel fronds, if desired. Serves 4 (serving size: about ⅔ cup)

CALORIES 47; **FAT** 1.3g (sat 0g); **SODIUM** 145mg

15. Sautéed Leeks & Radishes

Heat 2 tablespoons olive oil in a large skillet over medium heat. Add ¼ cup minced shallots, ½ teaspoon salt, ¼ teaspoon freshly ground black pepper, and 2 thinly sliced leeks; sauté just until tender (about 4 minutes). Add 2 bunches (1 pound) sliced radishes; sauté 3 minutes. Serves 4 (serving size: about ¾ cup)

CALORIES 113; **FAT** 7g (sat 1g); **SODIUM** 202mg

16. Broccoli Rabe with Golden Raisins

Combine 1 bunch (about 1 pound) trimmed broccoli rabe, cut into thirds; 1 cup unsalted chicken stock; and ½ cup golden raisins in a large skillet over medium-high heat. Cook 10 minutes. Drain, reserving stock; place rabe mixture in a bowl. Return stock to skillet; cook over medium-high heat until reduced by half. Pour over rabe mixture; sprinkle with ½ teaspoon freshly ground black pepper and ⅛ teaspoon kosher salt. Serves 4 (serving size: about ⅔ cup)

CALORIES 84; **FAT** 0.7g (sat 0.1g); **SODIUM** 237mg

17. Chopped Salad with Chive Vinaigrette

Combine 2 tablespoons fresh lemon juice, 1 tablespoon minced fresh chives, 1 teaspoon sugar, ⅜ teaspoon kosher salt, and ¼ teaspoon freshly ground black pepper; whisk in 3 tablespoons olive oil. Toss with 2 chopped romaine hearts, 1 diced cucumber, and 1 diced celery stalk. Serves 4 (serving size: about 1 cup)

CALORIES 123; **FAT** 10.2g (sat 1.4g); **SODIUM** 194mg

18. Herb Salad with Mustard Vinaigrette

Combine 1 teaspoon red wine vinegar, 1 teaspoon fresh orange juice, ½ teaspoon whole-grain

mustard, and ¼ teaspoon salt; whisk in 2 tablespoons olive oil. Pour over 1 (5-ounce) package herb salad; toss to coat. Serves 4 (serving size: about 1 cup)

CALORIES 61; **FAT** 6.8g (sat 0.9g); **SODIUM** 192mg

19. Toasty Tomatoes

Preheat broiler. Combine 1 teaspoon grated lemon rind, ⅛ teaspoon freshly ground black pepper, and 1 minced small garlic clove. Mix in 1½ tablespoons olive oil; toss in ½ cup panko. Arrange 8 halved Roma tomatoes, cut sides up, on a baking sheet; coat lightly with cooking spray. Top each with 1 teaspoon panko mixture; sprinkle 2 teaspoons grated Parmesan and ¼ teaspoon salt evenly over tomatoes; broil 3 minutes or until cheese is bubbly. Serves 4 (serving size: 2 tomato halves)

CALORIES 97; **FAT** 5.6g (sat 0.8g); **SODIUM** 178mg

20. Broiled Artichoke Hearts with Lemon Crumbs

Preheat broiler. Combine ½ cup panko, 1 tablespoon grated Parmesan cheese, 2 teaspoons melted butter, 1 teaspoon grated lemon rind, and ½ teaspoon freshly ground black pepper. Toss 2 (9-ounce) packages thawed frozen artichoke hearts with 1½ teaspoons olive oil and ⅛ teaspoon kosher salt on a baking sheet. Top with crumbs. Broil 6 inches from heat 5 to 6 minutes, until slightly browned. Serves 4 (serving size: about ⅔ cup)

CALORIES 127; **FAT** 5.8g (sat 1.7g); **SODIUM** 201mg

21. Warm-Spiced Okra

Toast ½ teaspoon curry powder, ⅛ teaspoon crushed red pepper, and 1 minced shallot in 2 teaspoons olive oil in a skillet over medium-low heat 2 minutes or until fragrant. Increase heat to high. Add 2 cups okra, halved lengthwise; cook 3 minutes or just until tender. Sprinkle with ¼ teaspoon salt. Serves 4 (serving size: ½ cup)

CALORIES 41; **FAT** 2.4g (sat 0.3g); **SODIUM** 153mg

22. Jicama Slaw

Combine 3 cups julienne-cut peeled jicama, 3 tablespoons chopped fresh cilantro, 3 tablespoons rice vinegar, 1 tablespoon fresh lime juice, ½ teaspoon kosher salt, ¼ teaspoon freshly ground black pepper, and 1 minced seeded jalapeño pepper. Serves 4 (serving size: ¾ cup)

CALORIES 65; **FAT** 0.2g (sat 0g); **SODIUM** 247mg

23. Shaved Yellow Beets and Mint

Shave 4 yellow beets very thinly with a chef's knife or mandoline; toss with 2 teaspoons walnut oil, ½ teaspoon sugar, ⅜ teaspoon kosher salt, ¼ teaspoon freshly ground black pepper, and 12 torn mint leaves. Serves 4 (serving size: about ½ cup)

CALORIES 59; **FAT** 2.4g (sat 0.2g); **SODIUM** 245mg

24. Shredded Cabbage Slaw

Shred ½ head red cabbage and ½ head green cabbage. Combine ½ cup 2% Greek yogurt, 2 tablespoons chopped fresh tarragon, 1½ tablespoons whole-grain Dijon mustard, 1 tablespoon cider vinegar, 1 teaspoon sugar, ½ teaspoon kosher salt, and ½ teaspoon freshly ground black pepper. Toss with cabbage. Serves 4 (serving size: about 1 cup)

CALORIES 92; **FAT** 0.9g (sat 0.4g); **SODIUM** 254mg

25. Steamed Snap Peas with Wasabi Butter

Stir together 1 tablespoon softened butter and 2 teaspoons wasabi powder until well combined. Microwave 1 pound sugar snap peas, covered, at HIGH 3 to 4 minutes, until crisp-tender. Toss with wasabi butter; sprinkle with ¼ teaspoon kosher salt. Serves 4 (serving size: about ¾ cup)

CALORIES 73; **FAT** 3.1g (sat 1.9g); **SODIUM** 170mg

26. Blasted Brussels Sprouts with Teriyaki Glaze

Preheat oven to 450°. Combine 2 tablespoons canola oil and 2 tablespoons lower-sodium teriyaki sauce with 1 pound halved Brussels sprouts on a jelly-roll pan. Bake at 450° for 12 to 15 minutes, until crisp-tender and slightly charred on the edges; stir after 6 minutes of cooking. Serves 4 (serving size: about 1 cup)

CALORIES 118; **FAT** 7.3g (sat 0.6g); **SODIUM** 188mg

27. Zucchini Ribbons with Lemon and Pecorino

Slice 2 zucchini into thin ribbons using a vegetable peeler; toss with 2 tablespoons fresh lemon juice, 2 teaspoons olive oil, ¼ teaspoon freshly ground black pepper, and ⅛ teaspoon kosher salt. Top with 3 tablespoons shaved pecorino Romano cheese. Serves 4 (serving size: about ½ cup)

CALORIES 60; **FAT** 4.3g (sat 1.7g); **SODIUM** 172mg

28. Buttery Mirin Mushrooms

Melt 1 tablespoon butter in a large skillet over medium heat. Add 8 ounces halved button mushrooms and 1 minced garlic clove; cook 3 minutes or until mushrooms release their liquid. Add ¼ cup unsalted chicken stock and 1 tablespoon mirin; cook 2 minutes or until liquid is syrupy. Sprinkle with ⅜ teaspoon kosher salt and ¼ teaspoon freshly ground black pepper. Serves 4 (serving size: about ½ cup)

CALORIES 49; **FAT** 3.1g (sat 1.9g); **SODIUM** 240mg

FROM THE CL GARDEN

PEAS, PLEASE

One of the season's most fleeting treats, fresh peas, with their tender tendrils, are a sweet revelation.

Thoughts of wrinkled peas usually cause wrinkled noses. Just like a minivan full of kids on a cross-country trip, peas lose their sweetness by their journey's end. As with corn, the sugars in peas begin turning to starch the moment you pluck the pod from the vine. That's why most folks just buy frozen and never know how amazingly sweet a fresh-picked pea can be.

Peas are the first seeds sown before winter fully thaws, when daffodils bloom or on St. Patrick's Day. They prefer colder weather, twirl tendrils of self-support as they climb and grow, and feed themselves and neighboring soil by capturing nitrogen from the air. Thomas Jefferson, who grew more than 300 varieties of fruits and vegetables in his Monticello garden, was famous for a friendly race to see who among his Colonial Virginia neighbors would have the pleasure of eating spring's first freshly grown pea.

Every part of the plant is edible, and tasty at that. Young shoots eaten raw or tossed in a stir-fry lend a bright, slight pea flavor. Young, immature pods of some varieties can be eaten whole. Even the white or violet blooms are edible. But the plump, sugar-sweet, faintly grassy peas are the real prize.

To maintain their sweetness for as long as you can after picking, keep your harvests cool. Shell, blanch, and freeze what you don't use immediately. If buying fresh from a local market, pop a few in your mouth before purchasing to test the sweetness level.

Other than providing initial support for tendrils to climb, the hardest part about growing peas is keeping paws off the precious loot. Those sweet shoots were a neon flag for night-grazing deer and rabbits in our garden. Of course, peas' most dangerous predator is the gardener herself. It's hard not to snack while tending to the pea patch.

TOM THUMB PEAS

Container gardeners favor this English heirloom; its dwarf, 8-inch vines need no trellis. The fast-producing pods are full size.

Kid Friendly • Quick & Easy
Gluten Free • Make Ahead

Green Goodness Dip

Hands-on: 10 min. Total: 10 min.
This dip is a riff on the classic green goddess dressing. It's made thicker with a base of pureed peas enriched with Greek yogurt and creamy avocado.

1 cup fresh or frozen, thawed green peas
1 cup plain fat-free Greek yogurt
½ cup flat-leaf parsley leaves
3 tablespoons chopped fresh chives
1 tablespoon chopped fresh tarragon
½ teaspoon kosher salt
¼ teaspoon freshly ground black pepper

2 tablespoons fresh lemon juice
3 canned anchovy fillets, drained
½ ripe peeled avocado

1. Place all ingredients in a food processor; process until smooth. Serves 8. (serving size: ¼ cup)

CALORIES 54; FAT 2.1g (sat 0.3g, mono 1.3g, poly 0.3g); PROTEIN 4g; CARB 5g; FIBER 2g; CHOL 1mg; IRON 1mg; SODIUM 207mg; CALC 35mg

Quick & Easy • Vegetarian

Orecchiette with Cress and Spring Pea Sauce

Hands-on: 12 min. Total: 20 min.
The fresh, vibrant flavors of sweet peas and peppery cress meld beautifully in this simple pasta dish. If you can't find orecchiette, small shell pasta is a good substitute.

1½ cups fresh or frozen green peas
8 ounces orecchiette rigate
3 tablespoons water
2 tablespoons tarragon leaves, divided
1 tablespoon extra-virgin olive oil
1½ teaspoons grated lemon rind
¼ teaspoon kosher salt
¼ teaspoon freshly ground black pepper
1 garlic clove
4 ounces watercress, trimmed
1 tablespoon fresh lemon juice
1 ounce feta cheese, crumbled (about ¼ cup)

1. Bring a large saucepan or Dutch oven of water to a boil. Place peas in a mesh strainer; set in boiling water for 1 minute. Rinse peas under cold water. Place 1 cup peas in a blender or food processor; reserve remaining peas.
2. Cook pasta in the boiling water according to package directions, omitting salt and fat; drain. Rinse under cold water until cool; drain.

3. Add 3 tablespoons water, 1 tablespoon tarragon, oil, rind, salt, pepper, and garlic to peas in blender. Process until smooth. Combine pea mixture and pasta in a large bowl; toss to coat. Add reserved peas, 1 tablespoon tarragon, watercress, and juice; toss gently to combine. Sprinkle with feta; serve immediately. Serves 4 (serving size: ¾ cup)

CALORIES 301; FAT 6g (sat 1.8g, mono 2.8g, poly 0.5g); PROTEIN 12g; CARB 51g; FIBER 4g; CHOL 6mg; IRON 3mg; SODIUM 268mg; CALC 99mg

TWO SPRING FAVORITES, PEAS AND WATERCRESS, COMBINE IN ONE EASY DISH.

TOM THUMB TENDRILS

There's more to peas than what's in the pods; the leaves and curlicue tendrils are edible, too.

THE LESSON: MOIST, FLAVORFUL BROILED FISH

Long before "local" had any cachet, The Cull House, a Long Island bayside hideaway, procured mussels, clams, flounder, and weakfish steps away from its kitchen doors. It's been successful and semisecret for more than 30 years, and one of its main draws is the Broiled Platter, a mainstay of coastal clam shacks.

The broiled platter is a dish that easily translates to home cooking, as broiling is basically the gloriously effortless absence of technique. Because it's so simple, it puts the spotlight on the food; you can't hide your ingredient selections, so make sure to select the superfresh. You need fast-cooking food, a touch of fat, and a good bit of moisture. Your technique is this: Pay attention, and don't burn the food. You'll be rewarded with a fast, easy, delicious dinner.

KEITH'S RECIPE BREAKDOWN

CLAM SHACK–STYLE BROILED FISH
(pictured on page 219)
Hands-on: 18 min. Total: 18 min.

INGREDIENT	AMOUNT	WHY
olive oil	1 tablespoon	The fish is mild. A little flavor from olive oil is welcome.
flounder	4 (6-ounce) fillets	It's dinner.
paprika	½ teaspoon	Honestly, for the color it gives. And it's a nostalgia thing.
shallots	½ cup, thinly sliced (about 2 shallots)	Shallots provide the savory contrast to the white wine in the dish.
melted butter	1 tablespoon	Because it's the universal flavor carrier for broiled fish.
garlic cloves	2, thinly sliced	Same as for shallots. If you want more textural contrast between garlic and shallots, mince the garlic.
dry white wine	½ cup	The moisture helps keep the fish, well, moist.
kosher salt	½ teaspoon	The salt is added at the end to finish. Seasoning the fish ahead of time would start drawing out moisture.
black pepper	¼ teaspoon, freshly ground	Add it with the salt. Grind fresh for best flavor.
flat-leaf parsley	1 tablespoon, coarsely chopped	Adds a fresh touch.
lemon wedges	4	Wedges are the norm for adding a fresh burst to your own taste.

Follow These Steps:

- Place oven rack in middle of oven. Preheat broiler to high.
- Drizzle olive oil in a roasting pan. Pat fish dry with paper towels; arrange fish in pan. Sprinkle fish evenly with paprika. Sprinkle shallots, butter, and garlic around pan. Pour wine into pan around fish. Broil 10 minutes or until fish flakes easily when tested with a fork, basting frequently. Arrange fish on a platter; sprinkle evenly with salt and pepper. Stir parsley into pan sauce; drizzle over fish. Serve with lemon wedges. Serves 4 (serving size: 1 fillet, about 2 tablespoons sauce, and 1 lemon wedge)

CALORIES 211; **FAT** 9.6g (sat 3.1g, mono 4.1g, poly 1.1g); **PROTEIN** 22g; **CARB** 4g; **FIBER** 0g; **CHOL** 84mg; **IRON** 1mg; **SODIUM** 404mg; **CALC** 42mg

BROILING IS ONE OF THE EASIEST, TASTIEST WAYS TO COOK LEAN FISH SUCH AS FLOUNDER.

Salsa Flounder

Omit the salt. Use ½ teaspoon salt-free Cajun/Creole seasoning in place of paprika. Use ¾ cup salsa (such as Herdez Salsa Casera) in place of wine. Swap in cilantro for parsley, and serve with lime wedges instead of lemon. Serves 4 (serving size: 1 fillet, about 2 tablespoons sauce, and 1 lime wedge)

CALORIES 201; **FAT** 9.6g (sat 3g); **SODIUM** 568mg

SKILLET ASPARAGUS AND GOAT CHEESE SALAD

From chef Linton Hopkins of Restaurant Eugene in Atlanta

If asparagus were a person in my life," says chef Linton Hopkins, "it'd have to be a beloved aunt." That's how much the James Beard Award–winning chef of Restaurant Eugene and Holeman & Finch in Atlanta looks forward to the annual visit of peak-season asparagus, and he accordingly shows it the utmost affection and respect. Hopkins stresses the importance of keeping things simple: Asparagus doesn't need a lot of embellishment for its uniquely verdant flavor to shine.

For this salad, Hopkins gives the asparagus a quick sear in a cast-iron skillet to put a little flavorful char on the stalks. A wine-spiked citrus vinaigrette contributes bright, zingy flavor, while creamy goat cheese and toasted pecans add richness and satisfying crunch. Try his original version of the dish this month at Restaurant Eugene.

**Quick & Easy • Gluten Free
Vegetarian**

Skillet Asparagus Salad with Goat Cheese

Hands-on: 25 min. Total: 25 min.

1 teaspoon olive oil
¼ teaspoon freshly ground black pepper
⅛ teaspoon salt
1½ pounds asparagus spears, trimmed (about 30 medium spears)
1 cup water
2 teaspoons julienne-cut orange rind
1 teaspoon julienne-cut lemon rind
¼ cup fresh orange juice
1 teaspoon sugar
1 tablespoon dry white wine
1½ teaspoons fresh lemon juice
½ teaspoon Dijon mustard
¼ teaspoon freshly ground black pepper
⅛ teaspoon salt
5 teaspoons olive oil
2 cups mixed baby salad greens
2 ounces goat cheese, crumbled (about ½ cup)
3 tablespoons chopped pecans, toasted
1 tablespoon tarragon leaves
1 teaspoon finely chopped fresh flat-leaf parsley

1. Combine first 4 ingredients in a large bowl; toss to coat. Heat a large cast-iron skillet over medium-high heat. Add one-third of asparagus mixture; cook 4 minutes or until lightly charred and crisp-tender, stirring occasionally. Remove from pan; set aside. Repeat procedure twice with remaining asparagus mixture.

2. Place 1 cup water in a microwave-safe measuring cup. Microwave at HIGH 2 minutes or until water just boils. Add orange rind; let stand 20 seconds. Drain, reserving rind. Repeat procedure with lemon rind.
3. Combine orange rind, orange juice, and sugar in a small saucepan. Bring to a boil. Reduce heat to medium-low; cook until juice mixture measures about 3 tablespoons (about 5 minutes). Combine wine, lemon juice, mustard, ¼ teaspoon pepper, and ⅛ teaspoon salt in a medium bowl; stir with a whisk. Gradually add 5 teaspoons oil, stirring constantly with a whisk. Stir in orange juice mixture.
4. Place ⅓ cup greens on each of 6 plates. Divide asparagus evenly among salads. Top evenly with cheese, pecans, and tarragon. Stir lemon rind and parsley into orange juice mixture; drizzle dressing over salads. Serves 6

CALORIES 117; **FAT** 8.4g (sat 2.2g, mono 4.6g, poly 1.2g); **PROTEIN** 5g; **CARB** 7g; **FIBER** 3g; **CHOL** 4mg; **IRON** 3mg; **SODIUM** 152mg; **CALC** 57mg

BLANCHING THE CITRUS RIND MELLOWS ITS FLAVOR AND TAMES BITTERNESS.

SHORTCUT STRAWBERRY SHORTCAKES

Whole grains, juicy berries, and a heavenly yogurt cream for 224 calories

There's something magical about a sweet, crumbly biscuit piled high with juicy-plump strawberries and light-as-air whipped cream—it's tasty proof that summer is just around the corner. If only the virtuous strawberry could erase those cream-filled, buttery calories—all 715 of them. When we did the math, project shortcake was on. Could we lighten it in a recipe that takes 25 minutes?

We start with the biscuit. Our trusty drop method reduces prep time by half with a simple trick: Stir cold nonfat buttermilk into melted butter. This creates pockets of butter throughout the whole wheat–flecked batter, allowing us to cut out an entire stick from the original recipe. A little canola oil keeps our shortcakes tender, while brown sugar and vanilla add notes of sweet caramel. Fresh strawberries need no attention; we just sprinkle them with a little sugar to draw out their juicy goodness. The true pleasure of strawberry shortcake, however, is the freshly whipped cream. We couldn't possibly deny this sweet treat its defining element. Heavy cream, though, packs in a hefty 3.5g sat fat per tablespoon, so we stretch each and every drop, adding volume with light, silky 2% reduced-fat Greek yogurt. A touch of sugar helps tame the tang. You get a truly delicious biscuit, berry, and decadent cream combo with almost 500 fewer calories than the original. And it's ready in just 25 minutes.

OURS SAVES
491 calories, 32g total fat, and 21g saturated fat over classic strawberry shortcake

Kid Friendly • Quick & Easy Make Ahead

Fresh Strawberry Shortcakes with Yogurt Cream

Hands-on: 25 min. Total: 25 min.
If you have a minute to spare, swap the vanilla extract for a vanilla bean. Split the bean lengthwise, scrape half of the seeds into the shortcake recipe, and whip the remaining half into the yogurt cream. It will add an extra level of flavor-packed intensity to the recipe.

5.6 ounces unbleached all-purpose flour (about 1¼ cups)
3.6 ounces whole-wheat flour (about ¾ cup)
¼ cup packed brown sugar
2 teaspoons baking powder
¾ teaspoon salt
½ teaspoon baking soda
¼ cup unsalted butter
1¼ cups very cold nonfat buttermilk
2 tablespoons canola oil
1 teaspoon vanilla extract
1½ pounds fresh strawberries
¼ cup sugar, divided
1 teaspoon fresh lemon juice
½ cup plain 2% reduced-fat Greek yogurt
⅓ cup heavy whipping cream

1. Preheat oven to 450°.
2. Weigh or lightly spoon flours into dry measuring cups; level with a knife. Combine flours, brown sugar, baking powder, salt, and baking soda in a large bowl, stirring with a whisk to combine.
3. Place butter in a medium microwave-safe bowl. Microwave at HIGH 1 minute or until melted. Add cold buttermilk, stirring until butter forms small lumps. Add oil and vanilla, stirring to combine.
4. Add buttermilk mixture to flour mixture, stirring just until incorporated (do not overmix) and batter pulls away from sides of bowl. (Batter will be very wet.)
5. Drop batter into 12 mounds (about 2 heaping tablespoonfuls each) onto a baking sheet lined with parchment paper. Bake at 450° for 12 minutes or until golden.
6. While biscuits bake, slice strawberries. Combine strawberries, 2 tablespoons sugar, and lemon juice; toss to coat. Set aside.
7. Place yogurt, cream, and 2 tablespoons sugar in a bowl; beat with a mixer at medium speed until soft peaks form. Split biscuits; fill with berry mixture and cream. Serves 12 (serving size: 1 biscuit, about ⅓ cup strawberries, and about 1½ tablespoons cream mixture).

CALORIES 224; FAT 9.3g (sat 4.3g, mono 3.2g, poly 1.1g); PROTEIN 5g; CARB 32g; FIBER 2g; CHOL 20mg; IRON 1mg; SODIUM 313mg; CALC 106mg

WHIP IT, WHIP IT BETTER

The real deal, with less fat and calories. Here's how.

There are times when nothing but a dollop will do: Plopped over a slice of fresh pie or spread between fudgy layers of cake, real whipped cream is sublime in a way that can't be copied. But with nearly 2 grams of saturated fat per whipped tablespoon, heavy cream can be heavy in ways a healthy cook wants to avoid.

The sexiness comes from the mouthfeel—a silky, butterfat-based texture that simply cannot be replaced. So we don't replace it. Instead, we fluff it up with a little reduced-fat Greek yogurt, whose thick, creamy texture complements the cream. A little sugar is added to maximize volume, and 40% of the calories and nearly half the sat fat are cut. This lighter heavy cream is clean, simple, and delicious—test it for yourself in our strawberry shortcake makeover, page 122.

OURS SAVES
11.5 calories, 1g saturated fat, over classic whipped cream

The Formula

Combine ⅓ cup heavy whipping cream, ½ cup 2% reduced-fat Greek yogurt, and 2 tablespoons sugar in a bowl; beat with a mixer at medium speed until soft peaks form.

MEXICO

A Los Angeles foodie gets a fresh view of the country's coastal cuisine after following his heart to Puerto Vallarta.

By Javier Cabral

Mexican coastal cuisine, with its reliance on vibrant, fresh flavors, has yet to be fully appreciated by the rest of the world. Though the country is surrounded by ocean, meaning a large percentage of its cuisine is seafood-based and inherently healthful, it's often belied by the cheesy, fried misrepresentations found in your average margarita joint stateside.

To put it in perspective, you can buy many types of fresh seafood as easily and cost effectively as you can a fast-food taco combo in the States. What does this mean for visitors in search of a local bite? A plethora of light, delicate seafood renditions of many Americanized Mexican dishes is always available, things like tacos with marinated mahimahi cut off the spit; burritos stuffed with smoked marlin, seared octopus or shrimp, and crisp veggies; and chiles rellenos filled with braised skate in tomato sauce.

I was first introduced to Mexican seafood via my girlfriend, Paola, who was raised in Puerto Vallarta. I'll never forget the first time I visited her family, not just because it was the first time she was bringing home an American boy (a Mexican-American boy, sure, since my parents are from Mexico) but also for the abundance of glorious seafood.

Of the many dishes I tasted that first trip, I quickly found a favorite: Pescado Sarandeado, Puerto Vallarta's specialty dish of wood-grilled fish marinated in a paste of dried chiles, spices, and achiote that you can find in most every restaurant, street-food stand by the beach, and fancy hotel.

Paola comes from a restaurant family. Her grandpa owned one of Puerto Vallarta's oldest seafood restaurants, which was known for its Pescado Sarandeado. Because of this, I experienced the dish there at such a personal level. Moist, wood-grilled snapper almost flaked itself into a taco over warm, pliable corn tortillas, especially when scantly drizzled with an oil-based salsa of crushed toasted chiles de árbol, peanuts, and cacao beans and even more fiery green salsa made of blended raw tomatillos and serrano chiles.

And there's nothing better to cut the heat of the dish (and of the day) than a chilled creamy Horchata de Coco. Here's a lightened-up take on these Puerto Vallarta classics, both ready in less than 25 minutes.

continued

Horchata de Coco

Hands-on: 10 min. Total: 25 min. *This typically sweet drink can be too sweet for some tastes. Feel free to dial back the sugar to 1/2 or 1/3 cup.*

1/2 cup flaked unsweetened coconut
1/2 cup uncooked long-grain white rice
2 cups boiling water
2 cups rice milk
2/3 cup sugar
1/2 teaspoon vanilla extract
1/4 teaspoon ground cinnamon

1. Place coconut and rice in a blender. Add 2 cups boiling water; let stand 15 minutes. Blend 1 minute or until smooth. Strain mixture through a fine sieve or cheesecloth into a pitcher, pressing mixture with the back of a spoon to remove as much liquid as possible. Discard solids. Stir in remaining ingredients, stirring until sugar dissolves. Serve over ice. Serves 6 (serving size: 2/3 cup)

CALORIES 178; **FAT** 2.9g (sat 2g, mono 0.1g, poly 0g); **PROTEIN** 1g; **CARB** 38g; **FIBER** 1g; **CHOL** 0mg; **IRON** 0mg; **SODIUM** 32mg; **CALC** 11mg

Pescado Sarandeado

Hands-on: 22 min. Total: 22 min. *You can let the pepper paste sit on the fish longer, up to two hours. The fish will stick to the pan, but preheating the pan to high will help it release.*

2 dried ancho chiles, stemmed and seeded
2 dried guajillo chiles, stemmed and seeded
3 cups water
1 1/2 tablespoons lower-sodium soy sauce
2 teaspoons lower-sodium Worcestershire sauce
2 teaspoons tomato paste
2 teaspoons fresh lime juice
1 teaspoon dried oregano
1/2 teaspoon ground cumin
4 garlic cloves, peeled
4 (6-ounce) skin-on snapper fillets
1/4 teaspoon salt
Cooking spray
8 lime wedges

1. Combine chiles and 3 cups water in a large microwave-safe bowl. Microwave at HIGH 2 minutes or until boiling; let stand 5 minutes. Strain chiles through a sieve into a bowl, reserving 2 tablespoons soaking liquid. Place chiles, reserved liquid, soy sauce, and next 6 ingredients in food processor; process until smooth.
2. Score skin of fillets. Sprinkle with salt. Coat with chile mixture; let stand 5 minutes. Heat a large grill pan over high heat. Coat pan with cooking spray. Add fillets to pan, skin side down. Grill 3 minutes, without moving. Turn and grill 3 minutes or until fish flakes easily when tested with a fork. Serve immediately with lime wedges. Serves 4 (serving size: 1 fillet and 2 lime wedges).

CALORIES 264; **FAT** 3.1g (sat 0.6g, mono 0.5g, poly 1.2g); **PROTEIN** 39g; **CARB** 18g; **FIBER** 3g; **CHOL** 63mg; **IRON** 3mg; **SODIUM** 472mg; **CALC** 95mg

GLOBAL PANTRY

POMEGRANATE MOLASSES

by Naomi Duguid

The tart ruby juice has a thicker, richer, even more tart cousin.

I love the cooked-down syrup made from pomegranate juice. It's tart and complex, a great flavoring ingredient. The thick, dark-red to brown liquid offers a quick and interesting way to add complexity of flavor—a cook's shortcut, you might say. I add a dash to vegetable soups, bean dishes, salad dressings, and marinades. Perhaps best of all, I blend pomegranate molasses with salt and oil (usually olive oil) to brush onto vegetables before grilling or to make a delicious glaze for grilled or roast chicken, lamb, or pork. The proportions are about two to one: two parts pomegranate molasses to one part oil. A touch of salt balances the flavor. Just whisk together and brush onto vegetables as they go on the grill (or into the oven under the broiler). When grilling meat, brush the molasses on lightly partway through grilling, or at the very end, as we do in the following recipe.

> CHOOSE THE PRODUCT WITH THE FEWEST INGREDIENTS– IDEALLY JUST POMEGRANATE JUICE, MAYBE SUGAR.

Slider Patties with Pomegranate Molasses

(pictured on page 221)

Hands-on: 25 min. Total: 25 min.
Here's an easy take on sliders that uses pomegranate molasses as a secret ingredient. It's available in Middle Eastern grocery stores and at large, well-stocked supermarkets. It is inexpensive and keeps well and for a long time at room temperature. I usually serve these slider patties with rice or bread, a salad, and one or two vegetable sides.

2 tablespoons pomegranate molasses, divided
¼ cup finely chopped fresh mint
¾ teaspoon kosher salt
½ teaspoon ground coriander
¼ teaspoon ground red pepper
¼ teaspoon ground turmeric
¼ teaspoon ground cinnamon
1 pound lean ground lamb
1 garlic clove, minced
Cooking spray

1. Combine 1 tablespoon pomegranate molasses, mint, and next 7 ingredients; stir to combine. Divide mixture into 16 equal portions; gently shape each into a ¼-inch-thick patty.
2. Heat a grill pan over high heat. Coat pan with cooking spray. Add patties to pan; cook 1½ minutes on each side or until desired degree of doneness. Place patties on a platter; lightly brush patties with 1 tablespoon molasses. Serves 4 (serving size: 4 patties)

CALORIES 282; **FAT** 15.2g (sat 6.3g, mono 6.4g, poly 1.1g); **PROTEIN** 19g; **CARB** 14g; **FIBER** 0g; **CHOL** 75mg; **IRON** 3mg; **SODIUM** 423mg; **CALC** 56mg

SAVORY CAKES TO FILL YOUR PLATE

Zucchini partners with whole grains, feta, nuts, and a cool, creamy cucumber sauce.

Zucchini, Walnut, and Feta Cakes with Cucumber-Yogurt Sauce

Hands-on: 25 min. Total: 25 min. *We use uncooked quinoa instead of flour to bind these tasty cakes. It's protein-rich, adding an extra 3 grams per serving. Simply pulse in a mini food processor until finely ground.*

½ cup uncooked quinoa
¼ cup chopped walnuts
4½ cups grated zucchini (about 2 medium)
½ teaspoon kosher salt, divided
¼ cup thinly sliced green onions
3 tablespoons chopped fresh dill
¾ teaspoon freshly ground black pepper, divided
3 ounces feta cheese, crumbled (about ⅔ cup)
2 large eggs, lightly beaten
2 tablespoons olive oil, divided
1 (6-ounce) container plain nonfat Greek yogurt
1 cucumber, halved lengthwise, seeded, and thinly sliced (about 1½ cups)
1 garlic clove, minced
4 cups mixed salad greens (about 2 ounces)

1. Place quinoa in a mini food processor; process 1 minute or until finely ground. Add chopped walnuts to processor; process until smooth.
2. Place zucchini in a colander, and sprinkle with ¼ teaspoon salt. Toss well. Let stand 10 minutes, tossing occasionally. Press zucchini between paper towels until barely moist.
3. Combine zucchini, green onions, dill, ½ teaspoon pepper, ¼ teaspoon salt, cheese, and eggs in a large bowl; stir to combine. Sprinkle quinoa mixture over zucchini mixture; stir well to combine.
4. Heat a large nonstick skillet over medium heat. Add 1 tablespoon oil to pan; swirl to coat. Add 4 (⅓-cup) zucchini batter mounds to pan; flatten into 3-inch cakes. Cook 4 minutes on each side or until browned. Remove from pan; keep warm. Repeat procedure with 1 tablespoon oil and batter to yield 8 cakes total.
5. Combine ¼ teaspoon pepper, yogurt, cucumber, and garlic in a small bowl. Divide greens evenly among 4 plates. Top each serving with 2 cakes and about ¼ cup cucumber mixture. Serve immediately. Serves 4

CALORIES 336; **FAT** 19.2g (sat 4.7g, mono 6.9g, poly 5.5g); **PROTEIN** 18g; **CARB** 27g; **FIBER** 5g; **CHOL** 101mg; **IRON** 3mg; **SODIUM** 589mg; **CALC** 175mg

EACH PLATE PACKS IN AN ENTIRE DAY'S WORTH OF VEGETABLES—ABOUT 2½ CUPS.

MOTHER'S DAY SWEETS

Treat your mom (and yourself) to a giant, chocolate-drizzled cookie.

Somewhere between candy, cookie, and nut brittle lies Hazelnut Lace—a recipe that combines hazelnut meal (very finely ground nuts), a splash of Frangelico, and chocolate-hazelnut spread for a triple hit of nutty goodness. It's a sophisticated dessert, with its large, pizza-sized shape and artfully pebbled texture. If hazelnuts aren't your mother's favorite, we have an almond variation that's just as pretty and delicious. And because both versions take only 21 minutes to make, baking a second batch couldn't be easier.

Kid Friendly • Quick & Easy
Make Ahead

Hazelnut Lace

Hands-on: 6 min. Total: 21 min.

⅓ cup packed brown sugar
2 tablespoons unsalted butter
1 tablespoon canola oil
1 tablespoon Frangelico
¼ cup hazelnut meal
2 tablespoons cake flour
⅛ teaspoon salt
2 tablespoons hazelnut-chocolate spread

1. Preheat oven to 350°.
2. Combine first 4 ingredients in a medium microwave-safe bowl. Microwave at HIGH 30 seconds; stir. Microwave at HIGH 30 more seconds (mixture will bubble); whisk until smooth. Stir in meal, flour, and salt. Scrape mixture into center of a baking sheet covered with parchment paper. Spread into a 12-inch circle. Bake at 350° for 9 minutes, rotating pan after 4

minutes. Lift parchment and cookie onto a wire rack.
3. Place spread in bottom of a zip-top plastic bag. Microwave at HIGH 15 seconds. Snip a tiny hole in bottom corner of bag; drizzle over cookie. Serves 8 (serving size: 1 wedge)

CALORIES 146; FAT 8.2g (sat 2.5g, mono 4.2g, poly 0.8g); PROTEIN 1g; CARB 17g; FIBER 1g; CHOL 8mg; IRON 0mg; SODIUM 41mg; CALC 19mg

Kid Friendly • Quick & Easy
Make Ahead
Almond Lace:
Substitute 1 tablespoon amaretto for the Frangelico, ¼ cup almond meal for the hazelnut meal, and 1 ounce finely chopped bittersweet chocolate for the hazelnut-chocolate spread. Serves 8 (serving size: 1 wedge)

CALORIES 129; FAT 7.7g (sat 2.9g); SODIUM 41mg

PACKAGE IN A COOKIE BOX FROM THE CRAFT STORE.

SUPERFAST 20-MINUTE COOKING

Kid Friendly • Quick & Easy
Gluten Free

Seared Salmon with Sweet Corn and Bacon Sauté

The corn sauté makes a sweet, tasty bed for the fish and almost makes this a complete meal. Let the fillets cook undisturbed over medium-high heat for a beautiful sear.

2 center-cut bacon slices, chopped
1 medium shallot, finely chopped
3 green onions, thinly sliced, white and green parts separated
2 tablespoons dry white wine
1 tablespoon sherry vinegar or cider vinegar
1 (10-ounce) package frozen corn kernels
½ teaspoon kosher salt, divided
½ teaspoon freshly ground black pepper, divided
1 tablespoon canola oil
4 (6-ounce) center-cut salmon fillets, skinned
1 teaspoon minced fresh thyme

1. Cook bacon in a skillet over medium heat 4 minutes or until crisp, stirring occasionally. Add shallot and white parts of onions; sauté 2 minutes. Add wine, scraping pan to loosen browned bits. Stir in vinegar, corn, ¼ teaspoon salt, and ¼ teaspoon pepper; cook 4 minutes or until thoroughly heated. Stir in green parts of onions.
2. Heat a large nonstick skillet over medium-high heat. Add oil; swirl to coat. Sprinkle fillets with ¼ teaspoon salt and ¼ teaspoon pepper. Add fillets to pan; cook 4 minutes. Turn

and cook 3 minutes or until desired degree of doneness. Divide corn mixture among 4 plates; top with fillets. Sprinkle thyme evenly over fillets. Serves 4 (serving size: ½ cup corn mixture and 1 fillet)

CALORIES 363; FAT 14.6g (sat 2.9g, mono 5.6g, poly 4.6g); PROTEIN 40g; CARB 17g; FIBER 2g; CHOL 94mg; IRON 1mg; SODIUM 392mg; CALC 31mg

Kid Friendly • Quick & Easy

Steak and Asparagus Stir-fry

Spring's favorite vegetable shines in this quick stir-fry. Serve with precooked jasmine rice, available in pouches on the rice aisle.

¼ cup unsalted chicken stock (such as Swanson)
1½ tablespoons oyster sauce
1½ tablespoons lower-sodium soy sauce
2 teaspoons grated peeled fresh ginger
2 teaspoons minced fresh garlic
1 teaspoon cornstarch
5 teaspoons canola oil, divided
12 ounces boneless sirloin steak, cut into ¼-inch strips
12 ounces medium asparagus, trimmed and cut into 2-inch pieces
1 medium-sized red bell pepper, cut into strips
½ teaspoon crushed red pepper
3 green onions, chopped

1. Combine first 6 ingredients in a small bowl, stirring well with a whisk.
2. Heat a large skillet over high heat. Add 1 tablespoon oil to pan; swirl to coat. Add beef; stir-fry until browned but not cooked through (about 1½ minutes). Place beef on a plate; discard liquid in pan.
3. Return pan to high heat. Add 2 teaspoons oil; swirl to coat. Add asparagus and bell pepper; stir-fry 2 minutes. Add crushed red pepper

and green onions; stir-fry 30 seconds. Reduce heat to medium-high. Add stock mixture; cook 3 minutes or until sauce is slightly thickened. Return beef and any juices to pan, and cook 1 minute. Serves 4 (serving size: 1 cup)

CALORIES 228; FAT 12.2g (sat 3g, mono 6.2g, poly 2g); PROTEIN 21g; CARB 9g; FIBER 3g; CHOL 55mg; IRON 4mg; SODIUM 444mg; CALC 59mg

Kid Friendly • Quick & Easy

Quick Rotini with Sausage and Tomato Sauce

You can substitute spinach for the arugula, if you like. For less heat, decrease or omit the crushed red pepper.

8 ounces uncooked rotini
Cooking spray
3 (4-ounce) sweet turkey Italian sausage links, casings removed
1½ cups finely chopped arugula, divided
1 cup minced onion
1 tablespoon chopped fresh oregano
½ teaspoon crushed red pepper
4 garlic cloves, thinly sliced
2 cups unsalted canned crushed tomatoes
½ teaspoon sugar
½ teaspoon freshly ground black pepper
¼ teaspoon kosher salt
4 teaspoons grated fresh Parmesan cheese

1. Bring a large saucepan of water to a boil. Add pasta; cook 7 minutes or until al dente. Drain pasta in a colander over a bowl, reserving 1 cup cooking liquid.
2. Heat a large skillet over medium-high heat. Coat pan with cooking spray. Add sausage to pan; cook 5 minutes or until browned, stirring to crumble. Add 1 cup arugula,

onion, oregano, crushed red pepper, and garlic; cook 2 minutes, stirring frequently.
3. Add reserved 1 cup cooking liquid, tomatoes, sugar, black pepper, and salt to pan; bring to a boil. Add pasta; cook 2 minutes. Stir in ½ cup arugula. Divide pasta mixture among 4 shallow bowls; top with Parmesan cheese. Serves 4 (serving size: 1½ cups pasta and 1 teaspoon cheese)

CALORIES 387; FAT 8.3g (sat 2.8g, mono 2.8g, poly 2.4g); PROTEIN 22g; CARB 55g; FIBER 5g; CHOL 39mg; IRON 5mg; SODIUM 558mg; CALC 101mg

Kid Friendly • Quick & Easy
Make Ahead • Vegetarian

Asparagus Farfalle

4 ounces uncooked mini farfalle
4 teaspoons olive oil, divided
8 ounces medium asparagus, trimmed and cut into 1-inch pieces
⅔ cup thinly sliced leek
2 garlic cloves, minced
3 tablespoons dry white wine
2 tablespoons chopped fresh mint
¼ teaspoon black pepper
⅛ teaspoon kosher salt
1 ounce pecorino Romano cheese, grated (about ¼ cup)

1. Cook pasta according to package directions; drain.
2. Heat a large skillet over medium-high heat. Add 2 teaspoons oil to pan; swirl to coat. Add asparagus to pan; sauté 4 minutes. Remove asparagus from pan. Add 2 teaspoons oil to pan; swirl to coat. Add leek; sauté 2 minutes. Add garlic; sauté 30 seconds. Add wine; cook 30 seconds. Add pasta, asparagus, mint, and remaining ingredients; toss. Serves 4 (serving size: ¾ cup)

CALORIES 203; FAT 7.3g (sat 2.5g, mono 3.3g, poly 0.5g); PROTEIN 7g; CARB 26g; FIBER 2g; CHOL 8mg; IRON 3mg; SODIUM 206mg; CALC 97mg

Peas, Pancetta, & Lemon

Add 1 cup frozen peas during last 2 minutes of cooking pasta; drain. Sauté 1 ounce diced pancetta 3 minutes. Add 2 minced garlic cloves; cook 30 seconds. Add 3 tablespoons dry white wine; cook 30 seconds. Add pasta, 1 tablespoon butter, ½ teaspoon lemon rind, and ¼ teaspoon salt and pepper. Serves 4 (serving size: ¾ cup)

CALORIES 194; FAT 5.7g (sat 3.1g); SODIUM 325mg

Pesto & Almonds

Add 6 ounces (1-inch) cut green beans during last 4 minutes of cooking pasta. Drain. Sauté 2 minced garlic cloves in 2 teaspoons olive oil 1 minute. Add pasta mixture, ¼ cup chopped almonds, 2 tablespoons pesto, ¼ teaspoon kosher salt, and 1 ounce grated fresh Parmesan cheese; toss. Serves 4 (serving size: 1 cup)

CALORIES 245; FAT 11.6g (sat 2.6g); SODIUM 300mg

Tomatoes, Feta, & Thyme

Cook pasta; drain. Sauté 1 cup sliced leek in 4 teaspoons olive oil over medium heat 2 minutes. Add 2 minced garlic cloves; sauté 30 seconds. Stir in 1 tablespoon fresh lemon juice, pasta, 1 cup quartered cherry tomatoes, 2 teaspoons minced fresh thyme, and ⅓ cup crumbled feta cheese. Serves 4 (serving size: ¾ cup)

CALORIES 195; FAT 7.3g (sat 2.4g); SODIUM 127mg

Kid Friendly • Quick & Easy

Grilled Turkey, Apple, and Cheddar Sandwiches

Mango chutney is more savory than sweet, with warm spices, onion, and vinegar. It adds a tangy note to the sandwiches, but you can omit it if you like. For extra toasty sandwiches, weigh them down with a plate or heavy pan as they cook.

½ cup flat-leaf parsley leaves
1 Granny Smith apple, grated (about 1 cup)
8 (1-ounce) slices multigrain bread
8 teaspoons mango chutney (such as Major Grey's)
4 (1-ounce) slices sharp cheddar cheese
4 ounces sliced lower-sodium turkey (such as Boar's Head)
Cooking spray

1. Combine parsley and apple in a bowl. Spread each of 4 bread slices with 2 teaspoons chutney. Top evenly with cheese, turkey, apple mixture, and remaining 4 bread slices. Coat sandwiches with cooking spray.
2. Heat a large skillet over medium heat. Coat pan with cooking spray. Add sandwiches to pan; cook 3 minutes or until browned. Turn sandwiches; cover and cook 2 minutes or until cheese melts. Serves 4 (serving size: 1 sandwich)

CALORIES 344; FAT 11.6g (sat 6g, mono 2.7g, poly 1.5g); PROTEIN 19g; CARB 41g; FIBER 4g; CHOL 40mg; IRON 2mg; SODIUM 674mg; CALC 390mg

---

Kid Friendly • Quick & Easy
Make Ahead

Chicken, Tortellini, and Spinach Soup with Pesto

Diced tomato and a dollop of garlicky pesto add freshness and color to this quick chicken-pasta soup. Searing the chicken thighs first creates browned bits that add savory richness to the broth.

2 teaspoons canola oil
1 pound skinless, boneless chicken thighs, cut into 1-inch pieces
4 garlic cloves, minced
4 cups unsalted chicken stock (such as Swanson)
1 (9-ounce) package whole-wheat cheese tortellini
1 (5-ounce) package spinach
½ teaspoon kosher salt
½ teaspoon freshly ground black pepper
½ cup diced seeded tomato
¼ cup refrigerated pesto (such as Buitoni)

1. Heat a Dutch oven over high heat. Add oil; swirl to coat. Add chicken; cook 4 minutes, browning on all sides. Add garlic; cook 30 seconds. Add stock; bring to a boil. Add tortellini; reduce heat to medium, and simmer 6 minutes or until tortellini are done. Stir in spinach, salt, and pepper. Divide soup among 6 bowls; top evenly with tomato and pesto. Serves 6 (serving size: 1 cup soup, about 1 tablespoon tomato, and 2 teaspoons pesto)

CALORIES 301; FAT 12g (sat 3.5g, mono 3.6g, poly 2g); PROTEIN 27g; CARB 20g; FIBER 3g; CHOL 92mg; IRON 6mg; SODIUM 551mg; CALC 83mg

A GOOD BREAKFAST EVERY DAY

Make the day's first meal more than just a to-do list item. Our heroes share tips to see that it's a stress-free, special moment for you and your family.

Without sounding too Pollyanna-ish about it, every day is a fresh start, and every good breakfast marks a new shot at eating well all day. Plus, as we all have heard, it's not wise to skip breakfast because concentration at school or work can flag on an empty stomach. Eat nothing at 8, and risk overeating at snacktime or lunch.

That's the philosophy that this month's Healthy Habits Heroes have adopted. For Maria and Josh Lichty, the bloggers behind TwoPeasAndTheirPod.com, breakfast is the ideal way to usher in a new day with their 2-year-old son, Caleb. "We want to start the morning having a conversation with one another and with our son," says Maria. "We like to talk about our upcoming day, go over our schedules, and start off on a good foot."

As with any family that has appointments to keep and commutes to make, they can't afford a lot of time for prep. For the Lichtys, the key to success lies with planning.

"People focus on being stocked for dinner, but really, you need to be equally stocked with healthy breakfast options so you're not starving at 10:30 a.m. and going to the vending machine," Maria says. "Have a breakfast game plan. That way, when your alarm goes off, you don't have to think about it."

A more leisurely approach to breakfast rules on weekends. "We turn on the music and have dance parties while we cook," Maria says.

Quick & Easy • Freezable
Make Ahead • Vegetarian

Lemon-Poppy Seed Pancakes with Blueberry Compote

Hands-on: 25 min. Total: 25 min.
Make a double batch on the weekends, and freeze one batch for grab-and-go breakfasts during the week. To reheat, microwave at HIGH 1 minute, or pop in the toaster until hot. If you have to cook the pancakes in batches, wrap the cooked pancakes in a moist paper towel to prevent them from drying out while you finish the second batch.

3 cups fresh blueberries
6 tablespoons sugar, divided
3 teaspoons grated lemon rind, divided
2 tablespoons fresh lemon juice, divided
1 tablespoon water
6.6 ounces white whole-wheat flour (about 1½ cups)
2 teaspoons baking powder
¼ teaspoon salt
1 cup fat-free milk
½ cup plain 2% reduced-fat Greek yogurt
2 tablespoons poppy seeds
1 tablespoon canola oil
1 teaspoon vanilla extract
2 large eggs, lightly beaten
Cooking spray

1. Combine blueberries, ¼ cup sugar, 1 teaspoon rind, 1 tablespoon juice, and 1 tablespoon water in a small saucepan; bring to a boil over medium-high heat. Cook 10 minutes or until blueberries break down, stirring frequently.
2. While compote cooks, combine 2 tablespoons sugar and 2 teaspoons rind in a large bowl. Using your fingers, rub rind mixture together for 15 seconds.

Weigh or lightly spoon flour into dry measuring cups; level with a knife. Add flour, baking powder, and salt to rind mixture, stirring with a whisk. Combine milk and next 5 ingredients in a small bowl, stirring with a whisk; add 1 tablespoon lemon juice. Add milk mixture to flour mixture, stirring just until moist.
3. Preheat a griddle to medium heat. Coat pan with cooking spray. Spoon ¼ cup batter per pancake onto griddle. Cook 3 minutes or until edges begin to bubble and bottom is browned. Turn pancakes over; cook 3 minutes or until done. Serve with blueberry compote. Serves 6 (serving size: 2 pancakes and about ¼ cup blueberry compote)

CALORIES 286; FAT 6.4g (sat 1.1g, mono 2.3g, poly 1.9g); PROTEIN 10g; CARB 46g; FIBER 6g; CHOL 64mg; IRON 2mg; SODIUM 279mg; CALC 219mg

---

MARIA AND JOSH'S 3 TIPS FOR SPEEDY BREAKFASTS

SIP ON A SMOOTHIE.
"Make a smoothie at night, and freeze it. When you're getting ready the next morning, set it out to thaw. Use whatever fruits and veggies you have. (I like bananas, blueberries, spinach, and kale.) Stock up and store produce while it's on sale."

TOP YOUR TOAST.
"Nut butter on whole-grain toast is great for busy mornings. Add a few banana slices and a drizzle of honey. Fold that up, and go. Leftovers from last night's dinner are OK to eat for breakfast, too—eating something is better than eating nothing."

DOUBLE UP AND FREEZE.
"If you're going to make breakfast once, make a double batch. We make baked oatmeal on Saturday or Sunday, and keep it in the fridge so we can reheat portions throughout the week. When we make pancakes or waffles, we put a stack in the freezer for the week."

DINNER TONIGHT

READY IN 25 MINUTES

GAME PLAN

While potatoes cook:
- Grill chicken.
- Prepare tomato mixture.
While tomato mixture cooks:
- Prepare vinaigrette for potatoes.

Kid Friendly • Quick & Easy
Gluten Free

Greek-Style Chicken Breasts + Herbed Gold Potatoes

If you have extra minutes, you can roast rather than boil the potatoes. Toss them in the vinaigrette, and bake at 400° for 30 minutes, stirring after 20 minutes.

Cooking spray
4 (6-ounce) skinless, boneless chicken breast halves
¼ teaspoon kosher salt
¼ teaspoon black pepper
1½ tablespoons olive oil
1¾ cups vertically sliced onion
1 tablespoon minced fresh garlic
1 ounce chopped pitted kalamata olives (about 14)
1 medium tomato, halved and sliced
¼ cup chopped fresh flat-leaf parsley
2 teaspoons chopped fresh oregano
2 teaspoons fresh lemon juice
1 ounce feta cheese, crumbled (about ¼ cup)

1. Heat a grill pan over medium-high heat. Coat pan with cooking spray. Sprinkle chicken with salt and pepper. Add chicken to pan; cook 6 minutes on each side or until done.
2. Heat a large skillet over medium-high heat. Add oil to pan; swirl to coat. Add onion and garlic; sauté 4 minutes. Add olives and tomato; cook 3 minutes or until tomato begins to break down, stirring occasionally. Remove pan from heat; stir in parsley, oregano, and juice. Top chicken with tomato and olive mixture; sprinkle feta evenly over chicken. Serves 4 (serving size: 1 chicken breast half, about ⅓ cup tomato mixture, and about 1 tablespoon feta)

CALORIES 311; FAT 13.2g (sat 3g, mono 6.8g, poly 1.5g); PROTEIN 38g; CARB 8g; FIBER 2g; CHOL 115mg; IRON 1mg; SODIUM 518mg; CALC 74mg

Herbed Gold Potatoes
Place 1¼ pounds (1½-inch) baby gold potatoes in a large saucepan. Cover with water to 2 inches above potatoes; bring to a boil. Cover and cook 14 minutes or until potatoes are tender; drain. Combine 1 tablespoon melted butter, 1 tablespoon white wine vinegar, 2 teaspoons extra-virgin olive oil, 2 teaspoons chopped oregano leaves, ½ teaspoon freshly ground black pepper, and ¼ teaspoon kosher salt in a large bowl, stirring with a whisk. Add potatoes; toss to coat. Garnish with oregano leaves, if desired. Serves 4 (serving size: about 4 potatoes)

CALORIES 146; FAT 5.4g (sat 2.2g); SODIUM 171mg

READY IN 25 MINUTES

While stock mixture comes to a boil:
- Make vinaigrette.

While soup simmers:
- Finish salad.

Kid Friendly • Quick & Easy

Shrimp Marinara Soup + Crumbled Feta + Simple Salad

Leftover Lunch: Add 1 cup baby spinach leaves to soup; then reheat, and stir until wilted.

Simple Sub: Use red wine vinegar in place of lemon juice in the salad dressing.

2 teaspoons olive oil
1/2 teaspoon dried oregano
1/4 teaspoon crushed red pepper
3 large garlic cloves, minced
1/4 cup dry white wine
2 cups unsalted chicken stock (such as Swanson)
1/2 cup water
1/2 cup uncooked orzo
2 cups lower-sodium marinara sauce
12 ounces large shrimp, peeled and deveined
2 tablespoons chopped fresh flat-leaf parsley
1 ounce feta cheese, crumbled (about 1/4 cup)

1. Heat a large saucepan over medium heat. Add oil; swirl to coat. Add oregano, pepper, and garlic; sauté 30 seconds. Add wine; cook 1 minute. Add stock and 1/2 cup water to pan; bring to a boil. Stir in orzo; cook 6 minutes or until al dente. Stir in marinara and shrimp; cook 4 minutes or until shrimp are done. Place 1 1/2 cups soup in each of 4 bowls; top each serving with 1 1/2 teaspoons

parsley and 1 tablespoon crumbled feta. Serves 4

CALORIES 269; **FAT** 6.2g (sat 1.5g, mono 2.6g, poly 1.2g); **PROTEIN** 20g; **CARB** 31g; **FIBER** 2g; **CHOL** 113mg; **IRON** 3mg; **SODIUM** 372mg; **CALC** 123mg

Simple Salad with Lemon Dressing
Combine 1 1/2 tablespoons fresh lemon juice, 1 1/2 tablespoons extra-virgin olive oil, 1/4 teaspoon freshly ground black pepper, and 1/8 teaspoon kosher salt in a large bowl, stirring with a whisk. Add 6 cups mixed greens, 1 cup halved cherry tomatoes, and 1/2 cup thinly sliced radishes; toss to coat. Serves 4 (serving size: 1 1/2 cups)

CALORIES 71; **FAT** 5.2g (sat 0.7g); **SODIUM** 98mg

Kid Friendly • Quick & Easy

Glazed Salmon + Couscous + Haricots Verts

Quick Tip: Glazing the fish before cooking keeps it moist. A second coat later lets the sweet-tangy sauce shine.

Prep pointer: Brown the butter in a stainless steel pan so you can monitor the change in color.

1 1/4 cups water
3/8 teaspoon kosher salt, divided
3/8 teaspoon freshly ground black pepper, divided
1 cup uncooked couscous
2 tablespoons chopped fresh dill
1/4 teaspoon grated lemon rind
1 teaspoon fresh lemon juice
2 teaspoons olive oil
1 teaspoon butter
3 tablespoons chopped shallots
1/4 cup dry white wine
2 tablespoons whole-grain mustard
1 tablespoon brown sugar
4 (6-ounce) salmon fillets (about 1 inch thick)
Cooking spray

1. Preheat broiler.
2. Bring 1 1/4 cups water to a boil in a medium saucepan. Stir in 1/8 teaspoon salt, 1/8 teaspoon pepper, and couscous; cover. Remove from heat; let stand 5 minutes. Stir in dill, rind, and juice.
3. Heat a small saucepan over medium-high heat. Add olive oil and butter; swirl until butter melts. Add shallots; cook 2 minutes, stirring occasionally. Add wine to pan; bring to a boil. Cook 2 minutes; stir in mustard and brown sugar. Remove pan from heat.
4. Arrange fillets, skin sides down, on a jelly-roll pan lined with foil coated with cooking spray. Sprinkle fillets with 1/4 teaspoon salt and 1/4 teaspoon pepper. Spread half of mustard mixture evenly over fillets. Broil 6 minutes or until desired degree of doneness. Spread remaining half of mustard mixture over fillets. Serve fish with couscous. Serves 4 (serving size: 1 fillet and about 1/2 cup couscous)

CALORIES 467; **FAT** 13.2g (sat 3g, mono 5.1g, poly 3.7g); **PROTEIN** 42g; **CARB** 40g; **FIBER** 2g; **CHOL** 93mg; **IRON** 1mg; **SODIUM** 455mg; **CALC** 36mg

Browned Butter Haricots Verts
Cook 2 (8-ounce) packages microwave-in-a-bag fresh haricots verts according to package directions. Combine 1 tablespoon butter and 3 tablespoons sliced almonds in a large skillet over medium heat; cook 3 minutes or until butter is lightly browned and almonds are lightly toasted. Add haricots verts to pan; toss to coat. Sprinkle with 1/4 teaspoon kosher salt and 1/4 teaspoon freshly ground black pepper. Serves 4 (serving size: 1/2 cup)

CALORIES 86; **FAT** 5.3g (sat 2g); **SODIUM** 152mg

continued

READY IN 25 MINUTES

SHOPPING LIST

Glazed Salmon and Couscous

Kosher salt
Uncooked couscous
Fresh dill
Lemon
Olive oil
Butter
Shallots
Dry white wine
Whole-grain mustard
Brown sugar
4 (6-ounce) salmon fillets

Browned Butter Haricots Verts

2 packages microwave-in-a-bag
  haricots verts
Butter
Sliced almonds
Kosher salt

GAME PLAN

While couscous cooks:
▪ Prepare brown sugar mixture.
While salmon cooks:
▪ Prepare haricots verts.

Quick & Easy

Moroccan Chicken Salad Pitas

with Orange-Carrot Salad

On the Go: A filled sandwich may get soggy by lunchtime. Pack the salad alone, and bring pita chips for dipping.
Budget Buy: Substitute sliced toasted almonds for the pine nuts.
Flavor Hit: Bell pepper adds color and crunch.

1 cup packed fresh spinach leaves
1/2 cup packed mint leaves
1 small shallot, coarsely chopped
1 garlic clove, peeled and crushed
1/2 cup plain nonfat Greek yogurt
3/8 teaspoon kosher salt, divided
1/4 teaspoon black pepper
1 tablespoon fresh lemon juice
1 tablespoon olive oil
1/4 teaspoon ground cinnamon
1/4 teaspoon ground cumin
1/4 teaspoon ground coriander
1/8 teaspoon ground red pepper
6 ounces chopped skinless, boneless
  rotisserie chicken breast
  (about 1 1/2 cups)
2 (6-inch) whole-wheat pitas, halved
1/4 cup prechopped red bell pepper
4 teaspoons pine nuts, toasted

1. Place first 4 ingredients in the bowl of a food processor, and process until coarsely chopped. Place spinach mixture in a bowl; stir in yogurt, ⅛ teaspoon salt, and black pepper.
2. Combine ¼ teaspoon salt, juice, and next 5 ingredients in a medium bowl. Add chicken; toss.

---

3. Spread 2 tablespoons spinach mixture in each pita half. Divide chicken mixture among pita halves; sprinkle with bell pepper and nuts. Serves 4 (serving size: 1 filled pita half)

CALORIES 227; FAT 7.8g (sat 1.1g, mono 3.7g, poly 1.9g); PROTEIN 19g; CARB 22g; FIBER 3g; CHOL 38mg; IRON 2mg; SODIUM 514mg; CALC 51mg

READY IN 25 MINUTES

SHOPPING LIST

Moroccan Chicken Salad Pitas

Fresh spinach leaves
Fresh mint leaves
Shallot (1)
Garlic clove (1)
Plain nonfat Greek yogurt
Kosher salt
Lemon
Olive oil
Ground cinnamon
Ground cumin
Ground coriander
Ground red pepper
6 ounces skinless, boneless rotisserie
  chicken breast
2 (6-inch) whole-wheat pitas
Prechopped red bell pepper
Pine nuts

Orange-Carrot Salad

Orange juice
Olive oil
Honey
Kosher salt
Matchstick-cut carrots
Fresh cilantro

GAME PLAN

While orange juice reduces:
▪ Prepare spinach mixture.
▪ Finish carrot salad.
▪ Assemble sandwiches.

Orange-Carrot Salad

Place ¼ cup orange juice in a small saucepan over high heat. Bring to a boil; cook 4 minutes or until reduced by half. Remove pan from heat; stir in 1 tablespoon olive oil, 1 teaspoon honey, ¼ teaspoon freshly ground black pepper, and a dash of kosher salt. Place 2 cups matchstick-cut carrots and ¼ cup chopped fresh cilantro in a bowl. Add juice mixture; toss. Serves 4 (serving size: about ½ cup)

CALORIES 65; **FAT** 3.5g (sat 0.5g); **SODIUM** 68mg

Kid Friendly • Quick & Easy
Make Ahead • Vegetarian

Tortellini with Snap Peas and Pesto

with Radicchio Caesar Salad

Make Ahead: The totellini and snap pea mixture can be prepared a couple of days ahead.
Kid Tweaks: Omit the anchovy in the dressing, and sub romaine for radicchio.

1 (9-ounce) package refrigerated three-cheese tortellini (such as Buitoni)
8 ounces sugar snap peas, trimmed and halved diagonally (about 1½ cups)
1 cup mint leaves
1 cup basil leaves
3 tablespoons sliced almonds, toasted
2 tablespoons grated fresh Parmesan cheese
1 teaspoon grated lemon rind
¼ teaspoon freshly ground black pepper
⅛ teaspoon kosher salt
1 garlic clove, minced
3 tablespoons olive oil
1 tablespoon fresh lemon juice

1. Cook tortellini according to package directions, omitting salt and fat. Add snap peas to pan during last 3 minutes of cooking; cook 3 minutes. Drain.
2. Place mint and next 7 ingredients in a mini food processor; process until finely chopped, scraping sides of bowl once. Combine oil and juice in a small bowl, stirring with a whisk. With processor on, slowly pour oil mixture through food chute; process until well blended. Combine tortellini mixture and mint mixture; toss gently to coat. Serves 4 (serving size: about 1¼ cups).

CALORIES 351; **FAT** 17.4g (sat 4.1g, mono 9g, poly 1.7g); **PROTEIN** 13g; **CARB** 37g; **FIBER** 5g; **CHOL** 26mg; **IRON** 3mg; **SODIUM** 392mg; **CALC** 191mg

Radicchio Caesar Salad

Combine 3 tablespoons canola mayonnaise, 1½ tablespoons fresh lemon juice, ½ teaspoon black pepper, 2 minced garlic cloves, and 1 minced anchovy fillet in a large bowl. Add 2½ cups very thinly sliced, cored radicchio and 2½ cups baby spinach leaves; toss to coat. Top with 5 teaspoons grated fresh Parmesan cheese. Serves 4 (serving size: about 1 cup)

CALORIES 77; **FAT** 4.5g (sat 0.4g); **SODIUM** 246mg

READY IN
35
MINUTES

SHOPPING LIST

Tortellini with Snap Peas and Pesto

1 package refrigerated three-cheese tortellini (such as Buitoni)
Sugar snap peas
Fresh mint leaves
Fresh basil leaves
Sliced almonds
Grated fresh Parmesan cheese
Lemon
Kosher salt
Garlic clove
Olive oil

Radicchio Caesar Salad

Canola mayonnaise
Lemon
Garlic cloves
Anchovy fillet
Radicchio
Baby spinach leaves
Grated fresh Parmesan cheese

GAME PLAN

While water comes to a boil:
■ Prepare pesto.
While tortellini cooks:
■ Prepare salad.

FEED 4 FOR LESS THAN $10

Simple dinners, big flavors: Mussels with smoky kielbasa, pasta with mint and Parmesan.

Quick & Easy

$2.49 PER SERVING

Smoky Portuguese-Style Mussels

Hands-on: 15 min. Total: 25 min.
Paprika and turkey sausage infuse the broth and lend a smoky flavor to the mussels, which are a sustainable, affordable choice.

2 teaspoons canola oil
2 ounces chopped turkey kielbasa
1¼ cups chopped onion
8 garlic cloves, minced
1 tablespoon smoked paprika
1 pound red potatoes, cut into
   ½-inch pieces (about 3 cups)
1¾ cups unsalted chicken stock
   (such as Swanson)
½ cup white wine
40 mussels (about 1½ pounds),
   scrubbed and debearded
2 tablespoons fresh lemon juice
¼ teaspoon freshly ground black
   pepper
⅛ teaspoon kosher salt
4 lemon wedges

1. Heat a large Dutch oven over medium-high heat. Add oil; swirl to coat. Add sausage; cook 3 minutes, stirring to brown on all sides. Add onion and garlic; cook 2 minutes, stirring frequently. Add paprika and potatoes; cook 1 minute. Add stock, scraping pan to loosen browned bits. Bring to a simmer; cover and cook 15 minutes, stirring occasionally. Add wine; simmer 5 minutes. Add mussels; cover and cook 5 minutes or until shells open. Discard unopened shells. Stir in lemon juice, pepper, and salt. Serve with lemon wedges. Serves 4 (serving size: about 10 mussels, ½ cup broth, and 1 lemon wedge)

CALORIES 284; **FAT** 6.6g (sat 1.2g, mono 2g, poly 1.5g); **PROTEIN** 20g; **CARB** 33g; **FIBER** 4g; **CHOL** 36mg; **IRON** 6mg; **SODIUM** 583mg; **CALC** 79mg

Kid Friendly
Quick & Easy • Vegetarian

$2.37 PER SERVING

Fettuccine with Squash Ribbons

Hands-on: 21 min. Total: 21 min.
Stirring olive oil into boiling water creates a quick emulsified sauce for this simple, summery pasta. For a refreshing side, cut half a peeled, seeded cantaloupe lengthwise into 4 wedges. Wrap ½ ounce very thinly sliced prosciutto around each wedge.

8 ounces uncooked fettuccine
2 small zucchini
1 large yellow squash
3 tablespoons olive oil, divided
1 cup grape tomatoes
½ teaspoon kosher salt
½ teaspoon crushed red pepper
6 garlic cloves, thinly sliced
1 ounce Parmesan cheese, shaved
   (about ¼ cup)
3 tablespoons torn fresh mint

1. Cook pasta according to package directions, omitting salt and fat. Drain in a colander over a bowl, reserving ¾ cup cooking liquid. Shave zucchini and squash into thin ribbons using a vegetable peeler; discard seeds. Place ribbons in a large bowl.
2. Heat a large skillet over medium heat. Add 1 tablespoon oil to pan; swirl to coat. Add tomatoes, salt, and pepper to pan; cook 8 minutes or until tomatoes begin to break down, stirring occasionally. Remove tomatoes from pan using a slotted spoon; add to squash ribbons. Add garlic to pan; cook 1 minute or until fragrant, stirring constantly. Stir in reserved ¾ cup cooking liquid; bring to a boil. Gradually add 2 tablespoons oil to pan, stirring constantly with a whisk.
3. Add pasta to pan; cook 1 minute, tossing to coat. Remove pan from heat. Add pasta mixture to squash mixture; toss. Sprinkle with Parmesan cheese and mint. Serves 4 (serving size: about 1¾ cups)

CALORIES 364; **FAT** 13.4g (sat 3g, mono 8g, poly 1.3g); **PROTEIN** 13g; **CARB** 50g; **FIBER** 4g; **CHOL** 6mg; **IRON** 3mg; **SODIUM** 361mg; **CALC** 128mg

FIVE-MINUTE FROZEN YOGURT

Matisse and friends whip up a quick, fruity treat.

"Today I made berry frozen yogurt that's quick, easy, and fun. You can use any frozen fruit you want, like blueberries, raspberries, or even bananas. I used strawberries. The yogurt balances out the sweet and tart strawberry flavor and makes it nice and creamy. You can also use any flavor of yogurt. I made a batch with Greek yogurt for my mom. It was a little sour for us kids, but my mom really enjoyed it. This recipe did not take long and was very healthy. I loved how the flavors blended together and that the texture of the yogurt was creamy and smooth—a melt-in-your-mouth experience like no other! This is definitely a summer treat you and your family will love."

Quick Berry Frozen Yogurt

Hands-on: 5 min. Total: 5 min.

2 cups frozen mixed berries, divided
1 cup vanilla low-fat frozen yogurt, divided
¼ cup fat-free milk
1 tablespoon chopped fresh mint
1 tablespoon agave syrup

1. Place 1 cup berries, ¾ cup yogurt, milk, mint, and agave syrup in the bowl of a food processor; process until smooth. Spoon into a freezer-safe container. Add 1 cup berries and ¼ cup yogurt to processor; process until smooth. Swirl berry mixture into yogurt mixture. Serve immediately, or freeze until firm. Serves 4 (serving size: about ½ cup)

CALORIES 150; FAT 2.5g (sat 1.3g, mono 0g, poly 0g); PROTEIN 6g; CARB 29g; FIBER 2g; CHOL 33mg; IRON 0mg; SODIUM 34mg; CALC 155mg

THE VERDICT

KAHLO (AGE 7)
She thought the frozen yogurt tasted like the fresh berry ice cream at our local farmers' market. **10/10**

JASPER (AGE 9)
He said, "I love fruit. This is super-yummy!" **10/10**

MATISSE (AGE 13)
I love summer berries but could have easily eaten this with any fruit. The mint adds a hint of freshness to the dish. **10/10**

FRESH RIGHT NOW

AVOCADO

Tuck into one of the season's top treasures. California avocado farmers owe their livelihoods to America's love of guacamole. But there's a lot beyond dip-making to do with this fruit, which is chock-full of healthy fats. Eaten alone, a sprinkle of salt and lime—or a few dashes of soy and sesame oil—makes them shine. In this grilled cheese sandwich, a few slices seem positively decadent.

Kid Friendly • Quick & Easy Vegetarian

Avocado and Tomato Grilled Cheese Sandwiches

Hands-on: 22 min. Total: 22 min. *Soft, buttery avocado amps up the irresistible gooeyness of this grilled cheese. Tomato brings a bright, acidic contrast to the richness of cheese and avocado. Firm, ripe tomatoes will perform best—giving off some, but not too much, juice as the sandwich grills.*

3 ounces white cheddar cheese, shredded (about ¾ cup)
8 (¾-ounce) slices multigrain bread
8 thin tomato slices, seeded
1 ripe peeled avocado, cut into thin slices
¼ teaspoon salt
¼ teaspoon black pepper
Cooking spray

1. Sprinkle 3 tablespoons cheddar cheese over each of 4 bread slices. Top each with 2 tomato slices. Arrange avocado slices evenly over tomato slices. Sprinkle evenly with salt and pepper. Top with remaining 4 bread slices. Lightly coat outsides of sandwiches with cooking spray.

2. Heat a grill pan over medium heat. Place sandwiches in pan; cook 3 minutes on each side or until bread is toasted and well marked and cheese melts. Cut each sandwich in half; serve immediately. Serves 4 (serving size: 1 sandwich)

CALORIES 275; FAT 15.7g (sat 6g, mono 6.1g, poly 1.8g); PROTEIN 11g; CARB 24g; FIBER 7g; CHOL 19mg; IRON 1mg; SODIUM 490mg; CALC 207mg

250-CALORIE WAFFLE COMBOS

These grab-and-go whole-grain breakfasts add easy morning variety.

The freezer aisle of your grocery store is stocked with a hearty selection of whole-grain toaster waffles that have less than 100 calories per serving. That's a low-calorie, grain-rich base for tasty combos that go way beyond butter and syrup. The fruity options are great, but we love savory ones, too. Nutrition information is for one Van's multigrain Belgian waffle plus toppings.

1. Chicken & Waffles
2 ounces shredded skinless rotisserie chicken breast + 1 cup arugula tossed in 1 teaspoon olive oil, ½ teaspoon honey, and ½ teaspoon balsamic vinegar + 2 tablespoons chopped red onion

CALORIES 228; FAT 9g (sat 1.1g); PROTEIN 19g; SODIUM 299mg

2. Berries & Browned Butter Waffle
⅔ cup sliced strawberries tossed in 1 teaspoon brown sugar + 2 teaspoons browned butter + 2 tablespoons fresh basil leaves + 1 tablespoon toasted sliced almonds

CALORIES 239; FAT 13.4g (sat 5.1g); PROTEIN 4g; SODIUM 109mg

3. Peaches & Cream Waffle

¼ cup vanilla light ice cream, softened + ⅔ cup sliced peaches + dash of cinnamon + 1½ tablespoons chopped pecans, toasted + 1 tablespoon fresh mint leaves

CALORIES 239; **FAT** 13.4g (sat 5.1g); **PROTEIN** 4g; **SODIUM** 109mg

4. Green, Egg & Ham Waffle

3 tablespoons thinly sliced avocado + 1 large egg, poached + ½ ounce slivered prosciutto + 1 tablespoon chopped fresh cilantro + ¼ cup chopped tomato

CALORIES 233; **FAT** 12.7g (sat 2.6g); **PROTEIN** 12g; **SODIUM** 392mg

5. Skinny Elvis Waffle

⅓ cup sliced banana + 2 teaspoons creamy peanut butter + 1 center-cut bacon slice, cooked and crumbled + 1 teaspoon honey

CALORIES 239; **FAT** 10g (sat 2.2g); **PROTEIN** 7g; **SODIUM** 290mg

6. Creamy Coconut-Citrus Waffle

1 tablespoon ⅓-less-fat cream cheese + ¼ cup orange sections + 2 teaspoons chopped unsalted macadamia nuts + 2 teaspoons maple syrup + 1 tablespoon toasted flaked sweetened coconut

CALORIES 238; **FAT** 11.5g (sat 3.9g); **PROTEIN** 4g; **SODIUM** 169mg

QUICK TRICKS

6 EASY VINAGRETTES

Match sweet dressings to tender lettuce like Bibb, acidic ones to hearty leaves like romaine.

Quick & Easy • Make Ahead
Cilantro-Chile

Combine 2 tablespoons olive oil, 4 teaspoons fresh lime juice, 1 tablespoon minced fresh Fresno or other red chile, 2 teaspoons fish sauce, 1 teaspoon grated peeled fresh ginger, ½ teaspoon sugar, and 1 garlic clove, mashed into a paste; stir with a whisk. Stir in 1 tablespoon finely chopped fresh cilantro. Toss with shredded green cabbage. Serves 4 (serving size: 1½ tablespoons)

CALORIES 67; **FAT** 6.8g (sat 0.9g); **SODIUM** 191mg

Quick & Easy • Gluten Free
Make Ahead • Vegetarian
Orange-Fennel

Combine 3 tablespoons fresh orange juice, 2 teaspoons white wine vinegar, 1 teaspoon crushed toasted fennel seeds, ¼ teaspoon grated orange rind, ⅛ teaspoon kosher salt, and ⅛ teaspoon freshly ground black pepper in a bowl, stirring with a whisk. Gradually add 2 tablespoons olive oil, stirring constantly with a whisk. Drizzle over Bibb lettuce. Serves 4 (serving size: 1 tablespoon)

CALORIES 67; **FAT** 6.9g (sat 0.9g); **SODIUM** 61mg

Kid Friendly • Quick & Easy
Make Ahead
Caesar

Place 2 tablespoons finely grated fresh Parmesan cheese, 1 tablespoon fresh lemon juice, ½ teaspoon anchovy paste, ¼ teaspoon freshly ground black pepper, ¼ teaspoon Worcestershire sauce, 1 large pasteurized egg yolk, and 1 minced garlic clove in a mini food processor; process 15 seconds. With the processor on, gradually add 2 tablespoons extra-virgin olive oil, processing until combined. Toss with romaine lettuce. Serves 4 (serving size: about 1 tablespoon)

CALORIES 88; **FAT** 8.7g (sat 1.8g); **SODIUM** 83mg

Kid Friendly • Quick & Easy
Gluten Free
Sweet & Sour Bacon

Cook 2 center-cut bacon slices until crisp. Remove bacon from pan; crumble. Add 1½ tablespoons cider vinegar, 1½ teaspoons brown sugar, 1½ teaspoons Dijon mustard, ⅛ teaspoon freshly ground black pepper, and a dash of kosher salt to drippings in pan, stirring with a whisk. Stir in bacon. Drizzle over spinach. Serves 4 (serving size: 1 tablespoon)

CALORIES 20; **FAT** 0.7g (sat 0.3g); **SODIUM** 119mg

Tomato-Basil

Place 2 tablespoons minced fresh basil, 2 tablespoons balsamic vinegar, 1 tablespoon minced shallots, 1 teaspoon Dijon mustard, 10 grape tomatoes, and 1 garlic clove in a mini food processor; process until smooth. With processor on, gradually add 2 tablespoons olive oil, processing until combined. Drizzle over mixed baby greens. Serves 4 (serving size: 2 tablespoons)

CALORIES 73; **FAT** 6.8g (sat 0.9g); **SODIUM** 33mg

Grapefruit-Poppy Seed

Combine 3 tablespoons fresh grapefruit juice, 4 teaspoons canola mayonnaise, 2 teaspoons white wine vinegar, 1 teaspoon honey, and ½ teaspoon grated grapefruit rind in a bowl, stirring with a whisk. Gradually add 2 tablespoons grapeseed oil, stirring constantly with a whisk. Stir in ½ teaspoon poppy seeds, ⅛ teaspoon kosher salt, and ⅛ teaspoon freshly ground black pepper. Drizzle over baby spinach. Serves 4 (serving size: 2 tablespoons)

CALORIES 85; **FAT** 8.3g (sat 0.7g); **SODIUM** 96mg

A TASTY WANDER THROUGH THE SUMMER GARDEN

Our midyear Summer Cookbook for peak-season vegetables and fruits

The bounty of the summer garden—such soulful pleasures! After careful planning and much hard working of shovel and hoe, this is the time for the juicy rewards. What a delight to walk out your back door and pluck a sun-splashed assortment of tomatoes for tonight's salad. What a joy to cozy up at a rustic garden table for an alfresco meal.

When you grow your own food, you're not at the mercy of long-haul trucks and supermarket produce buyers. You're the master of a broad variety of flavors, textures, and colors. Luckily, the national explosion of farmers' markets has brought so much more selection to those who don't have the land, or time, to garden.

For a fresh crop of new vegetable recipes, we turned to Deborah Madison, author of the wonderful book *Vegetable Literacy* and a national treasure when it comes to exciting plant cookery.

THE VEGETABLE RECIPES

Kid Friendly • Quick & Easy
Gluten Free • Vegetarian

Beefsteak Tomato Salad with Fried Tomato Skins

(pictured on page 222)

Hands-on: 20 min. Total: 20 min.
Ample beefsteak tomatoes are the ones you want to eat uncooked: They are fleshy, big, juicy, and so delicious. Saving the skins and frying them is a genius touch, creating a beautiful garnish with bacony qualities.

2¹/₂ pounds beefsteak tomatoes in assorted colors (about 4)
5 tablespoons olive oil, divided
³/₈ teaspoon kosher salt, divided
¹/₂ teaspoon freshly ground pepper
2 cups baby arugula

1. Bring a large pot of water to a boil. Core tomatoes; discard cores. Place tomatoes in boiling water for 15 seconds. Plunge tomatoes into ice water; drain. Peel; arrange skins flat on a jelly-roll pan. Cut peeled tomatoes into ½-inch-thick slices; arrange on a platter.
2. Heat a small skillet over medium-high heat. Add ¼ cup oil; swirl to coat. Add half of skins to oil; cook 2 minutes or until crisp, turning occasionally. Drain on a paper towel; repeat procedure with remaining skins. Discard oil in pan. Sprinkle skins with ⅛ teaspoon salt.
3. Drizzle tomatoes with 1 tablespoon oil; sprinkle with ¼ teaspoon salt and pepper. Top with tomato skins and arugula. Serves 4 (serving size: about 2 cups)

CALORIES 114; FAT 7.4g (sat 1g, mono 5g, poly 1g); PROTEIN 3g; CARB 12g; FIBER 4g; CHOL 0mg; IRON 1mg; SODIUM 197mg; CALC 46mg

LUSH AND BRIGHT— TAKE A BITE

Selection and storage tips for vegetables

PEPPERS
Choose the Best: You want a fresh-looking green stem and taut, glossy skin.
Keep It Fresh: Place uncut peppers in your crisper, along with a damp paper towel. Use within 10 days.

POLE BEANS
Choose the Best: Seek crisp pods that are not bulging
Keep It Fresh: Unwashed, they can be refrigerated in a plastic bag for 3 days. To use later, blanch and freeze.

OKRA
Choose the Best: Look for firm, bright pods no longer than 4 inches.
Keep It Fresh: Place unwashed okra in a paper bag, and store in the refrigerator for up to 3 days.

TOMATOES
Choose the Best: Ripe, juicy tomatoes will feel heavy for their size. When you give the area around their stems a sniff, there should be a sweet, earthy scent.
Keep It Fresh: Store at room temperature, away from direct sunlight, for 2 to 3 days. Avoid piling these delicate beauties on top of each other.

Roasted Peppers and Tomatoes with Herbs and Capers

Hands-on: 35 min. Total: 2 hr. *This dish is baked just long enough to bring out the juices of the tomatoes, and then chilled. Serve it as a salad or a side dish. Keep the colors of the tomatoes and peppers the same, or vary them wildly. Campari tomatoes are commonly available at supermarkets.*

2 red bell peppers
2 yellow bell peppers
1¹/₂ pounds Campari tomatoes, halved
³/₈ teaspoon kosher salt, divided
¹/₄ teaspoon freshly ground black pepper
¹/₃ cup flat-leaf parsley leaves
3 tablespoons extra-virgin olive oil
1 tablespoon chopped fresh oregano
1 tablespoon capers, rinsed and drained
2 teaspoons minced fresh garlic
12 niçoise olives, pitted and halved

1. Preheat broiler to high.
2. Cut bell peppers in half lengthwise; discard seeds and membranes. Place halves, skin sides up, on a foil-lined baking sheet; flatten with hand. Broil 10 minutes or until blackened. Wrap peppers in foil; let stand 10 minutes. Peel; cut into ½-inch strips.
3. Preheat oven to 400°.
4. Combine tomatoes, ¼ teaspoon salt, and black pepper in a medium bowl.
5. Combine ⅛ teaspoon salt, parsley, and remaining ingredients in a small bowl. Place one-third of tomatoes in bottom of a 1½-quart gratin dish. Top with one-third of peppers and one-third of parsley mixture. Repeat layers twice, ending with parsley mixture. Cover and bake at 400° for 30 minutes or until vegetables are

thoroughly heated. Cool to room temperature; cover and chill. Serves 8 (serving size: ¾ cup)

CALORIES 97; FAT 6.9g (sat 0.9g, mono 4.9g, poly 0.8g); PROTEIN 2g; CARB 8g; FIBER 2g; CHOL 0mg; IRON 1mg; SODIUM 222mg; CALC 23mg

Grilled Green Beans

Hands-on: 15 min. Total: 30 min.
Grilling green beans is a fantastic approach, kissing the vegetables with a little smoky char. Be sure not to skip the step of covering and letting the mixture stand; all steams to perfect doneness in that time. If you don't have a grill basket, grill on a large piece of heavy-duty foil.

3 large shallots or 1 small red onion, vertically sliced
2 garlic cloves, minced
1 pound green beans, trimmed
2 tablespoons canola oil
2 teaspoons lower-sodium soy sauce
1 teaspoon dark sesame oil
¹/₄ teaspoon kosher salt
¹/₄ teaspoon freshly ground black pepper

1. Preheat grill to medium-high heat.
2. Place a grill basket on hot grill; preheat for 5 minutes.
3. Place shallots, garlic, and green beans in a large bowl. Drizzle with canola oil; toss well to coat. Arrange mixture in hot grill basket; cover grill, and cook 7 minutes or until beans are lightly charred, tossing occasionally. Place bean mixture in a large bowl; cover and let stand 5 minutes. Add soy sauce and remaining ingredients; toss to combine. Serves 6 (serving size: about 1 cup)

CALORIES 84; FAT 5.6g (sat 0.5g, mono 3.3g, poly 1.7g); PROTEIN 2g; CARB 8g; FIBER 2g; CHOL 0mg; IRON 1mg; SODIUM 149mg; CALC 30mg

Corn Frittata with Pecorino-Romano Cheese

Hands-on: 34 min. Total: 34 min. *There isn't an herb that doesn't go well with crisp fresh corn—dill, basil, cilantro, lovage—but dark green Italian parsley is also good and bracing against the corn's sweetness. For an extra dose of smoky essence, sprinkle a pinch of smoked paprika over each serving.*

1 teaspoon olive oil
1¹/₂ cups fresh corn kernels (about 2 ears)
¹/₃ cup diced shallots
¹/₂ teaspoon kosher salt, divided
¹/₂ teaspoon freshly ground black pepper, divided
¹/₄ teaspoon smoked paprika (optional)
¹/₄ cup 1% low-fat milk
6 large eggs, lightly beaten
2 teaspoons butter
1 ounce pecorino Romano cheese, grated (about ¹/₄ cup)
2 tablespoons chopped fresh flat-leaf parsley

1. Heat a medium ovenproof skillet over medium-high heat. Add oil to pan; swirl to coat. Add corn and shallots to pan; cook 3 minutes, stirring frequently. Stir in ¼ teaspoon salt, ¼ teaspoon pepper, and paprika, if desired. Place corn mixture in a bowl; cool slightly. Wipe skillet clean with paper towels.
2. Place ¼ teaspoon salt, ¼ teaspoon pepper, milk, and eggs in a bowl; stir with a whisk until well combined. Add corn mixture to egg mixture, stirring to combine.
3. Preheat broiler to high.
4. Return pan to medium heat. Add butter to pan; swirl until butter melts. Add egg mixture to pan. Cook

1 minute, without stirring. Gently slide pan back and forth to keep eggs from sticking. Cover, reduce heat to low, and cook 4 minutes or until eggs are set and golden on the bottom. Sprinkle cheese evenly over eggs. Broil 1 minute or until eggs are just set and cheese browns. Sprinkle evenly with parsley. Serves 4 (serving size: 1 wedge)

CALORIES 227; FAT 13.4g (sat 5.8g, mono 4.4g, poly 1.9g); PROTEIN 14g; CARB 14g; FIBER 2g; CHOL 292mg; IRON 2mg; SODIUM 520mg; CALC 135mg

Quick & Easy • Vegetarian

Grilled Cheese and Green Chile Sandwiches

Hands-on: 10 min. Total: 35 min.

2 mild green chiles (such as Anaheim)
2 poblano chiles
1/4 teaspoon kosher salt
3 ounces cheddar cheese, shredded (about 3/4 cup)
1 1/2 ounces part-skim mozzarella cheese, shredded (about 1/3 cup)
8 (1-ounce) slices whole-wheat bread
Cooking spray

1. Preheat broiler to high.
2. Place chiles on a foil-lined baking sheet; broil 10 minutes or until blackened, turning once. Wrap in foil; let stand 10 minutes. Peel chiles; cut in half lengthwise. Discard seeds and membranes. Cut chiles into strips; place in a bowl. Add salt; toss.
3. Sprinkle half of cheeses evenly over 4 bread slices; top with chiles, remaining cheese, and remaining bread slices.
4. Heat a large cast-iron skillet over medium heat. Coat both sides of 2 sandwiches with cooking spray; place in pan. Cook 4 minutes or until golden brown and crisp. Turn over; cover and cook 3 minutes or until cheese melts. Remove from pan. Repeat procedure with remaining sandwiches and cooking spray. Serves 4 (serving size: 1 sandwich)

CALORIES 269; FAT 10.7g (sat 6g, mono 3.4g, poly 0.6g); PROTEIN 16g; CARB 28g; FIBER 4g; CHOL 29mg; IRON 2mg; SODIUM 585mg; CALC 304mg

Kid Friendly • Quick & Easy
Gluten Free • Vegetarian

Grilled Summer Squash Gremolata

Hands-on: 13 min. Total: 36 min. This all-purpose, easy summer side goes great with just about any main dish. You can keep the cooking indoors by using a grill pan; because of the smaller surface area, you'll need to cook the squash in two batches.

3 tablespoons finely chopped fresh parsley
2 teaspoons fresh lemon juice
1 1/2 teaspoons extra-virgin olive oil
1/2 teaspoon salt
1/4 teaspoon freshly ground black pepper
1 garlic clove, minced
4 yellow squash, cut lengthwise into 1/4-inch slices (about 1 1/2 pounds)
Cooking spray

1. Preheat grill to medium-high heat.
2. Combine first 6 ingredients in a large bowl.
3. Coat squash slices lightly with cooking spray. Place squash on grill rack coated with cooking spray; grill 1 1/2 minutes on each side or until tender. Add squash to parsley mixture; toss gently to coat. Serve immediately. Serves 5 (serving size: 2/3 cup)

CALORIES 38; FAT 1.8g (sat 0.3g, mono 1g, poly 0.3g); PROTEIN 2g; CARB 5g; FIBER 2g; CHOL 0mg; IRON 1mg; SODIUM 240mg; CALC 25mg

Quick & Easy

Indian-Spiced Grilled Shrimp and Okra
(pictured on page 223)

Hands-on: 25 min. Total: 25 min.
Here's a fun way to cook okra; it retains some crunch and doesn't even think of getting slimy. The fresh serrano chile and curry powder offer a good bit of heat; seed the chile or omit it for a milder dish.

3 tablespoons canola oil
1 teaspoon Madras curry powder
1/2 teaspoon ground coriander
1 serrano chile, minced
24 large shrimp, peeled and deveined (about 1 pound)
1 pound small okra pods, trimmed
Cooking spray
1/2 teaspoon kosher salt
2 tablespoons chopped fresh cilantro

1. Preheat grill to medium-high heat.
2. Combine first 4 ingredients in a small bowl. Place half of serrano mixture and shrimp in a bowl; toss to coat. Place remaining serrano mixture and okra in a bowl; toss to coat.
3. Thread shrimp onto 4 (8-inch) skewers. Thread okra onto 4 (8-inch) skewers. Place skewers on grill rack coated with cooking spray. Grill okra 3 minutes on each side or until well-marked and crisp-tender; sprinkle with salt. Grill shrimp 3 minutes on each side or until done; sprinkle with cilantro. Serves 4 (serving size: 1 shrimp skewer and 1 okra skewer)

CALORIES 211; FAT 11.9g (sat 1g, mono 6.8g, poly 3.2g); PROTEIN 18g; CARB 9g; FIBER 4g; CHOL 143mg; IRON 1mg; SODIUM 417mg; CALC 157mg

Cucumber and Herb Salad with Pine Nuts

Hands-on: 10 min. Total: 10 min. *For this salad, leave the skins on the cucumbers, and mix varieties. Lovage is a great cucumber herb—lively but not overwhelming. If you have it, use it in place of the celery leaves and flat-leaf parsley. Or change directions and go for dill, another natural with cukes.*

1 tablespoon lemon rind strips
2 tablespoons fresh lemon juice
1 tablespoon extra-virgin olive oil
½ teaspoon kosher salt
¼ teaspoon freshly ground black pepper
¼ cup coarsely chopped flat-leaf parsley leaves
¼ cup coarsely chopped celery leaves
4 green onions, thinly sliced
3 cups coarsely chopped or sliced cucumber
2 tablespoons pine nuts, toasted

1. Combine first 5 ingredients in a medium bowl, stirring with a whisk. Add parsley, celery leaves, onions, and cucumber; toss gently. Sprinkle with pine nuts. Serves 4 (serving size: about ¾ cup)

CALORIES 76; **FAT** 6.4g (sat 0.7g, mono 3.3g, poly 1.8g); **PROTEIN** 1g; **CARB** 5g; **FIBER** 1g; **CHOL** 0mg; **IRON** 1mg; **SODIUM** 245mg; **CALC** 26mg

Halibut with Charred Tomatoes and Dill

Hands-on: 12 min. Total: 12 min. *Who would believe this elegant dish takes only 12 minutes to make? For the prettiest presentation, choose small tomatoes in different colors. If some of your garden oregano is purple, by all means use it here.*

4 (6-ounce) halibut fillets, skinned
½ teaspoon salt, divided
¼ teaspoon freshly ground black pepper
2 tablespoons butter
½ cup dry white wine
1½ cups cherry, pear, or grape tomatoes
1 teaspoon olive oil
1 tablespoon chopped fresh dill
Oregano leaves (optional)

1. Heat a large skillet over medium-high heat. Sprinkle fish with ¼ teaspoon salt and pepper. Add butter to pan; swirl until butter melts. Add fish; cook 1 minute. Add wine; cover, reduce heat to medium-low, and cook 7 minutes or until fish flakes easily when tested with a fork.
2. Heat a small skillet over high heat. Combine tomatoes and oil. Add to pan; cook 3 minutes or until lightly charred and beginning to soften.
3. Place 1 fillet in each of 4 shallow bowls; spoon cooking liquid evenly over fillets. Divide tomatoes among servings. Sprinkle with ¼ teaspoon salt and dill. Garnish with oregano, if desired. Serves 4

CALORIES 252; **FAT** 9.4g (sat 4.3g, mono 3.1g, poly 0.9g); **PROTEIN** 32g; **CARB** 3g; **FIBER** 1g; **CHOL** 99mg; **IRON** 1mg; **SODIUM** 466mg; **CALC** 22mg

Zucchini and Onion Gratin

Hands-on: 21 min. Total: 45 min. *You can serve this side dish hot, but it's also great at room temperature.*

2 tablespoons olive oil, divided
1 large onion, quartered lengthwise and thinly sliced
1 tablespoon tomato paste
2 teaspoons grated lemon rind
1 teaspoon thyme leaves
⅜ teaspoon kosher salt, divided
¼ teaspoon freshly ground black pepper
1½ pounds zucchini, diagonally sliced into ¼-inch-thick pieces
1 ounce Parmesan cheese, grated (about ¼ cup)

1. Heat a large skillet over medium heat. Add 1 tablespoon oil to pan; swirl to coat. Add onion; cook 6 minutes, stirring occasionally. Stir in tomato paste; cook 2 minutes. Stir in rind, thyme, ⅛ teaspoon salt, and pepper; cook 2 minutes, stirring occasionally.
2. Preheat broiler to high.
3. Arrange zucchini on a jelly-roll pan. Drizzle with 1 tablespoon oil; toss. Broil 7 minutes or until lightly charred. Sprinkle with ¼ teaspoon salt.
4. Preheat oven to 375°.
5. Spread onion mixture in a 2-quart gratin dish. Arrange zucchini mixture over onion mixture. Sprinkle with cheese. Cover and bake at 375° for 25 minutes. Remove from oven.
6. Preheat broiler to high.
7. Uncover zucchini mixture; broil 1½ minutes or until lightly browned. Serves 6 (serving size: about 1 cup)

CALORIES 92; **FAT** 6.3g (sat 1.6g, mono 3.7g, poly 0.6g); **PROTEIN** 4g; **CARB** 7g; **FIBER** 2g; **CHOL** 4mg; **IRON** 1mg; **SODIUM** 224mg; **CALC** 79mg

THE FRUIT RECIPES

When it comes to just-plucked fruity goodness, even avid gardeners turn to farmers' market finds because it requires more land than most have to do justice to the varieties of peaches, cherries, and plums that are being rediscovered by American orchardists.

Fruit brings its wonderful tang, juice, and balance to far more than desserts. In these pages you'll find salads, main dishes, and appetizers. Not that we neglected the sweeter side of the meal; check out the marriage of almond and fruit in our Apricot-Amaretti Crisp on page 143.

Gluten Free

Grilled Chicken Thighs with Peach-Lime Salsa

Hands-on: 45 min. Total: 2 hrs. 15 min.

3 tablespoons olive oil
1 teaspoon ground cumin
6 garlic cloves, minced
6 (5-ounce) skinless bone-in chicken thighs, trimmed
2 tablespoons finely chopped red onion
1 tablespoon chopped fresh basil
1 1/2 teaspoons chopped fresh mint
1 1/2 teaspoons fresh lime juice
1/2 teaspoon sugar
2 ripe peaches (about 1/2 pound), peeled and chopped
1 red or green jalapeño pepper, minced
3/4 teaspoon salt, divided
1/2 teaspoon black pepper
Cooking spray
6 lime wedges (optional)

1. Place first 3 ingredients in a large bowl, stirring with a whisk. Add chicken; toss well to coat. Cover and refrigerate 1 hour.
2. To prepare salsa, combine onion and next 6 ingredients; stir in 1/4 teaspoon salt. Let stand 1 hour.
3. Preheat grill to medium-high heat.
4. Remove chicken from marinade; discard marinade. Let chicken stand at room temperature 30 minutes. Sprinkle chicken evenly with 1/2 teaspoon salt and black pepper. Place chicken on grill rack coated with cooking spray; grill 6 minutes on each side or until done. Serve with salsa and lime wedges, if desired. Serves 6 (serving size: 1 thigh and about 1/3 cup salsa)

CALORIES 194; **FAT** 10.4g (sat 2.3g, mono 5.2g, poly 1.7g); **PROTEIN** 20g; **CARB** 5g; **FIBER** 1g; **CHOL** 110mg; **IRON** 1mg; **SODIUM** 367mg; **CALC** 17mg

Quick & Easy • Gluten Free

Tequila-Watermelon Refresco

Hands-on: 10 min. Total: 10 min.

5 1/2 cups chopped seeded watermelon
3/4 cup tequila
6 tablespoons Triple Sec (orange-flavored liqueur)
5 tablespoons fresh lime juice
1/4 teaspoon salt
2 1/4 cups club soda, chilled
6 lime wedges

1. Place watermelon in a blender; process until smooth. Pour pureed watermelon into a sieve over a large bowl, pressing with the back of a spoon to extract as much liquid as possible; discard solids. Combine 3 cups watermelon juice, tequila, Triple Sec, lime juice, and salt in a pitcher; stir with a whisk. Gently stir in club soda. Serve over ice with lime wedges. Serves 6 (serving size: about 1 cup)

CALORIES 138; **FAT** 0.2g (sat 0g, mono 0g, poly 0.1g); **PROTEIN** 1g; **CARB** 13g; **FIBER** 0g; **CHOL** 0mg; **IRON** 0mg; **SODIUM** 119mg; **CALC** 12mg

Quick & Easy • Make Ahead Vegetarian

Farro, Cherry, and Walnut Salad

Hands-on: 25 min. Total: 25 min.

5 cups water
1 1/2 cups uncooked farro
1/2 teaspoon salt, divided
3/4 pound sweet cherries, pitted and halved (about 2 cups)
2/3 cup diced celery
1/2 cup coarsely chopped walnuts, toasted
1/4 cup packed flat-leaf parsley leaves
2 tablespoons fresh lemon juice
1 tablespoon whole-grain Dijon mustard
1 tablespoon honey
1/4 teaspoon black pepper
3 tablespoons extra-virgin olive oil

1. Bring 5 cups water to a boil in a large saucepan. Add farro and 1/4 teaspoon salt to boiling water; cook 15 minutes or until al dente. Drain; cool at room temperature 15 minutes. Combine farro, cherries, celery, walnuts, and parsley in a large bowl.
2. Combine lemon juice, mustard, honey, pepper, and 1/4 teaspoon salt, stirring with a whisk. Gradually add oil, stirring constantly with a whisk. Pour dressing over farro mixture; toss to coat. Serves 8 (serving size: 2/3 cup)

CALORIES 256; **FAT** 10.6g (sat 1.2g, mono 4.4g, poly 3.9g); **PROTEIN** 7g; **CARB** 37g; **FIBER** 5g; **CHOL** 0mg; **IRON** 2mg; **SODIUM** 201mg; **CALC** 34mg

Lemon Verbena– Buttermilk Sherbet

Hands-on: 10 min. Total: 3 hr. 10 min.
OK, so lemon verbena isn't a fruit—but it does add fruity flavor to this lovely dessert. Its floral aroma and taste soften the tang of the buttermilk.

1 cup granulated sugar
³/₄ cup water
3 tablespoons packed, coarsely chopped fresh lemon verbena
2¹/₂ cups cold whole-milk buttermilk
1 tablespoon grated lemon rind
Dash of salt
Lemon rind strips (optional)

1. Combine first 3 ingredients in a saucepan, stirring until sugar dissolves. Bring to a boil; boil 2 minutes. Remove from heat; let stand 30 minutes. Pour syrup through a fine sieve into a bowl; discard solids. Stir in buttermilk, rind, and salt; chill 1 hour.
2. Pour mixture into the freezer can of an ice-cream freezer; freeze according to manufacturer's instructions. Spoon sherbet into a freezer-safe container; cover and freeze 1 hour or until firm. Garnish with lemon rind strips, if desired. Serves 8 (serving size: about ½ cup)

CALORIES 145; **FAT** 2.5g (sat 1.5g, mono 0.6g, poly 0.2g); **PROTEIN** 2g; **CARB** 29g; **FIBER** 0g; **CHOL** 8mg; **IRON** 0mg; **SODIUM** 99mg; **CALC** 89mg

Raspberries with Peach-Basil Sorbet

Hands-on: 10 min. Total: 1 hr. 55 min.
Here's a twist on peach Melba, the classic dessert of poached peaches with raspberry sauce. We turn juicy summer peaches instead into a velvety sorbet spiked with basil and serve it with fresh raspberries for the perfect ending to a summer meal.

1 cup granulated sugar
³/₄ cup water
¹/₄ cup packed, coarsely chopped basil leaves
1¹/₂ pounds ripe peaches
1 tablespoon fresh lemon juice
Dash of salt
12 ounces fresh raspberries
Basil sprigs (optional)

1. Combine first 3 ingredients in a saucepan. Bring to a boil; stir until sugar dissolves. Let stand 15 minutes. Pour through a fine sieve into a bowl; discard solids.
2. Cook peaches in a large pot of boiling water for 1 minute. Place peaches in a bowl of ice water until cool. Peel peaches; remove pits and chop flesh. Place chopped peaches and lemon juice in a blender; process until smooth. Stir peach mixture and salt into basil mixture. Chill 1 hour.
3. Pour peach mixture into the freezer can of an ice-cream freezer; freeze according to manufacturer's instructions. Spoon sorbet into a freezer-safe container; cover and freeze until firm. Serve with raspberries. Garnish with basil sprigs, if desired. Serves 6 (serving size: ½ cup sorbet and about ⅓ cup raspberries)

CALORIES 199; **FAT** 0.6g (sat 0g, mono 0.1g, poly 0.3g); **PROTEIN** 2g; **CARB** 50g; **FIBER** 5g; **CHOL** 0mg; **IRON** 1mg; **SODIUM** 26mg; **CALC** 21mg

Duck Breasts with Blackberry-Port Sauce

Hands-on: 20 min. Total: 20 min.
Luscious, lean duck breasts make for a sophisticated but easy main dish, where the blackberry sauce provides a fruity counterpoint to the duck's meatiness. For a light dinner, serve over a bed of lettuce with a piece of crusty bread.

1 tablespoon olive oil
4 (6-ounce) boneless duck breast halves, skinned
³/₄ teaspoon kosher salt, divided
¹/₂ teaspoon freshly ground black pepper, divided
1¹/₂ cups blackberries
¹/₄ cup finely chopped shallots
1 tablespoon chopped fresh thyme
¹/₂ cup port or other sweet red wine
³/₄ cup unsalted chicken stock
1 teaspoon red wine vinegar

1. Heat a large nonstick skillet over medium-high heat. Add oil to pan; swirl to coat. Sprinkle duck with ½ teaspoon salt and ¼ teaspoon pepper. Add duck to pan; cook 3 minutes or until browned. Turn duck over; cook 3 minutes or until desired degree of doneness. Remove duck from pan; let stand 5 minutes.
2. Add blackberries, shallots, and thyme to pan; sauté 2 minutes or until slightly softened. Add port; cook 1 minute or until syrupy. Add stock and any juices from duck; cook 5 minutes or until thickened and reduced to about ½ cup. Stir in ¼ teaspoon salt, ¼ teaspoon pepper, and vinegar. Cut duck across grain into thin slices; serve with sauce. Serves 4 (serving size: 1 duck breast half and about 2 tablespoons sauce)

CALORIES 227; **FAT** 7.6g (sat 1.7g, mono 3.6g, poly 1.1g); **PROTEIN** 20g; **CARB** 11g; **FIBER** 3g; **CHOL** 71mg; **IRON** 5mg; **SODIUM** 441mg; **CALC** 32mg

Blueberry Coffeecake with Almond Streusel

Hands-on: 25 min. Total: 1 hr. 40 min.

9 ounces unbleached all-purpose
   flour (about 2 cups)
1½ teaspoons baking powder
½ teaspoon baking soda
½ teaspoon salt
2 cups fresh blueberries
⅓ cup packed brown sugar
¼ cup old-fashioned rolled oats
2 tablespoons sliced almonds
1 tablespoon unbleached
   all-purpose flour
¼ teaspoon ground cinnamon
2 tablespoons butter, melted
¾ cup granulated sugar
¼ cup butter, softened
2 tablespoons canola oil
1 large egg, lightly beaten
1 cup nonfat buttermilk
2 teaspoons grated lemon rind
1 tablespoon fresh lemon juice
Cooking spray

1. Preheat oven to 375°.
2. Weigh or lightly spoon 9 ounces flour into dry measuring cups; level with a knife. Combine 9 ounces flour and next 3 ingredients (through salt), stirring with a whisk. Remove 2 tablespoons flour mixture; sprinkle over blueberries, tossing to coat.
3. Combine brown sugar and next 4 ingredients (through cinnamon) in a medium bowl. Drizzle with 2 tablespoons melted butter; toss to combine.
4. Place granulated sugar, ¼ cup butter, and oil in a large bowl; beat with a mixer at medium speed until blended (about 2 minutes). Add egg; beat well. Add flour mixture and buttermilk alternately to sugar mixture, beginning and ending with flour mixture; mix after each addition. Stir in rind and juice.
5. Spoon half of batter into a 9-inch square light-colored metal baking pan coated with cooking spray (do not use a dark or nonstick pan). Sprinkle evenly with 1 cup blueberry mixture. Spoon remaining batter over blueberries. Sprinkle evenly with remaining 1 cup blueberry mixture. Sprinkle with brown sugar mixture. Bake at 375° for 45 minutes or until a wooden pick inserted in center comes out clean. Cool in pan 10 minutes on a wire rack; remove from pan. Cool completely on a wire rack. Serves 12 (serving size: 1 piece)

CALORIES 264; **FAT** 9.5g (sat 4.1g, mono 3.5g, poly 1.2g);
PROTEIN 4g; **CARB** 42g; **FIBER** 2g; **CHOL** 31mg;
IRON 1mg; **SODIUM** 280mg; **CALC** 73mg

Shaved Melon Salad with Lemon-Sherry Dressing

Hands-on: 20 min. Total: 20 min.
For the best flavor, choose a good bottle of sherry. If you don't have a mandoline, you can cube the melons or scoop them with a melon baller.

1 teaspoon grated lemon rind
2 tablespoons fresh lemon juice
1 tablespoon sherry
1 teaspoon honey
⅜ teaspoon kosher salt
¼ teaspoon freshly ground black
   pepper
2 tablespoons extra-virgin olive oil
½ medium cantaloupe
½ medium honeydew melon
3 tablespoons torn fresh mint

1. Combine first 6 ingredients in a large bowl, stirring with a whisk. Gradually add oil, stirring constantly with a whisk
2. Remove and discard seeds from cantaloupe and honeydew melon. Cut melons into 2-inch-wide wedges; remove rinds. Cut melon wedges into long, thin ribbons using a mandoline. Add melon ribbons to dressing; toss gently to coat. Sprinkle with mint. Serve immediately. Serves 6 (serving size: about 1 cup)

CALORIES 94; **FAT** 4.7g (sat 0.7g, mono 3.3g, poly 0.6g);
PROTEIN 1g; **CARB** 13g; **FIBER** 1g; **CHOL** 0mg;
IRON 0mg; **SODIUM** 143mg; **CALC** 12mg

Apricot-Amaretti Crisp

Hands-on: 10 min. Total: 40 min.

1½ pounds apricots, pitted and cut
   into eighths
⅓ cup packed brown sugar
½ teaspoon ground nutmeg, divided
Cooking spray
⅔ cup crushed amaretti cookies
2 tablespoons all-purpose flour
⅛ teaspoon ground cinnamon
Dash of ground cloves
2 tablespoons unsalted butter, melted
⅓ cup heavy whipping cream

1. Preheat oven to 375°.
2. Combine apricots, sugar, and ¼ teaspoon nutmeg; toss. Spoon apricot mixture evenly into 6 (8-ounce) ramekins coated with cooking spray.
3. Combine ¼ teaspoon nutmeg, cookies, and next 4 ingredients; sprinkle cookie mixture over apricot mixture. Arrange ramekins on a baking sheet. Bake at 375° for 25 minutes or until filling is bubbly.
4. Place cream in a medium bowl; beat with a mixer at high speed until soft peaks form. Dollop cream over crisps. Serves 6 (serving size: 1 crisp and 1½ tablespoons whipped cream)

CALORIES 247; **FAT** 10g (sat 5.6g, mono 2.6g, poly 0.4g);
PROTEIN 4g; **CARB** 39g; **FIBER** 3g; **CHOL** 28mg;
IRON 1mg; **SODIUM** 47mg; **CALC** 36mg

Grilled Ginger-Glazed Chicken Livers with Spicy Plum Sauce

Hands-on: 25 min. Total: 1 hr. 15 min.
This is a fantastic appetizer featuring rich chicken livers paired with a Southeast Asian-inspired sauce.

1/2 cup water
3 tablespoons rice vinegar
1 tablespoon sugar
1 tablespoon Sriracha (hot chile sauce)
4 plums, pitted and quartered (about 1 pound)
1 star anise
1 (1-inch) cinnamon stick
1/2 cup mirin
1 1/2 tablespoons minced peeled fresh ginger
1 tablespoon lower-sodium soy sauce
2 garlic cloves, minced
1 pound chicken livers
Cooking spray
1/2 English cucumber, thinly sliced

1. Combine first 7 ingredients in a saucepan. Bring to a simmer; cover and cook 15 minutes or until plums are tender. Discard star anise and cinnamon. Cool completely. Place in a blender; process until smooth.
2. Combine mirin, ginger, soy sauce, and garlic in a saucepan over medium heat. Bring to a simmer; cook 4 minutes or until reduced to 1/4 cup.
3. Trim excess fat and connective tissue from livers; separate livers into lobes. Pat livers dry with paper towels. Heat a grill pan over high heat. Coat pan with cooking spray. Add half of livers to pan; cook 7 minutes or until slightly firm (like a cooked chicken breast), turning once. Remove from pan; brush with half of glaze. Repeat procedure with remaining livers and glaze. Serve with plum sauce and cucumber. Serves 8 (serving size: about 1½ ounces livers, ¼ cup plum sauce, and about 3 cucumber slices)

CALORIES 141; FAT 2.8g (sat 1g, mono 0.7g, poly 0.8g); PROTEIN 10g; CARB 15g; FIBER 1g; CHOL 196mg; IRON 5mg; SODIUM 150mg; CALC 10mg

---

SUPPLE AND SWEET—READY TO EAT

Selection and storage tips for summer fruits

CHERRIES
Choose the Best: Check for deep color saturation and no wrinkled skin around the stems.
Keep It Fresh: Cherries are best eaten within 2 days of purchase. Refrigerate, unwashed, in a plastic bag; bring to room temperature before eating for best flavor.

BLUEBERRIES
Choose the Best: Go for plump berries with a lightly frosted hue.
Keep It Fresh: Keep unwashed blueberries in their original container, and refrigerate for up to a week.

CANTALOUPE AND HONEYDEW MELON
Choose the Best: Select cantaloupes with defined netting and tan/yellow undertones. Honeydew melons should have a pale, creamy rind and feel heavy for their size. Slight cracking around the stem signifies ripeness.
Keep It Fresh: Let ripen up to 2 days at room temperature. Store whole melons in the refrigerator up to 1 week. Wrap sliced melon in plastic wrap, and refrigerate up to 3 days.

PLUMS, PEACHES, AND NECTARINES
Choose the Best: Should yield to gentle squeezing. Peaches and nectarines emit a strong floral aroma when ripe.
Keep It Fresh: Keep handling to a minimum, and allow to ripen at room temperature; refrigerate once ripe. Ripe plums and yellow peaches should last 3 to 5 days, but nectarines and white peaches should be eaten within a day.

ZUCCHINI LASAGNA

A squash-loving Philly chef Marc Vetri shares his great recipe.

There's an easygoing quality to the sometimes-derided zucchini that Vetri loves. "It's just so versatile," says the chef-restaurateur, who presides over such restaurants as Vetri, Osteria, and Alla Spina. "It works with everything: fish, meat, salads, or on its own."

In his lasagna with zucchini, Vetri pairs the squash and his exquisite house-made pasta with ultrarich Burrata, a shell of fresh mozzarella with sweet cream and cheese curd at the center. In our lighter take, we combine mozzarella with fat-free ricotta and a little mozzarella liquid to mimic the creamy Burrata texture. Try the original dish at Vetri this month in Philadelphia's Center City East.

Kid Friendly • Make Ahead Vegetarian

Lasagna with Zucchini

Hands-on: 20 min. Total: 1 hr. 10 min.

2 tablespoons extra-virgin olive oil
3 cups julienne-cut zucchini
2 cups julienne-cut yellow squash
1 1/2 tablespoons chopped fresh thyme
6 garlic cloves, thinly sliced
3/4 teaspoon kosher salt, divided
1/2 teaspoon black pepper, divided
1 cup fat-free ricotta cheese
1/4 cup water from fresh mozzarella container
4 ounces fresh mozzarella cheese
2.5 ounces grated fresh Parmesan cheese (about 10 tablespoons)
1 (9-ounce) package refrigerated fresh lasagna noodles (6 noodles)
Cooking spray

1. Preheat oven to 375°. Heat a skillet over medium-high heat. Add oil; swirl. Add zucchini, squash, thyme, and garlic; sauté 5 minutes. Stir in ½ teaspoon salt and ¼ teaspoon pepper. Remove zucchini mixture; cool.

2. Place ¼ teaspoon salt, ¼ teaspoon pepper, ricotta, mozzarella water, and mozzarella in a food processor. Pulse until smooth. Combine ½ cup ricotta mixture and ½ cup Parmesan.

3. Arrange 2 noodles in an 8-inch square glass baking dish coated with cooking spray; trim to fit if needed. Top with half of zucchini mixture and half of ricotta mixture. Repeat layers, ending with noodles. Top with ricotta-Parmesan mixture. Cover dish with foil. Bake at 375° for 30 minutes; uncover. Bake, uncovered, 15 minutes.

4. Turn broiler to high. Sprinkle lasagna with 2 tablespoons Parmesan. Broil 2 minutes or until lightly browned. Let stand 5 minutes. Serves 6

CALORIES 326; FAT 14.2g (sat 6g, mono 4g, poly 0.7g); PROTEIN 17g; CARB 32g; FIBER 3g; CHOL 61mg; IRON 2mg; SODIUM 598mg; CALC 212mg

RECIPE MAKEOVER

CHIMICHANGA CHANGE-UP

All the cheesy goodness you want inside, plus crispy perfection outside.

The calorie count rises steeply when an overstuffed burrito hits the deep-fryer then gets covered in cheese. The classic chimichanga boasts 730 calories and 40g of fat.

To shave some calories off this classic, we start with a simple combination of salsa verde and chicken stock, reduce it until thick, and make it rich and creamy with ⅓-less-fat cream cheese. Sautéed kale, onion, and mushrooms add a delicious and nutrient-dense twist to our tender poached chicken breast, and all gets piled together on a tortilla and sprinkled with reduced-fat Mexican cheese.

We use an 8-inch flour tortilla instead of the traditional 10- or 12-incher; it's more portion-friendly and still holds plenty of meat and cheese. Instead of deep-frying, we pan-sear it in a hot skillet, turning until brown on all sides, to create a crunchy, fried-like coating. Fresh tomatoes and an avocado cream offer a bright finish. It's a crisp, flavor-packed wrap of veggies, meat, and cheese for less than 300 calories.

OURS SAVES
435 calories, 31g total fat, 11g sat fat, and 733mg sodium over the classic chimichanga

Kid Friendly

Chicken, Kale, and Mushroom Chimichangas

Hands-on: 60 min. Total: 60 min.

2 cups unsalted chicken stock
2 (6-ounce) skinless, boneless chicken breast halves
¾ cup salsa verde
2 ounces ⅓-less-fat cream cheese
½ teaspoon ground cumin
6 tablespoons chopped fresh cilantro, divided
1 tablespoon olive oil
1 cup chopped onion
4 garlic cloves, minced
8 ounces presliced cremini mushrooms
2 cups chopped Lacinato kale
¼ teaspoon black pepper
8 (8-inch) flour tortillas
3 ounces preshredded reduced-fat 4-cheese Mexican blend cheese (about ¾ cup)

Cooking spray
¾ cup ripe peeled avocado, chopped
3 tablespoons 1% low-fat milk
2 tablespoons fresh lime juice, divided
2 cups chopped grape tomatoes

1. Combine stock and chicken in a saucepan over medium heat; bring to a simmer. Cook 8 minutes or until done. Remove chicken with a slotted spoon; let stand 10 minutes. Shred chicken; set aside. Drain cooking liquid through a sieve over a bowl, reserving liquid; discard solids. Set aside 2 tablespoons liquid.

2. Return remaining cooking liquid to pan. Add salsa verde; bring to a boil. Cook until reduced to 1 cup (about 11 minutes). Reduce heat to low. Add cream cheese and cumin; stir with a whisk until smooth. Remove from heat; stir in chicken and ¼ cup cilantro.

3. Heat a large skillet over medium heat. Add oil to pan; swirl to coat. Add onion, garlic, and mushrooms; sauté 8 minutes or until tender. Add kale, black pepper, and reserved 2 tablespoons cooking liquid. Cook 2 minutes or until kale wilts, stirring occasionally. Add kale mixture to chicken mixture. Divide chicken mixture evenly among tortillas. Top each with about 1½ tablespoons cheese. Fold in edges of tortilla; roll up.

4. Heat a large nonstick skillet over medium-high heat. Coat all sides of each chimichanga evenly with cooking spray. Cook 6 to 8 minutes, turning to brown on all sides.

5. Place avocado, milk, and 1 tablespoon lime juice in a mini food processor; process until smooth.

6. Combine tomatoes, 2 tablespoons cilantro, and 1 tablespoon lime juice. To serve, top each chimichanga with 1½ tablespoons avocado cream and about ¼ cup tomato salad. Serves 8

CALORIES 296; FAT 10.3g (sat 3g, mono 3.9g, poly 0.9g); PROTEIN 20g; CARB 32g; FIBER 6g; CHOL 39mg; IRON 2mg; SODIUM 625mg; CALC 245mg

SUPER SIMPLE SUMMER PASTAS

Garden-fresh ingredients add a seasonal kick to our favorite comfort food. Casual suppers this good will be hits with family and friends.

Kid Friendly • Quick & Easy

Summer Vegetable Rigatoni with Chicken

(pictured on page 224)

Hands-on: 25 min. Total: 40 min.

12 ounces uncooked rigatoni
1½ cups diagonally sliced sugar snap peas
Cooking spray
3 (6-ounce) skinless, boneless chicken breast halves
1 teaspoon freshly ground black pepper, divided
¾ teaspoon kosher salt, divided
¼ cup olive oil
2 tablespoons sliced garlic
2 oregano sprigs
2 thyme sprigs
½ cup unsalted chicken stock
3 ounces Parmigiano-Reggiano cheese, grated and divided (about ¾ cup)
2 cups multicolored cherry tomatoes, halved
¼ cup small basil leaves
1 teaspoon oregano leaves
1 teaspoon thyme leaves

1. Cook pasta according to package directions 10 minutes, omitting salt and fat. Add peas; cook 2 minutes. Drain mixture over a bowl, reserving 1½ cups cooking liquid; rinse with cold water. Drain.
2. Heat a grill pan over medium-high heat; coat with cooking spray. Sprinkle chicken with ½ teaspoon pepper and ¼ teaspoon salt. Add chicken to pan; cook 5 minutes on each side or until done. Let stand 10 minutes; cut chicken into 1-inch pieces.
3. Combine oil, garlic, oregano sprigs, and thyme sprigs in a large skillet over medium heat; cook 4 minutes or just until garlic begins to brown. Add reserved 1½ cups cooking liquid, ¼ teaspoon pepper, ½ teaspoon salt, and stock to pan; bring to a boil. Cook until reduced to ¾ cup (about 10 minutes); discard herb sprigs. Stir in 2 ounces cheese; stir until cheese melts. Stir in pasta mixture. Stir in chicken, 1 ounce cheese, and tomatoes. Sprinkle with ¼ teaspoon pepper, basil, oregano, and thyme leaves. Serves 6 (serving size: about 1½ cups)

CALORIES 428; **FAT** 13.7g (sat 2.5g, mono 7.3g, poly 1.7g); **PROTEIN** 28g; **CARB** 47g; FIBER 3g; **CHOL** 56mg; **IRON** 3mg; **SODIUM** 370mg; **CALC** 69mg

Quick & Easy • Vegetarian

Linguine with Sweet Pepper Sauce

Hands-on: 29 min. Total: 33 min.

8 ounces uncooked linguine
1 pound red bell peppers, halved and seeded
1 pound yellow bell peppers, halved and seeded
3 tablespoons extra-virgin olive oil
6 garlic cloves, thinly sliced
¾ teaspoon kosher salt
¼ teaspoon black pepper
¼ cup small basil leaves
1 (4-ounce) ball Burrata cheese

1. Preheat broiler to high.
2. Cook pasta according to package directions until al dente, omitting salt and fat. Drain pasta, reserving ¼ cup cooking liquid.
3. While pasta cooks, place bell peppers, skin sides up, on a foil-lined baking sheet; flatten with hand. Broil 8 minutes or until blackened. Wrap peppers in foil. Let stand 10 minutes; peel. Set aside half of 1 of each color bell pepper. Puree remaining peppers in a food processor.
4. Heat a large skillet over medium-low heat. Add oil to pan; swirl. Add garlic; cook 2 minutes or until fragrant and soft, stirring occasionally. Add reserved ¼ cup cooking liquid, pureed bell pepper, salt, and black pepper; stir with a whisk. Simmer 5 minutes or until thickened. Add pasta; cook 1 minute, tossing to combine.
5. Thinly slice reserved bell pepper. Place about 1 cup pasta mixture in each of 4 bowls; top each serving with sliced bell peppers, 1 tablespoon basil, and 1 ounce cheese. Serve immediately. Serves 4

CALORIES 412; **FAT** 14.2g (sat 5.3g, mono 6.9g, poly 0.9g); **PROTEIN** 14g; **CARB** 55g; **FIBER** 6g; **CHOL** 20mg; **IRON** 3mg; **SODIUM** 442mg; **CALC** 187mg

Cavatappi with Salmon and Wilted Fennel

Hands-on: 22 min. Total: 22 min.

6 ounces uncooked cavatappi
**3 (6-ounce) skinless wild sockeye
    salmon fillets (about ³/₄ inch thick)**
1 teaspoon kosher salt, divided
**¹/₂ teaspoon freshly ground black
    pepper, divided**
**2 tablespoons extra-virgin olive oil,
    divided**
2 cups sliced fennel bulb
1 cup vertically sliced onion
3 cups grape tomatoes, halved
¹/₂ cup dry white wine
Fennel fronds (optional)

1. Cook pasta according to package directions until al dente, omitting salt and fat. Drain pasta, reserving ½ cup cooking liquid.
2. While pasta cooks, heat a large nonstick skillet over medium-high heat. Sprinkle salmon with ½ teaspoon salt and ¼ teaspoon pepper. Add 1 tablespoon oil to pan; swirl to coat. Add salmon; cook 3 minutes on each side or until desired degree of doneness. Remove salmon; flake into large pieces.
3. Add 1 tablespoon oil to pan; swirl to coat. Add fennel and onion; sauté 2 minutes. Reduce heat to medium; cook 10 minutes or until mixture begins to brown, stirring occasionally. Stir in tomatoes and wine; cook 2 minutes or until syrupy. Stir in pasta, reserved ½ cup cooking liquid, ½ teaspoon salt, and ¼ teaspoon pepper; cook 2 minutes or until slightly thickened. Gently stir in salmon. Top with fennel fronds, if desired. Serves 4 (serving size: 2 cups)

CALORIES 468; **FAT** 14.8g (sat 2.5g, mono 7.3g, poly 3.2g); **PROTEIN** 34g; **CARB** 42g; **FIBER** 4g; **CHOL** 68mg; **IRON** 2mg; **SODIUM** 573mg; **CALC** 66mg

Silky Pappardelle with Zucchini Ribbons

Hands-on: 20 min. Total: 20 min.

4 baby zucchini (about 1 pound)
³/₄ teaspoon kosher salt, divided
3 (1-pint) packages cherry tomatoes
**1¹/₂ tablespoons extra-virgin olive oil,
    divided**
8 ounces uncooked pappardelle
6 tablespoons crème fraîche
**1 tablespoon chopped fresh flat-leaf
    parsley**
2 teaspoons minced fresh chives
2 teaspoons chopped fresh thyme

1. Preheat broiler to high.
2. Shave zucchini into thin strips using a vegetable peeler; toss with ¼ teaspoon salt in a medium bowl.
3. Combine tomatoes and 1½ teaspoons oil in a large bowl. Arrange tomatoes in a single layer on a foil-lined baking sheet; broil 10 minutes or until blistered. Reserve juices.
4. Cook pasta according to package directions until almost al dente, omitting salt and fat; drain, reserving ½ cup cooking liquid.
5. Heat a large skillet over medium-high heat. Add reserved cooking liquid; bring to a boil. Add pasta, tomatoes, and tomato juices; cook 2 minutes or until slightly thickened. Remove from heat. Stir in 1 tablespoon oil, ½ teaspoon salt, crème fraîche, and herbs. Divide pasta mixture among 4 bowls; top with zucchini. Serves 4 (serving size: 1½ cups)

CALORIES 387; **FAT** 14.4g (sat 5.9g, mono 5.8g, poly 0.8g); **PROTEIN** 12g; **CARB** 54g; **FIBER** 6g; **CHOL** 21mg; **IRON** 3mg; **SODIUM** 390mg; **CALC** 53mg

Spaghetti with Toasty Garlic Tomato Sauce

Hands-on: 19 min. Total: 19 min.

4 ounces uncooked spaghetti
2 cups grape tomatoes
2 tablespoons extra-virgin olive oil
2 large garlic cloves, thinly sliced
¹/₈ teaspoon crushed red pepper
2 tablespoons thinly sliced fresh basil
³/₈ teaspoon kosher salt
**2 tablespoons grated fresh pecorino
    Romano cheese**

1. Cook pasta according to package directions until al dente, omitting salt and fat. Drain pasta, reserving ¼ cup cooking liquid.
2. Cut each tomato crosswise into 8 to 10 thin slices. Heat a large skillet over medium heat. Add oil; swirl to coat. Add garlic; cook 1 minute, stirring constantly. Add tomatoes and pepper; increase heat to medium-high. Cook 2 minutes or until tomatoes slightly soften, stirring occasionally. Stir in pasta, reserved ¼ cup cooking liquid, basil, and salt. Sprinkle with cheese. Serves 2 (serving size: 1 cup)

CALORIES 388; **FAT** 16.7g (sat 3.8g, mono 10g, poly 1.8g); **PROTEIN** 10g; **CARB** 49g; **FIBER** 4g; **CHOL** 8mg; **IRON** 2mg; **SODIUM** 510mg; **CALC** 107mg

Kid Friendly • Quick & Easy

Bacon and Shrimp Pasta Toss

Hands-on: 22 min. Total: 22 min.

8 ounces uncooked penne
2 applewood-smoked bacon slices
5 garlic cloves, minced
1 pound large shrimp, peeled and
   deveined
2 tablespoons extra-virgin olive oil
5 cups baby spinach leaves
½ teaspoon kosher salt

1. Cook pasta according to package directions until almost al dente, omitting salt and fat; drain, reserving ¾ cup cooking liquid.
2. Cook bacon in a large skillet over medium-high heat 10 minutes or until crisp, turning once. Remove from pan; reserve drippings. Crumble bacon. Add garlic to drippings in pan; cook 30 seconds, stirring constantly. Add shrimp; cook 1½ minutes on each side or until done. Remove shrimp from pan; set aside.
3. Add reserved ¾ cup cooking liquid and oil to pan; bring to a boil. Boil 30 seconds, stirring with a whisk. Add pasta to pan; cook 1 minute, tossing to combine. Stir in spinach, shrimp, and salt. Top with bacon. Serve immediately. Serves 4 (serving size: about 1¾ cups)

CALORIES 396; FAT 11g (sat 2.1g, mono 5.1g, poly 1.2g); PROTEIN 26g; CARB 48g; FIBER 3g; CHOL 148mg; IRON 3mg; SODIUM 570mg; CALC 101mg

THIS MONTH'S LESSON: FLAVOR BALANCE IN A CLASSIC THAI SALAD

Larb, the popular Thai salad of highly seasoned ground meat and herbs, offers cooks who like to go big a real opportunity to do so. In the main recipe, pan-toasted rice adds welcome crunch and depth of flavor. Piquant, salty, funky, tart, and sweet flavors all harmonize to near-addictive perfection. Pay attention to measurements here, as careful consideration was given to balance. Lime can be spiked after tasting if you like your food brighter (but only after tasting), and feel free to ramp up the chiles if you like a less restrained salad. The Isan people of Northern Thailand would smile upon you. For a playful, zero-percent-authentic interpretation, try the Yucatán variation.

Follow These Steps

• Heat a large skillet over medium heat. Add rice; cook 2½ minutes or until toasted, stirring occasionally. Pulse in a mini food processor until coarsely ground.
• Heat pan over medium-high heat. Coat with cooking spray. Add pork, and cook 3 minutes. Add mushrooms, and cook 3 minutes. Add turkey; spread into an even layer. Cook, without stirring, 4 minutes or until browned. Stir to crumble. Spread into an even layer; cook 3 minutes.

• Place garlic on a cutting board; sprinkle with sugar. Chop to a paste. Place paste in a large bowl. Stir in lime juice, fish sauce, shallots, and chiles. Add pork mixture and half of rice; toss. Cool slightly. Add mint, basil, and cilantro; toss.
• Place cabbage, onions, beans, and cucumber on a platter. Top with meat mixture. Sprinkle with remaining toasted rice and dried chiles. Serve with lime wedges. Serves 4 (serving size: 1¼ cups salad and ¾ cup meat mixture)

CALORIES 261; FAT 10g (sat 2.9g, mono 3.6g, poly 2.3g); PROTEIN 23g; CARB 21g; FIBER 4g; CHOL 69mg; IRON 3mg; SODIUM 607mg; CALC 127mg

KEITH'S RECIPE BREAKDOWN
ISAN-INSPIRED LARB
Hands-on: 25 min. Total: 30 min.

INGREDIENT	AMOUNT	WHY
jasmine rice	2 tablespoons, uncooked	For crunch. You'll see.
cooking spray		
ground pork	2 ounces	For some fat and additional flavor
button mushrooms	1 cup, minced	To bulk up the meat mixture and balance the sweet, acid, and spice with some earthiness
ground turkey	¾ pound	The main substance
garlic	3 cloves	Essential in this style of larb
sugar	1 tablespoon	To facilitate mashing the garlic and lend sweetness against the punchy heat of the dish
fresh Key or Mexican lime juice	3 tablespoons	These limes simply taste different. Persian limes sold in supermarkets have their place, but not here. We need boldness.
fish sauce	1½ tablespoons	For salt and to offer depth of flavor
shallots	4, very thinly sliced	For welcome pungency
Thai bird chiles	3, minced	The right kind of chile for larb
mint leaves	1 bunch, torn	This is critical; its freshness is absolutely incredible against the fish sauce and toasted rice.
Thai basil leaves	1 bunch, torn	Movement two of this herb symphony
cilantro	½ bunch	Ties the herbs in one big, flavorful knot
napa (Chinese) cabbage	2 cups, thinly sliced	Its ruffled texture traps liquids beautifully.
green onions	½ cup, thinly sliced	Now we're building the "salad."
green beans	½ cup, diagonally sliced in half	Crunch
cucumber	1 large, peeled and julienne-cut	Relief from the heat
dried crushed Thai-style chiles or gochugaru	1 teaspoon	Toasty capsaicin punch. As the salad is mixed, the dried chile rehydrates and announces its presence forcefully.
Key limes	2, cut into wedges	For a dose of freshness, à la minute

FEED 4 FOR LESS THAN $10

Star ingredients make the meal: smoked salmon in chowder, fresh cherries on pork.

**Kid Friendly • Quick & Easy
Make Ahead**

Smoked Salmon Chowder

$2.24
PER
SERVING

Hands-on: 25 min. Total: 25 min.

1 tablespoon butter
2 tablespoons canola oil
1 cup finely chopped onion
1/2 cup chopped carrot
1/3 cup chopped celery
1/2 teaspoon kosher salt
1/8 teaspoon ground red pepper
2 cups water
1 cup 2% reduced-fat milk
1/3 cup half-and-half
2 1/2 tablespoons all-purpose flour
1 cup precooked brown and wild rice
1 (3.5-ounce) package cold-smoked salmon, torn into small pieces
2 tablespoons chopped green onions

1. Melt butter in a large saucepan over medium-high heat. Add oil; swirl. Add onion, carrot, celery, salt, and red pepper; sauté 4 minutes. Add 2 cups water; bring to a boil. Reduce heat to medium; cook until tender.
2. Combine milk, half-and-half, and flour in a bowl. Add milk mixture to pan; bring to a boil. Cook 1 minute or until slightly thickened, stirring constantly. Stir in rice and salmon; cook 1 minute or until thoroughly heated. Sprinkle evenly with green onions. Serves 4 (serving size: 1 cup)

CALORIES 270; **FAT** 15.6g (sat 4.9g, mono 6g, poly 2.4g); **PROTEIN** 10g; **CARB** 23g; **FIBER** 2g; **CHOL** 26mg; **IRON** 1mg; **SODIUM** 518mg; **CALC** 119mg

**Kid Friendly • Quick & Easy
Gluten Free**

Pork Tenderloin with Roasted Cherries and Shallots

$2.45
PER
SERVING

Hands-on: 39 min. Total: 39 min.
Serve with a quick cabbage slaw: Combine 4 cups thinly sliced green cabbage, 1/4 cup coarsely chopped fresh flat-leaf parsley, 1 tablespoon olive oil, 1 tablespoon cider vinegar, 1/4 teaspoon kosher salt, and 1/4 teaspoon freshly ground black pepper.

2 tablespoons canola oil, divided
3/4 teaspoon kosher salt, divided
1/2 teaspoon freshly ground black pepper
1/2 teaspoon ground cumin
1/8 teaspoon ground cinnamon
1 (1-pound) pork tenderloin, trimmed
3 large shallots, quartered
8 ounces fresh cherries, pitted and halved
1/4 cup unsalted chicken stock
2 tablespoons balsamic vinegar
1/2 teaspoon brown sugar
1 tablespoon butter
1/4 cup coarsely chopped fresh flat-leaf parsley

1. Preheat oven to 425°.
2. Heat a large ovenproof skillet over medium-high heat. Add 1 table-spoon oil; swirl to coat. Combine 1/2 teaspoon salt, pepper, cumin, and cinnamon. Rub pork evenly with spice mixture. Add pork to pan; sauté 4 minutes. Turn pork over; place pan in oven and bake at 425° for 15 minutes or until a thermome-ter registers 140°. Remove pork from pan; place on a cutting board (do not wipe out pan). Let pork stand 10 minutes. Cut into thin slices.
3. Add 1 tablespoon oil to pan; swirl to coat. Add shallots and cherries to pan, and sprinkle with 1/4 teaspoon salt. Place pan in oven, and bake at 425° for 10 minutes (do not turn cherries). Carefully remove pan from oven; place over medium-high heat. Stir in stock, vinegar, and sugar; bring to a boil. Cook 4 minutes or until liquid is syrupy. Remove from heat; stir in butter. Serve cherry mixture with pork; sprinkle with parsley. Serves 4 (serving size: 3 ounces pork and about 2/3 cup sauce)

CALORIES 270; **FAT** 12.5g (sat 3.2g, mono 6.1g, poly 2.5g); **PROTEIN** 25g; **CARB** 14g; **FIBER** 2g; **CHOL** 81mg; **IRON** 2mg; **SODIUM** 458mg; **CALC** 27mg

COOL, CRUNCHY SUMMER ROLLS

Chewy-silky rice paper sheets make for fun, low-calorie wraps perfect for dipping.

Quick & Easy • Vegetarian

Basil Summer Rolls with Peanut Dipping Sauce

Hands-on: 35 min. Total: 35 min.
Made from a simple combination of rice flour, water, and salt, rice paper has about 30 calories per 8-inch round—that's 80% less than the same size flour tortilla. While filling one summer roll, let another rice paper soak.

8 ounces extra-firm tofu, drained
1 1/2 ounces uncooked rice vermicelli noodles
5 teaspoons rice vinegar, divided

2 tablespoons lower-sodium
   soy sauce, divided
2 tablespoons dark sesame oil
1½ tablespoons hoisin sauce,
   divided
2 teaspoons sambal oelek (ground
   fresh chile paste)
1 cup very thinly sliced napa
   (Chinese) cabbage
¾ cup matchstick-cut carrot
½ cup presliced shiitake mushroom
   caps
2 tablespoons mint leaves
8 (8-inch) round rice paper sheets
8 large basil leaves
4 green onions, each cut into
   2 (4-inch) slices
1½ tablespoons chunky peanut
   butter
1 tablespoon water

1. Cut tofu crosswise into 4 slices. Place tofu on several layers of paper towels. Cover with additional paper towels. Let stand 10 minutes, pressing down occasionally. Cut each slice in half to form 8 (3-inch) strips.
2. Cook noodles according to package directions. Drain and rinse with cold water; drain.
3. Combine 1 tablespoon vinegar, 1 tablespoon soy sauce, oil, 1½ teaspoons hoisin sauce, and sambal oelek in a medium bowl, stirring with a whisk. Stir in cabbage, carrot, mushrooms, and mint; toss gently to coat.
4. Add hot water to a large shallow dish to a depth of 1 inch. Place 1 rice paper sheet in dish; let stand 30 seconds or until soft. Place a dry kitchen towel on a work surface. Place rice paper sheet on towel. Place 1 basil leaf on bottom third of sheet, leaving a 2-inch border; top with 1 tofu strip, about 3 tablespoons cabbage mixture, about 2 tablespoons noodles, and 1 onion slice. Fold bottom of sheet over filling. Fold sides of sheet over filling; starting with filled side, roll up, jelly-roll fashion. Gently press seam to seal. Place roll, seam side down, on a serving platter

(cover to keep from drying). Repeat procedure with remaining wrappers, basil, tofu, cabbage mixture, noodles, and onion.
5. Combine 2 teaspoons vinegar, 1 tablespoon soy sauce, 1 tablespoon hoisin, peanut butter, and 1 tablespoon water in a small bowl, stirring with a whisk. Serve with summer rolls. Serves 4 (serving size: 2 rolls and 1½ tablespoons sauce)

CALORIES 287; FAT 13.5g (sat 1.8g, mono 6.6g, poly 4.2g); PROTEIN 11g; CARB 33g; FIBER 2g; CHOL 0mg; IRON 2mg; SODIUM 498mg; CALC 132mg

SLOW COOKER

ALL-DAY VEGETARIAN CHILI

Simmer a crockful of fresh produce, earthy spices, and beans for a great Sunday dinner.

Kid Friendly • Make Ahead Vegetarian

White Bean Chili with Corn Chip Crunch

Hands-on: 30 min. Total: 9 hr.

3 cups chopped onion, divided
3 cups chopped red bell pepper,
   divided
½ cup chopped fresh cilantro stems
1½ tablespoons dried oregano
6 garlic cloves
3 dried ancho chile peppers,
   stemmed, seeded, and finely
   chopped
¼ cup olive oil
1 tablespoon ground cumin
2 tablespoons tomato paste

1 teaspoon ground coriander
1¾ teaspoons kosher salt
1 teaspoon freshly ground black
   pepper
½ teaspoon ground cinnamon
1 bay leaf
4½ cups organic vegetable broth
1 (16-ounce) package dried white
   beans
1 (26.46-ounce) container unsalted
   tomato puree
1 (12-ounce) bottle stout beer (such
   as Guinness)
4 cups chopped zucchini (about
   2 large)
1 (15-ounce) can unsalted fire-
   roasted diced tomatoes, undrained
¾ cup reduced-fat sour cream
3 ounces corn chips, crushed
   (such as Fritos)

1. Place 1 cup onion, 1 cup bell pepper, cilantro, oregano, garlic, and ancho chile peppers in a food processor; process until almost smooth. Heat a large skillet over medium heat. Add oil to pan; swirl to coat. Add onion mixture to pan; cook 8 minutes or until liquid nearly evaporates, stirring frequently. Add cumin and next 6 ingredients (through bay leaf); cook 2 minutes, stirring frequently.
2. Transfer mixture to a 6-quart electric slow cooker. Stir in 2 cups onion, 1 cup bell pepper, broth, beans, tomato puree, and beer; cover and cook on LOW 8 hours.
3. Stir in 1 cup bell pepper, zucchini, and diced tomatoes; cook on LOW 30 minutes or until vegetables are tender. Discard bay leaf. Top chili with sour cream and crushed corn chips. Serves 12 (serving size: about 1½ cups chili, 1 tablespoon sour cream, and about 1 tablespoon crushed corn chips)

CALORIES 319; FAT 10.1g (sat 2.5g, mono 4.6g, poly 2.1g); PROTEIN 13g; CARB 46g; FIBER 12g; CHOL 5mg; IRON 4mg; SODIUM 592mg; CALC 148mg

SUPERFAST 20-MINUTE COOKING

Kid Friendly • Quick & Easy
Freezable • Gluten Free
Make Ahead

Gluten-Free Peanut Butter-Chocolate Chip Cookies

To fit the cookies on a single sheet pan, divide cookies into 5 rows of 4. Pressing the cookies flat helps them bake quickly and get lovely crisp edges; otherwise they'll be too round and undercooked.

¼ teaspoon salt
1 large egg white
1 cup reduced-fat chunky peanut butter
⅓ cup granulated sugar
¼ cup brown sugar
¼ cup semisweet chocolate minichips

1. Preheat oven to 375°.
2. Place salt and egg white in a medium bowl; stir with a whisk until white is frothy. Add peanut butter, granulated sugar, brown sugar, and chocolate chips, stirring to combine.
3. Divide dough into 20 equal portions (about 1 tablespoon each); arrange dough 2 inches apart on a baking sheet lined with parchment paper. Gently press the top of each cookie with a fork; press the top of each cookie again to form a crisscross pattern, and flatten to a 2-inch diameter. Bake at 375° for 10 minutes or until lightly browned. Serves 20 (serving size: 1 cookie)

CALORIES 111; FAT 5.6g (sat 1.4g, mono 2.6g, poly 1.4g); PROTEIN 3g; CARB 13g; FIBER 1g; CHOL 0mg; IRON 0mg; SODIUM 121mg; CALC 3mg

---

Quick & Easy • Gluten Free

Grilled Lemon-Dijon Chicken Thighs with Arugula Salad

This light, quick main is perfect for warmer months. If you have 5 extra minutes, grill some vegetables to toss into the salad; try asparagus or red onion.

4 (4-ounce) skinless, boneless chicken thighs
½ teaspoon salt, divided
¼ teaspoon black pepper, divided
2½ tablespoons extra-virgin olive oil, divided
2 teaspoons fresh lemon juice
2 teaspoons Dijon mustard
1 teaspoon minced fresh garlic
Cooking spray
2 tablespoons thinly sliced shallots
1 tablespoon balsamic vinegar
2 teaspoons honey
1 cup grape tomatoes, halved
1 (5-ounce) package baby arugula

1. Sprinkle chicken with ¼ teaspoon salt and ⅛ teaspoon pepper. Combine chicken, 1½ teaspoons oil, juice, Dijon, and garlic in a bowl; toss to coat. Let stand 4 minutes. Heat a grill pan over medium-high heat. Coat pan with cooking spray. Add chicken to pan; grill 5 minutes on each side or until done. Place chicken on a cutting board. Cut chicken into ¼-inch-thick slices.
2. Combine ¼ teaspoon salt, ⅛ teaspoon pepper, 2 tablespoons oil, shallots, vinegar, and honey in a large bowl, stirring with a whisk to dissolve honey. Add tomatoes and arugula; toss to coat. Place 1½ cups arugula mixture on each of 4 plates; top evenly with sliced chicken. Serves 4

CALORIES 249; FAT 13.5g (sat 2.4g, mono 7.8g, poly 2g); PROTEIN 23g; CARB 8g; FIBER 1g; CHOL 108mg; IRON 2mg; SODIUM 469mg; CALC 78mg

---

Kid Friendly • Quick & Easy

Open-Faced Salmon and Avocado BLTs

Coarsely chop leftover salmon and combine with any remaining mayo mixture. Top toasted bread and garnish with arugula for a quick lunch.

4 (1-ounce) slices diagonally cut ciabatta or rustic Italian bread
4 center-cut bacon slices
4 (4-ounce) sustainable salmon fillets, skinned (about ¾ inch thick)
¼ cup canola mayonnaise
2 tablespoons water
1 tablespoon minced fresh chives, divided
1½ teaspoons Dijon mustard
4 Bibb lettuce leaves
4 (½-inch-thick) slices tomato, halved
½ peeled ripe avocado, cut into 8 slices
4 lemon wedges

1. Preheat broiler to high.
2. Arrange bread slices on a baking sheet; broil 1 minute on each side or until toasted.
3. Cook bacon in a large nonstick skillet over medium heat until crisp. Remove bacon from pan. Add fillets to drippings in pan; cook 4 minutes on each side or until desired degree of doneness.
4. Combine canola mayonnaise, 2 tablespoons water, 2 teaspoons minced chives, and Dijon mustard in a small bowl, stirring with a whisk. Spread mayonnaise mixture evenly over bread slices; top each with 1 lettuce leaf, 1 bacon slice, 1 halved tomato slice, 2 avocado slices, and 1 fish fillet. Sprinkle evenly with 1 teaspoon chives. Serve with lemon wedges. Serves 4 (serving size: 1 sandwich)

CALORIES 345; FAT 16.4g (sat 2.5g, mono 8.4g, poly 4.4g); PROTEIN 29g; CARB 19g; FIBER 3g; CHOL 65mg; IRON 2mg; SODIUM 488mg; CALC 21mg

Sweet Sesame Noodles with Chicken and Broccoli

1 (8-ounce) package uncooked soba
1 (8-ounce) package broccoli florets
Cooking spray
2 (6-ounce) skinless, boneless
  chicken breast halves
1/8 teaspoon salt
1/4 teaspoon freshly ground black
  pepper
2 tablespoons rice vinegar
2 tablespoons dark sesame oil
2 tablespoons lower-sodium soy
  sauce
1 tablespoon creamy peanut butter
2 teaspoons toasted sesame seeds,
  divided
1 teaspoon brown sugar
1/4 teaspoon crushed red pepper
1 garlic clove, minced
3 green onions, chopped

1. Bring a large saucepan of water to a boil. Add soba; cook 3 minutes. Add broccoli to pan; cook 3 minutes or until soba and broccoli are done. Drain.
2. Heat a grill pan over medium-high heat. Coat pan with cooking spray. Sprinkle chicken evenly with salt and pepper. Add chicken to pan; grill 6 minutes on each side or until done. Remove chicken from pan. Cut into 1-inch pieces.
3. Combine vinegar, sesame oil, soy sauce, peanut butter, 1 teaspoon sesame seeds, sugar, crushed red pepper, and garlic in a large bowl, stirring with a whisk. Stir in noodle mixture and chicken. Sprinkle with 1 teaspoon sesame seeds and green onions. Serves 4 (serving size: 1½ cups)

CALORIES 429; **FAT** 12.4g (sat 2.1g, mono 4.7g, poly 4.3g); **PROTEIN** 32g; **CARB** 52g; **FIBER** 3g; **CHOL** 54mg; **IRON** 2mg; **SODIUM** 602mg; **CALC** 69mg

Red Pepper Couscous

³/₄ cup chopped red bell pepper
¹/₂ cup chopped red onion
4 teaspoons olive oil
³/₄ cup Israeli couscous
1¹/₄ cups water
¹/₄ teaspoon salt
¹/₄ teaspoon black pepper
3 tablespoons fresh lime juice
2 tablespoons chopped fresh cilantro
1 jalapeño pepper, seeded and finely
  chopped

1. Sauté bell pepper and onion in oil 3 minutes. Add couscous, 1¼ cups water, salt, and black pepper; bring to a boil. Reduce heat to medium-low; cover and simmer 8 minutes. Stir in juice, cilantro, and jalapeño. Serves 4 (serving size: about ½ cup)

CALORIES 179; **FAT** 4.9g (sat 0.6g, mono 3.3g, poly 0.5g); **PROTEIN** 5g; **CARB** 29g; **FIBER** 1g; **CHOL** 0mg; **IRON** 0mg; **SODIUM** 150mg; **CALC** 9mg

**Kid Friendly • Quick & Easy
Make Ahead • Vegetarian
Pecorino and Parsley**
Bring 1¼ cups water to a boil. Add ¾ cup Israeli couscous. Reduce heat to medium-low; cover and simmer 8 minutes. Stir in ¼ cup chopped fresh flat-leaf parsley, 2 tablespoons shaved pecorino Romano cheese, 1 tablespoon toasted pine nuts, 1 teaspoon grated lemon rind, ¼ teaspoon salt, and ¼ teaspoon black pepper. Serves 4 (serving size: about ½ cup)

CALORIES 148; **FAT** 2.9g (sat 1g); **SODIUM** 219mg

**Kid Friendly • Quick & Easy
Make Ahead • Vegetarian
Tomato and Cucumber**
Bring 1¼ cups water to a boil. Add ¾ cup Israeli couscous. Reduce heat to medium-low; cover and simmer 8 minutes or until liquid is absorbed. Stir in ½ cup halved grape tomatoes, ½ cup diced seeded cucumber, ¼ cup chopped red onion, 1 tablespoon fresh lemon juice, ¼ teaspoon salt, and 1½ ounces crumbled feta cheese. Serves 4 (serving size: about ½ cup)

CALORIES 156; **FAT** 2.6g (sat 1.6g); **SODIUM** 268mg

**Kid Friendly • Quick & Easy
Make Ahead • Vegetarian
Nectarine and Basil**
Bring 1¼ cups water to a boil. Add ¾ cup Israeli couscous. Reduce heat to medium-low; cover and simmer 8 minutes or until liquid is absorbed. Stir in ⅓ cup chopped Vidalia or other sweet onion, 3 tablespoons chopped fresh basil, 2 tablespoons fresh orange juice, ¼ teaspoon salt, and 1 medium nectarine, diced. Serves 4 (serving size: about ½ cup)

CALORIES 143; **FAT** 0.4g (sat 0g); **SODIUM** 148mg

**Kid Friendly • Quick & Easy
Gluten Free • Make Ahead
Vegetarian**

Roasted Garlic and Chive Dip

¹/₂ cup unpeeled garlic cloves
¹/₂ cup plain fat-free Greek yogurt
¹/₂ cup light sour cream
2 tablespoons minced fresh chives
³/₈ teaspoon salt
Dash of freshly ground black pepper

1. Heat a large nonstick skillet over medium heat. Add garlic cloves to pan; cover and cook 8 minutes or until lightly browned and tender when pierced with a fork, stirring occasionally. Cool slightly. Squeeze garlic from skins into the bowl of a mini food processor. Discard skins. Puree garlic until smooth.
2. Combine yogurt, sour cream, chives, salt, and pepper in a medium bowl, stirring well with a whisk. Add garlic to yogurt mixture, stirring with a whisk to combine. Serves 8 (serving size: about 2 tablespoons)

CALORIES 42; **FAT** 1.7g (sat 1g, mono 0.5g, poly 0.1g); **PROTEIN** 2g; **CARB** 5g; **FIBER** 0g; **CHOL** 5mg; **IRON** 0mg; **SODIUM** 128mg; **CALC** 47mg

Quick Fried Brown Rice with Shrimp and Snap Peas

1½ (8.8-ounce) pouches precooked brown rice (such as Uncle Ben's)
2 tablespoons lower-sodium soy sauce
1 tablespoon sambal oelek (ground fresh chile paste)
1 tablespoon honey
2 tablespoons peanut oil, divided
10 ounces medium shrimp, peeled and deveined
3 large eggs, lightly beaten
1½ cups sugar snap peas, diagonally sliced
⅓ cup unsalted, dry-roasted peanuts
⅛ teaspoon salt
3 garlic cloves, crushed

1. Heat rice according to package directions.
2. Combine soy sauce, sambal oelek, and honey in a large bowl. Combine 1 teaspoon peanut oil and shrimp in a medium bowl; toss to coat. Heat a wok or large skillet over high heat. Add shrimp to pan, and stir-fry 2 minutes. Add shrimp to soy sauce mixture; toss to coat shrimp. Add 1 teaspoon peanut oil to pan; swirl to coat. Add eggs to pan; cook 45 seconds or until set. Remove eggs from pan; cut into bite-sized pieces.
3. Add 1 tablespoon oil to pan; swirl to coat. Add rice; stir-fry 4 minutes. Add rice to shrimp mixture. Add remaining 1 teaspoon oil to pan; swirl to coat. Add sugar snap peas, peanuts, salt, and garlic to pan; stir-fry for 2 minutes or until peanuts begin to brown. Add shrimp mixture and egg to pan, and cook for 2 minutes or until thoroughly heated. Serves 4. (serving size: 1½ cups)

CALORIES 418; FAT 19.8g (sat 3.6g, mono 8.5g, poly 5.9g); PROTEIN 22g; CARB 39g; FIBER 3g; CHOL 229mg; IRON 2mg; SODIUM 587mg; CALC 82mg

Warm Brown Rice and Chickpea Salad

1 (8.8-ounce) pouch precooked brown rice (such as Uncle Ben's)
¼ cup chopped green onions
¼ cup chopped fresh basil
3 tablespoons extra-virgin olive oil
2 tablespoons white balsamic vinegar
½ teaspoon salt
¼ teaspoon black pepper
32 cherries, pitted and quartered
1 (15-ounce) can unsalted chickpeas, rinsed and drained
2 ounces goat cheese, crumbled

1. Heat rice according to package directions. Place rice in a medium bowl. Stir in onions and next 7 ingredients. Sprinkle with goat cheese. Serves 4. (serving size: 1 cup)

CALORIES 359; FAT 16.8g (sat 4.6g, mono 8.4g, poly 1.2g); PROTEIN 10g; CARB 43g; FIBER 5g; CHOL 11mg; IRON 2mg; SODIUM 389mg; CALC 100mg

12 HEALTHY HABITS

GET STRONGER

Look beyond the barbells and bench presses. This month's hero shares ways you can build muscle from head to toe.

Strength training does so much more than just help you look better. It makes daily activities easier and supports your entire system.

"Yoga and Pilates help you get stronger all over, not just in your arms," says Kristin McGee, a celebrity yoga and Pilates instructor. "When you focus on strength, you'll notice you have more longevity in your workouts, your body won't ache for days after a good workout, and you can do things like pick up your baby without hurting your back."

Grilled Tuna over Green Bean, Tomato, and Chickpea Salad

Hands-on: 23 min. Total: 23 min.

12 ounces haricots verts
2 tablespoons toasted walnut oil
1½ tablespoons fresh lemon juice
1 tablespoon white balsamic vinegar
1 tablespoon water
2 teaspoons minced fresh garlic
1½ teaspoons Dijon mustard
2 teaspoons honey
½ teaspoon kosher salt, divided
1 (15½-ounce) can unsalted chickpeas (garbanzo beans), rinsed and drained
2 cups grape tomatoes, halved
¼ cup chopped walnuts, toasted
2 tablespoons shaved Parmigiano-Reggiano cheese
1 ounce sliced pitted kalamata olives
2 (8-ounce) tuna steaks (about 1½ inches thick)
⅛ teaspoon black pepper
Cooking spray

1. Cook green beans in boiling water 4 minutes or until crisp-tender. Drain and rinse with cold water; drain well.
2. Combine oil, next 6 ingredients, and ¼ teaspoon salt. Stir in beans, chickpeas, and tomatoes; toss. Sprinkle with walnuts, cheese, and olives.
3. Sprinkle tuna with ¼ teaspoon salt and pepper. Heat a grill pan over medium-high heat. Coat pan with cooking spray. Add tuna; cook 3 minutes on each side or until desired degree of doneness. Divide bean mixture evenly among 4 plates; top with sliced tuna. Serves 4 (serving size: 3 ounces tuna and about 1 cup bean mixture)

CALORIES 381; FAT 14.7g (sat 1.6g, mono 3.1g, poly 7.4g); PROTEIN 37g; CARB 27g; FIBER 6g; CHOL 46mg; IRON 3mg; SODIUM 518mg; CALC 120mg

QUICK TRICKS

6 TASTY ZUCCHINI TOPPERS

Grill two medium sliced zucchini two minutes on each side. Top with a favorite flavor.

Kid Friendly • Quick & Easy Gluten Free • Vegetarian
Caprese Zucchini
Preheat broiler. Combine ½ cup diced seeded tomato, 2 tablespoons chopped fresh basil, 2 teaspoons olive oil, 1 teaspoon red wine vinegar, ¼ teaspoon kosher salt, and ¼ teaspoon freshly ground black pepper in a bowl. Arrange grilled zucchini on a foil-lined baking sheet; top evenly with tomato mixture and 1 ounce shredded part-skim mozzarella cheese (about ¼ cup). Broil 2 minutes or until cheese melts. Serves 4 (serving size: 4 zucchini slices, 2 tablespoons tomato mixture, and 1 tablespoon cheese)

CALORIES 64; FAT 4.2g (sat 1.2g); SODIUM 175mg

Quick & Easy
Shiitake and Ponzu Zucchini
Combine ¼ cup unsalted chicken stock, 1 tablespoon lower-sodium soy sauce, 2 teaspoons mirin (sweet rice wine), and ¼ teaspoon crushed red pepper. Sauté 1 (3.5-ounce) package shiitake mushroom caps, thinly sliced, in 2 teaspoons olive oil over medium-high heat 8 minutes. Stir in stock mixture and ¼ cup chopped green onions; cook 2 minutes. Spoon mushroom mixture over zucchini. Serves 4 (serving size: 4 zucchini slices and 2 tablespoons mushroom mixture)

CALORIES 55; FAT 2.8g (sat 0.4g); SODIUM 152mg

Quick & Easy • Gluten Free Vegetarian
Walnut and Gorgonzola Zucchini
Grill 2 (½-inch-thick) slices red onion 5 minutes on each side or until tender. Remove from grill; coarsely chop. Combine onion, ¼ cup chopped toasted walnuts, 2 teaspoons olive oil, 1 teaspoon balsamic vinegar, ¼ teaspoon kosher salt, and ¼ teaspoon freshly ground black pepper. Spoon walnut mixture evenly over zucchini; sprinkle with 3 tablespoons crumbled Gorgonzola cheese. Serves 4 (serving size: 4 zucchini slices, 3 tablespoons walnut mixture, and 2 teaspoons cheese)

CALORIES 109; FAT 9g (sat 2g); SODIUM 200mg

Quick & Easy • Gluten Free Vegetarian
Chickpea and Red Pepper Zucchini
Combine ½ cup canned unsalted chickpeas, rinsed, drained, and chopped; ¼ cup chopped fresh parsley; ¼ cup chopped bottled roasted red bell peppers; 2 tablespoons finely chopped red onion; 2 tablespoons crumbled feta cheese; 1 tablespoon olive oil; 1 tablespoon lemon juice; ¼ teaspoon kosher salt; and ¼ teaspoon black pepper. Spoon chickpea mixture over zucchini. Serves 4 (serving size: 4 zucchini slices and ¼ cup chickpea mixture)

CALORIES 99; FAT 5.1g (sat 1.3g); SODIUM 210mg

Kid Friendly • Quick & Easy Vegetarian
Olive and Orange Zucchini
Combine 2 tablespoons minced fresh flat-leaf parsley, 1 tablespoon minced shallot, 1 tablespoon olive oil, ¼ teaspoon grated orange rind, 2 teaspoons fresh orange juice, 1 teaspoon minced fresh garlic, ½ teaspoon chopped fresh thyme, 10 finely chopped pitted kalamata olives, and 8 finely chopped Castelvetrano olives in a small bowl. Spoon olive mixture evenly over zucchini. Serves 4 (serving size: 4 zucchini slices and 2 tablespoons olive mixture)

CALORIES 89; FAT 7.3g (sat 1g); SODIUM 227mg

Kid Friendly • Quick & Easy Vegetarian
Pine Nut and Raisin Zucchini
Pulse 1 ounce torn French bread baguette in a food processor until crumbly. Sauté in 1 tablespoon olive oil over medium heat until golden. Combine breadcrumbs, ¼ cup golden raisins, 3 tablespoons toasted pine nuts, 1 teaspoon minced fresh dill, ¼ teaspoon grated lemon rind, ¼ teaspoon kosher salt, and ¼ teaspoon pepper; spoon over zucchini. Serves 4 (serving size: 4 zucchini slices and 3 tablespoons breadcrumb mixture)

CALORIES 139; FAT 8.3g (sat 0.9g); SODIUM 166mg

FATHER'S DAY BREAKFAST

Just for Dad, gutsy beer-spiked muffins that pack some sweet heat

Double up and bake an extra dozen of these streusel muffins for Dad. He'll get a kick out of the cayenne and candied-bacon topping that lends crunch to each bite. It may seem odd to find beer in a breakfast treat, but creamy, Irish-style stout adds mellow notes of chocolate and coffee to the tender crumb. Muffin batter doesn't hold well, so only double the batter if you have enough tins to bake 24 muffins at once; if not, make a second batch of batter when your tins are free. Deliver with a note that they're great at room temperature or gently warmed in the microwave.

Freezable • Make Ahead

Spicy Bacon and Brew Muffins

Hands-on: 22 min. Total: 50 min.

Streusel:
3 tablespoons dark brown sugar
2 teaspoons water
1/2 teaspoon ground red pepper
3 applewood-smoked bacon slices
3 tablespoons old-fashioned rolled oats
1 tablespoon all-purpose flour
1 tablespoon unsalted butter, melted
Muffins:
7.9 ounces all-purpose flour (about 1 3/4 cups)
1/2 cup packed dark brown sugar
2 teaspoons baking powder
1/4 teaspoon salt
1/4 teaspoon baking soda
2/3 cup Guinness Stout or other stout beer
3 tablespoons canola oil
1 teaspoon vanilla extract
1 large egg, lightly beaten

1. Preheat oven to 400°. Line a baking sheet with foil; place a wire rack on the baking sheet.
2. To prepare streusel, combine 3 tablespoons sugar, 2 teaspoons water, and pepper in a small bowl. Spread mixture evenly over both sides of bacon. Place coated bacon on rack; bake at 400° for 18 minutes or until done. Cool; finely chop.
3. Combine oats and 1 tablespoon flour in a small bowl. Stir in butter. Stir in 2 tablespoons chopped bacon; reserve remaining bacon. Set aside.
4. Reduce oven temperature to 350°. Line 12 muffin cups with paper liners.
5. To prepare muffins, weigh or lightly spoon 7.9 ounces (about 1¾ cups) flour into dry measuring cups; level with a knife. Combine 7.9 ounces flour, remaining bacon, ½ cup sugar, baking powder, salt, and baking soda in a large bowl; stir well. Combine beer, oil, vanilla, and egg in another bowl, gently stirring with a whisk. Add beer mixture to flour mixture, stirring just until combined. Evenly divide batter among muffin cups. Sprinkle streusel evenly over batter.
6. Bake at 350° for 18 minutes or until a wooden pick inserted in the center of muffins comes out clean. Cool in pan 5 minutes. Remove muffins from pan; serve warm, or cool completely on a wire rack. Serves 12 (serving size: 1 muffin)

CALORIES 176; FAT 5.9g (sat 1.3g, mono 2.9g, poly 1.3g); PROTEIN 3g; CARB 27g; FIBER 1g; CHOL 20mg; IRON 1mg; SODIUM 200mg; CALC 52mg

KID IN THE KITCHEN

SAUCY, SMOKY, PORKY

A bit of spicy heat (or not) makes these tacos a hit with the kids.

"Today I made this delicious taco dish. It was one of the more difficult recipes I've made (I recommend taking a little extra time to prep the ingredients), but it was worth it and a real hit with my friends. We had fun putting together our own tacos. The sauce is a bit on the spicy side, but you can use less chipotle or replace it with milder chili powder mixed with smoked paprika (my favorite spice). This way you get less heat without compromising the smoky flavor.

I added a dollop of sour cream to my taco, which completed the dish nicely. The leftover shredded pork was great in wraps for lunch the next day, as the flavor only intensifies over time. I am always up for a challenge with a new recipe, and the results of this one were incredible!"

BRING THE PORK TO ROOM TEMPERATURE FOR MORE EVEN COOKING.

Smoky Shredded Pork Tacos

Hands-on: 27 min. Total: 1 hr. 10 min.

4 teaspoons olive oil, divided
⅓ cup minced fresh onion
1 tablespoon chopped fresh garlic
2 tablespoons tomato paste
1 tablespoon brown sugar
1 teaspoon ground cumin
½ teaspoon ground cinnamon
½ teaspoon chipotle chile powder
1½ cups unsalted chicken stock
1 cup plus 2 tablespoons fresh orange juice, divided
1 (1-pound) pork tenderloin, trimmed and cut into 2-inch pieces
1 teaspoon honey
¼ teaspoon kosher salt
⅛ teaspoon freshly ground black pepper
1 cup shredded carrot
1 cup thinly sliced peeled jicama
¼ cup chopped fresh cilantro
8 (6-inch) corn tortillas, warmed
4 lime wedges

1. Heat a Dutch oven over medium heat. Add 2 teaspoons oil; swirl. Add onion; sauté 2 minutes. Add garlic; sauté 30 seconds. Stir in tomato paste and next 4 ingredients (through chile powder); cook 2 minutes. Add stock and 1 cup orange juice; bring to a boil. Add pork to pan; cover, reduce heat, and simmer 20 minutes. Place pork on a cutting board. Bring orange juice mixture to a boil; cook 23 minutes or until reduced to 1 cup. Shred pork with 2 forks. Return pork to pan; toss.
2. Combine 2 teaspoons olive oil, 2 tablespoons orange juice, honey, salt, and pepper in a medium bowl, stirring with a whisk. Stir in carrot, jicama, and cilantro. Top each tortilla with ½ cup pork mixture and ½ cup jicama mixture. Serve with lime wedges. Serves 4 (serving size: 2 tacos)

CALORIES 373; FAT 8.7g (sat 1.7g, mono 4.6g, poly 1.7g); PROTEIN 30g; CARB 45g; FIBER 7g; CHOL 74mg; IRON 3mg; SODIUM 349mg; CALC 92mg

---

THE VERDICT

MONICA (AGE 10)
She had not tasted a taco like this before and really enjoyed it. **9/10**

SADE (AGE 13)
She said, "It might be spicy for some kids, but I loved everything about it!" **10/10**

MATISSE (AGE 13)
The crunchy jicama brought together all the flavors, making each bite as delicious as the last. Yum! **9/10**

FRESH RIGHT NOW

THE COOLEST CUCUMBER

Give props to Kirbys: popular as pickles and just as great raw.

It's Kirby cucumbers' earthy flavor that sets them apart from other grocery varieties—they just taste like the garden. The hearty meat stands up to a brine, but eaten fresh, they are a revelation: crisp, never watery, pure cucumber taste. And that bumpy-looking skin? It's totally tender. No need to peel; just slice and go. Mixed into a bold salsa (like pineapple-lime) or sprinkled with pungent za'atar, salt, and olive oil, their full-bodied flavor shines. By contrast, in our gazpacho Kirbys blend in for a beautifully balanced chilled soup.

Cucumber Gazpacho with Toasted Rye Croutons

Hands-on: 25 min. Total: 8 hr. 40 min.

2 garlic cloves, divided
3 cups chopped peeled Kirby cucumber (about 1 pound)
2 cups chopped green tomato (about 1 large)
1½ cups chopped honeydew melon
½ cup finely chopped sweet onion
⅓ cup finely chopped celery
2½ tablespoons red wine vinegar
2 tablespoons chopped fresh mint
4 teaspoons olive oil, divided
1 teaspoon chopped fresh tarragon
½ teaspoon salt
2 seedless rye bread slices, cubed (about 2 ounces)
1 teaspoon finely minced serrano chile
½ cup water (optional)

1. Finely chop 1 garlic clove; place in an 11-cup food processor. Add cucumber and next 6 ingredients. Add 1 tablespoon oil, tarragon, and salt; process 1 minute or until almost smooth. (For smaller food processor bowls, work in 2 batches.) Cover and chill up to 8 hours.
2. Preheat oven to 450°.
3. Smash remaining garlic clove; place in a bowl with 1 teaspoon oil. Microwave at HIGH 15 seconds; let stand 5 minutes. Drizzle garlic oil over bread cubes; toss to coat. Place bread on a jelly-roll pan. Bake at 450° for 8 minutes or until browned, turning once. Stir chile into chilled soup. Add up to ½ cup water to thin soup, if desired. Ladle soup into bowls; top with croutons. Serves 6 (serving size: ⅔ cup soup and about ¼ cup croutons)

CALORIES 97; FAT 3.7g (sat 0.5g, mono 1.6g, poly 1.2g); PROTEIN 2g; CARB 15g; FIBER 2g; CHOL 0mg; IRON 1mg; SODIUM 277mg; CALC 37mg

DINNER TONIGHT

One week, five fast meals

....

SHOPPING LIST

Charred Flank Steak with Grilled Tomato Bruschetta

Cherry tomatoes (1 pint)
Fresh basil
Shallot
Garlic
Smoked paprika
Creole seasoning
Canola oil
Olive oil
Whole-wheat French bread baguette
Flank steak (1 pound)

Tarragon Green Beans

Green beans (1 pound)
Fresh tarragon
Celery seeds
White balsamic vinegar
Butter

....

GAME PLAN

While water for beans comes to a boil:
▪ Cook steak.
While steak rests:
▪ Grill bread slices.

Kid Friendly • Quick & Easy

Charred Flank Steak with Grilled Tomato Bruschetta

With Tarragon Green Beans

2 teaspoons canola oil
½ teaspoon smoked paprika
½ teaspoon kosher salt, divided
½ teaspoon freshly ground black pepper, divided
¼ teaspoon Creole seasoning
1 (1-pound) flank steak, trimmed
Cooking spray
2 cups cherry tomatoes
4 teaspoons olive oil, divided
2 tablespoons chopped fresh basil
1 small shallot, chopped
4 (1-ounce) slices whole-wheat French bread baguette
1 garlic clove, halved

1. Preheat grill to medium-high heat.
2. Combine canola oil, paprika, ¼ teaspoon salt, ¼ teaspoon pepper, and Creole seasoning. Rub spice mixture over steak. Place steak on grill rack coated with cooking spray; grill 4 minutes on each side or until desired degree of doneness. Place steak on a cutting board; let stand 5 minutes. Cut across the grain into thin slices. Thread tomatoes onto 4 skewers; grill 5 minutes, turning once after 3 minutes. Remove tomatoes from grill.
3. Remove tomatoes from skewers; coarsely chop. Place tomatoes, 2 teaspoons olive oil, ¼ teaspoon salt, ¼ teaspoon pepper, basil, and shallots in a small bowl, stirring to combine.
4. Drizzle bread slices evenly with 2 teaspoons olive oil. Grill 30 seconds on each side or until toasted. Rub cut sides of garlic over one side of bread slices; top evenly with tomato mixture. Serves 4 (serving size: 3 ounces steak and 1 bruschetta)

CALORIES 325; FAT 13.9g (sat 3.3g, mono 7.1g, poly 1.7g); PROTEIN 29g; CARB 21g; FIBER 2g; CHOL 70mg; IRON 3mg; SODIUM 490mg; CALC 53mg

---

Tarragon Green Beans
Add 1 pound trimmed green beans to 2 quarts boiling water; cook 4 minutes. Drain. Stir in 1 tablespoon butter, 1 teaspoon finely chopped fresh tarragon, 1 teaspoon white balsamic vinegar, ¼ teaspoon celery seeds, ¼ teaspoon kosher salt, and ¼ teaspoon freshly ground black pepper. Serves 4 (serving size: 1 cup)

CALORIES 63; FAT 3.2g (sat 1.9g); SODIUM 153mg

....

SHOPPING LIST

Seared Tilapia with Pineapple Salsa and Tomato-Avocado Salad

Lime (2)
Pineapple
Tomato (1 medium)
Avocado (1)
Fresh basil
Fresh cilantro
Jalapeño pepper (1)
Red onion (1)
Ground cumin
Chipotle chile powder
Extra-virgin olive oil
Tilapia fillets (1½ pounds)

Black Bean–Cilantro Rice

Jalapeño pepper (1)
Fresh cilantro
Red onion (1)
Garlic
Ground cumin
Olive oil
Unsalted chicken stock
(15-ounce) can unsalted black beans (1)
(3.5-ounce) bag boil-in-bag brown rice (1)
Queso fresco

While rice cooks:
- Prepare black bean mixture.
- Prepare salsa and salad.

While bean mixture cooks:
- Cook tilapia.

Kid Friendly • Quick & Easy
Gluten Free

Seared Tilapia with Pineapple Salsa and Tomato-Avocado Salad

With Black Bean-Cilantro Rice

More For Later: Double the pineapple salsa, and use it to top salads, tacos, or grilled steak or chicken during the week.

1 cup chopped pineapple
2 tablespoons finely chopped red onion
½ jalapeño pepper, seeded and finely chopped
2 tablespoons chopped fresh cilantro
3 tablespoons fresh lime juice, divided
¾ teaspoon kosher salt, divided
½ cup thinly vertically sliced red onion
¼ cup thinly sliced fresh basil
1 medium tomato, cut into thin wedges
1 peeled ripe avocado, cut into 8 wedges
2 tablespoons extra-virgin olive oil, divided
4 (6-ounce) tilapia fillets
½ teaspoon ground cumin
¼ teaspoon chipotle chile powder

1. Combine pineapple, chopped red onion, jalapeño, cilantro, 1 tablespoon lime juice, and ¼ teaspoon salt in a small bowl.
2. Combine 2 tablespoons lime juice, sliced red onion, basil, tomato, avocado, and 1 tablespoon oil in a bowl; sprinkle with ¼ teaspoon salt.
3. Heat a large nonstick skillet over medium-high heat. Add 1 tablespoon oil to pan; swirl to coat. Sprinkle fish with ¼ teaspoon salt, cumin, and chipotle chile powder. Add fish to pan; cook 3 minutes on each side or until fish flakes easily when tested with a fork. Spoon pineapple salsa over fish. Serve with tomato and avocado salad. Serves 4 (serving size: 1 fillet, 1 cup salad, and ¼ cup salsa)

CALORIES 342; FAT 17.2g (sat 3g, mono 10.7g, poly 2.3g); PROTEIN 36g; CARB 14g; FIBER 5g; CHOL 85mg; IRON 2mg; SODIUM 461mg; CALC 44mg

Black Bean-Cilantro Rice

Cook 1 (3.5-ounce) bag boil-in-bag brown rice according to directions. Sauté ¾ cup chopped red onion; 5 thinly sliced garlic cloves; ¼ teaspoon ground cumin; and ½ jalapeño pepper, seeded and minced, in 1 tablespoon olive oil over medium-high heat 2 minutes. Add 1 (15-ounce) can unsalted black beans, rinsed and drained; 1 cup unsalted chicken stock; and ¼ teaspoon kosher salt. Cook 6 minutes. Lightly mash with a fork. Top rice with bean mixture, 2 tablespoons queso fresco, and ¼ cup chopped fresh cilantro. Serves 4 (serving size: ⅓ cup rice and ⅔ cup bean mixture)

CALORIES 205; FAT 5.1g (sat 1g); SODIUM 191mg

READY IN
40
MINUTES

SHOPPING LIST

Summer Veggie Salad
Lemon (1)
Portobello mushroom caps (4)
Red bell pepper (1)
Zucchini (1 medium)
Yellow squash (1 large)
Corn (2 ears)
Fresh thyme
Red onion (1)
Olive oil
Pine nuts
Dijon mustard
Manchego cheese (2 ounces)

Green Onion and Dill Quinoa
Lemon (1)
Fresh dill
Green onions
Quinoa

GAME PLAN

While water for quinoa comes to a boil:
- Grill vegetables.

While quinoa simmers:
- Cut vegetables into bite-sized pieces.
- Prepare vinaigrette.

continued

Summer Veggie Salad

With Green Onion and Dill Quinoa

4 (4-inch) portobello mushroom caps
2 (½-inch-thick) slices red onion
2 ears shucked corn
1 large red bell pepper, quartered
  and seeded
1 medium zucchini, halved lengthwise
1 large yellow squash, halved
  lengthwise
Cooking spray
2 tablespoons olive oil
2 teaspoons fresh lemon juice
1 teaspoon minced fresh thyme
½ teaspoon Dijon mustard
¼ teaspoon kosher salt
¼ teaspoon freshly ground black
  pepper
2 ounces Manchego cheese, shaved
  (about ½ cup)
1 ounce pine nuts, toasted (about
  ¼ cup)

1. Preheat grill to medium-high heat.
2. Coat mushrooms, onion, corn, bell pepper, zucchini, and yellow squash with cooking spray. Arrange vegetables on grill rack coated with cooking spray. Grill 5 minutes on each side or until tender.
3. Combine oil and next 5 ingredients in a bowl, stirring with a whisk. Cut kernels from ears of corn; add to oil mixture. Cut remaining vegetables into bite-sized pieces; add to oil mixture. Toss gently to combine. Top with cheese and pine nuts. Serves 4 (serving size: about 1¼ cups)

CALORIES 270; FAT 18.2g (sat 5.1g, mono 6.5g, poly 3.6g); PROTEIN 10g; CARB 22g; FIBER 5g; CHOL 15mg; IRON 2mg; SODIUM 244mg; CALC 213mg

Green Onion and Dill Quinoa

Rinse and drain 1 cup uncooked quinoa. Bring 1¼ cups water to a boil in a medium saucepan. Add quinoa to pan; cover, reduce heat, and simmer 13 minutes or until liquid is absorbed. Stir in ¼ cup chopped green onions, 3 tablespoons chopped fresh dill, 2 teaspoons fresh lemon juice, ½ teaspoon minced fresh garlic, ¼ teaspoon kosher salt, and ¼ teaspoon freshly ground black pepper. Serves 4 (serving size: about ½ cup)

CALORIES 160; FAT 2.6g (sat 0.3g); SODIUM 123mg

READY IN
25
MINUTES

SHOPPING LIST

Grilled Shrimp with Miso-Ginger Sauce
Lime (1)
Fresh flat-leaf parsley
Green onions
Garlic
Fresh ginger
Sesame seeds
Dark sesame oil
Soba noodles (8 ounces)
Rice vinegar
White miso
Honey
Large shrimp, peeled
  and deveined (12 ounces)

Cucumber and Shaved Carrot Salad
Carrot (2 medium)
English cucumber (1)
Shallot
Crushed red pepper
Olive oil
Rice vinegar
Sugar

GAME PLAN

While noodles cook:
■ Prepare cucumber and carrot salad.
While shrimp cooks:
■ Prepare miso mixture.

Grilled Shrimp with Miso-Ginger Sauce

With Cucumber and Shaved Carrot Salad

8 ounces uncooked soba (buckwheat
  noodles)
2 tablespoons chopped fresh flat-leaf
  parsley
2 tablespoons white miso (soybean
  paste)
2 tablespoons water
1 tablespoon rice vinegar
1 teaspoon honey, divided
1 teaspoon grated peeled fresh
  ginger
1 teaspoon minced fresh garlic
¼ teaspoon kosher salt
¼ teaspoon freshly ground black
  pepper
12 ounces large shrimp, peeled and
  deveined
Cooking spray
4 green onions
2 teaspoons dark sesame oil
1 teaspoon fresh lime juice
1 teaspoon sesame seeds

1. Cook noodles according to package directions; drain. Rinse with cold water; drain.
2. Combine parsley, miso, 2 tablespoons water, vinegar, and ½ teaspoon honey in a small bowl, stirring with a whisk until smooth.
3. Combine ½ teaspoon honey, ginger, garlic, salt, pepper, and shrimp in a medium bowl; toss to coat. Heat a grill pan over high heat. Coat pan with cooking spray. Add shrimp to pan; cook 2 minutes on each side or until done. Remove shrimp from pan. Add onions to pan; cook 1 minute on each side or until well marked. Coarsely chop onions. Combine noodles, onions, oil, and juice in a medium bowl; toss to

coat. Sprinkle noodle mixture with sesame seeds. Top noodle mixture with shrimp. Drizzle miso mixture over shrimp. Serves 4 (serving size: ½ cup noodles, ¾ cup shrimp, and 1 tablespoon sauce)

CALORIES 323; FAT 4g (sat 0.5g, mono 1.3g, poly 1.4g); PROTEIN 24g; CARB 52g; FIBER 2g; CHOL 107mg; IRON 2mg; SODIUM 646mg; CALC 77mg

Cucumber and Shaved Carrot Salad

Combine 1 tablespoon olive oil, 1 tablespoon rice vinegar, ¼ teaspoon sugar, ¼ teaspoon kosher salt, and ⅛ teaspoon crushed red pepper in a large bowl, stirring with a whisk until sugar dissolves. Shave 2 peeled medium carrots into thin strips using a vegetable peeler. Combine carrot, 1½ cups shaved English cucumber, and 2 tablespoons thinly sliced shallot. Add carrot and cucumber mixture to rice vinegar mixture; toss to coat. Serve immediately. Serves 4 (serving size: about ½ cup)

CALORIES 53; FAT 3.5g (sat 0.5g); SODIUM 143mg

Kid Friendly • Quick & Easy

Peach-Glazed Chicken and Peach-Studded Bulgur

With Arugula, Tomato, and Almond Salad

1⅓ cups water
¾ cup uncooked bulgur
2 tablespoons canola oil, divided
2½ tablespoons white wine vinegar, divided
2 teaspoons chopped fresh thyme
1 teaspoon grated peeled fresh ginger
2 cups chopped peaches
¼ cup thinly sliced green onions
½ teaspoon kosher salt, divided

½ teaspoon black pepper, divided
1 ounce goat cheese, crumbled (about ¼ cup)
4 (6-ounce) skinless, boneless chicken breast halves
½ cup unsalted chicken stock (such as Swanson)
¼ cup peach preserves
2 teaspoons whole-grain mustard

1. Combine 1⅓ cups water and bulgur in a small saucepan; bring to a boil. Cover, reduce heat, and simmer 12 minutes; drain. Rinse with cold water; drain. Combine 1 tablespoon oil, 1½ tablespoons vinegar, thyme, and ginger in a large bowl. Add bulgur, peaches, onions, ¼ teaspoon salt, and ¼ teaspoon pepper. Sprinkle with goat cheese.
2. Heat a large skillet over medium-high heat. Add 1 tablespoon oil to pan; swirl. Sprinkle chicken with ¼ teaspoon salt and ¼ teaspoon pepper; cook 5 minutes on each side or until done. Remove chicken from pan; keep warm.
3. Add chicken stock to pan; cook 2 minutes, scraping pan to loosen browned bits. Stir in 1 tablespoon vinegar, peach preserves, and mustard; cook 1 minute. Spoon glaze over chicken. Serve chicken with bulgur mixture. Serves 4 (serving size: 1 chicken breast half, 1½ tablespoons sauce, and 1 cup bulgur mixture)

CALORIES 461; FAT 14.1g (sat 3g, mono 6.3g, poly 2.9g); PROTEIN 42g; CARB 42g; FIBER 6g; CHOL 115mg; IRON 2mg; SODIUM 556mg; CALC 53mg

Arugula, Tomato, and Almond Salad

Combine 2 tablespoons balsamic vinegar, 1 tablespoon extra-virgin olive oil, ½ teaspoon Dijon mustard, ¼ teaspoon freshly ground black pepper, and ⅛ teaspoon kosher salt in a medium bowl. Add 6 ounces baby arugula, 2 cups halved grape tomatoes, and 3 tablespoons sliced toasted almonds; toss to coat. Serves 4 (serving size: 1½ cups)

CALORIES 87; FAT 5.8g (sat 0.7g); SODIUM 92mg

READY IN 30 MINUTES

SHOPPING LIST

Peach-Glazed Chicken and Peach-Studded Bulgur

Peaches (2)
Fresh thyme
Green onions
Fresh ginger
Canola oil
Unsalted chicken stock
Bulgur
White wine vinegar
Peach preserves
Whole-grain mustard
Goat cheese
Boneless, skinless chicken breast halves (1½ pounds)

Arugula, Tomato, and Almond Salad

Baby arugula (6 ounces)
Grape tomatoes (1 pint)
Extra-virgin olive oil
Sliced toasted almonds
Balsamic vinegar
Dijon mustard

GAME PLAN

While water for bulgur comes to a boil:
■ Prepare salad.
While bulgur simmers:
■ Cook chicken.

FUN FOODS FOR A SIZZLING SUMMER

It's time to cut loose and play with your food. Turn a cocktail into a kebab, a potato salad into portable "poppers." Add fun drinks to keep the kids happy and the parents totally chill.

Freezable • Gluten Free

Lemon-Caper-Parmesan Potato Salad Bites

Hands-on: 20 min. Total: 1 hr. 20 min.
Turn "jacket potatoes" into irresistible potato salad bites.

12 small red potatoes, halved (about 1¼ pounds)
2 teaspoons olive oil
½ cup light sour cream
2 tablespoons minced fresh chives, divided
2 tablespoons butter, melted
2 tablespoons finely chopped drained capers
1½ teaspoons fresh lemon juice
½ teaspoon kosher salt
½ teaspoon freshly ground black pepper
2 tablespoons grated fresh Parmesan cheese

1. Preheat oven to 450°.
2. Combine potatoes and oil; toss to coat. Arrange potatoes, cut sides down, in a single layer on a parchment paper–lined baking sheet. Bake at 450° for 20 minutes. Turn potatoes; bake 10 minutes. Remove and cool 20 minutes.
3. Preheat broiler to high.
4. Using a paring knife, carefully cut a circle in the cut side of potatoes. Using a melon baller or small spoon, remove pulp from potato, leaving a thin shell. Combine pulp, sour cream, 1 tablespoon chives, and next 5 ingredients. Evenly fill potato shells with filling; sprinkle with cheese and 1 tablespoon chives.
5. Broil potatoes 2 minutes or until cheese is lightly browned. Serves 12 (serving size: 2 potato halves)

CALORIES 85; FAT 3.9g (sat 2.2g, mono 1.2g, poly 0.2g); PROTEIN 2g; CARB 10g; FIBER 1g; CHOL 6mg; IRON 0mg; SODIUM 182mg; CALC 20mg

Kid Friendly

BLT Pizza with White Sauce

(pictured on page 227)

Hands-on: 15 min. Total: 50 min.
All the components of America's favorite summer sandwich are here—even the mayonnaise. Yes, it turns out adding some oil to the mayo makes a creamy sauce that fully covers the pie and gives a richer taste to the pizza.

1 pound ripe tomatoes, seeded and cut into ¼-inch-thick slices
1 teaspoon dried oregano
½ teaspoon freshly ground black pepper
¼ cup canola mayonnaise
1 tablespoon extra-virgin olive oil
1 tablespoon minced fresh chives
2 garlic cloves, grated
4 center-cut bacon slices
10 ounces fresh pizza dough
1 tablespoon cornmeal
2 ounces part-skim mozzarella cheese, shredded
Cooking spray
1 cup baby arugula

1. Place a pizza stone on bottom oven rack. Preheat oven to 400°.
2. Arrange tomato slices on a parchment-lined baking sheet; sprinkle with oregano and pepper. Place baking sheet directly on pizza stone. Bake at 400° for 20 minutes or until tomatoes are no longer wet. Remove tomatoes; keep stone in oven.
3. Increase oven temperature to 500°.
4. Combine mayonnaise, oil, chives, and garlic in a small bowl.
5. Cook bacon in a skillet over medium heat until crisp; drain on paper towels. Break into pieces.
6. Using well-floured hands, pat dough into a 10-inch circle. Place dough on a pizza peel or baking sheet sprinkled with cornmeal. Pierce dough with a fork; transfer to preheated pizza stone. Bake at 500° for 5 minutes.
7. Carefully remove pizza stone from the oven. Brush mayonnaise mixture over crust, leaving a 1-inch border; top with tomatoes and bacon. Top with cheese; coat crust edge with cooking spray. Bake 10 minutes or until cheese melts and crust browns. Top with arugula. Cut into 8 slices. Serves 4 (serving size: 2 slices)

CALORIES 353; FAT 14g (sat 3.3g, mono 6.7g, poly 2.3g); PROTEIN 13g; CARB 41g; FIBER 7g; CHOL 15mg; IRON 1mg; SODIUM 658mg; CALC 134mg

Berry Pie Pops

Hands-on: 25 min. Total: 1 hr. 30 min.

2 tablespoons sugar
1/4 teaspoon grated orange rind
1 tablespoon fresh orange juice
2 teaspoons cornstarch
1 (6-ounce) package raspberries
1 (6-ounce) package blueberries
Cooking spray
1 (14.1-ounce) package refrigerated pie dough
1 tablespoon milk
1 large egg white

1. Combine first 6 ingredients in a saucepan over medium heat. Bring to a boil; cook 8 minutes or until juices thicken. Pour mixture into a medium bowl; cool to room temperature.
2. Preheat oven to 450°.
3. Line a baking sheet with parchment paper; coat paper with cooking spray. Roll 1 dough portion into a 12-inch circle. Cut out 8 (3½-inch) rounds; arrange in a single layer on prepared pan. Reroll scraps; cut out 4 more rounds. Place on pan. Cover dough rounds; refrigerate. Repeat with remaining dough portion for 12 more dough rounds; place on work surface.
4. Cut 3 small slits in center of 12 dough rounds on work surface; set aside. Place 1 craft stick on each of remaining 12 rounds on pan, pressing slightly; top each with 4 teaspoons filling, leaving a ¼-inch border. Moisten borders with water using your finger. Place rounds with slits over filling; press edges with a fork to seal. Mix milk and egg white; brush gently over pie pops.
5. Bake at 450° for 14 minutes or until golden brown. Cool on pan 3 minutes; carefully place pie pops on a wire rack; cool completely. Serves 12 (serving size: 1 pie pop)

CALORIES 164; **FAT** 8.8g (sat 3.7g, mono 3.2g, poly 1.7g); **PROTEIN** 2g; **CARB** 21g; **FIBER** 1g; **CHOL** 4mg; **IRON** 0mg; **SODIUM** 178mg; **CALC** 6mg

BE THE BACKYARD SLUSHIE QUEEN

Dazzle guests with made-to-order icy beverages that couldn't be easier. All were developed to go in the Magic Bullet—that inexpensive blender that whips up one drink at a time. (If you don't have one, use a regular blender; just start with ⅔ cup ice and add more as needed). Load ingredients into the 8-ounce cup in the order specified on the chart (it's important to really fill the cup up). Use bagged, small-piece ice over large, hard chunks. For kids, nix the liquor.

	Blueberry-Mint Frozen Gimlet	Raspberry Summer Freeze	Orange-Cream Refresher	Icy Vanilla-Rum Malted Milkshake	Mint Margarita Slushie
FLAVOR	½ cup fresh blueberries + 6 mint leaves	½ cup fresh raspberries	¼ cup 1% low-fat milk	¼ cup 1% low-fat milk + 1 tablespoon malted milk powder	5 mint leaves
BOOZE	1½ ounces dry London-style gin	1½ ounces raspberry vodka	1½ ounces white rum	1½ ounces golden rum	1½ ounces tequila
SWEETENER	¾ ounce simple syrup	¾ ounce simple syrup	⅓ cup orange sorbet	⅓ cup vanilla low-fat ice cream	1½ ounces simple syrup
ACID	1 ounce fresh lime juice	1 ounce fresh lime juice	1 teaspoon fresh lime juice	None	2 ounces fresh lime juice
SLUSH	Ice to fill cup	Ice to fill cup	Ice to fill cup	Ice to fill cup	Ice to fill cup
NUMBERS	**SERVES 1** (serving size: 1¼ cups) **CALORIES** 185	**SERVES 1** (serving size: 1¼ cups) **CALORIES** 180	**SERVES 1** (serving size: 1¼ cups) **CALORIES** 185	**SERVES 1** (serving size: 1¼ cups) **CALORIES** 274; **FAT** 3.6g (sat 2.1g)	**SERVES 1** (serving size: 1¼ cups) **CALORIES** 188

Watermelon-Lime Soda

Combine ¾ cup sugar, ½ cup water, and ¼ cup chopped peeled fresh ginger in a small saucepan over high heat. Cook until sugar dissolves, stirring with a whisk. Remove from heat; cover and let stand 15 minutes. Strain; discard solids. Working in batches, place 10 cups diced watermelon and ¾ cup fresh lime juice in a blender; process until smooth. Strain watermelon mixture through a fine sieve into a pitcher; discard solids. Stir in sugar syrup and 4 cups chilled club soda. Serve over ice; garnish with mint sprigs, if desired. Serves 8 (serving size: about 1⅓ cups)

CALORIES 136; **FAT** 0.3g (sat 0g); **SODIUM** 3mg

Citrus-Honey Beer Shandy

Combine 3 tablespoons water and 1½ tablespoons honey, stirring well. Pour honey mixture, 4.5 ounces vodka, ¼ cup fresh orange juice, and 2 tablespoons fresh lemon juice into a cocktail shaker filled with ice; shake vigorously. Strain into a small pitcher; add 1 (12-ounce) hefeweizen beer. Serve over ice; garnish each drink with an orange slice, if desired. Serves 4 (serving size: about ⅔ cup)

CALORIES 147; **FAT** 0.1g (sat 0g); **SODIUM** 3mg

HOW TO MAKE
GRILLED CHICKEN DRUMSTICKS

Preheat grill to high heat. Combine ½ teaspoon freshly ground black pepper, ⅛ teaspoon kosher salt, and ⅛ teaspoon ground red pepper; sprinkle over 8 skinless chicken drumsticks. Place drumsticks on grill rack coated with cooking spray. Cover and grill 3 minutes or until charred; reduce heat to medium. Grill 18 minutes or until a thermometer inserted into the thickest part registers 160°, turning occasionally. Serve sauces on the side for dipping. Or for glazes, divide the sauce in half; brush drumsticks with half of the glaze during the last 4 minutes of cooking, and use the rest for dipping.

THE SAUCES

1 Singapore Sauce
Combine ¼ cup Sriracha, 2 tablespoons unsalted chicken stock, 2 tablespoons fresh lime juice, 1 tablespoon grated peeled fresh ginger, 2 teaspoons sugar, and 4 grated garlic cloves. Serves 4 (serving size: 2 drumsticks and 1 tablespoon dipping sauce)

CALORIES 321; FAT 10.7g (sat 2.7g); SODIUM 594mg

2 Cilantro Pesto
Place 2½ tablespoons crumbled Cotija cheese, 2 tablespoons water, 4 teaspoons fresh lime juice, 4 teaspoons olive oil, ⅜ teaspoon ground cumin, ¼ teaspoon kosher salt, ¼ teaspoon freshly ground black pepper, 3 garlic cloves, 1 seeded serrano chile, and ½ bunch cilantro (including stems) in a blender. Process until sauce is smooth. Serves 4 (serving size: 2 drumsticks and about 2 tablespoons pesto)

CALORIES 353; FAT 16.6g (sat 4g); SODIUM 448mg

3 Sesame Glaze
Combine 3 tablespoons finely chopped green onions, 3 tablespoons unsalted chicken stock, 2 tablespoons lower-sodium soy sauce, 2 tablespoons honey, 2 tablespoons dark sesame oil, 1 tablespoon sesame seeds, ¾ teaspoon crushed red pepper, and 3 grated fresh garlic cloves. Serves 4 (serving size: 2 glazed drumsticks and about 4 teaspoons leftover glaze)

CALORIES 407; FAT 18.7g (sat 3.9g); SODIUM 565mg

4 Dill-icious Dipping Sauce
Combine ¼ cup canola mayonnaise, 3 tablespoons water, 2 tablespoons reduced-fat sour cream, 1 tablespoon chopped fresh dill, 2 teaspoons hot sauce, 1 teaspoon cider vinegar, ¼ teaspoon garlic powder, and ¼ teaspoon onion powder; let stand 30 minutes. Serves 4 (serving size: 2 drumsticks and 2 tablespoons dipping sauce)

CALORIES 345; FAT 15.3g (sat 3.3g); SODIUM 464mg

5 Bourbon-Dijon Glaze
Combine ½ cup unsalted chicken stock, ¼ cup bourbon, ¼ cup honey, and 4 thyme sprigs in a small saucepan. Bring to a boil; reduce heat, and simmer 15 minutes or until liquid is syrupy and reduced to ⅓ cup. Discard thyme. Whisk in 3 tablespoons whole-grain Dijon mustard and 2 tablespoons minced green onions. Serves 4 (serving size: 2 glazed drumsticks and about 4 teaspoons leftover glaze)

CALORIES 394; FAT 10.7g (sat 2.7g); SODIUM 578mg

Quick & Easy
Buffalo Chicken Sliders

Hands-on: 26 min. Total: 26 min.
For this slider, we tuck the usual Buffalo wing accompaniments—carrots and celery—inside the patty. This gives you all the flavors of a wing plate while also helping to keep the lean breast meat moist.

2 tablespoons canola mayonnaise
1 tablespoon 2% reduced-fat milk
1 ounce blue cheese, crumbled
1 pound ground chicken breast
⅓ cup panko (Japanese breadcrumbs)
⅓ cup shredded carrot
⅓ cup shredded celery
½ teaspoon paprika
1 large egg, lightly beaten
1 garlic clove, grated
Cooking spray
3 tablespoons hot sauce
1 tablespoon butter, melted
8 whole-grain slider buns, split and toasted
16 celery leaves

1. Combine first 3 ingredients in a small bowl; set aside.
2. Place chicken in a medium bowl; add panko, carrot, celery, paprika, egg, and garlic. Mix just until combined. Divide into 8 portions; shape each into a 3-inch patty.
3. Heat a grill pan over medium-high heat. Lightly coat pan with cooking spray. Add patties to pan; cook 3 minutes on each side or until done. Combine hot sauce and butter in a medium bowl; add patties to bowl, turning to coat. Layer bottom half of each bun with 1 patty, about 1 teaspoon blue cheese mixture, 2 celery leaves, and top half of bun. Serves 4 (serving size: 2 sliders)

CALORIES 392; FAT 12.7g (sat 4.5g, mono 3.7g, poly 3.2g); PROTEIN 31g; CARB 42g; FIBER 3g; CHOL 109mg; IRON 0mg; SODIUM 796mg; CALC 60mg

Quinoa-Arugula Layered Salad

Hands-on: 15 min. Total: 35 min.

2 tablespoons extra-virgin olive oil, divided
¾ cup uncooked quinoa
1 cup unsalted chicken stock
½ teaspoon salt, divided
2 tablespoons fresh lemon juice
¼ teaspoon black pepper
Dash of sugar
1 garlic clove, minced
2 cups baby arugula leaves
1 cup diced English cucumber
½ cup diced red onion
1 cup grape tomatoes, halved
¾ cup chopped fresh flat-leaf parsley

1. Heat a small saucepan over medium-high heat. Add 1 teaspoon oil; swirl to coat. Add quinoa; cook 2 minutes or until lightly toasted, stirring frequently. Gradually stir in stock; bring to a boil. Cover, reduce heat, and simmer 13 minutes or until quinoa is tender. Remove from heat; stir in ¼ teaspoon salt. Cool the quinoa to room temperature.
2. Combine 5 teaspoons oil, ¼ teaspoon salt, juice, pepper, sugar, and garlic in a small bowl; stirring with a whisk.
3. Place about 1 tablespoon dressing in each of 4 pint-sized jars with lids. Layer ½ cup arugula, one-fourth of quinoa mixture, ¼ cup cucumber, 2 tablespoons onion, ¼ cup tomato, and 3 tablespoons parsley in each jar. Close lid; refrigerate up to 24 hours. Shake before serving. Serves 4 (serving size: 1 jar)

CALORIES 216; FAT 9.2g (sat 1.2g, mono 5.9g, poly 1.7g); PROTEIN 7g; CARB 27g; FIBER 4g; CHOL 0mg; IRON 2mg; SODIUM 339mg; CALC 75mg

Deep-Dish Strawberry Ice Dream Pie

Hands-on: 20 min. Total: 5 hr. 20 min.

30 chocolate wafers
5 teaspoons unsalted butter, melted
1 large egg white, lightly beaten
Dash of salt
Cooking spray
1 pound fresh strawberries, divided
¼ cup seedless strawberry jam, divided
1 teaspoon fresh lemon juice
⅔ cup fat-free sweetened condensed milk
4 cups frozen low-fat whipped topping, thawed

1. Preheat oven to 350°.
2. Finely grind wafers in a food processor. Add butter, egg white, and salt; process until well combined. Gently press mixture into bottom and up sides of a 9.5-inch deep-dish pie plate coated with cooking spray. Bake at 350° for 10 minutes. Cool 10 minutes on a wire rack. Freeze 30 minutes or until well chilled.
3. Slice 1 cup of strawberries; place in large bowl. Add 1 tablespoon jam and lemon juice; gently stir. Stir in milk. Gently fold in whipped topping. Spoon mixture into prepared crust, smoothing top. Freeze 4 hours or up to overnight.
4. Quarter remaining strawberries lengthwise; combine with 3 tablespoons jam. Arrange mixture over pie. Serve immediately. Serves 10 (serving size: 1 slice)

CALORIES 264; FAT 8.5g (sat 5.5g, mono 1.7g, poly 0.5g); PROTEIN 4g; CARB 43g; FIBER 2g; CHOL 11mg; IRON 1mg; SODIUM 196mg; CALC 83mg

TWO AWESOME COBS

Preheat grill to high heat. Place 4 ears shucked corn on grill rack coated with cooking spray; grill 8 minutes or until lightly charred, turning occasionally. Pick a topping below, and spread on hot ears.

SMOKY RED PEPPER MAYO AND BASIL

Place 2 tablespoons chopped bottled roasted red bell pepper, 1½ tablespoons canola mayonnaise, ½ teaspoon minced garlic, ½ teaspoon fresh lemon juice, ⅛ teaspoon smoked paprika, ⅛ teaspoon kosher salt, and a dash of ground red pepper in a mini food processor; process until smooth. Drizzle mixture over corn. Sprinkle with 4 teaspoons chopped fresh basil. Serves 4 (serving size: 1 corn cob)

CALORIES 105; FAT 2.9g (sat 0.3g); SODIUM 126mg

FETA AND MINT BUTTER

Place 2 tablespoons crumbled feta, 1 tablespoon softened unsalted butter, 1 tablespoon minced fresh mint, and 1½ teaspoons fresh lime juice in a small bowl. Mash with a fork to combine. Press mixture onto cobs using hands. Serves 4 (serving size: 1 corn cob)

CALORIES 128; FAT 5.4g (sat 2.9g); SODIUM 68mg

Gluten Free • Make Ahead

Piña Colada on a Stick

Hands-on: 56 min. Total: 4 hr. 56 min.

1½ cups shredded unsweetened coconut
¼ cup heavy whipping cream
1 (13.5-ounce) can light coconut milk
⅔ cup sugar
⅜ teaspoon salt
1 cup coconut water
2 envelopes plus 1 teaspoon unflavored gelatin
½ teaspoon vanilla extract
Cooking spray
½ cup white rum
2 tablespoons fresh lime juice
1 whole pineapple, peeled, cored, and cut into 72 chunks
18 strawberries, halved lengthwise

1. Preheat oven to 350°.
2. Spread coconut on a baking sheet. Bake at 350° for 7 minutes or until golden, stirring after 4 minutes. Combine coconut, cream, coconut milk, sugar, and salt in a saucepan. Bring to a simmer over medium heat (do not boil). Remove from heat; cover and let stand 20 minutes.
3. Place coconut water in a medium bowl; sprinkle gelatin over top. Let stand 5 minutes or until solid.
4. Strain coconut milk mixture through a sieve over a bowl, pressing to extract liquid. Discard coconut. Gradually add coconut milk mixture to gelatin mixture, stirring with a whisk. Return mixture to pan; heat over medium heat just until gelatin dissolves (do not boil). Remove from heat; stir in vanilla. Pour mixture into an 8-inch square baking dish coated with cooking spray. Cool to room temperature. Cover and chill 4 hours or up to overnight. (The layers should separate naturally.)
5. While coconut mixture chills, combine rum and lime juice in a large zip-top plastic bag; add pineapple, and seal bag. Refrigerate 4 hours or up to overnight, turning bag occasionally.
6. Drain pineapple mixture. Cut coconut mixture into 72 cubes. Thread 2 pineapple chunks, 2 coconut cubes, and 1 strawberry half alternately onto each of 36 skewers. Serves 12 (serving size: 3 skewers)

CALORIES 160; FAT 4.7g (sat 3.6g, mono 0.6g, poly 0.2g); PROTEIN 3g; CARB 26g; FIBER 2g; CHOL 7mg; IRON 1mg; SODIUM 92mg; CALC 22mg

Kid Friendly • Quick & Easy

Tropical Fruit Nachos

Hands-on: 15 min. Total: 30 min.

Cooking spray
16 wonton wrappers, cut in half diagonally
¼ cup sugar, divided
¼ teaspoon cinnamon
½ cup light coconut milk
Dash of salt
1 teaspoon cornstarch
1 tablespoon cold water
2 teaspoons fresh lime juice
½ cup diced pineapple
½ cup diced mango
½ cup diced strawberries
1 diced peeled kiwifruit
¼ cup unsweetened coconut flakes, toasted
2 tablespoons sliced fresh mint

1. Preheat oven to 400°.
2. Coat a baking sheet with cooking spray. Arrange wontons on baking sheet; coat with cooking spray. Combine 3 tablespoons sugar and cinnamon in a small bowl. Sprinkle wontons evenly with sugar mixture. Bake at 400° for 10 minutes or until golden brown, rotating pan after 5 minutes. Cool completely on pan.
3. Combine 1 tablespoon sugar, coconut milk, and salt in a small saucepan; bring to a boil. Combine cornstarch and water in a small bowl. Add cornstarch mixture to milk mixture; cook 1 minute or until mixture thickens, stirring constantly with a whisk. Remove pan from heat; stir in lime juice.
4. Combine pineapple, mango, strawberries, and kiwifruit in a bowl; toss gently. Place wontons on a platter; top with pineapple mixture. Drizzle with sauce; sprinkle with coconut and mint. Serve immediately. Serves 4 (serving size: 8 chips, ½ cup fruit mixture, and about 2½ tablespoons sauce)

CALORIES 235; FAT 5.4g (sat 3.6g, mono 0.1g, poly 0.3g); PROTEIN 4g; CARB 44g; FIBER 3g; CHOL 3g; IRON 1g; SODIUM 224mg; CALC 33mg

Kid Friendly

Bourbon-Peach Barbecue Pulled Pork Sliders

Hands-on: 10 min. Total: 10 min.

1½ tablespoons canola mayonnaise
1 teaspoon sugar
1½ teaspoons cider vinegar
⅛ teaspoon kosher salt
1 cup cabbage-and-carrot coleslaw
¼ cup thinly vertically sliced red onion
8 ounces Slow Cooker Pulled Pork with Bourbon-Peach Barbecue Sauce (recipe on page 188)
8 slider buns, split and toasted

1. Combine first 4 ingredients in a medium bowl. Add coleslaw and onion; toss well to combine.
2. Divide pork among bottom halves of buns; top each slider with 2 heaping tablespoons slaw and top half of bun. Serves 4 (serving size: 2 sliders)

CALORIES 363; FAT 9.3g (sat 1.4g, mono 4.3g, poly 3.1g); PROTEIN 21g; CARB 50g; FIBER 3g; CHOL 36mg; IRON 3mg; SODIUM 650mg; CALC 116mg

Classic Bacon Cheeseburger Sliders

Hands-on: 22 min. Total: 22 min.

4 center-cut bacon slices, cut in
   half crosswise
1 pound 93% lean ground beef
1½ teaspoons olive oil
½ teaspoon garlic powder
½ teaspoon freshly ground black
   pepper
⅛ teaspoon kosher salt
Cooking spray
2 2% reduced-fat American slices
   cheese, quartered
8 teaspoons ketchup
8 slider buns, split and toasted
4 teaspoons minced fresh onion,
   rinsed and drained
8 green leaf lettuce leaves

1. Cook bacon in a skillet over
medium heat until crisp; drain.
2. Place beef in a medium bowl.
Drizzle with oil, and sprinkle with
garlic powder, pepper, and salt; mix
well to combine. Divide mixture into
8 equal portions, shaping each into
a 3-inch patty.
3. Heat a grill pan or cast-iron skillet
over medium-high heat. Coat pan
with cooking spray. Add patties;
cook 3 minutes or until seared. Turn
patties over; top each with 1 piece of
cheese. Cover and cook 2 additional
minutes or until beef is done and
cheese melts.
4. Spread 1 teaspoon ketchup on top
half of each bun; top each with
½ teaspoon onion. Layer bottom half
of bun with 1 lettuce leaf, 1 patty,
1 bacon piece, and top half of bun.
Serves 4 (serving size: 2 sliders)

CALORIES 406; FAT 15g (sat 5.4g, mono 4.4g, poly 3.4g);
PROTEIN 32g; CARB 38g; FIBER 2g; CHOL 66mg;
IRON 4mg; SODIUM 803mg; CALC 215mg

MASTERING YOUR GRILL WITH THE KING OF FIRE

Amid a gaggle of hip grilling stars, Steven Raichlen still rules the roost for home cooks.

Salt Slab Chicken al Mattone

Hands-on: 15 min. Total: 45 min.
*Pollo al mattone (chicken grilled under a
brick) is one of Italy's great gifts to global
barbecue. The weight of the brick gives the
chicken a crisp, compact texture. Himalayan
pink salt slabs are available at cookware
shops or online at amazon.com. If you'd
prefer to use a foil-wrapped brick instead,
sprinkle the chicken with an additional ¼
teaspoon salt.*

1 tablespoon finely chopped fresh
   rosemary
3 tablespoons fresh lemon juice
3 tablespoons extra-virgin olive
   oil
1 teaspoon crushed red pepper
⅜ teaspoon coarse sea salt
¼ teaspoon freshly ground black
   pepper
2 garlic cloves, minced
4 (6-ounce) skinless, boneless
   chicken breast halves
Cooking spray
1 (12 x 8-inch) salt slab
Lemon wedges (optional)

1. Preheat grill to high heat.
2. Combine first 7 ingredients in a
small bowl, stirring with a whisk.
Place chicken in a large zip-top
plastic bag. Add juice mixture; seal
bag. Turn bag to completely coat
chicken. Refrigerate 20 minutes.
3. Remove chicken from bag; discard
marinade. Place chicken on grill rack
coated with cooking spray. Place salt
slab on top of chicken; grill 5 minutes on each side or until chicken
is done. Serve with lemon wedges,
if desired. Serves 4 (serving size: 1
breast half)

CALORIES 292; FAT 14.8g (sat 2.4g, mono 8.7g, poly 1.8g);
PROTEIN 36g; CARB 2g; FIBER 0g; CHOL 109mg;
IRON 1mg; SODIUM 554mg; CALC 15mg

HIGH, DIRECT
HEAT (600°)
IS PERFECT FOR
QUICK-COOKING
CUTS LIKE
BONELESS
CHICKEN BREASTS.
RAICHLEN GIVES
MEAT A QUARTER-
TURN HALFWAY
THROUGH COOK-
ING EACH SIDE
FOR ATTRACTIVE
GRILL MARKS.

Grilled Gazpacho

Hands-on: 30 min. Total: 1 hr. 50 min.
Grilling adds a smoky dimension to Spain's favorite summertime soup. The trick is to grill the veggies over a screaming-hot fire, just long enough to char the exterior while leaving the vegetables raw in the center.

1½ cups apple or oak wood chips
Cooking spray
4 green onions, trimmed
1 small red onion, peeled and
    quartered
2 garlic cloves, peeled
⅓ cup extra-virgin olive oil, divided
1 (½-inch-thick) slice country-style
    bread (about 2 ounces)
6 ripe tomatoes (2½ pounds)
1 red bell pepper
1 green bell pepper
1 cucumber, peeled
3 tablespoons chopped fresh basil
3 tablespoons chopped fresh flat-leaf
    parsley
1 tablespoon chopped fresh oregano
1 tablespoon chopped fresh tarragon
1 teaspoon chopped fresh thyme
2 tablespoons red wine vinegar
¾ teaspoon sea salt
¼ teaspoon freshly ground black
    pepper

1. Soak wood chips in water 30 minutes; drain.
2. Remove grill rack; set aside. Preheat grill to high heat. Place wood chips on hot coals; heat wood chips 10 minutes. Coat grill rack with cooking spray; place grill rack on grill.
3. Finely chop green onion tops; set aside. Thread white parts of green onions onto a skewer. Thread red onion quarters onto skewers. Thread garlic cloves onto a skewer. Lightly brush vegetables with oil.
4. Place green onion, red onion, and garlic skewers on the grill, and grill 1 minute on each side or until darkly browned on the outside but still raw in the center. Remove from grill; cool. Place bread on grill; grill 1 minute on each side or until darkly toasted. Remove from grill. Place tomatoes and bell peppers on grill; grill tomatoes 2 minutes on each side or until skins are charred. Grill peppers 3 minutes on each side or until charred. Remove from grill; cool. Scrape and discard charred skins from 3 tomatoes and both peppers with a paring knife. Remove and discard seeds and membranes from peppers.
5. Place grilled vegetables, bread, remaining oil, cucumber, and remaining ingredients in a blender or food processor; process until smooth. Chill 1 hour. Ladle ¾ cup gazpacho into each of 8 bowls; sprinkle with green onion tops. Serves 8

CALORIES 137; FAT 9.6g (sat 1.3g, mono 6.6g, poly 1.1g); PROTEIN 2g; CARB 12g; FIBER 3g; CHOL 0mg; IRON 1mg; SODIUM 251mg; CALC 32mg

Smoked Salmon, Barbecue University-Style

Hands-on: 40 min. Total: 6 hr. 10 min.
This whisky-scented smoked salmon combines the virtues of hot smoking and cedar planking. The dry brine in a sugar-salt mixture seasons the fish wonderfully. Cedar planks are available at grill stores and cookware shops. For gas grilling, place drained, soaked wood chips in a disposable aluminum pan directly on the burner of your grill.

½ cup Scotch whisky
1 (1½-pound) ¾-inch-thick,
    center-cut skinless salmon fillet
    (preferably wild)
1 cup brown sugar
2 tablespoons coarsely cracked black
    peppercorns
1 tablespoon kosher salt
1 teaspoon grated lemon rind
1 (15 x 6½ x ⅜-inch) cedar grilling
    plank
1½ cups hickory wood chips
Coarsely cracked black peppercorns
    (optional)
Lemon slices (optional)

1. Combine whisky and salmon in a large zip-top plastic bag. Refrigerate 1 hour, turning occasionally. Drain; pat salmon dry.
2. Combine brown sugar, pepper, salt, and rind in a large bowl. Place one-third of sugar mixture in bottom of an 11 x 7–inch baking dish. Add fish; top evenly with remaining sugar mixture. Cover with plastic wrap; refrigerate 4 hours. Rinse fish well; pat dry.
3. While fish marinates, soak grilling plank in water 1 hour; drain. Soak wood chips in water 30 minutes; drain.
4. Remove grill rack; set aside. Prepare grill for indirect grilling, heating both sides to medium and leaving center with no heat. Maintain temperature at medium (325°). Toss wood chips on coals. Place grill rack on grill. Place salmon, skinned-side down, on plank in center of hot rack, away from the heat. Cover; grill 30 minutes or until desired degree of doneness. Serve with cracked peppercorns and lemon slices, if desired. Serves 4 (serving size: 5 ounces cooked salmon)

CALORIES 312; FAT 9.6g (sat 2g, mono 3.2g, poly 3.3g); PROTEIN 36g; CARB 14g; FIBER 0g; CHOL 90mg; IRON 1mg; SODIUM 444mg; CALC 32mg

EIGHT SIZZLING SUMMER KEBABS

Tasty combos that really please, with less than 250 calories per serving

Kid Friendly • Quick & Easy
Gluten Free
Mediterranean Lamb, Tomato & Mint
Combine 2 teaspoons fresh ginger, 2 teaspoons olive oil, 1½ teaspoons ground cumin, 1 teaspoon ground coriander, ¼ teaspoon kosher salt, 2 minced garlic cloves, and 1 pound boneless lean leg of lamb (cut into 24 pieces); toss. Thread lamb, 16 cherry tomatoes, 16 (½-inch) slices cucumber, and 16 mint leaves onto skewers. Coat with cooking spray; sprinkle with ¼ teaspoon salt. Grill 6 minutes (for medium-rare) or until done. Serves 4 (serving size: 2 skewers)

CALORIES 185; **FAT** 8.5g (sat 2.4g); **SODIUM** 201mg

Kid Friendly • Quick & Easy
Gluten Free
Tuscany Chicken, Red Onion & Prosciutto-Wrapped Plums
Combine 1 pound skinless, boneless chicken thighs (cut into 32 cubes); 1 tablespoon olive oil; 1 tablespoon fresh lime juice; ¼ teaspoon kosher salt; ¼ teaspoon black pepper; and 2 minced garlic cloves. Toss. Wrap 24 plum wedges with 1½ ounces prosciutto, torn into pieces. Thread chicken, 16 basil leaves, 16 (1-inch) wedges red onion, and plums onto skewers. Grill 8 minutes or until chicken is done. Sprinkle with 2 tablespoons chopped fresh basil. Serves 4 (serving size: 2 skewers)

CALORIES 205; **FAT** 9.1g (sat 2.3g); **SODIUM** 474mg

Kid Friendly • Quick & Easy
Gluten Free
Middle East Yogurt-Marinated Chicken & Zucchini
Combine ½ cup 2% Greek yogurt, 1 tablespoon olive oil, 1 tablespoon fresh lemon juice, ½ teaspoon ground cumin, ¼ teaspoon ground ginger, ¼ teaspoon ground coriander, and 2 minced garlic cloves. Add 1 pound skinless, boneless chicken breasts (cut into 32 cubes); toss. Thread chicken and 32 (½-inch) slices zucchini coated with cooking spray onto skewers. Sprinkle with ½ teaspoon kosher salt. Grill 8 minutes. Sprinkle with chopped fresh dill. Serves 4 (serving size: 2 skewers)

CALORIES 193; **FAT** 7.1g (sat 1.7g); **SODIUM** 313mg

Quick & Easy
Pacific Northwest Salmon, Asparagus & Fresh Lemon
Combine 1 tablespoon rice vinegar, 1 tablespoon lower-sodium soy sauce, 1 tablespoon honey, 2 teaspoons canola oil, 2 grated garlic cloves, 1 pound skinless salmon fillet (cut into 1-inch pieces), and 32 (1½-inch) slices asparagus; toss. Thread fish, asparagus, and 16 lemon slices onto skewers. Coat with cooking spray; sprinkle with ¼ teaspoon kosher salt and ¼ teaspoon freshly ground black pepper. Grill 6 minutes or until done. Serves 4 (serving size: 2 skewers)

CALORIES 220; **FAT** 8.9g (sat 1g); **SODIUM** 327mg

Kid Friendly • Quick & Easy
Gluten Free
Italy Pesto Shrimp
Combine 3 tablespoons pesto, 1 tablespoon fresh lemon juice, and 32 peeled and deveined large shrimp; toss. Let stand 5 minutes. Thread shrimp and 32 (1-inch) squares red and yellow bell pepper onto skewers. Sprinkle evenly with ¼ teaspoon kosher salt. Grill 7 minutes. Serves 4 (serving size: 2 skewers)

CALORIES 125; **FAT** 6.3g (sat 1.5g); **SODIUM** 295mg

Quick & Easy • Vegetarian
Berkeley BBQ Tempeh & Mushroom
Combine 1 tablespoon olive oil, 1 tablespoon lower-sodium soy sauce, and 8 ounces organic soy tempeh (cut into 16 pieces). Let stand 20 minutes. Add ¼ cup barbecue sauce; toss. Thread tempeh, 16 mushrooms, 16 grape tomatoes, and 16 (1-inch) squares yellow bell pepper onto skewers. Grill 9 minutes or until browned. Sprinkle with chopped green onions. Serve with barbecue sauce. Serves 4 (serving size: 2 skewers)

CALORIES 214; **FAT** 10g (sat 1.8g); **SODIUM** 291mg

Kid Friendly • Quick & Easy
Gluten Free
Southwest Steak & Avocado
Combine 1 teaspoon olive oil, ¼ teaspoon kosher salt, ½ teaspoon chipotle chile powder, and ¼ teaspoon black pepper; rub evenly over 1 pound top sirloin. Cut steak into 32 cubes. Thread steak, 16 ripe avocado cubes, 16 cherry tomatoes, and 16 (1-inch) squares red onion onto skewers. Coat with cooking spray; sprinkle with ¼ teaspoon kosher salt. Grill 5 minutes or until done. Serves 4 (serving size: 2 skewers)

CALORIES 227; **FAT** 11.3g (sat 2.6g); **SODIUM** 294mg

Kid Friendly • Quick & Easy
Hawaii Pork & Pineapple
Combine 1½ tablespoons brown sugar, 1½ tablespoons lower-sodium soy sauce, 1 tablespoon fresh orange juice, 2 teaspoons fresh lemon juice, 1 seeded minced jalapeño, and ¼ teaspoon black pepper. Divide mixture between 2 bowls. Add 1 pound pork tenderloin (cut into 16 cubes) to first bowl; toss. Add 16 pineapple cubes to second bowl; toss. Thread pork, pineapple, and 16 (1-inch) pieces poblano pepper onto skewers. Grill 14 minutes or until done. Sprinkle with chopped fresh cilantro. Serves 4 (serving size: 2 skewers)

CALORIES 194; **FAT** 3.3g (sat 1g); **SODIUM** 250mg

CORN AND SHRIMP SUCCOTASH

The Miami star chef Michelle Bernstein puts summer produce to spectacular use.

The James Beard Award–winning chef, who specializes in what she calls luxurious comfort food at her lauded Miami restaurant, Michy's, considers corn one of the most comforting produce ingredients on the market.

"Corn has been a staple in our house forever. I adore it," Bernstein says. "And it's so versatile, I can't think of anything it doesn't go with. You can make it savory or sweet." Indeed, it can go into everything from breakfast eggs, tangy relishes, and fiery salsas to a cool, clean salad or custardy dessert flan.

In this succotash, Bernstein sought a dish that was richly satisfying yet healthy and not heavy. Omitting the bacon that many folks include in succotash, Bernstein makes a quick shrimp stock from shells for a savory umami boost. Fresh beans bring verdant brightness, while briny shrimp marry perfectly with sweet corn. A touch of sour cream adds velvety mouthfeel.

Kid Friendly • Gluten Free

Summer Corn and Shrimp Succotash

Hands-on: 1 hr. 10 min. Total: 1 hr. 10 min.

³/₄ pound jumbo shrimp
2 tablespoons olive oil, divided
1 cup unsalted chicken stock
8 cups water
3 cups shelled fava beans (about 4¹/₂ pounds unshelled beans)
1 cup (1-inch) diagonally cut green beans (about ¹/₄ pound)
2 tablespoons butter, divided
3 garlic cloves, minced
2 shallots, minced
1¹/₂ cups fresh corn kernels (about 3 ears)
¹/₂ teaspoon kosher salt
1 tablespoon chopped fresh dill
1 tablespoon chopped fresh tarragon
¹/₂ teaspoon hot sauce
2 tablespoons reduced-fat sour cream
¹/₂ teaspoon freshly ground black pepper

1. Peel and devein shrimp, reserving shells. Set shrimp aside.
2. Heat a medium saucepan over medium-high heat. Add 1 tablespoon oil to pan. Add shrimp shells; sauté 5 minutes. Add stock. Bring to a boil; cook until liquid is reduced to ¹/₂ cup. Strain liquid through a sieve into a bowl; discard shells. Reserve liquid.
3. Fill a large bowl with ice water. Bring 8 cups water to a boil in a large saucepan or Dutch oven. Add fava beans; cook 1 minute. Remove with a slotted spoon. Plunge fava beans into ice water; cool completely. Drain well. Remove and discard tough outer shell from fava beans. Add green beans to boiling water; cook 2 minutes. Plunge green beans into ice water; cool completely. Drain well.
4. Heat a large skillet over medium-high heat. Add remaining oil and 1 tablespoon butter. Add garlic and shallots; sauté 2 minutes. Add corn; sauté 2 minutes. Add shrimp, reserved shrimp liquid, and salt; cook 3 minutes. Add fava beans, green beans, 1 tablespoon butter, dill, tarragon, and hot sauce; cook 3 minutes or until shrimp are done. Remove from heat. Stir in sour cream and pepper. Serves 4 (serving size: 1½ cups)

CALORIES 340; FAT 15.8g (sat 5.6g, mono 7g, poly 1.8g); PROTEIN 22g; CARB 30g; FIBER 7g; CHOL 125mg; IRON 4mg; SODIUM 534mg; CALC 120mg

KEY LIME TIME

A few of these petite citrus fruits leave a big, bold impression.

Summer is peak season for Key limes—a fruit no bigger than a walnut but mighty in intensity. In our panna cotta, we use the aromatic juice with restraint to highlight the fruit's floral notes along with its distinct tang. While tarter and more acidic than Persian limes, Key limes are actually a little sweeter. The juice adds zing to marinades for fish, pork, and chicken and is delightful in a juicy cocktail. The zested skin will add flavor to icings or salad dressings. About four Key limes give you as much juice as one Persian lime, and with the skyrocketing price of the latter, Key limes may be the better buy. Get 'em now—while they're fresh.

Kid Friendly • Make Ahead

Key Lime Panna Cotta

Hands-on: 25 min. Total: 8 hr. 50 min. We used only enough gelatin for the creamy texture and wobbly jiggle panna cotta is known for.

¹/₂ cup half-and-half
¹/₂ cup low-fat sweetened condensed milk
2 tablespoons grated Key lime rind
¹/₄ teaspoon salt, divided
1 cup 2% reduced-fat milk, divided
1¹/₄ teaspoons unflavored gelatin
2 tablespoons Key lime juice, divided (about 4)
Cooking spray
1¹/₂ tablespoons honey
1 teaspoon unsalted butter
1 low-fat graham cracker sheet, crushed into coarse crumbs

1. Combine first 3 ingredients and ⅛ teaspoon salt in a small saucepan; bring to a boil. Remove pan from heat; cover and let stand 30 minutes.
2. Place ¼ cup 2% milk in a medium bowl. Sprinkle gelatin over milk; let stand 10 minutes.
3. Return pan to medium-high heat; bring to a simmer. Add hot milk mixture to gelatin mixture, stirring until gelatin dissolves. Add remaining ¾ cup 2% milk. Strain mixture through a fine sieve into a medium bowl; discard solids. Stir in 1 tablespoon Key lime juice. Divide mixture evenly among 4 (4-ounce) ramekins or custard cups lightly coated with cooking spray. Cover with plastic wrap, and refrigerate overnight.
4. Combine 1 tablespoon juice and honey.
5. Melt butter in a small skillet over medium heat. Add crumbs and ⅛ teaspoon salt. Cook 1 minute or until lightly toasted, stirring constantly. Cool completely. To serve, loosen edges of panna cotta with a knife or rubber spatula. Invert ramekins onto dessert plates. Drizzle each with about 2 teaspoons honey mixture, and top with about 2 teaspoons graham cracker crumbs. Serves 4

CALORIES 251; FAT 7.3g (sat 4.5g, mono 1.6g, poly 0.2g); PROTEIN 7g; CARB 37g; FIBER 0g; CHOL 24mg; IRON 0mg; SODIUM 250mg; CALC 224mg

ALL YOU NEED FOR A FANTASTIC SAUCE IS A DRIZZLE OF HONEY AND A SPLASH OF ZINGY LIME JUICE.

BLUEPRINT FOR A BETTER SANDWICH

Six boldly updated versions of America's signature regional treats

Kid Friendly • Quick & Easy

Indiana Pork Tenderloin Sandwiches with Creamy Corn Relish

Hands-on: 35 min. Total: 35 min.
Wondra flour adds to the coating's crisp texture, but all-purpose flour will work just fine.

2 teaspoons butter
½ cup fresh corn kernels (about 1 ear)
⅛ teaspoon ground red pepper
1 tablespoon 2% reduced-fat milk
1 tablespoon cider vinegar
2 ounces ⅓-less-fat cream cheese, softened (about ¼ cup)
3 tablespoons diced red bell pepper
1 tablespoon diced red onion
1 tablespoon chopped fresh parsley
4 (3-ounce) slices pork tenderloin
½ teaspoon salt
½ teaspoon freshly ground black pepper
1 large egg
1 teaspoon water
2 tablespoons quick-mixing flour (such as Wondra)
⅔ cup panko (Japanese breadcrumbs)
2 tablespoons canola oil
4 green leaf lettuce leaves
4 white-wheat hamburger buns

1. Melt butter in a small skillet over medium-high heat. Add corn and ground red pepper; sauté 3 minutes or until crisp-tender. Add milk, vinegar, and cream cheese; cook 1 minute or until cream cheese melts, stirring constantly. Remove pan from heat. Stir in bell pepper, onion, and parsley. Let stand at room temperature.
2. Place pork slices between 2 sheets of plastic wrap; pound to an even ¼-inch thickness using a meat mallet or a small heavy skillet. Discard plastic wrap. Sprinkle pork evenly with salt and pepper. Combine egg and 1 teaspoon water in a shallow dish, stirring with a whisk. Place flour and panko in separate dishes. Dredge pork in flour. Dip in egg mixture; dredge in panko. Heat a large nonstick skillet over medium-high heat. Add oil to pan. Add pork; cook 4 minutes on each side or until browned and done.
3. Place 1 lettuce leaf on bottom half of each bun; top with 1 pork slice. Spread about 3 tablespoons corn relish on each; top each with top half of bun. Serves 4 (serving size: 1 sandwich)

CALORIES 386; FAT 17.6g (sat 5.1g, mono 7g, poly 3.7g); PROTEIN 28g; CARB 33g; FIBER 6g; CHOL 118mg; IRON 2mg; SODIUM 658mg; CALC 301mg

Louisville Hot Browns with Cauliflower Mornay

Hands-on: 32 min. Total: 32 min.

1¹/₂ cups chopped cauliflower
1 cup unsalted chicken stock
  (such as Swanson)
¹/₃ cup 2% reduced-fat milk
1¹/₂ tablespoons unsalted butter
¹/₂ teaspoon freshly ground black
  pepper, divided
¹/₄ teaspoon kosher salt
1 ounce pecorino Romano cheese,
  grated (about ¹/₄ cup)
4 (1¹/₂-ounce) slices multigrain bread
4 center-cut bacon slices, chopped
12 ounces turkey breast cutlets
  (about ¹/₄ inch thick)
4 (¹/₂-inch-thick) slices heirloom
  beefsteak tomatoes
1 tablespoon chopped fresh flat-leaf
  parsley
1 tablespoon chopped fresh chives

1. Preheat broiler to high.
2. Combine cauliflower and stock in
a medium saucepan. Bring to a boil;
cook 10 minutes or until tender.
Place cauliflower mixture in a
blender. Add milk, butter, ¼ teaspoon
pepper, salt, and cheese. Remove
center piece of blender lid (to allow
steam to escape); secure blender lid
on blender. Place a clean towel over
opening in blender lid; process until
smooth.
3. Place bread on a baking sheet.
Broil 2 minutes or until toasted.
4. Cook bacon in a large ovenproof
skillet over medium-high heat until
crisp. Remove bacon with a slotted spoon. Sprinkle turkey with ¼
teaspoon pepper. Add turkey to pan;
cook 2 minutes on each side or
until done. Remove turkey from pan;

let stand 5 minutes. Shred turkey
into large pieces. Arrange bread
slices in a single layer, toasted side
down, in pan. Top bread slices evenly
with turkey. Pour cauliflower mixture
evenly over turkey; broil 3 minutes
or until sauce begins to bubble. Top
each serving with 1 tomato slice,
one-fourth of the bacon, and herbs.
Serves 4 (serving size: 1 sandwich)

CALORIES 331; FAT 11.7g (sat 5.5g, mono 3.4g, poly 1.4g);
PROTEIN 33g; CARB 24g; FIBER 5g; CHOL 78mg;
IRON 3mg; SODIUM 640mg; CALC 162mg

Vegetarian

Nor-Cal Veggie Sandwiches with Hazelnut Butter

Hands-on: 43 min. Total: 43 min.

1 large garlic clove
¹/₂ cup hazelnuts, toasted
2 tablespoons canola mayonnaise
2 tablespoons water
¹/₄ teaspoon salt, divided
6 cups water
3 tablespoons fresh lemon juice,
  divided
4 trimmed fresh globe artichoke
  hearts, halved crosswise
2 teaspoons olive oil
1¹/₂ cups baby arugula
8 (1-ounce) slices whole-wheat
  sunflower bread, toasted
1 ounce radish sprouts
1 ripe peeled avocado, thinly sliced

1. Place garlic in bowl of a mini
food processor; process until finely
chopped. Add nuts; process until a
coarse butter forms. Add mayonnaise, 2 tablespoons water, and ⅛
teaspoon salt; process until smooth.
2. Combine 6 cups water and 2½
tablespoons juice in a medium saucepan. Bring to a boil. Add artichoke
hearts; cook 6 minutes or until tender. Drain; dry with a paper towel.

3. Heat a large skillet over medium-
high heat. Add oil to pan; swirl. Add
artichokes. Sprinkle with remaining
⅛ teaspoon salt; cook 2 minutes on
each side or until well browned.
4. Combine 1½ teaspoons juice and
arugula; toss to coat.
5. Spread 2 tablespoons hazelnut
mixture on 1 side of each of 4 bread
slices. Top hazelnut butter with 2
artichoke pieces, about ⅓ cup arugula
mixture, ¼ ounce sprouts, about 4
avocado slices, and 1 bread slice.
Serves 4 (serving size: 1 sandwich)

CALORIES 359; FAT 22.4g (sat 2g, mono 14.6g, poly 4.1g);
PROTEIN 10g; CARB 35g; FIBER 9g; CHOL 0mg;
IRON 2mg; SODIUM 417mg; CALC 66mg

NYC Melting Pot Reubens

Hands-on: 24 min. Total: 24 min.

3 tablespoons canola mayonnaise
2 tablespoons minced shallots
2 tablespoons minced dill pickles
1 tablespoon unsalted ketchup
¹/₂ teaspoon black pepper
8 (³/₄-ounce) slices rye bread
4 ounces thinly sliced lower-sodium
  roast beef (such as Boar's Head)
2 ounces thinly sliced lower-sodium
  corned beef (such as Boar's Head)
2 ounces Swiss cheese, shredded
  (about ¹/₂ cup)
²/₃ cup kimchi, drained and thinly
  sliced
Cooking spray

1. Combine first 5 ingredients. Spread
1½ tablespoons mayonnaise mixture
over 1 side of each of 4 bread slices.
Top each with 1 ounce roast beef, ½
ounce corned beef, and 2 tablespoons
cheese. Top each sandwich with one-
fourth of kimchi and 1 bread slice.
2. Heat a large skillet over medium
heat. Generously coat both sides of
sandwiches with cooking spray.

Arrange sandwiches in pan; cook 6 minutes or until lightly browned on both sides, turning once. Serves 4 (serving size: 1 sandwich)

CALORIES 270; FAT 10.2g (sat 3.6g, mono 3.8g, poly 1.5g); PROTEIN 18g; CARB 25g; FIBER 3g; CHOL 36mg; IRON 2mg; SODIUM 799mg; CALC 147mg

Quick & Easy
Oven-Fried Shrimp and Okra Louisiana Po'Boys

Hands-on: 33 min. Total: 33 min.

2 tablespoons finely chopped green onions
1 tablespoon drained chopped capers
2 tablespoons canola mayonnaise
1½ teaspoons fresh lemon juice
1 teaspoon Creole mustard
⅛ teaspoon ground red pepper
1 small garlic clove, grated
15 small okra pods, trimmed and halved lengthwise (about 6 ounces)
½ cup fat-free buttermilk, divided
½ teaspoon kosher salt, divided
10 ounces medium shrimp, peeled and deveined
1 tablespoon all-purpose flour
⅔ cup yellow cornmeal
1½ teaspoons salt-free Cajun/Creole seasoning
3 tablespoons canola oil
4 top-split hot dog buns, toasted
½ cup thinly sliced iceberg lettuce
1 medium tomato, cut in half lengthwise and thinly sliced

1. Place a jelly-roll pan in oven. Preheat oven to 450° (leave pan in oven).
2. Combine first 7 ingredients in a small bowl. Chill until ready to use.
3. Combine okra and 2 tablespoons buttermilk; toss to coat. Sprinkle with ¼ teaspoon salt; toss to coat.
4. Place shrimp in a bowl. Sprinkle with flour; toss well to coat. Drizzle with 6 tablespoons buttermilk, and

sprinkle with ¼ teaspoon salt; toss to coat. Drain okra and shrimp through a sieve; discard liquid.
5. Combine cornmeal and Cajun/Creole seasoning in a large zip-top plastic bag. Add okra and shrimp; seal bag, and shake well to coat.
6. Carefully remove pan from oven; drizzle with oil, tilting pan to spread oil. Remove shrimp and okra from cornmeal, shaking off excess; arrange in a single layer on pan. Bake at 450° for 5 minutes; carefully stir and turn over. Bake 4 minutes or until done.
7. Spread about 1 tablespoon rémoulade on one side of buns; divide lettuce and tomato among buns. Divide shrimp mixture among buns. Serves 4 (serving size: 1 sandwich)

CALORIES 396; FAT 15.7g (sat 1.4g, mono 8.5g, poly 4.8g); PROTEIN 18g; CARB 46g; FIBER 4g; CHOL 90mg; IRON 3mg; SODIUM 754mg; CALC 194mg

Vegetarian
"New" New Mexican Green Chile Cheeseburgers

Hands-on: 45 min. Total: 45 min. .

4 garlic cloves
1 Cubanelle pepper
1 serrano chile
1 medium tomatillo, papery skin removed
Cooking spray
2 tablespoons chopped fresh cilantro
1 tablespoon finely diced red onion
1 tablespoon fresh lime juice
1 tablespoon olive oil
½ teaspoon sugar
¼ teaspoon kosher salt
6 (½-inch-thick) slices small red onion
1½ tablespoons olive oil, divided
4 ounces cremini mushrooms
2 garlic cloves

1 (15-ounce) can unsalted black beans, rinsed and drained
½ cup plus 1 tablespoon whole-wheat panko (Japanese breadcrumbs)
1 tablespoon chopped fresh oregano
1 teaspoon ground cumin
½ teaspoon kosher salt
¼ teaspoon ancho chile powder
1 large egg
2 ounces aged white cheddar cheese, thinly sliced
6 romaine lettuce leaves
6 whole-wheat hamburger buns, toasted

1. Preheat broiler to high.
2. Place first 4 ingredients on a foil-lined baking sheet. Coat vegetables with cooking spray. Broil 14 minutes, turning vegetables once. Wrap Cubanelle and serrano in foil; let stand 10 minutes. Peel and cut into 1-inch strips; discard peels and seeds. Place tomatillo, Cubanelle, serrano, garlic, cilantro, and next 5 ingredients in a mini food processor; pulse until combined.
3. Brush onion slices with 1½ teaspoons oil. Arrange onion in a single layer on a foil-lined baking sheet. Broil 6 minutes or until lightly charred, turning once.
4. Place mushrooms, 2 garlic cloves, and black beans in a food processor; pulse until mixture is coarsely chopped. Add panko and next 5 ingredients; pulse until combined. Divide mixture into 6 equal portions; shape each portion into a ½-inch-thick patty.
5. Heat a large cast-iron skillet over medium heat. Add 1 tablespoon olive oil; swirl. Add patties; cook 12 minutes, turning once. Add cheese to patties during last 2 minutes of cooking; cover pan to melt cheese. Place 1 lettuce leaf on bottom half of each bun. Top each lettuce leaf with 1 patty, 1 charred onion slice, and about 1½ tablespoons relish. Top with top halves of buns. Serves 6 (serving size: 1 sandwich)

CALORIES 286; FAT 11.1g (sat 3.3g, mono 4.4g, poly 1.7g); PROTEIN 12g; CARB 38g; FIBER 7g; CHOL 41mg; IRON 2mg; SODIUM 502mg; CALC 86mg

THE LESSON: HOMEMADE SRIRACHA

Cook like a genius as Keith Schroeder reveals the science behind his art.

The hot red sauce from the green-topped bottle now squeezed on everything from Thai noodles to tacos to burgers is the breakout condiment star of the last 10 years. Sriracha as we know it is a California-made, amped-up version of a sweet, semitranslucent, slightly viscous chile sauce from the coastal town of Si Racha, Thailand. With so much product available, you might wonder why it's worth the bother to make at home. Answer: It's quick, it's easy, and it tastes amazingly fresh—the essence of bright chile heat softened by the perfect amount of sweetness and tang.

KEITH'S RECIPE BREAKDOWN
MAD-FRESH SRIRACHA
Hands-on: 5 min. Total: 40 min.

INGREDIENT	AMOUNT	WHY
red chiles, such as Fresno, serrano, and/ or jalapeño, in any ratio	2 cups, split and seeded (about 8 ounces whole)	It's a chile sauce.
garlic cloves	½ cup (about 10 peeled)	We're nodding to both iterations of Sriracha, and they both have garlic. Without the garlic, it's just another hot sauce.
sugar	3 tablespoons	The sweetness is a signature of both Srirachas. Oddly, the U.S. version is actually less sugar-forward than the original Thai sauce.
salt	¾ teaspoon	To balance. This is a sauce for savories.
white vinegar	¼ cup	The acid is what ties all the flavors together. White vinegar provides straightforward, midtone, neutral acid. We want to highlight the chiles. This does that.
hot water	¼ cup	Because we need more liquid to blend things up, and a half-cup of vinegar would make the sauce too strong.

Follow These Steps:

• Combine chiles, garlic, sugar, salt, and vinegar in a small saucepan. Cover and heat gently, as if to steep, over very low heat for 30 minutes.
• Add chile mixture and ¼ cup hot water to a blender. Remove center piece of blender lid (to allow steam to escape); secure blender lid on blender. Place a clean towel over opening in blender lid (to avoid splatters). Blend until smooth, adding more hot water if necessary.
• Store in refrigerator in an airtight container for 7 to 10 days. If sauce separates, give it a good stir or shake. Serves 16 (serving size: 1 tablespoon)

CALORIES 19; **FAT** 0.1g (sat 0g, mono 0g, poly 0.1g); **PROTEIN** 0g; **CARB** 5g; **FIBER** 0g; **CHOL** 0mg; **IRON** 0mg; **SODIUM** 112mg; **CALC** 9mg

STACKED SUMMER TREAT

Matisse and friends have a mess of fun whipping up this dessert.

"Today I made Berry-Ginger Mess. The meringues take several hours to bake and set, so I would make them ahead of time (even a day before). It's important that no yolk gets in the egg whites before beating them, so make sure you separate the eggs carefully. I also left the meringues in the oven until they had completely cooled. The extra time makes them crispier and not so sticky. If you want to make this a true 'messy' dessert, you can break up your beautiful meringues and gently stir the pieces into the berries and cream. Yum!"

Berry-Ginger Mess

Hands-on: 30 min. Total: 5 hr. 30 min.

5 tablespoons sugar, divided
1/8 teaspoon ground ginger
3 large egg whites, at room
   temperature
1/4 teaspoon cream of tartar
1/4 teaspoon salt, divided
1/2 teaspoon vanilla extract
2 tablespoons honey
1 cup strawberries, hulled and
   halved
1 cup blueberries
1 cup raspberries
1/3 cup chilled heavy cream

1. Preheat oven to 225°. Line a baking sheet with parchment paper; tape paper to baking sheet.
2. Combine ¼ cup sugar and ginger. Place egg whites in a large bowl; beat with a mixer at medium-low speed until foamy. Add cream of tartar and ⅛ teaspoon salt; beat at medium speed until soft peaks form. Add sugar mixture, 1 tablespoon at a time, beating just until stiff peaks form. Add vanilla; beat just until combined. Spoon mixture by 2 table-spoons into mounds onto baking sheet (about 18 total). Bake at 225° for 4 hours or until meringues are straw-colored, rotating pan once after 2 hours. Turn off oven (do not remove pan). Cool meringues to room temperature.
3. Combine 1 tablespoon sugar, ⅛ teaspoon salt, and honey in a bowl. Add berries; toss. Let stand 1 hour.
4. Beat cream with a mixer at high speed until stiff peaks form. Place 1 meringue in each of 6 dessert glasses; divide half of berry mixture among glasses. Top each serving with 1 meringue. Divide remaining berry mixture among glasses. Top each with 2 tablespoons whipped

cream. Crumble 1 meringue over each serving. Serves 6

CALORIES 150; FAT 5.3g (sat 3.1g, mono 1.5g, poly 0.3g); PROTEIN 3g; CARB 25g; FIBER 2g; CHOL 18mg; IRON 0mg; SODIUM 132mg; CALC 21mg

THE VERDICT

MADDIE (AGE 13)
She said, "This is the best dessert, so creamy and yummy." **10/10**

FRAANZ (AGE 9)
He thought it was delicious, but he would leave the ginger out next time. **9/10**

MATISSE (AGE 13)
I love the berries and cream and the crunch and sweetness of the meringue. **10/10**

MEATLESS MONDAYS

TOSTADA: TOWER OF FLAVORS

This open-faced taco is piled high with beans, roasted veggies, and crisp radish.

Roasted Zucchini and Black Bean Tostadas with Crisp Radish Relish

Hands-on: 35 min. Total: 35 min.

1 cup thinly sliced radishes
¼ cup chopped fresh cilantro
2 tablespoons thinly sliced green
   onions
2 tablespoons unsalted pumpkinseed
   kernels, toasted

1 teaspoon honey
4 teaspoons fresh lime juice, divided
¾ teaspoon kosher salt, divided
2 large zucchini (about 1 pound),
   quartered lengthwise and cut into
   ½-inch pieces
1 large poblano chile, stemmed,
   seeded, and cut into ½-inch pieces
1 tablespoon olive oil
1 teaspoon ground cumin
3 garlic cloves, chopped
1 (15-ounce) can unsalted black
   beans, undrained
8 (6-inch) corn tortillas
Cooking spray
3 tablespoons light sour cream
2 teaspoons 1% low-fat milk
4 teaspoons picante sauce

1. Combine first 5 ingredients and 1 tablespoon lime juice in a medium bowl; toss to coat. Sprinkle with ¼ teaspoon salt.
2. Preheat oven to 450°.
3. Place zucchini and poblano on a jelly-roll pan; drizzle with oil. Sprinkle with cumin and ¼ teaspoon salt; toss to coat. Bake at 450° for 20 minutes or until tender and lightly browned.
4. Combine garlic, beans, and ¼ teaspoon salt in a small saucepan over medium heat; bring to a simmer. Cook 10 minutes or until slightly thickened. Coarsely mash with a potato masher.
5. Lightly coat both sides of tortillas with cooking spray. Arrange in a single layer on a baking sheet. Bake at 450° for 6 minutes. Turn tortillas over; bake 3 minutes or until crispy.
6. Combine sour cream, milk, and 1 teaspoon lime juice in a small bowl.
7. Layer each tortilla with about 2 tablespoons bean mixture, ¼ cup zuc-chini mixture, 1 teaspoon sour cream mixture, ½ teaspoon picante sauce, and about 2 tablespoons radish mixture. Serve immediately. Serves 4 (serving size: 2 tostadas)

CALORIES 300; FAT 8.6g (sat 19g, mono 3.8g, poly 2g); PROTEIN 12g; CARB 47g; FIBER 10g; CHOL 4mg; IRON 3mg; SODIUM 469mg; CALC 151mg

SUPERFAST 20-MINUTE COOKING

Grilled Lemon Chicken with Tomato Salad

1 teaspoon grated lemon rind
4 tablespoons fresh lemon juice, divided
3 tablespoons extra-virgin olive oil, divided
4 (6-ounce) skinless, boneless chicken breasts
½ teaspoon kosher salt, divided
½ teaspoon freshly ground black pepper, divided
2 cups baby heirloom tomatoes, halved
1.5 ounces feta cheese, crumbled (about ⅓ cup)
Cooking spray

1. Combine rind, 2 tablespoons juice, and 1 tablespoon oil in a large zip-top plastic bag. Add chicken; turn to coat. Let stand 8 minutes.
2. Combine 2 tablespoons juice, 2 tablespoons oil, ¼ teaspoon salt, and ¼ teaspoon pepper in a bowl. Stir in tomatoes and feta cheese.
3. Heat a grill pan over medium-high heat. Coat pan with cooking spray. Sprinkle chicken with ¼ teaspoon salt and ¼ teaspoon pepper; grill 5 minutes on each side or until done. Top chicken with tomato mixture. Serves 4 (serving size: 1 chicken breast half and ½ cup tomato mixture)

CALORIES 304; FAT 14.1g (sat 3.6g, mono 7g, poly 1.6g); PROTEIN 38g; CARB 5g; FIBER 1g; CHOL 118mg; IRON 1mg; SODIUM 560mg; CALC 71mg

Seared Scallops with Snap Peas and Pancetta

Sautéed snap peas, pancetta, and shallots make a speedy but sophisticated accompaniment to seared scallops.

3 teaspoons canola oil, divided
12 ounces sugar snap peas, trimmed and diagonally sliced
¼ teaspoon kosher salt, divided
¼ teaspoon freshly ground black pepper, divided
1½ ounces diced pancetta (such as Boar's Head)
2 large shallots, sliced
1½ pounds large sea scallops
4 lemon wedges

1. Heat a large cast-iron skillet over medium-high heat. Add 1 teaspoon oil; swirl to coat. Add peas, ⅛ teaspoon salt, and ⅛ teaspoon pepper; sauté 2 minutes. Place snap peas in a bowl. Heat pan over medium heat. Add pancetta; cook 1 minute. Add shallots; cook 1 minute, stirring constantly. Add pancetta mixture to pea mixture.
2. Return pan to medium-high heat. Pat scallops dry with paper towels; sprinkle evenly with ⅛ teaspoon salt and ⅛ teaspoon pepper. Add 1 teaspoon oil to pan; swirl to coat. Add half of scallops to pan; cook 2 minutes. Turn and cook 1 minute or until desired degree of doneness. Place cooked scallops on a plate. Repeat procedure with 1 teaspoon oil and remaining scallops. Serve scallops with snap pea mixture and lemon wedges. Serves 4 (serving size: about 5 scallops and ¾ cup pea mixture)

CALORIES 237; FAT 7.9g (sat 2.2g, mono 2.3g, poly 1.3g); PROTEIN 25g; CARB 15g; FIBER 3g; CHOL 48mg; IRON 3mg; SODIUM 568mg; CALC 52mg

Grilled Shrimp Tostadas with Lime

Shrimp:
24 large shrimp, peeled and deveined (about 1½ pounds)
½ teaspoon garlic powder
½ teaspoon ground cumin
¼ teaspoon kosher salt
Black bean salsa:
¼ cup chopped green onions
¼ cup chopped fresh cilantro
1 tablespoon olive oil
1 tablespoon red wine vinegar
1 tablespoon minced chipotle chiles in adobo sauce
1 teaspoon minced fresh garlic
¼ teaspoon kosher salt
1 (15-ounce) can unsalted black beans, rinsed and drained
Avocado topping:
¼ cup plain fat-free Greek yogurt
1 teaspoon fresh lime juice
1 ripe peeled avocado
1 cup chopped seeded tomato
Cooking spray
8 corn tostadas
4 lime wedges

1. To prepare shrimp, combine shrimp, garlic powder, cumin, and ¼ teaspoon salt. Let stand 10 minutes.
2. To prepare black bean salsa, combine green onions and next 7 ingredients in a bowl; toss to coat.
3. To prepare avocado topping, combine yogurt, juice, and avocado in a small bowl, mashing with a fork until smooth. Stir in tomato.
4. Heat a grill pan over medium-high heat. Coat pan with cooking spray. Add shrimp to pan; grill 2 minutes on each side. Top each tostada with ¼ cup bean mixture, 3 shrimp, and 1 tablespoon avocado mixture. Serve with lime wedges. Serves 4 (serving size: 2 tostadas)

CALORIES 302; FAT 10.8g (sat 1.5g, mono 6.2g, poly 1.8g); PROTEIN 15g; CARB 40g; FIBER 10g; CHOL 53mg; IRON 2mg; SODIUM 384mg; CALC 118mg

Kid Friendly • Quick & Easy
Gluten Free • Make Ahead
Vegetarian

Chickpea and Vegetable Tagine

1 cup water
¾ cup uncooked quinoa, rinsed and drained
½ teaspoon kosher salt, divided
1 tablespoon extra-virgin olive oil
1½ cups chopped onion
1 teaspoon ground cumin
1 teaspoon ground coriander
½ teaspoon ground cinnamon
½ teaspoon turmeric
4 garlic cloves, chopped
3 cups Sun Gold or cherry tomatoes, halved
1 (15-ounce) can unsalted chickpeas (garbanzo beans), rinsed and drained
1 medium zucchini, halved lengthwise and thinly sliced
¼ teaspoon freshly ground black pepper

1. Bring 1 cup water, quinoa, and ¼ teaspoon salt to a boil in a small saucepan over medium-high heat. Cover, reduce heat, and simmer 13 minutes or until liquid is absorbed.
2. Heat a large saucepan over medium-high heat. Add oil to pan; swirl to coat. Add onion to pan; sauté 4 minutes. Add cumin, coriander, cinnamon, turmeric, and garlic; cook 1 minute, stirring constantly. Add tomatoes; cook 2 minutes or until tomatoes begin to release their liquid. Add chickpeas and zucchini. Cover, reduce heat to medium, and cook 5 minutes. Stir in ¼ teaspoon salt and pepper. Serve zucchini mixture with quinoa. Serves 4 (serving size: ½ cup quinoa and 1 cup zucchini mixture)

CALORIES 278; **FAT** 6.5g (sat 0.8g, mono 3g, poly 1.6g); **PROTEIN** 11g; **CARB** 46g; **FIBER** 8g; **CHOL** 0mg; **IRON** 3mg; **SODIUM** 271mg; **CALC** 90mg

Kid Friendly • Quick & Easy
Gluten Free • Vegetarian

Tomato and Peach Salad with Almonds

1 tablespoon canola oil
2 teaspoons white wine vinegar
1 teaspoon honey
2 medium tomatoes, cut into ¼-inch-thick slices
1 medium peach, pitted and sliced
2 tablespoons sliced toasted almonds
1 tablespoon fresh mint leaves
⅛ teaspoon kosher salt
⅛ teaspoon black pepper

1. Combine oil, vinegar, and honey in a bowl. Divide tomato and peach slices among 4 plates. Top with almonds, mint, salt, and pepper. Drizzle with honey mixture. Serves 4

CALORIES 79; **FAT** 5.1g (sat 0.4g, mono 3.2g, poly 1.4g); **PROTEIN** 2g; **CARB** 8g; **FIBER** 2g; **CHOL** 0mg; **IRON** 0mg; **SODIUM** 63mg; **CALC** 17mg

Kid Friendly • Quick & Easy
Tomato Salad with Caesar Breadcrumbs
Heat 4 teaspoons olive oil, 1 minced garlic clove, and ¼ teaspoon anchovy paste in a skillet over medium heat 1 minute. Add ½ cup fresh bread-crumbs; cook 1½ minutes. Combine 2 teaspoons olive oil, 2 cups arugula, and 1½ teaspoons balsamic vinegar. Top with 2 sliced tomatoes, ⅛ tea-spoon kosher salt, and breadcrumbs. Serves 4

CALORIES 95; **FAT** 7.2g (sat 1g); **SODIUM** 120mg

Kid Friendly • Quick & Easy
Gluten Free • Vegetarian
Tomato Salad with Halloumi and Oregano
Heat 2 teaspoons canola oil in a nonstick skillet over medium heat. Add 1.5 ounces thinly sliced halloumi cheese; cook 2 minutes on each side or until browned. Top 2 sliced tomatoes with halloumi, 1 tablespoon fresh lemon juice,

1 teaspoon fresh oregano leaves, ⅛ teaspoon kosher salt, and ⅛ teaspoon pepper. Serves 4

CALORIES 67; **FAT** 5.5g (sat 2.1g); **SODIUM** 176mg

Kid Friendly • Quick & Easy
Gluten Free • Vegetarian
Tomato Salad with Avocado and Onion
Arrange 2 sliced tomatoes and 1 sliced avocado on a platter; top with ¼ cup thinly vertically sliced white onion, 1 tablespoon chopped fresh cilantro, 1 tablespoon fresh lemon juice, ¼ teaspoon chipotle chile powder, ¼ teaspoon kosher salt, and ⅛ teaspoon black pepper. Serves 4

CALORIES 72; **FAT** 5.4g (sat 0.7g); **SODIUM** 131mg

Kid Friendly • Quick & Easy

Quick Banana and Milk Chocolate S'mores

4 honey graham cracker sheets, halved (8 squares)
1 ounce milk chocolate, divided into 4 pieces
1 small banana, peeled and sliced
¼ cup marshmallow crème

1. Preheat broiler to high.
2. Place graham cracker squares on a foil-lined baking sheet. Divide chocolate among 4 squares; top with banana slices. Spread 1 tablespoon marshmallow crème on each of 4 remaining squares. Broil 1½ minutes or until chocolate just begins to melt and marshmallow crème lightly browns. Carefully top banana with the marshmallow-topped squares. Serves 4 (serving size: 1 s'more)

CALORIES 140; **FAT** 3.6g (sat 1.6g, mono 1.1g, poly 0.7g); **PROTEIN** 2g; **CARB** 26g; **FIBER** 1g; **CHOL** 2mg; **IRON** 1mg; **SODIUM** 78mg; **CALC** 18mg

Halibut and Peach Salad with Lemon-Mint Vinaigrette

- **3 tablespoons extra-virgin olive oil, divided**
- **4 (6-ounce) halibut fillets**
- **½ teaspoon kosher salt, divided**
- **½ teaspoon black pepper, divided**
- **2 tablespoons chopped fresh mint**
- **2 tablespoons fresh lemon juice**
- **1 teaspoon maple syrup**
- **6 cups baby spinach leaves**
- **2 medium peaches, halved and sliced**
- **½ English cucumber, halved lengthwise and sliced**
- **¼ cup toasted sliced almonds**

1. Heat a large nonstick skillet over medium-high heat. Add 1 tablespoon oil; swirl to coat. Sprinkle fish evenly with ¼ teaspoon salt and ¼ teaspoon pepper. Add fish to pan; cook 3 minutes on each side or until fish flakes easily when tested with a fork.

2. Combine remaining ¼ teaspoon salt, remaining ¼ teaspoon pepper, remaining 2 tablespoons oil, mint, juice, and syrup in a large bowl, stirring with a whisk. Add spinach, peaches, and cucumber; toss gently to coat. Divide spinach mixture among 4 plates; top with fish. Sprinkle with almonds. Serves 4 (serving size: 2 cups salad, 1 fillet, and 1 tablespoon almonds)

CALORIES 332; **FAT** 15.5g (sat 2.1g, mono 10g, poly 2.3g); **PROTEIN** 35g; **CARB** 15g; **FIBER** 4g; **CHOL** 83mg; **IRON** 2mg; **SODIUM** 415mg; **CALC** 66mg

ONE COOLER, ONE WEEKEND

This menu plan is a real, tested party in a box, a prescription for full, carry-in enjoyment. Lots of perfectly peak-season produce, which hardly needs cooking at all. Ingredients like pancetta, Greek yogurt, figs, and anchovies deliver bold flavor.

FIVE MEALS FROM ONE MAGIC BOX (AND A TOTE)

FRIDAY DINNER:
Mojito Cooler, Pancetta-Wrapped Pork Tenderloin with Cantaloupe–Red Pepper Salsa, Shaved Zucchini and Parsley Salad

SATURDAY BREAKFAST:
Orange, Pumpkin Seed, and Smoked Almond Granola with Greek Yogurt

SATURDAY LUNCH:
Figgy Pork Tenderloin Sandwiches, Yogurt "Romesco" Dip

SATURDAY DINNER:
Grilled Romaine Hearts with Pepper, Grilled Vegetable Pizzas with Anchovies, Cantaloupe Granita

SUNDAY BRUNCH:
Farro Salad with Cherry Tomato, Onion, and Almonds

Orange, Pumpkin Seed, and Smoked Almond Granola

Hands-on: 5 min. Total: 61 min.

- **½ cup old-fashioned rolled oats**
- **¼ cup roasted, unsalted pumpkin seed kernels**
- **1 ounce lightly salted, smoked almonds, chopped**
- **5 teaspoons brown sugar**
- **1½ tablespoons canola oil**
- **1 teaspoon grated orange rind**
- **1 tablespoon fresh orange juice**
- **¼ teaspoon vanilla extract**
- **⅛ teaspoon salt**

1. Preheat oven to 325°.

2. Combine all ingredients in a bowl. Spread mixture on a parchment paper–lined baking sheet. Bake at 325° for 26 minutes. Cool completely. Serves 4 (serving size: 3 tablespoons)

CALORIES 195; **FAT** 13.4g (sat 1.4g, mono 6.9g, poly 4g); **PROTEIN** 5g; **CARB** 16g; **FIBER** 2g; **CHOL** 0mg; **IRON** 1mg; **SODIUM** 107mg; **CALC** 24mg

Multipurpose Vinaigrette

Hands-on: 10 min. Total: 10 min..

3 tablespoons red wine vinegar
2 tablespoons finely chopped shallots
2 teaspoons chopped fresh thyme
 leaves
1½ teaspoons Dijon mustard
½ teaspoon light agave nectar
½ teaspoon freshly ground black
 pepper
¼ teaspoon kosher salt
2 garlic cloves, minced
¼ cup extra-virgin olive oil

1. Combine first 8 ingredients in a small bowl, stirring with a whisk. Slowly drizzle olive oil into vinegar mixture, stirring constantly with a whisk. Serves 8 (serving size: 1 tablespoon)

CALORIES 69; FAT 6.7g (sat 0.9g, mono 4.9g, poly 0.7g);
PROTEIN 0g; CARB 2g; FIBER 0g; CHOL 0mg;
IRON 0mg; SODIUM 144mg; CALC 4mg

Mojito Cooler

Hands-on: 5 min. Total: 5 min.

⅔ cup fresh mint
¾ cup white rum
½ cup fresh lime juice
10 teaspoons agave nectar
1½ cups club soda

1. Muddle mint in a pitcher. Stir in rum, juice, and nectar. Strain mixture, if desired, and add club soda before serving. Serve over ice. Serves 4 (serving size: ¾ cup)

CALORIES 169; FAT 0.1g (sat 0g, mono 0g, poly 0.1g);
PROTEIN 0g; CARB 17g; FIBER 1g; CHOL 0mg;
IRON 2mg; SODIUM 74mg; CALC 51mg

FRIDAY

DINNER: Mix up a pitcher of cocktails (OK, two), and relax for a while before starting dinner. Then, once the grill is going, take advantage of it—grill the pork and bell pepper you'll use for tomorrow's lunch while you're preparing tonight's menu.

Pancetta-Wrapped Pork Tenderloin

(pictured on page 225)

Hands-on: 5 min. Total: 25 min.
Prep both tenderloins before you pack the cooler. Season both with ¼ teaspoon each kosher salt and black pepper, and then wrap one with pancetta. Tightly seal each in plastic wrap. Grill both on Friday (the cooking instructions are the same, minus the pork-on-pork wrapping). Serve one for dinner; cool, wrap, and refrigerate the other to use in Saturday's lunch.

1 (1-pound) pork tenderloin, trimmed
¼ teaspoon kosher salt
¼ teaspoon freshly ground black
 pepper
2 ounces thinly sliced pancetta
 (about 6 slices)
Cooking spray

1. Preheat grill to medium-high heat.
2. Pat pork tenderloin dry with paper towels.
3. Sprinkle pork evenly with salt and pepper. Wrap pork in pancetta, with slices slightly overlapping.
4. Place pork on grill rack coated with cooking spray; cover. Grill 18 minutes or until a thermometer registers 145°, turning occasionally to brown all sides. Let pork stand 10 minutes before slicing. Serves 4 (serving size: 3½ ounces cooked)

CALORIES 137; FAT 3.6g (sat 1.2g, mono 0.9g, poly 0.4g);
PROTEIN 24g; CARB 0g; FIBER 0g; CHOL 76mg;
IRON 1mg; SODIUM 238mg; CALC 6mg

Cantaloupe-Red Pepper Salsa

Hands-on: 12 min. Total: 1 hr. 12 min.
Sweet with a little bit of heat, this salsa is delicious with the pancetta-wrapped pork.

1 cup finely chopped fresh cantaloupe
½ cup finely chopped red bell pepper
¼ cup finely chopped red onion
3 tablespoons chopped fresh mint
1 tablespoon finely chopped seeded
 jalapeño pepper
1 tablespoon fresh lime juice
¼ teaspoon kosher salt

1. Combine all ingredients in a medium bowl, stirring well. Cover and chill at least 1 hour. Serves 4 (serving size: about ⅓ cup)

CALORIES 28; FAT 0g; PROTEIN 1g; CARB 6g;
FIBER 1g; CHOL 0mg; IRON 1mg; SODIUM 129mg;
CALC 17mg

Shaved Zucchini and Parsley Salad

Hands-on: 9 min. Total: 9 min.

3 medium zucchini
¼ cup chopped fresh flat-leaf parsley
¼ cup thinly vertically sliced red onion
¼ cup Multipurpose Vinaigrette
 (page 178)
3 tablespoons crumbled feta cheese

1. Slice zucchini into thin ribbons using a vegetable peeler; toss with parsley, onion, and vinaigrette. Sprinkle with cheese. Serves 4 (serving size: about ⅔ cup)

CALORIES 132; FAT 9.1g (sat 2.2g, mono 5.3g, poly 1g);
PROTEIN 4g; CARB 10g; FIBER 3g; CHOL 6mg;
IRON 1mg; SODIUM 244mg; CALC 84mg

PACKING LIST

TOTE BAG
Make-Ahead:
Orange, Pumpkin Seed, and Smoked Almond Granola
Multipurpose Vinaigrette

2 cartons cherry tomatoes
5 limes
2 lemons
2 red onions
1 head garlic
1 large cantaloupe
4 onion rolls
1 small container cornmeal
1 bag lightly salted, smoked almonds
1 bag pearled farro
1 small container or jar anchovies
1 small bottle agave nectar
1 large bottle club soda
1 small bottle white rum
Wines
1 small bottle extra-virgin olive oil
Salt and pepper
Kosher salt
Cooking spray

COOLER
2 packages fresh mint

1 bunch fresh flat-leaf parsley
1 bunch fresh basil
1 large red bell pepper
1 jalapeño pepper
4 zucchini
2 cucumbers
2 romaine lettuce hearts
1 head lettuce
1 carton fresh figs
2 (1-pound) pork tenderloins
2 ounces pancetta
1 container feta cheese
1 container mascarpone cheese
1 large container 2% reduced-fat Greek yogurt
1 small piece Parmigiano-Reggiano cheese
1 ball fresh mozzarella
1 small container homemade pesto
1 ball pizza dough

Kid Friendly • Make Ahead
Vegetarian

Orange, Pumpkin Seed, and Smoked Almond Granola with Greek Yogurt

Hands-on: 5 min. Total: 5 min.
If you have surplus cantaloupe not used in Friday's salsa and Saturday's dessert, serve it here. One melon wedge has about 35 calories, plus vitamin C, folate, and potassium.

2 cups plain 2% reduced-fat Greek yogurt
¾ cup Orange, Pumpkin Seed, and Smoked Almond Granola (page 178)

1. Top yogurt with granola. Serves 4 (serving size: ½ cup yogurt and about 3 tablespoons granola)

CALORIES 270; **FAT** 15.7g (sat 2.9g, mono 6.9g, poly 4g); **PROTEIN** 15g; **CARB** 20g; **FIBER** 2g; **CHOL** 8mg; **IRON** 1mg; **SODIUM** 145mg; **CALC** 100mg

---

Kid Friendly • Quick & Easy

Figgy Pork Tenderloin Sandwiches

Hands-on: 28 min. Total: 38 min.
Onion rolls usually come eight to a pack. Take four with you, and freeze the rest. Fire up the broiler to toast the bread and warm the pork, if you like.

2 cups torn lettuce leaves
2 teaspoons Multipurpose Vinaigrette (page 179)
2 tablespoons mascarpone cheese
4 onion rolls, halved and toasted
4 teaspoons prepared or homemade basil pesto

12 ounces grilled pork tenderloin, thinly sliced
4 fresh figs, stemmed and sliced

1. Combine lettuce and vinaigrette; toss.
2. Spread 1½ teaspoons mascarpone evenly over bottom half of each roll. Spread 1 teaspoon pesto over top half of each roll. Divide sliced pork evenly among bottom halves of rolls. Top with lettuce mixture, figs, and top halves of rolls. Serves 4

CALORIES 382; **FAT** 16.6g (sat 5.8g, mono 4.2g, poly 2.2g); **PROTEIN** 26g; **CARB** 33g; **FIBER** 3g; **CHOL** 77mg; **IRON** 3mg; **SODIUM** 522mg; **CALC** 191mg

---

*Kid Friendly • **Quick & Easy***
*Gluten Free • **Make Ahead***
Vegetarian

Yogurt "Romesco" Dip

Hands-on: 11 min. Total: 11 min.
Grill the bell pepper half with Friday night's dinner until it's nicely charred, and then peel, chop, and refrigerate it in a zip-top plastic bag. It'll be ready to go for this quick dip served with Saturday lunch.

½ large red bell pepper, grilled, peeled, and chopped
2 ounces lightly salted, smoked almonds
2 tablespoons Multipurpose Vinaigrette (page 179)
½ cup plain 2% reduced-fat Greek yogurt

1. Place bell pepper, almonds, and vinaigrette in a mini food processor; process until smooth. Stir bell pepper mixture into yogurt. Serve with vegetables or whole-grain crackers. Serves 4 (serving size: about ¼ cup)

CALORIES 144; **FAT** 11.6g (sat 1.7g, mono 6.8g, poly 2.1g); **PROTEIN** 6g; **CARB** 6g; **FIBER** 2g; **CHOL** 2mg; **IRON** 1mg; **SODIUM** 143mg; **CALC** 52mg

Quick & Easy • Gluten Free
Vegetarian

Grilled Romaine Hearts with Pepper

Hands-on: 13 min. Total: 13 min.
Be sure to leave the lettuce on the grill long enough to get nice grill marks.

2 romaine lettuce hearts, halved
   lengthwise
Cooking spray
1½ tablespoons extra-virgin olive oil
½ teaspoon freshly ground black
   pepper
¼ teaspoon kosher salt

1. Preheat grill to medium-high heat.
2. Place lettuce, cut side down, on grill rack lightly coated with cooking spray. Grill 1 minute on each side or until grill marks appear. Remove lettuce. Drizzle with oil, and sprinkle with pepper and salt. Serves 4 (serving size: 1 piece)

CALORIES 63; **FAT** 5.3g (sat 0.7g, mono 4g, poly 0.5g); **PROTEIN** 1g; **CARB** 3g; **FIBER** 1g; **CHOL** 0mg; **IRON** 1mg; **SODIUM** 125mg; **CALC** 41mg

SATURDAY

BREAKFAST: Prep work before the trip yields its first payoff with orange-scented granola served over yogurt. Breakfast is ready in less time than it takes to brew a pot of coffee.

LUNCH: With two elements (pork tenderloin and bell pepper) grilled at the same time as Friday night's dinner, today's lunch is a leisurely affair for the cook. Assemble the sandwiches, and give the dip ingredients a quick spin. Let someone else do the washing up—there's a hammock somewhere calling your name.

DINNER: Once the grill is going, use it for both the salad and the pizzas. An amazingly simple, frozen, four-ingredient dessert provides a cool counterpoint to all that work over the fire.

Quick & Easy

Grilled Vegetable Pizzas with Anchovies

Hands-on: 30 min. Total: 30 min.
If your companions simply can't be convinced to try anchovies, sub prosciutto. (It has twice the calories and fat—120 calories and 6g fat per ounce, compared to 60 calories and 3g fat for anchovies.)

10 ounces refrigerated fresh pizza
   dough
Cooking spray
1 tablespoon cornmeal
1 large zucchini, sliced lengthwise
   into ¼-inch-thick slices
1 tablespoon olive oil
3 garlic cloves, grated
2 ounces Parmigiano-Reggiano
   cheese, grated (about ½ cup)
⅔ cup chopped red onion
1½ cups halved cherry tomatoes
1.5 ounces anchovies, drained and cut
   into ½-inch pieces
2 ounces fresh mozzarella cheese,
   thinly sliced
¼ cup thinly sliced fresh basil leaves
1½ teaspoons fresh lemon juice
½ teaspoon freshly ground black
   pepper

1. Preheat grill to high heat.
2. Divide dough into 4 equal portions. Roll each portion into a 7-inch circle on a floured surface. Place dough on a baking sheet coated with cooking spray and sprinkled with 1 tablespoon cornmeal. Place pizza dough rounds, cornmeal side up, on a grill rack coated with cooking spray. Grill 90 seconds or until blistered. Turn dough; grill 1 minute. Remove from grill. Place zucchini on grill rack coated with cooking spray. Grill 2 minutes on each side. Remove to a cutting board; cut into 1-inch pieces.
3. Combine oil and garlic in a small bowl; brush evenly over top of dough

rounds. Sprinkle rounds evenly with Parmigiano-Reggiano. Top with zucchini, onion, and tomatoes, leaving a ½-inch border. Arrange anchovies over tomatoes; top with mozzarella cheese.
4. Reduce grill temperature to medium. Carefully return pizzas to grill; grill 4 minutes or until cheese melts and toppings are hot. Remove from grill. Sprinkle with basil, lemon juice, and black pepper before serving. Serves 4 (serving size: 1 pizza)

CALORIES 329; **FAT** 10.9g (sat 3.8g, mono 3.7g, poly 1.1g); **PROTEIN** 15g; **CARB** 42g; **FIBER** 7g; **CHOL** 21mg; **IRON** 2mg; **SODIUM** 760mg; **CALC** 94mg

Kid Friendly • Freezable
Gluten Free • Make Ahead

Cantaloupe Granita

Hands-on: 10 min. Total: 8 hr. 10 min.
Start this recipe after breakfast Saturday morning; it can freeze all day long while you're busy doing other things—or nothing at all.

4 cups cubed peeled cantaloupe
2 tablespoons fresh lime juice
⅓ cup agave nectar
⅛ teaspoon salt

1. Place cantaloupe in a food processor or blender; process until smooth. Strain through a fine sieve over a bowl; discard solids. Stir in juice, nectar, and salt. Pour mixture into an 8-inch square dish. Freeze at least 8 hours. Remove mixture from freezer; scrape entire mixture with a fork until fluffy. Serves 4 (serving size: about 1 cup)

CALORIES 136; **FAT** 0.3g (sat 0.1g, mono 0g, poly 0.1g); **PROTEIN** 1g; **CARB** 35g; **FIBER** 1g; **CHOL** 0mg; **IRON** 0mg; **SODIUM** 100mg; **CALC** 15mg

Farro Salad with Cherry Tomato, Onion, and Almonds

Hands-on: 10 min. Total: 38 min.
If you have any remaining ingredients—figs, lettuce—that you don't want to pack for the return trip, use them here as sides.

9 ounces uncooked pearled farro
1¹/₂ cups sliced, halved cucumber (half moon)
1¹/₂ cups quartered cherry tomatoes
¹/₂ cup vertically sliced red onion
¹/₂ cup chopped fresh flat-leaf parsley
¹/₄ cup Multipurpose Vinaigrette (page 178)
1 tablespoon mascarpone cheese
¹/₄ cup lightly salted, smoked almonds, chopped

1. Cook farro according to package directions, omitting salt; drain in a colander. Rinse with cold water for 30 seconds; drain. Cool to room temperature.
2. Combine cooked farro, cucumber, tomatoes, onion, and parsley in a large bowl.
3. Combine vinaigrette and mascarpone in a bowl, stirring with a whisk. Pour over farro mixture, tossing to combine. Top with almonds. Serves 4 (serving size: 1½ cups salad)

CALORIES 375; FAT 16.7g (sat 3.3g, mono 7.7g, poly 1.8g); PROTEIN 12g; CARB 48g; FIBER 8g; CHOL 9mg; IRON 3mg; SODIUM 217mg; CALC 67mg

THE FACTS OF LIFE WITH CHICKENS

So you want to raise a hip urban flock? *Cooking Light* Garden Gurus Mary Beth and David Shaddix keep dozens at a time. Here, wise words about the birds.

The *Cooking Light* Garden has killer tillers. Our hens prey upon unwanted insects, wanted earthworms, and sometimes a coveted red tomato. But even so, they win us over every day with their personalities, not to mention their fresh eggs. Visitors are wooed by the girls, soon wanting hens of their own. Nationwide, cooping is cool. Urban bylaws are loosening. Hens are popping up in backyards from San Francisco to Brooklyn. Chickens are both fun and useful. But it takes pluck and planning, as I have learned the hard way, to tend your flock.

Zucchini and Red Pepper Frittata

Hands-on: 9 min. Total: 62 min. *This recipe also uses another ingredient many gardeners have in abundance: zucchini.*

1 large red bell pepper
1 tablespoon olive oil
1 large zucchini, thinly sliced (about 2 cups)
³/₄ cup 2% reduced-fat milk
¹/₄ teaspoon salt
¹/₄ teaspoon freshly ground black pepper
4 ounces white cheddar cheese, shredded (about 1 cup)
4 large eggs, lightly beaten

1. Preheat broiler to high.
2. Cut bell pepper in half lengthwise; discard seeds and membranes. Place, skin sides up, on a foil-lined baking sheet; flatten with hand. Broil 8 minutes or until blackened. Wrap pepper in foil; let stand 15 minutes. Peel and slice.
3. Preheat oven to 350°.
4. Heat a 9-inch nonstick, ovenproof skillet over medium-high heat. Add oil; swirl to coat. Add zucchini; cook 6 minutes. Stir in bell pepper; reduce heat to medium.
5. Combine remaining ingredients in a large bowl. Add to zucchini mixture; cook 2 minutes or until edges are set. Bake at 350° for 16 minutes or until center is set. Let stand 15 minutes. Cut into 6 wedges. Serves 6 (serving size: 1 wedge)

CALORIES 175; FAT 12.4g (sat 5.2g, mono 3g, poly 1g); PROTEIN 11g; CARB 6g; FIBER 1g; CHOL 147mg; IRON 1mg; SODIUM 294mg; CALC 201mg

WISE WORDS ABOUT THE BIRDS

Know Your Endgame

Figure out how you're likely to view your birds—as pets or urban livestock? It will be six months until Henrietta lays an egg; then she'll lay one every day or so for about three years. Production decreases with age and with winter's shorter days. Old Henrietta might live for seven more years and not reliably pay the rent with fresh eggs. Of course, she could be converted to dinner. But if you've named her Henrietta, is that likely? The breed you pick should reflect your goal. A few fuzzy, fashionable Silkies and mini-hens known as bantams can be fun, but they won't keep you in eggs. If you dream of green, blue, pink, brown, speckled, and white eggs by the basketful, choose breeds known for reliable production and by egg color. Ameraucanas or Araucanas lay blue eggs, Australorps lay a pinkish brown, and Cuckoo Marans dazzle with dark cocoa-brown shells.

Break Eggs, Not the Law

Before you collect that first flock of fuzzy peeps, ask: Is the neighborhood association into feathered residents? Call your city zoning officials to see if regulations allow backyard birds. If the local municipality does approve, it might be polite to check with neighbors, too. Hens are allowed more often than roosters, but they also cluck and squawk out a proud song after laying an egg (well-deserved airtime, in my opinion, but a little different from your average barking dog).

Keep It to Just the Girls

Many think a hen needs a rooster to make an egg. Not so. You only need a rooster if you want fertilized eggs—that is, future chickens. Hens will lay eggs regardless. Roosters are great protection for the flock, sounding an alarm when they spot predators such as hawks or dogs. But that alarm can irk neighbors. Although roosters may herald the sun's rising, they also crow randomly and quite loudly throughout the day, every day.

Get the Scoop on Coops

Whether they're city girls or free-ranging country girls, your flock will need a coop. Make no mistake—keeping chickens is hard work. A smart coop design helps make daily care easier.

First, build larger than you think you need (chickens are addictive; you've been warned). Make access easy, for you and the birds. My coop has laying bays with hinged lids, so I can easily reach in for eggs. We have a gravity-fed trough that keeps food flowing from a 50-gallon bucket, although our chickens also forage outside under my watchful eye when I'm working nearby in the garden. The smartest coup in our design happened when my husband solved the problem of changing water bowls daily. His creation of a rain barrel container with beak-activated drippers supplies fresh water on demand. Also, place your coop away from those prized petunias, which might not survive a hunting-and-pecking raid. Like bulls, chickens charge ahead when they see red. This is when you see how aggressive they can be. It's funny when a cherry tomato results in a game of chicken soccer. It's not so funny when you wanted that tomato for your lunch.

Grow a Garden, Too

You'll have a continuous supply of wonderful fertilizer. In our coop, we use the deep litter method, a lazy chicken tender's secret. Pile leaves from the yard at least 12 inches deep on an earthen floor. It works much like a compost heap: Debris breaks down into nitrogen-rich matter while serving as warm, fluffy flooring. Change it twice a year, and use the aged litter later as a superb amendment for your garden's soil.

You'll Need a Lot of Egg Recipes

Golden-yolked eggs will be laid, sometimes at your feet. If you have 10 hens, you may be collecting 10 eggs a day, if you're lucky. Yes, they're delicious, and the richly hued yolks from free-range hens are high in omega-3s and vitamins A and E. But you'll have *lots* of eggs. Soon, you will have a new Pinterest board called "Uses for Eggs." After scores of frittatas, omelets, quiches, and deviled eggs eight ways, try angel food cake and lemon curd. This is a smart one-two punch because the cake batter uses a million whites and the curd is enriched by all the yolks. Still have too many eggs? Here's another trick: Buy your neighbors' approval with regular deliveries of fresh, local, lovingly cultivated eggs.

Kid Friendly • Quick & Easy

Open-Faced Fried Egg BLT Sandwiches

Hands-on: 15 min. Total: 15 min.

1 teaspoon olive oil
4 large eggs
1 cup packed baby arugula
4 (1-ounce) slices focaccia, toasted
1 medium tomato, cut into 4 slices
¼ teaspoon kosher salt
¼ teaspoon freshly ground black pepper
4 applewood-smoked bacon slices, cooked and crumbled

1. Heat a large nonstick skillet over medium heat. Add oil to pan; swirl to coat. Crack eggs into pan; cook 2 minutes. Cover and cook an additional 2 minutes or until whites are set. Remove pan from heat.
2. Arrange ¼ cup packed arugula on each bread slice. Top each bread slice with 1 tomato slice and 1 egg; sprinkle evenly with salt and pepper. Sprinkle bacon evenly over eggs. Serve immediately. Serves 4 (serving size: 1 sandwich)

CALORIES 204; FAT 10g (sat 2.9g, mono 4.7g, poly 1.6g); PROTEIN 12g; CARB 16g; FIBER 1g; CHOL 195mg; IRON 2mg; SODIUM 482mg; CALC 39mg

DINNER TONIGHT

READY IN 35 MINUTES

SHOPPING LIST

Turkey Pitas with Tahini-Yogurt Sauce

Ground cumin
Paprika
Kosher salt
Ground turmeric
Turkey cutlets
Whole-wheat pitas
Cucumber
Red bell pepper
Tahini
Plain low-fat yogurt
Lemon

Chopped Romaine Salad

Olive oil
Red wine vinegar
Oregano
Lemon
Kosher salt
Romaine lettuce
Cherry tomatoes
Red onion

GAME PLAN

While turkey grills:
- Prepare salad.
- Slice vegetables.
- Prepare tahini mixture.

Kid Friendly • Quick and Easy

Turkey Pitas with Tahini-Yogurt Sauce + Chopped Romaine Salad

Cooking spray
1 teaspoon ground cumin
1 teaspoon paprika
¼ teaspoon kosher salt
¼ teaspoon ground turmeric
4 (4-ounce) turkey cutlets
4 (6-inch) whole-wheat pitas
1 cup thinly sliced cucumber
1 cup thinly sliced red bell pepper
2 tablespoons tahini (sesame seed paste)
2 tablespoons plain low-fat yogurt
1½ tablespoons fresh lemon juice
1 tablespoon water
½ teaspoon freshly ground black pepper

1. Heat a grill pan over medium-high heat. Coat pan with cooking spray. Combine cumin, paprika, salt, and turmeric in a small bowl. Rub spice mixture evenly over turkey. Add turkey to pan; cook 3 minutes on each side or until done. Remove turkey from pan.
2. Cut off top third of each pita; reserve for another use. Add pitas to pan; grill 30 seconds on each side or until marked. Cut turkey into slices. Divide turkey, cucumber, and bell pepper evenly among pitas.
3. Combine tahini and remaining ingredients in a small bowl, stirring with a whisk. Serve tahini mixture with sandwiches. Serves 4 (serving size: 1 filled pita and about 1½ tablespoons sauce)

CALORIES 341; **FAT** 6.4g (sat 1.1g, mono 1.7g, poly 2.4g); **PROTEIN** 36g; **CARB** 37g; **FIBER** 6g; **CHOL** 71mg; **IRON** 4mg; **SODIUM** 487mg; **CALC** 77mg

---

Chopped Romaine Salad
Combine 1 tablespoon olive oil, 1 tablespoon red wine vinegar, ½ teaspoon chopped fresh oregano, ¼ teaspoon grated lemon rind, and ¼ teaspoon kosher salt in a large bowl, stirring with a whisk. Add 3 cups chopped romaine lettuce, 1 cup quartered cherry tomatoes, and ¼ cup vertically sliced red onion; toss gently to coat. Serves 4 (serving size: 1 cup)

CALORIES 49; **FAT** 3.6g (sat 0.5g); **SODIUM** 126mg

READY IN 40 MINUTES

SHOPPING LIST

Chipotle Chicken with Coriander Rice

Long-grain white rice
Olive oil
Onion
Coriander seeds
Kosher salt
Flat-leaf parsley
Lemon
Skinless, boneless chicken breast halves
Unsalted chicken stock (such as Swanson)
Cherry preserves
Canned chipotle chiles in adobo sauce
Garlic
Ground cumin

Simple Salad with Parmesan

Lemon
Canola mayonnaise
Extra-virgin olive oil
Sugar
Mixed baby greens
Cherry tomatoes
Parmesan cheese

GAME PLAN

While oven preheats:
- Cook rice.
- Sear chicken in pan.

While chicken bakes:
- Prepare sauce.
- Finish rice.

Kid Friendly • Quick and Easy

Chipotle Chicken with Coriander Rice + Simple Salad with Parmesan

³/₄ cup uncooked long-grain white rice

1 tablespoon olive oil, divided

¹/₂ cup chopped onion

1 teaspoon coriander seeds

¹/₂ teaspoon kosher salt, divided

¹/₄ cup chopped fresh flat-leaf parsley

1 tablespoon fresh lemon juice

4 (6-ounce) skinless, boneless chicken breast halves

¹/₂ teaspoon freshly ground black pepper, divided

¹/₂ cup unsalted chicken stock (such as Swanson)

¹/₄ cup cherry preserves

2 teaspoons chopped canned chipotle chiles in adobo sauce

1 teaspoon minced fresh garlic

¹/₂ teaspoon ground cumin

1. Preheat oven to 450°.

2. Cook rice according to package directions, omitting salt and fat.

3. Heat a large skillet over medium-high heat. Add 1 teaspoon oil to pan; swirl to coat. Add onion and coriander; sauté 1 minute. Stir in rice and ¼ teaspoon salt; sauté 1½ minutes. Stir in parsley and lemon juice.

4. Sprinkle chicken with ¼ teaspoon salt and ¼ teaspoon black pepper. Heat a large skillet over medium-high heat. Add 2 teaspoons oil to pan; swirl to coat. Add chicken; cook 4 minutes on each side. Place chicken on a baking sheet. Bake at 450° for 5 minutes or until done. Return skillet to medium-high heat. Add stock; cook 1 minute, scraping pan to loosen browned bits. Stir in ¼ teaspoon black pepper, cherry preserves, and remaining ingredients; cook 3 minutes or until reduced to about ¼ cup. Serve sauce with chicken and rice. Serves 4 (serving size: ½ cup rice, 1 chicken breast half, and about 1 tablespoon sauce)

CALORIES 419; FAT 8.2g (sat 1.5g, mono 3.9g, poly 1.1g); PROTEIN 40g; CARB 44g; FIBER 1g; CHOL 109mg; IRON 3mg; SODIUM 486mg; CALC 38mg

Simple Salad with Parmesan

Combine 2½ tablespoons fresh lemon juice, 2 tablespoons canola mayonnaise, 1 teaspoon extra-virgin olive oil, ½ teaspoon sugar, and ½ teaspoon freshly ground black pepper, stirring with a whisk. Add 6 cups mixed baby greens; toss to coat. Sprinkle with ½ cup halved cherry tomatoes and 1 ounce shaved Parmesan cheese. Serves 4 (serving size: about 1½ cups)

CALORIES 83; FAT 5.1g (sat 1.4g); SODIUM 193mg

READY IN 40 MINUTES

SHOPPING LIST

Paprika Pork Chops with Zucchini
Paprika
Brown sugar
Kosher salt
Crushed red pepper
Bone-in, center-cut pork chops
Zucchini
Extra-virgin olive oil
Whole-grain mustard

Grilled Corn with Lime
Butter
Lime
Corn
Kosher salt

GAME PLAN

While corn grills:
- Grill pork chops.
- Halve zucchini.

While zucchini grills:
- Prepare lime-butter mixture.

continued

Paprika Pork Chops with Zucchini + Grilled Corn with Lime

2 teaspoons paprika
¾ teaspoon brown sugar
¾ teaspoon freshly ground black pepper, divided
½ teaspoon kosher salt, divided
¼ teaspoon crushed red pepper
4 (6-ounce) bone-in, center-cut pork chops
Cooking spray
3 medium zucchini, halved lengthwise
2 teaspoons extra-virgin olive oil
2 teaspoons whole-grain mustard

1. Preheat grill to medium-high heat.
2. Combine paprika, sugar, ½ teaspoon black pepper, ¼ teaspoon salt, and crushed red pepper in a small bowl. Rub paprika mixture evenly over pork. Place pork on grill rack coated with cooking spray. Grill 3 minutes on each side or until desired degree of doneness. Remove pork from grill.
3. Add zucchini to grill; grill 4 minutes on each side or until well marked. Cut zucchini into ½-inch pieces. Combine zucchini and ¼ teaspoon black pepper, ¼ teaspoon salt, oil, and mustard; toss to coat. Serves 4 (serving size: 1 pork chop and about ⅔ cup zucchini mixture)

CALORIES 271; FAT 11.7g (sat 3g, mono 4.8g, poly 1.4g); PROTEIN 34g; CARB 7g; FIBER 2g; CHOL 100mg; IRON 2mg; SODIUM 379mg; CALC 56mg

Grilled Corn with Lime
Preheat grill to medium-high heat. Combine 1 tablespoon melted butter, 1 teaspoon grated lime rind, and 1 tablespoon fresh lime juice, stirring with a whisk. Place 4 ears shucked corn on grill. Grill 15 minutes or un-til lightly charred, turning occasionally. Place corn on a serving plate; brush with juice mixture. Sprinkle with ¼ teaspoon kosher salt. Serves 4 (serving size: 1 ear)

CALORIES 114; FAT 4.3g (sat 2.2g); SODIUM 161mg

READY IN
35
MINUTES

SHOPPING LIST

Catfish with Corn Hash
Center-cut bacon slice
Olive oil
Onion
Green bell pepper
Celery
Thyme
Garlic
Fresh or frozen corn kernels
Ground red pepper
Kosher salt
Paprika
Catfish fillets
Canola oil

Heirloom Tomato and Zucchini Salad
Heirloom tomatoes
Zucchini
Kosher salt
Chives
Olive oil
Red wine vinegar
Sugar

GAME PLAN

While corn hash cooks:
■ Cook fish.
While fish cooks:
■ Prepare salad.

Catfish with Corn Hash + Heirloom Tomato and Zucchini Salad

1 center-cut bacon slice, chopped
2 teaspoons olive oil
¾ cup chopped onion
¾ cup chopped green bell pepper
½ cup finely chopped celery
2 teaspoons chopped fresh thyme
2 garlic cloves, minced
2 cups fresh or frozen corn kernels
¼ teaspoon ground red pepper
½ teaspoon kosher salt, divided
½ teaspoon paprika
½ teaspoon freshly ground black pepper
4 (6-ounce) catfish fillets
2 teaspoons canola oil

1. Heat a large skillet over medium heat. Add bacon to pan; cook 3 minutes or until crisp, stirring frequently. Remove bacon from pan. Add olive oil, onion, bell pepper, celery, and thyme to drippings in pan; cook 5 minutes or until vegetables are crisp-tender. Add garlic; cook 30 seconds, stirring constantly. Stir in corn, red pepper, and ¼ teaspoon salt. Cover, reduce heat to low, and cook 8 minutes, stirring occasionally. Stir in bacon.
2. Combine ¼ teaspoon salt, paprika, and black pepper in a small bowl. Rub spice mixture evenly over fish. Heat a large skillet over medium-high heat. Add canola oil to pan; swirl to coat. Add fish to pan; cook 3 to 4 minutes on each side or until fish flakes easily when tested with a fork. Serve with corn mixture. Serves 4 (serving size: 1 fillet and about ¾ cup corn mixture)

CALORIES 332; FAT 15.7g (sat 3g, mono 7.7g, poly 3.1g); PROTEIN 29g; CARB 20g; FIBER 3g; CHOL 95mg; IRON 1mg; SODIUM 443mg; CALC 37mg

Heirloom Tomato and Zucchini Salad

Divide 1 pound heirloom tomatoes, cut into ¼-inch-thick slices, and 1 small zucchini, cut into ⅛-inch-thick rounds, evenly among 4 plates. Sprinkle with ¼ teaspoon kosher salt and ¼ teaspoon freshly ground black pepper. Combine 2 tablespoons finely chopped fresh chives, 1 tablespoon olive oil, 1 tablespoon red wine vinegar, and 1 teaspoon sugar in a bowl, stirring with a whisk. Drizzle vinegar mixture evenly over salads. Serves 4 (serving size: about 1 cup salad and 1 tablespoon vinaigrette)

CALORIES 61; FAT 3.7g (sat 0.5g); SODIUM 128mg

READY IN 35 MINUTES

SHOPPING LIST

London Broil with Chimichurri

Flat-leaf parsley
Olive oil
Oregano
Sherry vinegar or white wine vinegar
Crushed red pepper
Garlic
Green onion
Flank steak
Kosher salt
Whole-grain bread or Italian bread

Grilled Pepper, Onion, and Blue Cheese Salad

Anaheim chiles
Red bell peppers
Red onion
Sherry vinegar
Kosher salt
Blue cheese

GAME PLAN

While steak marinates:
- Grill peppers.

While steak rests:
- Grill bread slices.
- Finish salad.

Kid Friendly • Quick & Easy

London Broil with Chimichurri + Grilled Pepper, Onion, and Blue Cheese Salad

1 cup flat-leaf parsley leaves
2½ tablespoons olive oil, divided
1 tablespoon oregano leaves
2 teaspoons sherry vinegar or white wine vinegar
⅛ teaspoon crushed red pepper
2 garlic cloves, divided
1 green onion, coarsely chopped
1 (1-pound) flank steak, trimmed
½ teaspoon kosher salt
½ teaspoon freshly ground black pepper
Cooking spray
4 (1-ounce) slices whole-grain bread or Italian bread

1. Preheat grill to medium-high heat.
2. Place parsley, 1½ tablespoons oil, oregano, vinegar, red pepper, 1 garlic clove, and green onion in a food processor; process until finely chopped. Rub 2 tablespoons parsley mixture evenly over steak; reserve remaining parsley mixture. Let steak stand at room temperature 15 minutes.
3. Sprinkle steak with salt and pepper. Place steak on grill rack coated with cooking spray. Grill, covered, 4 minutes on each side or until desired degree of doneness. Place steak on a cutting board; let stand 10 minutes. Cut across the grain into thin slices.
4. Brush both sides of bread slices with 1 tablespoon oil; grill 2 minutes on each side or until toasted. Cut remaining garlic clove in half; rub cut sides of garlic over toasted bread. Serve toast with steak and reserved parsley mixture. Serves 4 (serving size: 3 ounces beef, about 1½ tablespoons chimichurri, and 1 bread slice)

CALORIES 323; FAT 16g (sat 3.8g, mono 8.6g, poly 1.7g); PROTEIN 29g; CARB 14g; FIBER 3g; CHOL 70mg; IRON 4mg; SODIUM 431mg; CALC 89mg

Grilled Pepper, Onion, and Blue Cheese Salad

Preheat grill to medium-high heat. Place 2 Anaheim chiles, 2 quartered red bell peppers, and ½ medium red onion, cut into 1-inch wedges, on grill rack coated with cooking spray. Grill 10 minutes, turning occasionally. Remove tops and seeds from Anaheim; thinly slice. Combine peppers, onion, 2 teaspoons sherry vinegar, 2 teaspoons olive oil, ¼ teaspoon freshly ground black pepper, and a dash of kosher salt; toss to coat. Sprinkle with 2 tablespoons crumbled blue cheese. Serves 4 (serving size: about ½ cup)

CALORIES 70; FAT 3.8g (sat 1.1g); SODIUM 93mg

SMOKED CHERRY BOMBS

Stunning and unforgettable—a second set of this treat is a must.

Some flavor fireworks and fun surprises help light up the Fourth, and this whimsical dessert delivers. We free the main ingredient, maraschino cherries, from the cocktail garnish tray and flavor them with cherry wood smoke; then we wrap them up with a creamy almond filling in buttery layers of phyllo. They're an easy potluck dish, and they'll make anyone who receives them feel just as special as they are.

Kid Friendly • Make Ahead
Smoked Cherry Bombs

Hands-on: 20 min. Total: 65 min.

½ cup cherry wood chips
12 dye-free maraschino cherries with
    stems (such as Tillen Farms)
2 ounces almond paste
5 teaspoons sugar, divided
2 ounces ⅓-less-fat cream cheese,
    softened
¼ teaspoon vanilla extract
Dash of salt
4 (14 x 9-inch) sheets frozen phyllo
    dough, thawed
3 tablespoons butter, melted

1. Preheat oven to 375°.
2. Pierce 10 holes on one side of the bottom of a 13 x 9–inch disposable aluminum foil pan. Place holes over element on cooktop; place wood chips over holes inside pan. Heat element under holes to medium-high; let burn 1 minute or until chips begin to smoke. Arrange cherries on opposite end of pan. Cover pan with foil.

Reduce heat to low; smoke cherries 5 minutes. Remove from heat; uncover.
3. Combine almond paste and 1 tablespoon sugar; beat with a mixer at medium speed until mixture resembles damp sand. Add cream cheese, vanilla, and salt; beat until combined.
4. Place 1 phyllo sheet on a work surface (cover remaining dough to keep from drying); lightly brush with butter. Sprinkle with ½ teaspoon sugar. Repeat layers with remaining phyllo, butter (save a little butter for the outsides), and sugar. Cut 12 (3½ x 3–inch) rectangles through phyllo layers using a pizza cutter or sharp knife. Place 1 teaspoon almond mixture in the center of each phyllo stack; press 1 cherry, stem up, into almond mixture. Gather corners of phyllo, and press around stem to seal, forming a pouch. Gently brush pouch with remaining butter. Place pouches on a baking sheet lined with parchment paper. Bake at 375° for 13 minutes or until crisp. Cool on pan on a wire rack. Serves 12 (serving size: 1 piece)

CALORIES 93; FAT 5.7g (sat 2.7g, mono 2.1g, poly 0.5g); PROTEIN 1g; CARB 10g; FIBER 1g; CHOL 11mg; IRON 0mg; SODIUM 84mg; CALC 18mg

PULLED PORK ON YOUR COUNTERTOP

Kid Friendly • Freezable
Make Ahead
Slow Cooker Pulled Pork with Bourbon-Peach Barbecue Sauce

Hands-on: 30 min. Total: 7 hr. 10 min.
Smoked paprika comes from a centuries-old tradition in which chile peppers are slowly dried over low-burning fires of Spanish oak and then ground into powder. In the slow cooker, this earthy, aromatic spice adds outdoor smoked barbecue flavor.

2 teaspoons Spanish smoked paprika
1¼ teaspoons kosher salt, divided
1 teaspoon freshly ground black
    pepper
1 (3½-pound) bone-in pork shoulder
    roast (Boston butt), trimmed
Cooking spray
½ cup unsalted chicken stock (such
    as Swanson)
⅓ cup balsamic vinegar
⅓ cup molasses
2 tablespoons lower-sodium soy
    sauce
1 teaspoon crushed red pepper
½ cup peach preserves
2 cups vertically sliced onion
5 garlic cloves, thinly sliced
¼ cup bourbon
2 tablespoons cold water
2 teaspoons cornstarch

1. Heat a large skillet over medium-high heat. Combine paprika, ½ teaspoon salt, and black pepper; rub evenly over pork. Coat pan with

cooking spray. Add pork to pan; cook 10 minutes, turning to brown on all sides. Place pork in a 6-quart electric slow cooker.

2. Add stock and next 4 ingredients to pan; bring to a boil, scraping pan to loosen browned bits. Add preserves, stirring with a whisk. Pour mixture over pork; top with onion and garlic. Cover and cook on LOW 6½ hours or until pork is very tender. Remove pork from pan, reserving liquid; cool slightly. Shred with 2 forks. Remove onion with a slotted spoon; add to pork.

3. Place a large zip-top plastic bag inside a 4-cup glass measuring cup. Pour cooking liquid into bag; let stand 10 minutes (fat will rise to the top). Seal bag; carefully snip off 1 bottom corner of bag. Drain drippings into skillet, stopping before fat layer reaches opening; discard fat. Stir bourbon into drippings; bring to a boil. Cook 10 minutes or until mixture is reduced to about 1½ cups. Combine 2 tablespoons cold water and cornstarch in a small bowl, stirring with a whisk; add cornstarch mixture to sauce, stirring constantly until thickened. Stir in ¾ teaspoon salt. Drizzle sauce over pork; toss gently to coat. Serves 12 (serving size: about 3 ounces meat and about 2 tablespoons sauce)

CALORIES 206; FAT 5.9g (sat 2g, mono 2.6g, poly 0.7g); PROTEIN 17g; CARB 20g; FIBER 1g; CHOL 54mg; IRON 2mg; SODIUM 369mg; CALC 41mg

LEFTOVERS FREEZE WELL. PACK SHREDDED MEAT IN SAUCE, AND WARM GENTLY.

FIVE FROSTY ICE POPS

For sugar syrup: Boil 1 cup water and ⅔ cup sugar in a saucepan over medium-high heat until sugar dissolves. Cool and stir in 2 tablespoons light-colored corn syrup.

Freezable • Gluten Free
Melon Mimosa
Add 4 torn mint leaves and 4 torn basil leaves to sugar mixture before bringing it to a boil. Pour cooled sugar syrup through a sieve; discard solids. Place 2 (1-inch) cantaloupe balls and 2 (1-inch) honeydew balls in each of 8 (⅓-cup) icepop molds. Combine 1 cup sugar syrup and 1 cup Champagne. Divide Champagne mixture among ice pop molds. Cover and insert craft sticks; freeze 4 hours or until thoroughly frozen. Serves 8 (serving size: 1 ice pop)

CALORIES 94; FAT 0.1g (sat 0g); SODIUM 12mg

Freezable • Gluten Free
Cappuccino
Reserve ¼ cup sugar syrup; set aside. Dissolve 2 tablespoons instant espresso granules in 1¼ cups sugar syrup while still warm; cool to room temperature. Combine 1 cup half-and-half with reserved ¼ cup syrup. Divide half-and-half mixture evenly among 10 (⅓-cup) ice pop molds. Divide espresso mixture among molds. Cover and insert craft sticks; freeze 6 hours or until thoroughly frozen. Serves 10 (serving size: 1 ice pop)

CALORIES 97; FAT 2.8g (sat 1.7g); SODIUM 13mg

Freezable • Gluten Free
Vanilla Yogurt and Spiced Plum
Place 1½ cups chopped red-fleshed plums, ¾ cup sugar syrup, ⅛ teaspoon salt, and a dash of ground allspice in a blender or food processor; process until smooth. Strain mixture over a bowl, pressing to extract juices; discard solids. Combine remaining ¾ cup sugar syrup, 1 cup plain 2% reduced-fat Greek yogurt, and ½ teaspoon vanilla extract. Place about 1½ tablespoons plum mixture in each of 8 (⅓-cup) ice pop molds; cover and freeze 30 minutes. Top each serving with about 2 tablespoons yogurt mixture; cover and insert craft sticks. Freeze 30 minutes or until set. Top each serving with about 2 tablespoons plum mixture. Cover and freeze 8 hours or until thoroughly frozen. Serves 8 (serving size: 1 ice pop)

CALORIES 114; FAT 0.7g (sat 0.4g); SODIUM 49mg

Freezable • Gluten Free
Cucumber-Chili-Lime
Place 3 cups chopped peeled English cucumber, ⅓ cup fresh lime juice, ¼ teaspoon salt, and ¼ teaspoon ground red pepper in a blender or food processor; process until smooth. Combine cucumber mixture and sugar syrup; pour into 9 (⅓-cup) ice pop molds. Cover and insert craft sticks; freeze 4 hours or until thoroughly frozen. Serves 9 (serving size: 1 ice pop)

CALORIES 79; FAT 0.1g (sat 0g); SODIUM 69mg

Freezable • Gluten-Free
Strawberry-Balsamic
Combine ½ cup balsamic vinegar, 2 tablespoons honey, and 4 thyme sprigs in a small saucepan. Bring to a simmer over medium heat; cook 8 minutes or until liquid is thickened and reduced by half. Discard thyme; cool. Place ¾ cup sugar syrup, balsamic mixture, and 4 cups hulled strawberries in a blender or food processor; process until smooth. Divide mixture evenly among 8 (⅓-cup) icepop molds. Cover and insert craft sticks; freeze for 6 hours or until thoroughly frozen. Serves 8 (serving size: 1 ice pop)

CALORIES 94; FAT 0.2g (sat 0g); SODIUM 6mg

CRUNCHY "FRIED" GREEN TOMATOES

Pickled, pan-seared, and perfectly crisp with 75% less fat and calories

Pickled "Fried" Green Tomatoes

Hands-on: 37 min. Total: 40 min.

1 cup water
1 cup cider vinegar
2 tablespoons sugar
³/₄ teaspoon kosher salt, divided
16 (¹/₄-inch-thick) slices green tomato (about 4 tomatoes)
7 tablespoons nonfat buttermilk, divided
2 tablespoons finely chopped basil
3 tablespoons canola mayonnaise
1 teaspoon finely chopped thyme
2 teaspoons cider vinegar
1 garlic clove, minced
¹/₂ teaspoon black pepper, divided
³/₄ cup panko
¹/₃ cup masa harina
1 large egg
1 large egg white
1 ounce all-purpose flour (about ¹/₄ cup)
3 tablespoons extra-virgin olive oil, divided
Cooking spray

1. Combine 1 cup water, 1 cup vinegar, sugar, and ½ teaspoon salt in a medium saucepan; bring to a boil. Add tomatoes; cook 2 minutes. Remove from heat; let stand 15 minutes, stirring occasionally. Drain tomatoes; pat dry.
2. Combine 5 tablespoons buttermilk and next 5 ingredients. Stir in ¼ teaspoon pepper.

OURS SAVES
420 calories, 33g total fat, and 502mg sodium over deep-fried green tomatoes

3. Heat a large skillet over medium heat. Add panko to pan; cook 2 minutes or until toasted, stirring frequently. Remove from heat; stir in masa harina, ¼ teaspoon salt, and ¼ teaspoon pepper. Place panko mixture in a shallow dish. Combine 2 tablespoons buttermilk, egg, and egg white. Place flour in another shallow dish. Dredge tomato slices in flour; dip in egg mixture, and dredge in panko mixture, turning to coat.
4. Heat a large nonstick skillet over medium-high heat. Add 1 tablespoon oil; swirl to coat. Add half of tomatoes; cook 4 minutes. Coat tops of tomatoes with cooking spray. Turn; add 1½ teaspoons oil to pan. Cook 4 minutes or until golden. Repeat procedure with 1½ tablespoons oil, tomatoes, and cooking spray. Serves 8 (serving size: 2 tomato slices and about 1 tablespoon sauce)

CALORIES 154; **FAT** 7.7g (sat 0.9g, mono 4.8g, poly 1.2g); **PROTEIN** 4g; **CARB** 16g; **FIBER** 1g; **CHOL** 23mg; **IRON** 1mg; **SODIUM** 215mg; **CALC** 41mg

12 HEALTHY HABITS

EVOLVE YOUR VIEW ON FAT

Fat fears are outdated. Learn how to deftly use all fats—yes, even butter.

Scientific views about dietary fats have changed tremendously—from a time when fat was supposed to take up no more than 30% of your daily calories to now, when butter sales are at an all-time high.

Jennifer McGruther, this month's Healthy Habits hero and author of the blog and cookbook *The Nourished Kitchen*, is an advocate for whole, traditional foods, with a focus on natural sources of fat. Online and in workshops around the country, she shows cooks how to find high-quality, unadulterated olive oils and how to make their own butter.

McGruther believes, as we do, that there is a place for all kinds of fats in a healthy diet, even saturated ones. The emphasis is on quality, both for flavor and for health.

Roasted Beet Hummus

Hands-on: 15 min. Total: 1 hr. 10 min.

1 small red beet
¹/₄ cup coarsely chopped walnuts
4 garlic cloves, halved
1 teaspoon grated lemon rind
¹/₄ cup water
2 tablespoons fresh lemon juice
2 tablespoons walnut oil
³/₄ teaspoon black pepper
¹/₂ teaspoon kosher salt
1 (15-ounce) can chickpeas (garbanzo beans), rinsed and drained

1. Preheat oven to 450°.
2. Leave root and 1 inch stem on beet; scrub with a brush. Wrap beet in foil. Place on a rimmed baking sheet. Bake at 450° for 35 minutes. Add walnuts and garlic to pan. Bake 7 minutes or until nuts are toasted. Cool 10 minutes. Trim off beet root; rub off skin. Cut beet into quarters.
3. Place garlic in a food processor; process until finely chopped. Add beet; process until very finely chopped. Add walnuts, lemon rind, and remaining ingredients. Process until smooth. Serves 12 (serving size: about 2½ tablespoons)

CALORIES 73; **FAT** 4.4g (sat 0.4g, mono 0.9g, poly 2.8g); **PROTEIN** 2g; **CARB** 7g; **FIBER** 2g; **CHOL** 0mg; **IRON** 0mg; **SODIUM** 134mg; **CALC** 16mg

THE AMAZING FIVE-INGREDIENT ENTRÉE

Turn a handful of ingredients into simple yet stunning mains, from roasted fish to a centerpiece roast.

Gluten Free

Roasted Orange-Fennel Striped Bass

Hands-on: 15 min. Total: 45 min.
Roasting the fish whole keeps it tender and succulent. If you can't find striped bass, you can substitute whole white fish or yellowtail snapper, which are both sustainable options.

1 large fennel bulb with stalks
2 tablespoons extra-virgin olive oil, divided
6 garlic cloves, minced
¾ teaspoon kosher salt, divided
2 (1¾-pound) whole cleaned striped bass (heads and tails intact)
3 tablespoons fresh lemon juice
¼ teaspoon freshly ground black pepper
Cooking spray
1 orange, cut into 8 slices

1. Preheat oven to 400°.
2. Remove fronds from fennel bulb; finely chop fronds to measure 1 tablespoon. Remove and discard stalks. Thinly slice fennel bulb. Heat a large nonstick skillet over medium-high heat. Add 1 tablespoon oil; swirl to coat. Add sliced fennel and garlic to pan; sauté 6 minutes or until lightly browned, stirring frequently. Stir in ¼ teaspoon salt. Remove pan from heat; cool 5 minutes.
3. Score skin of each fish with 3 diagonal cuts. Combine 1 tablespoon oil and lemon juice, stirring with a whisk. Rub inside flesh of each fish with half of lemon juice mixture; drizzle outside of each fish with remaining half of lemon juice mixture. Sprinkle inside flesh evenly with ½ teaspoon salt and pepper. Place both fish on a parchment-lined jelly-roll pan coated with cooking spray. Place half of fennel mixture and 4 orange slices inside each fish.
4. Roast at 400° for 30 minutes or until fish flakes easily when tested with a fork; let stand 5 minutes. Sprinkle reserved fennel fronds over fish. Serves 4 (serving size: 6 ounces fish and ⅔ cup fennel mixture)

CALORIES 271; **FAT** 10.5g (sat 1.8g, mono 5.7g, poly 2g); **PROTEIN** 33g; **CARB** 11g; **FIBER** 3g; **CHOL** 70mg; **IRON** 1mg; **SODIUM** 507mg; **CALC** 70mg

Quick & Easy

Cilantro Burgers with Sriracha Mayo

Hands-on: 20 min. Total: 20 min.
Sriracha has rightfully become an all-purpose condiment—its sweet chile heat and its vinegar punch go well beyond burgers, perking up brothy soups, meat marinades, and dipping sauces.

1 pound 90% lean ground sirloin
3 tablespoons chopped fresh cilantro
¼ teaspoon kosher salt
¼ teaspoon freshly ground black pepper
Cooking spray
4 (1½-ounce) hamburger buns
3 tablespoons canola mayonnaise
1 tablespoon Sriracha
⅓ cup cilantro sprigs

1. Combine ground sirloin, chopped cilantro, salt, and pepper in a bowl; mix just until combined. Divide sirloin mixture into 4 equal portions, gently shaping each into a ½ inch-thick patty (about 3½ inches in diameter).
2. Heat a grill pan over medium-high heat. Coat pan with cooking spray. Add patties to pan; grill 4 minutes. Carefully turn patties; grill 4 minutes or until desired degree of doneness. Remove patties from pan. Add buns, cut sides down, to pan; grill 1 minute or until toasted.
3. Combine mayonnaise and Sriracha in a small bowl, stirring with a whisk. Spread 1 tablespoon mayonnaise mixture on bottom half of each bun; top each with 1 patty. Divide cilantro sprigs evenly among servings; top with top halves of buns. Serves 4 (serving size: 1 burger)

CALORIES 329; **FAT** 14.1g (sat 4.2g, mono 6.2g, poly 2.1g); **PROTEIN** 26g; **CARB** 22g; **FIBER** 1g; **CHOL** 69mg; **IRON** 4mg; **SODIUM** 543mg; **CALC** 85mg

Mesquite-Smoked Beer Can Chicken

Hands-on: 45 min. Total: 2 hr. 30 min.
If using a charcoal grill, heap lit coals to the right side of the grill and add chips directly to the coals. Place chicken on left side of grill rack. Add additional charcoal to the fire as needed during grilling.

2 cups mesquite wood chips
1 (4-pound) whole chicken
1 tablespoon olive oil
2 teaspoons chili powder
2 teaspoons brown sugar
1 teaspoon ground cumin
³/₄ teaspoon kosher salt
¹/₂ teaspoon freshly ground black pepper
1 (12-ounce) can beer

1. Soak wood chips in water 30 minutes; drain well.
2. Preheat grill to medium-high heat using both burners. After preheating, turn the left burner off (leave the right burner on). Pierce the bottom of an aluminum foil pan liberally with the tip of a knife. Place pan on heat element on heated side of grill; add wood chips to pan.
3. Remove giblets and neck from chicken, and discard. Starting at the neck cavity, loosen skin from breasts and drumsticks by inserting fingers, gently pushing between skin and meat.
4. Combine oil and next 5 ingredients (through black pepper) in a bowl. Rub spice mixture under loosened skin and over drumsticks and breasts; let stand 20 minutes.
5. Discard 6 ounces beer from can. Holding chicken upright with the body cavity facing down, insert beer can into cavity. Place chicken, upright, on grill rack covering left burner, spreading legs out to form a tripod. Cover and grill 1½ hours or until a thermometer inserted in thigh registers 165°. Place chicken and can on cutting board; let stand 10 minutes. Discard can and skin. Serves 4 (serving size: 5 ounces chicken)

CALORIES 375; **FAT** 16.6g (sat 4.1g, mono 7.1g, poly 3.4g); **PROTEIN** 51g; **CARB** 3g; **FIBER** 1g; **CHOL** 155mg; **IRON** 3mg; **SODIUM** 533mg; **CALC** 37mg

BLT Pasta

Hands-on: 24 min. Total: 24 min.
We love the look of mezze penne, a smaller version of regular penne, but you can use any short pasta you like. The "lettuce" in this BLT is actually tender baby spinach. You could also substitute peppery arugula or even baby kale.

8 ounces uncooked mezze penne pasta
6 center-cut bacon slices
2 cups grape tomatoes, halved
¹/₄ teaspoon kosher salt
1 (6-ounce) package baby spinach
¹/₂ teaspoon freshly ground black pepper
1 ounce fresh Romano cheese, finely grated (about ¹/₄ cup)

1. Cook pasta according to package directions, omitting salt and fat. Drain.
2. Heat a large nonstick skillet over medium-high heat. Add bacon; cook 6 minutes or until crisp. Remove bacon from pan; crumble. Add tomatoes and salt to drippings in pan; cook 3 minutes or until tomatoes are tender, stirring occasionally. Add spinach and pasta to pan; cook 1 minute or just until spinach begins to wilt, stirring occasionally. Sprinkle pasta with bacon, pepper, and cheese. Serves 4 (serving size: about 1⅔ cups)

CALORIES 302; **FAT** 5.7g (sat 3.1g, mono 1.9g, poly 0.4g); **PROTEIN** 14g; **CARB** 50g; **FIBER** 5g; **CHOL** 16mg; **IRON** 3mg; **SODIUM** 512mg; **CALC** 137mg

Cherry-Port Glazed Pork Loin Roast

Hands-on: 15 min. Total: 45 min. *Port reduces to an intensely fruity, syrupy glaze.*

³/₄ cup ruby port
¹/₂ cup cherry preserves
1 teaspoon chopped fresh thyme
1 teaspoon garlic powder
1¹/₄ teaspoons kosher salt
¹/₂ teaspoon freshly ground black pepper
1 (3-pound) boneless pork loin, trimmed
1 tablespoon olive oil
Cooking spray
Thyme sprigs (optional)

1. Preheat oven to 425°.
2. Bring port to a boil in a small saucepan over medium-high heat; cook 10 minutes or until reduced to 2 tablespoons. Stir in cherry preserves; cook 45 seconds. Remove pan from heat; stir in chopped thyme.
3. Combine garlic powder, salt, and pepper in a small bowl. Rub spice mixture evenly over pork. Heat a large skillet over medium-high heat. Add oil; swirl to coat. Add pork to pan; cook 8 minutes, turning to brown on all sides.
4. Place pork on a jelly-roll pan coated with cooking spray. Roast at 425° for 20 minutes. Brush pork with half of port mixture; roast at 425° for 5 minutes or until a thermometer registers 135°. Remove pork from oven; brush with remaining half of port mixture. Let stand 10 minutes before cutting into slices. Top with thyme sprigs, if desired. Serves 12 (serving size: 3 ounces pork)

CALORIES 191; **FAT** 7g (sat 1.9g, mono 2.9g, poly 0.8g); **PROTEIN** 21g; **CARB** 9g; **FIBER** 0g; **CHOL** 66mg; **IRON** 1mg; **SODIUM** 245mg; **CALC** 20mg

**Kid Friendly • Quick & Easy
Vegetarian**

Asparagus, Ricotta, and Egg Pizza

Hands-on: 20 min. Total: 40 min.
Arranging the dough on a hot pizza stone or skillet will get the crust nice and crisp.

**12 ounces refrigerated fresh pizza
 dough**
2/3 cup part-skim ricotta cheese
1/8 teaspoon kosher salt
**1 1/2 cups asparagus, trimmed and cut
 into 1-inch pieces**
2 teaspoons extra-virgin olive oil
4 large eggs
**1/4 teaspoon freshly ground black
 pepper**
**1 ounce Parmesan cheese, grated
 (about 1/4 cup)**

1. Place a pizza stone or heavy baking sheet in oven. Preheat oven to 500° (keep pizza stone or baking sheet in oven as it preheats).
2. Let dough stand at room temperature 30 minutes.
3. Combine ricotta and salt in a small bowl.
4. Roll dough into an 11-inch circle on a floured surface. Carefully remove pizza stone from oven. Arrange dough on pizza stone. Spread ricotta mixture over dough, leaving a 1/2-inch border. Combine asparagus and oil in a bowl. Top ricotta mixture with asparagus mixture, gently pressing asparagus into ricotta. Bake at 500° for 5 minutes.
5. Crack eggs over top of pizza (do not remove pizza from oven). Bake 4 minutes or until whites are set. Sprinkle with pepper and Parmesan. Cut into 8 slices. Serves 4 (serving size: 2 slices)

CALORIES 402; **FAT** 13.9g (sat 5.2g, mono 5.9g, poly 1.8g);
PROTEIN 22g; **CARB** 44g; **FIBER** 7g; **CHOL** 205mg;
IRON 3mg; **SODIUM** 657mg; **CALC** 232mg

SUPER SIMPLE GRILLING

The grill is the healthy cook's tool of choice for low-fat, high-flavor food. These delightful dishes come together in a snap, and a little smoke and char make them shine.

Quick & Easy • Gluten Free

Spicy Flank Steak Tacos with Watermelon Salsa

Hands-on: 28 min. Total: 38 min.
The three-pepper spice rub gives the steak wonderful complexity.

5/8 teaspoon kosher salt, divided
**1/4 teaspoon freshly ground black
 pepper**
1/4 teaspoon ground white pepper
1/4 teaspoon ground red pepper
**1 (1-pound) flank steak, trimmed
 and halved lengthwise**
Cooking spray
8 green onions, roots trimmed
**2 cups finely chopped fresh
 watermelon**
2 tablespoons chopped fresh mint
2 tablespoons fresh lime juice
2 teaspoons olive oil
**1 serrano chile, seeded and
 chopped**
8 (6-inch) corn tortillas
**2 ounces feta cheese, crumbled
 (about 1/2 cup)**

1. Preheat grill to medium-high heat.
2. Combine 1/2 teaspoon salt, black pepper, white pepper, and red pepper in a small bowl. Score steak with a sharp knife in a diamond pattern on both sides (1/4 inch deep). Lightly coat steak with cooking spray; sprinkle steak evenly with pepper mixture. Arrange steak on grill rack coated with cooking spray; grill 4 minutes on each side or until desired degree of doneness. Let stand 5 minutes; cut steak across the grain into thin slices.
3. Arrange green onions on grill rack coated with cooking spray; grill 3 minutes or until slightly charred and tender.
4. Combine watermelon, mint, juice, oil, chile, and 1/8 teaspoon salt in a medium bowl.
5. Place tortillas on grill rack coated with cooking spray; grill 1 minute on each side or until lightly charred. Arrange onions evenly down the center of each tortilla; divide steak, salsa, and cheese evenly among tortillas. Serves 4 (serving size: 2 tacos)

CALORIES 335; **FAT** 12.8g (sat 4.8g, mono 4.6g, poly 1.1g);
PROTEIN 30g; **CARB** 28g; **FIBER** 3g; **CHOL** 83mg;
IRON 3mg; **SODIUM** 537mg; **CALC** 152mg

Cedar Plank Salmon with Tomato Salsa

Hands-on: 30 min. Total: 40 min.

1 (18-inch) cedar plank
1 poblano chile, seeded and halved
1 jalapeño pepper, seeded and halved
1 small red onion, cut into (¹⁄₂-inch-thick) slices
Cooking spray
2 cups chopped seeded heirloom tomato
3 tablespoons chopped fresh cilantro
¹⁄₂ teaspoon kosher salt, divided
¹⁄₂ teaspoon freshly ground black pepper, divided
1 diced peeled avocado
1 lime, divided
4 (6-ounce) sustainable skinless salmon fillets

1. Soak plank in water 25 minutes.
2. Preheat grill to medium-high heat.
3. Place poblano, jalapeño, and onion on grill rack coated with cooking spray; grill 10 minutes, turning occasionally. Remove from grill; cool. Coarsely chop poblano and onion; finely chop jalapeño. Combine peppers, onion, tomato, cilantro, ¼ teaspoon salt, ¼ teaspoon pepper, avocado, and juice from half of lime.
4. Sprinkle salmon with ¼ teaspoon salt and ¼ teaspoon black pepper. Place plank on grill rack; grill 3 minutes or until lightly charred. Turn plank over; place fish on charred side. Cover; grill 8 minutes or until desired degree of doneness. Cut remaining lime half into 4 wedges. Top each fillet with ½ cup tomato salsa. Serve with lime wedges. Serves 4

CALORIES 386; **FAT** 20.7g (sat 4.2g, mono 10.6g, poly 4.2g); **PROTEIN** 38g; **CARB** 12g; **FIBER** 6g; **CHOL** 87mg; **IRON** 1mg; **SODIUM** 330mg; **CALC** 48mg

Grilled Shrimp and Summer Vegetables with Buttermilk Dressing

Hands-on: 32 min. Total: 32 min. *A full meal from the grill in about half an hour.*

3 tablespoons buttermilk
2 tablespoons canola mayonnaise
7 teaspoons extra-virgin olive oil, divided
3 tablespoons minced fresh chives, divided
1 tablespoon chopped fresh dill
1 teaspoon cider vinegar
1 teaspoon freshly ground black pepper, divided
³⁄₄ teaspoon kosher salt, divided
1 teaspoon honey
16 large shrimp, peeled and deveined (about 1 pound)
20 large okra pods
2 ears corn, shucked
Cooking spray
12 medium heirloom tomato slices

1. Preheat grill to high heat.
2. Combine buttermilk, mayonnaise, 2 tablespoons oil, 2 tablespoons chives, dill, vinegar, ½ teaspoon pepper, and ¼ teaspoon salt in a bowl, stirring with a whisk.
3. Combine 1 teaspoon oil, honey, and shrimp in a small bowl; toss to coat. Thread shrimp onto 4 (6-inch) skewers. Thread okra pods onto 4 (6-inch) skewers. Lightly coat shrimp, okra, and corn with cooking spray. Place shrimp, okra, and corn on grill rack coated with cooking spray. Grill corn 14 minutes, turning occasionally. Grill okra 4 minutes on each side. Grill shrimp 3 minutes on each side or until done. Cut corn crosswise into 8 pieces.
4. Place tomatoes on a large platter; sprinkle with ¼ teaspoon salt and ¼ teaspoon pepper. Arrange shrimp, okra, and corn over tomatoes. Drizzle with dressing; sprinkle with 1 tablespoon chives, ¼ teaspoon salt, and ¼ teaspoon pepper. Serves 4 (serving size: 4 shrimp, 5 okra pods, 3 tomato slices, 2 corn pieces, and about 2 tablespoons dressing)

CALORIES 262; **FAT** 12.7g (sat 3g, mono 7.5g, poly 2.1g); **PROTEIN** 19g; **CARB** 20g; **FIBER** 4g; **CHOL** 144mg; **IRON** 1mg; **SODIUM** 609mg; **CALC** 135mg

Herbaceous Grilled Pork Tenderloin

Hands-on: 15 min. Total: 45 min.

3 tablespoons chopped fresh chives
1 tablespoon chopped fresh thyme
2 tablespoons fresh lemon juice
2 tablespoons olive oil
1 teaspoon chopped fresh rosemary
1 teaspoon black pepper
1 (1-pound) pork tenderloin, trimmed
¹⁄₂ teaspoon kosher salt
Cooking spray

1. Preheat grill to medium-high heat.
2. Combine first 6 ingredients in a large zip-top plastic bag. Add pork to bag, turning to coat well. Let stand at room temperature 20 minutes.
3. Remove pork from bag, and discard marinade. Sprinkle pork evenly with salt. Place pork on grill rack coated with cooking spray, and grill 20 minutes or until a thermometer registers 140°. Remove pork from grill, and let stand 5 minutes. Thinly slice the pork. Serves 4 (serving size: about 3 ounces pork)

CALORIES 144; **FAT** 4.6g (sat 1g, mono 2.1g, poly 0.6g); **PROTEIN** 24g; **CARB** 0g; **FIBER** 0g; **CHOL** 74mg; **IRON** 1mg; **SODIUM** 300mg; **CALC** 8mg

Jerk Chicken with Grilled Pineapple Salsa

Hands-on: 37 min. Total: 1 hr. 57 min.
Traditional jerk recipes have you marinate the meat for a day or more. Here, just an hour-long marinade lends huge flavor to the chicken.

1¹⁄₃ cups sliced green onions, divided
3 tablespoons fresh lime juice, divided
2¹⁄₂ tablespoons olive oil, divided
2 tablespoons dark brown sugar
1 tablespoon thyme leaves
1 tablespoon lower-sodium soy sauce
1 tablespoon minced peeled fresh ginger
1¹⁄₄ teaspoons ground allspice
¹⁄₂ teaspoon freshly ground black pepper
3 garlic cloves, crushed
2 bay leaves, finely crumbled
1 small habanero pepper, chopped
4 (6-ounce) skinless, boneless chicken breast halves
2 (1-inch) slices fresh pineapple
Cooking spray
¹⁄₂ cup diced red bell pepper
³⁄₄ teaspoon kosher salt, divided

1. Place 1 cup sliced onions, 2 tablespoons lime juice, 2 tablespoons olive oil, sugar, and next 8 ingredients (through habanero pepper) in a mini food processor; process until almost smooth. Pour mixture into a large zip-top plastic bag. Add chicken to bag; seal bag. Marinate in refrigerator 1 hour, turning occasionally.
2. Preheat grill to medium-high heat.
3. Remove chicken from bag; discard marinade. Let chicken stand at room temperature 20 minutes.
4. Place pineapple on grill rack coated with cooking spray; grill pineapple 6 minutes, turning once. Cool 5 minutes. Chop pineapple; place in a medium bowl. Add ¹⁄₃ cup onions, 1 tablespoon lime juice, 1¹⁄₂ teaspoons oil, bell pepper, and ¹⁄₄ teaspoon salt; toss to combine.
5. Sprinkle chicken with ¹⁄₂ teaspoon salt. Place chicken on grill rack; grill chicken 5 minutes on each side or until done. Remove chicken from grill; let stand 5 minutes. Cut chicken into slices. Serve with pineapple salsa. Serves 4 (serving size: 1 breast half and about ¹⁄₄ cup salsa)

CALORIES 268; **FAT** 8.1g (sat 1.5g, mono 3.8g, poly 1.1g); **PROTEIN** 37g; **CARB** 11g; **FIBER** 2g; **CHOL** 109mg; **IRON** 1mg; **SODIUM** 595mg; **CALC** 33mg

SUPERFAST 20 MINUTE COOKING

Quick & Easy • Gluten Free

Crab and Heirloom Tomato Salad

¹⁄₃ cup cilantro leaves
4 mini sweet bell peppers, thinly diagonally sliced
1 large shallot, thinly sliced
1 jalapeño pepper, thinly diagonally sliced
12 ounces jumbo lump crabmeat, shell pieces removed
2¹⁄₂ tablespoons canola mayonnaise
1 teaspoon grated lime rind
1 tablespoon fresh lime juice
2 pounds heirloom tomatoes, sliced
1¹⁄₂ tablespoons extra-virgin olive oil
¹⁄₄ teaspoon kosher salt
¹⁄₄ teaspoon freshly ground black pepper
¹⁄₄ cup small basil leaves

1. Combine first 5 ingredients in a large bowl. Combine mayonnaise, rind, and juice in a small bowl, stirring with a whisk. Add mayonnaise mixture to crab mixture; toss gently to coat. Arrange tomatoes on a serving platter; drizzle with oil. Sprinkle tomatoes with salt and pepper. Mound crab mixture over tomatoes. Sprinkle with basil leaves. Serves 4 (serving size: ³⁄₄ cup crab mixture and about one-fourth tomato salad)

CALORIES 200; **FAT** 8.6g (sat 1g, mono 5.3g, poly 1.9g); **PROTEIN** 18g; **CARB** 13g; **FIBER** 4g; **CHOL** 83mg; **IRON** 1mg; **SODIUM** 536mg; **CALC** 109mg

Kid Friendly • Quick & Easy
Make Ahead

Greek-Style Chicken Wraps

(pictured on page 228)

Look for plain rotisserie chicken in the deli section of your supermarket. Use the breast meat for pastas and sandwiches, and the leg and thigh meat for salads, soups, or tacos.

1 cup grape tomatoes, halved
3 tablespoons pitted kalamata olives, coarsely chopped
2 tablespoons crumbled feta cheese
1¹⁄₂ tablespoons fresh lemon juice
1 tablespoon chopped fresh oregano
1 tablespoon olive oil
¹⁄₈ teaspoon ground red pepper
4 ounces shredded skinless, boneless rotisserie chicken breast (about 1 cup)
2 Kirby or small cucumbers, chopped
6 tablespoons plain hummus
6 (8-inch) whole-wheat flour tortillas

1. Place tomatoes, olives, feta, juice, oregano, oil, pepper, chicken, and cucumber in a large bowl; toss to combine. Spread 1 tablespoon hummus over 1 side of each tortilla. Top each tortilla with about ¹⁄₂ cup chicken mixture. Roll up wraps; cut in half. Serves 6 (serving size: 1 wrap)

CALORIES 237; **FAT** 9.9g (sat 2.3g, mono 5g, poly 2.4g); **PROTEIN** 12g; **CARB** 27g; **FIBER** 5g; **CHOL** 20mg; **IRON** 1mg; **SODIUM** 556mg; **CALC** 40mg

Creamy Blueberry Chicken Salad

Red onion and celery add crunch to this quick chicken salad. Blueberries have thick skins, so they won't break apart when tossed with the chicken.

1/2 cup thinly vertically sliced red
   onion
1/3 cup diced celery
1/4 cup torn fresh basil
12 ounces shredded skinless, boneless
   rotisserie chicken (about 3 cups)
1/2 teaspoon kosher salt, divided
1/2 cup plain 2% reduced-fat Greek
   yogurt
2 1/2 tablespoons fresh lemon juice,
   divided
1 tablespoon honey
2 cups fresh blueberries
1 (5-ounce) package baby arugula
2 teaspoons extra-virgin olive oil
1/4 teaspoon freshly ground black
   pepper

1. Combine first 4 ingredients in a medium bowl; sprinkle with 1/4 teaspoon salt. Combine yogurt, 1 tablespoon lemon juice, and honey in a small bowl, stirring with a whisk. Add yogurt mixture to chicken mixture; toss to coat. Gently stir in blueberries. Place arugula, 1 1/2 tablespoons lemon juice, oil, 1/4 teaspoon salt, and pepper in a bowl; toss to coat. Divide arugula mixture evenly among 6 plates; top each serving with about 3/4 cup chicken mixture. Serves 6

CALORIES 188; **FAT** 8.5g (sat 2.1g, mono 3.9g, poly 1.3g); **PROTEIN** 16g; **CARB** 13g; **FIBER** 2g; **CHOL** 75mg; **IRON** 1mg; **SODIUM** 369mg; **CALC** 69mg

Tangy Tomato-Basil Soup

3/4 cup fat-free buttermilk
1/4 cup basil leaves
2 tablespoons extra-virgin olive oil
2 tablespoons fresh lemon juice
1 tablespoon sugar
5/8 teaspoon kosher salt
1/4 teaspoon freshly ground black
   pepper
3 medium ripe red beefsteak
   tomatoes, cored and quartered
2 green onions, chopped
1 garlic clove
2 tablespoons plain 2% reduced-fat
   Greek yogurt
Basil leaves

1. Place first 10 ingredients in a blender; blend until smooth.
2. Place 3/4 cup soup in each of 6 bowls. Top evenly with yogurt and basil leaves. Serves 6

CALORIES 78; **FAT** 4.8g (sat 0.7g, mono 3.3g, poly 0.5g); **PROTEIN** 2g; **CARB** 7g; **FIBER** 1g; **CHOL** 1mg; **IRON** 0mg; **SODIUM** 236mg; **CALC** 55mg

Middle Eastern:
Omit basil, sugar, and red tomatoes. Add 1/2 cup cilantro, 1/4 teaspoon ground cumin, 2 seeded yellow bell peppers, and 3 large yellow beefsteak tomatoes, quartered, to mixture in blender. Blend until smooth. Combine yogurt, 3 tablespoons plain hummus, and 1 tablespoon water. Top each serving with yogurt mixture and cilantro leaves. Serves 6

CALORIES 94; **FAT** 5.6g (sat 0.8g); **SODIUM** 266mg

Berry-Balsamic:
Omit lemon juice, green onions, and garlic. Increase pepper to 3/4 teaspoon. Add 2 tablespoons white balsamic vinegar and 1 cup quartered strawberries to mixture in blender. Blend until very smooth. Top each serving

with 1 teaspoon yogurt, 1 tablespoon sliced strawberries, and cracked black pepper. Serves 6

CALORIES 91; **FAT** 4.8g (sat 0.7g); **SODIUM** 236mg

Tomato-Melon:
Omit basil, red tomatoes, green onion, and garlic. Add 2 cups cubed honeydew melon, 1/2 cup fresh mint leaves, and 3 large yellow beefsteak tomatoes, quartered, to mixture in blender. Blend until very smooth. Top each serving with 1 teaspoon yogurt, 1 tablespoon diced honeydew melon, and fresh mint leaves. Serves 6

CALORIES 99; **FAT** 4.8g (sat 0.7g); **SODIUM** 247mg

Almond-Date Bars

Marcona almonds are blanched and roasted—you won't need to toast them. You can also substitute regular whole almonds. For the best texture, use whole pitted dates, not chopped; you need the sticky texture of the whole fruit.

1 cup Marcona almonds
1 1/4 cups pitted dates (about 15)
3/4 cup dried apples (about 2 ounces)
1/4 cup flaked sweetened coconut
1 tablespoon honey
1/8 teaspoon kosher salt
3/4 cup crispy rice cereal
Cooking spray

1. Place first 6 ingredients in the bowl of a food processor; process until finely chopped. Add cereal; pulse to combine. Press date mixture into bottom of an 8-inch square glass or ceramic baking dish coated with cooking spray. Cut into 12 pieces. Serves 12 (serving size: 1 bar)

CALORIES 142; **FAT** 6.3g (sat 1g, mono 3.7g, poly 1.5g); **PROTEIN** 3g; **CARB** 22g; **FIBER** 3g; **CHOL** 0mg; **IRON** 1mg; **SODIUM** 76mg; **CALC** 36mg

Kale and Beet Salad with Blue Cheese and Walnuts

A bag of baby kale leaves saves the time of washing, stemming, and chopping larger leaves. Treat these small, tender leaves like baby spinach—as the base for salads or stirred into soups and stews at the end.

1 cup torn mint leaves
¹/₃ cup thinly vertically sliced red onion
1 (6-ounce) package baby kale
¹/₄ cup plain 2% reduced-fat Greek yogurt
2 tablespoons fat-free buttermilk
2 teaspoons white wine vinegar
1¹/₂ teaspoons extra-virgin olive oil
¹/₄ teaspoon kosher salt
¹/₄ teaspoon freshly ground black pepper
4 hard-cooked large eggs, quartered lengthwise
1 (8-ounce) package peeled and steamed baby beets, quartered (such as Melissa's)
¹/₂ cup coarsely chopped walnuts
2 ounces blue cheese, crumbled (about ¹/₂ cup)

1. Combine mint, onion, and kale in a large bowl. Combine yogurt, buttermilk, vinegar, oil, salt, and pepper in a bowl, stirring with a whisk. Drizzle yogurt mixture over kale mixture; toss gently to coat. Arrange eggs and beets over salad; sprinkle with nuts and cheese. Serves 6 (serving size: 1½ cups)

CALORIES 202; **FAT** 14.2g (sat 3.8g, mono 3.8g, poly 5.4g); **PROTEIN** 10g; **CARB** 11g; **FIBER** 2g; **CHOL** 132mg; **IRON** 1mg; **SODIUM** 287mg; **CALC** 139mg

Kale, Quinoa, and Cherry Salad

Use leftover quinoa-rice blend for fried rice, or stir into soup.

3 tablespoons extra-virgin olive oil
3 tablespoons cider vinegar
1 tablespoon honey
2 teaspoons Dijon mustard
¹/₄ teaspoon freshly-ground black pepper
¹/₄ teaspoon kosher salt
1¹/₂ (6-ounce) packages baby kale
1¹/₂ (8.5-ounce) packages precooked quinoa and brown rice blend (such as Seeds of Change)
³/₄ cup fresh sweet cherries, pitted and halved
²/₃ cup chopped fresh flat-leaf parsley
¹/₃ cup thinly sliced shallots
1 (15-ounce) can unsalted chickpeas, rinsed and drained
2 ounces goat cheese, crumbled (about ¹/₂ cup)

1. Combine first 6 ingredients in a medium bowl. Combine 1½ tablespoons oil mixture and kale. Place kale mixture on a platter. Stir quinoa blend, cherries, parsley, shallots, and chickpeas into remaining oil mixture. Top kale mixture with quinoa mixture and cheese. Serves 6 (serving size: about ⅔ cup kale mixture, ⅔ cup quinoa mixture, and about 1 tablespoon cheese)

CALORIES 296; **FAT** 11.8g (sat 3.2g, mono 5.6g, poly 0.9g); **PROTEIN** 9g; **CARB** 40g; **FIBER** 5g; **CHOL** 7mg; **IRON** 3mg; **SODIUM** 369mg; **CALC** 135mg

Tomato and Prosciutto Sandwiches with Pea Pesto

Toast the leftover torn bread from the baguette for breadcrumbs (which you can freeze), or add to the tomato soups on page 196 for a slightly thicker soup.

1 cup frozen peas, thawed
¹/₄ cup mint leaves
2 tablespoons water
1 tablespoon extra-virgin olive oil
¹/₂ teaspoon freshly ground black pepper, divided
¹/₄ teaspoon kosher salt, divided
1 (8-ounce) French bread baguette, halved lengthwise
2 ounces thinly sliced prosciutto
¹/₂ cup very thinly sliced red onion
3 medium tomatoes, thinly sliced
2 ounces goat cheese, crumbled (about ¹/₂ cup)

1. Place peas, mint, 2 tablespoons water, oil, ¼ teaspoon pepper, and ⅛ teaspoon salt in the bowl of a food processor; process until smooth.
2. Hollow out bottom and top halves of bread, leaving a ¾-inch-thick shell; reserve torn bread for another use. Cut bread halves in half crosswise. Spread pea mixture evenly over cut sides of bread; top evenly with prosciutto, onion, and tomatoes. Sprinkle with ¼ teaspoon pepper, ⅛ teaspoon salt, and goat cheese. Serves 4 (serving size: 1 sandwich)

CALORIES 244; **FAT** 10g (sat 4.1g, mono 3.6g, poly 0.8g); **PROTEIN** 13g; **CARB** 26g; **FIBER** 4g; **CHOL** 19mg; **IRON** 2mg; **SODIUM** 760mg; **CALC** 80mg

TWO SIDES TO EVERY PEACH

Explore both sweet and savory recipes—and make the most of summer's fleeting, fragrant fruit.

With Alabama's peach capital, Chilton County, practically in our Test Kitchen's backyard, we have plenty of opportunity to find peaches that will be perfectly ripe. Notice the "will be." With peach cookery, you often have to buy a day or two ahead of when you want to serve. Even during the June-to-August peak season, we often find peaches at our local markets that are firm and not yet ready to yield their full succulence. This is because farmers pick the fruit before it fully softens: The skin and flesh are so delicate they would not survive the journey to market if boxed up when completely soft and ready to eat. So plan ahead. A firm peach can become perfectly ripe, although that's not guaranteed. To make sure, choose peaches that are already very aromatic and give slightly when gently pressed. Avoid those that are green and hard with no give. To get your peaches to perfection, place them in a single layer on a kitchen towel, and cover loosely with another towel; keep at room temperature for up to three days. Then store in the fridge. Whenever possible, buy local. Nonlocal and off-season peaches travel far and are more likely to have been picked before the sugars have developed. They will be pretty, and they will soften, but they will never increase in flavor or sweetness. These are fruits that break your heart and fall flat in recipes, that will never reach peachy ideal.

Quick & Easy • Gluten Free
Make Ahead

Bourbon-Peach Limeades
(pictured on page 230)

Hands-on: 10 min. Total: 30 min.
Freeze fresh peach and lime slices on a parchment-lined pan, and drop a few into your drink for a frosty garnish.

2¹/₂ cups water
²/₃ cup sugar
3 peeled peaches, chopped

1¹/₄ cups bourbon
1 cup fresh lime juice

1. Combine first 3 ingredients in a medium saucepan over medium-high heat; bring to a boil. Reduce heat, and simmer 10 minutes, stirring occasionally. Remove from heat; transfer to a bowl set over ice water, and cool to room temperature. Transfer peach mixture to a blender; process until smooth. Combine peach mixture, bourbon, and lime juice; serve over ice. Serves 8 (serving size: about ¾ cup)

CALORIES 175; **FAT** 0.2g (sat 0g, mono 0g, poly 0.1g); **PROTEIN** 1g; **CARB** 25g; **FIBER** 1g; **CHOL** 0mg; **IRON** 0mg; **SODIUM** 1mg; **CALC** 8mg

Quick & Easy • Gluten Free
Make Ahead • Vegetarian

Quick Pickled Peaches

Hands-on: 10 min. Total: 40 min.
These gorgeously spiced, tangy-sweet peaches make a fantastic addition to a summer relish tray, or serve them on pound cake or alongside grilled pork or chicken. Look for peaches that are still a little firm; they will soften some in the warm liquid. If you start with very ripe peaches, they may oversoften by the time they are finished pickling.

1¹/₂ cups cider vinegar
1¹/₂ cups water
1 cup sugar
1 tablespoon kosher salt
1 tablespoon crushed red pepper
2 teaspoons whole black peppercorns
6 whole cloves
1 (2-inch) cinnamon stick, broken into small pieces
4 large, slightly firm peeled peaches

1. Combine first 8 ingredients in a large saucepan; bring to a boil. Cook 2 minutes, stirring until sugar dissolves. Remove from heat; let stand 10 minutes. Cut each peach into 12 wedges. Add peaches to vinegar mixture; let stand 20 minutes. Remove peaches with a slotted spoon. Serves 8 (serving size: 6 wedges)

CALORIES 45; **FAT** 0.2g (sat 0g, mono 0.1g, poly 0.1g); **PROTEIN** 1g; **CARB** 11g; **FIBER** 1g; **CHOL** 0mg; **IRON** 0mg; **SODIUM** 72mg; **CALC** 6mg

SWEET:
A TANGY BRINE GETS PEACHES QUICKLY PICKLED FOR A SUMMER RELISH TRAY.

Peach Salad with Tomatoes and Beets

Hands-on: 25 min. Total: 1 hr. 15 min.
Golden beets and a mix of colorful tomatoes (like Purple Cherokee and red heirlooms) offer a dramatic contrast on the plate and are a beautiful and tasty base for the tangy-sweet peaches on top— but red beets and any garden tomatoes would also work.

2 medium-sized golden beets
2 medium-sized ripe tomatoes
³/₄ teaspoon kosher salt, divided
¹/₂ teaspoon freshly ground black pepper
3 tablespoons extra-virgin olive oil
2 tablespoons fresh lemon juice, divided
1 tablespoon honey
1 medium shallot, thinly sliced
3 medium peeled peaches, sliced
3 tablespoons small mint leaves
2 teaspoons thyme leaves
2 ounces goat cheese, crumbled (about ¹/₂ cup)

1. Preheat oven to 425°.
2. Scrub beets and trim tops to 1 inch. Place beets in a glass or ceramic baking dish; fill dish one-third full with water. Cover with foil; bake at 425° for 1 hour or until beets are tender. Cool. Peel beets, and cut into ¼-inch-thick slices. Core tomatoes; cut into ¼-inch-thick slices. Arrange beet and tomato slices on a platter; sprinkle with ½ teaspoon salt and pepper.
3. Combine ¼ teaspoon salt, oil, 1 tablespoon juice, honey, and shallot in a medium bowl. Toss peach slices with 1 tablespoon juice. Add peach mixture to honey mixture; toss. Mound peach mixture on top of beet and tomato slices; sprinkle salad with mint, thyme, and goat cheese.

Serves 8 (serving size: about 2 beet slices, 2 tomato slices, ½ cup peach mixture, and 1 tablespoon cheese)

CALORIES 112; FAT 6.8g (sat 1.8g, mono 4.1g, poly 0.7g); PROTEIN 3g; CARB 12g; FIBER 2g; CHOL 3mg; IRON 1mg; SODIUM 164mg; CALC 23mg

SAVORY: FRAGRANT PEACHES MINGLE WITH THE SALT OF CHÈVRE, THE BITE OF SHALLOT, THE FRAGRANCE OF MINT AND THYME.

Kid Friendly • Freezable
Make Ahead

No-Bake Peach Pie

Hands-on: 24 min. Total: 3 hr. 44 min.
This luscious dessert comes together easily and is the perfect ending to summer supper with friends. Use the softest and juiciest peaches you have, even slightly overripe fruit. For added peach oomph, chop some of the topping and stir it into the filling.

³/₄ cup graham cracker crumbs (about 5 cookie sheets)
¹/₄ teaspoon salt, divided
1 tablespoon unsalted butter
3¹/₂ ounces white chocolate, finely chopped
Cooking spray
5 ounces ¹/₃-less-fat cream cheese, softened
¹/₃ cup powdered sugar
¹/₂ teaspoon vanilla extract
2 cups frozen fat-free whipped topping, thawed
2 tablespoons seedless peach spread
1 tablespoon peach schnapps
¹/₂ teaspoon fresh lemon juice
3 medium peeled peaches, pitted and cut into ¹/₂-inch wedges

1. Place crumbs and ⅛ teaspoon salt in a food processor; process until combined. Place butter and chocolate in a microwave-safe bowl. Microwave at HIGH 30 seconds, stirring until chocolate is smooth. Add to processor; pulse until combined. Press mixture into bottom and up sides of a 9-inch pie plate coated with cooking spray. Freeze 20 minutes or until set.
2. Place cream cheese, sugar, and vanilla in a medium bowl; beat with a mixer at medium speed until smooth. Gently fold in whipped topping. Carefully spread filling over bottom of crust. Place peach spread in a large microwave-safe bowl; microwave at HIGH 30 seconds or until bubbly. Stir in ⅛ teaspoon salt, schnapps, and juice. Add peach wedges; toss to combine. Arrange peach wedges over pie. Chill 3 hours before serving. Serves 10 (serving size: 1 wedge)

CALORIES 195; FAT 8.3g (sat 4.6g, mono 2.3g, poly 1g); PROTEIN 3g; CARB 27g; FIBER 1g; CHOL 16mg; IRON 0mg; SODIUM 155mg; CALC 41mg

SWEET: A GORGEOUS PILE OF SYRUPY FRUIT TOPS A CREAMY CONCOCTION THAT FALLS SOME-WHERE BETWEEN DECADENT CHEESECAKE AND BILLOWY CHIFFON PIE.

Peaches-and-Cream Frozen Pops

(pictured on page 229)

Hands-on: 20 min. Total: 7 hr. 20 min.
Our version of the Creamsicle is silky, with distinct peachy flavor. It's a not-too-sweet pop that grown-ups will love but that's playful enough for all ages.

1/4 cup sugar
1 tablespoon corn syrup
1/2 teaspoon vanilla extract
1/4 teaspoon salt
3 large, slightly firm peeled peaches, chopped
1 tablespoon fresh lemon juice
1/3 cup heavy whipping cream

1. Combine first 5 ingredients in a medium saucepan over medium-high heat; bring to a boil. Reduce heat to medium, and simmer 5 minutes or until peaches are very tender, stirring frequently. Place peach mixture and lemon juice in a food processor; process until smooth. Refrigerate 1 hour. Stir in cream.
2. Divide peach mixture evenly among 8 (4-ounce) ice-pop molds. Top with lid, and insert a craft stick into center of each mold; freeze 6 hours or until thoroughly frozen. Serves 8 (serving size: 1 pop)

CALORIES 93; **FAT** 3.9g (sat 2.3g, mono 1.1g, poly 0.2g); **PROTEIN** 1g; **CARB** 15g; **FIBER** 1g; **CHOL** 14mg; **IRON** 0mg; **SODIUM** 79mg; **CALC** 11mg

SAVORY:
THE CLASSIC HAM AND FRUIT COMBO, BUT WITH PEACHES SUBBED FOR MELON

Peach and Prosciutto Canapés

Hands-on: 22 min. Total: 22 min.
Make-ahead tip: Toast the baguette slices and combine the cheese mixture well in advance, but assemble just before serving.

1 (6-ounce) French bread baguette, cut diagonally into 16 slices
Cooking spray
2 tablespoons mascarpone cheese
2 teaspoons finely minced shallots
1/4 teaspoon grated lemon rind
1 ounce fat-free cream cheese, softened
1 1/2 tablespoons coarsely chopped fresh basil, divided
1 large ripe peach, cut into 16 wedges
1 ounce prosciutto, cut into 16 thin slices

1. Preheat broiler to high.
2. Lightly coat bread slices with cooking spray; broil 2 minutes on each side or until toasted. Combine mascarpone and next 3 ingredients in a small bowl. Stir in 1 tablespoon basil. Spread cheese mixture evenly among bread slices.
3. Wrap each peach wedge with 1 prosciutto piece. Top each bread slice with 1 wrapped peach wedge. Sprinkle with 1 1/2 teaspoons basil. Serve immediately. Serves 8 (serving size: 2 canapés)

CALORIES 104; **FAT** 3.7g (sat 1.9g, mono 0.2g, poly 0.1g); **PROTEIN** 4g; **CARB** 15g; **FIBER** 1g; **CHOL** 11mg; **IRON** 1mg; **SODIUM** 220mg; **CALC** 24mg

Sautéed Black Grouper with Peach Relish

Hands-on: 20 min. Total: 20 min.
Black grouper, a mild white-fleshed fish, comes from the Gulf of Mexico and is a sustainable seafood choice, but not all kinds of grouper are. If you can't find black grouper, you can substitute sustainably caught halibut, cod, or salmon.

4 (6-ounce) black grouper fillets
1/2 teaspoon kosher salt, divided
1/4 teaspoon freshly ground black pepper
1 1/2 tablespoons canola oil
1/3 cup thinly sliced radishes
2 tablespoons chopped fresh chives
2 ripe peaches, peeled and cut into 1/2-inch chunks
1 serrano chile, thinly sliced
2 tablespoons extra-virgin olive oil
1 tablespoon fresh lime juice
2 teaspoons honey

1. Heat a large skillet over medium-high heat. Sprinkle both sides of fish evenly with 1/4 teaspoon salt and pepper. Add canola oil to pan; swirl to coat. Add fish to pan; sauté 4 minutes or until golden. Turn fish over; sauté 2 minutes or until desired degree of doneness.
2. Combine radishes and next 3 ingredients in a medium bowl. Combine 1/4 teaspoon salt, olive oil, juice, and honey in a small bowl, stirring with a whisk. Drizzle dressing over peach mixture; toss gently. Serve relish with fish. Serves 4 (serving size: 1 fillet and about 1/2 cup relish)

CALORIES 290; **FAT** 13.8g (sat 1.7g, mono 8.6g, poly 2.8g); **PROTEIN** 32g; **CARB** 8g; **FIBER** 1g; **CHOL** 60mg; **IRON** 2mg; **SODIUM** 312mg; **CALC** 35mg

UPSIDE-DOWN AND GLUTEN-FREE

Fresh pineapple, caramelized in its own juices, sits atop a tender base.

Upside-down cake is one of the happiest desserts in America—that classic brown sugar–soaked mosaic of canned pineapple rings and maraschino cherries set atop an all-butter yellow cake, the whole package densely glazed in rich, buttery-sweet caramel. It's a bit less smile-inducing, though, when you tally up 700 sugar-loaded calories and 10g sat fat in a generous slice. We decided to develop a cake that's not only lighter in calories but also gluten-free.

Cakes made without gluten are notoriously dense (in wheat-flour cakes, this magic protein inflates like a hot-air balloon, yielding the fluffy and light texture that's so prized). To create the right crumb, structure, and flavor, you can't just sub in a gluten-free flour from one source; you need a blend of flours, plus added starches. We default to King Arthur Flour's multipurpose gluten-free flour, whose well-tested blend yields fluffy results. For a hint of nuttiness, we add a little almond flour to the mix, too.

Half the butter in the batter is replaced with heart-healthy canola oil, which is whisked with light sour cream until fluffy to create a moist, tender result. Canned pineapple gets swapped for fresh, and instead of drowning it in glaze, we caramelize the fruit in its own juices, using half the amount of butter and brown sugar called for in the original. A vanilla bean and a splash of rum add richness. This cake is delicate, moist, and tender, delivering all those happy upside-down pleasures—with a lot less heft.

Kid Friendly • Gluten Free
Make Ahead

Gluten-Free Caramelized Pineapple Upside-Down Cake

OURS SAVES
446 calories, 10g total fat, and 5.6g saturated fat over classic pineapple upside-down cake

Hands-on: 29 min. Total: 1 hr. 25 min.

½ cup packed brown sugar
¼ cup unsalted butter, divided
1 vanilla bean, split lengthwise
6 (½-inch-thick) slices fresh pineapple
¼ cup dark rum
Cooking spray
5 ounces gluten-free multipurpose flour (such as King Arthur Flour; about 1 cup)
¼ cup almond flour
½ teaspoon baking powder
½ teaspoon kosher salt
¼ teaspoon baking soda
½ cup light sour cream
2 tablespoons canola oil
⅔ cup granulated sugar
2 large eggs

1. Preheat oven to 350°.
2. Combine brown sugar, 2 tablespoons butter, and vanilla bean in a large skillet over medium heat; cook 6 minutes or until butter melts and sugar dissolves, stirring frequently. Add pineapple in a single layer. Carefully pour rum over pineapple; tilt pan to ignite. Simmer 5 minutes on each side or until slightly tender and caramelized. Remove vanilla bean.
3. Coat a 9-inch cake pan with cooking spray. Arrange pineapple in a single layer in bottom of pan; pour sugar mixture over pineapple, tilting pan to coat bottom evenly.
4. Weigh or lightly spoon multipurpose flour into a dry measuring cup; level with a knife. Combine multipurpose flour, almond flour, baking powder, salt, and baking soda; stir with a whisk. Melt 2 tablespoons butter in a microwave-safe dish at HIGH 35 seconds. Place melted butter, sour cream, and oil in a bowl, stirring well with a whisk until fluffy.
5. Place granulated sugar and eggs in a large bowl; beat with a mixer at high speed 5 minutes or until fluffy. Reduce speed to medium. Add flour mixture and sour cream mixture alternately to egg mixture, beginning and ending with flour mixture. Spoon batter over pineapple, spreading evenly. Bake at 350° for 38 minutes or until a wooden pick inserted in center comes out clean. Cool in pan 15 minutes on a wire rack. Loosen cake from edges of pan with a knife; invert onto a plate. Serves 10 (serving size: 1 wedge)

CALORIES 292; FAT 11.2g (sat 4.4g, mono 3.7g, poly 1.2g); PROTEIN 4g; CARB 44g; FIBER 1g; CHOL 54mg; IRON 1mg; SODIUM 177mg; CALC 87mg

THE RUM WILL IGNITE WHEN YOU TILT THE PAN; THIS BURNS OFF THE ALCOHOL.

FEED 4 FOR LESS THAN $10

Sweet caramelized onions form a creamy pizza "sauce." Intense spices make chicken kickin'.

**Make Ahead
Vegetarian**

$2.23
PER
SERVING

Caramelized Onion and Olive Pizza with Goat Cheese

Hands-on: 35 min. Total: 59 min.
Peppery arugula dressed with lemon vinaigrette complements this rich pizza. Toss 4 cups arugula, 1 cup rinsed and drained unsalted canned chickpeas, and 1 shaved carrot with 1 tablespoon extra-virgin olive oil, 1 1/2 tablespoons fresh lemon juice, and 1/8 teaspoon each of salt and pepper.

**12 ounces refrigerated fresh pizza
    dough
4 teaspoons olive oil, divided
2 cups vertically sliced yellow onion
1 cup vertically sliced red onion
1 cup vertically sliced white onion
2 tablespoons thinly sliced garlic
3/4 teaspoon dried thyme
1 tablespoon white wine vinegar
1 1/2 ounces Castelvetrano olives,
    chopped
1 1/2 ounces goat cheese, crumbled
1/2 teaspoon freshly ground black
    pepper
1/8 teaspoon kosher salt**

1. Place a pizza stone or heavy baking sheet in oven. Preheat oven to 450° (keep pizza stone or baking sheet in oven as it preheats).

2. Let dough stand at room temperature 30 minutes.
3. While dough stands, heat a large nonstick skillet over medium-low heat. Add 2 teaspoons oil; swirl to coat. Add onions, garlic, and thyme; cook 25 minutes or until onions are very soft and browned, stirring occasionally. Stir in vinegar.
4. Place dough on a floured surface; roll into a 14-inch circle. Pierce entire surface liberally with a fork. Remove pizza stone from oven. Place dough on pizza stone. Spread 2 teaspoons oil over dough. Spread onion mixture and olives evenly over dough. Sprinkle with cheese, pepper, and salt. Bake at 450° for 15 minutes or until crust is browned. Cut into 8 slices. Serves 4 (serving size: 2 slices)

CALORIES 363; **FAT** 11.1g (sat 2.9g, mono 4.9g, poly 1g);
PROTEIN 11g; **CARB** 52g; **FIBER** 8g; **CHOL** 8mg;
IRON 2mg; **SODIUM** 697mg; **CALC** 71mg

Make Ahead

$2.49
PER
SERVING

Spiced Chicken Thighs and Parsley Couscous

Hands-on: 30 min. Total: 55 min. Sip on a cool glass of ginger lemonade for just 32 cents per serving: Bring 4 cups water and 1/3 cup sliced fresh ginger to a boil in a medium saucepan; remove from heat. Steep 30 minutes. Strain; discard solids. Mix the liquid with the juice of 2 large lemons and 3 tablespoons honey. Serve over ice.

**2 teaspoons ground cumin
2 teaspoons brown sugar
1 teaspoon chili powder
1 teaspoon ground ginger
3/4 teaspoon kosher salt, divided
1/2 teaspoon crushed red pepper
1/2 teaspoon grated lemon rind
1/4 teaspoon black pepper**

**8 bone-in chicken thighs, trimmed
    and skinned (about 2 1/2 pounds)
1 1/2 tablespoons canola oil, divided
2/3 cup uncooked couscous
2 teaspoons minced fresh garlic
3/4 cup unsalted chicken stock
1/4 cup chopped fresh flat-leaf parsley
1 tablespoon fresh lemon juice**

1. Preheat oven to 425°.
2. Combine cumin, sugar, chili powder, ginger, 1/2 teaspoon salt, red pepper, lemon rind, and black pepper in a small bowl; rub spice mixture over both sides of chicken. Heat a large ovenproof skillet or cast-iron pan over medium-high heat. Add 1 tablespoon oil to pan; swirl to coat. Add chicken to pan, placing it skin side down; cook 5 minutes on each side or until chicken is browned. (If necessary, work in batches to avoid overcrowding the pan.) Transfer pan to oven. Bake chicken at 425° for 14 minutes or until done. Remove chicken from pan; let stand 10 minutes before serving.
3. While chicken rests, heat a small saucepan over medium-high heat. Add 1 1/2 teaspoons oil to pan; swirl to coat. Add couscous and garlic to pan; cook 2 minutes or until toasted and fragrant, stirring frequently. Carefully stir in 1/4 teaspoon salt and chicken stock. Bring liquid to a boil. Remove from heat; cover and let stand 4 minutes (avoid opening the lid). Fluff couscous with a fork, and stir in parsley and lemon juice. Serves 4 (serving size: 2 thighs and about 1/2 cup couscous)

CALORIES 468; **FAT** 19.3g (sat 4.2g, mono 8.9g, poly 4.3g);
PROTEIN 44g; **CARB** 27g; **FIBER** 2g; **CHOL** 219mg;
IRON 3mg; **SODIUM** 544mg; **CALC** 48mg

THE SECRETS OF A TENNESSEE PICKLE PREACHER

Shannon Walker, the chief preservationist and beekeeper at Blackberry Farm in East Tennessee, visits the *Cooking Light* garden to share his simple, delicious techniques.

Shannon Walker's pickles have a muted, juicy sweetness and elusive complexity of flavor. White balsamic vinegar is one of the secret ingredients that make his pickles so memorably delicious. According to Walker, plain white vinegar, a common choice for pickles (which require a certain pH level), "can be harsh and really bring some heat" to the product. In his pickling kitchen, armed with a pH meter, Walker tested lots of vinegars before settling on white balsamic, which has the acid to do the job but also "has that slight bit of sweetness that really makes a great base for pickling." It's used in three of his recipes here.

Southern food traditions are rich with pickling, canning, curing, all sorts of "putting up." Walker recalls, as a child, pulling strings from beans, slicing cucumbers—"whatever Granny had for you to do"—in preparation for pickling and canning. "You don't see that much anymore, where you have three generations of people sitting around with a common goal in mind," he says. But those are some of his fondest memories from childhood, and he'd love for this sort of thing, or some version of it, to come back. Certainly the boom in farmers' markets and gardens (urban and backyard) points in the pickling direction. Every summer brings more glorious things to put up: multicolored beets, tender okra pods, graceful pole beans, thin-skinned cucumbers.

Even if you don't have three generations on hand, you can take a haul of local produce and host a pickling party with friends, using a pitch-in and take-home model: They help with prep and canning, everyone enjoys a meal at the end, and everyone gets a few jars of goodies to take home.

Be not afraid of the canning process. It's easy to master the basic safety principles (see page 205). Then, Walker says, "just have fun with it." Begin with recipes; follow with experiments. Few are the fruits and vegetables he would not try to pickle.

Bottom line: Pickling falls somewhere between a project and play, and here's a new-timey way to get in the mood for old-timey cooking: a pickling party playlist. Walker suggests downloading the song "Pickles" by the Gourds for inspiration. Then just pile on your favorite high-spirited tunes.

Kid Friendly • Gluten Free
Make Ahead • Vegetarian

Dilly Beans

Hands-on: 30 min. Total: 3 weeks
These addictively crunchy sticks would make a mighty fine Bloody Mary garnish. Wide-mouth jars are your friend here. When placing beans into jars, try squeezing them into a tight bunch before pushing them down inside.

4 cups white balsamic vinegar
3 cups water
1 tablespoon salt
1 tablespoon dill seeds
6 garlic cloves
3 pounds wax or green beans, trimmed
18 fresh dill sprigs

1. Combine vinegar, 3 cups water, and salt in a medium saucepan; bring to a boil.
2. Place ½ teaspoon dill seeds and 1 garlic clove in each of 6 (1-pint) hot sterilized jars. Divide beans and dill sprigs among jars.
3. Divide hot vinegar mixture among jars, filling to ½ inch from top. Remove air bubbles; wipe jar rims. Cover with metal lids; screw on bands.
4. Process in boiling-water bath 5 minutes. Remove jars from water bath; cool completely, and check for proper seal (see page 205). For best flavor, allow 3 weeks before eating. Store in a cool, dark place up to 1 year. Serves 24 (serving size: about 12 beans)

CALORIES 31; FAT 0.1g (sat 0g, mono 0g, poly 0.1g); PROTEIN 1g; CARB 7g; FIBER 2g; CHOL 0mg; IRON 1mg; SODIUM 77mg; CALC 21mg

Dill Pickle Spears

Hands-on: 50 min. Total: 2 weeks
Considering that the average supermarket dill pickle spears contain 313mg sodium each, these are downright saintly, with only 193mg in 4 spears.

2 gallons water
1/2 cup pickling salt
40 pickling cucumbers, quartered lengthwise (about 8 pounds)
1/2 cup mustard seeds
24 fresh dill sprigs
6 garlic cloves, halved
1 1/2 quarts white vinegar
4 cups water
1/4 cup sugar
2 tablespoons pickling spice

1. Combine 2 gallons water and salt in a large container, stirring with a whisk until salt dissolves. Add cucumbers; let stand at room temperature 12 hours.
2. Place 2 teaspoons mustard seeds, 2 dill sprigs, and 1 garlic clove half in each of 12 (1-pint) hot sterilized jars. Drain cucumbers; divide among jars.
3. Combine vinegar, 4 cups water, sugar, and pickling spice in a large saucepan. Bring to a boil; cook 10 minutes. Divide hot vinegar mixture evenly among jars, filling to 1/2 inch from top. Remove air bubbles; wipe jar rims. Cover with metal lids; screw on bands.
4. Process in boiling-water bath 20 minutes. Remove jars from water bath; cool completely, and check for proper seal (see page 205). For best flavor, allow 2 weeks before eating. Store pickles in a cool, dark place for up to 1 year. Serves 40 (serving size: 4 spears)

CALORIES 15; FAT 0.1g (sat 0.1g, mono 0g, poly 0g); PROTEIN 1g; CARB 4g; FIBER 0g; CHOL 0mg; IRON 0mg; SODIUM 193mg; CALC 15mg

Spiced Pickled Beets

Hands-on: 50 min. Total: 2 weeks
What a sweet addition to a summer veggie plate! Any kind of beets will work; we used golden ones for their lovely color. Although we love the softer flavor of white balsamic vinegar, you can also make this using 2 1/2 cups water mixed with 2 1/2 cups cider vinegar.

18 (2 1/2-inch-wide) whole beets (about 5 pounds)
5 cups white balsamic vinegar
2 cups sugar
1 tablespoon salt
10 whole cloves
2 (3-inch) cinnamon sticks

1. Leave root and 1-inch stem on beets; scrub with a brush. Place beets in a large Dutch oven; cover with water. Bring to a boil; reduce heat, and simmer 15 minutes or until almost tender. Drain beets; cover with cool water. When beets are cool enough to handle, drain. Trim off beet roots; rub off skins. Cut beets lengthwise into quarters.
2. Combine vinegar and remaining ingredients in Dutch oven. Bring to a boil; reduce heat, and simmer 10 minutes. Discard spices.
3. Divide beets evenly among 6 (1-pint) hot sterilized jars. Divide hot vinegar mixture evenly among jars, filling to 1/2 inch from top. Remove air bubbles; wipe jar rims. Cover with metal lids; screw on bands.
4. Process in boiling-water bath 15 minutes. Remove jars from water bath; cool completely, and check for proper seal (see page 205). For best flavor, allow 2 weeks before eating. Store in a cool, dark place up to 1 year. Serves 24 (serving size: 3 pieces)

CALORIES 74; FAT 0.2g (sat 0g, mono 0g, poly 0.1g); PROTEIN 2g; CARB 17g; FIBER 3g; CHOL 0mg; IRON 1mg; SODIUM 148mg; CALC 15mg

Chowchow

Hands-on: 60 min. Total: 1 week *Serve this crunchy-sweet-tangy relish on burgers or hot dogs, on a pile of black-eyed peas, in deviled eggs, or over steaks or grilled fish.*

20 cups chopped green cabbage (about 4 pounds)
2 cups chopped yellow squash
2 cups chopped zucchini
1 1/2 cups chopped onion
1 1/4 cups chopped green bell pepper
1 1/4 cups chopped red bell pepper
1/4 cup kosher salt
2 cups cider vinegar
1 1/2 cups rice wine vinegar
1 1/4 cups sugar
1 1/2 tablespoons mustard seeds
2 teaspoons celery seeds, toasted
2 teaspoons dry mustard
1/2 teaspoon ground ginger
1/4 teaspoon turmeric

1. Combine first 7 ingredients; toss to coat with salt. Place mixture in a large colander. Place colander in sink; drain 3 hours.
2. Combine cider vinegar and remaining ingredients in a large Dutch oven; bring to a boil. Gradually add vegetables, one handful at a time; cook 10 minutes or until cabbage just begins to wilt. Using a slotted spoon, divide hot cabbage mixture among 7 (1-pint) hot sterilized jars. Divide hot vinegar mixture among jars, filling to 1/2 inch from top. Remove air bubbles; wipe jar rims. Cover with metal lids; screw on bands.
3. Process in boiling-water bath 15 minutes. Remove from water bath; cool completely, and check for proper seal (see page 205). For best flavor, allow 1 week before eating. Store in a cool, dark place for up to 1 year. Serves 40 (serving size: about 1/3 cup)

CALORIES 27; FAT 0.1g (sat 0.1g, mono 0g, poly 0g); PROTEIN 1g; CARB 6g; FIBER 2g; CHOL 0mg; IRON 0mg; SODIUM 196mg; CALC 23mg

Refrigerator Pickled Blackberries

Hands-on: 35 min. Total: 8 hr. 35 min.
Because heat processing might damage the fragile berries, we skip the canning method and instead make what's called refrigerator pickles; they're not shelf-stable like the other pickles in this story, but they'll keep in the fridge for two weeks. The glistening jewels would be incredible as a sauce for duck breast, as part of a cheese platter, spooned onto ricotta-topped crostini, draped over yogurt, or plopped into cocktails.

3 cups white balsamic vinegar
2 whole cloves
2 (3-inch) cinnamon sticks
1 gallon fresh blackberries
2 cups honey

1. Combine first 3 ingredients in a Dutch oven; bring to a boil. Cover; reduce heat, and simmer 10 minutes. Remove from heat, and let stand 5 minutes. Add berries; cover and chill 8 hours.
2. Drain berries in a colander over a bowl, reserving liquid. Discard spices. Divide berries among 12 (half-pint) jars.
3. Bring vinegar mixture and honey to a boil in a saucepan. Divide hot vinegar mixture among jars, filling to ¼ inch from top. Cover with metal lids; screw on bands. Cool to room temperature. Refrigerate up to 2 weeks. Serves 32 (serving size: about ⅓ cup)

CALORIES 78; **FAT** 0.4g (sat 0g, mono 0g, poly 0.2g); **PROTEIN** 1g; **CARB** 19g; **FIBER** 4g; **CHOL** 0mg; **IRON** 0mg; **SODIUM** 1mg; **CALC** 22mg

BASIC GUIDE TO A PICKLE CANNING PARTY

Make sure you have the proper equipment. For a canning party, it's ideal to have two complete setups: two canners or deep stockpots, two canning racks, two jar lifters, and plenty of canning jars with new lids. These recipes are written for pint-sized glass jars with metal lids and bands (such as Ball), which will provide plenty of goodies for guests to take home and the host to keep; if you'd like to use jars with rubber canning rings (such as Weck), go to weckjars.com for slightly different instructions.

1. READ Study recipes so you know what's required.

2. STERILIZE The party host should wash jars, bands, and lids in hot, soapy water; dry; and then heat jars and lids (not bands) in a large pot of simmering water until ready to use. Do not boil lids, as doing so may prevent them from sealing properly.

3. PREP When guests arrive, cut food as specified, and cook mixtures as necessary.

4. SEAL AND PROCESS Fill hot jars with hot food. Use a rubber spatula to release air bubbles from jars, and wipe rims clean. Immediately affix lids, and screw on bands just until closed (so remaining air bubbles can escape). Place jars on canning rack in boiling water in canner, making sure water covers jars by 1 to 2 inches. Return water to a rolling boil, and start timing; boil for the time specified in recipe.

5. COOL Remove jars from canner, placing on a towel. Let jars stand at room temperature 12 to 24 hours. (Guests can take warm jars home and follow steps 6 and 7 on their own.)

6. CHECK Press center of each lid; lids should not flex or "pop." Remove bands; gently try to lift lid with gentle pressure. If lid stays on, you have a good seal.

7. STORE Label properly sealed jars; store in a cool, dark place for up to 1 year. For any jars that did not seal, immediately reprocess in boiling water, or store in refrigerator for 2 to 4 weeks.

For more information, including high-altitude instructions, go to usda.gov and search "canning," or visit freshpreserving.com.

PREPARE SNACKS OR A SIMPLE MEAL FOR GUESTS TO NOSH ON, INCLUDING A PICKLE YOU'VE MADE AHEAD OF TIME. A COCKTAIL NEVER HURTS, EITHER.

PEPPERS, SWEET AND HOT

Our crop comes in all shapes and sizes, boasts a kaleidoscope of colors, and runs the gamut from fruity to flame-throwing.

Sweet and hot peppers are summer garden superheroes, flourishing in full sun and high heat. This time of year, the harvests are a huge payoff for 80-plus days of waiting.

Consider their beauty: Deep green foliage hides brilliant orange, yellow, red, green, purple, and striped fruits in twisted horns or fat bell shapes. It's why savvy gardeners plant peppers among front-yard flower patches for a naturally ornamental element.

There's a saying in some regions: "If you don't like the weather, wait five minutes." It's similar with peppers. If you want a colorful harvest, wait awhile. Peppers that begin deep green mature to reds and purples. Sweet peppers also have better flavor and nutrition when allowed to color. Jalapeños and poblanos, like varieties in our garden, are picked green and glossy, before woody nicks appear in aged skins. If blessed with a bumper crop, let some age to a fiery red, then roast or smoke them.

Quick & Easy • Gluten Free
Vegetarian

Peppery Potato Omelet

Hands-on: 20 min. Total: 30 min.

1½ pounds Yukon gold potatoes, peeled and cut into ½-inch pieces
1 large red bell pepper
1 tablespoon extra-virgin olive oil
2½ cups thinly vertically sliced onion
3 large eggs, lightly beaten
3 large egg whites, lightly beaten
1 teaspoon kosher salt, divided
¼ teaspoon freshly ground black pepper
1 tablespoon chopped fresh parsley

1. Preheat broiler to high.
2. Place potatoes in a saucepan; cover with water. Bring to a boil. Reduce heat; simmer 8 minutes or until tender. Drain well.
3. Cut bell pepper in half lengthwise; discard seeds and membranes. Place halves, skin sides up, on a foil-lined baking sheet; flatten with hand. Broil 8 minutes or until blackened. Wrap in foil; let stand 10 minutes. Peel and chop.
4. Reduce oven temperature to 350°.
5. Heat a large ovenproof, nonstick skillet over medium-high heat. Add oil; swirl to coat. Add onion; sauté 5 minutes. Combine eggs, egg whites, and ½ teaspoon salt in a large bowl; stir with a whisk. Pour egg mixture over onions; top with potatoes.

Sprinkle potatoes with bell pepper, ½ teaspoon salt, and black pepper. Cook 2 minutes, shaking pan. Place pan in oven; bake 8 minutes or until eggs are set. Sprinkle with parsley. Serves 8 (serving size: 1 wedge)

CALORIES 149; **FAT** 3.8g (sat 0.9g, mono 2g, poly 0.6g); **PROTEIN** 6g; **CARB** 23g; **FIBER** 3g; **CHOL** 70mg; **IRON** 1mg; **SODIUM** 295mg; **CALC** 32mg

Gluten Free

Carne Tampiqueña

Hands-on: 55 min. Total: 55 min.

1½ pounds skirt steak, cut into 3-inch pieces
¾ cup fresh lime juice (about 10 limes)
1 teaspoon salt, divided
Cooking spray
2 poblano chiles
1 serrano chile
1 small onion, cut horizontally into ½-inch-thick slices
1 small tomato
2 ounces queso fresco, cut into 4 slabs
1 tablespoon extra-virgin olive oil
2 teaspoons minced fresh garlic
12 (6-inch) corn tortillas
1 ripe peeled avocado, sliced
1 jalapeño pepper, thinly sliced
6 lime wedges

1. Preheat grill to high heat.
2. Combine steak and juice in a large zip-top bag; let stand 30 minutes, turning occasionally. Remove steak from marinade; discard marinade. Sprinkle steak with ½ teaspoon salt. Lightly coat grill rack with cooking spray. Place chiles on grill rack; grill 12 minutes or until charred on all sides, turning occasionally. Wrap chiles in foil; let stand 10 minutes. Place onion slices on grill; grill 10 minutes, turning once. Place tomato on grill; grill 6 minutes or until softened. Place steak on grill;

grill 3 minutes on each side or until desired degree of doneness. Lightly coat cheese with cooking spray. Add cheese to grill; grill 1 minute on each side or until browned.

3. Peel, seed, and chop grilled chiles; place in a medium bowl. Chop onion and tomato; add to chiles. Stir in ½ teaspoon salt, olive oil, and minced garlic. Cut steak across the grain into thin slices.

4. Warm tortillas according to package directions. Divide steak, onion mixture, cheese, avocado, and jalapeño among tortillas. Serve with lime wedges. Serves 6 (serving size: 2 tacos)

CALORIES 356; **FAT** 16.3g (sat 4.6g, mono 8.6g, poly 1.6g); **PROTEIN** 27g; **CARB** 28g; **FIBER** 5g; **CHOL** 75mg; **IRON** 3mg; **SODIUM** 492mg; **CALC** 80mg

Gluten Free • Vegetarian

Summery Stuffed Poblanos

Hands-on: 30 min. Total: 60 min.

6 poblano chiles
2 ears shucked corn
Cooking spray
2 cups chopped seeded tomato, divided
1 cup hot cooked brown rice
¼ cup chopped fresh cilantro, divided
2 tablespoons pine nuts, toasted
2 tablespoons ⅓-less-fat cream cheese
2 teaspoons fresh lime juice
¼ teaspoon kosher salt
3 garlic cloves, minced
3 ounces Monterey Jack cheese, shredded (about ¾ cup)
2 ounces queso fresco, crumbled (about ½ cup)
Jalapeño pepper sauce (optional)

1. Preheat grill to high heat.
2. Lightly coat poblanos and corn with cooking spray. Place poblanos and corn on grill rack. Grill poblanos 12 minutes or until charred, turning occasionally. Grill corn 10 minutes or until lightly charred, turning occasionally. Wrap poblanos in foil; let stand 15 minutes. Peel and discard skins. Cut a lengthwise slit in each chile; discard seeds and membranes. Set aside.
3. Preheat oven to 400°.
4. Cut kernels from ears of corn. Combine kernels, 1 cup tomato, rice, 2 tablespoons cilantro, pine nuts, and next 5 ingredients (through Monterey Jack); toss well to combine. Open each poblano; divide rice mixture evenly among chiles (chiles will be very full). Place on a baking sheet. Bake at 400° for 7 minutes or until hot. Turn broiler to high. Sprinkle chiles with queso fresco. Broil 3 minutes or until cheese is lightly browned. Place chiles on a platter. Sprinkle with 1 cup tomato and 2 tablespoons cilantro. Serve with hot sauce, if desired. Serves 6 (serving size: 1 stuffed chile)

CALORIES 210; **FAT** 9.6g (sat 4.2g, mono 2.2g, poly 1.4g); **PROTEIN** 10g; **CARB** 25g; **FIBER** 5g; **CHOL** 19mg; **IRON** 1mg; **SODIUM** 197mg; **CALC** 165mg

12 HEALTHY HABITS

GO MEATLESS ONCE A WEEK

Embracing meat-free meals requires a simple shift in plate balance.

The country's collective culinary focus is shifting from the meat to the potatoes (and kale, quinoa, and cauliflower). Chefs, many of whom have spent the past decade in a bacon-fat-fueled haze, are waking up to the pleasures of all things vegetal. Home cooks, whether driven by environmental or economic reasons, are also fueling the Meatless Monday momentum. The plant-centric plate is having its day—and that is a very good thing for anyone who enjoys cooking and eating.

"We're learning to stop looking at the plate as a big hunk of meat and three little side dishes," says Ivy Manning, this month's Healthy Habits Hero and author of several cookbooks, including *The Adaptable Feast: Satisfying Meals for the Vegetarians, Vegans, and Omnivores at Your Table.*

Manning's affinity for meat-free plates comes from a diverse culinary background, as well as a more personal place: her home. "I'm Mrs. Pork Chop, and I married Mr. Tofu," she says. "Everybody said we wouldn't work because he is a vegetarian, and I can do amazing things with pork." At first, she cooked two meals each night, one for her and one for her husband. But that couldn't last.

Over the years, she began devising cook-savvy ways to make meatless dishes easier and equally appetizing for all—and none of them involve whipping up entirely separate plates. "I try to keep flavors similar. If I'm doing a tri-tip with a Mediterranean rub on the grill, I'll brush the same garlicky cumin oil on eggplant, tomatoes, and zucchini, and everyone shares the same sides, like a high-protein grain salad, so the meal feels cohesive for everyone," she says. "When you're including a vegetarian, you want them to enjoy the wine and food in the same way, instead of having it be like 'We're having Mediterranean, and you get mac and cheese.'"

Today, Manning has made peace with being meatless most days. "Meat to me now is more like a condiment—it's only one part of the meal," she says. And there's a bonus to thinking in this veggie-centric way: "If you use vegetables at their peak, regardless of what the season is, you're doing less work to get great flavor."

continued

Quinoa-Stuffed Heirloom Tomatoes with Romesco

Hands-on: 60 min. Total: 1 hr. 30 min.

Romesco:
1 cup bottled roasted red bell
    peppers, rinsed and drained (about
    5 ounces)
¼ cup unsalted dry-roasted almonds
2 tablespoons water
1 tablespoon olive oil
1½ teaspoons red wine vinegar
1 teaspoon minced fresh garlic
⅛ teaspoon kosher salt
⅛ teaspoon ground red pepper
⅛ teaspoon black pepper
Filling:
1 tablespoon olive oil
¼ cup thinly sliced onion
1 teaspoon minced fresh garlic
1 teaspoon minced peeled ginger
¾ cup uncooked quinoa
1¾ cups organic vegetable broth
⅜ teaspoon kosher salt
¼ teaspoon black pepper
3 tablespoons chopped fresh Italian
    parsley
2 tablespoons chopped fresh dill
1 (15-ounce) can unsalted chickpeas
    (garbanzo beans), drained and
    coarsely chopped
8 medium heirloom tomatoes

1. To prepare romesco sauce, place first 9 ingredients in a blender or food processor; process until smooth.
2. To prepare filling, heat a medium saucepan over medium-high heat. Add 1 tablespoon oil to pan; swirl to coat. Add onion; sauté 4 minutes or until onion begins to brown. Add 1 teaspoon garlic and ginger; sauté 30 seconds, stirring constantly. Stir in quinoa; cook 1 minute, stirring constantly. Add broth, ⅜ teaspoon salt, and ¼ teaspoon black pepper; bring to a boil. Cover and simmer 20 minutes or until quinoa is tender and liquid is absorbed.
3. Combine quinoa mixture, parsley, dill, and chickpeas in a bowl. Cut tops off tomatoes; set aside. Carefully scoop out tomato pulp, leaving shells intact; discard pulp. Divide quinoa mixture evenly among tomato shells; replace tomato tops. Spoon romesco sauce around stuffed tomatoes. Serves 4 (serving size: 2 stuffed tomatoes and about ¼ cup sauce)

CALORIES 387; FAT 15.4g (sat 1.7g, mono 8.7g, poly 3.8g); PROTEIN 14g; CARB 52g; FIBER 11g; CHOL 0mg; IRON 3mg; SODIUM 614mg; CALC 102mg

IVY'S IDEAS FOR GOING MEATLESS

1 MANAGE YOUR MESSAGES.
"If you tell your kids they have to eat meatless because it's right for the planet, they may not be excited about it. But if you tell them it's pizza night, and they love pizza, they will be. It's so easy to make a delicious pizza that doesn't contain meat."

2 EXPLORE MORE.
"Eating meatless is pretty easy when you start looking around the globe for inspiration. Look at countries like India, where a huge percentage of the population does not eat meat for both religious and economic reasons. Mexico is a bean, rice, and corn culture. Middle Eastern food has some lamb, but they also have many delicious chickpea- and fava bean–based dishes."

3 AMP UP UMAMI.
"A food's texture, or mouthfeel, goes a long way toward satisfying you. I always keep dried shiitake mushrooms and reconstitute them. They're chewy, and they have lots of umami. So do cheese, brewer's yeast, and ripe tomatoes. These foods give you the kind of big, round, gutsy flavor that meat typically provides."

NUTRITION MADE EASY

GLUTEN-FREE GRAINS BEYOND QUINOA

Simple recipes and techniques for five tasty whole-grain options
    Reaching six daily whole-grain servings can be tricky. Subtract all things wheat, and it gets even more challenging. But the rapid growth of the quinoa market has been followed by a wealth of alternative grains. Whether you have to avoid gluten or just want to expand your whole-grain recipe repertoire, they're well worth exploring.

Gluten Free • Make Ahead

Sorghum with Summer Corn, Tomatoes, and Tarragon

Hands-on: 18 min. Total: 1 hr. 30 min.
Combine 3 cups unsalted chicken stock and 1 cup uncooked sorghum in a medium saucepan. Bring to a boil; cover, reduce heat to low, and simmer 1 hour and 10 minutes or until tender. Drain; cool. Combine 8 teaspoons olive oil, 1 tablespoon chopped fresh tarragon, 2 tablespoons vinegar, 1 teaspoon Dijon mustard, 1 teaspoon garlic, ½ teaspoon kosher salt, and ¼ teaspoon black pepper in a large bowl, stirring well with a whisk. Add cooked sorghum, 8 ounces roasted asparagus, 2 cups halved cherry tomatoes, and 1½ cups fresh corn kernels; toss. Serves 6 (serving size: 1 cup)

CALORIES 234; FAT 8.6g (sat 1.2g, mono 5.4g, poly 1.4g); PROTEIN 9g; CARB 35g; FIBER 4g; SODIUM 256mg

Cranberry-Pistachio Energy Bars, *page 79*

Orange-Mustard Glazed Pork Chops,
page 34

Coconut Curry Halibut with Cashew Rice and Stir-Fried Vegetables, *page 25*

Grapefruit and Hearts of Palm Salad, *page 34*

Mu Shu Chicken Lettuce Wraps, *page 33*

Chicken Parmesan with Spaghetti with Sauteed Broccoli Rabe, *page 24*

Chewy Meringues with Tangerine-Lemon Curd, *page 36*

Tahini Swirl Brownies,
page 73

Chicken Cutlets with Mushrooms and Pearl Onions, *page 48*

Tortilla Soup with Chorizo and Turkey Meatballs,
page 59

Individual White Chicken Pizzas,
page 55

Pork and Shiitake Pot Stickers,
page 52

White Bean, Sage, and Sausage Soup,
page 54

Pasta with Shrimp and Tomato-Caper Sauce, *page 92*

Spicy Bean and Quinoa Salad with "Mole" Vinaigrette, *page 78*

Creamy Asparagus, Herb and Pea Pasta,
page 93

Clam Shack-Style
Broiled Fish,
page 120

**Chicken-Broccoli Mac and
Cheese with Bacon,**
page 104

Slider Patties with Pomegranate Molasses, *page 125*

Beefsteak Tomato Salad with Fried Tomato Skins, *page 137*

Indian-Spiced Grilled Shrimp and Okra,
page 140

**Summer Vegetable
Rigatoni with Chicken,**
page 150

**Pancetta-Wrapped
Pork Tenderloin with
Cantaloupe-Red Pepper
Salsa,** *page 179*

Halibut & Peach Salad with Lemon-Mint Vinaigrette,
page 178

BLT Pizza with White Sauce,
page 162

Greek-Style Chicken Wraps,
page 195

Peaches-and-Cream Frozen Pops,
page 200

229

Bourbon-Peach Limeades,
page 198

Black Bean–Quinoa Salad with Chipotle Steak, *page 255*

Caprese Mac anc Cheese with Chopped Tricolor Salad, *page 268*

Banana–Almond Butter French Toast Sandwiches, *page 266*

Lemon-Pepper Flank Steak Tacos, *page 261*

Deep-Dish Mushroom and Onion Pizza,
page 252

Smoky Tilapia Tacos,
page 261

233

Cheesy Nachos with Pinto Bean Salsa and
Pickled Jalapeños,
page 281

**Pork Chops Simmered in
Spiced Tomato Sauce,**
page 285

**Tuscan-Style Garlic-Herb
Pork Chops,**
page 284

Classic Lasagna with Meat Sauce,
page 279

Sautéed Chard Agrodolce,
page 336

237

Moroccan-Spiced Turkey with Aromatic Orange Pan Jus,
page 309

Farro Stuffing with Butternut Squash, Red Onion, and Almonds, *page 308*

Roasted Fennel with Rosemary Breadcrumbs, *page 308*

Hazelnut Rye Rolls, *page 308*

Five-Ingredient Chocolate Cakes,
page 327

Creamy Gorgonzola Teff with Herb-Roasted Tomatoes

Hands-on: 15 min. Total: 30 min.
Combine 1½ cups unsalted chicken stock and 1½ cups 2% milk in a medium saucepan; bring to a boil. Stir in 1 cup uncooked teff and ½ teaspoon kosher salt. Cover and simmer 20 minutes or until liquid is absorbed, stirring occasionally. Remove pan from heat; stir in 2 ounces crumbled Gorgonzola cheese, ¼ cup fat-free sour cream, and ¼ teaspoon black pepper. Divide teff mixture evenly among 6 plates. Top each with ¼ cup oven-roasted cherry tomatoes; sprinkle with fresh thyme. Serves 6 (serving size: about ½ cup teff and about ¼ cup tomato mixture)

CALORIES 219; FAT 7g (sat 3.1g, mono 2g, poly 0.4g); PROTEIN 10g; CARB 30g; FIBER 5g; SODIUM 375mg

5 WHOLE-GRAIN OPTIONS

TEFF is a tiny grain that cooks in 20 minutes. It's porridgy, like polenta, with a deep, toasty flavor.

MILLET is fast, nearly foolproof, and fluffy. Its corn-forward flavor makes it perfect for highly seasoned recipes.

AMARANTH cooks up creamy and tender; don't expect it to fluff. It's ideal for breakfast with fruit, vanilla, and warm spices.

SORGHUM is mild and slightly sweet, like a chewier version of Israeli couscous when cooked. It needs at least an hour to simmer.

BUCKWHEAT is earthy and pairs well with smoky flavors. It tends to clump when simply boiled in water. To keep it fluffy, beat an egg into the grain to coat each groat, toast in a pan until dry, and then add liquid.

Vanilla Amaranth with Peach Compote

Hands-on: 20 min. Total: 20 min
Melt 2 teaspoons butter in a saucepan over medium heat. Add 1 cup uncooked amaranth; cook 2 minutes. Stir in 2 cups 1% milk, a dash of salt, and ½ vanilla bean (split lengthwise); bring to a boil. Cover, reduce heat, and simmer 20 minutes or until liquid is absorbed. Discard vanilla bean. Combine ¾ pound sliced peaches (fresh or frozen), ¼ cup water, 2 tablespoons sugar, ⅛ teaspoon cinnamon, and a dash of ground ginger in a saucepan over medium-high heat; bring to a boil. Simmer 12 minutes or until peaches are tender and thick. Serve peaches over amaranth. Serves 4 (serving size: ½ cup amaranth and ⅓ cup fruit)

CALORIES 310; FAT 6.7g (sat 2.7g, mono 1.7g, poly 1.5g); PROTEIN 11g; CARB 53g; FIBER 5g; SODIUM 58mg

Toasted Millet with Cilantro Vinaigrette

Hands-on: 30 min. Total: 40 min.
Heat 1½ teaspoons olive oil in a saucepan over medium heat. Add ½ cup chopped onion; sauté 3 minutes. Add 1 cup uncooked millet and 1 tablespoon minced garlic to pan; cook 2 minutes. Stir in 1 cup unsalted chicken stock, 1 cup water, and ½ teaspoon kosher salt; bring to a boil. Cover, reduce heat, and simmer 25 minutes or until liquid is absorbed. Combine 2½ tablespoons olive oil, ¼ teaspoon kosher salt, ½ cup fresh cilantro, 2 tablespoons lime juice, 1 teaspoon honey, ½ teaspoon cumin, and ¼ teaspoon black pepper. Add millet mixture, 1 cup chopped red bell pepper, ¾ cup diced avocado, and 1½ cups unsalted black beans; toss to coat. Sprinkle with 2 ounces crumbled feta. Serves 8 (serving size: ¾ cup)

CALORIES 225; FAT 9.8g (sat 2.3g, mono 5.6g, poly 1.4g); PROTEIN 7g; CARB 28g; FIBER 5g; SODIUM 283mg

Cheesy Buckwheat with Kale and Mushrooms

Hands-on: 33 min. Total: 33 min.
Combine 1 cup uncooked buckwheat and 1 lightly beaten large egg in a bowl; toss. Heat a saucepan over medium heat. Add buckwheat mixture to pan; cook 3 minutes or until grains are dry and separated, stirring frequently. Stir in 1½ cups water and ½ teaspoon kosher salt; bring to a boil. Cover, reduce heat, and simmer 15 minutes or until water is absorbed. Remove from heat; stir in 2 ounces shredded Gruyère cheese and 2 tablespoons grated Parmesan cheese. Heat 1 tablespoon oil in a large nonstick skillet over medium heat. Add ½ cup diced onion, 1 tablespoon sliced garlic, and 8 ounces presliced mushrooms; cook 7 minutes. Add 6 cups chopped kale and ¼ teaspoon black pepper to pan; cook 2 minutes. Add kale mixture to buckwheat mixture. Sprinkle with ¼ cup toasted walnuts and 2 center-cut bacon slices, cooked and crumbled. Serves 6 (serving size: ¾ cup)

CALORIES 268; FAT 11.6g (sat 3.4g, mono 3.5g, poly 3.1g); PROTEIN 13g; CARB 32g; FIBER 4g; SODIUM 309mg

THIS MONTH'S LESSON: CREAMY DRESSING ON GRILLED SALAD

It's high time for grilled salads. This one is rendered luxurious with a generous amount of sweet lump crabmeat and a cream-based vinaigrette. It may sound counterintuitive, but heavy cream actually has fewer calories and less total fat than an equal measure of oil (though it does increase saturated fat). That's because cream is somewhere between 36% and 40% fat, whereas oils are fat. Just a splash is all you need for creamy richness and incredible flavor.

KEITH'S RECIPE BREAKDOWN

GRILLED CORN, CRAB, AND ASPARAGUS SALAD

Hands-on: 30 min. Total: 40 min.

INGREDIENT	AMOUNT	WHY
fresh sweet corn	4 ears, shucked	It's corn season, no?
asparagus	1 pound, trimmed	For a gently bitter, almost bulby contrast to the corn.
sweet onion (such as Vidalia)	½ cup, diced	You're not cooking the onion, so keep it subtle with this small amount.
jalapeño pepper	¼ cup, diced	Spicy and sweet work nicely together.
chives	1 tablespoon, finely chopped	Chives add an oniony quality while offering grassy notes.
heavy cream	3 tablespoons	For your vinaigrette. Think *oil*.
tarragon	1 teaspoon, chopped	Once you have corn with tarragon, you'll be a believer.
white wine vinegar	1 teaspoon	To mimic the flavor profile of a béarnaise.
black pepper	½ teaspoon	Black pepper shines in cream.
kosher salt	¼ teaspoon	There's a lot of sweet going on. This balances it.
garlic cloves	2, minced	Garlic softens against cream yet adds a pronounced raw punch to the dish. Raw garlic deserves love.
lump crabmeat	8 ounces	You're worth it.

Follow These Steps:

• Heat a grill or grill pan over medium-high heat.
• Place corn on grill rack; grill 20 minutes or until here-and-there charred, turning occasionally. Place in a large bowl; cover with foil. Leave in a warm location 10 minutes.
• Place asparagus on grill rack, and grill 3 minutes or until crisp-tender, carefully turning occasionally.
• Cut corn kernels off cobs, encouraging clusters to stay intact, if possible. Cut grilled asparagus into ¾-inch pieces.
• Combine onion, jalapeño, chives, cream, tarragon, vinegar, black pepper, salt, and garlic in a large bowl. Add asparagus and corn; toss gently to coat. Gently fold in crabmeat. Serve warm. Serves 4 (serving size: about 1 cup)

CALORIES 209; FAT 6.2g (sat 3.1g, mono 1.7g, poly 0.9g); PROTEIN 17g; CARB 27g; FIBER 5g; CHOL 70mg; IRON 3mg; SODIUM 367mg; CALC 99mg

Variation: Grilled Corn, Chicken, and Bell Pepper Salad

Sub 1 red and 1 yellow bell pepper, halved and seeded, for asparagus. Grill 4 minutes on each side; cut into 1-inch pieces. Sub 2 (½-inch) onion slices for diced onion. Grill 3 minutes on each side; chop. Sub oregano for tarragon. Sub 2 teaspoons sherry vinegar for white wine vinegar. Sub 6 ounces shredded skinless rotisserie chicken (dark and white meat) for crab. Serves 4 (serving size: about 1 cup)

CALORIES 233; FAT 8.8g (sat 3.8g); SODIUM 314mg

HANDS-FREE JAM

Use your slow cooker to make peak-of-the-season preserves without stirring.

Gluten Free • Make Ahead Vegetarian

Strawberry-Riesling Jam

Hands-on: 20 min. Total: 21 hr. 20 min.

2 pounds very ripe hulled strawberries
1 cup sugar
½ cup riesling wine
1 medium peeled Macintosh apple, grated
1 (1.75-ounce) box Sure-Jell fruit pectin for less- or no-sugar recipes*
1 rosemary sprig

1. Place first 5 ingredients in a 6-quart electric slow cooker. Cover and cook on LOW for 8 hours.
2. Mash the fruit to a chunky puree with a potato masher. Increase heat to HIGH; cook, uncovered, 4 hours. Turn off heat, and nestle rosemary sprig into fruit mixture; let stand 1 hour. Remove and discard rosemary sprig and any loose needles. Place jam in a bowl; cover and chill 8 hours. Store, refrigerated, for up to 3 weeks. Serves 26 (serving size: 2 tablespoons)

CALORIES 53; FAT 0.1g (sat 0g, mono 0g, poly 0.1g); PROTEIN 0g; CARB 13g; FIBER 1g; CHOL 0mg; IRON 0mg; SODIUM 4mg; CALC 6mg

*A number of manufacturers make pectin for low-sugar recipes; depending on the brand, you may need to use more or less than we call for. Read the instructions on the package, and use the recommended amount for the quantity of fruit being used.

6 SNAZZY SALSAS

Not just for chips, these salsas dress up fish or chicken and give rice and grains pizzazz.

Smoky Black Bean & Mango
Combine 1 (15-ounce) can unsalted black beans, rinsed and drained; ¾ cup chopped mango; ½ cup chopped seeded tomato; ¼ cup chopped red bell pepper; ¼ cup finely chopped red onion; 3 tablespoons chopped fresh cilantro; 2 tablespoons fresh lime juice; 1 tablespoon olive oil; 1 teaspoon minced chipotle chile in adobo sauce; 1 teaspoon adobo sauce; and ¼ teaspoon kosher salt. Serves 10 (serving size: ¼ cup)

CALORIES 45; FAT 1.5g (sat 0.2g); SODIUM 63mg

Salsa Verde
Place 2½ cups chopped tomatillos, ⅓ cup chopped white onion, ¼ cup chopped fresh cilantro, 2 tablespoons fresh lime juice, 1 tablespoon olive oil, ¼ teaspoon kosher salt, 2 garlic cloves, and 1 chopped seeded serrano chile in a food processor; pulse to finely chop. Serves 8 (serving size: ¼ cup)

CALORIES 75; FAT 3.5g (sat 0.5g); SODIUM 62mg

Chunky Strawberry-Avocado
Combine 1½ cups quartered ripe strawberries, ⅔ cup chopped radish, ½ cup chopped green onions, 1 tablespoon white balsamic vinegar, ¼ teaspoon kosher salt, and 1 diced ripe avocado. Serves 12 (serving size: ¼ cup)

CALORIES 37; FAT 2.5g (sat 0.4g); SODIUM 44mg

Golden Pico de Gallo
Combine 2 cups chopped seeded yellow tomato, 1 cup chopped orange bell pepper, ¾ cup chopped peeled cucumber, ½ cup minced fresh onion, 3 tablespoons chopped hot pickled banana pepper, 2 tablespoons chopped fresh cilantro, ¼ teaspoon kosher salt, ¼ teaspoon freshly ground black pepper, and juice of ½ lime. Serves 12 (serving size: ¼ cup)

CALORIES 14; FAT 0.1g (sat 0g); SODIUM 129mg

Summer Squash and Zucchini
Sauté 1½ cups diced zucchini, 1½ cups diced yellow squash, 2 tablespoons minced shallots, and 1 tablespoon olive oil in a skillet over medium-high heat 2 minutes. Combine squash mixture, ½ cup chopped green onions, ¼ cup chopped walnuts, 1 teaspoon grated lemon rind, 2 tablespoons fresh lemon juice, 1 teaspoon chopped fresh tarragon, and ¼ teaspoon kosher salt. Cool slightly. Serves 12 (serving size: ¼ cup)

CALORIES 38; FAT 2.8g (sat 0.3g); SODIUM 44mg

Red Onion, Olive & Feta
Preheat broiler. Cut 2 large red onions crosswise into ¼-inch-thick slices; arrange in a single layer on a baking sheet coated with cooking spray. Coat onions lightly with cooking spray. Broil 4 minutes on each side or until onions begin to brown; cool to room temperature. Chop onions; combine with ¼ cup chopped fresh parsley, ¼ cup sliced pitted kalamata olives, 2 tablespoons red wine vinegar, 1 teaspoon chopped fresh oregano, and ¼ teaspoon kosher salt. Stir in ¼ cup crumbled feta cheese. Serves 6 (serving size: ¼ cup)

CALORIES 45; FAT 2.1g (sat 1g); SODIUM 234mg

DINNER TONIGHT

Kid Friendly • Quick & Easy
Gluten Free • Vegetarian

Vegetable Hash with Poached Eggs

with Multigrain Toast and Red Pepper Tapenade

4 teaspoons olive oil
1 cup chopped Vidalia or other sweet onion
1 cup (1/4-inch-thick) slices fingerling or small red potatoes
1 teaspoon dried herbes de Provence
1 cup diced zucchini
1 cup diced yellow squash
1 cup green beans, trimmed and cut into 1/2-inch pieces
1/2 teaspoon kosher salt
1/2 teaspoon freshly ground black pepper, divided
2 cups chopped seeded tomato
2 tablespoons thinly sliced fresh chives
2 tablespoons chopped fresh flat-leaf parsley
1 tablespoon white vinegar
4 large eggs
1 ounce Parmesan cheese, shredded (about 1/4 cup)

1. Heat a large nonstick skillet over medium-high heat. Add oil; swirl to coat. Add onion, potatoes, and herbes de Provence; spread mixture in a single layer in pan. Cook 4 minutes, without stirring, or until potatoes are lightly browned.

2. Reduce heat to medium. Stir in zucchini, yellow squash, beans, salt, and 3/8 teaspoon pepper; cook 3 minutes. Remove pan from heat; cover and let stand 5 minutes. Stir in tomato, chives, and parsley.

3. Add water to a large skillet, filling two-thirds full; bring to a boil. Reduce heat; simmer. Stir in vinegar. Break each egg into a custard cup. Gently pour eggs into pan; cook 3 minutes or until desired degree of doneness. Carefully remove eggs from pan using a slotted spoon. Divide squash mixture evenly among 4 plates; top each serving with 1 egg. Sprinkle eggs evenly with 1/8 teaspoon pepper and Parmesan cheese. Serves 4 (serving size: about 1 1/3 cups squash mixture, 1 egg, and 1 tablespoon cheese)

CALORIES 221; FAT 11.8g (sat 3.5g, mono 5.8g, poly 1.7g); PROTEIN 12g; CARB 18g; FIBER 4g; CHOL 192mg; IRON 2mg; SODIUM 438mg; CALC 156mg

Multigrain Toast and Red Pepper Tapenade

Preheat broiler to high. Arrange 4 (1-ounce) multigrain bread slices on a baking sheet. Broil 1 minute on each side or until toasted. Place 2 tablespoons slivered almonds, 1 tablespoon olive oil, 1 small garlic clove, 2 ounces drained bottled roasted red bell peppers, and 1/2 ounce pitted kalamata olives in the bowl of a food processor. Pulse until mixture is finely chopped. Spread tapenade evenly over bread slices. Serves 4 (serving size: 1 bread slice and 1 1/2 tablespoons tapenade)

CALORIES 132; FAT 6.9g (sat 0.7g); SODIUM 202mg

READY IN
40
MINUTES

SHOPPING LIST

Vegetable Hash with Poached Eggs
Zucchini
Yellow squash
Green beans
Tomato
Fresh flat-leaf parsley
Fresh chives
Vidalia onion
Fingerling potatoes
Herbes de Provence
Olive oil
White vinegar
Parmesan cheese
Eggs

Multigrain Toast and Red Pepper Tapenade
Garlic
Olive oil
7-ounce jar roasted red bell peppers
Kalamata olives
Slivered almonds
Multigrain bread

GAME PLAN

While water for eggs comes to a boil:
■ Cook squash mixture.
■ Prepare tapenade.
While squash mixture rests:
■ Poach eggs.
■ Toast bread.

Quick & Easy

Olive and Pesto-Crusted Cod

with Summer Bread Salad

4 (6-ounce) cod fillets
Cooking spray
¹/₂ teaspoon kosher salt
¹/₄ teaspoon freshly ground black
**   pepper**
2 tablespoons refrigerated pesto
**   (such as Buitoni)**
1 teaspoon grated lemon rind
1¹/₂ ounces pitted Castelvetrano
**   olives, chopped**
1 (1-ounce) whole-grain bread slice,
**   toasted**

1. Preheat oven to 400°.
2. Arrange fish on a parchment paper–lined baking sheet coated with cooking spray. Sprinkle fish evenly with salt and pepper.
3. Place pesto, rind, olives, and bread in the bowl of a mini food processor; pulse until finely chopped. Spoon olive mixture evenly over fish, pressing to adhere. Bake at 400° for 12 minutes or until fish flakes easily when tested with a fork. Serves 4 (serving size: 1 fillet)

CALORIES 188; **FAT** 5.8g (sat 1g, mono 3.1g, poly 0.8g); **PROTEIN** 28g; **CARB** 5g; **FIBER** 1g; **CHOL** 82mg; **IRON** 1mg; **SODIUM** 536mg; **CALC** 50mg

Summer Bread Salad

Combine 2 tablespoons fresh lemon juice, 4 teaspoons olive oil, ¼ teaspoon kosher salt, and ¼ teaspoon black pepper in a large bowl. Stir in 3 cups toasted whole-grain bread cubes, 2 cups halved cherry tomatoes, 1 cup chopped seeded cucumber, 1 cup chopped green bell pepper, ¼ cup chopped green onions, and ¼ cup chopped fresh basil. Serves 4 (serving size: about 1½ cups)

CALORIES 163; **FAT** 6.3g (sat 1g); **SODIUM** 276mg

READY IN
35
MINUTES

SHOPPING LIST

Olive and Pesto-Crusted Cod
Lemon
Castelvetrano olives
Refrigerated pesto
Whole-grain bread
Cod fillets

Summer Bread Salad
Lemon
Cherry tomatoes
Cucumber
Green bell pepper
Green onions
Fresh basil
Olive oil
Whole-grain bread

GAME PLAN

While oven preheats:
■ Prepare olive mixture.
■ Cut bread into cubes.
While fish cooks:
■ Toast bread cubes in oven.
■ Prepare salad.

Kid Friendly • Quick & Easy
Gluten Free

Beef and Bell Pepper Kebabs

with Mushroom-Ginger Noodles

¹/₄ cup lower-sodium soy sauce
2 tablespoons orange juice
2 teaspoons honey
1 teaspoon minced garlic
1 teaspoon minced peeled fresh
**   ginger**
³/₄ teaspoon five-spice powder
¹/₈ teaspoon ground red pepper
2 (8-ounce) sirloin steaks, cut against
**   the grain into ¹/₄-inch-thick strips**
2 red or yellow bell peppers, seeded
**   and cut into 1-inch pieces**
Cooking spray
1 teaspoon sesame seeds, toasted

1. Combine first 7 ingredients, stirring with a whisk. Add beef; let stand 15 minutes. Remove beef from marinade; discard marinade. Thread beef and peppers onto 8 (8-inch) skewers.
2. Heat a grill pan over medium-high heat. Coat pan with cooking spray. Add kebabs to pan; grill 3 minutes on each side or until desired degree of doneness. Sprinkle with sesame seeds. Serves 4 (serving size: 2 kebabs)

CALORIES 173; **FAT** 5.2g (sat 1.8g, mono 1.9g, poly 0.4g); **PROTEIN** 24g; **CARB** 7g; **FIBER** 1g; **CHOL** 60mg; **IRON** 2mg; **SODIUM** 316mg; **CALC** 33mg

Mushroom-Ginger Noodles

Prepare 5 ounces rice noodles; drain. Sauté 1 teaspoon minced fresh garlic and 1 teaspoon minced peeled fresh ginger in 2 teaspoons dark sesame oil over medium-high heat for 30 seconds. Add 1½ cups sliced shiitake mushrooms and ½ cup sliced onion; sauté 4 minutes. Stir in rice noodles, 1 tablespoon lower-sodium soy sauce, and ¼ teaspoon kosher salt. Sprinkle with ½ cup sliced green onions. Serves 4 (serving size: about 1 cup)

CALORIES 164; **FAT** 2.4g (sat 0.4g); **SODIUM** 261mg

continued

READY IN
40
MINUTES

SHOPPING LIST

Beef and Bell Pepper Kebabs
Red or yellow bell peppers
Garlic
Ginger
Orange juice
Five-spice powder
Ground red pepper
Sesame seeds
Lower-sodium soy sauce
Honey
Sirloin steak

Mushroom-Ginger Noodles
Shiitake mushroom caps
Green onions
Onion
Garlic
Ginger
Dark sesame oil
Lower-sodium soy sauce
Rice noodles

GAME PLAN

While beef marinates:
- Prepare noodles.
- Sauté mushrooms and onion.
While beef grills:
- Finish noodle mixture.

Kid Friendly • Quick & Easy
Gluten Free

Honey-Glazed Pork Chops

with Tomato Salad and Silver Dollar Corn Cakes

2 cups grape tomatoes, halved
1 tablespoon olive oil, divided
2 teaspoons thyme leaves
1 teaspoon minced fresh garlic
2 tablespoons honey
2 tablespoons cider vinegar
1 tablespoon Dijon mustard
4 (6-ounce) bone-in center-cut pork chops
1/4 teaspoon kosher salt
1/4 teaspoon freshly ground black pepper
1/2 cup unsalted chicken stock
3 cups baby spinach leaves
2 teaspoons balsamic vinegar

1. Preheat oven to 425°.
2. Combine tomatoes, 1 teaspoon oil, thyme, and garlic on a foil-lined jelly-roll pan. Roast at 425° for 17 minutes.
3. Combine honey, cider vinegar, and mustard, stirring with a whisk. Heat a large skillet over medium-high heat. Add 2 teaspoons oil to pan; swirl to coat. Sprinkle pork evenly with salt and pepper. Add pork to pan; cook 3 minutes on each side or until desired degree of doneness. Remove pork from pan. Add stock to pan; cook 2 minutes or until reduced by half. Remove pan from heat; stir in honey mixture.
4. Place tomatoes, spinach, and balsamic vinegar in a bowl; toss to coat. Serve salad with pork and sauce. Serves 4 (serving size: 1 pork chop, about 2 teaspoons sauce, and about 3/4 cup salad)

CALORIES 247; FAT 9.5g (sat 2.3g, mono 4.7g, poly 1.1g); PROTEIN 24g; CARB 15g; FIBER 2g; CHOL 71mg; IRON 1mg; SODIUM 307mg; CALC 52mg

Silver Dollar Corn Cakes
Combine 1/2 cup yellow cornmeal, 1/4 cup all-purpose flour, 1 teaspoon sugar, 1/2 teaspoon baking powder, and 1/4 teaspoon kosher salt. Combine 1/2 cup low-fat buttermilk and 1 large egg in a bowl, stirring with a whisk. Stir in cornmeal mixture, 1 cup fresh corn kernels, and 2 tablespoons chopped green onions. Heat a nonstick skillet over medium heat. Add 8 (1-tablespoon) mounds batter to pan; cook 2 minutes on each side. Remove corn cakes from pan. Repeat with remaining batter to yield 16 corn cakes total. Serves 4 (serving size: 4 corn cakes)

CALORIES 170; FAT 2.3g (sat 0.7g); SODIUM 239mg

READY IN
40
MINUTES

SHOPPING LIST

Honey-Glazed Pork Chops with Tomato Salad
5-ounce package baby spinach
Grape tomatoes
Fresh thyme
Garlic
Olive oil
Unsalted chicken stock
Balsamic vinegar
Cider vinegar
Dijon mustard
Honey
Bone-in, center-cut pork chops

Silver Dollar Corn Cakes
Corn
Green onions
Yellow cornmeal
All-purpose flour
Sugar
Baking powder
Low-fat buttermilk
Egg

While oven preheats:
- Prepare honey mixture.
- Prepare corn cake batter.

While tomatoes roast:
- Cook pork.
- Cook corn cakes.

Kid Friendly • Quick & Easy

Chicken Schnitzel

with Smashed Mustard Potatoes
and Apple, Fennel, and Celery Slaw

1 pound small red potatoes, halved
1/3 cup unsalted chicken stock (such as Swanson)
1/4 cup chopped green onions
1 tablespoon whole-grain mustard
1 teaspoon freshly ground black pepper, divided
4 (6-ounce) skinless, boneless chicken breast halves, pounded to 1/4-inch thickness
1/4 teaspoon kosher salt
1/4 cup all-purpose flour
1/4 cup fat-free milk
1 large egg, lightly beaten
1 cup panko (Japanese breadcrumbs)
2 tablespoons chopped fresh flat-leaf parsley
1/2 teaspoon garlic powder
Cooking spray
4 teaspoons olive oil, divided

1. Place potatoes in a large saucepan; cover with water. Bring to a boil. Cook 12 minutes or until tender; drain. Return potatoes to pan; mash to desired consistency. Stir in stock, green onions, mustard, and 1/2 teaspoon pepper.

2. Sprinkle chicken with 1/2 teaspoon pepper and salt. Place flour in a shallow dish. Combine milk and egg in a shallow dish. Combine panko, parsley, and garlic powder in a shallow dish. Dredge chicken in flour. Dip in milk mixture; dredge in panko mixture, shaking off excess. Lightly coat breaded chicken with cooking spray.

3. Heat a large nonstick skillet over medium-high heat. Add 2 teaspoons oil to pan; swirl to coat. Add 2 chicken breast halves to pan; cook 3 minutes on each side or until chicken is done. Remove chicken from pan; keep warm. Repeat procedure with 2 teaspoons oil and remaining 2 chicken breast halves. Serves 4 (serving size: 1 chicken breast half and 1/2 cup potatoes)

CALORIES 433; **FAT** 11g (sat 2g, mono 5.1g, poly 1.5g); **PROTEIN** 44g; **CARB** 37g; **FIBER** 3g; **CHOL** 156mg; **IRON** 2mg; **SODIUM** 508mg; **CALC** 58mg

Apple, Fennel, and Celery Slaw

Combine 1 tablespoon olive oil, 1 tablespoon cider vinegar, 1 teaspoon honey, 1/2 teaspoon freshly ground black pepper, and 1/4 teaspoon kosher salt in a medium bowl, stirring with a whisk. Add 1 1/2 cups julienne-cut Granny Smith apple, 1 1/2 cups thinly sliced fennel bulb, 1 cup thinly sliced celery, and 1 tablespoon chopped fennel fronds. Toss to coat. Serves 4 (serving size: 1 cup)

CALORIES 71; **FAT** 3.5g (sat 0.5g); **SODIUM** 158mg

READY IN 40 MINUTES

SHOPPING LIST

Chicken Schnitzel with Smashed Mustard Potatoes
Fresh flat-leaf parsley
Green onions
Small red potatoes
Garlic powder
Olive oil
Unsalted chicken stock
Whole-grain mustard
All-purpose flour
Panko
Fat-free milk
Egg
Skinless, boneless chicken breast halves

Apple, Fennel, and Celery Slaw
Granny Smith apple
Fennel bulb
Celery
Olive oil
Cider vinegar
Honey

GAME PLAN

While potatoes cook:
- Bread chicken.
- Cut apple, fennel, and celery.

While chicken cooks:
- Finish slaw.

YELLOW WAX BEANS

These pale pole beans have a character all their own.

Some may tell you yellow wax beans taste just like green beans—heresy! Their unique grassy flavor is one of summer's distinct delights. Plus, these translucent, supersmooth pods need no stringing. In our salad, their flavor is mild but doesn't disappear against peppery radishes, pungent blue cheese, salty bacon, or tangy buttermilk dressing.

These beans are at their peak from midsummer through early September. Choose firm, uniformly yellow pods with small beans inside—bulging beans are too mature and will be tough.

DITCH THE BACON AND CRUMBLE IN SMOKED BLUE CHEESE IN PLACE OF REGULAR. YOU'LL GET MEAT-FREE SMOKED FLAVOR.

Quick & Easy • Gluten Free Make Ahead

Wax Bean and Radish Salad with Creamy Parsley Dressing

Hands-on: 18 min. Total: 18 min. Here is a salad that will hold, creamy buttermilk dressing and all, for several hours. Just sprinkle the blue cheese and bacon on right before serving.

¼ cup low-fat buttermilk
¼ cup plain 2% reduced-fat Greek yogurt
2 tablespoons finely chopped fresh flat-leaf parsley
1½ tablespoons fresh lemon juice
1 tablespoon finely chopped shallots
1½ teaspoons Dijon mustard
¼ teaspoon kosher salt
8 cups water
1 pound fresh yellow wax beans
1 cup thinly sliced radishes
1 tablespoon extra-virgin olive oil
1 ounce crumbled blue cheese (about ¼ cup)
¼ teaspoon freshly ground black pepper
3 center-cut bacon slices, cooked, drained, and crumbled

1. Combine first 7 ingredients in a small bowl.
2. Bring 8 cups water to a boil in a large saucepan. Add wax beans; cook 5 minutes or until crisp-tender. Drain and plunge into ice water; drain. Combine beans, radishes, and oil in a large bowl; toss to coat. Place bean mixture on a serving platter; drizzle with buttermilk dressing. Top with cheese, pepper, and bacon. Serves 6 (serving size: about 1 cup bean mixture and 1½ tablespoons dressing)

CALORIES 89; FAT 4.9g (sat 1.6g, mono 2g, poly 0.3g); PROTEIN 5g; CARB 8g; FIBER 3g; CHOL 8mg; IRON 1mg; SODIUM 244mg; CALC 76mg

---

CRISPY FISH STICKS

A fun twist on a top kid fave gets raves from Matisse and friends.

"Today I made Crispy Fish Sticks. These are in no way similar to the boring store-bought kind. The fish is coated in cornflakes for extra crunch, which you don't usually get from regular breadcrumbs. We used tilapia for this recipe, but you could probably use any kind of firm white fish—just make sure to buy it the day you plan to cook so it's really fresh. I cut mine into bite-sized nuggets, but you can also use whole fillets or strips. The ketchup was a nice change from the tartar sauce I would normally have with fish. We used it on barbecue chicken a few days later. I also think it would go well on a burger. This was a hit with my friends and family, and I hope it is with yours, too!"

THE VERDICT

BETHANY (AGE 13)
She loves pineapple and thought the ketchup was a great addition. **10/10**

MANDY (AGE 12)
She said, "The cornflake crust was really good!" **10/10**

MATISSE (AGE 13)
The fish was amazing. I enjoyed the crunch of the cornflakes and the hit of lemon from the rind. **10/10**

Kid Friendly • Quick & Easy

Crispy Fish Sticks with Pineapple Ketchup

Hands-on: 10 min. Total: 25 min.

Cooking spray
2 cups cornflakes
1 teaspoon grated lemon rind
1 teaspoon freshly ground black pepper, divided
1 tablespoon fresh lemon juice
1 large egg
1 pound tilapia fillets, cut into 4 x 1–inch pieces (about 12 pieces)
1/4 teaspoon kosher salt
1/2 cup cubed fresh pineapple
1/3 cup reduced-sugar ketchup (such as Heinz)
1 teaspoon lower-sodium soy sauce

1. Preheat oven to 425°.
2. Place a wire rack on a large baking sheet. Coat rack with cooking spray. Place cereal in a large zip-top bag; roll with a rolling pin until crushed. Place crushed cereal, rind, and 1/4 teaspoon pepper in a shallow dish. Combine juice and egg in a shallow dish, stirring with a whisk.
3. Sprinkle fish evenly with 1/4 teaspoon pepper and salt. Dip fish in egg mixture; dredge in cereal mixture. Arrange fish on prepared rack; bake at 425° for 12 minutes or until fish flakes easily when tested with a fork.
4. Place 1/2 teaspoon pepper, pineapple, ketchup, and soy sauce in the bowl of a mini food processor; process until smooth. Serve ketchup mixture with fish sticks. Serves 4 (serving size: about 3 fish sticks and 2 tablespoons ketchup mixture)

CALORIES 204; FAT 3.3g (sat 1.1g, mono 1g, poly 0.7g); PROTEIN 26g; CARB 18g; FIBER 2g; CHOL 103mg; IRON 1mg; SODIUM 533mg; CALC 24mg

MEATLESS MONDAYS

CREAMY, CRUNCHY, JUICY, CRISP

Pickled onions, feta, and capers add bright, briny pop to an earthy beet and broccoli salad.

Gluten Free • Vegetarian

Broccoli, Beet, and Pickled Onion Salad

Hands-on: 30 min. Total: 1 hr.
Steam the broccoli while you are cooling and peeling the beets. Look for beets that are about 2 inches in diameter to match our steaming cook time.

Vinaigrette:
3 tablespoons red wine vinegar
2 tablespoons olive oil
1 tablespoon diced shallots
1 teaspoon Dijon mustard
1/8 teaspoon kosher salt
Salad:
1 cup thinly vertically sliced red onion
1/2 cup cider vinegar
1/4 teaspoon kosher salt, divided
4 golden beets, trimmed (about 1 pound)
1 pound broccoli with stalks
1/4 teaspoon freshly ground black pepper
1/4 cup chopped walnuts, toasted
1/4 cup broccoli sprouts
1 tablespoon capers, rinsed and drained
2 ounces feta cheese, crumbled (about 1/2 cup)

1. To prepare vinaigrette, combine first 5 ingredients in a small bowl, stirring well with a whisk.
2. To prepare salad, combine onion, cider vinegar, and 1/8 teaspoon salt in a zip-top plastic bag. Let stand 30 minutes. Drain.
3. Steam beets, covered, 35 minutes or until tender. Rinse under cold water. Drain; peel and cut into 1/4-inch-thick slices. Combine 2 tablespoons vinaigrette and beets, tossing to coat.
4. Peel broccoli stalks; cut into quarters lengthwise. Steam broccoli, covered, 8 minutes or until crisp-tender. Combine remaining vinaigrette, broccoli, 1/8 teaspoon salt, and pepper in a bowl; toss to coat.
5. Place broccoli on each of 4 plates. Top evenly with beets and onions. Sprinkle with walnuts, sprouts, capers, and cheese. Serves 4 (serving size: about 1 beet, 3 pieces broccoli, 3 tablespoons onion, 1 tablespoon nuts, 1 tablespoon sprouts, 1/2 teaspoon capers, and 2 tablespoons cheese)

CALORIES 251; FAT 15.3g (sat 3.6g, mono 6.3g, poly 4.4g); PROTEIN 9g; CARB 24g; FIBER 7g; CHOL 13mg; IRON 2mg; SODIUM 531mg; CALC 159mg

DON'T TOSS THE BROCCOLI STALKS. THEY STEAM UP EVEN MORE TENDER AND JUICY THAN THE FLORETS.

FRESH PIZZA

Six fantastic pies hearty enough for fall, delicious and simple enough for tonight

Kid Friendly • Quick & Easy

Grilled Individual Hawaiian Pizzas

Hands-on: 22 min. Total: 35 min.
Here's a supersimple grilled pizza your kids will love. Don't feel like grilling? No problem: Bake them. Cook the dough on a hot pizza stone at 500° for 4 minutes, add toppings, and bake an additional 8 minutes or until done.

12 ounces refrigerated fresh pizza dough
1 tablespoon honey
1 teaspoon water
3 (½-inch-thick) slices fresh pineapple
1 (4-ounce) slice 33%-less-sodium ham (about ¼ inch thick)
Cooking spray
⅔ cup lower-sodium marinara sauce
4 ounces fresh mozzarella cheese, torn into small pieces
½ teaspoon freshly ground black pepper

1. Remove dough from refrigerator. Let stand at room temperature, covered, 30 minutes.
2. Preheat grill to high heat.
3. While dough stands, combine honey and 1 teaspoon water in a medium bowl. Add pineapple and ham; toss to coat. Add pineapple and ham to grill rack coated with cooking spray; grill 3 minutes on each side or until well marked. Remove from grill; cut into 1-inch pieces.

4. Divide dough into 4 portions. Roll each portion into a 7-inch circle on a lightly floured surface. Lightly coat dough with cooking spray. Place dough on grill rack; grill 2 minutes on each side or until lightly browned.
5. Reduce grill temperature to medium.
6. Spread marinara evenly over pizzas, leaving a ½-inch border. Arrange pineapple and ham over pizzas, and sprinkle with cheese. Place pizzas on grill rack; grill pizzas 3 minutes or until cheese melts. Sprinkle with pepper. Serves 4 (serving size: 1 pizza)

CALORIES 401; **FAT** 10.9g (sat 4.8g, mono 2.1g, poly 0.7g); **PROTEIN** 19g; **CARB** 54g; **FIBER** 7g; **CHOL** 40mg; **IRON** 2mg; **SODIUM** 690mg; **CALC** 17mg

Kid Friendly • Vegetarian

Caprese Pizza

Hands-on: 20 min. Total: 45 min.

12 ounces refrigerated fresh pizza dough
1½ cups grape tomatoes, halved
2 tablespoons olive oil, divided
3 tablespoons balsamic vinegar
1 tablespoon cornmeal
3 garlic cloves, minced
3.25 ounces fresh mozzarella cheese, thinly sliced
Cooking spray
½ teaspoon kosher salt
¼ teaspoon freshly ground black pepper
¼ cup very thinly sliced fresh basil leaves

1. Remove dough from refrigerator. Let stand at room temperature, covered, for 30 minutes.
2. Preheat broiler to high.
3. While dough stands, combine tomatoes and 1 tablespoon oil on a parchment-lined baking sheet; toss to coat tomatoes. Broil 10 minutes or until tomatoes begin to brown.
4. Bring vinegar to a simmer in a saucepan over medium heat; simmer 10 minutes or until reduced by half.
5. Place a pizza stone or heavy baking sheet in oven. Preheat oven to 500° (keep pizza stone or baking sheet in oven as it preheats).
6. Roll dough into a 14-inch circle on a lightly floured surface; pierce dough liberally with a fork. Remove pizza stone from oven. Sprinkle cornmeal over pizza stone. Place dough on pizza stone; bake at 500° for 5 minutes.
7. Remove stone from oven. Combine 1 tablespoon oil and garlic; brush evenly over crust, leaving a 1-inch border. Top with tomatoes and cheese. Spray border of crust with cooking spray. Bake 12 minutes or until cheese melts and crust browns. Sprinkle with salt and pepper. Drizzle with vinegar; sprinkle with basil. Cut into 8 wedges. Serves 4 (serving size: 2 wedges)

CALORIES 385; **FAT** 15.2g (sat 5.1g, mono 7.3g, poly 1.5g); **PROTEIN** 12g; **CARB** 47g; **FIBER** 7g; **CHOL** 17mg; **IRON** 1mg; **SODIUM** 676mg; **CALC** 22mg

TANGY-SWEET BALSAMIC DRIZZLE MAKES FRESH TOMATOES SING.

BBQ Pizza with Slaw

Hands-on: 19 min. Total: 40 min.
The sweet, tangy, spicy barbecue topping comes together in a snap with the help of supermarket rotisserie chicken.

12 ounces refrigerated fresh pizza dough
⅓ cup unsalted ketchup
¼ cup lower-sodium marinara sauce
3 tablespoons water
1 tablespoon honey mustard
1 teaspoon ground ancho chile pepper
1 teaspoon lower-sodium Worcestershire sauce
¾ teaspoon smoked paprika
¾ teaspoon garlic powder
½ teaspoon onion powder
3 ounces shredded skinless, boneless rotisserie chicken breast
2 teaspoons cornmeal
3 ounces reduced-fat sharp cheddar cheese, grated (about ¾ cup)
2 teaspoons cider vinegar
2 teaspoons extra-virgin olive oil
Dash of sugar
¼ cup thinly sliced green cabbage
¼ cup thinly sliced red onion
3 tablespoons grated carrot
2 tablespoons chopped fresh flat-leaf parsley
½ teaspoon crushed red pepper

1. Remove dough from refrigerator. Let stand at room temperature, covered, 30 minutes.
2. While dough stands, place a pizza stone or heavy baking sheet in oven. Preheat oven to 500° (keep pizza stone or baking sheet in oven as it preheats).
3. Combine ketchup and next 8 ingredients in a small saucepan; bring to a simmer. Reduce heat; cook 6 minutes. Combine 2 tablespoons ketchup mixture and chicken in a small bowl; toss to coat.
4. Roll dough into a 14-inch circle on a lightly floured surface; pierce liberally with a fork. Carefully remove pizza stone from oven. Sprinkle cornmeal over stone; place dough on stone. Spread remaining ketchup mixture over crust, leaving a ½-inch border. Arrange chicken mixture over dough. Sprinkle with cheese. Bake at 500° for 9 minutes or until crust and cheese are browned.
5. Combine vinegar, oil, and sugar in a medium bowl. Stir in cabbage, onion, and carrot; toss to coat. Top pizza with cabbage mixture, parsley, and red pepper. Cut into 8 wedges. Serves 4 (serving size: 2 wedges)

CALORIES 399; **FAT** 9.7g (sat 3.6g, mono 3g, poly 0.8g); **PROTEIN** 20g; **CARB** 55g; **FIBER** 7g; **CHOL** 34mg; **IRON** 2mg; **SODIUM** 702mg; **CALC** 170mg

Carne Asada Pizza

Hands-on: 40 min. Total: 1 hr. 15 min.

12 ounces refrigerated fresh pizza dough
2 small poblano peppers
8 ounces flank steak, trimmed
½ teaspoon ground cumin
½ teaspoon chipotle chile powder
⅛ teaspoon salt
Cooking spray
1 small red onion, cut into ½-inch-thick rings
½ cup lower-sodium marinara sauce
1 tablespoon adobo sauce from 1 can chipotle chiles in adobo sauce
1 tablespoon cornmeal
1 ounce part-skim mozzarella cheese, shredded (about ¼ cup)
1 ounce cheddar cheese, shredded (about ¼ cup)
1 ounce queso fresco, crumbled (about ¼ cup)
1 cup chopped seeded tomato
2 tablespoons fresh lime juice
2 tablespoons minced red onion
Cilantro sprigs (optional)

1. Remove dough from refrigerator. Let stand at room temperature, covered, 30 minutes.
2. Preheat broiler to high.
3. While dough stands, arrange poblanos on a foil-lined baking sheet. Broil 8 minutes or until charred on all sides, turning occasionally. Wrap peppers in foil, and close tightly. Let stand 15 minutes. Peel and seed peppers; discard skin, membrane, and seeds. Cut into ¼-inch-thick strips.
4. Place a pizza stone or heavy baking sheet in oven. Preheat oven to 500° (keep pizza stone or baking sheet in oven as it preheats).
5. Sprinkle steak with cumin, chipotle powder, and salt. Heat a grill pan over high heat. Coat pan with cooking spray. Add steak to pan; cook 4 minutes on each side or until well marked. Let stand 10 minutes. Thinly slice steak across the grain.
6. Add onion rings to pan; grill 4 minutes on each side or until well marked. Place in a bowl; cover with plastic wrap. Combine marinara and adobo sauce.
7. Roll dough into a 15 x 9–inch rectangle on a lightly floured surface. Pierce dough liberally with a fork. Sprinkle cornmeal on pizza stone. Place dough on hot stone; bake at 500° for 5 minutes. Remove stone from oven. Spread sauce mixture over dough, leaving a ½-inch border, and top evenly with mozzarella and cheddar. Arrange poblano and onion slices over pizza, and top with steak. Sprinkle with queso fresco. Return stone to oven; bake pizza for 9 minutes or until crust is done.
8. Combine tomato, juice, and minced red onion; sprinkle tomato mixture over pizza. Top with cilantro sprigs, if desired. Serves 4 (serving size: 2 slices)

CALORIES 419; **FAT** 10.2g (sat 4.8g, mono 3.7g, poly 1g); **PROTEIN** 26g; **CARB** 54g; **FIBER** 9g; **CHOL** 49mg; **IRON** 3mg; **SODIUM** 685mg; **CALC** 153mg

Ratatouille Pizza

Hands-on: 30 min. Total: 55 min.

12 ounces refrigerated fresh pizza dough
1 red bell pepper
1 tablespoon olive oil
2 cups (1/2-inch) cubed eggplant
1/4 teaspoon kosher salt
6 garlic cloves, thinly sliced
1 cup thinly sliced zucchini rounds
1 cup thinly sliced yellow squash rounds
1 tablespoon chopped fresh oregano
1/2 cup lower-sodium marinara sauce
2 tablespoons balsamic vinegar
1 tablespoon cornmeal
3 ounces fresh mozzarella cheese, torn into small pieces
3/4 cup thinly sliced red onion rings
1/2 ounce Parmesan cheese, grated (about 1/4 cup)
1/3 cup torn basil leaves
1/2 teaspoon crushed red pepper

1. Remove dough from refrigerator. Let stand at room temperature, covered, 30 minutes.
2. Preheat broiler to high.
3. Cut bell pepper in half lengthwise; discard seeds and membranes. Place pepper halves, skin sides up, on a foil-lined baking sheet; flatten with hand. Broil 12 minutes or until blackened. Wrap pepper in foil; close tightly. Let stand 10 minutes. Peel and cut into 1/4-inch-thick strips.
4. Place a pizza stone or heavy baking sheet in oven. Heat to 500° (keep stone or sheet in oven as it preheats).
5. Heat a nonstick skillet over medium-high heat. Add 1 tablespoon oil; swirl. Add eggplant; sauté 3 minutes. Add 1/4 teaspoon salt and garlic; sauté 2 minutes. Remove eggplant mixture from pan; set aside. Add zucchini, squash, and oregano to pan; sauté 3 minutes. Remove zucchini mixture; set aside.
6. Combine marinara and vinegar.
7. Roll dough into a 14-inch circle. Pierce liberally with a fork. Remove stone from oven. Sprinkle cornmeal on stone. Place dough on stone; bake at 500° for 5 minutes. Remove from oven. Spread marinara mixture over dough, leaving a 1/2-inch border; top with half of mozzarella. Arrange zucchini mixture over cheese. Top with remaining mozzarella, eggplant mixture, peppers, and onion rings. Sprinkle with Parmesan. Bake 10 minutes or until crust is done. Top with basil and crushed red pepper. Serves 4 (serving size: 2 wedges)

CALORIES 392; **FAT** 11.6g (sat 4.9g, mono 4.6g, poly 1.2g); **PROTEIN** 15g; **CARB** 55g; **FIBER** 10g; **CHOL** 20mg; **IRON** 3mg; **SODIUM** 585mg; **CALC** 102mg

Deep-Dish Mushroom and Onion Pizza

(pictured on page 232)

Hands-on: 35 min. Total: 2 hr. 30 min.

1 1/4 teaspoons dry yeast
1/2 teaspoon sugar
3/4 cup warm water (100°)
3 tablespoons olive oil
9 ounces all-purpose flour, divided (about 2 cups)
1/4 cup semolina flour
3/8 teaspoon salt
Cooking spray
1 tablespoon olive oil
1 1/2 cups thinly vertically sliced onion
1 tablespoon minced garlic
1/2 teaspoon dried oregano
1/4 teaspoon salt, divided
1/4 teaspoon black pepper
1 (8-ounce) package sliced mushrooms
3/4 cup lower-sodium marinara sauce
1 bay leaf
1 tablespoon olive oil
1 ounce Parmesan cheese, grated (about 1/4 cup)
5 ounces part-skim mozzarella cheese, shredded (about 1 1/4 cups)

1. Dissolve yeast and sugar in 3/4 cup warm water in the bowl of a stand mixer; let stand 5 minutes. Add 3 tablespoons oil. Weigh or lightly spoon 7.9 ounces (about 1 3/4 cups) all-purpose flour into dry measuring cups; level with a knife. Add 7.9 ounces flour, semolina, and 3/8 teaspoon salt to yeast mixture; mix at medium-low speed with a dough hook until smooth (about 4 minutes). Turn dough out onto a lightly floured surface. Knead until smooth and elastic (about 5 minutes), gradually adding remaining 1/4 cup all-purpose flour. Place dough in a large bowl coated with cooking spray, turning to coat top. Cover and let rise in a warm place (85°), free from drafts, 1 1/2 hours or until doubled in size.
2. Heat a large skillet over medium-high heat. Add 1 tablespoon oil; swirl. Add onion; cook 3 minutes or just until tender. Stir in garlic; cook 30 seconds, stirring constantly. Add oregano, 1/8 teaspoon salt, pepper, and mushrooms. Cook 6 minutes or until mushrooms release their moisture.
3. Combine 1/8 teaspoon salt, marinara, and bay leaf in a saucepan. Bring to a boil; reduce heat, and simmer 5 minutes. Discard bay leaf.
4. Preheat oven to 425°. Place oven rack in bottom third of oven.
5. Coat bottom and sides of a 10-inch springform pan with 1 tablespoon oil. Punch dough down, and turn dough out onto a lightly floured surface. Gently press dough into a 13-inch circle. Carefully lift dough and place in prepared pan. Press dough into bottom and halfway up sides of pan. Sprinkle Parmesan over dough. Top with mushroom mixture. Spread marinara mixture over mushroom mixture. Sprinkle with mozzarella. Bake at 425° for 28 minutes or until browned. Let stand 5 minutes. Serves 6 (serving size: 1 wedge)

CALORIES 410; **FAT** 18g (sat 4.9g, mono 9.8g, poly 1.6g); **PROTEIN** 15g; **CARB** 47g; **FIBER** 3g; **CHOL** 19mg; **IRON** 3mg; **SODIUM** 663mg; **CALC** 266mg

EASIEST RED BEANS AND RICE

Big, bold N'awlins flavor builds in the slow cooker while you're at work.

Kid Friendly • Freezable Make Ahead

Slow Cooker Red Beans and Rice

Hands-on: 30 min. Total: 16 hr. 30 min. *Because dried kidney beans contain a toxin that's not killed at the low temperatures of the slow cooker, we boil them briskly for 10 minutes first; don't be tempted to skip this step.*

1 pound dried red kidney beans
1 tablespoon olive oil
1 pound andouille sausage, quartered lengthwise and cut crosswise into ³/₄-inch pieces
1½ cups chopped onion
1½ cups chopped poblano chile
1 cup diced celery
2 tablespoons chopped fresh thyme
½ teaspoon kosher salt
10 garlic cloves, crushed
1 (12-ounce) can lager-style beer (such as Budweiser)
4 cups unsalted chicken stock (such as Swanson)
½ teaspoon ground red pepper
¼ teaspoon freshly ground black pepper
3 bay leaves
½ cup thinly sliced green onions, divided
2 tablespoons cider vinegar
4 cups hot cooked long-grain rice

1. Sort and wash beans; place in a large saucepan. Cover with water to 2 inches above beans; cover and let stand 8 hours. Drain beans.
2. Return beans to saucepan. Cover with water to 2 inches above beans; bring to a boil. Cook 10 minutes; drain.
3. Heat a large skillet over medium-high heat. Add oil to pan; swirl to coat. Add sausage; cook 6 minutes or until browned. Add onion and next 5 ingredients; cook 8 minutes. Stir in beer; bring to a boil. Cook 2 minutes, scraping pan to loosen browned bits. Place sausage mixture in a 6-quart electric slow cooker. Add beans, stock, red pepper, black pepper, and bay leaves. Cover and cook on LOW for 8 hours.
4. Discard bay leaves. Stir in ¼ cup green onions and vinegar. Serve over rice; sprinkle with ¼ cup green onions. Serves 8 (serving size: 1 cup bean mixture, ½ cup rice, and 1½ teaspoons green onions)

CALORIES 486; FAT 10.1g (sat 3.3g, mono 5.2g, poly 0.8g); PROTEIN 30g; CARB 65g; FIBER 16g; CHOL 33mg; IRON 7mg; SODIUM 634mg; CALC 117mg

> DON'T BE TURNED OFF BY THE TOTAL TIME THIS RECIPE REQUIRES: EIGHT HOURS ARE SIMPLY FOR SOAKING BEANS OVERNIGHT, AND ANOTHER EIGHT ARE FOR HANDS-OFF COOKING.

TODAY'S SPECIAL: MARINATED BEET SALAD

From Chef Josh Habiger of Pinewood Social in Nashville, TN

Beets have become a hugely popular, ubiquitous item on restaurant menus. But just because they're a hearty root veggie doesn't mean they don't need careful treatment: They can run the gamut from steamed and bland to deliciously roasty and caramelized. "Well-roasted beets can be eye-opening," chef Josh Habiger says. "A lot of chefs use beets as a really colorful ingredient that brightens up a plate. But if you don't do the ingredient justice, you could be ruining it for that person forever." The distinctive flavor of beets lends itself to simple preparations. "You can make a salad of roasted beets and vinegar; you don't even need to add oil," he says. Habiger was a founding chef of the celebrated Catbird Seat in Nashville and now runs the kitchen at Pinewood Social, one of the country's most buzz-worthy restaurants. He also worked in such world-renowned kitchens as The Fat Duck in England and Alinea in Chicago. Though well versed in some of the planet's most elaborate cooking, Habiger shows restraint when needed, as with this salad. Roasted beets get tossed in a full-bodied, citrus-spiked vinaigrette made with pureed roasted leek. In his original version—available this month at Pinewood Social—he grills the leeks for added complexity.

continued

Marinated Beet Salad

Hands-on: 22 min. Total: 1 hr. 45 min.

1 pound red baby beets, trimmed
1/2 cup water, divided
1/8 teaspoon kosher salt, divided
6 thyme sprigs, divided
2 rosemary sprigs, divided
1 pound gold baby beets, trimmed
1 medium leek, white and light green parts only, halved lengthwise
Cooking spray
1 teaspoon grated orange rind
3 tablespoons fresh orange juice
1 teaspoon grated lime rind
2 tablespoons fresh lime juice
2 tablespoons sherry vinegar
2 tablespoons olive oil
1 teaspoon thyme leaves
1/8 teaspoon salt
6 cups herb salad mix
3 tablespoons plain fat-free Greek yogurt
1 tablespoon toasted unsalted sunflower seeds

1. Preheat oven to 375°.
2. Place red beets, ¼ cup water, a dash of salt, 3 thyme sprigs, and 1 rosemary sprig in an 11 x 7–inch glass baking dish; cover with foil. Repeat procedure with gold beets, ¼ cup water, dash of salt, 3 thyme sprigs, and 1 rosemary sprig. Roast at 375° for 1 hour and 15 minutes or until a knife inserted into center of a beet meets little resistance. Remove from oven; uncover. Let stand until cool enough to handle; rub skins from beets with a kitchen towel. Discard skins.
3. Coat leek with cooking spray. Place leek, cut side down, on a foil-lined baking sheet. Roast at 375° for 25 minutes or until very tender. Cool slightly. Place leek, orange rind, and next 7 ingredients in a blender. Process until smooth.

4. Place beets in a large bowl with half of vinaigrette; toss to combine. Add salad mix and remaining vinaigrette; toss gently to coat. Place 1⅔ cups salad on each of 6 plates. Top each serving with 1½ teaspoons yogurt; sprinkle each with ½ teaspoon sunflower seeds. Serves 6

CALORIES 144; FAT 5.6g (sat 0.8g, mono 3.5g, poly 1g); PROTEIN 4g; CARB 21g; FIBER 6g; CHOL 0mg; IRON 2mg; SODIUM 233mg; CALC 45mg

BUDGET COOKING

FEED 4 FOR LESS THAN $10

Go big, go bold: Turn up the flavor with vibrant accents of citrus, chiles, and herbs.

Make Ahead

Vietnamese Barbecue Pork and Noodle Salad

$2.45 PER SERVING

Hands-on: 20 min. Total: 1 hr. 35 min.
Sambal oelek is a condiment you'll be happy to have on hand. Made by grinding together chiles, vinegar or lime, a touch of sugar, and salt, it's great in marinades and salad dressings, or it can add heat and complexity to a fruity mango salsa.

5 teaspoons dark sesame oil, divided
2 tablespoons lower-sodium soy sauce
1½ tablespoons sambal oelek (ground fresh chile paste)
1 tablespoon brown sugar
6 garlic cloves, chopped
1 large shallot, chopped
1 (12-ounce) pork tenderloin
Cooking spray
6 ounces uncooked rice vermicelli
1 tablespoon fresh lime juice

2 cups sliced romaine lettuce
1 cup thinly sliced cucumber
1/2 cup julienne-cut carrot
2 tablespoons chopped dry-roasted, unsalted peanuts
4 lime wedges

1. Place 1 tablespoon sesame oil and next 5 ingredients (through shallot) in a mini food processor; process until smooth. Place pork in a large zip-top plastic bag. Set aside ¼ cup marinade; add remaining marinade to bag, and seal. Marinate pork in refrigerator 1 hour, turning after 30 minutes.
2. Preheat oven to 450°.
3. Remove pork from bag; discard remaining marinade. Place pork on a broiler pan coated with cooking spray. Cook 25 minutes or until a thermometer inserted in thickest portion registers 140°. Let pork stand 10 minutes; thinly slice.
4. Cook noodles according to the package directions; drain and toss with 2 teaspoons sesame oil and lime juice. Divide noodles evenly among 4 bowls, and top each serving with ½ cup lettuce, ¼ cup cucumber, and 2 tablespoons carrot. Drizzle each serving with 1 tablespoon reserved marinade. Divide pork slices evenly among bowls; top each serving with 1½ teaspoons chopped peanuts and 1 lime wedge. Serves 4 (serving size: 1 salad)

CALORIES 373; FAT 10.1g (sat 1.8g, mono 4.1g, poly 3.5g); PROTEIN 21g; CARB 51g; FIBER 2g; CHOL 55mg; IRON 3mg; SODIUM 455mg; CALC 53mg

Grilled Chicken Thighs with Cilantro-Mint Chutney

$2.34 PER SERVING

Hands-on: 31 min. Total: 2 hr. 41 min.
Serve this moist chicken dish over brown rice.

3 tablespoons grated fresh onion
1/2 teaspoon ground red pepper
10 garlic cloves, minced
2 1/2 tablespoons canola oil, divided
2 teaspoons ground cumin, divided
4 (6-ounce) bone-in chicken thighs
1/2 teaspoon kosher salt, divided
Cooking spray
1 cup cilantro leaves
1/2 cup mint leaves
1/3 cup chopped green onions
2 teaspoons chopped seeded jalapeño pepper

1. Combine first 3 ingredients in a large zip-top plastic bag; stir in 2 tablespoons oil and 1¾ teaspoons cumin. Add chicken to bag, seal, and massage marinade into chicken. Marinate in refrigerator 2 hours.
2. Preheat grill to medium-high heat.
3. Remove chicken from bag. Sprinkle chicken with ¼ teaspoon salt. Place on grill rack coated with cooking spray; grill 8 minutes on each side.
4. Place cilantro, mint, onions, and jalapeño in a food processor. Add 1½ teaspoons oil, ¼ teaspoon cumin, and ¼ teaspoon salt; process until smooth. Serve chicken topped with chutney. Serves 4 (serving size: 1 chicken thigh and about 1½ table-spoons chutney)

CALORIES 331; **FAT** 24g (sat 4.8g, mono 11.8g, poly 5.5g); **PROTEIN** 24g; **CARB** 5g; **FIBER** 1g; **CHOL** 135mg; **IRON** 2mg; **SODIUM** 332mg; **CALC** 46mg

---

FOOD ON THE MOVE

2 GREAT GRAINS, 10 HEALTHY LUNCHES

It's tasty. It's easy. It's built for speed.

Quick & Easy • Make Ahead
Gluten Free

Black Bean–Quinoa Salad with Chipotle Steak

(pictured on page 231)

Hands-on: 28 min. Total: 28 min.

5 teaspoons olive oil, divided
1/2 teaspoon kosher salt, divided
1/4 teaspoon chipotle chile powder
1/4 teaspoon freshly ground black pepper
2 (6-ounce) top sirloin steaks
2 tablespoons fresh orange juice
2 tablespoons red wine vinegar
1 tablespoon adobo sauce from canned chipotle chiles in adobo sauce
1/2 teaspoon ground cumin
1/4 teaspoon honey
1 1/2 cups cooked quinoa
1 cup unsalted black beans, rinsed and drained
3/4 cup chopped red bell pepper
1/4 cup chopped fresh cilantro
1/4 cup thinly sliced green onions
1 1/2 cups baby spinach leaves
1 ounce crumbled feta cheese (about 1/4 cup)
1/2 cup ripe peeled avocado, sliced

1. Heat a grill pan over medium-high heat. Combine 1 teaspoon oil, ¼ teaspoon salt, chipotle chile powder, and black pepper; rub evenly over steaks. Add steaks to pan; cook 4 minutes on each side or until desired degree of doneness. Let stand 10 minutes. Cut steaks diagonally across the grain into thin slices.
2. Combine 4 teaspoons oil, ¼ teaspoon salt, juice, and next 4 in-gredients (through honey) in a large bowl, stirring with a whisk. Stir in quinoa, beans, bell pepper, cilantro, green onions, and spinach; toss to coat. Sprinkle with feta. Divide quinoa mixture evenly among 4 shallow bowls; top evenly with steak and avocado. Serves 4 (serving size: about 1½ cups)

CALORIES 340; **FAT** 14.8g (sat 3.5g, mono 7.6g, poly 1.2g); **PROTEIN** 24g; **CARB** 27g; **FIBER** 7g; **CHOL** 51mg; **IRON** 4mg; **SODIUM** 421mg; **CALC** 103mg

WE LOVE THE CHIPOTLE-RUBBED SIRLOIN, BUT THIS SALAD IS A WONDERFUL USE FOR ANY LEFTOVER STEAK.

Kale Caesar Quinoa Salad with Roasted Chicken

Hands-on: 23 min. Total: 23 min.

2 tablespoons hot water
2 tablespoons canola mayonnaise
1½ tablespoons olive oil
1 tablespoon fresh lemon juice
½ teaspoon anchovy paste
¼ teaspoon freshly ground black pepper
1 garlic clove, grated
1.5 ounces shaved Parmesan cheese, divided (about 6 tablespoons)
5 cups thinly sliced stemmed Lacinato kale
1½ cups cooked quinoa
1½ cups chopped skinless, boneless rotisserie chicken breast
2 tablespoons chopped toasted walnuts

1. Combine first 7 ingredients in a bowl, stirring well with a whisk. Stir in 3 tablespoons Parmesan cheese. Add kale, quinoa, and chicken; toss to coat. Top with 3 tablespoons Parmesan cheese and walnuts. Serves 4 (serving size: 1½ cups)

CALORIES 344; **FAT** 16.3g (sat 3.3g, mono 6.9g, poly 3.6g); **PROTEIN** 27g; **CARB** 25g; **FIBER** 4g; **CHOL** 61mg; **IRON** 3mg; **SODIUM** 487mg; **CALC** 256mg

Asian Stir-Fry Quinoa Bowl

Hands-on: 28 min. Total: 28 min.

8 ounces extra-firm tofu
2 tablespoons toasted sesame oil, divided
1 cup (1-inch) slices green onions
1 tablespoon minced peeled fresh ginger
5 ounces thinly sliced shiitake mushroom caps
5 garlic cloves, thinly sliced
1 red bell pepper, thinly sliced
3 tablespoons lower-sodium soy sauce, divided
2 tablespoons rice vinegar, divided
¼ teaspoon kosher salt
2 cups cooked quinoa
2 cups thinly sliced napa cabbage
¼ cup chopped fresh cilantro
½ teaspoon sugar

1. Arrange tofu on several layers of heavy-duty paper towels. Cover with additional paper towels; let stand 15 minutes. Cut into ½-inch-thick cubes.
2. Heat a large nonstick skillet over medium-high heat. Add 1 tablespoon oil to pan; swirl to coat. Add tofu; sauté 4 minutes or until browned. Place tofu in a bowl. Return pan to medium-high heat. Add 1 tablespoon oil to pan. Add onions and next 4 ingredients (through bell pepper); stir-fry 4 minutes or just until tender. Add 2 tablespoons soy sauce, 1 tablespoon vinegar, and salt; cook 30 seconds. Add mushroom mixture to tofu.
3. Stir in 1 tablespoon soy sauce, 1 tablespoon vinegar, quinoa, cabbage, cilantro, and sugar. Toss well to combine. Serves 4 (serving size: 1¼ cups)

CALORIES 283; **FAT** 12.5g (sat 1.7g, mono 3.7g, poly 5.1g); **PROTEIN** 12g; **CARB** 32g; **FIBER** 5g; **CHOL** 0mg; **IRON** 3mg; **SODIUM** 540mg; **CALC** 99mg

Roasted Carrot, Chicken, and Grape Quinoa Bowl

Hands-on: 20 min. Total: 30 min.
Caramelized carrots and fresh, juicy grapes lend a welcome sweetness to this quinoa.

2 cups (¾-inch) diagonally cut carrot
2 teaspoons olive oil
½ teaspoon kosher salt, divided
Cooking spray
5 tablespoons plain 2% reduced-fat Greek yogurt
3 tablespoons fresh lemon juice
2 tablespoons water
1½ tablespoons honey
¾ teaspoon ground cumin
½ teaspoon black pepper
1½ cups cooked quinoa
1½ cups shredded skinless, boneless rotisserie chicken breast
1½ cups seedless red grapes, halved
½ cup thinly sliced green onions
½ cup flat-leaf parsley leaves
½ cup toasted sliced almonds
4 cups mixed salad greens

1. Preheat oven to 450°.
2. Combine carrot, oil, and ¼ teaspoon salt on a jelly-roll pan coated with cooking spray; toss to coat. Bake at 450° for 15 minutes or until tender.
3. Combine ¼ teaspoon salt, yogurt, and next 5 ingredients (through pepper) in a large bowl, stirring with a whisk. Add carrot, quinoa, and next 5 ingredients (through almonds); toss. Place 1 cup salad greens in each of 4 shallow bowls; top each serving with about 1½ cups quinoa mixture. Serves 4

CALORIES 371; **FAT** 12.3g (sat 1.6g, mono 6.2g, poly 2g); **PROTEIN** 25g; **CARB** 44g; **FIBER** 7g; **CHOL** 51mg; **IRON** 3mg; **SODIUM** 502mg; **CALC** 142mg

Kid Friendly • Quick & Easy
Make Ahead • Vegetarian

Cauliflower and Chickpea Quinoa with Tahini Drizzle

Hands-on: 18 min. Total: 40 min.
Roasting adds an earthy depth of flavor to the veggies, but you can save time by keeping them raw—just toss right into the quinoa.

2½ cups chopped cauliflower florets
⅔ cup chopped onion
1 (15-ounce) can organic chickpeas, rinsed, drained, and patted dry
2 tablespoons olive oil, divided
1½ cups cooked quinoa
¼ cup chopped fresh flat-leaf parsley
½ teaspoon kosher salt
¼ teaspoon freshly ground black pepper
¼ cup pine nuts, toasted
2 tablespoons tahini
2 tablespoons water
2 tablespoons plain nonfat Greek yogurt
1 tablespoon fresh lemon juice
2 teaspoons lower-sodium soy sauce
1 garlic clove, minced

1. Preheat oven to 400°.
2. Combine first 3 ingredients on a jelly-roll pan. Drizzle with 1 tablespoon oil; toss to coat. Bake at 400° for 20 minutes or until cauliflower is tender, stirring once. Place 1 tablespoon oil, cauliflower mixture, quinoa, and next 4 ingredients (through nuts) in a large bowl; toss.
3. Combine tahini and remaining ingredients in a small bowl, stirring with a whisk. Drizzle tahini mixture over cauliflower mixture. Serves 4 (serving size: about 1 cup)

CALORIES 374; **FAT** 19.8g (sat 2.1g, mono 8.4g, poly 6g); **PROTEIN** 13g; **CARB** 40g; **FIBER** 11g; **CHOL** 0mg; **IRON** 3mg; **SODIUM** 507mg; **CALC** 87mg

Kid Friendly • Quick & Easy
Make Ahead

Cherry, Chicken, and Pecan Wheat Berry Salad

Hands-on: 28 min. Total: 28 min.
What a fantastic combo! If you can't find fresh cherries, add ¼ cup boiling water to ¼ cup dried cherries. Let stand 10 minutes; drain and chop.

3 tablespoons olive oil, divided
2 tablespoons apple cider vinegar
¾ teaspoon kosher salt
½ teaspoon freshly ground black pepper
¼ teaspoon sugar
1½ cups cooked wheat berries
¼ cup pecan halves and pieces, toasted
6 ounces shredded skinless, boneless chicken breast
½ cup chopped onion
1 tablespoon chopped fresh thyme
1 cup fresh cherries, pitted and halved
1 ounce baby arugula leaves
2 ounces goat cheese, crumbled

1. Combine 2½ tablespoons oil, vinegar, salt, pepper, and sugar in a large bowl, stirring well with a whisk. Add wheat berries, nuts, and chicken; toss.
2. Heat a medium nonstick skillet over medium heat. Add 1½ teaspoons oil to pan; swirl to coat. Add onion and thyme; cook 3 minutes or until tender. Add to wheat berry mixture; toss. Stir in cherries and arugula; toss. Sprinkle with cheese. Serves 4 (serving size: about 1¼ cups)

CALORIES 397; **FAT** 20.1g (sat 4.4g, mono 12g, poly 2.8g); **PROTEIN** 21g; **CARB** 37g; **FIBER** 7g; **CHOL** 44mg; **IRON** 1mg; **SODIUM** 570mg; **CALC** 49mg]

Quick & Easy • Make Ahead

Smoked Salmon Wheat Berry Salad with Caper-Yogurt Dressing

Hands-on: 13 min. Total: 13 min.

3 tablespoons water
2 tablespoons capers, drained
2 tablespoons plain 2% Greek yogurt
2 tablespoons cider vinegar
1 teaspoon Dijon mustard
¾ teaspoon freshly ground black pepper
½ teaspoon sugar
3 ounces ⅓-less-fat cream cheese
2 cups cooked wheat berries
1½ cups thinly sliced English cucumber
¾ cup thinly vertically sliced red onion
⅓ cup fresh chopped dill
3½ ounces cold-smoked salmon, cut into thin strips, divided
4 cups baby spinach leaves

1. Combine first 8 ingredients in a bowl, stirring well with a whisk. Stir in wheat berries, cucumber, onion, dill, and 1½ ounces salmon; toss to coat. Place 1 cup spinach in each of 4 bowls; top each serving with 1 cup wheat berry mixture and ½ ounce salmon. Serves 4

CALORIES 275; **FAT** 7.1g (sat 3g, mono 1.3g, poly 0.6g); **PROTEIN** 15g; **CARB** 41g; **FIBER** 7g; **CHOL** 29mg; **IRON** 1mg; **SODIUM** 581mg; **CALC** 87mg

Wheat Berry Salad with Melon and Feta

Hands-on: 22 min. Total: 22 min.
We were blown away by this intriguing mix of fresh, crunchy, and juicy produce with chewy wheat berries and creamy cheese.

3 tablespoons extra-virgin olive oil
2 tablespoons white wine vinegar
1/2 teaspoon kosher salt
1/2 teaspoon freshly ground black pepper
1/2 teaspoon tomato paste
1 1/2 cups cooked wheat berries
1 cup sliced English cucumber
1 cup chopped watermelon
1 cup yellow grape tomatoes, halved
3 tablespoons chopped fresh mint
2 ounces feta cheese, crumbled (about 1/2 cup)
2 tablespoons unsalted sunflower seed kernels

1. Combine first 5 ingredients in a large bowl, stirring well with a whisk. Stir in wheat berries; toss to coat. Stir in cucumber, watermelon, tomato, and mint; toss to coat. Sprinkle with cheese and sunflower seeds. Serves 4 (serving size: about 1¼ cups)

CALORIES 306; **FAT** 16.5g (sat 3.8g, mono 9.2g, poly 2.4g); **PROTEIN** 9g; **CARB** 31g; **FIBER** 5g; **CHOL** 13mg; **IRON** 2mg; **SODIUM** 411mg; **CALC** 103mg

Cashew Chicken Wheat Berry Salad with Peas

Hands-on: 14 min. Total: 14 min. *The thigh meat lends an especially moist, rich flavor, but you can use any leftover chicken.*

4 teaspoons hoisin sauce
1 tablespoon rice vinegar
1 tablespoon lower-sodium soy sauce
1 tablespoon minced fresh garlic
1/2 teaspoon freshly ground black pepper
1/4 teaspoon kosher salt
2 cups cooked wheat berries
1 1/2 cups chopped cooked chicken thighs
3/4 cup sugar snap peas, halved diagonally
1/2 cup dry-roasted, unsalted cashews
1/3 cup thinly sliced green onions

1. Combine first 6 ingredients in a medium bowl, stirring well with a whisk. Add wheat berries, chicken, and peas; toss well to coat. Stir in cashews and onions. Serves 4 (serving size: 1 cup)

CALORIES 376; **FAT** 13.3g (sat 3g, mono 6.6g, poly 2.6g); **PROTEIN** 22g; **CARB** 46g; **FIBER** 7g; **CHOL** 71mg; **IRON** 2mg; **SODIUM** 393mg; **CALC** 32mg

Tuna, Olive, and Wheat Berry Salad

Hands-on: 9 min. Total: 9 min. *Be sure to seek out a sustainable type of tuna. We like Wild Planet's wild albacore tuna in extra-virgin olive oil; a 5-ounce can, once drained, gives you the correct amount here.*

2 tablespoons chopped fresh parsley
2 tablespoons extra-virgin olive oil
2 tablespoons fresh lemon juice
2 teaspoons chopped fresh thyme
1/2 teaspoon freshly ground black pepper
1/4 teaspoon kosher salt
2 1/2 cups cooked wheat berries
1/2 cup thinly vertically sliced red onion
10 pitted Castelvetrano olives, sliced
4 ounces canned or jarred white tuna packed in oil, drained

1. Combine first 6 ingredients in a medium bowl, stirring well with a whisk. Stir in wheat berries and onion; toss to coat. Place about ¾ cup wheat berry mixture on each of 4 plates. Sprinkle with olives; top with tuna. Serves 4

CALORIES 348; **FAT** 12.8g (sat 1.6g, mono 6.4g, poly 1.9g); **PROTEIN** 15g; **CARB** 46g; **FIBER** 8g; **CHOL** 9mg; **IRON** 0mg; **SODIUM** 535mg; **CALC** 10mg

FRIDAY NIGHTS LIGHT!

Three casual meals that let the eaters pile on their own fave toppings

Even as the deceleration of the weekend begins, many families find Friday night eating just as chaotic as on any weekday: After all, it's a workday, a soccer day, a get-stuff-done day. Friday dinner needs to be flexible, with a menu that will hold up over a few hours and can be dished out easily. With that end in mind, we've got you covered: three nourishing, serve-yourself supper bars with enough options to appeal to everyone's tastes.

THE CHILI BAR

For meat lovers, you can add ground beef to our vegetarian chili.

Kid Friendly • Freezable
Gluten Free • Make Ahead
Vegetarian

Five-Bean Chili

Hands-on: 30 min. Total: 1 hr. 15 min.
This chili packs in all the classic flavors you want and is loaded with beans. Serving this chili the next day lets flavors meld—if the beans soak up a lot of liquid overnight, you can add more vegetable broth or even water to thin out the stew.

1 tablespoon canola oil
2 cups prechopped onion
1 cup chopped carrot
2 tablespoons unsalted tomato paste
2 tablespoons minced fresh garlic
1 1/2 teaspoons dried oregano
1 1/2 teaspoons chili powder
1 teaspoon kosher salt
1/2 teaspoon Spanish smoked paprika
4 cups stemmed and torn kale
3 cups organic vegetable broth
2 red bell peppers, chopped
1 jalapeño pepper, seeded and chopped
1 (14.5-ounce) can unsalted diced tomatoes, undrained
1 (15-ounce) can unsalted black beans, rinsed and drained
1 (15-ounce) can unsalted kidney beans, rinsed and drained
1 (15.5-ounce) can unsalted chickpeas (garbanzo beans), rinsed and drained
1 (15.8-ounce) can unsalted Great Northern beans, rinsed and drained
1 (16-ounce) can unsalted pinto beans, rinsed and drained

1. Heat a large Dutch oven over medium heat. Add oil; swirl to coat. Add onion and carrot; sauté 10 minutes or until tender. Stir in tomato paste and next 5 ingredients (through paprika); cook 2 minutes, stirring constantly. Add kale and remaining ingredients. Cover and simmer 45 minutes. Serves 8 (serving size: about 1 1/2 cups)

CALORIES 221; FAT 2.8g (sat 0.2g, mono 1.2g, poly 0.7g); PROTEIN 11g; CARB 39g; FIBER 12g; CHOL 0mg; IRON 3mg; SODIUM 520mg; CALC 153mg

TOPPING OPTION

Kid Friendly • Freezable
Make Ahead • Vegetarian

Cheesy Corn Bread Croutons

Hands-on: 17 min. Total: 1 hr. 15 min.
These toasted corn bread cubes are crispy and hearty enough to top a bowl of chili without falling apart into crumbs.

1 cup fine cornmeal
1.5 ounces all-purpose flour (about 1/3 cup)
1 teaspoon baking powder
1/2 teaspoon salt
1/2 teaspoon baking soda
1/2 cup low-fat buttermilk
2 tablespoons butter, melted and cooled
2 ounces sharp cheddar cheese, shredded (about 1/2 cup)
1 large egg, lightly beaten
Cooking spray

1. Preheat oven to 400°.
2. Combine first 5 ingredients in a medium bowl, stirring with a whisk. Stir in remaining ingredients except cooking spray. Spread batter in an 8-inch square metal baking pan coated with cooking spray. Bake at 400° for 20 minutes or until a wooden pick inserted in center comes out clean. Cool in pan on a wire rack 10 minutes. Invert onto rack, and cool completely. Leave oven on.
3. Cut corn bread into 36 (1 1/3-inch) cubes. Spread in an even layer on a baking sheet; bake 10 minutes or until bread is toasted. Serves 12 (serving size: 3 croutons)

CALORIES 107; FAT 4.2g (sat 2.4g, mono 1.2g, poly 0.3g); PROTEIN 3g; CARB 14g; FIBER 1g; CHOL 26mg; IRON 1mg; SODIUM 237mg; CALC 72mg

**Kid Friendly • Quick & Easy
Gluten Free • Make Ahead
Vegetarian**

Toasted Corn and Tomato Chili Topping

Hands-on: 15 min. Total: 25 min. Toasting the corn kernels brings the sugars forward and adds a sweet caramel-y element to this salsa. For a shortcut, you can thaw frozen fire-roasted corn kernels instead.

**1½ cups fresh corn kernels
Cooking spray
⅓ cup finely chopped onion
2 tablespoons chopped fresh cilantro
1 tablespoon chopped pickled jalapeño
1 tablespoon pickled jalapeño juice
¼ teaspoon kosher salt
2 medium tomatoes, seeded and diced**

1. Preheat oven to 400°.
2. Arrange corn in a single layer on a baking sheet coated with cooking spray. Bake at 400° for 10 minutes or until corn is golden and lightly toasted. Combine corn and remaining ingredients in a medium bowl, tossing to combine. Serves 6 (serving size: ⅓ cup)

CALORIES 43; FAT 0.7g (sat 0.1g, mono 0.2g, poly 0.2g); PROTEIN 2g; CARB 9g; FIBER 1g; CHOL 0mg; IRON 0mg; SODIUM 139mg; CALC 7mg

THE STUFFED POTATO BAR

Try our hearty barley or chicken option, or go for your own custom creation.

**Kid Friendly • Gluten Free
Vegetarian**

Perfect Roasted Sweet Potatoes

Hands-on: 10 min. Total: 1 hr. 10 min.

Preheat oven to 400°. Pierce 6 (8-ounce) sweet potatoes with a fork. Rub potatoes with 1½ teaspoons olive oil; wrap each in foil. Place potatoes on a jelly-roll pan; bake at 400° for 1 hour or until tender. Partially split potatoes in half lengthwise; fluff the flesh with a fork. Sprinkle evenly with ⅜ teaspoon kosher salt and ¼ teaspoon freshly ground black pepper. Serves 6 (serving size: 1 potato)

CALORIES 205; FAT 1.2g (sat 0.2g); SODIUM 245mg

Kid Friendly • Vegetarian

Cheddar, Broccoli, and Barley Sweet Potatoes

Hands-on: 12 min. Total: 1 hr. 10 min.

**6 Roasted Sweet Potatoes (recipe above)
⅓ cup uncooked pearl barley
1½ tablespoons olive oil
1 tablespoon finely chopped garlic
4½ cups coarsely chopped broccoli florets (about 1 large head)
¼ cup water
¼ teaspoon kosher salt**

**¼ teaspoon crushed red pepper
2 ounces cheddar cheese, shredded (about ½ cup)**

1. Preheat oven to 400°. Bake potatoes according to recipe instructions.
2. Cook barley according to package directions, omitting salt and fat.
3. Heat a large nonstick skillet over medium-high heat. Add oil; swirl to coat. Add garlic; cook 30 seconds, stirring constantly. Add broccoli and ¼ cup water to pan. Cover and cook 4 minutes or until crisp-tender. Stir in cooked barley, salt, and pepper; uncover and cook 1 minute. Stir in cheese. Top potatoes with barley-broccoli mixture. Serves 6 (serving size: ½ cup topping and 1 potato)

CALORIES 409; FAT 17.1g (sat 4g, mono 10.8g, poly 1.7g); PROTEIN 9g; CARB 58g; FIBER 10g; CHOL 10mg; IRON 2mg; SODIUM 399mg; CALC 168mg

Kid Friendly • Gluten Free

Sweet Potatoes with Cinnamon Chicken and Cashews

Hands-on: 20 min. Total: 1 hr. 10 min.

**6 Roasted Sweet Potatoes (recipe at left)
1 tablespoon olive oil
¼ cup finely chopped celery
¼ cup dried tart cherries
¼ cup golden raisins
3 tablespoons fresh orange juice
¼ teaspoon ground cinnamon
⅛ teaspoon ground red pepper
⅛ teaspoon kosher salt
2 cups shredded skinless, boneless rotisserie chicken breast
½ cup dry-roasted cashews, unsalted
¼ cup thinly sliced green onions**

1. Preheat oven to 400°. Bake potatoes according to recipe instructions.
2. Heat a large nonstick skillet over medium heat. Add oil; swirl to coat. Add celery; cook 2 minutes, stirring frequently. Add cherries and next 5 ingredients (through salt); cook 1 minute. Stir in chicken and cashews; cook 2 minutes. Sprinkle with onions. Top potatoes with chicken mixture. Serves 6 (serving size: about ⅓ cup topping and 1 potato)

CALORIES 412; FAT 10.6g (sat 2g, mono 6.3g, poly 1.5g); PROTEIN 20g; CARB 61g; FIBER 8g; CHOL 44mg; IRON 3mg; SODIUM 462mg; CALC 97mg

THE TACO BAR

These toppings are hearty enough to make tacos a complete meal.

TACO OPTION 1
Kid Friendly • Quick & Easy

Lemon-Pepper Flank Steak Tacos
(pictured on page 231)

Hands-on: 5 min. Total: 20 min.

1 (1¼-pound) flank steak, trimmed
2 teaspoons grated lemon rind
¾ teaspoon freshly ground black pepper
Cooking spray
2 tablespoons fresh lemon juice
1 tablespoon olive oil
1 tablespoon lower-sodium soy sauce
3 garlic cloves, minced
¼ teaspoon kosher salt
12 (6-inch) corn tortillas
1 ounce queso fresco, crumbled (about ¼ cup)

1. Sprinkle steak with rind and pepper, pressing to adhere.
2. Heat grill pan over medium-high

heat. Coat pan with cooking spray. Add steak to pan; grill 6 minutes on each side or until desired degree of doneness. Place steak on a cutting board; let stand 5 minutes.
3. Combine juice, oil, soy sauce, and garlic in a small bowl. Cut steak diagonally across grain into thin slices. Drizzle steak with soy sauce mixture; sprinkle with salt.
4. Heat tortillas on grill pan coated with cooking spray 20 seconds on each side or until lightly charred. Divide steak among tortillas. Sprinkle each taco with about 1 teaspoon cheese. Serves 6 (serving size: 2 tacos)

CALORIES 245; FAT 9.4g (sat 2.9g, mono 4g, poly 1g); PROTEIN 22g; CARB 20g; FIBER 2g; CHOL 56mg; IRON 1mg; SODIUM 230mg; CALC 49mg

TOPPING OPTION
Kid Friendly • Gluten Free
Make Ahead • Vegetarian

Cabbage and Mango Slaw

Hands-on: 5 min. Total: 5 min. We made this slaw to top tacos, but the tangy-sweet-hot salad can stand on its own as a side dish. Serve it alongside broiled pork chops or with your favorite jerk chicken. For extra heat, you can mix in a whole minced serrano chile rather than half.

3 cups thinly sliced Savoy cabbage
1 cup ripe peeled julienne-cut mango
½ cup vertically sliced red onion
2 tablespoons cider vinegar
1 tablespoon olive oil
⅛ teaspoon kosher salt
⅛ teaspoon freshly ground black pepper
½ serrano chile, seeded and minced

1. Combine all ingredients in a medium bowl; toss to coat. Serves 6 (serving size: ⅔ cup)

CALORIES 51; FAT 2.4g (sat 0.4g, mono 1.7g, poly 0.3g); PROTEIN 1g; CARB 7g; FIBER 2g; CHOL 0mg; IRON 0mg; SODIUM 51mg; CALC 18mg

TACO OPTION 2
Kid Friendly • Quick & Easy
Gluten Free

Smoky Tilapia Tacos
(pictured on page 233)

Hands-on: 10 min. Total: 21 min.
Inexpensive tilapia is readily available and sustainable. Broiling makes this a no-fuss fish dish. The tilapia cooks fast, so make sure all the other components for the taco are ready before you put it under the heat.

1 teaspoon garlic powder
1 teaspoon Spanish smoked paprika
¼ teaspoon ground coriander
¼ teaspoon freshly ground black pepper
⅜ teaspoon kosher salt, divided
2 pounds tilapia fillets
1 tablespoon olive oil
1 tablespoon finely chopped fresh cilantro
2 teaspoons canned chopped green chiles
1 diced peeled avocado
12 (6-inch) corn tortillas
Cooking spray
6 lime wedges

1. Preheat broiler to high.
2. Combine first 4 ingredients and ¼ teaspoon salt. Brush fillets with oil, and sprinkle with spice mixture. Place fillets on a baking sheet. Broil 6 minutes or until fish flakes easily when tested with a fork.
3. Combine ⅛ teaspoon salt, cilantro, chiles, and avocado in a bowl; lightly mash with a fork.
4. Heat tortillas on a grill pan coated with cooking spray 20 seconds on each side or until lightly charred. Divide avocado mixture and fish among tortillas. Serve with lime wedges. Serves 6 (serving size: 2 tacos and 1 lime wedge)

CALORIES 304; FAT 10.8g (sat 1.9g, mono 5.7g, poly 1.9g); PROTEIN 33g; CARB 22g; FIBER 5g; CHOL 76mg; IRON 1mg; SODIUM 258mg; CALC 42mg

Simmered Pinto Beans with Chipotle Sour Cream

Hands-on: 5 min. Total: 15 min. Refried beans can be high in fat; instead serve these pinto beans simmered with earthy cumin. Like the slaw, this topping can be served as a side dish, too.

2 teaspoons olive oil
1/2 cup chopped onion
1/2 cup chopped red bell pepper
1/2 teaspoon ground cumin
2 garlic cloves, minced
1/2 cup unsalted chicken stock
1/8 teaspoon kosher salt
1/8 teaspoon freshly ground black pepper
1 (15-ounce) can unsalted pinto beans, rinsed and drained
1 tablespoon fresh lemon juice
2 tablespoons chopped fresh flat-leaf parsley
3/4 cup reduced-fat sour cream
3 tablespoons low-fat buttermilk
1 1/2 teaspoons minced chipotle chiles, canned in adobo sauce

1. Heat a saucepan over medium-high heat. Add oil; swirl to coat. Add onion, bell pepper, cumin, and garlic, and; sauté 2 minutes. Add stock, salt, black pepper, and beans; simmer 7 minutes. Stir in juice and parsley.
2. Combine remaining ingredients; serve with beans. Serves 6 (serving size: about 1/4 cup beans and 2 tablespoons cream)

CALORIES 128; FAT 5.4g (sat 2.6g, mono 1.1g, poly 0.2g); PROTEIN 5g; CARB 14g; FIBER 4g; CHOL 16mg; IRON 1mg; SODIUM 100mg; CALC 99mg

BUNCHES AND BUNCHES OF BROCCOLI

This brassica thrives in cool weather. We grow it twice a year, and find our autumn harvest sweeter by a head.

Broccoli gets a bad rap as a veggie that kids, and even some adults, can't learn to love. Overcooked, it's a khaki-colored, limp, gassy disappointment. But broccoli deserves a fresh look. It's a versatile vegetable—it's great raw as a fresh snack with a zesty dip; steamed and sprinkled with fresh lemon juice; stir-fried (where the florets soak up flavor); or shaved into slaw or salad. No need to hide it in a cheesy casserole: Minimal cooking and a light hand make the most of the homegrown harvest.

Charred Broccoli with Orange Browned Butter

Hands-on: 10 min. Total: 25 min.

10 ounces broccoli florets (2 1/2 cups)
Cooking spray
1 tablespoon butter
1 teaspoon grated orange rind
2 tablespoons fresh orange juice
1/4 teaspoon salt
1/4 teaspoon freshly ground black pepper

1. Preheat oven to 450°.
2. Arrange broccoli on a foil-lined baking sheet; coat with cooking spray. Bake at 450° for 12 minutes or until crisp-tender and lightly browned, stirring once. Heat broiler to high, leaving pan in oven; broil 2 minutes or until lightly charred.
3. Melt butter in a small skillet over medium heat; cook 3 minutes or until browned. Remove from heat. Stir in rind and juice. Combine broccoli and butter mixture in a large bowl. Sprinkle with salt and pepper; toss to coat. Serves 4 (serving size: about 2/3 cup)

CALORIES 50; FAT 3.2g (sat 1.9g, mono 0.8g, poly 0.2g); PROTEIN 2g; CARB 5g; FIBER 2g; CHOL 8mg; IRON 1mg; SODIUM 192mg; CALC 37mg

Broccoli, Pancetta, and Parmesan Frittata

Hands-on: 25 min. Total: 34 min. *To save time, you can microwave the broccoli florets in a covered microwave-safe bowl at HIGH for 2 minutes or until crisp-tender.*

6 ounces small broccoli florets (about 2 cups)
1 teaspoon thyme leaves
1/2 teaspoon kosher salt
1/4 teaspoon freshly ground black pepper
Dash of grated whole nutmeg
8 large eggs, lightly beaten
1 ounce Parmesan cheese, grated (about 1/4 cup)
1 teaspoon olive oil
1 1/2 ounces pancetta, chopped
1 cup sliced sweet onion

1. Preheat oven to 350°.
2. Cook broccoli florets in boiling water 2 minutes. Drain and plunge into ice water; drain broccoli well.
3. Combine thyme, salt, pepper, nutmeg, eggs, and cheese in a medium bowl, stirring with a whisk.
4. Heat a 10-inch ovenproof non-stick skillet over medium heat. Add oil; swirl to coat. Add pancetta; cook 4 minutes or until crisp, stirring occasionally. Remove pancetta. Increase heat to medium-high. Add onion; sauté 3 minutes or until tender. Add broccoli; sauté 1 minute. Add egg mixture; cook 3 minutes, stirring occasionally. Sprinkle with pancetta. Place pan in oven; bake at 350° for 12 minutes or until center is set. Cut into 8 wedges. Serves 4 (serving size: 2 wedges)

CALORIES 221; **FAT** 13.7g (sat 4.9g, mono 5.1g, poly 2.2g); **PROTEIN** 17g; **CARB** 7g; **FIBER** 2g; **CHOL** 380mg; **IRON** 2mg; **SODIUM** 547mg; **CALC** 166mg

Shaved Broccoli-Apple Salad with Tarragon Dressing and Bacon

Hands-on: 15 min. Total: 3 hr. 15 min. *This is a refreshing new twist on the broccoli-and-bacon picnic standard that sometimes gets drenched in mayonnaise dressing.*

3 tablespoons cider vinegar
1 teaspoon whole-grain Dijon mustard
1/2 teaspoon freshly ground black pepper
1/4 teaspoon kosher salt
1 shallot, thinly sliced
1/3 cup plain fat-free Greek yogurt
3 tablespoons canola mayonnaise
1 tablespoon plus 1 teaspoon chopped fresh tarragon
12 ounces broccoli florets
1 tablespoon fresh lemon juice
2 Jazz or Gala apples, cored and cut into wedges
2 applewood-smoked bacon slices, cooked and crumbled

1. Combine first 5 ingredients in a bowl, and let stand 10 minutes. Add yogurt, mayonnaise, and tarragon; stir with a whisk.
2. With processor on, add broccoli through the food chute of a food processor fitted with the slicer attachment. Transfer broccoli to a bowl. Add juice to bowl of food processor. Repeat procedure with apples; add apples to bowl with broccoli.
3. Combine dressing and broccoli mixture; toss well to coat. Cover and refrigerate 3 hours. Stir in bacon just before serving. Serves 9 (serving size: about 1 cup)

CALORIES 68; **FAT** 2.5g (sat 0.4g, mono 0.8g, poly 0.6g); **PROTEIN** 3g; **CARB** 9g; **FIBER** 2g; **CHOL** 2mg; **IRON** 0mg; **SODIUM** 164mg; **CALC** 31mg

Green Broccoli Spread

Hands-on: 10 min. Total: 10 min. *This simple spread is great slathered over grilled bread, as a dip for raw veggies, or as a sandwich condiment. Make ahead and keep for up to three days, but leave out the lemon juice until you're ready to serve so it doesn't turn the broccoli brown.*

6 ounces broccoli florets (about 2 cups)
1/3 cup canola mayonnaise
2 teaspoons fresh lemon juice
1/4 teaspoon kosher salt
6 basil leaves
3 garlic cloves, peeled
1 (1 1/4-ounce) slice bread, torn
1 anchovy fillet

1. Cook broccoli in boiling water 3 minutes or until crisp-tender. Drain. Rinse under cold water until cool. Drain well.
2. Place broccoli, mayonnaise, and remaining ingredients in a food processor; process until smooth. Serves 10 (serving size: 2 tablespoons)

CALORIES 36; **FAT** 2.2g (sat 0g, mono 1.3g, poly 0.8g); **PROTEIN** 1g; **CARB** 3g; **FIBER** 1g; **CHOL** 0mg; **IRON** 0mg; **SODIUM** 142mg; **CALC** 21mg

THIS MONTH'S LESSON: SUGARED GRILLED TOAST

Cook like a genius as Keith Schroeder reveals the science behind his art.

I grew up with French toast here in the States, but toast became something altogether different during my trips to Southeast Asia. There I kept stumbling across "toast places," where a piece of bread becomes an elegant dessert. Shibuya Honey Toast is particularly popular—pillowy, butter-rich bread that's block-cut, toasted, and topped with ice cream. It's my starting point for these recipes.

KEITH'S RECIPE BREAKDOWN
GRILLED BANANAS ON SUGARED RUM TOAST
Hands-on: 15 min. Total: 15 min.

INGREDIENT	AMOUNT	WHY
dark rum	¼ cup	Bananas. Rum.
brown sugar	3 tablespoons	The molasses gives depth and is welcome with charred things.
butter	2½ tablespoons, melted and divided	Some for the toast. Some for the sauce.
black pepper	1 teaspoon, freshly ground	Methinks sugar and black pepper are more natural partners than salt and pepper.
kosher salt	⅛ teaspoon	Salt heightens flavors and helps combat cloying sweetness.
bananas	4, peeled and cut in half lengthwise	Use mini bananas or Manzanos if you can find them. Any perfectly ripe banana will work, though.
cooking spray		To keep things moving.
challah bread	4 (¾-ounce) "blocks," crusts removed	You'll be sugar-dredging this. Then you'll grill. You may never bake again.
granulated sugar	2 tablespoons	This will bind with the butter and create something between a glaze and a candy on the bread.

Follow These Steps:

• Combine rum, brown sugar, and 1 tablespoon butter in a saucepan. Bring to a simmer over medium-high heat. (Be careful; rum will flame up when it comes to a boil.) When flames subside, stir with a whisk until syrupy. Remove from heat; stir in pepper and salt. Keep warm.

• Heat a grill pan over medium heat. Coat bananas with cooking spray. Place on grill pan; grill 2 minutes on each side or until lightly charred Remove from pan.

• Brush bread with 1½ tablespoons butter. Sprinkle granulated sugar onto a small plate. Dredge bread evenly in sugar. Place bread in pan; grill 15 seconds on each side or until lightly charred, being careful not to scorch. Serve bread with bananas and sauce. Serves 4 (serving size: 1 bread block, 1 banana, and 1 tablespoon sauce)

CALORIES 304; FAT 10g (sat 4.9g, mono 2.8g, poly 0.9g); PROTEIN 3g; CARB 50g; FIBER 3g; CHOL 38mg; IRON 1mg; SODIUM 236mg; CALC 18mg

Variation: Grilled Fig Toast

Use turbinado sugar in place of brown sugar and Saba* in place of rum; omit salt. Replace bananas with 6 fresh figs, halved. Arrange on a platter; drizzle with 1 teaspoon extra-virgin olive oil. Sprinkle with ¼ teaspoon coarse sea salt. (*Saba is a sweet-tart condiment made from grape must; you can substitute balsamic syrup.) Serves 4 (serving size: 1 bread block, 3 fig halves, about 2 teaspoons sauce, ¼ teaspoon oil, and dash of salt)

CALORIES 288; FAT 11g (sat 5g); SODIUM 315mg

FAST, FAMILY-FRIENDLY BREAKFASTS

From our new kid-authored book, four easy recipes for busy mornings.

Twelve-year-old identical twins Lilly and Audrey Andrews are real cooks who know the joys of playing around in the kitchen; they've been doing so since they were 3 years old. In their first book, *We "Heart" Cooking* ($21.95, amazon.com), they share more than 80 of their favorite tried-and-true recipes that are guaranteed to please kids and their parents. The book is loaded with tips for making recipes easier for kids to prepare, plus ideas on how to riff on dishes by using different ingredients. Here's a tasty sampling from the breakfast chapter.

Kid Friendly • Quick & Easy
Gluten Free

Creamy, Dreamy Tropical Smoothie

Hands-on: 5 min. Total: 5 min. *Wish you were on the beach right now? One sip of our smoothie, and you'll be there before you can say "aloha." Coconut milk and Greek yogurt make this smoothie supercreamy, and pineapple gives it a sweeeeet tropical kick.*

4 teaspoons unsweetened shredded coconut (optional)
2 cups fresh or frozen pineapple chunks
1 cup plain low-fat Greek yogurt
1 cup light coconut milk
1 cup crushed ice or ice cubes
3 tablespoons honey

1. If you would like to garnish with coconut, toast it first. Heat a small skillet over medium heat. Add coconut flakes; cook, stirring frequently, for 1 to 2 minutes or until golden brown.
2. Place pineapple, yogurt, coconut milk, ice, and honey in a blender. Process on high speed for 60 seconds or until smooth or desired consistency.
3. Pour into tall glasses. Garnish each serving with 1 teaspoon toasted shredded coconut, if desired. Serve smoothies immediately. Serves 4 (serving size: about 1 cup)

CALORIES 140; **FAT** 2.1g (sat 1.6g, mono 0.2g, poly 0.2g); **PROTEIN** 6g; **CARB** 27g; **FIBER** 1g; **CHOL** 3mg; **IRON** 0mg; **SODIUM** 25mg; **CALC** 140mg

Kid Friendly • Make Ahead
Vegetarian

Jammin' Oat Muffins

Hands-on: 10 min. Total: 46 min.
Hi! It's me, Lilly. When I was 6, I went to an amazing bakery called Muffin Street, and I fell in love … with a Raspberry Cheesecake muffin! In honor of that life-changing muffin, meet the Jammin' Oat Muffin.

Cooking spray
6 ounces unbleached all-purpose flour (about 1 1/3 cups)
3/4 cup quick-cooking steel-cut oats
1/3 cup packed brown sugar
2 teaspoons baking powder
1/8 teaspoon salt
1 large egg
3/4 cup 1% low-fat milk
1/4 cup canola oil
1/4 cup maple syrup
1/4 cup raspberry preserves or jam

1. Preheat oven to 400°.
2. Lightly coat a 12-cup muffin tin with cooking spray; set aside. Weigh or lightly spoon flour into dry measuring cups; level with a knife. Combine flour, oats, brown sugar, baking powder, and salt in a large bowl.
3. Crack egg into a medium bowl, and beat lightly with a fork. Add milk, oil, and maple syrup; mix well.
4. Pour egg mixture into flour mixture, and stir until combined (mixture should still be lumpy and very wet). Spoon 1/3 cup batter into each muffin cup. Spoon 1 teaspoon preserves or jam into center of each cup of batter. Bake at 400° for 16 minutes or until muffins spring back when touched lightly in centers. Cool in pan for 5 minutes. Place muffins on a wire rack. Cool 15 minutes before serving. Serves 12 (serving size: 1 muffin)

CALORIES 243; **FAT** 6g (sat 0.7g, mono 3.4g, poly 1.7g); **PROTEIN** 4g; **CARB** 44g; **FIBER** 2g; **CHOL** 16mg; **IRON** 2mg; **SODIUM** 133mg; **CALC** 83mg

Chilaquiles and Eggs

Kid Friendly • Quick & Easy
Vegetarian • Gluten Free

Hands-on: 27 min. Total: 27 min.
If you're making this for dinner, use shredded chicken instead of eggs. Save a little extra tomato for more color in the garnish.

2 large tomatoes, chopped
2 jalapeño peppers, seeded
1 cup organic vegetable broth
¼ teaspoon salt
2 garlic cloves, peeled
1 tablespoon olive oil
¼ cup chopped red onion
4 cups tortilla chips (about 40 chips)
6 large eggs
1 ripe avocado, peeled and sliced
¼ cup light sour cream
1 tablespoon finely chopped fresh
   cilantro

1. Place tomatoes and jalapeños in a blender. Add broth, salt, and garlic. Cover and process on high speed for 1 minute or until smooth; set aside.
2. Heat a 12-inch sauté pan over medium-high heat. Add oil; swirl to coat. Add onion; sauté 2 minutes or until just tender, stirring occasionally. Add tomato mixture to pan. Bring to a simmer. Reduce heat to medium-low, and continue to simmer, uncovered, for 10 minutes, stirring occasionally.
3. Add chips to pan, and stir to coat with tomato mixture. Crack eggs, 1 at a time, over chips, evenly spacing them in a circle inside pan. Reduce heat to medium-low, cover, and cook for 5 to 7 minutes or until eggs are set but still runny in the centers. Remove pan from heat. Arrange avocado slices over eggs. Top with dollops of sour cream and a sprinkle of cilantro. Serve immediately. Serves 6

CALORIES 312; FAT 19.6g (sat 4.1g, mono 9g, poly 6.1g); PROTEIN 10g; CARB 26g; FIBER 5g; CHOL 186mg; IRON 2mg; SODIUM 394mg; CALC 89mg

Banana-Almond Butter French Toast Sandwiches

Kid Friendly • Quick & Easy
Vegetarian

(pictured on page 231)

Hands-on: 20 min. Total: 20 min.

2 large eggs
¼ cup unsweetened almond milk
2 teaspoons vanilla extract
¼ teaspoon ground cinnamon
2 tablespoons almond butter
4 teaspoons maple syrup
1 banana
4 (1.5-ounce) slices multigrain
   bread
Cooking spray

1. Crack eggs into a shallow bowl. Add almond milk, vanilla extract, and cinnamon; stir with a whisk to combine.
2. Combine almond butter and maple syrup in a small bowl. Cut banana lengthwise into 4 thin slices; cut crosswise into halves. Spread almond butter mixture evenly across bread slices. Top 2 bread slices with 4 banana pieces. Place remaining 2 bread slices over banana, sandwiching almond butter and bananas inside.
3. Heat a panini press to 425° or high heat. Dip sandwiches in egg mixture, and let excess drip off. Lightly coat grill plates of panini press with cooking spray, if needed. Arrange sandwiches on press. Close panini press, pushing down gently to flatten. Cook 3 to 4 minutes or until sandwiches are browned on the outside and hot in the center.
4. Place sandwiches on a cutting board. Cut in half diagonally. Serve hot. Serves 4 (serving size: ½ sandwich)

CALORIES 228; FAT 8.3g (sat 0.8g, mono 5g, poly 2g); PROTEIN 9g; CARB 33g; FIBER 6g; CHOL 47mg; IRON 2mg; SODIUM 228mg; CALC 69mg

FRESH RIGHT NOW

GREAT GRAPES

Fall's red fruits offer the sweetest rewards.

Though you can get grapes year-round, now is peak season for late summer's red seedless varieties. Flames are round and mildly sweet; oval-shaped Crimsons are juicy and crisp; Scarlet Royals' elongated berries have thick skin; and tightly clustered Rubys have a mild flavor. You'll taste the difference this time of year, when these fruits are at their sweetest. Frozen, they make an addictive snack; fresh, they complement most cheeses, from pungent blue to mild Brie. We roast them to bring out deep, rich, grapy flavor, and then toss with earthy kale and salty Manchego cheese in a memorable salad.

Kid Friendly • Gluten Free

Chicken and Roasted Grape Salad

Hands-on: 15 min. Total: 1 hr. 40 min
Roasting mellows the tartness, deepens the flavor, and intensifies the sweetness of fresh grapes. The result? A midpoint between a raisin and a juicy fresh grape.

3 cups seedless red grapes
Cooking spray
3 tablespoons extra-virgin olive oil
2 teaspoons finely chopped rosemary
6 cups cut prewashed kale, stemmed
2 tablespoons white wine vinegar
¼ teaspoon coarse sea salt
4 cups shredded skinless, boneless
   rotisserie chicken breast
2 teaspoons fresh lemon juice
4 green onions, thinly sliced
2 celery stalks, thinly diagonally
   sliced
2 ounces Manchego cheese, shaved

1. Preheat oven to 325°.
2. Arrange grapes in a single layer on a wire rack set in a jelly-roll pan coated with cooking spray. Bake at 325° for 1 hour and 15 minutes or until slightly shriveled. Cool on wire rack.
3. While grapes bake, combine oil and rosemary in a small microwave-safe dish; microwave at HIGH 40 seconds. Remove from microwave, and let stand 20 minutes. Strain through a sieve into a bowl; discard solids.
4. Place kale in a large bowl; massage kale with hands until tender and dark green. Add strained oil, vinegar, and salt; toss to coat. Add roasted grapes, chicken, lemon juice, green onions, and celery; toss. Top with cheese. Serves 6 (serving size: about 1¼ cups)

CALORIES 342; FAT 14.3g (sat 4.3g, mono 6.4g, poly 1.5g); PROTEIN 34g; CARB 22g; FIBER 3g; CHOL 98mg; IRON 2mg; SODIUM 541mg; CALC 255mg

RECIPE MAKEOVER

HASH BROWN CASSEROLE, DONE LIGHT

We drop the butter, trim the cheese, and create a luscious mushroom cream.

Homey shredded potatoes get cozy with butter, cream soup, sour cream, and plenty of cheese. It's a workingman's day-starter. But unless you're the wood-chopping type, you likely won't be able to burn off nearly 500 calories of cheesy potatoes by lunch. The challenge: Keep the mighty comfort-filled portion and whack the calorie count.

One of the key players in classic hash brown casserole is canned cream of mushroom soup, which is packed with sodium and thickeners. We make our own by simmering fresh mushrooms and garlic in savory chicken stock, and then we puree it with light sour cream to create a rich, velvety sauce. The cheddar remains, but in reduced-fat form; a little is stirred into the mushroom cream, and the rest is saved for a gooey, melty topping. We brown the frozen hash browns in olive oil and bacon drippings, and then bake the casserole in a cast-iron skillet to create a crisp, caramelized crust. Sautéed mushrooms and onions add texture and moisture. As if that weren't enough, we top it all off with extra-crunchy reduced-fat kettle potato chips—a salty, crispy topper for the creamy, cheese-filled casserole. Voilà: less than 300 calories, and mighty good.

OURS SAVES
207 calories, 15g saturated fat, and 493mg sodium over classic hash brown casserole

Kid Friendly • Gluten Free
Make Ahead

Creamy, Cheesy Double-Potato Hash Brown Casserole

Hands-on: 30 min. Total: 45 min.

1 cup unsalted chicken stock
2 cups chopped onion, divided
2 (8-ounce) packages presliced white mushrooms, divided
6 garlic cloves
½ cup light sour cream
1 teaspoon black pepper
½ teaspoon kosher salt
4 ounces reduced-fat sharp cheddar cheese, shredded and divided
3 center-cut bacon slices
1 (30-ounce) package frozen shredded hash brown potatoes, thawed
1 tablespoon olive oil, divided
2 large eggs, lightly beaten
2 ounces 40% less fat original kettle-style potato chips, crushed
3 tablespoons chopped fresh flat-leaf parsley

1. Preheat oven to 400°.
2. Combine stock, 1 cup onion, half of mushrooms, and garlic in a saucepan; bring to a boil. Cover, reduce heat, and simmer 10 minutes or until mushrooms are tender. Place mixture in a blender. Remove center piece of blender lid (to allow steam to escape); secure blender lid on blender. Place a clean towel over opening in blender lid (to avoid splatters); blend until smooth. Stir in sour cream, pepper, salt, and 2 ounces cheese; blend until smooth.
3. Cook bacon in a large cast-iron skillet over medium heat until crisp. Remove bacon from pan; crumble. Add half of potatoes to drippings in pan; cover and cook 4 minutes on each side or until browned. Remove potatoes from pan. Repeat procedure with remaining potatoes and 2 teaspoons oil. Remove from pan.
4. Add 1 teaspoon oil to pan; swirl to coat. Add 1 cup onion and remaining half of mushrooms to pan; cook 6 minutes or until tender, stirring occasionally. Return potatoes to pan; add eggs, stirring well to combine. Pour sour cream mixture evenly over potato mixture. Sprinkle with bacon, 2 ounces cheese, chips, and parsley. Bake at 400° for 10 minutes or until cheese melts. Turn broiler on (do not remove pan from oven); broil 1½ minutes or until lightly browned. Serves 8 (serving size: 1 wedge)

CALORIES 273; FAT 9.7g (sat 4g, mono 2.9g, poly 0.7g); PROTEIN 13g; CARB 34g; FIBER 3g; CHOL 63mg; IRON 1mg; SODIUM 379mg; CALC 178mg

DINNER TONIGHT

READY IN 30 MINUTES

....

SHOPPING LIST

Caprese Mac and Cheese
Grape tomatoes (1 pint)
Fresh basil
Garlic
Crushed red pepper
Extra-virgin olive oil
Penne (6 ounces)
All-purpose flour
Panko (Japanese breadcrumbs)
Part-skim mozzarella cheese (3 ounces)
Parmesan cheese (1.5 ounces)
1% low-fat milk

Chopped Tri Color Salad
Garlic
Extra-virgin olive oil
White wine vinegar
Baby spinach
Romaine lettuce
Radicchio
Sugar

....

GAME PLAN

While water for pasta comes to a boil:
- Broil tomatoes.
While pasta cooks:
- Prepare sauce.

Kid Friendly • Quick & Easy
Make Ahead • Vegetarian

Caprese Mac and Cheese with Chopped Tricolor Salad

(pictured on page 231)

2 cups grape tomatoes, halved
4 teaspoons extra-virgin olive oil, divided
6 ounces uncooked penne
2 teaspoons minced fresh garlic
5 teaspoons all-purpose flour
1³/₄ cups 1% low-fat milk
¹/₂ teaspoon kosher salt
¹/₂ teaspoon freshly ground black pepper
3 ounces part-skim mozzarella cheese, shredded (about ³/₄ cup)
1.5 ounces Parmesan cheese, grated (about ¹/₃ cup)
¹/₂ cup torn basil leaves
Cooking spray
3 tablespoons panko
¹/₈ teaspoon crushed red pepper

1. Preheat broiler to high.
2. Combine tomatoes and 2 teaspoons oil on a jelly-roll pan. Broil 3 minutes or until tomatoes begin to break down.
3. Cook pasta in a large saucepan according to package directions, omitting salt and fat. Drain. Return pasta to pan.
4. Heat a saucepan over medium heat. Add 2 teaspoons oil; swirl. Add garlic; cook 1 minute, stirring frequently. Stir in flour. Add milk, salt, and black pepper, stirring with a whisk. Bring to a simmer; cook 1 minute or until thickened, stirring frequently. Remove pan from heat; stir in cheeses. Add cheese mixture to pasta; toss. Stir in tomato mixture and basil. Spoon pasta mixture into 4 (6-ounce) gratin dishes coated with cooking spray. Sprinkle panko and red pepper over pasta mixture.

Broil 2 minutes or until browned. Serves 4 (serving size: about 2 cups)

CALORIES 391; FAT 13.9g (sat 5.7g, mono 5.5g, poly 0.9g); PROTEIN 21g; CARB 46g; FIBER 3g; CHOL 26mg; IRON 2mg; SODIUM 603mg; CALC 436mg

Quick & Easy • Vegetarian
Gluten Free
Chopped Tricolor Salad
Combine 2 tablespoons extra-virgin olive oil, 2 tablespoons white wine vinegar, 1 teaspoon minced garlic, ¹/₂ teaspoon sugar, ¹/₄ teaspoon kosher salt, and ¹/₄ teaspoon freshly ground black pepper in a large bowl, stirring with a whisk. Add 2 cups thinly sliced baby spinach leaves, 1¹/₂ cups thinly sliced romaine lettuce, and 1 cup thinly sliced radicchio; toss to coat. Let stand 10 minutes before serving. Serves 4 (serving size: 1¹/₄ cups)

CALORIES 74; FAT 6.8g (sat 1g); SODIUM 143mg

READY IN 35 MINUTES

....

SHOPPING LIST

Ginger Steak with Sesame Brown Rice
Green onions
Ginger
Garlic
Toasted sesame seeds
Dark sesame oil
Lower-soduim soy sauce
8.8-ounce package precooked brown rice (1)
1 pound sirloin steak

Chili-Basil Slaw
Napa (Chinese) cabbage (1)
Carrots (1 large)
Fresh basil
Dark sesame oil
Lower-sodium soy sauce
Rice vinegar
Sweet chili sauce

While steak marinates:
- Prepare slaw.

While steak grills:
- Prepare rice.

Kid Friendly • Quick & Easy

Ginger Steak with Sesame Brown Rice and Chili-Basil Slaw

2½ tablespoons lower-sodium soy sauce
1 tablespoon grated peeled ginger
1 tablespoon finely minced garlic, mashed into a paste
¼ teaspoon black pepper
1 (1-pound) sirloin steak, trimmed
Cooking spray
1 (8.8-ounce) package precooked brown rice (such as Uncle Ben's)
4 green onions, thinly sliced
1½ tablespoons toasted sesame seeds
2 teaspoons dark sesame oil

1. Combine first 4 ingredients. Reserve half of soy sauce mixture. Add steak to remaining soy sauce mixture; toss to coat. Let stand at room temperature 15 minutes.
2. Heat a grill pan over medium-high heat. Coat pan with cooking spray. Add steak to pan; grill 4 minutes on each side or until desired degree of doneness. Place steak on a cutting board; let stand 5 minutes. Cut across the grain into thin slices.
3. Prepare rice according to package directions. Stir in green onions, sesame seeds, and oil. Serve rice mixture with steak. Drizzle with reserved soy sauce mixture. Serves 4 (serving size: 3½ ounces steak, ½ cup rice, and 2 teaspoons sauce)

CALORIES 285; **FAT** 10.3g (sat 2.5g, mono 3.3g, poly 1.9g); **PROTEIN** 26g; **CARB** 21g; **FIBER** 2g; **CHOL** 60mg; **IRON** 3mg; **SODIUM** 385mg; **CALC** 64mg

---

Quick & Easy • Vegetarian
Chili-Basil Slaw
Combine 1 tablespoon rice vinegar, 2 teaspoons sweet chili sauce, 1 teaspoon dark sesame oil, and ½ teaspoon lower-sodium soy sauce in a large bowl, stirring with a whisk. Add 3 cups thinly sliced napa (Chinese) cabbage and 1 large peeled and grated carrot; toss to coat. Sprinkle with ½ cup small fresh basil leaves. Serves 4 (serving size: 1 cup)

CALORIES 32; **FAT** 1.3g (sat 0.2g); **SODIUM** 44mg

READY IN
40
MINUTES

SHOPPING LIST

Dijon-Herb Chicken Thighs
Fresh parsley
Fresh chives
Garlic
Olive oil
Dijon mustard
1½ pounds bone-in chicken thighs, skinned

Tomato-Basil Bread Salad
English cucumber (1 medium)
Tomato (1 large)
Fresh basil
Fresh chives
Olive oil
Red wine vinegar
Dijon mustard
Whole-grain bread (5 ounces)

GAME PLAN

While oven preheats:
- Prepare chicken.

While chicken bakes:
- Prepare salad.

Kid Friendly • Quick & Easy
Gluten Free

Dijon-Herb Chicken Thighs and Tomato-Basil Bread Salad

2 tablespoons chopped fresh flat-leaf parsley
2 tablespoons chopped fresh chives
2 tablespoons olive oil
2 teaspoons Dijon mustard
2 garlic cloves, minced
4 (6-ounce) bone-in chicken thighs (about 1½ pounds), skinned
½ teaspoon kosher salt
½ teaspoon black pepper
Cooking spray

1. Preheat oven to 450°.
2. Combine parsley, chives, olive oil, Dijon mustard, and garlic. Rub herb mixture over meaty side of chicken thighs; sprinkle with salt and pepper.
3. Arrange chicken on a baking sheet coated with cooking spray. Bake at 450° for 25 minutes or until done.
4. Preheat broiler to high (do not remove pan from oven). Broil chicken 3 minutes or until browned. Serves 4 (serving size: 1 chicken thigh)

CALORIES 270; **FAT** 13.9g (sat 2.7g, mono 7.4g, poly 2.3g); **PROTEIN** 33g; **CARB** 1g; **FIBER** 0g; **CHOL** 162mg; **IRON** 2mg; **SODIUM** 453mg; **CALC** 23mg

---

Kid Friendly • Quick & Easy
Vegetarian
Tomato-Basil Bread Salad
Combine 2 tablespoons olive oil, 1½ tablespoons red wine vinegar, 1 teaspoon Dijon mustard, and ¼ teaspoon black pepper, stirring with a whisk. Add 3 cups toasted whole-grain bread cubes, 2 cups chopped English cucumber, 2 cups chopped seeded tomato, ¼ cup chopped fresh basil, and 2 tablespoons chopped fresh chives. Serves 4 (serving size: 1½ cups)

CALORIES 182; **FAT** 8.6g (sat 1.3g); **SODIUM** 185mg

SHOPPING LIST

Tilapia and Fennel-Yogurt Sauce
Lemon (1)
Fennel
Garlic
Ground coriander
Ground red pepper
Olive oil
White wine vinegar
Panko (Japanese breadcrumbs)
Honey
Plain fat-free Greek yogurt
1 pound tilapia fillets
Ground cumin

Red Pepper Couscous
Red bell pepper (1 medium)
Red onion
Olive oil
Israeli couscous
Unsalted chicken stock (such as
   Swanson)
Unsalted tomato paste

Shaved Carrot Salad
Lemon (1)
Carrots (1 pound)
Red onion
Fresh parsley
Crushed red pepper
Olive oil
Honey

GAME PLAN

While couscous simmers:
■ Prepare salad.
While salad stands:
■ Prepare yogurt sauce.
■ Cook fish.

Kid Friendly • Quick & Easy

Tilapia and Fennel-Yogurt Sauce with Red Pepper Couscous and Shaved Carrot Salad

½ cup finely chopped fennel bulb
½ cup plain fat-free Greek yogurt
1 tablespoon chopped fennel fronds
1½ teaspoons white wine vinegar
1 teaspoon honey
¾ teaspoon kosher salt, divided
½ cup panko (Japanese
   breadcrumbs)
1 tablespoon grated lemon rind
½ teaspoon freshly ground black
   pepper
5 teaspoons olive oil
1 garlic clove, thinly sliced
½ teaspoon ground coriander
½ teaspoon ground cumin
¼ teaspoon ground red pepper
4 (4-ounce) tilapia fillets
2 tablespoons fresh lemon juice

1. Combine fennel bulb, yogurt, fronds, vinegar, 1 teaspoon honey, and ¼ teaspoon salt in a bowl.
2. Preheat broiler to high.
3. Combine ¼ teaspoon salt, panko, rind, and black pepper in a bowl. Heat oil and garlic in an ovenproof skillet 1 minute or until garlic is golden. Remove garlic with a slotted spoon; discard. Add 2 teaspoons oil from pan to panko mixture; toss to coat.

4. Return pan to medium-high heat. Combine coriander, cumin, red pepper, and ¼ teaspoon salt in a bowl. Sprinkle one side of fillets with spice mixture. Add fillets, spice side down, to remaining oil in pan; cook 3 minutes. Turn fillets; top evenly with panko mixture. Add lemon juice to pan. Place pan in oven; broil 90 seconds or until topping is golden and fillets are done. Serve with yogurt sauce. Serves 4 (serving size: 1 fillet and ¼ cup yogurt sauce)

CALORIES 216; **FAT** 8g (sat 1.5g, mono 4.7g, poly 1g); **PROTEIN** 27g; **CARB** 10g; **FIBER** 1g; **CHOL** 57mg; **IRON** 1mg; **SODIUM** 457mg; **CALC** 44mg

Kid Friendly • Quick & Easy
Red Pepper Couscous
Heat 1 tablespoon olive oil in a saucepan over medium heat. Add 1 cup uncooked Israeli couscous; sauté 3 minutes. Add ¾ cup chopped red bell pepper and ½ cup chopped red onion; sauté 4 minutes. Add 1½ cups unsalted chicken stock and 1 tablespoon unsalted tomato paste; bring to a boil. Cover, reduce heat, and simmer 10 minutes. Serves 4 (serving size: ½ cup)

CALORIES 217; **FAT** 3.9g (sat 0.5g); **SODIUM** 53mg

Kid Friendly • Quick & Easy
Vegetarian • Gluten Free
Shaved Carrot Salad
Combine 4 cups shaved carrots, ½ cup thinly sliced red onion, ¼ cup chopped fresh parsley, 1 tablespoon olive oil, 1 tablespoon fresh lemon juice, 1 teaspoon honey, and ¼ teaspoon crushed red pepper. Let stand 10 minutes. Serves 4 (serving size: ¾ cup)

CALORIES 90; **FAT** 3.7g (sat 0.5g); **SODIUM** 81mg

Kid Friendly • Quick & Easy
Make Ahead • Gluten Free

Spinach and Ham Stuffed Baked Potatoes with Apple and Almond Salad

4 (8-ounce) baking potatoes
2 tablespoons water
1 (5-ounce) bag baby spinach
2 tablespoons plain fat-free Greek yogurt
¼ teaspoon kosher salt
¼ teaspoon freshly ground black pepper
2 ounces lower-sodium ham, diced (such as Boar's Head; about ½ cup)
2 ounces cheddar cheese, shredded (about ½ cup)
¼ cup chopped green onions

1. Pierce potatoes liberally with a fork. Microwave at HIGH 14 minutes or until tender. Remove potatoes from microwave, and cool 10 minutes.
2. While potatoes cook, bring 2 tablespoons water to a simmer in a large skillet over medium-high heat. Add spinach to pan; cook 2 minutes, stirring until spinach wilts. Cool 5 minutes. Place spinach in a paper towel, and squeeze out any excess liquid. Coarsely chop spinach.
3. Cut one-third off each potato lengthwise. Remove pulp from potato, leaving a ⅛-inch-thick shell. Combine potato pulp, yogurt, salt, pepper, ham, cheese, and spinach in a large bowl, stirring to combine. Evenly fill potato shells with spinach mixture; sprinkle with green onions. Serves 4 (serving size: 1 potato)

CALORIES 272; **FAT** 5.2g (sat 3.1g, mono 1.5g, poly 0.2g); **PROTEIN** 12g; **CARB** 46g; **FIBER** 5g; **CHOL** 21mg; **IRON** 3mg; **SODIUM** 429mg; **CALC** 166mg

Apple and Almond Salad

Combine 1½ tablespoons olive oil, 1½ tablespoons white wine vinegar, 1 teaspoon Dijon mustard, ¼ teaspoon freshly ground black pepper, and ⅛ teaspoon kosher salt in a large bowl, stirring with a whisk. Add 6 cups mixed spring greens, ¼ cup toasted sliced almonds, and 1 thinly sliced medium apple. Toss to coat. Serves 4 (serving size: 1½ cups)

CALORIES 110; **FAT** 8g (sat 0.9g); **SODIUM** 120mg

READY IN
30
MINUTES

SHOPPING LIST

Spinach and Ham Stuffed Baked Potatoes
Green onions
5-ounce package baby spinach (1)
8-ounce baking potatoes (4)
Cheddar cheese (2 ounces)
Plain fat-free Greek yogurt
Lower-sodium ham (such as Boar's Head)

Apple and Almond Salad
Apple (1)
Mixed spring greens (6 cups)
Olive oil
White wine vinegar
Dijon mustard
Sliced almonds

GAME PLAN

While potatoes cook:
■ Prepare spinach mixture.
While potatoes cool:
■ Prepare salad.

12 HEALTHY HABITS

EAT MORE FISH

It's a good source of protein and healthy fat, and we could all use a little more of it. This month's hero shares his favorite ways to get three servings of seafood into weekly meals.

Despite the "eat more fish" push, Americans are eating less seafood each year, while red meat and poultry consumption climb. Does it matter? Well, it very well might. The primary fats in fish have been shown to protect the body against heart disease, reduce blood pressure and inflammation, and possibly lessen your chances of some cancers.

But many fisheries are in trouble, and "more fish" needs to be "sustainable fish." Fortunately, a multitude of smartphone apps, websites, and insignia on labels help pinpoint seafood that has been caught—or raised—using planet-friendly means.

Apps in hand, all that's left to decide is what type of seafood to cook and how to cook it. However, for some people, that's precisely the problem. "We get a lot of customers asking for fish that's 'not so fishy' or wanting to know how to cook it so it won't taste fishy," says Lyf Gildersleeve, this month's hero and owner of Portland, Oregon's Flying Fish Company. "No fish is 'fishy' unless it's bad." That's not to say there aren't stronger and milder fish. "Everybody's got a different palate," says Gildersleeve, "and unfortunately, one bad experience with fish sometimes turns people off. People say they don't like fish, but I think they just haven't had the right fish."

continued

Crab Cake Sliders with Yogurt-Dill Sauce

Hands-on: 35 min. Total: 35 min.

8 whole-wheat slider buns
5 tablespoons rice vinegar, divided
1 tablespoon sugar
½ cup thinly vertically sliced red
   onion
3 tablespoons canola mayonnaise,
   divided
3 tablespoons plain fat-free Greek
   yogurt
1 tablespoon chopped fresh dill
¾ cup finely chopped red bell pepper
¼ teaspoon black pepper
⅛ teaspoon kosher salt
2 green onions, chopped
1 large egg, lightly beaten
1 large egg yolk, lightly beaten
⅔ cup whole-wheat panko
8 ounces lump crabmeat, drained
   and shell pieces removed
4 teaspoons canola oil
1½ cups baby arugula

1. Preheat broiler to high. Hollow out buns, leaving a ½-inch-thick shell. Arrange buns in a single layer on a baking sheet. Broil 1½ minutes on each side or until lightly toasted.
2. Place ¼ cup vinegar and sugar in a microwave-safe bowl. Microwave at HIGH 45 seconds. Stir in onion. Let stand 15 minutes. Drain.
3. Combine 1 tablespoon vinegar, 1 tablespoon mayonnaise, yogurt, and dill in a small bowl.
4. Combine 2 tablespoons mayonnaise, bell pepper, and next 5 ingredients. Add panko and crab; stir. Working with damp hands, divide crab mixture into 8 equal portions, shaping each into a ¾-inch-thick patty.
5. Heat a large nonstick skillet over medium-high heat. Add oil to pan; swirl to coat. Add crab cakes to pan;

cook 4 minutes on each side or until golden and thoroughly heated.
6. Spread 1 teaspoon yogurt mixture on bottom half of each bun. Top with 1 patty. Divide onions and arugula among sliders. Top with top halves of buns. Serves 4 (serving size: 2 sliders)

CALORIES 387; **FAT** 14.5g (sat 1.2g, mono 5.7g, poly 2.8g); **PROTEIN** 22g; **CARB** 45g; **FIBER** 4g; **CHOL** 143mg; **IRON** 3mg; **SODIUM** 731mg; **CALC** 128mg

KID IN THE KITCHEN

APPLE STREUSEL MUFFINS

For these irresistible whole-grain goodies, it's all about the drizzle.

"If you don't have buttermilk, you can make your own by adding 1 tablespoon lemon juice or vinegar to 1 cup milk. The maple drizzle gave these a dessert-style twist; I loved the sweet hit it added. My mom is pretty good at making muffins, but I think these beat hers. You'll love them, too."

**Kid Friendly • Freezable
Make Ahead**

Apple Streusel Muffins with Maple Drizzle

Hands-on: 25 min. Total: 45 min.

2 tablespoons old-fashioned rolled oats
2 tablespoons spelt flour
1 tablespoon brown sugar
1 tablespoon butter, melted
½ teaspoon ground cinnamon
5 ounces spelt flour (about 1 cup)
2.5 ounces whole-wheat pastry flour
   (about ½ cup)
2 teaspoons ground cinnamon

1½ teaspoons baking powder
½ teaspoon baking soda
¼ teaspoon kosher salt
¾ cup low-fat buttermilk
½ cup brown sugar
2 tablespoons canola oil
1 tablespoon butter, melted
1 large egg, lightly beaten
1 Granny Smith apple, diced
½ cup powdered sugar
2 tablespoons maple syrup
½ teaspoon water

1. Preheat oven to 400°.
2. Combine first 5 ingredients in a bowl; set aside.
3. Weigh or spoon 5 ounces spelt flour and whole-wheat pastry flour into dry measuring cups; level with a knife. Combine flours, cinnamon, baking powder, baking soda, and salt.
4. Combine buttermilk, ½ cup sugar, oil, 1 tablespoon melted butter, and egg. Add buttermilk mixture to flour mixture, stirring just until combined. Fold in apple. Divide batter among 12 paper-lined muffin cups; top with streusel. Bake at 400° for 16 minutes or until a wooden pick inserted in the center comes out with moist crumbs clinging. Cool in pan 5 minutes. Remove from pan; cool completely.
5. Combine powdered sugar, syrup, and ½ teaspoon water in a bowl; stir until smooth. Drizzle over muffins. Serves 12 (serving size: 1 muffin)

CALORIES 194; **FAT** 5.2g (sat 1.6g, mono 2.2g, poly 0.8g); **PROTEIN** 4g; **CARB** 35g; **FIBER** 2g; **CHOL** 21mg; **IRON** 1mg; **SODIUM** 196mg; **CALC** 77mg

THE VERDICT

MICA (AGE 12)
She thought the muffins tasted great. She especially liked the maple drizzle on top. **9/10**

KATY (AGE 14)
She said, "I wished there was more. Next time, make a double batch." **10/10**

MATISSE (AGE 13)
These muffins were light and fluffy with just enough sweetness and tartness from the apple. **10/10**

SIX STELLAR SOUP TOPPERS

Simple butternut squash soup is a perfect base for both creamy and crunchy toppers.

For Simple Butternut Soup:

Place 3½ pounds cooked peeled butternut squash; 4 cups fat-free, lower-sodium chicken broth; 1 cup water; and ¾ teaspoon salt in a blender. Puree until smooth. Ladle soup into 8 bowls; top with one of these finishers. Serves 8.

CALORIES 92; **FAT** 0.2g (sat 0g); **SODIUM** 294mg

Fontina and Basil Croutons

Preheat oven to 400°. Cut 3 ounces baguette into 8 (½-inch-thick) slices; rub each with sliced garlic. Place on a baking sheet coated with cooking spray; coat tops of bread with cooking spray. Bake 5 minutes, turning once. Combine ⅓ cup grated fontina cheese, 1½ tablespoons chopped fresh basil, and ¼ teaspoon crushed red pepper. Divide among toasted bread rounds. Bake 4 minutes. Serves 8 (serving size: 1 crouton)

CALORIES 41; **FAT** 1.5g (sat 0.9g); **SODIUM** 98mg

Beet Cream with Goat Cheese and Chives

Place ¼ cup pickled beets, 3 tablespoons light whipping cream, 3 tablespoons water, and ½ teaspoon honey in a blender. Process until smooth. Swirl 1 tablespoon cream into each bowl; top with 1½ teaspoons goat cheese and ½ teaspoon chopped fresh chives. Serves 8 (serving size: 1 tablespoon beet cream, 1½ teaspoons goat cheese, and ½ teaspoon chives)

CALORIES 33; **FAT** 2.4g (sat 1.6g); **SODIUM** 35mg

Spiced Popcorn and Bacon

Cook 1 bacon slice in a nonstick skillet until crisp. Remove bacon from pan, reserving drippings; crumble bacon. Toss 1 cup hot air-popped popcorn in reserved drippings with crumbled bacon, 1 tablespoon brown sugar, ½ teaspoon chili powder, ¼ teaspoon kosher salt, and ¼ teaspoon ground red pepper. Serves 8 (serving size: 2 tablespoons)

CALORIES 37; **FAT** 2.8g (sat 1g); **SODIUM** 95mg

Parmesan and Shallot Crisps

Preheat oven to 300°. Sauté 1 large sliced shallot in 1 teaspoon olive oil until lightly browned. Grate 3 ounces Parmigiano-Reggiano cheese (about ¾ cup) into a bowl. Spoon cheese into 8 equal mounds on a parchment-lined baking sheet. Flatten mounds with the back of a spoon, and gently press shallot slices into each. Bake 20 minutes or until golden. Serves 8 (serving size: 1 crisp)

CALORIES 53; **FAT** 3.6g (sat 1.9g); **SODIUM** 163mg

Chipotle Kale Chips

Preheat oven to 425°. Toss 1 cup chopped kale leaves (stemmed) with 1 teaspoon olive oil, ¼ teaspoon kosher salt, and ¼ teaspoon chipotle chile powder. Arrange kale on a baking sheet. Bake 8 minutes. Serves 8 (serving size: 1 tablespoon)

CALORIES 9; **FAT** 0.6g (sat 0.1g); **SODIUM** 66mg

Roasted Red Pepper and Cream

Place ½ cup bottled roasted red bell peppers, 1½ teaspoons extra-virgin olive oil, ½ teaspoon ground cumin, and 1 garlic clove in a food processor; process until smooth. Drizzle 1 tablespoon puree over soup in each bowl; top with 1 tablespoon light sour cream and freshly ground black pepper. Serves 8 (serving size: 1 tablespoon puree and 1 tablespoon sour cream)

CALORIES 34; **FAT** 2.7g (sat 1.3g); **SODIUM** 30mg

THREE SIMPLE CEREAL RULES

The breakfast aisle is noisy with health claims. Remember "5-5-10" when reading box labels.

5 GRAMS OF FIBER

There's no better time to get ahead on your daily fiber goal of 25 to 38 grams than at breakfast. It's your number one satiety factor. Five grams is the baseline; more is better. Whole grains are the best source—they should always be the first item on the ingredient list.

5 GRAMS OF PROTEIN

Choose cereals full of naturally occurring protein—like whole grains, nuts, and seeds—instead of ones that contain added proteins or "isolates," which are often highly processed. A half cup of fat-free milk adds 4 more grams of protein.

10 GRAMS OF SUGAR

That's the max you want in a serving: equal to 2 heaping teaspoons. Some complicated "healthy" cereals contain as much as 16g per serving—more sugar than a glazed doughnut. Added sugars should be low on the ingredient list, never first. Lots of dried fruit can also add lots of sugar.

YUP, A LIGHTLY SUGARED WHOLE-GRAIN CEREAL CAN BE A GOOD CHOICE IF YOU TEND TO ADD TOO MUCH SUGAR AT HOME.

CREAMY, LIGHT FETTUCCINE ALFREDO

Kid Friendly • Quick & Easy Vegetarian

Fettuccine Alfredo with Asparagus

Hands-on: 23 min. Total: 23 min.

8 ounces uncooked fettuccine
1 teaspoon olive oil
1 pound fresh asparagus spears, trimmed and cut into 2-inch pieces
³/₄ teaspoon kosher salt, divided
½ teaspoon black pepper, divided
1 teaspoon grated lemon rind
2 teaspoons fresh lemon juice
1 tablespoon butter
1 tablespoon vodka or water
4 garlic cloves, minced
2 ounces ¹/₃-less-fat cream cheese
¼ cup fat-free milk
1.5 ounces vegetarian Parmesan cheese, grated (about 6 tablespoons)
1 tablespoon chopped fresh chives

1. Cook pasta according to package directions. Drain in a colander over a bowl. Reserve ¼ cup pasta water.
2. Heat a large skillet over medium-high heat. Add oil to pan; swirl to coat. Add asparagus, ¼ teaspoon salt, and ¼ teaspoon pepper; sauté 6 minutes or until crisp-tender. Remove from heat. Add rind and juice; toss. Keep warm.
3. Melt butter in a medium saucepan over medium heat. Add vodka and garlic; cook 1 minute. Add cream cheese, stirring until smooth. Stir in milk, Parmesan cheese, ½ teaspoon salt, and ¼ teaspoon pepper.

Stir in reserved pasta water, pasta, and asparagus; toss to coat noodles. Sprinkle with chives. Serves 4 (serving size: about 2 cups)

CALORIES 365; **FAT** 11.2g (sat 5.9g, mono 3.3g, poly 0.6g); **PROTEIN** 16g; **CARB** 50g; **FIBER** 4g; **CHOL** 28mg; **IRON** 4mg; **SODIUM** 609mg; **CALC** 212mg

NUTRITION MADE EASY

FAST AND FUN FRITTATA COMBOS

The frittata is a high-wow, low-difficulty dish. Here are six easy variations for under 250 calories. They're quick, easy, kid friendly, and delicious hot or cold. Each serves four.

Frittatas in Five Easy Steps
1. Preheat broiler to high. Combine 2 large egg whites, 6 large eggs, ¼ teaspoon kosher salt, ¼ teaspoon pepper, and ⅓ cup 1% milk; stir with a whisk.
2. Heat a 9-inch cast-iron skillet over medium heat. Sauté any specified ingredients until tender (some recipes skip this step).
3. Layer in veggies and cooked protein.
4. Sprinkle with cheese.
5. Pour egg mixture over cheese. Cook over medium heat 5 to 6 minutes or until eggs are partially set; then broil 5 inches from heat for 2 to 3 minutes or until browned and almost set.

Gluten Free • Vegetarian
Two-Tomato, Basil & Goat Cheese
Sauté 1 pint grape tomatoes and 2 teaspoons chopped fresh thyme in 1½ teaspoons olive oil. Layer in 3 plum tomatoes, seeded and thinly sliced, and ½ cup finely chopped fresh basil. Sprinkle with 2 ounces crumbled goat cheese.

CALORIES 201; **FAT** 12.2g (sat 4.5g); **PROTEIN** 16g; **SODIUM** 321mg

Gluten Free • Vegetarian
Feta, Green Onion & Asparagus
Layer in 8 ounces raw asparagus, ¼ cup thinly sliced shallots, and 3 tablespoons chopped green onions. Sprinkle with 2 ounces crumbled feta cheese.

CALORIES 183; **FAT** 10.5g (sat 4.6g); **PROTEIN** 15g; **SODIUM** 426mg

Gluten Free
Creamy Smoked Salmon & Dill
Layer in ½ cup thinly sliced red onion, 2 tablespoons chopped fresh dill, 1 tablespoon chopped fresh chives, and 2 ounces thinly sliced smoked salmon. Sprinkle with 2 ounces diced ⅓-less-fat cream cheese. Serve with lemon.

CALORIES 190; **FAT** 11.3g (sat 4.3g); **PROTEIN** 17g; **SODIUM** 506mg

Gluten Free
Spinach, Ham & Gruyère
Sauté 3 cups spinach and 2 cloves minced garlic in 1½ teaspoons olive oil. Layer in 1 ounce prosciutto, crisped and crumbled; ¼ cup caramelized onions; and 1 tablespoon chopped fresh chives. Sprinkle with 2 ounces shredded Gruyère cheese.

CALORIES 237; **FAT** 15.4g (sat 5.7g); **PROTEIN** 18g; **SODIUM** 402mg

Gluten Free • Vegetarian
Mushroom, Leek & Fontina
Sauté 8 ounces sliced mushrooms and ½ cup sliced leeks in 2 teaspoons olive oil. Layer in 2 teaspoons chopped fresh thyme and ¼ cup chopped green onions. Sprinkle with 2 ounces shredded fontina cheese.

CALORIES 222; **FAT** 14.3g (sat 5.5g); **PROTEIN** 17g; **SODIUM** 384mg

Sausage, Feta & Kale
Sauté 3 cups thinly sliced kale in 1½ teaspoons olive oil. Layer in 4 ounces turkey Italian sausage, cooked and crumbled, and ½ cup chopped red bell pepper. Sprinkle with 1 ounce crumbled feta cheese.

CALORIES 224; **FAT** 13.6g (sat 4.7g); **PROTEIN** 19g; **SODIUM** 519mg

SUPERFAST 20-MINUTE COOKING

Kid Friendly • Quick & Easy
Vegetarian

Broccoli and Pecorino Pesto Pasta

8 ounces uncooked whole-wheat
  angel hair pasta
1 (12-ounce) package microwave-in-
  bag fresh broccoli florets
1/4 cup basil leaves
3 tablespoons extra-virgin olive oil
1 tablespoon grated fresh lemon rind
3 tablespoons fresh lemon juice
1/4 teaspoon kosher salt
1/4 teaspoon crushed red pepper
2 garlic cloves
2 anchovy fillets, drained
1 ounce pecorino Romano cheese,
  grated (about 1/4 cup)

1. Cook pasta according to package
directions, omitting salt and
fat. Drain pasta in a colander over
a bowl, reserving 1 cup cooking
liquid.
2. Cook broccoli according to
package directions; cool 5 minutes.
Place broccoli and remaining ingredients in the bowl of a food processor; pulse until finely chopped. With
processor on, slowly add
reserved 1 cup cooking liquid
through food chute until sauce
reaches desired consistency. Place
broccoli mixture in a large bowl; add
pasta, and toss to combine. Serve
immediately. Serves 4 (serving size:
about 1½ cups)

CALORIES 364; FAT 14.5g (sat 3.3g, mono 7.7g, poly 1.9g);
PROTEIN 12g; CARB 49g; FIBER 8g; CHOL 9mg;
IRON 3mg; SODIUM 366mg; CALC 139mg

Quick & Easy

Smoky Pork Stir-Fry

*Smoked paprika and dark sesame oil add
depth to this stir-fry. Serve over precooked
brown rice or soba noodles.*

2 teaspoons canola oil
10 ounces pork tenderloin, trimmed
  and cut into bite-sized pieces
1/2 teaspoon smoked paprika
1/4 teaspoon kosher salt
2 teaspoons dark sesame oil
1½ cups thinly sliced orange bell
  pepper (1 medium)
1 cup snow peas
1 tablespoon minced peeled fresh
  ginger
1 garlic clove, minced
3 tablespoons rice vinegar
1 tablespoon lower-sodium soy sauce
2 teaspoons sugar
1 teaspoon chili garlic sauce
3 cups tricolor coleslaw
3 green onions, thinly sliced

1. Heat a large skillet over high
heat. Add canola oil; swirl to coat.
Sprinkle pork with paprika and salt.
Add pork to pan; sauté 3 minutes or
until browned. Remove pork from
pan.
2. Return pan to medium-high heat.
Add sesame oil; swirl to coat. Add
bell pepper, peas, ginger, and garlic;
stir-fry 3 minutes or until vegetables
are crisp-tender, stirring frequently.
Combine vinegar, soy sauce, sugar,
and chili garlic sauce in a bowl, stirring with a whisk. Add pork and soy
sauce mixture to pan; cook 1 minute.
Stir in coleslaw; cook 1 minute or
until slightly wilted. Remove pan
from heat; sprinkle with green
onions. Serves 4 (serving size: about
1 cup)

CALORIES 165; FAT 6.4g (sat 1g, mono 3g, poly 1.9g);
PROTEIN 17g; CARB 10g; FIBER 3g; CHOL 46mg;
IRON 2mg; SODIUM 323mg; CALC 44mg

Kid Friendly • Quick & Easy

Two-Pea Pasta with Bacon Breadcrumbs

*You can use any short pasta in place
of the ziti.*

8 cups water
8 ounces uncooked ziti
1 cup frozen green peas
8 ounces sugar snap peas, trimmed
  and halved diagonally
2 center-cut bacon slices, chopped
1/3 cup panko (Japanese
  breadcrumbs)
1 tablespoon unsalted butter
1 cup thinly sliced green onions
2 large garlic cloves, sliced
1 cup unsalted chicken stock (such
  as Swanson)
1/4 teaspoon kosher salt
1/4 teaspoon freshly ground black
  pepper
1 tablespoon fresh lemon juice
1 ounce Parmesan cheese, grated
  (about 1/4 cup)

1. Bring 8 cups water to a boil in a
large saucepan. Add pasta; cook
5 minutes. Add green peas and sugar
snap peas; cook 1 minute or until
pasta is done. Drain.
2. Heat a large nonstick skillet over
medium heat. Add bacon to pan;
cook 3 minutes or until bacon
begins to brown. Add panko; cook
1½ minutes or until browned.
Remove panko mixture from pan.
Add butter to pan; swirl until butter
melts. Add green onions and garlic;
cook 1½ minutes. Stir in stock, salt,
and pepper; cook 3 minutes. Stir in
pasta mixture, juice, and Parmesan
cheese; toss. Top with panko mixture.
Serves 4 (serving size: 1¼ cups)

CALORIES 365; FAT 7.5g (sat 3.8g, mono 2g, poly 0.5g);
PROTEIN 17g; CARB 58g; FIBER 6g; CHOL 17mg;
IRON 4mg; SODIUM 394mg; CALC 148mg

Root Beer Sloppy Joes

Root beer adds a warm caramel note to these fun sandwiches. Serve with baked sweet potato chips.

2 teaspoons canola oil
¾ cup prechopped onion
12 ounces 90% lean ground sirloin
½ cup unsalted tomato sauce
¼ cup bottled chili sauce (such as Heinz)
¼ cup root beer
1 tablespoon Worcestershire sauce
2 teaspoons minced fresh garlic
1 teaspoon dry mustard
1 teaspoon chili powder
1 teaspoon tomato paste
4 (1½-ounce) hamburger buns, toasted

1. Heat a large nonstick skillet over medium heat. Add oil; swirl to coat. Add onion; cook 3 minutes. Add beef; cook 4 minutes or until beef begins to brown, stirring to crumble. Stir in tomato sauce and next 7 ingredients; bring to a simmer. Cook 5 minutes or until slightly thickened, stirring occasionally. Divide beef mixture evenly among bottom halves of buns; top with top halves of buns. Serves 4 (serving size: 1 sandwich)

CALORIES 331; FAT 11.6g (sat 3.5g, mono 4.9g, poly 1.7g); PROTEIN 21g; CARB 35g; FIBER 2g; CHOL 52mg; IRON 4mg; SODIUM 555mg; CALC 105mg

Greek-Style Edamame Salad

8 cups water
1½ cups frozen shelled edamame
1½ tablespoons extra-virgin olive oil
1½ tablespoons red wine vinegar
2 teaspoons minced fresh oregano
¼ teaspoon kosher salt
1 cup chopped English cucumber
2 tablespoons sliced kalamata olives
2 tablespoons crumbled feta cheese

1. Bring 8 cups water to a boil in a saucepan. Add edamame; cook 3 minutes or until tender. Drain.
2. Combine oil, vinegar, oregano, and salt in a medium bowl. Stir in edamame and cucumber. Sprinkle with olives and feta cheese. Serves 4 (serving size: 1 cup)

CALORIES 121; FAT 9.1g (sat 1.8g, mono 5.1g, poly 1.5g); PROTEIN 5g; CARB 5g; FIBER 2g; CHOL 4mg; IRON 1mg; SODIUM 234mg; CALC 59mg

**Kid Friendly • Quick & Easy
Gluten Free • Make Ahead
Vegetarian
Sesame-Carrot Edamame Salad**
Boil 1½ cups frozen shelled edamame 3 minutes or until tender. Drain. Combine 2 tablespoons chopped fresh cilantro, 1½ tablespoons rice vinegar, 1½ tablespoons dark sesame oil, ½ teaspoon sesame seeds, and ¼ teaspoon kosher salt in a medium bowl, stirring with a whisk. Stir in edamame, 1 cup shredded carrot, and ¼ cup sliced green onions. Serves 4 (serving size: ½ cup)

CALORIES 109; FAT 7.5g (sat 1g); SODIUM 143mg

SOY LOVE: THIS PROTEIN-PACKED LEGUME IS ALSO A GOOD TOPPING FOR LETTUCE SALADS. OR ADD TO STIR-FRIES OR BLEND INTO A DIP.

**Kid Friendly • Quick & Easy
Gluten Free • Make Ahead
Vegetarian
Edamame Succotash Salad**
Boil 1½ cups frozen shelled edamame 3 minutes or until tender. Drain. Melt 2 teaspoons butter in a large skillet over medium-high heat. Add 1 cup fresh corn kernels, ½ cup chopped sweet onion, and 1 minced garlic clove; sauté 4 minutes. Stir in edamame, 1 pint halved cherry tomatoes, ½ teaspoon freshly ground black pepper, and ⅜ teaspoon kosher salt; sauté 1 minute. Stir in ¼ cup chopped fresh basil. Serves 4 (serving size: ¾ cup)

CALORIES 121; FAT 4.7g (sat 1.6g); SODIUM 210mg

**Kid Friendly • Quick & Easy
Gluten Free • Make Ahead
Vegetarian
Radish and Chive Edamame Salad**
Boil 1½ cups frozen shelled edamame 3 minutes or until tender. Drain. Combine 1½ tablespoons extra-virgin olive oil, 1½ tablespoons white wine vinegar, ½ teaspoon Dijon mustard, ¼ teaspoon kosher salt, and ¼ teaspoon freshly ground black pepper in a medium bowl, stirring with a whisk. Stir in edamame, 1 cup thinly sliced radishes, and ¼ cup chopped fresh chives. Serves 4 (serving size: ½ cup)

CALORIES 100; FAT 7.2g (sat 1g); SODIUM 149mg

Apricot-Rosemary Chicken Thighs with Roasted Almond Couscous

Fresh herbs turn a couple of pantry basics into a beautiful glaze for chicken.

1 cup unsalted chicken stock (such as Swanson)
1/2 teaspoon kosher salt, divided
1 cup uncooked couscous
1/3 cup chopped fresh flat-leaf parsley
2 tablespoons dry-roasted, unsalted almonds, coarsely chopped
1/3 cup apricot preserves
1 1/2 tablespoons white wine vinegar
1 teaspoon finely chopped fresh rosemary
Cooking spray
1 1/2 pounds skinless, boneless chicken thighs, trimmed
1/2 teaspoon freshly ground black pepper

1. Bring stock and 1/8 teaspoon salt to a boil in a small saucepan. Stir in couscous. Remove pan from heat; cover and let stand 5 minutes. Stir in parsley and almonds.
2. Combine 1/8 teaspoon salt, apricot preserves, vinegar, and rosemary in a 2-cup glass measure. Microwave at HIGH 2 minutes, stirring after 1 minute.
3. Heat a grill pan over medium-high heat. Coat pan with cooking spray. Sprinkle chicken with 1/4 teaspoon salt and pepper. Add chicken to pan; grill 3 minutes on each side or until almost done. Brush chicken with half of apricot mixture. Grill chicken 1 minute on each side or until done; brush with remaining half of apricot mixture. Serve with couscous. Serves 4 (serving size: 4 ounces chicken and about 1/2 cup couscous)

CALORIES 466; FAT 9.8g (sat 2g, mono 3.9g, poly 2.2g); PROTEIN 41g; CARB 52g; FIBER 3g; CHOL 162mg; IRON 3mg; SODIUM 442mg; CALC 56mg

Vietnamese Caramel Chicken

Serve with steamed, quartered baby bok choy and precooked jasmine rice.

4 teaspoons canola oil
1 1/2 pounds skinless, boneless chicken thighs, cut into 2-inch pieces
1 tablespoon minced peeled fresh ginger
3 garlic cloves, minced
1 large shallot, thinly sliced
1/4 cup unsalted chicken stock
3 tablespoons dark brown sugar
1 tablespoon fish sauce
1 tablespoon fresh lime juice
1/4 teaspoon kosher salt
1/4 teaspoon black pepper
1/4 teaspoon crushed red pepper
6 green onions, cut into 1-inch pieces

1. Heat a large nonstick skillet over medium-high heat. Add canola oil; swirl to coat. Add chicken; cook 2 minutes. Turn chicken; add ginger, garlic, and shallot. Cook 1 minute, stirring frequently.
2. Combine 1/4 cup stock, sugar, and next 5 ingredients in a bowl. Add to pan; cook 1 minute. Reduce heat to medium-low; simmer 7 minutes or until sauce has thickened and chicken is done. Stir in green onions. Serves 4 (serving size: 1 cup chicken mixture)

CALORIES 306; FAT 11.8g (sat 2.1g, mono 5.4g, poly 2.9g); PROTEIN 34g; CARB 15g; FIBER 1g; CHOL 162mg; IRON 2mg; SODIUM 648mg; CALC 50mg

Shrimp and Corn Chowder

Serve this hearty chowder with a crusty baguette. Use fresh corn, if available.

4 center-cut bacon slices, chopped
4 green onions
1 tablespoon chopped fresh thyme
4 garlic cloves, minced
1.1 ounces all-purpose flour (about 1/4 cup)
2 1/2 cups 2% reduced-fat milk
1 1/4 cups unsalted chicken stock
1 bay leaf
1/4 teaspoon kosher salt
1/4 teaspoon freshly ground black pepper
1/8 teaspoon ground red pepper
24 medium shrimp, peeled and deveined (about 1 pound)
1 (10-ounce) package frozen corn kernels, thawed

1. Cook bacon in a large saucepan over medium heat 6 minutes or until crisp. Remove bacon from pan with a slotted spoon, reserving drippings.
2. Thinly slice green onions; reserve 2 tablespoons dark green parts. Add white and light green onion parts, thyme, and garlic to drippings in pan; sauté 2 minutes. Weigh or lightly spoon flour into a dry measuring cup; level with a knife. Sprinkle over onion mixture; cook 1 minute, stirring constantly. Stir in milk, stock, and bay leaf; bring to a boil. Reduce heat to medium, and cook 2 minutes. Stir in salt, black pepper, red pepper, shrimp, and corn; simmer 4 minutes or until shrimp are done. Discard bay leaf. Divide soup evenly among 4 bowls; sprinkle with bacon and reserved 2 tablespoons green onions. Serves 4 (serving size: 1 1/2 cups)

CALORIES 300; FAT 7.5g (sat 3g, mono 2.2g, poly 0.9g); PROTEIN 28g; CARB 32g; FIBER 2g; CHOL 162mg; IRON 2mg; SODIUM 552mg; CALC 274mg

DRIED RED LENTILS

By Naomi Duguid

These legumes cook to a creamy texture that enriches many dishes.

I love having a stash of red lentils (actually they are a gorgeous orange-pink color) in a glass jar in my pantry—they are just so beautiful. They are also a flexible go-to ingredient: They cook quickly in boiling water (about 20 minutes), provide protein and substance (especially valuable if cooking for vegetarians or vegans), and lend themselves to many dishes. And because they are dried, they keep almost indefinitely when stored in a dry, airtight container.

In India, red lentils are known as masoor dal and often boiled until soft (usually in a proportion of 3 cups water to 1 cup lentils), and then flavored with fried minced onions and spices. This is traditionally eaten with rice and chapati (Indian flatbread), but you can also serve it as a soup course in a Western meal. I like to knead cooked mashed red lentils into a standard yeast dough to give more protein heft to the bread. It's delicious.

But one of the most interesting ways to prepare red lentils is to make meatless "burgers," spiced with onion and a little tomato paste, as well as a generous squeeze of lemon juice. You can make them ahead and serve them at room temperature as an appetizer or as a vegetarian main course. Or, you can shape them ahead, and then pan-fry and serve them hot.

Kid Friendly • Freezable
Make Ahead • Vegetarian
Gluten Free

Red Lentil Burgers

*Hands-on: **40 min.** Total: **60 min.** The classic version of these meatless burgers comes from Turkey, where cooked lentils are combined with fine bulgur to make the "meat" for the patties. You could also use rice. Lightly wet your hands before shaping the patties; the water helps prevent the mixture from sticking to your skin. Serve cooked burgers on leaf lettuce if you wish, sprinkled with fresh herbs, and put out lemon wedges, a bowl of chopped cucumber, and a chile sauce or a creamy yogurt-based sauce as accompaniments. Cooked patties freeze well; reheat in the oven at 350° for 10 minutes or until heated.*

1 cup dried small red lentils
1 cup uncooked long-grain white rice
3 tablespoons olive oil, divided
3 tablespoons chopped green onions
1 tablespoon tomato paste
½ teaspoon ground red pepper
¼ cup chopped fresh cilantro, divided
2 tablespoons fresh lemon juice
1¼ teaspoons kosher salt
¾ cup diced English cucumber
6 lemon wedges

1. Rinse and drain lentils; place lentils and rice in a large saucepan. Cover with water to 3 inches above lentil mixture; bring to a boil. Cover, reduce heat, and simmer 20 minutes or until lentils and rice are tender. Drain.
2. Place lentil mixture in a food processor; pulse until finely chopped. Set aside (keep mixture in processor).
3. Heat a large skillet over medium heat. Add 1 tablespoon oil to pan; swirl to coat. Add green onions to pan; cook 2 minutes or until softened. Stir in tomato paste and red pepper; cook 1 minute, stirring frequently. Add green onion mixture, 2 tablespoons cilantro, lemon juice, and salt to food processor; process until combined.
4. Divide mixture into 12 equal portions, gently shaping each into a ½-inch-thick patty. Return skillet to medium-high heat. Add 1 tablespoon oil to pan; swirl to coat. Add 6 patties to pan; cook 3 minutes on each side or until browned. Remove cooked patties from pan. Repeat procedure with 1 tablespoon oil and 6 patties. Sprinkle with 2 tablespoons cilantro. Serve patties with cucumber and lemon wedges. Serves 6 (serving size: 2 patties, 2 tablespoons cucumber, and 1 lemon wedge)

CALORIES 249; **FAT** 7.6g (sat 1g, mono 5g, poly 0.8g); **PROTEIN** 10g; **CARB** 35g; **FIBER** 5g; **CHOL** 0mg; **IRON** 3mg; **SODIUM** 414mg; **CALC** 24mg

MICROWAVE TIP: EASIEST TECHNIQUE FOR CLEAN COBS

We're at the tail end of sweet corn season, so get in as much fresh corn goodness as you can. It's a whole grain, after all. But those silks and husks can be a mess to deal with, right? Not if you use this cooking method, perhaps the easiest way to cook corn I've ever tried. Simply place two unshucked ears in the microwave—seriously, don't prep them in any way. Microwave at HIGH for 7 to 8 minutes. Let the corn cool slightly, and then remove husks and silks; they come right off cleanly and effortlessly. You can also try this for a showier reveal: Cut off the fatter base end of the corn. Hold the cob by the top, where the silks come out, and give it a squeeze. The pristine cob will slide out cleanly. Brush with a little melted butter, and you're good to go.

THE CHEESIEST RECIPES EVER!

Yum! Who can resist a casserole blanketed in melted cheddar or a pizza that oozes with mozza goodness?

The pleasures of cheese are many: Parm's salty nuttiness, mozzarella's milky richness, sharp cheddar's tangy splendor. Cheese is simply a fantastic ingredient, so we made it our mission to develop some smart strategies for delivering full cheese satisfaction in lighter, healthier dishes.

Kid Friendly • Make Ahead

Classic Lasagna with Meat Sauce

(pictured on page 236)

Hands-on: 16 min. Total: 66 min.

1¹/₂ cups fat-free ricotta cheese
6 ounces part-skim mozzarella cheese, shredded and divided (about 1¹/₂ cups)
¹/₄ cup flat-leaf parsley leaves, divided
1¹/₂ tablespoons unsalted butter, melted
1 tablespoon finely chopped fresh oregano
5 garlic cloves, minced and divided
1 large egg, lightly beaten
12 ounces extra-lean ground beef (93% lean)
¹/₂ teaspoon freshly ground black pepper
¹/₄ teaspoon crushed red pepper
1 (25-ounce) jar lower-sodium marinara sauce
Cooking spray
6 lasagna noodles, cooked
1 ounce Parmigiano-Reggiano cheese, grated (about ¹/₄ cup)

1. Preheat oven to 375°.
2. Combine ricotta, 2 ounces (about ½ cup) mozzarella, 2 tablespoons parsley, butter, oregano, 1 garlic clove, and egg; set aside.
3. Place ground beef in a large non-stick skillet over medium-high heat; sprinkle with peppers and 4 garlic cloves. Cook 9 minutes or until beef is browned, stirring to crumble; drain. Return beef mixture to pan; stir in marinara sauce, and remove from heat.
4. Spread ½ cup meat sauce in the bottom of a broiler-safe 11 x 7–inch glass or ceramic baking dish coated with cooking spray. Cut bottom third off each noodle to form 6 long and 6 short noodles; cut short noodles in half to form 12 pieces. Arrange 2 long noodles along outside edges of dish; arrange 4 short noodle pieces along center of dish. Top noodles with 1 cup meat sauce. Top with 2 long noodles and 4 short noodle pieces, all of ricotta mixture, and 1 cup meat sauce. Arrange remaining 2 long noodles and 4 short noodle pieces on top. Spread remaining meat sauce over top noodles. Sprinkle evenly with 4 ounces (1 cup) mozzarella cheese and Parmigiano-Reggiano cheese. Cover with foil coated with cooking spray. Bake at 375° for 30 minutes. Uncover and bake for an additional 10 minutes or until bubbly.
5. Preheat broiler to high. (Keep lasagna in oven.)
6. Broil lasagna 1 to 2 minutes or until cheese is golden brown and sauce is bubbly. Remove from oven; let stand 10 minutes. Sprinkle with 2 tablespoons parsley; cut into 6 pieces. Serves 6 (serving size: 1 piece)

CALORIES 378; **FAT** 15.3g (sat 6.8g, mono 6.3g, poly 1g); **PROTEIN** 27g; **CARB** 30g; **FIBER** 3g; **CHOL** 92mg; **IRON** 1mg; **SODIUM** 591mg; **CALC** 395mg

OUR STRATEGY

We stick to part-skim mozzarella for our lasagna and add just a touch of Parm-Regg to the top so its salty flavor is prominent. In the filling, we use fat-free ricotta but stir in a bit of melted butter to enrich it—it tastes great and still has less fat and sat fat than part-skim ricotta.

CLASSIC VERSION
493 calories
27g fat, 14g sat fat
1,144mg sodium

OUR VERSION
378 calories
15.3g fat, 6.8g sat fat
591mg sodium

Grilled Cheese with Roasted Tomato Spread

Hands-on: 24 min. Total: 44 min.

1 tablespoon olive oil, divided
4 plum tomatoes, halved and seeded
2 garlic cloves, unpeeled
6 to 8 basil leaves
Dash of kosher salt
Dash of black pepper
4 teaspoons canola mayonnaise
2 ounces ⅓-less-fat cream cheese
4 ounces 2% reduced-fat sharp
   cheddar cheese, finely shredded
8 (1-ounce) slices whole-grain bread
Cooking spray

1. Preheat oven to 400°.
2. Combine 1 teaspoon oil, tomatoes, and garlic on a baking sheet. Bake at 400° for 20 minutes. Remove skins from tomatoes; discard skins. Squeeze garlic to extract pulp; discard garlic skins. Place tomatoes, garlic pulp, basil, salt, and pepper in a mini food processor; pulse 10 times.
3. Combine mayonnaise and cream cheese. Add cheddar, stirring well (mixture will be very thick). Spread one-fourth of cheese mixture over each of 4 bread slices; top each with about 1½ tablespoons tomato mixture and 1 bread slice. Lightly coat outsides of sandwiches with cooking spray.
4. Heat a large skillet over medium heat. Add 1 teaspoon oil; swirl. Cook sandwiches 3 minutes or until lightly browned (do not flip). Remove sandwiches from pan. Add 1 teaspoon oil; swirl. Turn sandwiches over, and add to pan; cook 3 minutes or until lightly browned and cheese melts. Serve immediately. Serves 4 (serving size: 1 sandwich)

CALORIES 312; **FAT** 15.1g (sat 6g, mono 6.4g, poly 1.6g); **PROTEIN** 17g; **CARB** 27g; **FIBER** 5g; **CHOL** 26mg; **IRON** 2mg; **SODIUM** 590mg; **CALC** 345mg

---

Three-Cheese White Pizza with Fresh Arugula

Hands-on: 20 min. Total: 40 min.

12 ounces refrigerated fresh pizza
   dough
2 teaspoons extra-virgin olive oil
6 garlic cloves, crushed
⅔ cup fat-free ricotta cheese
2 tablespoons canola mayonnaise
2 teaspoons chopped fresh thyme
¼ teaspoon black pepper
1.5 ounces Parmigiano-Reggiano
   cheese, finely shredded (about ⅓
   cup)
3 ounces fresh mozzarella cheese,
   very thinly sliced
1 teaspoon fresh lemon juice
1 teaspoon balsamic vinegar
1½ cups baby arugula

1. Remove dough from refrigerator. Let stand at room temperature, covered, 20 minutes.
2. Place a pizza stone or heavy baking sheet in oven. Preheat oven to 500° (keep pizza stone or baking sheet in oven as it preheats).
3. Heat a small skillet over medium heat. Add oil to pan; swirl to coat. Add garlic; cook 2 minutes or until garlic is lightly browned. Remove garlic with a slotted spoon. Finely chop garlic. Reserve oil.
4. Place chopped garlic, ricotta, mayonnaise, thyme, pepper, and Parmigiano-Reggiano cheese in a medium bowl. Beat with a mixer at medium-high speed until almost smooth (about 2 minutes).
5. Roll dough into a 14-inch circle on a lightly floured surface; pierce entire surface of dough liberally with a fork. Carefully remove pizza stone from oven. Arrange dough on pizza stone. Bake at 500° for 5 minutes. Spread ricotta mixture over crust, leaving a ½-inch border. Arrange mozzarella over ricotta mixture. Bake at 500° for 10 minutes or until crust and cheese are browned.
6. Combine reserved oil, juice, and vinegar in a bowl. Add arugula; toss to coat. Top pizza with arugula mixture. Cut pizza into 4 large pieces. Serves 4 (serving size: 1 piece)

CALORIES 402; **FAT** 13.3g (sat 5.2g, mono 4.6g, poly 1.5g); **PROTEIN** 19g; **CARB** 46g; **FIBER** 6g; **CHOL** 31mg; **IRON** 1mg; **SODIUM** 688mg; **CALC** 321mg

---

Cheesy Nachos with Pinto Bean Salsa and Pickled Jalapeños

(pictured on page 234)

Hands-on: 40 min. Total: 40 min. *Be sure to shred the cheese yourself; pre-shredded strands are often coated in an anticaking agent that could make the sauce grainy. You'll want to build the nachos on a sturdy base—nothing too thin and fragile, as the chips need to stand up to those tasty toppings.*

¼ cup cider vinegar
¼ cup water
2 tablespoons sugar
2 jalapeño peppers, stemmed and thinly sliced
6 tablespoons chopped fresh cilantro, divided
2 tablespoons fresh lime juice
1 teaspoon extra-virgin olive oil
½ teaspoon kosher salt
¼ teaspoon chili powder
2 garlic cloves, minced
½ cup chopped tomato
½ cup diced red bell pepper
¼ cup diced red onion
2 center-cut bacon slices, cooked and crumbled
1 (15-ounce) can unsalted pinto beans, rinsed and drained
5 ounces 2% reduced-fat sharp cheddar cheese (such as Cracker Barrel), shredded (about 1¼ cups)
1 tablespoon cornstarch
1 cup evaporated fat-free milk
1½ teaspoons hot pepper sauce (such as Tabasco)
6 ounces brown rice tortilla chips (such as Lundberg Sea Salt Rice Chips)
⅔ cup diced peeled avocado

1. Combine first 3 ingredients in a medium microwave-safe bowl; microwave at HIGH 2 minutes or until mixture comes to a boil. Stir in jalapeño peppers. Let stand 25 minutes.
2. Combine 2 tablespoons cilantro, lime juice, and next 4 ingredients in a medium bowl, stirring with a whisk. Add tomato and next 4 ingredients; toss gently to coat.
3. Place cheese in a medium saucepan; sprinkle with cornstarch, and toss to combine. Add milk. Cook over low heat until cheese melts and mixture thickens, stirring constantly with a whisk. Add hot sauce, stirring with a whisk.
4. Drain jalapeño mixture; discard liquid. Arrange chips in a single layer on a large platter. Reserve ½ cup bean salsa; arrange remaining salsa evenly over chips. Drizzle with cheese sauce; top evenly with avocado. Top evenly with remaining ½ cup bean salsa, ¼ cup cilantro, and jalapeños. Serve immediately. Serves 6 (serving size: ½ cup bean mixture, ¼ cup cheese sauce, and 1 cup chips)

CALORIES 340; FAT 15.5g (sat 4.1g, mono 4.4g, poly 5.9g); PROTEIN 15g; CARB 36g; FIBER 5g; CHOL 17mg; IRON 1mg; SODIUM 554mg; CALC 367mg

OOPS! COMMON CHEESETASTROPHIES AND HOW TO AVOID THEM

YOUR CHEESE SAUCE GOES GRAINY
It's so sad when instead of luscious, silky cheese sauce, you end up with a broken, grainy mess. When adding cheese to a thickened white sauce, finely shred it (so it melts quickly), let it come to room temp, and add it to the sauce gradually. If using hard or aged cheeses, cool the sauce down to about 155° before stirring it in; high temps lead to separation and graininess.

YOUR SAUCE IS A LUMPY MESS
When making sauces, sometimes the cheese agglomerates, leaving you with clumps that don't incorporate into the sauce. That happens when you add too much cheese at once, at too high a heat. Follow the advice above for the smoothest sauce.

THE CHEESE OVERCOOKS
We're not talking about cheese burning under the broiler; those charred bits are rather tasty. But when you're hoping for a soft, melty topping on your pizza or lasagna but get a crusty, dry, hard surface, that's the pits. Just watch carefully, and don't overcook. If the food has to be in the oven for a long time (lasagna), keep it covered for much of the cooking.

YOU DON'T ACHIEVE MELTDOWN
First, know which cheeses are melting champs (fontina, Gruyère, mozzarella, cheddar) and those that just won't melt (halloumi, ricotta, feta, Parmigiano-Reggiano). Also be careful of reduced-fat versions: When we use reduced-fat cheddar, we mix it with moister, meltier ingredients (as in our grilled cheese recipe); if you use reduced-fat cheddar atop a casserole, though, the results will be rubbery and plasticky.

CHEESE SOGS OUT YOUR PIZZA
Fresh mozzarella, especially buffalo mozza, is moisture-rich and can water out on your pizza. If you can, opt for fresh mozza that's not packed in water. For either type, pat slices dry with paper towels. Prebake the crust, and avoid sauces that are loose (reduce marinara, or thicken with some tomato paste).

OUR STRATEGY

We transform reduced-fat cheddar into a creamy, silky, lighter sauce by melting it into evaporated fat-free milk. This technique allows less cheese to cover more chips than using shredded cheddar alone.

CLASSIC VERSION
463 calories
32.4g fat, 16g sat fat
1,041mg sodium

OUR VERSION
340 calories
15.5g fat, 4.1g sat fat
554mg sodium

Kid Friendly • Make Ahead

Broccoli-Quinoa Casserole with Chicken and Cheddar

Hands-on: 20 min. Total: 55 min. In our updated riff on chicken-rice casserole, whole-grain quinoa stands in for the typical white rice. It's a modern interpretation that still has loads of old-school comfort-food appeal.

1¹⁄₂ tablespoons canola oil
1 cup uncooked quinoa, rinsed and drained
1¹⁄₄ cups water
1 (12-ounce) package microwave-in-bag fresh broccoli florets
Cooking spray
12 ounces skinless, boneless chicken breast, cut into bite-sized pieces
¹⁄₂ teaspoon kosher salt, divided
¹⁄₂ teaspoon freshly ground black pepper, divided
1¹⁄₂ cups chopped onion
6 garlic cloves, minced
¹⁄₂ cup 1% low-fat milk
2¹⁄₂ tablespoons all-purpose flour
1¹⁄₂ cups unsalted chicken stock
2 ounces Parmesan cheese, grated (about ¹⁄₂ cup)
¹⁄₂ cup canola mayonnaise
4 ounces sharp cheddar cheese, shredded (1 cup)

1. Heat a medium saucepan over medium-high heat. Add 1¹⁄₂ teaspoons oil; swirl to coat. Add quinoa; cook 2 minutes or until toasted, stirring frequently. Add 1¹⁄₄ cups water; bring to a boil. Cover, reduce heat, and simmer 15 minutes or until quinoa is tender. Remove from heat; let stand 5 minutes. Fluff with a fork.
2. Preheat oven to 400°.
3. Cook broccoli in microwave according to package directions, reducing cook time to 2¹⁄₂ minutes.
4. Heat a Dutch oven over medium-high heat. Coat pan with cooking spray. Add chicken to pan; sprinkle with ¹⁄₈ teaspoon salt and ¹⁄₈ teaspoon pepper. Cook 5 minutes or until browned, turning occasionally; remove from pan.
5. Add 1 tablespoon oil to pan; swirl to coat. Add onion and garlic; sauté 5 minutes. Combine milk and flour, stirring with a whisk. Add milk mixture, stock, ³⁄₈ teaspoon salt, and ³⁄₈ teaspoon pepper to pan. Bring to a boil, stirring frequently; cook 2 minutes or until thickened. Remove from heat; cool slightly. Add Parmesan, stirring until cheese melts. Stir in quinoa, broccoli, chicken, and mayonnaise. Spoon mixture into a 2-quart glass or ceramic baking dish coated with cooking spray. Sprinkle with cheddar. Bake at 400° for 15 minutes or until casserole is bubbly and cheese melts. Serves 6 (serving size: 1¹⁄₃ cups)

CALORIES 449; FAT 21.3g (sat 6.7g, mono 9g, poly 4.5g); PROTEIN 34g; CARB 29g; FIBER 4g; CHOL 75mg; IRON 3mg; SODIUM 668mg; CALC 333mg

---

OUR STRATEGY

Instead of using condensed cream soup and processed cheese, we make a luscious white sauce with a touch of Parmesan to bind the casserole, and we use all the cheddar on top.

CLASSIC VERSION
562 calories
30.7g fat, 15.3g sat fat
1,544mg sodium

OUR VERSION
449 calories
21.3g fat, 6.7g sat fat
668mg sodium

Kid Friendly • Quick & Easy Vegetarian

Roasted Garlic Mac and Cheese

Hands-on: 24 min. Total: 24 min. We boost nutrition by using whole-grain pasta. We prefer whole-grain pasta over whole-wheat pasta here; the flavor of the latter is rather strong—sometimes a touch bitter—and would overwhelm the nice garlic notes.

2 whole garlic heads
1 tablespoon olive oil
3 tablespoons water
10 ounces whole-grain penne (such as Barilla)
2³⁄₄ cups 1% low-fat milk
3¹⁄₂ tablespoons all-purpose flour
1 teaspoon kosher salt
¹⁄₂ teaspoon freshly ground black pepper
4 ounces sharp cheddar cheese, shredded and divided (about 1 cup)
2 ounces part-skim mozzarella cheese, shredded (about ¹⁄₂ cup)
Cooking spray

1. Preheat broiler to high.
2. Remove white papery skin from garlic heads (do not peel or separate the cloves). Place garlic heads in a microwave-safe bowl; rub garlic heads with oil. Pour 3 tablespoons water into bottom of bowl. Cover with plastic wrap. Microwave at HIGH 4 minutes and 30 seconds or until garlic is very tender; cool slightly.
3. Cook pasta according to package directions, omitting salt and fat; drain.
4. Combine milk and flour in a medium saucepan, stirring with a whisk. Bring to a boil over medium-high heat, stirring frequently. Cook 3 minutes or until thickened; remove from heat. Stir in salt, pepper, 1 ounce cheddar, and mozzarella.

5. Separate garlic cloves; squeeze to extract garlic pulp. Discard skins. Place garlic pulp and 2 cups milk mixture in a blender; process until smooth. Stir garlic mixture into milk mixture. Add pasta; stir to coat. Spoon pasta mixture into 6 (10-ounce) ramekins or gratin dishes or a broiler-safe 11 x 7–inch glass or ceramic baking dish coated with cooking spray. Sprinkle evenly with 3 ounces cheddar. Broil 2 minutes or until cheese melts and begins to brown. Let stand 5 minutes. Serves 6 (serving size: about 1⅓ cups)

CALORIES 376; FAT 12.9g (sat 6g, mono 4.2g, poly 0.5g); PROTEIN 20g; CARB 45g; FIBER 4g; CHOL 31mg; IRON 1mg; SODIUM 568mg; CALC 386mg

OUR STRATEGY

We simply use less cheese—but it's where we use it that makes the difference. Lean part-skim mozzarella gives the sauce a wonderfully creamy texture; sharp cheddar goes on top so the mac looks super-cheesy, and you perceive it as cheesier than—from a fat and calorie stance—it really is.

CLASSIC VERSION
908 calories
59.3g fat, 35.8g sat fat
984mg sodium

OUR VERSION
376 calories
12.9g fat, 6g sat fat
568mg sodium

SUPER SIMPLE PORK CHOPS

Pork chops can be succulent, or they can be dry. These foolproof recipes get you to the right side of the equation, using supermarket ingredients.

Kid Friendly • Gluten Free

Oven Pork Chop Pan Roast

Hands-on: 15 min. Total: 55 min. Delicata squash, as the name implies, has skin so tender you don't have to peel it and makes this dish just that much faster to prep. You can substitute butternut or acorn squash—just peel it (or buy butternut prechopped).

1 tablespoon chopped fresh thyme leaves
12 dried plums, pitted and halved
6 shallots, peeled and halved
3 garlic cloves, sliced
½ delicata squash, seeded and cut into 1½-inch pieces (about 5 cups)
2 tablespoons plus 1 teaspoon olive oil, divided
½ teaspoon kosher salt, divided
4 (6-ounce) bone-in center-cut loin pork chops
¼ teaspoon freshly ground black pepper
3 cups baby arugula
2 teaspoons fresh lemon juice

1. Preheat oven to 425°. Place a jelly-roll pan in oven while it preheats.
2. Combine thyme, dried plums, shallots, garlic, and squash in a large bowl. Drizzle with 1 tablespoon olive oil, and sprinkle with ¼ teaspoon salt; toss to coat. Remove pan from oven. Arrange squash mixture in an even layer on pan. Return pan to oven; roast vegetables at 425° for 10 minutes.
3. While vegetables cook, sprinkle pork chops with ¼ teaspoon salt and pepper. Heat a large skillet over medium-high heat. Add 1½ teaspoons oil to pan; swirl to coat. Add 2 pork chops; cook 3 minutes or until browned on one side. Transfer to a plate. Repeat procedure with 1½ teaspoons oil and remaining pork chops. Remove squash mixture from oven, and place pork chops, browned side up, over vegetables; return to oven. Roast an additional 20 minutes or until vegetables are tender and pork chops are desired degree of doneness.
4. Combine arugula, lemon juice, and 1 teaspoon olive oil in a large bowl; toss gently to combine. Divide arugula mixture among 4 plates. Top with pork chops and roasted squash mixture; pour any pan juices over the top. Serves 4 (serving size: 1 pork chop, ¾ cup squash mixture, and ¾ cup arugula mixture)

CALORIES 444; FAT 14.7g (sat 3g, mono 8g, poly 1.8g); PROTEIN 28g; CARB 55g; FIBER 9g; CHOL 71mg; IRON 4mg; SODIUM 315mg; CALC 212mg

Kid Friendly • Gluten Free

Oven-Baked Pork and Apples

Hands-on: 25 min. Total: 50 min. *This is a delicious version of classic baked pork and apples. Serve with a simple broccoli slaw mixed with toasted walnuts and parsley and tossed with a light mayonnaise dressing.*

Cooking spray
1 tablespoon unsalted butter
4 (6-ounce) bone-in center-cut loin pork chops
2 large crisp apples (such as Honeycrisp), cored and each cut into 12 wedges
1 red onion, cut into 12 wedges
1 teaspoon chopped fresh thyme
1/3 cup unsalted chicken stock
3 tablespoons cider vinegar
1 tablespoon extra-virgin olive oil
1/4 teaspoon kosher salt
1/4 teaspoon freshly ground black pepper

1. Preheat oven to 425°. Coat a jelly-roll pan with cooking spray.
2. Heat a large nonstick skillet over medium-high heat. Add butter; swirl until butter melts. Add 2 pork chops to pan; cook 3 minutes on each side or until browned. Remove from pan. Repeat procedure with remaining 2 pork chops. Transfer pork to center of jelly-roll pan; scatter apple, onion, and thyme around pork chops. Combine stock, vinegar, and oil; drizzle over meat and vegetables. Sprinkle with salt and pepper. Roast at 425° for 25 minutes or until apples are golden brown and pork chops are desired degree of doneness. Serves 4 (serving size: 1 pork chop, 6 apple wedges, 3 onion wedges, and 2 tablespoons pan sauce)

CALORIES 285; **FAT** 12.4g (sat 4.1g, mono 5.4g, poly 1.2g); **PROTEIN** 24g; **CARB** 20g; **FIBER** 3g; **CHOL** 78mg; **IRON** 1mg; **SODIUM** 180mg; **CALC** 40mg

Kid Friendly

Red-Hot Currant-Glazed Pork Chops

Hands-on: 20 min. Total: 1 hr. 20 min. *If you want to use up some of the preserves in your fridge, you can sub them in for the red currant jelly. Seedless raspberry or apricot jam will work well; to balance the sweetness, add a little lemon juice to the sauce. Orange marmalade will work, too, putting a mild, pleasantly bitter spin on the dish.*

1/2 cup red currant jelly
1 teaspoon lower-sodium soy sauce
3/4 teaspoon hot sauce
1/4 teaspoon crushed red pepper
4 (6-ounce) bone-in center-cut loin pork chops (about 1/2 inch thick)
1/4 teaspoon kosher salt
1/4 teaspoon freshly ground black pepper
1 pound carrots, diagonally cut into 1-inch pieces
2 tablespoons chopped fresh parsley
1 tablespoon unsalted butter, melted
2 teaspoons stone-ground mustard

1. Combine first 4 ingredients in a small bowl, stirring with a whisk.
2. Place pork and 1/4 cup jelly mixture on a jelly-roll pan; toss to coat. Cover and marinate in refrigerator 1 hour. Reserve remaining jelly mixture.
3. Preheat broiler to high.
4. Sprinkle pork with salt and pepper. Broil 4 minutes or until desired degree of doneness (do not turn over).
5. Steam carrots 10 minutes or until tender. Combine carrots, parsley, butter, and mustard in a bowl; toss to coat. Serve pork chops with reserved jelly mixture and steamed carrots. Serves 4 (serving size: 1 pork chop, 1 tablespoon sauce, and about 3/4 cup carrots)

CALORIES 328; **FAT** 9.3g (sat 3.7g, mono 3g, poly 1g); **PROTEIN** 24g; **CARB** 38g; **FIBER** 3g; **CHOL** 78mg; **IRON** 1mg; **SODIUM** 375mg; **CALC** 61mg

Kid Friendly • Quick & Easy Gluten Free

Tuscan-Style Garlic-Herb Pork Chops

(pictured on page 235)

Hands-on: 8 min. Total: 20 min. *These grilled chops rest in and absorb an herb vinaigrette for a few minutes while you mix what might be the easiest side dish ever—a toss of white beans, briny green olives, and fresh spinach that matches up beautifully with the juicy pork chops.*

4 teaspoons olive oil, divided
1/4 cup chopped fresh flat-leaf parsley, divided
2 tablespoons thinly sliced sage leaves
1 tablespoon balsamic vinegar
1 teaspoon finely chopped rosemary
3 garlic cloves, minced and divided
4 (6-ounce) bone-in center-cut loin pork chops
1/2 teaspoon freshly ground black pepper, divided
1/4 teaspoon salt
Cooking spray
1 teaspoon grated lemon rind
3 tablespoons fresh lemon juice
2 (15-ounce) cans unsalted cannellini beans or other white beans, rinsed and drained
1 packed cup baby spinach leaves, thinly sliced
1/2 cup thinly sliced green onions
12 green olives, pitted and finely chopped (2 ounces)

1. Preheat a grill or grill pan to high heat.
2. Combine 2 teaspoons oil, 2 tablespoons parsley, sage, vinegar, rosemary, and half of garlic on a large plate or serving platter; set aside.
3. Sprinkle pork chops with 1/4 teaspoon pepper and salt. Place pork on grill rack coated with cooking spray; grill 5 minutes. Turn pork

chops over; grill 3 minutes or until done. Transfer chops to serving platter; turn to coat in herb mixture.

4. Combine lemon rind, juice, 2 teaspoons oil, and ¼ teaspoon pepper in a medium bowl; stir with a whisk. Add beans, remaining garlic, spinach, green onions, and olives; stir to combine. Serve with pork chops. Sprinkle with 2 tablespoons parsley to garnish. Serves 4 (serving size: 1 pork chop, 1 tablespoon dressing, and about ¾ cup beans)

CALORIES 328; FAT 14.8g (sat 2.5g, mono 7.8g, poly 2g); PROTEIN 29g; CARB 20g; FIBER 5g; CHOL 71mg; IRON 3mg; SODIUM 570mg; CALC 89mg

Kid Friendly • Quick & Easy

Pork Chops Simmered in Spiced Tomato Sauce

(pictured on page 235)

Hands-on: 22 min. Total: 22 min.
To get a good, brown sear on the pork, dry it with paper towels before adding it to the pan.

4 ounces uncooked whole-wheat spaghetti
2 teaspoons canola oil, divided
4 (6-ounce) bone-in center-cut loin pork chops (about ½ inch thick)
³⁄₈ teaspoon kosher salt, divided
¼ teaspoon freshly ground black pepper
1 cup vertically sliced sweet onion
1 cup sliced fennel bulb
1 teaspoon curry powder
½ teaspoon ground coriander
¼ cup dry white wine
2 tablespoons chopped fresh oregano, divided
1 (28-ounce) can whole tomatoes, undrained and chopped
1 ounce Parmesan cheese, shaved

1. Cook pasta according to package directions, omitting salt and fat. Drain.
2. While pasta cooks, heat a large stainless steel skillet over high heat. Add 1 teaspoon oil to pan; swirl to coat. Sprinkle pork with ¼ teaspoon salt and pepper. Add pork to pan; cook 2 minutes on each side or until browned. Remove pork from pan. Reduce heat to medium-high. Add 1 teaspoon oil to pan; swirl to coat. Add onion and fennel; sauté 3 minutes or just until vegetables begin to brown. Add curry powder and coriander; cook 30 seconds, stirring constantly. Add wine; cook 30 seconds. Stir in ⅛ teaspoon salt, 1 tablespoon oregano, and tomatoes; bring to a simmer. Cook 5 minutes or until liquid is slightly reduced. Return pork to pan; nestle in tomato sauce. Cook 4 minutes or until desired degree of doneness. Remove ½ cup sauce, and toss with pasta. Sprinkle with 1 tablespoon oregano and cheese. Serve with remaining sauce. Serves 4 (serving size: 1 pork chop, about ½ cup pasta, and about ½ cup sauce)

CALORIES 393; FAT 11.2g (sat 3.4g, mono 4.5g, poly 1.2g); PROTEIN 32g; CARB 41g; FIBER 8g; CHOL 76mg; IRON 5mg; SODIUM 666mg; CALC 236mg

Kid Friendly

Creamy Pork Chops and Mushrooms

Hands-on: 30 min. Total: 50 min.

1 cup unseasoned long-grain and wild rice blend
1 tablespoon unsalted butter
4 (6-ounce) bone-in center-cut loin pork chops
½ teaspoon kosher salt, divided
½ teaspoon freshly ground black pepper, divided
1 tablespoon finely chopped fresh rosemary
12 ounces fresh cremini mushrooms, cut into ½-inch-thick slices
1 medium onion, halved and thinly sliced
2 tablespoons all-purpose flour
¼ cup dry white wine
1½ cups unsalted chicken stock
¼ cup chopped roasted hazelnuts
¼ cup chopped fresh flat-leaf parsley
2 tablespoons reduced-fat sour cream

1. Cook rice according to package directions, omitting salt and fat.
2. While rice cooks, melt butter in a large skillet over medium-high heat. Sprinkle pork chops with ¼ teaspoon salt and ¼ teaspoon pepper. Add chops to pan; cook 3 minutes on each side or until browned. Transfer to a plate.
3. Add rosemary, mushrooms, and onion to pan; cook 8 minutes, stirring occasionally. Sprinkle mushrooms with flour; toss to coat. Stir in wine and chicken stock, scraping pan to loosen browned bits. Return pork chops and any accumulated juices to pan. Cover and simmer 10 minutes or until desired degree of doneness.
4. Stir hazelnuts, parsley, ¼ teaspoon salt, and ¼ teaspoon pepper into rice. Arrange pork chops on a serving platter. Simmer sauce, uncovered, 2 additional minutes. Remove from heat, and stir in sour cream. Serve pork chops with mushroom sauce and rice. Serves 4 (serving size: 1 pork chop, ½ cup mushroom sauce, and ¾ cup rice)

CALORIES 352; FAT 14.8g (sat 4.7g, mono 6.3g, poly 1.4g); PROTEIN 30g; CARB 23g; FIBER 2g; CHOL 82mg; IRON 3mg; SODIUM 538mg; CALC 90mg

THE NEW POTLUCK SOCIAL CLUB

Here's a plan for a soup-and-stew party that's fun, easy, and mighty good.

Now, while the weather calls for comfort food, invite friends over for a soup-and-stew potluck party. Add another layer of fun with a challenge to compete for the title of the best dish of the bunch. Encourage all, from the timid cook to the trendsetter, to join in. And feel free to dip into the recipes we've provided here, which cover all the style bases.

Kid Friendly

Chicken Stew and Dumplings

Hands-on: 60 min. Total: 1 hr. 45 min.

Stew:
- 3 center-cut bacon slices, cut into 1/2-inch pieces
- 6 skinless, boneless chicken thighs (about 1 1/4 pounds)
- 1.5 ounces cake flour (about 6 tablespoons), divided
- 1 cup chopped onion
- 1 1/2 tablespoons chopped fresh thyme
- 5 celery stalks, cut into 1/2-inch-thick pieces
- 4 garlic cloves, chopped
- 5 large carrots, cut into 1-inch-thick pieces
- 2 leeks, trimmed and cut into 1/2-inch-thick pieces
- 1/3 cup white wine
- 4 1/2 cups unsalted chicken stock
- 1/4 teaspoon kosher salt
- 1/2 teaspooon freshly ground black pepper

Dumplings:
- 8 ounces cake flour (about 2 cups)
- 1 teaspoon baking powder
- 1/8 teaspoon kosher salt
- 3 tablespoons unsalted butter
- 2 tablespoons chopped fresh chives
- 2/3 cup nonfat buttermilk
- 2 tablespoons chopped fresh parsley

1. To prepare stew, cook bacon in an 8-quart Dutch oven over medium-low heat until crisp. Remove bacon from pan with a slotted spoon; reserve 1 tablespoon bacon drippings.
2. Increase heat to medium-high. Sprinkle chicken on both sides with 3 tablespoons flour. Add 3 thighs to pan; cook 4 minutes on each side or until thighs are browned. Remove from pan. Repeat procedure with remaining thighs.
3. Reduce heat to medium. Add onion, thyme, celery, and garlic; cook 5 minutes or until onion is golden. Add carrots and leeks; cook 8 minutes, stirring frequently. Stir in 3 tablespoons flour; cook 5 minutes or until golden brown, stirring constantly. Stir in wine; cook 1 minute, scraping pan to loosen browned bits. Add stock, 1/4 teaspoon salt, and browned chicken to pan; bring to a boil. Cover, reduce heat, and simmer 30 minutes. Remove chicken from pan; shred into large pieces. Return shredded meat and cooked bacon to pan; stir in pepper.
4. To prepare dumplings, weigh or lightly spoon 8 ounces (about 2 cups) flour into dry measuring cups; level with a knife. Combine flour, baking powder, and salt in a medium bowl; cut in butter with a pastry blender or your fingers until mixture resembles coarse meal. Add chives and buttermilk; stir just until moist. Divide dough into 12 (1-tablespoon) portions, shaping each into a slightly flattened ball. Place dumplings on stew; cover and simmer 15 minutes or until dumplings are thoroughly cooked. Divide stew and dumplings among 6 shallow bowls; sprinkle with parsley. Serves 6 (serving size: 1 1/3 cups stew and 2 dumplings)

CALORIES 458; FAT 13.2g (sat 5.8g, mono 3.9g, poly 1.7g); PROTEIN 29g; CARB 52g; FIBER 4g; CHOL 110mg; IRON 6mg; SODIUM 520mg; CALC 172mg

Kid Friendly • Quick & Easy
Gluten Free • Make Ahead

Loaded Mashed Potato Soup

Hands-on: 10 min. Total: 30 min.

- Cooking spray
- 3/4 cup chopped onion
- 3 garlic cloves, minced
- 1 thyme sprig
- 1 (25-ounce) package unsalted chicken stock
- 1/4 teaspoon freshly ground black pepper
- 1 (24-ounce) package refrigerated mashed potatoes (such as Simply Potatoes)
- 1/4 cup plain 2% reduced-fat Greek yogurt
- 2 tablespoons chopped fresh dill
- 1/3 cup sliced green onion tops
- 1.5 ounces sharp cheddar cheese, shredded (about 1/3 cup)
- 3 bacon slices, cooked and crumbled

1. Heat a Dutch oven over medium heat. Coat pan with cooking spray. Add onion; cook 8 minutes or until tender, stirring frequently. Add garlic and thyme; cook 2 minutes, stirring frequently. Add stock; simmer 20 minutes. Remove and discard thyme sprig. Place half of stock mixture in a blender. Remove center piece of blender lid (to allow steam to escape); secure blender lid on blender. Place a clean towel over opening in blender lid (to avoid splatters). Blend until smooth. Pour into a large bowl. Repeat procedure with remaining stock mixture.

2. Return stock mixture to pan; add pepper and potatoes, stirring with a whisk until combined. Bring to a simmer; cook 5 minutes. Remove from heat; stir in yogurt and dill. Ladle into serving bowls; top with green onions, cheese, and crumbled bacon. Serves 6 (serving size: 1 cup soup, about 1 tablespoon cheese, 1½ teaspoons bacon, and about 2½ teaspoons green onions)

CALORIES 200; FAT 9.7g (sat 5.8g, mono 1.4g, poly 0.3g); PROTEIN 10g; CARB 19g; FIBER 2g; CHOL 31mg; IRON 1mg; SODIUM 588mg; CALC 117mg

THIS IS THE PERFECT RECIPE FOR A NOVICE, YIELDING DELICIOUS RESULTS WITH BASIC SKILLS.

Gluten Free • Make Ahead

Beefy Pressure Cooker Borscht with Dill Cream

Hands-on: 60 min. Total: 1 hr. 40 min.
The pressure cooker turns homemade stock from an hours-long affair into a 45-minute one, and cooks beets and celery root in just 7 minutes.

Dill cream:
½ cup heavy whipping cream
6 dill sprigs
Stock:
2¼ pounds cross-cut beef shanks
¼ teaspoon kosher salt
Cooking spray
7 cups water
3 parsley sprigs
3 thyme sprigs
2 bay leaves
1 medium onion, peeled and quartered
1 carrot, coarsely chopped
Soup:
1 tablespoon canola oil
2 cups chopped onion
4 garlic cloves, crushed
2 tablespoons tomato paste
4 cups thinly sliced red cabbage
3 cups coarsely chopped peeled red beets (about 1½ pounds)
1½ cups chopped peeled celeriac (celery root)
1 cup chopped carrot
12 ounces Yukon gold potato, coarsely chopped
3 tablespoons red wine vinegar
2 teaspoons kosher salt
¾ teaspoon freshly ground black pepper
Chopped fresh dill (optional)

1. To prepare dill cream, place whipping cream in a medium microwave-safe bowl. Microwave at HIGH 1 minute or until heated. Add dill; cover and chill.

2. To prepare stock, heat a 6-quart pressure cooker over medium-high heat. Sprinkle beef with ¼ teaspoon salt. Coat pan with cooking spray. Add beef to pan; cook 4 minutes on each side or until well browned. Add 7 cups water and next 5 ingredients. Close lid securely; bring to high pressure over high heat. Adjust heat to medium or level needed to maintain high pressure; cook 45 minutes. Remove from heat; release pressure by placing cooker under cold running water. Remove lid. Strain stock through a colander over a large bowl. Place beef on a cutting board; discard remaining solids. Cool beef slightly. Shred meat; discard bones, fat, and gristle. Set meat aside.

3. To prepare soup, heat cooker over medium-high heat. Add oil to pan; swirl to coat. Add chopped onion and garlic; sauté 3 minutes. Add tomato paste; sauté 1 minute. Add stock, cabbage, and next 4 ingredients (through potato). Close lid securely; bring to high pressure over high heat. Adjust heat to medium or level needed to maintain high pressure; cook 7 minutes. Remove from heat; release pressure by placing cooker under cold running water. Remove lid. Stir in beef, vinegar, 2 teaspoons salt, and pepper.

4. Remove cream from refrigerator; discard dill. Beat cream with a mixer at high speed until soft peaks form. Spoon over soup; garnish with dill, if desired. Serves 12 (serving size: about 1⅓ cups soup and 2 teaspoons cream)

CALORIES 224; FAT 10.7g (sat 4.6g, mono 4.3g, poly 0.8g); PROTEIN 14g; CARB 18g; FIBER 4g; CHOL 38mg; IRON 2mg; SODIUM 503mg; CALC 62mg

Braised Oxtail and Short Rib Stew

Kid Friendly • Freezable
Gluten Free • Make Ahead

Hands-on: 25 min. Total: 2 hr. 30 min.

1 tablespoon canola oil
1 pound (3-inch) bone-in short ribs, trimmed
½ pound oxtail
2 cups chopped onion
½ cup sliced shallots
6 garlic cloves, crushed
2 tablespoons tomato paste
1 cup dry red wine
3 cups unsalted beef stock
1¼ teaspoons black pepper
¾ teaspoon kosher salt
4 thyme sprigs
2 bay leaves
1 pound small Dutch yellow potatoes, halved
¾ pound carrots, cut diagonally into 2-inch-thick pieces
2 tablespoons chopped fresh flat-leaf parsley
2 teaspoons thyme leaves

1. Preheat oven to 300°.
2. Heat a large Dutch oven over medium-high heat. Add oil; swirl. Add short ribs and oxtail to pan; cook 10 minutes, browning on all sides. Remove from pan; place on a plate.
3. Add onion, shallots, and garlic to pan; cook 3 minutes. Add tomato paste; cook 1 minute. Stir in wine; cook 2 minutes, scraping pan to loosen browned bits. Add meat, stock, and next 6 ingredients; bring to a boil. Cover and bake at 300° for 2 hours or until beef is tender. Remove and discard bay leaves and thyme sprigs. Remove meat from bones; shred. Discard bones. Return shredded meat to pan; top with parsley and thyme leaves. Serves 8 (serving size: about 1 cup)

CALORIES 328; FAT 15.3g (sat 5.5g, mono 7.5g, poly 1g); PROTEIN 19g; CARB 23g; FIBER 4g; CHOL 51mg; IRON 3mg; SODIUM 344mg; CALC 51mg

Curried Cauliflower Soup

Gluten Free • Make Ahead
Vegetarian

Hands-on: 25 min. Total: 1 hr. 25 min.

1¾ pounds cauliflower (1 large head), cut into ½-inch-thick slices
Cooking spray
¼ cup slivered almonds
1½ teaspoons unsalted butter
¾ cup chopped yellow onion
3 garlic cloves, crushed
1 Granny Smith apple, peeled and chopped (about 1½ cups)
1½ teaspoons curry powder
4 cups water
½ teaspoon kosher salt
¼ teaspoon black pepper
1 bay leaf
⅔ cup half-and-half
¼ cup plain 2% reduced-fat Greek yogurt
2 teaspoons chopped fresh chives
Cracked black pepper

1. Preheat oven to 375°.
2. Place cauliflower on a baking sheet coated with cooking spray. Lightly coat cauliflower with cooking spray. Bake at 375° for 30 minutes or until cauliflower begins to brown on the bottom. Turn cauliflower over; bake 5 minutes. Add almonds to pan; bake an additional 5 minutes or until almonds are browned.
3. Melt butter in a large saucepan over medium heat. Add onion and garlic; cook 4 minutes, stirring occasionally. Add apple; cook 3 minutes. Add curry powder; cook 2 minutes, stirring frequently. Stir in cauliflower, almonds, 4 cups water, salt, pepper, and bay leaf; bring to a simmer. Cover and cook 30 minutes or until cauliflower and apple are very tender. Discard bay leaf. Place half of soup in a blender. Remove center piece of blender lid (to allow steam to escape); secure blender lid on blender. Place a clean towel over opening in blender lid (to avoid splatters). Blend until smooth. Pour into a large bowl. Repeat procedure with remaining soup. Return soup to pan; stir in half-and-half. Top soup with yogurt and chives; sprinkle with cracked black pepper. Serves 10 (serving size: ⅔ cup and about 1 teaspoon yogurt)

CALORIES 82; FAT 4.3g (sat 1.8g, mono 1.6g, poly 0.5g); PROTEIN 4g; CARB 9g; FIBER 3g; CHOL 8mg; IRON 1mg; SODIUM 131mg; CALC 57mg

West African Beef, Plantain, and Okra Stew

Gluten Free • Make Ahead

Hands-on: 30 min. Total: 1 hr. 25 min.

2 tablespoons olive oil, divided
1½ pounds beef stew meat, cut into 1½-inch cubes
1½ teaspoons kosher salt, divided
¾ teaspoon black pepper
1½ cups chopped onion
8 garlic cloves, sliced
1 tablespoon mustard seeds, divided
1½ teaspoons coriander seeds
1½ teaspoons ground cumin
4 cups (1-inch) cubed peeled sweet potato (about 1¼ pounds)
4 cups unsalted beef stock
1 (28-ounce) can plum tomatoes, drained
3 cups (½-inch-thick) slices okra
1 large green plantain, peeled and cubed
¼ cup chopped fresh cilantro

1. Heat a large Dutch oven over high heat. Add 1 tablespoon oil; swirl. Sprinkle beef with ½ teaspoon salt and pepper. Add half of beef to pan; cook 4 minutes, browning on all sides. Remove from pan. Repeat procedure with 1 tablespoon oil and beef.

2. Reduce heat to medium. Add onion and garlic; cook 3 minutes or until soft, scraping pan to loosen browned bits. Add 2 teaspoons mustard seeds, coriander, and cumin; cook 1 minute. Stir in 1 teaspoon salt, beef, sweet potato, stock, and tomatoes; stir to break up tomatoes. Cover; bring to a boil. Reduce heat to medium-low; simmer 25 minutes. Stir in okra and plantain; simmer an additional 25 minutes. Stir in 1 teaspoon mustard seeds and fresh cilantro. Serves 8 (serving size: 1½ cups)

CALORIES 287; FAT 7.6g (sat 1.9g, mono 4g, poly 0.6g); PROTEIN 23g; CARB 31g; FIBER 5g; CHOL 55mg; IRON 3mg; SODIUM 628mg; CALC 88mg

---

Kid Friendly • Quick & Easy Vegetarian

Quick Walnut-Sage Bread Knots

Hands-on: 15 min. Total: 35 min. *With just a few pantry items and ready-to-bake bread dough, you can whip up company-ready rolls in about half an hour.*

Preheat oven to 350°. Remove 1 (11-ounce) can refrigerated French bread dough (such as Pillsbury Crusty French Loaf) from package; lightly sprinkle with flour. Cut dough in half crosswise; cut each half lengthwise into 4 strips to form 8 (8-inch) strips total. Roll strips to 12-inch lengths; gently tie each strip in a knot. Arrange knots on a parchment-lined baking sheet. Brush knots evenly with 2 teaspoons walnut oil. Sprinkle with ¼ teaspoon kosher salt and 4 teaspoons minced fresh sage. Bake at 350° for 16 minutes or until knots are golden. Serves 8 (serving size: 1 knot)

CALORIES 102; FAT 2.3g (sat 0.5g); SODIUM 285mg

Kid Friendly • Quick & Easy Vegetarian
Asiago–Black Pepper variation
Omit walnut oil, salt, and sage. Brush knots with 2 teaspoons olive oil. Sprinkle knots with 1 ounce grated Asiago cheese and ½ teaspoon cracked black pepper before baking. Serves 8 (serving size: 1 knot)

CALORIES 115; FAT 3.4g (sat 1.2g); SODIUM 259mg

Kid Friendly • Quick & Easy Vegetarian
Three-Seed variation
Omit walnut oil and sage. Combine 1 teaspoon sesame seeds, 1 teaspoon flaxseed, ½ teaspoon instant minced onion, and ½ teaspoon poppy seeds in a small bowl. Brush knots with 1 tablespoon beaten egg; sprinkle with ¼ teaspoon kosher salt. Sprinkle with seed mixture before baking. Serves 8 (serving size: 1 knot)

CALORIES 97; FAT 1.6g (sat 0.5g); SODIUM 288mg

Kid Friendly • Quick & Easy Vegetarian
Honey-Pecan variation
Omit walnut oil, salt, and sage. Combine 2 tablespoons honey and 1 tablespoon melted butter. Brush honey mixture over dough; sprinkle with ¼ cup finely chopped pecans before baking. Serves 8 (serving size: 1 knot)

CALORIES 142; FAT 5g (sat 1.5g); SODIUM 238mg

FRESH RIGHT NOW

RADICCHIO

Enjoy this cool-weather leafy vegetable for its spicy, bold flavor.

Red- and white-veined radicchio is loved and sometimes feared for its bitter edge. The intensity of that bitterness can be mediated by the cook. Tossed into a salad, radicchio is bright and assertive. Sautéed, grilled, or baked, its sharp character mellows.

In our recipe, roasted radicchio wedges pair with tangy vinegar, salty Gorgonzola cheese, and sweet pears—a lesson in balancing the bitter.

Vegetarian • Gluten Free

Roasted Balsamic Radicchio and Pears

Hands-on: 20 min. Total: 65 min.

3 tablespoons balsamic vinegar
2 tablespoons extra-virgin olive oil
2 teaspoons chopped fresh thyme
2 teaspoons Dijon mustard
¼ teaspoon crushed red pepper
2 small heads radicchio, cored and cut into quarters
Cooking spray
2 Bosc pears, cored and each cut into 6 wedges
⅛ teaspoon kosher salt
1 ounce Gorgonzola cheese, crumbled

1. Preheat oven to 400°.
2. Combine first 5 ingredients in a large bowl; stir with a whisk until well blended. Add radicchio; toss gently to coat and allow mixture to seep between leaves. Place radicchio wedges, cut sides down, on a baking sheet coated with cooking spray; drizzle with any remaining vinegar mixture. Place pear wedges, cut sides down, on another baking sheet coated with cooking spray. Roast pears and radicchio at 400° for 12 minutes. Turn radicchio and pears over; roast an additional 12 minutes or until pears are golden and radicchio is browned. Place 2 radicchio wedges and 3 pear wedges on each of 4 plates, and sprinkle evenly with salt. Top radicchio evenly with cheese; serve immediately. Serves 4

CALORIES 148; FAT 9.1g (sat 2.4g, mono 5g, poly 1g); PROTEIN 2g; CARB 16g; FIBER 3g; CHOL 6mg; IRON 0mg; SODIUM 222mg; CALC 51mg

LIGHTER LAVA CAKES

Molten texture and chocolate intensity—but with whole grains and less butter.

Quite possibly the sexiest item on the dessert menu, the now-classic chocolate lava cake is all about decadence. A dense batter of chocolate, butter, sugar, and eggs is slightly underbaked to create a gooey, liquid center. These indulgent flavor bombs come in single servings, but even one little cake may contain more than 600 calories and a day's worth of saturated fat. Our plan: Keep the portion-savvy, chocolate-filled simplicity of the original, but cut the calories in half.

This proved not to be an easy task: Where does one begin when the recipe ingredients are simply fat and sugar? We decided to lighten the cake with whole-wheat pastry flour, which adds a bit of structure to preserve texture when we removed fat. Cocoa powder, which has been pressed to remove some of the cocoa butter, lends an intensely deep chocolate flavor with fewer calories. Canola oil subs in for some of the butter, tenderizing the cake with less saturated fat (leaving more room for chocolate). A dash of salt balances the sweet.

Then comes the trick: After the batter goes into the ramekins, we spoon a bit of reserved melted-chocolate mixture onto the top. As the cakes bake, this liquid sinks into the middle, providing a molten flow when you fork into the finished cakes. Still sexy and indulgent, with 60% fewer calories.

OURS SAVES
382 calories, 27.7g total fat, and 17.9g sat fat over traditional molten lava cake.

Kid Friendly

Chocolate Molten Lava Cakes

Hands-on: 20 min. Total: 2 hr. *If you prefer a more soufflé-like cake, add all the chocolate into the egg mixture during step 3. Use a high-quality chocolate. It will make all the difference.*

3 tablespoons unsalted butter
2 tablespoons canola oil
3 ounces high-quality dark or bittersweet chocolate (60% to 70% cacao), chopped
3 ounces whole-wheat pastry flour (about ⅔ cup)
½ cup unsweetened cocoa
1½ teaspoons baking powder
¼ teaspoon kosher salt
½ cup granulated sugar
½ cup packed brown sugar
½ teaspoon vanilla extract
3 large eggs
Baking spray with flour
Powdered sugar (optional)

1. Combine butter, oil, and chocolate in the top of a double boiler. Cook over simmering water until chocolate almost fully melts, stirring gently with a spatula. Remove top of double boiler; stir until chocolate fully melts.
2. Weigh or lightly spoon flour into a dry measuring cup; level with a knife. Combine flour, cocoa, baking powder, and salt in a bowl; stir well with a whisk.

3. Place granulated sugar, brown sugar, vanilla, and eggs in a large bowl; beat with a mixer at medium speed until light and fluffy (about 2 minutes). Set aside 2½ tablespoons chocolate mixture. Gradually pour remaining chocolate mixture in a thin stream over egg mixture, beating at medium speed. Gently fold flour mixture into egg mixture. Divide batter evenly among 10 (5-ounce) ramekins coated with baking spray. Working with 1 ramekin at a time, spoon ¾ teaspoon reserved chocolate mixture into center, pushing teaspoon toward center of batter. Repeat with remaining ramekins and chocolate mixture. Arrange ramekins on a jelly-roll pan. Cover and refrigerate 1 hour.
4. Preheat oven to 400°.
5. Let ramekins stand at room temperature 15 minutes. Uncover and bake at 400° for 13 minutes or until cakes are puffy and slightly crusty on top (centers will not be set). Place a dessert plate on top of ramekin. Using a dry kitchen towel to steady ramekin, invert each cake onto plate. Garnish with powdered sugar, if desired. Serve immediately. Serves 10 (serving size: 1 cake)

CALORIES 249; **FAT** 11.8g (sat 5.1g, mono 4.4g, poly 1.3g); **PROTEIN** 4g; **CARB** 35g; **FIBER** 3g; **CHOL** 65mg; **IRON** 2mg; **SODIUM** 135mg; **CALC** 71mg

KOHLRABI AND BOK CHOY

Cool-season crops with a funky look, these versatile veggies are prized for their healthy crunch.

As the weather turns a little cooler, we turn our attention to kohlrabi and bok choy. Both crops are coveted for their colorful, shapely stalks and richly verdant leaves that lend crunch and nutrients to slaws, salads, and sides.

Kid Friendly • Make Ahead
Vegetarian • Gluten Free

Kohlrabi Slaw

Hands-on: 14 min. Total: 1 hr. 14 min.
Crunchy kohlrabi is ideal for simple slaws because it stays crisp long after it's dressed.

⅓ cup canola mayonnaise
¼ cup red wine vinegar
1 tablespoon fennel seeds
2 teaspoons brown mustard
½ teaspoon sugar
½ teaspoon freshly ground black pepper
¼ teaspoon kosher salt
1½ pounds red kohlrabi, peeled
⅓ cup minced fresh parsley
4 green onions, thinly sliced

1. Combine first 7 ingredients in a medium bowl, stirring with a whisk.
2. Cut kohlrabi into ⅛-inch-thick slices. Cut each slice into thin slices to make about 5 cups julienne-cut kohlrabi. Add kohlrabi, parsley, and onions to mayonnaise mixture; toss to coat. Refrigerate at least 1 hour. Serves 6 (serving size: about ⅔ cup)

CALORIES 77; **FAT** 3.6g (sat 0g, mono 2.2g, poly 1.3g); **PROTEIN** 2g; **CARB** 9g; **FIBER** 5g; **CHOL** 0mg; **IRON** 1mg; **SODIUM** 219mg; **CALC** 52mg

Quick & Easy

Bok Choy Salad with Fried Shallots

Hands-on: 15 min. Total: 15 min.

5 tablespoons canola oil, divided
½ cup thinly sliced shallots, separated into rings
1 tablespoon cornstarch
1 tablespoon rice vinegar
1 tablespoon lower-sodium soy sauce
2 teaspoons fresh lime juice
1 teaspoon fish sauce
¼ teaspoon crushed red pepper
1 small shallot, minced
1 garlic clove, minced
1 pound baby bok choy, rinsed and cut into (1-inch) slices
¼ cup torn fresh mint leaves

1. Heat a medium skillet over medium-high heat. Add 1 tablespoon oil to pan; swirl to coat. Combine shallot rings and cornstarch in a bowl; toss to coat. Add shallots to pan; sauté 5 minutes or until crisp.
2. Combine vinegar and next 6 ingredients in a bowl; drizzle in ¼ cup oil, stirring with a whisk. Add bok choy and mint; toss to coat. Top with fried shallots. Serves 6 (serving size: 1 cup salad and 2 teaspoons shallots)

CALORIES 132; **FAT** 11.5g (sat 1.1g, mono 1.8g, poly 8g); **PROTEIN** 2g; **CARB** 7g; **FIBER** 1g; **CHOL** 0mg; **IRON** 1mg; **SODIUM** 219mg; **CALC** 91mg

Quick & Easy

Mirin-Braised Bok Choy with Shiitake Mushrooms

Hands-on: 20 min. Total: 32 min.

2 tablespoons peanut oil, divided
1 cup thinly sliced shiitake mushrooms
½ cup thinly sliced shallots
6 baby bok choy, halved lengthwise
½ cup unsalted chicken stock
¼ cup mirin (sweet rice wine)
1 tablespoon lower-sodium soy sauce
2 slices peeled fresh ginger

1. Heat a large skillet over medium-high heat. Add 2 teaspoons oil; swirl to coat. Add mushrooms and shallots to pan; cook 5 minutes or until mushrooms begin to brown, stirring occasionally. Remove mushroom mixture from pan.
2. Add 2 teaspoons oil to pan; swirl. Add half of bok choy, cut sides down, to pan; cook 3 minutes. Remove bok choy from pan. Repeat procedure with 2 teaspoons oil and remaining bok choy. Return mushroom mixture and bok choy to pan.
3. Stir in stock, mirin, soy sauce, and ginger; bring to a boil. Reduce heat to medium-low; partially cover, and cook 10 minutes or until bok choy is crisp-tender. Uncover and remove bok choy from pan. Bring liquid to a boil; cook 6 minutes or until reduced to about ¼ cup. Drizzle liquid over bok choy. Serves 4 (serving size: 3 bok choy halves and about 1 tablespoon sauce)

CALORIES 118; **FAT** 7g (sat 1.2g, mono 3.1g, poly 2.2g); **PROTEIN** 2g; **CARB** 9g; **FIBER** 1g; **CHOL** 0mg; **IRON** 1mg; **SODIUM** 199mg; **CALC** 66mg

Honey-Glazed Kohlrabi with Onions and Herbs

Hands-on: 22 min. Total: 1 hr. 25 min.
Kohlrabi offers the same dense texture and lightly peppery taste as turnips. But it's a touch sweeter, which we accent here with a luscious butter-honey glaze.

2 teaspoons olive oil
5 small green or red kohlrabi bulbs, cut lengthwise into wedges (about 1½ pounds)
1 teaspoon yellow mustard seeds
³⁄₈ teaspoon kosher salt
¼ teaspoon freshly ground black pepper
½ cup water
2½ tablespoons honey
1 tablespoon white wine vinegar
2 teaspoons butter
1 medium sweet onion, vertically sliced into wedges
2 tablespoons chopped fresh flat-leaf parsley

1. Preheat oven to 300°.
2. Heat a large ovenproof skillet over medium-high heat. Add oil; swirl to coat. Add kohlrabi to pan; cook 2 minutes or until browned, stirring occasionally. Stir in mustard seeds, salt, and pepper; cook 1 minute. Add ½ cup water, honey, vinegar, butter, and onion; bring mixture to a boil.
3. Cover and bake at 300° for 1 hour or until kohlrabi is tender. Uncover and remove kohlrabi from pan; place on a serving platter. Return pan to medium-high heat. Bring to a boil; cook 6 minutes or until syrupy. Drizzle kohlrabi with syrup; sprinkle evenly with chopped parsley. Serves 4 (serving size: about 1 cup)

CALORIES 155; **FAT** 4.7g (sat 1.6g, mono 2.2g, poly 0.4g); **PROTEIN** 4g; **CARB** 28g; **FIBER** 7g; **CHOL** 5mg; **IRON** 1mg; **SODIUM** 224mg; **CALC** 70mg

KID IN THE KITCHEN

STUFFED!

Dress up humble bakers with a cheesy, veggie-rich filling.

"Today I made amazing cheesy stuffed potatoes. This recipe was loaded with lots of my favorites: cheddar, broccoli, and ham. The cheesy sauce starts with a mixture of milk and flour that you stir into the pan. It is important to stir well so the sauce doesn't get lumpy. (Once you've mastered this technique, you can make all kinds of thick sauces and gravies.) I love the broccoli florets in this dish. Remember not to throw away the stems, though; they're the best part! Instead, carefully cut off the outer skin; then slice and steam them until tender. You can microwave the potatoes at HIGH for two or three minutes before baking in the oven. Microwaving speeds up the cook time, and baking makes the potato skins crispy. Next time I'll try this recipe with sweet potatoes. I bet that would be really good!"

Kid Friendly

Broccoli and Cheddar Stuffed Potatoes

Hands-on: 20 min. Total: 1 hr. 15 min.
To save time, you can also microwave the potatoes until tender: Pierce the potatoes liberally with a fork, and microwave at HIGH for 13 minutes or until tender, turning after 7 minutes.

4 (6-ounce) baking potatoes
1 tablespoon canola oil
3 ounces thick-cut ham slices, cut into ½-inch pieces
2 tablespoons minced fresh onion
1 cup 1% low-fat milk, divided
2 tablespoons all-purpose flour
½ teaspoon Dijon mustard
¼ teaspoon kosher salt
¼ teaspoon freshly ground black pepper
2 ounces mild cheddar cheese, shredded (about ½ cup)
2 cups water
2 cups broccoli florets

1. Preheat oven to 450°.
2. Place potatoes on a foil-lined baking sheet. Bake at 450° for 50 minutes or until tender. Let stand 10 minutes.
3. Heat a saucepan over medium heat. Add oil; swirl to coat. Add ham; sauté 3 minutes or until lightly browned. Add onion to pan; sauté 2 minutes. Combine ¼ cup milk and flour in a small bowl, stirring with a whisk. Add flour mixture and ¾ cup milk to pan, stirring constantly with a whisk. Cook 4 minutes or until slightly thickened. Remove pan from heat. Stir in mustard, salt, pepper, and cheese.
4. Bring 2 cups water to a boil in a medium saucepan. Add broccoli; cook 4 minutes or until crisp-tender. Drain.
5. Cut a lengthwise slit in each potato. Gently squeeze potatoes at both ends to open. Divide broccoli among potatoes; top evenly with sauce. Serves 4 (serving size: 1 potato, ½ cup broccoli, and about ⅓ cup sauce)

CALORIES 349; **FAT** 11.9g (sat 4.7g, mono 5g, poly 1.6g); **PROTEIN** 16g; **CARB** 45g; **FIBER** 5g; **CHOL** 29mg; **IRON** 3mg; **SODIUM** 578mg; **CALC** 230mg

THE VERDICT

KELLY (AGE 14)
She thought the dish was really filling and didn't need anything. **10/10**

MADDIE (AGE 13)
She said, "The cheesy sauce gave the bland potato lots of flavor." **9/10**

MATISSE (AGE 13)
The flavors worked really well together. I added some garlic to the onions and a dash of paprika on top. Yum! **10/10**

THIS MONTH'S LESSON: SLOW-BAKED CHICKEN THIGHS

It's safe to say that a chicken thigh is done when its internal temperature reaches 165°, but for rich dark meat that's tender and buttery, you have to push higher. Thighs are well-worked muscles, with more collagen and connective tissue. That means getting the meat to 180° or higher for at least an hour. Use the method here, in which the meat cooks for nearly two hours; you'll be rewarded with moist chicken that almost melts in your mouth.

KEITH'S RECIPE BREAKDOWN

SLOW-BAKED CHICKEN THIGHS WITH TOMATO, FENNEL, AND LEMON
Hands-on: 20 min. Total: 2 hr. 5 min.

INGREDIENT	AMOUNT	WHY
butter	2 tablespoons, divided	To tilt this in a rounder, richer direction.
fennel bulb	2 cups, shaved (about 2 bulbs)	The fennel will nearly melt into the dish. That's elegant.
kosher salt	½ teaspoon	To season.
skinless, boneless chicken thighs	2 pounds	They're easy, rich-tasting, and affordable.
canned whole plum tomatoes	1 (28-ounce) can, drained	They provide most of the moisture in the dish making for what's essentially an oven simmer.
garlic	12 cloves, cut into ¼-inch-thick slices	Sliced thick so they hold up, and you can experience the gloriousness of a sweet chunk of garlic on your fork.
lemons	3, sectioned	We're not looking for structure from the lemon. Indeed, we section here so the lemon flesh collapses fully into the sauce. That's why it's being removed from any white membrane.
fresh thyme leaves	1 tablespoon	It seems like a lot, but with the long cook time, the flavor softens and becomes more foundational, less punchy.
whole-wheat bread	1 tablespoon	For some color and more depth of flavor than white.
Parmesan cheese	2 tablespoons, grated	Tomatoes. Parmesan. Delicious!
fresh flat-leaf parsley	3 tablespoons, chopped	To finish fresh.

Follow These Steps:

- Preheat oven to 325°.
- Melt 1 tablespoon butter. Pour into a 13 x 9–inch glass or ceramic baking dish; tilt to coat bottom of dish. Top with fennel.
- Rub salt into chicken; arrange chicken over fennel. Hand-crush tomatoes; tuck between thighs. Scatter garlic and lemon over chicken; sprinkle with thyme.
- Cut 1 tablespoon butter into pieces; scatter over dish. Cover; bake at 325° for 1 hour or until a thermometer registers 180°.
- Uncover; bake 45 minutes, basting every 5 to 10 minutes.
- Place bread and cheese in a food processor; pulse for coarse crumbs. Sprinkle over chicken; drizzle with basting juices. Bake 10 minutes. Top with parsley.

CALORIES 267; FAT 10.7g (sat 4.2g, mono 3.3g, poly 1.6g); PROTEIN 32g; CARB 11g; FIBER 2g; CHOL 154mg; IRON 3mg; SODIUM 503mg; CALC 84mg

Kid Friendly • Gluten Free
Tomatillo and Chayote Chicken
Sub onion for fennel, 3 cups diced chayote for tomatoes, and 3 chopped tomatillos for lemons. Use 1½ teaspoons oregano in place of thyme, increase salt to ¾ teaspoon, and add 2 sliced serrano chiles with veggies. Rather than bread and Parm, use 3 tablespoons Cotija cheese. Top with cilantro instead of parsley; serve with lime wedges. Serves 6 (serving size: 4 ounces meat and about ⅔ cup vegetables)

CALORIES 270; FAT 11.4g (sat 4.7g); SODIUM 467mg

NUT BUTTER SANDWICHES, SIX NEW WAYS

Spread flavor and good health with a nutty twist: all under 350 calories.

Peanut butter now has plenty of company in the supermarket—nearly every nut has a spreadable counterpart that's both tasty and full of healthy plant-based fats and protein. You can make your own, too: Whir toasted nuts, a pinch of salt, and drizzle of oil in a food processor until smooth. Extra layers of complexity—macadamia is buttery, pecan is pleasantly bitter—make sandwich pairings way more fun. Start with 2 (1-ounce) slices of whole-grain bread; pile on the goods.

Quick & Easy • Vegetarian
Mango-Avocado Hazelnut
1 tablespoon hazelnut butter + ¼ cup sliced avocado + 2 tablespoons alfalfa sprouts + ¼ cup baby spinach leaves + 2 red onion rings + 2 teaspoons mango chutney

CALORIES 323; **FAT** 15.3g (sat 1.7g); **SODIUM** 365mg

Quick & Easy
Thai Chicken Peanut Crunch
1 tablespoon unsweetened creamy peanut butter + 2 ounces rotisserie chicken breast + ¼ cup thinly sliced cucumber + 3 tablespoons shredded carrot + 2 tablespoons chopped red onion + ½ teaspoon Sriracha

CALORIES 343; **FAT** 12.1g (sat 2.6g); **SODIUM** 602mg

Quick & Easy
Cran-Turkey, Greens, and Walnut
2 teaspoons walnut butter + 2 ounces oven-roasted turkey breast + 1 tablespoon crumbled blue cheese + ¼ cup arugula + 1 tablespoon cranberry sauce + Dash of black pepper

CALORIES 342; **FAT** 11.4g (sat 2.8g); **SODIUM** 419mg

Kid Friendly • Quick & Easy
Pecan, Prosciutto, and Brie
1 tablespoon roasted pecan butter + 4 large spinach leaves + 2 teaspoons pepper jelly + ½ ounce Brie cheese + ½ ounce thinly sliced prosciutto

CALORIES 342; **FAT** 17.5g (sat 4.4g); **SODIUM** 770mg

Kid Friendly • Quick & Easy
Cherry Cashew Pork
2 teaspoons cashew butter + 2 ounces thinly sliced grilled pork tenderloin + 2 tablespoons caramelized onions + 1 tablespoon chopped dried cherries + ¼ cup arugula

CALORIES 349; **FAT** 10.9g (sat 2.6g); **SODIUM** 388mg

Kid Friendly • Quick & Easy
Apple Almond Cheddar
1 tablespoon unsweetened almond butter + ¼ cup thinly sliced apple + 1 (½-ounce) thin slice sharp cheddar + 1 ounce lower-sodium deli ham + 1 romaine lettuce leaf

CALORIES 328; **FAT** 16g (sat 4.1g); **SODIUM** 623mg

NUT BUTTER PRIMER

WALNUT BUTTER
Richest in omega-3 fatty acids with about 1.3g per tablespoon, which meets 100% of your daily recommendation.

PEANUT BUTTER
Contains the most protein of the nut butters, with 4g per tablespoon.

HAZELNUT BUTTER
Mild in flavor but highest in fiber, with 2g per tablespoon.

ALMOND BUTTER
Highest in monounsaturated fatty acids and vitamin E—a powerful antioxidant.

SUPERFAST 20 MINUTE COOKING

Kid Friendly • Quick & Easy

Seared Tilapia with Spinach and White Bean Orzo

Feel free to sub another sustainable fish, such as flounder or red snapper, for the tilapia in this versatile dish.

¾ cup uncooked orzo pasta
4 (6-ounce) tilapia fillets
½ teaspoon salt, divided
½ teaspoon freshly ground black pepper, divided
1½ tablespoons olive oil, divided
½ teaspoon crushed red pepper
3 garlic cloves, minced
1 (5-ounce) package fresh baby spinach
1 cup halved grape tomatoes
1 (15-ounce) can unsalted cannellini beans, rinsed and drained
4 lemon wedges (optional)

1. Cook orzo according to package directions, omitting salt and fat.
2. While pasta cooks, sprinkle fish with ¼ teaspoon salt and ¼ teaspoon black pepper. Heat a large nonstick skillet over medium-high heat. Add 1 tablespoon oil to pan; swirl to coat. Add fish to pan; cook 3 minutes on each side or until desired degree of doneness. Remove fish from pan; keep warm.
3. Add 1½ teaspoons oil to pan. Add crushed red pepper and garlic; sauté 30 seconds. Add spinach; sauté 1 minute or just until spinach wilts. Stir in tomatoes, beans, ¼ teaspoon salt, and ¼ teaspoon black pepper; cook 1 minute or just until thoroughly heated. Remove pan from

heat. Add pasta to pan; toss to coat. Divide pasta mixture among 4 plates, and top with fish fillets. Serve with lemon wedges, if desired. Serves 4 (serving size: 1¼ cups pasta mixture and 1 fillet)

CALORIES 399; **FAT** 9g (sat 1.7g, mono 4.6g, poly 1.2g); **PROTEIN** 42g; **CARB** 38g; **FIBER** 6g; **CHOL** 85mg; **IRON** 3mg; **SODIUM** 455mg; **CALC** 71mg

Shrimp Farfalle with Arugula Pesto

Arugula instills this pesto with a peppery bite that pairs beautifully with supple, slightly sweet shrimp.

1 cup uncooked mini farfalle
1½ cups arugula
¼ cup basil leaves, plus more for garnish
3 tablespoons grated Parmigiano-Reggiano cheese
2 tablespoons pine nuts
½ teaspoon freshly ground black pepper
¼ teaspoon kosher salt
1 garlic clove
2½ tablespoons extra-virgin olive oil, divided
1½ pounds medium shrimp, peeled and deveined
¼ cup white wine

1. In a large saucepan, cook farfalle according to package directions, omitting salt and fat. Drain in a colander over a bowl, reserving ⅓ cup pasta cooking liquid.
2. Place arugula, basil, cheese, pine nuts, pepper, salt, and garlic in the bowl of a food processor; pulse 6 times. With the processor running, add 2 tablespoons olive oil through food chute, and process until smooth.
3. Heat a large skillet over medium-high heat. Add ½ tablespoon oil to pan; swirl to coat. Add shrimp; cook

5 minutes or until golden, turning occasionally. Remove shrimp from pan with a slotted spoon. Add wine to pan, and cook until mostly evaporated. Add basil mixture and reserved pasta water; bring to a simmer. Remove pan from heat. Top farfalle with sauce and shrimp. Garnish with basil. Serves 4 (serving size: 1 cup)

CALORIES 404; **FAT** 15g (sat 2.2g, mono 7.4g, poly 2.6g); **PROTEIN** 31g; **CARB** 33g; **FIBER** 7g; **CHOL** 218mg; **IRON** 1mg; **SODIUM** 432mg; **CALC** 158mg

Apple and Bacon Pita Pizzas

Smoky bacon, rich walnuts, and woodsy thyme give depth to these quick personal pizzas.

4 (6-inch) whole-wheat pitas
2 teaspoons olive oil
2 ounces cheddar cheese, shredded (about ½ cup)
2 cups thinly sliced Fuji apple
3 tablespoons grated fresh Parmesan cheese
2 tablespoons chopped walnuts, toasted
1 teaspoon chopped fresh thyme
2 applewood-smoked bacon slices, chopped and cooked

1. Preheat broiler to high.
2. Broil pitas 1 minute or until lightly golden. Remove from oven; carefully flip pitas over. Brush evenly with olive oil. Sprinkle cheddar over pitas; arrange apple slices over cheese.
3. Sprinkle Parmesan cheese, walnuts, thyme, and bacon evenly over apples. Return to oven; broil 1 to 2 minutes. Serves 4 (serving size: 1 pizza)

CALORIES 341; **FAT** 14.4g (sat 5.3g, mono 3.8g, poly 2.8g); **PROTEIN** 14g; **CARB** 43g; **FIBER** 6g; **CHOL** 23mg; **IRON** 2mg; **SODIUM** 596mg; **CALC** 160mg

Chicken and Edamame Couscous Salad

Dried cranberries complement the sweet and tangy dressing on this salad, while roasted peanuts contribute a nice crunch.

¾ cup water
⅔ cup uncooked whole-wheat couscous
¾ cup frozen shelled edamame
3 tablespoons fresh orange juice
2 tablespoons extra-virgin olive oil
1 tablespoon cider vinegar
2 teaspoons honey
½ teaspoon salt
½ teaspoon freshly ground black pepper
2 cups coarsely chopped baby spinach
2 cups shredded skinless, boneless rotisserie chicken breast
⅓ cup thinly sliced green onions
¼ cup coarsely chopped dried cranberries
3 tablespoons chopped unsalted, dry-roasted peanuts

1. Bring ¾ cup water to a boil in a saucepan; stir in couscous. Remove from heat; cover and let stand 5 minutes. Fluff couscous with a fork. Transfer to a bowl.
2. Cook edamame according to package directions; drain. Rinse with cold water; drain.
3. While edamame cooks, combine orange juice and next 5 ingredients, stirring well with a whisk. Add edamame, spinach, and next 3 ingredients to couscous. Pour orange juice mixture over salad; toss to coat. Sprinkle with chopped peanuts. Serves 6 (serving size: 1 cup)

CALORIES 272; **FAT** 9.7g (sat 1.4g, mono 5.1g, poly 1.5g); **PROTEIN** 22g; **CARB** 27g; **FIBER** 5g; **CHOL** 44mg; **IRON** 2mg; **SODIUM** 374mg; **CALC** 45mg

Pecan and Blue Cheese Brussels Sprout Salad

2 tablespoons minced shallots
1½ tablespoons extra-virgin olive oil
2 teaspoons Dijon mustard
2 teaspoons balsamic vinegar
1 garlic clove, minced
¼ teaspoon freshly ground black pepper
⅛ teaspoon kosher salt
½ pound Brussels sprouts, very thinly sliced
¼ cup chopped toasted pecans
2 tablespoons crumbled blue cheese

1. Combine first 7 ingredients in a small bowl. Place Brussels sprouts and pecans in a large bowl; toss to combine. Add vinaigrette; toss to coat. Sprinkle with blue cheese. Serves 4 (serving size: 1 cup)

CALORIES 141; FAT 11.4g (sat 1.9g, mono 6.8g, poly 2.1g); PROTEIN 4g; CARB 8g; FIBER 3g; CHOL 3mg; IRON 1mg; SODIUM 194mg; CALC 55mg

Peanut and Chile

Combine 2 tablespoons minced shallots, 1½ tablespoons olive oil, 2 teaspoons fresh lime juice, 1 teaspoon lower-sodium soy sauce, ¼ teaspoon kosher salt, ¼ teaspoon sugar, and 1 minced garlic clove in a small bowl. Combine ½ pound thinly sliced Brussels sprouts, ¼ cup unsalted peanuts, and 1 sliced red chile in a large bowl. Add vinaigrette; toss to coat. Serves 4 (serving size: 1 cup)

CALORIES 134; FAT 9.8g (sat 1.4g); SODIUM 181mg

Kale and Almond

Combine 2 tablespoons minced shallots, 1½ tablespoons olive oil, 2 teaspoons fresh lemon juice, 2 teaspoons Dijon mustard, ¼ teaspoon black pepper, ⅛ teaspoon kosher salt, and 1 minced garlic clove in a small bowl. Combine ½ pound thinly sliced Brussels sprouts, 1 cup stemmed chopped kale, and ¼ cup sliced almonds. Add vinaigrette; toss to coat. Top with 2 tablespoons grated Parmesan cheese. Serves 4 (serving size: about 1 cup)

CALORIES 134; FAT 9.2g (sat 1.6g); SODIUM 196mg

Apple and Pistachio

Combine 2 tablespoons minced shallots, 1½ tablespoons extra-virgin olive oil, 1 tablespoon Dijon mustard, 2 teaspoons cider vinegar, ¼ teaspoon kosher salt, ¼ teaspoon black pepper, and 1 minced garlic clove in a small bowl. Combine ½ pound thinly sliced Brussels sprouts, ¼ cup shelled unsalted pistachios, and ½ cup thinly sliced apple. Add vinaigrette; toss to coat. Serves 4 (serving size: 1 cup)

CALORIES 129; FAT 8.7g (sat 1.2g,); SODIUM 226mg

Chicken Paillards with Romaine Caesar Slaw

3 tablespoons plain 2% reduced-fat Greek yogurt
2 tablespoons grated Parmesan cheese
4 teaspoons fresh lemon juice
1 tablespoon water
2 teaspoons extra-virgin olive oil
1¼ teaspoons Worcestershire sauce
1 teaspoon Dijon mustard
¾ teaspoon anchovy paste
1 small garlic clove, minced
½ teaspoon freshly ground black pepper, divided
4 cups thinly sliced romaine lettuce
4 (6-ounce) skinless, boneless chicken breast halves
¼ teaspoon kosher salt
Cooking spray
1 ounce Parmesan cheese, shaved (about ¼ cup)

1. Combine first 9 ingredients and ¼ teaspoon pepper in a large bowl. Add lettuce; toss to coat.
2. Place chicken between 2 sheets of plastic wrap; pound to ¼-inch thickness. Sprinkle chicken evenly with ¼ teaspoon pepper and salt.
3. Heat a grill pan over high heat. Coat pan with cooking spray. Add chicken; cook 3 minutes. Turn and cook 2 minutes. Remove from pan. Place 1 chicken breast on each of 4 plates; top each with 1 cup slaw. Sprinkle evenly with 1 ounce Parmesan. Serves 4

CALORIES 279; FAT 10.1g (sat 3.1g, mono 3.8g, poly 1.1g); PROTEIN 42g; CARB 4g; FIBER 1g; CHOL 121mg; IRON 1mg; SODIUM 578mg; CALC 142mg

Chicken Cutlets with Tarragon-Mustard Sauce

1 tablespoon extra-virgin olive oil
1 pound chicken breast cutlets (about 4 cutlets)
½ teaspoon salt
¼ teaspoon black pepper
3 tablespoons chopped shallots
1 teaspoon all-purpose flour
½ cup dry white wine
¼ cup light sour cream
1 tablespoon Dijon mustard
1 tablespoon finely chopped fresh tarragon

1. Heat a large skillet over medium heat. Add oil to pan; swirl to coat. Sprinkle chicken with salt and pepper; cook 3 minutes on each side. Place chicken on a platter.
2. Return pan to medium heat. Add shallots; sauté 1 minute. Sprinkle flour over shallots; cook 1 minute, stirring constantly. Add wine; bring to a boil. Cook 1 minute, scraping pan to loosen browned bits. Remove

from heat; stir in sour cream and mustard. Return chicken and juices to pan. Sprinkle with tarragon. Serves 4 (serving size: 1 cutlet and 3 tablespoons sauce)

CALORIES 205; **FAT** 8g (sat 2.1g, mono 3.8g, poly 0.9g); **PROTEIN** 25g; **CARB** 4g; **FIBER** 0g; **CHOL** 78mg; **IRON** 1mg; **SODIUM** 529mg; **CALC** 33mg

Kid Friendly • Quick & Easy
Make Ahead • Vegetarian

White Bean and Pumpkin Hummus with Pita Chips

3 (6-inch) whole-wheat pitas, each split in half horizontally to form 2 rounds
2 teaspoons olive oil
1/2 teaspoon kosher salt
1 cup canned pumpkin puree
2 tablespoons tahini (sesame seed paste)
2 1/2 tablespoons fresh lemon juice
1 tablespoon extra-virgin olive oil
1 teaspoon ground cumin
1/2 teaspoon smoked paprika
1/8 teaspoon salt
1 (15-ounce) can cannellini or other white beans, rinsed and drained
2 garlic cloves, chopped

1. Preheat oven to 400°.
2. Lightly brush rough sides of pitas with olive oil; sprinkle with kosher salt. Cut each pita half into 8 wedges; arrange wedges in a single layer on baking sheets. Bake at 400° for 5 minutes; rotate pans, and bake 5 additional minutes or until crisp and golden.
3. While chips bake, place pumpkin puree and remaining ingredients in a food processor; process until smooth (about 30 seconds). Serve pumpkin spread with pita chips. Serves 12 (serving size: 3 tablespoons hummus and 4 pita chips)

CALORIES 98; **FAT** 3.9g (sat 0.5g, mono 1.9g, poly 1g); **PROTEIN** 3g; **CARB** 14g; **FIBER** 3g; **CHOL** 0mg; **IRON** 1mg; **SODIUM** 197mg; **CALC** 19mg

DINNER TONIGHT

READY IN
40
MINUTES

SHOPPING LIST

Eggplant and Zucchini Parmesan
Eggplant (1 pound)
Zucchini (1 medium)
Extra-virgin olive oil
Whole-wheat panko (Japanese breadcrumbs)
Lower-sodium marinara sauce (such as Dell'Amore)
Eggs (2)
Vegetarian Parmesan cheese
Part-skim mozzarella cheese

Lemon-Parsley Pasta
Lemon (1)
Fresh parsley
Extra-virgin olive oil
Whole-wheat spaghetti

GAME PLAN

While oven preheats:
■ Bread eggplant and zucchini.
■ Bring water for pasta to a boil.
While eggplant and zucchini bake:
■ Prepare pasta.

Kid Friendly • Quick & Easy
Vegetarian

Eggplant and Zucchini Parmesan

with Lemon-Parsley Pasta

Cooking spray
1 (1-pound) eggplant
2 teaspoons water
2 large eggs, lightly beaten
1 1/2 cups whole-wheat panko
3 tablespoons grated vegetarian Parmesan cheese
1 medium zucchini, trimmed and cut diagonally into 12 slices
1/4 teaspoon kosher salt
3/4 cup lower-sodium marinara sauce
2 ounces part-skim mozzarella cheese, shredded (about 1/2 cup)
4 teaspoons extra-virgin olive oil

1. Preheat oven to 475°.
2. Place a wire rack on a baking sheet. Coat rack with cooking spray. Cut top and bottom off eggplant. Partially peel eggplant lengthwise with a vegetable peeler, leaving long purple stripes. Cut eggplant crosswise into 8 slices. Combine 2 teaspoons water and eggs in a shallow dish, stirring with a whisk. Combine panko and Parmesan in a shallow dish. Dip eggplant and zucchini in egg mixture. Dredge in panko mixture, gently pressing mixture to adhere. Arrange eggplant and zucchini on prepared rack; coat with cooking spray. Sprinkle evenly with salt. Bake at 475° for 10 minutes.
3. Turn eggplant and zucchini; top eggplant and zucchini slices evenly with marinara sauce and mozzarella. Bake at 475° for 10 minutes or until cheese is melted and lightly browned. Arrange on a serving platter; drizzle with oil. Serves 4 (serving size: 2 eggplant slices and 3 zucchini slices)

CALORIES 291; **FAT** 12.4g (sat 3.7g, mono 5.2g, poly 1.2g); **PROTEIN** 15g; **CARB** 32g; **FIBER** 8g; **CHOL** 104mg; **IRON** 3mg; **SODIUM** 384mg; **CALC** 185mg

continued

Kid Friendly • Quick & Easy
Make Ahead • Vegetarian
Lemon-Parsley Pasta

Cook 6 ounces whole-wheat spaghetti according to package directions, omitting salt and fat. Drain. Combine pasta with ¼ cup chopped fresh parsley, 1½ tablespoons extra-virgin olive oil, 1 teaspoon grated lemon rind, 1 tablespoon fresh lemon juice, ¼ teaspoon kosher salt, and ¼ teaspoon freshly ground black pepper; toss. Serves 4 (serving size: ⅔ cup)

CALORIES 196; **FAT** 5.7g (sat 0.8g); **SODIUM** 126mg

SHOPPING LIST

Coconut-Curry Salmon with Brown Basmati Rice

Lime (1)
Fresh cilantro
Red curry paste
15-ounce can light coconut milk
Brown sugar
Salmon fillets (1½ pounds)
8.8-ounce package precooked brown basmati rice (1, such as Uncle Ben's)

Sautéed Sesame Snow Peas

Snow peas (12 ounces)
Sesame seeds
Dark sesame oil
Rice vinegar

GAME PLAN

While fish simmers:
- Cook snow peas.
While sauce reduces:
- Prepare rice.

Kid Friendly • Quick & Easy
Gluten Free

Coconut-Curry Salmon with Brown Basmati Rice

with Sautéed Sesame Snow Peas

1 tablespoon brown sugar
2 teaspoons fresh lime juice
1½ teaspoons red curry paste
1 (15-ounce) can light coconut milk
4 (6-ounce) salmon fillets, skinned (about 1 inch thick)
¼ teaspoon kosher salt
1 tablespoon chopped fresh cilantro
1 (8.8-ounce) package precooked brown basmati rice (such as Uncle Ben's)

1. Place brown sugar, lime juice, red curry paste, and coconut milk in a large skillet, stirring to combine. Add fish to pan; bring to a simmer over medium-high heat. Cover, reduce heat to medium-low, and cook 9 minutes or until desired degree of doneness, turning once after 5 minutes. Place fish on a plate; sprinkle with salt and cilantro.
2. Prepare rice according to package directions.
3. Bring remaining sauce to a boil in skillet; boil 6 minutes or until reduced to ½ cup. Serve sauce with rice and fish. Serves 4 (serving size: 1 fillet, 2 tablespoons sauce, and about ⅓ cup rice)

CALORIES 356; **FAT** 12.1g (sat 3.1g, mono 3.2g, poly 3.3g); **PROTEIN** 39g; **CARB** 22g; **FIBER** 1g; **CHOL** 90mg; **IRON** 1mg; **SODIUM** 261mg; **CALC** 20mg

---

Kid Friendly • Quick & Easy
Vegetarian • Gluten Free
Sautéed Sesame Snow Peas

Heat a large skillet over medium-high heat. Add 2 teaspoons dark sesame oil to pan; swirl to coat. Add 12 ounces trimmed snow peas; sauté 3 minutes. Stir in 1 tablespoon rice vinegar and 1 teaspoon toasted sesame seeds. Serves 4 (serving size: about ¾ cup)

CALORIES 60; **FAT** 2.8g (sat 0.4g); **SODIUM** 3mg

SHOPPING LIST

Chicken and Bell Pepper Sauté

Tomatoes (2)
Orange bell pepper (1 medium)
Fresh oregano
Garlic
Olive oil
Unsalted chicken stock (such as Swanson)
Pitted green olives
Feta cheese
Skinless, boneless chicken breast halves (1 pound)

Lemony Kale Quinoa

Lemon (1)
Kale
Quinoa
Butter

GAME PLAN

While chicken breast halves cook:
- Prepare quinoa.
While quinoa cooks:
- Finish chicken mixture.

Kid Friendly • Quick & Easy

Chicken and Bell Pepper Sauté

with Lemony Kale Quinoa

1 tablespoon olive oil
1 pound skinless, boneless chicken breast halves, cut into 1-inch pieces
½ teaspoon freshly ground black pepper
¼ teaspoon kosher salt
1 cup sliced orange bell pepper
1 tablespoon chopped fresh oregano
2 garlic cloves, minced
1½ cups chopped tomato
¼ cup unsalted chicken stock (such as Swanson)
1½ ounces pitted green olives, sliced
1 ounce feta cheese, crumbled (about ¼ cup)

1. Heat a large skillet over medium-high heat. Add oil; swirl to coat. Sprinkle chicken with black pepper and salt. Add chicken to pan; cook 7 minutes or until done, stirring occasionally. Remove chicken from pan. Add bell pepper, oregano, and garlic to pan; sauté 2 minutes. Stir in chicken, tomato, and stock; cook 1 minute. Sprinkle with olives and feta. Serves 4 (serving size: ¾ cup)

CALORIES 219; FAT 9.7g (sat 2.2g, mono 4.9g, poly 1.3g); PROTEIN 26g; CARB 6g; FIBER 1g; CHOL 79mg; IRON 1mg; SODIUM 523mg; CALC 59mg

Kid Friendly • Quick & Easy
Make Ahead • Vegetarian
Gluten Free
Lemony Kale Quinoa
Heat a medium saucepan over medium heat. Add 1 cup rinsed and drained quinoa; cook 4 minutes or until toasted, stirring frequently. Add 1¼ cups water, 2 teaspoons butter, and ¼ teaspoon kosher salt to pan; bring to a boil. Cover and cook 13 minutes or until liquid is absorbed and quinoa is tender. Combine

quinoa mixture, 2 cups stemmed chopped kale, 1 teaspoon grated lemon rind, and 2 teaspoons fresh lemon juice in a medium bowl; toss to coat. Serves 4 (serving size: about ¾ cup)

CALORIES 191; FAT 4.7g (sat 1.6g); SODIUM 153mg

READY IN
35
MINUTES

SHOPPING LIST

Lamb and Butternut Squash Stew
Kale
Fresh flat-leaf parsley
Butternut squash (1 medium)
Onion (1 medium)
Garlic
Ground cinnamon
Ground coriander
Ground cumin
Ground paprika
All-purpose flour
Unsalted beef stock (such as Swanson)
Tomato paste
90% lean ground sirloin (8 ounces)
Ground lamb (8 ounces)

Roasted Cauliflower with Pine Nuts
Lemon (1)
Cauliflower (1 large head)
Olive oil
Pine nuts

GAME PLAN

While oven preheats:
■ Prepare cauliflower.
■ Prepare lamb mixture.
While cauliflower roasts:
■ Bake lamb mixture.

Quick & Easy • Make Ahead

Lamb and Butternut Squash Stew

with Roasted Cauliflower with Pine Nuts

8 ounces ground lamb
8 ounces 90% lean ground sirloin
½ teaspoon kosher salt, divided
1½ cups chopped peeled butternut squash
1 cup chopped onion
2 garlic cloves, minced
1 tablespoon tomato paste
2 teaspoons all-purpose flour
½ teaspoon ground coriander
½ teaspoon ground cumin
¼ teaspoon ground paprika
¼ teaspoon ground cinnamon
1 cup unsalted beef stock (such as Swanson)
3 cups chopped kale
2 tablespoons chopped fresh flat-leaf parsley

1. Preheat oven to 450°.
2. Heat a large Dutch oven over medium-high heat. Add lamb, beef, and ¼ teaspoon salt; cook 5 minutes or until browned, stirring to crumble. Remove lamb mixture from pan. Add squash, onion, and garlic to pan; cook 3 minutes, stirring occasionally. Add tomato paste and next 5 ingredients (through cinnamon); cook 1 minute, stirring frequently. Stir in ¼ teaspoon salt and stock; bring to a boil. Stir in kale; cook 1 minute or until kale begins to wilt. Stir in lamb mixture. Cover and bake at 450° for 15 minutes. Sprinkle with chopped parsley. Serves 6 (serving size: ⅔ cup)

CALORIES 244; FAT 12.3g (sat 4.9g, mono 5g, poly 0.8g); PROTEIN 22g; CARB 12g; FIBER 2g; CHOL 69mg; IRON 3mg; SODIUM 279mg; CALC 89mg

continued

Kid Friendly • Quick & Easy
Vegetarian • Gluten Free
Roasted Cauliflower with Pine Nuts
Preheat oven to 450°. Combine
8 cups cauliflower florets (1 large
head), 2 tablespoons olive oil, 1 teaspoon grated lemon rind, ¼ teaspoon
kosher salt, and ¼ teaspoon freshly
ground black pepper on a jelly-roll
pan; toss to coat. Bake at 450° for 25
minutes or until browned, stirring
once after 10 minutes. Sprinkle with
2 tablespoons toasted pine nuts.
Serves 6 (serving size: about ¾ cup)

CALORIES 94; FAT 6.8g (sat 0.9g); SODIUM 122mg

READY IN
25
MINUTES

SHOPPING LIST

Cheesy Skillet Gnocchi
Tomatoes (2)
Fresh basil
Garlic
Extra-virgin olive oil
Unsalted chicken stock (such as
    Swanson)
Whole-wheat gnocchi (16 ounces)
Part-skim mozzarella cheese
Mild Italian sausage (4 ounces)

Grape and Hazelnut Salad
Seedless red grapes
Mixed salad greens (5 ounces)
Extra-virgin olive oil
White balsamic vinegar
Dijon mustard
Hazelnuts

GAME PLAN

While gnocchi cooks:
■ Chop tomato and basil.
■ Slice garlic.
While sausage cooks:
■ Prepare salad.

Kid Friendly • Quick & Easy
Make Ahead

Cheesy Skillet Gnocchi

with Grape and Hazelnut Salad

2 teaspoons extra-virgin olive oil
**1 (16-ounce) package prepared
    whole-wheat gnocchi**
**4 ounces mild Italian sausage,
    casings removed**
1½ cups chopped tomato
2 garlic cloves, sliced
¼ cup unsalted chicken stock
**2 ounces part-skim mozzarella
    cheese, shredded (about ½ cup)**
¼ cup chopped fresh basil

1. Preheat broiler to high.
2. Heat a large ovenproof skillet over
medium heat. Add oil; swirl. Add
gnocchi; cook 7 minutes or until
lightly browned, stirring occasionally.
Place gnocchi in a large bowl. Add
sausage to pan; cook 6 minutes or until browned, stirring to crumble. Add
sausage to gnocchi. Add tomato and
garlic to pan; cook 2 minutes. Add
gnocchi mixture and stock to pan;
sprinkle with cheese. Place pan in
oven; broil 2 minutes or until cheese
lightly browned. Sprinkle with basil.
Serves 4 (serving size: about ¾ cup)

CALORIES 301; FAT 8.6g (sat 2.8g, mono 3.4g, poly 0.5g);
PROTEIN 14g; CARB 40g; FIBER 8g; CHOL 16mg;
IRON 4mg; SODIUM 691mg; CALC 128mg

Kid Friendly • Quick & Easy
Vegetarian • Gluten Free
Grape and Hazelnut Salad
Combine 1 tablespoon extra-virgin
olive oil, 1 tablespoon white balsamic
vinegar, and ½ teaspoon Dijon mustard
in a bowl, stirring with a whisk. Add 1
(5-ounce) package mixed salad greens,
⅓ cup halved seedless red grapes, and 2
tablespoons coarsely chopped toasted
hazelnuts; toss to coat. Serves 4 (serving size: about 1 cup)

CALORIES 71; FAT 5.6g (sat 0.6g); SODIUM 29mg

BUDGET COOKING

FEED 4 FOR LESS THAN $10

Barley in risotto, horseradish in potato
salad: Little surprises make meals more
exciting.

Kid Friendly

$2.37
PER
SERVING

Barley and Butternut Risotto

Hands-on: 65 min. Total: 65 min.

**2 pounds butternut squash, peeled,
    seeded, and cut into ½-inch cubes**
Cooking spray
4 cups unsalted chicken stock
1 cup water
2 teaspoons olive oil
1 cup chopped onion
¼ teaspoon salt
**¼ teaspoon freshly ground black
    pepper**
1¼ cups uncooked pearl barley
3 garlic cloves, minced
**1.5 ounces shaved Parmesan cheese
    (about ⅓ cup), divided**
1 teaspoon dried sage

1. Preheat oven to 425°.
2. Place squash on a jelly-roll pan
coated with cooking spray. Bake at
425° for 25 minutes.
3. Bring stock and 1 cup water to a
simmer in a saucepan. Keep warm.
4. Heat a large saucepan over medium-high heat. Add oil to pan; swirl.
Add onion, salt, and pepper; cook
4 minutes. Add barley and garlic;
cook 2 minutes. Stir in ½ cup stock
mixture; cook 4 minutes, stirring
frequently. Reduce heat to medium-
low. Reserve ¼ cup stock. Add
remaining stock, ½ cup at a time,
stirring frequently until each portion
is absorbed. Remove from heat. Stir
in reserved ¼ cup stock and 1 ounce

cheese. Fold in squash. Sprinkle with remaining cheese and sage. Serves 4 (serving size: about 1¼ cups)

CALORIES 421; FAT 6.2g (sat 2.3g, mono 2.6g, poly 0.8g); PROTEIN 17g; CARB 79g; FIBER 15g; CHOL 8mg; IRON 4mg; SODIUM 438mg; CALC 263mg.

Kid Friendly • Gluten Free

Grilled Pork Medallions with Spicy Potato Salad

$2.16 PER SERVING

Hands-on: 25 min. Total: 45 min.

1 pound small red potatoes (about 1½ inches wide)
¼ cup canola mayonnaise
¼ cup plain low-fat yogurt
¼ cup sliced green onions
2 tablespoons prepared horseradish
2 teaspoons cider vinegar
½ teaspoon salt, divided
½ teaspoon freshly ground black pepper, divided
½ cup thinly sliced radishes
2 hard-cooked large eggs, diced
1 (1-pound) pork tenderloin, trimmed and cut into 12 (1-inch-thick) medallions
2 garlic cloves, minced
Cooking spray

1. Place potatoes in a large saucepan; cover with cold water. Bring to a boil. Reduce heat, and simmer 20 minutes or until tender; drain and cool.
2. Combine mayonnaise, yogurt, green onions, horseradish, vinegar, ¼ teaspoon salt, and ¼ teaspoon pepper in a medium bowl. Stir in potatoes. Gently fold in radishes and eggs.
3. Heat a grill pan over medium-high heat. Sprinkle pork medallions with ¼ teaspoon salt and ¼ teaspoon pepper. Spread garlic evenly over pork. Lightly coat pan with cooking spray. Add pork; grill 4 minutes on each side or until desired degree of doneness. Let stand 5 minutes before

serving. Serve with potato salad. Serves 4 (serving size: 3 ounces pork and 1 cup potato salad)

CALORIES 298; FAT 9.2g (sat 1.8g, mono 4.2g, poly 2.4g); PROTEIN 31g; CARB 22g; FIBER 3g; CHOL 168mg; IRON 3mg; SODIUM 550mg; CALC 60mg

BAKE A SECOND BATCH

BLACK AND BOO COOKIES

No tricks, only treats. Double up to share these Halloween sweets.

Everyday ingredients are all it takes to mix up a couple of batches of our spooktacular Halloween-themed cookies for you and a special group of treat-or-treaters. These chocolate, buttery cookies resemble both a classic sugar cookie and shortbread: They break with a crisp snap yet are melt-in-your-mouth tender. But don't let that fool you: The dough can be doubled without a hitch and is firm enough to roll and cut into fun shapes. The orange-flavored icing sets hard enough to slip one cookie into a cellophane bag or to box up a batch for delivery without smudging the black and orange seasonal effects.

Kid Friendly • Make Ahead

Chocolate Halloween Cutout Cookies

Hands-on: 56 min. Total: 2 hr. 44 min.

5.6 ounces all-purpose flour (about 1¼ cups)
½ cup unsweetened cocoa
¼ teaspoon salt
½ cup unsalted butter, softened
⅔ cup granulated sugar

2 large egg whites
¼ teaspoon vanilla extract
2 cups powdered sugar
1 teaspoon grated orange rind
2 tablespoons plus 2 teaspoons fresh orange juice
6 to 10 drops orange food coloring

1. Weigh or lightly spoon flour into dry measuring cups; level with a knife. Combine flour, cocoa, and salt in a bowl, stirring with a whisk.
2. Place butter and granulated sugar in a medium bowl. Beat with a mixer at medium speed 3 minutes or until light and fluffy. Add egg whites and vanilla; beat 1 minute or until well combined. Add flour mixture; beat at low speed just until combined. Spoon dough onto a 12-inch-long sheet of plastic wrap; gently press mixture into a ball. Wrap and chill dough for 1 hour.
3. Preheat oven to 350°.
4. Divide dough in half (wrap and refrigerate 1 dough portion to keep it chilled). Working with 1 portion at a time, roll dough to ¼-inch thickness on a lightly floured surface; cut into desired shapes with 2¼- to 3¾-inch cookie cutters. Place cookies on baking sheets lined with parchment paper. Bake at 350° for 10 minutes or until cookies are firm in the center. Cool 2 minutes on pan. Remove cookies from pan, and cool completely on a wire rack.
5. Combine powdered sugar and remaining ingredients in a small bowl; stir with a whisk until smooth. Scrape icing into a heavy-duty zip-top plastic bag. Snip a tiny hole in 1 corner of bag with scissors; decorate cookies as desired with icing. Serves 26 (serving size: 1 cookie)

CALORIES 115; FAT 3.8g (sat 2.4g, mono 1g, poly 0.2g); PROTEIN 1g; CARB 20g; FIBER 1g; CHOL 9mg; IRON 1mg; SODIUM 28mg; CALC 5mg

DROP BISCUIT CHICKEN POTPIE FROM CORY BAHR

A Cajun Country chef finds his roots in turnips.

Among fall's root veggie heroes, humble turnips rarely get their due. But there's so much to praise: Toothy and succulent, peppery and sweet, turnips add amazing complexity to hearty cool-weather cooking. "Growing up, they were a big part of my life, and now as a chef, I really appreciate how versatile they are," says chef Cory Bahr of Cotton in Monroe, Louisiana, and a 2012 winner on Chopped! "This time of year, they're at their best, so full of natural sweetness with a real balance of flavor."

On the Cotton menu, Bahr takes full advantage of the peak season for turnips: "We use them raw in coleslaws, fry them like French fries, work them into soups, pair them with seafood or red meat, serve them glazed along with duck breast— you name it." In his potpie, which features local rabbit at Cotton (we've subbed chicken), turnips are part of a fantastic seasonal veggie blend in the filling, along with sweet carrots, pleasantly bitter Brussels sprouts, and meaty shiitakes. Try Bahr's original dish at Cotton this month.

Kid Friendly

Drop Biscuit Chicken Potpie

Hands-on: 60 min. Total: 2 hr. 30 min. Cooking the chicken bone-in makes it more flavorful and moist, but for convenience, you can substitute 4 cups diced skinless, boneless chicken thighs. Brown them first, and then mix into the filling to bake in the last step.

6.75 ounces self-rising flour (about 1 1/2 cups)
6 tablespoons cold unsalted butter, cubed
9 tablespoons nonfat buttermilk
Cooking spray
2 tablespoons canola oil, divided
1 (3 1/2-pound) chicken, cut into 6 pieces and skinned
1 teaspoon kosher salt, divided
3/4 teaspoon freshly ground black pepper, divided
2 1/2 cups chopped peeled carrot (4 medium)
2 1/2 cups chopped peeled turnip (2 medium)
1 tablespoon chopped fresh thyme
1 tablespoon chopped fresh sage
5 garlic cloves, thinly sliced
2 shallots, thinly sliced
1/2 cup riesling or other white wine
4 cups unsalted chicken stock (such as Swanson)
5 tablespoons all-purpose flour
8 Brussels sprouts, trimmed and halved lengthwise
3 cups halved shiitake mushroom caps (about 12)

1. Preheat oven to 500°.
2. Weigh or lightly spoon self-rising flour into dry measuring cups; level with a knife. Place self-rising flour in a bowl. Cut in butter with a pastry blender or 2 knives until mixture resembles coarse meal. Add buttermilk; toss with a fork until moist. Drop dough by tablespoonfuls onto a foil-lined baking sheet coated with cooking spray to make 32 biscuits. Bake at 500° for 12 minutes or until edges are browned. Cool on wire racks. Reduce oven temperature to 350°.
3. Heat a large Dutch oven over medium-high heat. Add 1 tablespoon oil to pan; swirl to coat. Sprinkle chicken with 1/2 teaspoon salt and 1/2 teaspoon pepper. Add half of chicken to pan; cook 5 minutes on each side or until browned. Remove from pan. Repeat procedure with remaining chicken. Remove from pan.
4. Add carrot and next 5 ingredients to pan; cook 5 minutes or until lightly browned, stirring occasionally. Add wine; cook until liquid is reduced to 1/4 cup (about 2 minutes). Add stock; bring to a boil. Add browned chicken. Cover and place in oven; bake at 350° for 45 minutes or until chicken is very tender. Remove from oven. Remove chicken from pan, and let stand 5 minutes.
5. Remove chicken from bones; discard bones. Strain liquid over a bowl; reserve solids. Combine 1/2 cup cooking liquid and all-purpose flour in a small bowl, stirring with a whisk until smooth. Add flour mixture and remaining cooking liquid to pan. Bring to a boil; cook 3 minutes or until slightly thickened.
6. Heat a large skillet over medium-high heat. Add 1 tablespoon oil; swirl to coat. Add Brussels sprouts, cut sides down, to pan; cook 3 minutes or until lightly browned. Add 1/2 teaspoon salt, 1/4 teaspoon pepper, and mushrooms to pan; sauté 5 minutes.
7. Combine chicken, carrot mixture, cooking liquid, and mushroom mixture in a 13 x 9–inch glass or ceramic baking dish. Arrange biscuits evenly over chicken mixture. Bake at 350° for 20 minutes or until bubbly. Serves 8 (serving size: 1 1/2 cups chicken mixture and 4 biscuits)

CALORIES 381; FAT 15.5g (sat 6.6g, mono 5.5g, poly 2.1g); PROTEIN 23g; CARB 34g; FIBER 4g; CHOL 76mg; IRON 3mg; SODIUM 712mg; CALC 159mg

EAT LESS SALT

As experts scrutinize the oversalting of restaurant food, a leading chef shares his best sodium-moderating tips.

The U.S. Food and Drug Administration is focusing its attention on the notoriously high sodium levels found in some restaurant food. Fast-food meals can exceed the whole-day sodium recommendations for adults. Chain restaurants publish their nutrition numbers, but few chefs have been taught to watch sodium when turning out their latest masterpieces. One exception is this month's Healthy Habits Hero, chef Jeremy Bearman. Until recently, Bearman helmed New York City's Rouge Tomate, the leading health-forward fine dining restaurant in America. The restaurant's dishes adhered to strict nutrition parameters—including sodium—based on the United States Department of Agriculture's 2010 Dietary Guidelines for Americans. Yet there was nothing about Bearman's dishes that tasted "low sodium."

Bearman employs several strategies to prevent oversalted food, including saving some of the recipe's allowable salt until right when the dish is ready to be served. This way, the salt flavor hasn't had the chance to diminish, and you get a perfectly seasoned dish without big sodium numbers.

Another salt-savvy point to consider when you're cooking at home is tasting as you go: "The first bite of a soup might taste good, but think in terms of eating the entire bowl. At the end, you're probably going to notice that it's saltier than you wanted it to be."

Bearman's approach comes down to considering a food's natural sodium level and adjusting the salt accordingly. For example, pasta sauce is often salty enough that you don't need to salt the pasta water. The same can't be said for naturally low-sodium foods like beans.

"When I cook beans, I put salt in the liquid to get some seasoning inside the bean. That way you don't have to put so much salt in whatever you're dressing them with because the beans are actually well seasoned on their own," says Bearman.

In light of these strategies, Bearman is not suggesting cooks abandon the saltshaker. "You're not going to eat things that are completely, utterly bland, but you have to wean yourself off salt use in a smart way," he says. "You can actually decrease your desire for salt by using a step-down approach to minimize the amount you use."

**Kid Friendly • Gluten Free
Make Ahead**

Roasted Tomato and Garlic Soup

Hands-on: 12 min. Total: 60 min.

3 (10-ounce) beefsteak tomatoes, halved
8 garlic cloves
Cooking spray
1½ teaspoons butter
¼ cup uncooked long-grain brown rice
2 cups unsalted chicken stock
1 (14.5-ounce) can unsalted fire-roasted diced tomatoes, undrained
³⁄₈ teaspoon kosher salt
2 tablespoons half-and-half
¾ teaspoon black pepper
2 tablespoons minced fresh chives (optional)

1. Preheat oven to 400°.
2. Working with 1 beefsteak tomato at a time, squeeze halves into a bowl; reserve seeds and juice. Arrange garlic and tomatoes, cut sides down, in a single layer on a foil-lined jelly-roll pan; coat with cooking spray. Bake at 400° for 50 minutes or until tomatoes are lightly charred. Reserve juices.

3. Melt butter in a large Dutch oven over medium-high heat. Add rice; sauté 1 minute or until toasted. Add reserved tomato juices, tomato mixture, stock, canned tomatoes, and salt to pan. Bring to a boil. Reduce heat, and simmer 40 minutes.
4. Place half of soup mixture in a blender. Remove center piece of blender lid (to allow steam to escape); secure blender lid on blender. Place a clean towel over opening in blender lid (to avoid splatters). Blend until smooth. Strain through a fine sieve over a bowl; discard solids. Pour into a large bowl. Repeat procedure with remaining soup mixture. Stir in half-and-half and pepper. Sprinkle with chives, if desired. Serves 4 (serving size: 1¼ cups)

CALORIES 152; **FAT** 3.3g (sat 1.6g, mono 0.8g, poly 0.4g); **PROTEIN** 7g; **CARB** 25g; **FIBER** 4g; **CHOL** 7mg; **IRON** 1mg; **SODIUM** 273mg; **CALC** 55mg

CHEF BEARMAN'S SALT-SMART STRATEGIES

1. MAKE YOUR OWN LOW-SODIUM SAUCES. Condiments, such as mustard and mayo, are loaded with salt. Make a few favorite sauces yourself to reduce the sodium.

2. EXPERIMENT WITH FLAVOR INTENSIFIERS. "Vinegar is one of those foods that sometimes people mistake for salt. Most of the time, pickles are made by adding salt to the cucumbers and letting them ferment. That fermentation process brings out acid, so the pickle ends up tasting acidic. It also ends up being incredibly salty. We actually did a lot of our pickles without salt and just vinegar with a small ratio of sugar."

3. BEWARE HEALTH-FOOD HALOS. Salt can be high in otherwise healthy foods. "Some whole-wheat hamburger buns have almost double the sodium of traditional options," Bearman says. Leafy greens, like kale, have a lot of naturally occurring sodium, too.

A TASTY TWIST FOR TOMATO SAUCE

Everyday pasta sauce goes to an exotic level when simmered with earthy spices.

Kid Friendly • Freezable Make Ahead

Turkey Sausage and Spicy Tomato Sauce

Hands-on: 25 min. Total: 8 hr. 30 min.
Stir leftovers into cooked brown rice or farro for a whole-grain dinner with a jambalaya feel. To amp up the veggies, serve over a bed of roasted cauliflower.

1 tablespoon olive oil
1¼ pounds smoked turkey sausage, cut into 1-inch pieces
2 cups chopped onion
15 garlic cloves, chopped (about 1 head)
2 carrots, very thinly sliced
2 Fresno chiles, thinly sliced
3 tablespoons chopped fresh thyme
2 teaspoons ground coriander
2 teaspoons ground cumin
1 teaspoon ground cinnamon
1 teaspoon ground turmeric
½ teaspoon crushed red pepper
1 cup dry white wine
2 (28.5-ounce) cans unsalted whole tomatoes
1 tablespoon mustard seeds
1 tablespoon lower-sodium soy sauce
6 (2-inch) strips lemon rind (about 1 lemon)
3 bay leaves
8 cups cooked penne pasta (about 1 pound uncooked)
¼ cup chopped fresh cilantro
2 ounces Cotija cheese, crumbled (about ½ cup)

1. Heat a large Dutch oven over medium-high heat. Add oil; swirl to coat. Add sausage; cook 8 minutes or until browned, stirring occasionally. Transfer sausage to a 6-quart electric slow cooker.
2. Add onion, garlic, carrots, and chiles to pan; sauté 6 minutes or until tender. Add thyme and next 5 ingredients to pan; cook 1 minute. Add wine; bring to a boil. Cook 2 minutes or until wine is reduced by half. Place onion mixture in slow cooker.
3. Drain 1 can of tomatoes. Add drained tomatoes, remaining 1 can tomatoes with liquid, mustard seeds, soy sauce, rind, and bay leaves to slow cooker. Stir to combine and break up tomatoes. Cover and cook on LOW 8 hours. Remove and discard rind and bay leaves. Ladle sauce over pasta; sprinkle with cilantro and cheese. Serves 12 (serving size: ⅔ cup pasta and 1 cup sauce)

CALORIES 304; FAT 7.7g (sat 3g, mono 2.3g, poly 1g); PROTEIN 15g; CARB 41g; FIBER 4g; CHOL 30mg; IRON 7mg; SODIUM 582mg; CALC 149mg

CHEESY! SAUCY! LIGHT!

A simple real-cheese sauce, made with less fat and salt. Here's how.

Few things can elevate green veggies or a pile of nachos quite like cheese that's been melted down with butter into a rich, creamy sauce, and then slathered on top. Sauces, however, can be calorie-packed: A from-scratch cheese-and-butter sauce contains about 90 calories in just 2 tablespoons. Go the convenience route with processed cheese, and you're looking at more than 400mg of sodium.

We wanted something as rich as a traditional cheese-and-butter sauce but almost as simple as opening a jar of processed stuff. Borrowing an idea from our Help Me, Kenji columnist, Kenji Lopez-Alt, we whisked together cheese, cornstarch, and evaporated milk over low heat until smooth. By subbing fat-free milk and using less cheese than Kenji, we created a richly dense sauce, ready in minutes, with half the calories of full-fat sauce and less salt than jarred.

Cooking Light Cheese Sauce
Toss 5 ounces shredded reduced-fat sharp cheddar cheese and 1 tablespoon cornstarch together in a medium saucepan. Add 1 cup evaporated fat-free milk. Cook over low heat, stirring constantly with a whisk until melted and thickened. For a spicy nacho-style kick, stir in 1½ teaspoons hot sauce. Makes 1½ cups (serving size: 2 tablespoons)

CALORIES 53 FAT 2.2g (1.4g sat fat) SODIUM 114mg

QUICK TRICKS

5 CRAVEABLE CARAMEL APPLES

Start with the basic caramel at the bottom, and customize with our tasty combos.

START HERE: Ready Your Apples

Push a wooden craft stick into the tops of 8 small apples. Bring 1 cup sugar, ¼ cup light-colored corn syrup, and ¼ cup water to a boil in a medium, heavy saucepan, stirring until sugar dissolves. Bring to a boil over medium-high heat. Cook, without stirring, 9 minutes or until lightly golden (about 260°). Follow one of the variations for a whimsical spin on this fall favorite.

Kid Friendly • Gluten Free
Make Ahead
Hummingbird

Stir ½ cup half-and-half, ½ cup light coconut milk, 1 teaspoon vanilla, and ⅛ teaspoon salt into caramel mixture. Simmer until candy thermometer registers 235°, stirring frequently. Place ⅓ cup dried pineapple and ⅓ cup toasted pecans in a food processor; pulse. Combine pineapple mixture and ½ cup toasted flaked sweetened coconut in a large bowl. Pour caramel into a bowl sitting in a hot water bath. Swirl bottom halves of apples in caramel; dip in pineapple mixture. Serves 8 (serving size: 1 apple)

CALORIES 301; FAT 6.9g (sat 3g); SODIUM 69mg

Kid Friendly • Make Ahead
Granola and Rosemary Cider

Stir ¾ cup half-and-half, ¼ cup apple cider, 1 teaspoon vanilla, and ⅛ teaspoon salt into caramel mixture. Simmer until candy thermometer registers 235°, stirring frequently. Stir in 1 teaspoon chopped fresh rosemary. Place 1 cup honey-oat granola in a bowl. Pour caramel into a bowl sitting in a hot water bath. Swirl bottom halves of apples in caramel; dip in granola. Serves 8 (serving size: 1 apple)

CALORIES 296; FAT 4.9g (sat 1.8g); SODIUM 108mg

Kid Friendly • Quick & Easy
Gluten Free • Make Ahead
Pistachio-Orange

Stir ¾ cup half-and-half, ¼ cup fresh orange juice, ½ teaspoon grated orange rind, and ⅛ teaspoon salt into caramel mixture. Simmer until candy thermometer registers 235°, stirring frequently. While caramel cooks, combine ½ cup chopped pistachios and ⅓ cup semisweet chocolate minichips in a large bowl, and set aside. Pour caramel into a bowl sitting in a hot water bath. Swirl bottom halves of apples in caramel; dip in the pistachio mixture. Serves 8 (serving size: 1 apple)

CALORIES 300; FAT 8.5g (sat 3.3g); SODIUM 56mg

Kid Friendly • Make Ahead
White Chocolate-Pumpkin Pie

Stir 1 cup half-and-half, 1 teaspoon vanilla, and ⅛ teaspoon salt into caramel mixture. Simmer until candy thermometer registers 235°, stirring frequently. Stir in 1 teaspoon pumpkin pie spice. Pour caramel into a bowl sitting in a hot water bath. Place ⅔ cup graham cracker crumbs in a bowl. Combine 1½ ounces white chocolate chips and ½ teaspoon canola oil in a microwave-safe bowl. Microwave at HIGH until melted, stirring every 20 seconds. Swirl bottom halves of apples in caramel; dip in crumbs. Drizzle with white chocolate. Serves 8 (serving size: 1 apple)

CALORIES 308; FAT 6.5g (sat 3.4g); SODIUM 96mg

Kid Friendly • Make Ahead
Bacon-Pretzel-Peanut Butter

Stir 1 cup half-and-half, ½ teaspoon vanilla, and ⅛ teaspoon salt into caramel. Simmer until candy thermometer registers 235°, stirring frequently. Combine 2 slices cooked and crumbled bacon and 2 ounces crushed pretzels in a bowl. Stir 2½ tablespoons creamy peanut butter into caramel; pour mixture into a bowl sitting in a hot water bath. Swirl bottom halves of apples in caramel; dip in pretzel mixture. Serves 8 (serving size: 1 apple)

CALORIES 309; FAT 6.8g (sat 2.8g); SODIUM 249mg

DOUBLE-CHICKPEA CREPES

Chickpea flour imbues crepes with nutty flavor; canned garbanzos make a tasty filling.

Make Ahead • Vegetarian

Chickpea-Rosemary Crepes with Pepper Relish

Hands-on: 55 min. Total: 55 min.

Crepes:
3.13 ounces chickpea (garbanzo bean) flour (about ³/₄ cup)
3 tablespoons all-purpose flour
2 teaspoons chopped fresh rosemary
1 teaspoon grated lemon rind
¹/₄ teaspoon kosher salt
¹/₈ teaspoon baking soda
³/₄ cup water
2 tablespoons olive oil
2 large eggs, lightly beaten

Filling:
1 cup canned chickpeas (garbanzo beans), rinsed and drained
1 tablespoon 2% reduced-fat milk
2 teaspoons olive oil
2 teaspoons fresh lemon juice
¹/₄ teaspoon freshly ground black pepper
Dash of salt
2 ounces goat cheese
¹/₂ garlic clove

Relish:
¹/₄ cup diced yellow bell pepper
¹/₄ cup diced red bell pepper
¹/₄ cup diced orange bell pepper
2 tablespoons finely diced onion
1 teaspoon extra-virgin olive oil
¹/₂ teaspoon balsamic vinegar
¹/₄ teaspoon kosher salt
¹/₄ teaspoon freshly ground black pepper

1. To prepare crepes, weigh or lightly spoon chickpea flour into dry measuring cups; level with a knife. Combine flours, rosemary, rind, ¼ teaspoon salt, and baking soda in a large bowl, stirring with a whisk. Add ¾ cup water, 2 tablespoons oil, and eggs, and stir with a whisk. Let stand 30 minutes.
2. To prepare filling, place chickpeas and next 7 ingredients in a food processor; process until smooth.
3. To prepare relish, place yellow pepper and remaining ingredients in a medium bowl; toss gently to combine.
4. Heat an 8-inch crepe pan or nonstick skillet over medium-high heat. Pour about 2 tablespoons batter into pan; quickly tilt pan in all directions so batter covers pan with a thin film. Cook 30 seconds. Carefully lift edge of crepe with a spatula to test for doneness. Turn crepe over when it can be shaken loose from pan and the underside is lightly browned; cook 10 seconds. Place crepe on a clean towel; keep warm. Repeat procedure until all the batter is used. Stack crepes between single layers of paper towels to prevent sticking.
5. Spread 1 heaping tablespoon filling down the center of each crepe; roll up. Top with relish. Serves 4 (serving size: 3 crepes and 3 tablespoons relish)

CALORIES 319; **FAT** 17.8g (sat 4.5g, mono 9.5g, poly 2.6g); **PROTEIN** 13g; **CARB** 26g; **FIBER** 3g; **CHOL** 100mg; **IRON** 2mg; **SODIUM** 492mg; **CALC** 71mg

CHICKPEA FLOUR HAS MORE PROTEIN THAN WHEAT FLOUR, A BONUS FOR VEGETARIANS. MAKE THE CREPES IN ADVANCE FOR SPEEDIER PREP, AND GARNISH WITH ADDITIONAL ROSEMARY, IF DESIRED.

THE ANNUAL HOLIDAY COOKBOOK

Mix and match recipes for a perfect Thanksgiving

ADVENTUROUS

Please your thrill-seeking palate with vibrant, fun flavors. For the traditionalist in all of us, mix and match new dishes with familar ones.

Make Ahead

Port-Glazed Pear Tart with Rosemary-Cornmeal Crust

Hands-on: 45 min. Total: 1 hr. 50 min.
Prepare the crust and pears up to 1 day ahead and refrigerate. Assemble just before serving.

4.5 ounces all-purpose flour (about 1 cup)
½ cup yellow cornmeal
½ cup plus 2 tablespoons sugar, divided
½ teaspoon salt, divided
½ teaspoon finely chopped fresh rosemary
⅓ cup olive oil

Cooking spray
1 cup port wine
¾ cup water
1 (2-inch) strip lemon rind
3 small peeled Bosc pears, cored and halved lengthwise
¾ cup 1% low-fat milk, divided
4 teaspoons cornstarch
1 large egg yolk
½ cup part-skim ricotta cheese
⅓ cup plain 2% reduced-fat Greek yogurt
1 teaspoon grated lemon rind
½ teaspoon vanilla extract

1. Preheat oven to 375°.
2. Weigh or lightly spoon flour into a dry measuring cup. Place flour, cornmeal, ¼ cup sugar, ¼ teaspoon salt, and rosemary in the bowl of a food processor; pulse 2 times to combine. With processor on, slowly add oil through food chute; process until crumbly. Press cornmeal mixture into bottom and up sides of a 9-inch round fluted removable-bottom tart pan coated with cooking spray. Chill 10 minutes. Line bottom of dough with a piece of foil coated with cooking spray; arrange pie weights or dried beans on foil. Bake at 375° for 20 minutes.

Remove weights and foil; cool on a wire rack.
3. Combine ¼ cup sugar, port, ¾ cup water, and lemon rind strip in a medium saucepan, stirring with a whisk. Add pears; bring to a boil. Cover, reduce heat, and simmer 9 minutes or until pears are tender when pierced with a knife. Remove pears with a slotted spoon; cool slightly. Cut lengthwise into wedges. Increase heat to high. Bring port mixture to a boil; cook 6 minutes or until reduced to ¼ cup. Discard lemon rind strip.
4. Combine 2 tablespoons sugar, ¼ teaspoon salt, ¼ cup milk, cornstarch, and yolk in a small saucepan, stirring with a whisk. Bring to a boil over medium heat, stirring frequently. Stir in ½ cup milk; cook 1 minute, stirring constantly. Remove pan from heat; stir in ricotta, yogurt, 1 teaspoon grated rind, and vanilla. Cover and chill at least 1 hour.
5. Spread ricotta mixture evenly over bottom of crust. Arrange pear wedges over ricotta mixture. Drizzle with port mixture. Serves 10 (serving size: 1 wedge)

CALORIES 288; FAT 9.4g (sat 2g, mono 5.8g, poly 1g); PROTEIN 5g; CARB 42g; FIBER 2g; CHOL 24mg; IRON 1mg; SODIUM 148mg; CALC 73mg

THE SHORTBREAD-LIKE CRUST STANDS UP WELL TO A LUSCIOUS RICOTTA FILLING THAT'S TOPPED WITH PRETTY PORT-STAINED PEARS. LARGER PEAR WEDGES ARE STUNNING; YOU CAN ALSO CUT THE PEARS INTO THIN SLICES AND ARRANGE SPOKELIKE ON TOP.

Farro Stuffing with Butternut Squash, Red Onion, and Almonds

Hands-on: 15 min. Total: 40 min.

4 cups unsalted chicken stock
 (such as Swanson)
2 cups uncooked farro
2 tablespoons olive oil
2 cups diced peeled butternut squash
1 cup chopped red onion
1 cup thinly sliced carrot
³/₄ cup thinly sliced celery
³/₄ cup almonds, toasted and coarsely
 chopped
³/₄ cup chopped fresh flat-leaf
 parsley
1 tablespoon thyme leaves
1 tablespoon minced fresh sage
1¹/₄ teaspoons kosher salt
¹/₂ teaspoon freshly ground black
 pepper

1. Bring stock and farro to a boil in a large saucepan; cover, reduce heat, and simmer 25 minutes or until farro is al dente. Drain in a colander over a bowl, reserving cooking liquid.
2. Heat a large nonstick skillet over medium heat. Add oil; swirl to coat. Add squash, onion, carrot, and celery; sauté 5 minutes. Stir in ¼ cup reserved cooking liquid. Reduce heat to low; cover and cook 7 minutes or until vegetables are tender. Stir squash mixture into farro mixture. Stir in almonds, parsley, thyme, sage, salt, and pepper. Spoon into an 11 x 7–inch glass or ceramic baking dish. Cover and keep warm until ready to serve. Stir in additional reserved cooking liquid as needed just before serving. Serves 12 (serving size: ¾ cup)

CALORIES 216; FAT 7.5g (sat 0.7g, mono 4.4g, poly 1.4g); PROTEIN 9g; CARB 31g; FIBER 6g; CHOL 0mg; IRON 2mg; SODIUM 259mg; CALC 71mg

Hazelnut Rye Rolls

Hands-on: 27 min. Total: 2 hr.

1 cup 1% low-fat milk
1 tablespoon honey
1 package active dry yeast (about
 2¹/₄ teaspoons)
2 tablespoons olive oil
9.5 ounces bread flour, divided
 (about 2 cups)
3.5 ounces light rye flour (about 1
 cup)
¹/₄ cup chopped hazelnuts, toasted
1¹/₂ teaspoons salt
Cooking spray
1 tablespoon water
1 large egg white, lightly beaten

1. Heat milk in a small saucepan over medium heat; keep warm. Combine ¼ cup milk, honey, and yeast in the bowl of a stand mixer fitted with the dough hook. Let stand 5 minutes or until mixture is bubbly. Stir in ¾ cup milk and olive oil.
2. Weigh or lightly spoon 8.3 ounces (1¾ cups) bread flour and rye flour into dry measuring cups; level with a knife. Add 1¾ cups bread flour, rye flour, hazelnuts, and salt to stand mixer; mix at medium-low speed just until combined. With mixer at low speed, gradually add remaining 1.2 ounces (¼ cup) bread flour. Mix at low speed 5 minutes or until a soft dough forms, scraping sides of bowl once. Place dough in a bowl coated with cooking spray, turning to coat. Cover and let rise in a warm place (85°), free from drafts, 1 hour or until doubled in size.
3. Punch dough down; turn out onto a lightly floured surface. Cut dough into 16 equal pieces. Working with 1 piece at a time, roll dough into a ball by cupping your hand and pushing against dough and surface while rolling. Arrange dough balls 1 inch apart on a baking sheet coated with cooking spray. Cover and let rise 45 minutes or until the dough is doubled in size.
4. Preheat oven to 375°.
5. Combine 1 tablespoon water and egg white in a small bowl; brush evenly over rolls. Bake at 375° for 14 minutes or until golden. Remove rolls from pan; cool on a wire rack. Serves 16 (serving size: 1 roll)

CALORIES 122; FAT 3.4g (sat 0.5g, mono 2.2g, poly 0.5g); PROTEIN 4g; CARB 19g; FIBER 1g; CHOL 1mg; IRON 1mg; SODIUM 232mg; CALC 25mg

Roasted Fennel with Rosemary Breadcrumbs

Hands-on: 12 min. Total: 60 min.
Instead of roasted root vegetables or Brussels sprouts, try roasted fennel. Fennel has licorice notes that mellow in the oven, becoming slightly sweet.

2 tablespoons chopped walnuts
2 (1-ounce) slices whole-grain bread,
 torn into pieces
2 tablespoons olive oil, divided
2 teaspoons finely chopped fresh
 rosemary
4 medium fennel bulbs, trimmed and
 halved lengthwise (about 4 pounds)
¹/₄ teaspoon kosher salt
¹/₄ teaspoon black pepper
2 tablespoons cider vinegar

1. Preheat oven to 375°.
2. Place walnuts and bread in the bowl of a mini food processor; pulse 3 to 4 times or until coarse crumbs form. Heat a large nonstick skillet over medium heat. Add 1 tablespoon oil to pan; swirl to coat. Add rosemary; cook 30 seconds. Add nut mixture; cook 4 minutes, stirring frequently.
3. Cut each fennel half into 4 wedges. Combine fennel, 1 tablespoon oil,

salt, and pepper on a foil-lined baking sheet; toss. Bake at 375° for 45 minutes or until edges are lightly browned, turning after 20 minutes. Drizzle with vinegar. Sprinkle with walnut mixture; toss to coat. Serves 8 (serving size: about ⅔ cup)

CALORIES 98; **FAT** 5.1g (sat 0.6g, mono 2.7g, poly 1.4g); **PROTEIN** 3g; **CARB** 12g; **FIBER** 4g; **CHOL** 0mg; **IRON** 1mg; **SODIUM** 151mg; **CALC** 68mg

Quick & Easy • Make Ahead
Vegetarian • Gluten Free

Spiced Cranberry-Mango Chutney

Hands-on: 23 min. Total: 23 min.

1½ tablespoons canola oil
½ cup finely chopped shallots
2 teaspoons mustard seeds
1 teaspoon minced peeled fresh ginger
1 teaspoon minced fresh garlic
1 teaspoon minced serrano chile
⅓ cup sugar
¼ cup golden raisins
2 tablespoons red wine vinegar
¼ teaspoon kosher salt
1 (12-ounce) package fresh cranberries
2 cups chopped mango (about 2 large)
⅓ cup finely chopped toasted walnuts

1. Heat a large skillet over medium heat. Add oil; swirl. Add shallots; sauté 2 minutes. Add mustard seeds, ginger, garlic, and serrano; sauté 2 minutes. Stir in sugar and next 4 ingredients (through cranberries); bring to a simmer. Reduce heat and cook 4 minutes. Add mango; cook 1 minute. Stir in walnuts. Serves 12 (serving size: about ¼ cup)

CALORIES 105; **FAT** 4.2g (sat 0.4g, mono 1.4g, poly 2.1g); **PROTEIN** 1g; **CARB** 17g; **FIBER** 2g; **CHOL** 0mg; **IRON** 0mg; **SODIUM** 42mg; **CALC** 17mg

Moroccan-Spiced Turkey with Aromatic Orange Pan Jus

Hands-on: 50 min. Total: 2 hr. 40 min.
A fragrant spice rub infuses the turkey with subtle Middle Eastern flavor.

1 (12-pound) fresh or frozen turkey, thawed
2 tablespoons extra-virgin olive oil
1 tablespoon grated orange rind
1 tablespoon ground cumin
1 tablespoon honey
2 teaspoons garlic powder
2 teaspoons ground coriander
1¼ teaspoons kosher salt, divided
⅝ teaspoon freshly ground black pepper, divided
½ teaspoon ground ginger
½ teaspoon ground cinnamon
½ teaspoon ground red pepper
2 medium onions, chopped
2 celery stalks, chopped
2 carrots, chopped
2 cups unsalted chicken stock
¾ cup dry sherry
Cooking spray
½ cup fresh orange juice

1. Preheat oven to 425°.
2. Remove giblets and neck from turkey; discard liver. Pat turkey dry with paper towels; trim and discard excess fat. Starting at neck cavity, loosen skin from breast and drumsticks by inserting fingers, gently pushing between skin and meat. Combine oil, rind, cumin, honey, garlic powder, coriander, 1 teaspoon salt, ½ teaspoon black pepper, ginger, cinnamon, and red pepper, stirring with a whisk. Rub spice mixture under loosened skin and over breast and drumsticks. Lift wing tips up and over back; tuck under turkey. Tie legs together with kitchen string. Place giblets, neck, onions, celery, and car-

rots in the bottom of a large roasting pan; add stock and sherry to pan. Place roasting rack in pan. Coat rack with cooking spray. Arrange turkey, breast side up, on roasting rack. Bake at 425° for 30 minutes. Cover turkey loosely with foil. Reduce oven temperature to 325° (do not remove turkey from oven). Bake an additional 1 hour and 10 minutes or until a thermometer inserted into meaty part of thigh registers 165°. Remove pan from oven; place turkey on a cutting board. Let stand, covered, 20 minutes. Carve turkey; discard skin.
3. Place a zip-top plastic bag inside a 4-cup glass measure. Pour stock mixture through a sieve into bag; discard solids. Let stand 10 minutes. Seal bag; snip off 1 bottom corner of bag. Drain stock mixture into a medium saucepan, stopping before fat layer reaches opening. Add orange juice to pan; bring to a boil. Cook 3 minutes or until slightly thickened. Stir in ¼ teaspoon salt and ⅛ teaspoon black pepper. Serve sauce with turkey. Serves 16 (serving size: 4 ounces turkey and about 2 tablespoons sauce)

CALORIES 274; **FAT** 8.2g (sat 2.1g, mono 2.7g, poly 2.1g); **PROTEIN** 39g; **CARB** 6g; **FIBER** 1g; **CHOL** 97mg; **IRON** 3mg; **SODIUM** 338mg; **CALC** 49mg

Sautéed Green Beans with Miso Butter

***Hands-on: 8 min. Total: 15 min.** Super-savory miso elevates crisp beans beyond their humble goodness.*

2 **tablespoons unsalted butter, softened**
2 **tablespoons white miso**
2 **pounds green beans, trimmed**
¼ **cup sliced almonds, toasted**

1. Combine butter and miso in a small bowl; refrigerate 5 minutes.
2. Place beans in a large saucepan of boiling water; cook 4 minutes. Drain; plunge beans into ice water. Drain.
3. Heat a large nonstick skillet over medium-high heat. Add beans, and sauté 4 minutes. Add butter mixture, and cook 3 minutes. Top with almonds. Serves 12 (serving size: about ¾ cup)

CALORIES 56; FAT 3g (sat 1.3g, mono 1.1g, poly 0.4g); PROTEIN 2g; CARB 7g; FIBER 3g; CHOL 5mg; IRON 1mg; SODIUM 95mg; CALC 34mg

---

Make Ahead

Leek and Pancetta Potato Rösti

***Hands-on: 15 min. Total: 60 min.** This rösti, essentially a large potato pancake, is perfect for hash brown lovers. If making ahead, cool on a wire rack, wrap in plastic wrap, and refrigerate. Reheat in an oven-proof skillet at 350° for 10 minutes.*

4½ **cups shredded peeled baking potato (about 2 pounds)**
3 **ounces diced pancetta**
1 **large leek, halved lengthwise and thinly sliced (white and light green parts only)**
3 **tablespoons all-purpose flour**
2 **tablespoons chopped fresh sage**
½ **teaspoon kosher salt**
¼ **teaspoon black pepper**
1 **large egg**
2 **tablespoons olive oil**

1. Place shredded potato on a double layer of cheesecloth. Gather edges of cheesecloth together; squeeze cheesecloth to extract excess moisture. Place potato in a bowl.
2. Heat a large nonstick skillet over medium-high heat. Add pancetta; cook 4 minutes or until lightly browned and crisp. Stir in leek; cook 4 minutes or until tender. Add pancetta mixture, flour, sage, salt, pepper, and egg to potato; stir well to combine.
3. Return pan to medium-high heat. Add oil; swirl to coat. Add potato mixture to pan; flatten with a spatula into an even layer. Cook 12 minutes or until bottom is golden brown. Place a large plate upside down on top of pan; invert onto plate. Carefully slide potato cake into pan, browned side up; cook 10 minutes or until golden brown. Place potato cake on a cutting board; cool slightly. Cut into 8 wedges. Serves 8 (serving size: 1 wedge)

CALORIES 159; FAT 5.8g (sat 1.5g, mono 2.7g, poly 0.5g); PROTEIN 4g; CARB 23g; FIBER 2g; CHOL 27mg; IRON 1mg; SODIUM 220mg; CALC 18mg

---

MODERN TWIST ON TRADITIONAL

Tried-and-true dishes have earned their place, but that doesn't mean they can't be jazzed up. Fun riffs on classic flavors bring family favorites to a new level.

Kid Friendly • Quick & Easy
Make Ahead • Vegetarian
Gluten Free

Cardamom-Glazed Carrots

Hands-on: 15 min. Total: 15 min.

1 **tablespoon butter**
1 **tablespoon canola oil**
2 **teaspoons minced peeled fresh ginger**
⅜ **teaspoon ground cardamom**
½ **cup water**
2 **tablespoons light brown sugar**
1 **pound carrots, peeled and cut diagonally into ½-inch pieces**
¼ **teaspoon kosher salt**
¼ **teaspoon black pepper**
2 **tablespoons cilantro leaves (optional)**

1. Cut a circle from parchment paper to fit a large nonstick skillet.
2. Heat skillet over medium heat. Add butter and oil to pan; swirl until butter melts. Add ginger and cardamom to pan; cook 2 minutes. Add ½ cup water, sugar, and carrot; bring to a boil. Cover with parchment circle, reduce heat, and simmer 9 minutes or until carrot is crisp-tender. Remove parchment circle; discard. Sprinkle carrot mixture with salt, pepper, and cilantro, if desired. Serves 6 (serving size: ½ cup)

CALORIES 87; FAT 4.5g (sat 1.4g, mono 2g, poly 0.8g); PROTEIN 1g; CARB 12g; FIBER 2g; CHOL 5mg; IRON 0mg; SODIUM 150mg; CALC 30mg

Cracked Wheat and Barley Pull-Aparts

Hands-on: 40 min. Total: 3 hr.

2 cups boiling water
$1/3$ cup medium-grain bulgur
(cracked wheat)
$1^1/2$ teaspoons salt, divided
1 tablespoon honey
1 package active dry yeast (about
$2^1/4$ teaspoons)
13.5 ounces all-purpose flour (about
3 cups)
3.25 ounces barley flour (about 1
cup)
2 tablespoons extra-virgin olive oil
2 large eggs, lightly beaten
Cooking spray

1. Combine 2 cups water, bulgur, and
¼ teaspoon salt in a bowl; let stand
30 minutes or until bulgur is tender.
Drain in a colander over a bowl, reserving soaking liquid. Add water to
soaking liquid if needed to measure
1 cup. Heat liquid in a small saucepan over medium-low heat 1 minute
or until warm; keep liquid warm.
2. Place ¼ cup soaking liquid, honey,
and yeast in the bowl of a stand
mixer fitted with the dough hook.
Let yeast mixture stand 5 minutes or
until bubbly.
3. Weigh or lightly spoon flours
into dry measuring cups; level with
a knife. Add flours, ¾ cup soaking
liquid, bulgur, 1¼ teaspoons salt,
olive oil, and eggs to stand mixer.
Mix at low speed 5 minutes or until
a soft dough forms. Place dough in
a bowl coated with cooking spray,
turning to coat. Cover and let rise in
a warm place (85°), free from drafts,
45 minutes or until doubled in size.
4. Punch dough down; turn out onto
a lightly floured surface. Cut dough
into 16 equal pieces. Working with 1
piece at a time, roll dough into a ball
by cupping your hand and pushing
against dough and surface while rolling. Arrange dough balls 1 inch apart
on a jelly-roll pan coated with cooking
spray. Cover; let rise 40 minutes or
until doubled in size (rolls will be
touching).
5. Preheat oven to 375°.
6. Bake rolls at 375° for 20 minutes
or until rolls are golden. Remove rolls
from pan, and cool on a wire rack.
Serves 16 (serving size: 1 roll)

CALORIES 147; FAT 2.7g (sat 0.5g, mono 1.5g, poly 0.5g);
PROTEIN 4g; CARB 26g; FIBER 2g; CHOL 23mg;
IRON 1mg; SODIUM 232mg; CALC 10mg

Cherry-Port Cranberry Sauce

Hands-on: 15 min. Total: 20 min. *Port
adds a grown-up twist, but you can sub unsweetened cherry or pomegranate juice,
if you like.*

2 cups fresh cranberries (about
8 ounces)
¾ cup dried sweetened cherries
¾ cup port wine
$1/3$ cup brown sugar
1 tablespoon red wine vinegar
¼ teaspoon freshly ground black
pepper

1. Bring all ingredients to a boil in a
medium saucepan over medium-high
heat, stirring until sugar melts. Reduce
heat to medium-low; simmer 5 minutes or until cranberries begin to pop.
Cool slightly before serving. Serves 12
(serving size: about 2½ tablespoons)

CALORIES 80; FAT 0g; PROTEIN 0g; CARB 16g;
FIBER 1g; CHOL 0mg; IRON 0mg; SODIUM 3mg;
CALC 7mg

Maple-Walnut Cranberry Pie

Hands-on: 13 min. Total: 1 hr. 26 min.
*While the buttery, maple-scented filling is
inspired by classic pecan pie, we swap in
toasted walnuts and add chopped fresh
cranberries for a beautiful pop of color and
tart flavor contrast that cuts the sweetness.*

½ (14.1-ounce) package refrigerated
pie dough (such as Pillsbury)
Cooking spray
½ cup maple syrup
½ cup dark corn syrup
2 tablespoons butter, melted
2 teaspoons cornstarch
½ teaspoon vanilla extract
¼ teaspoon salt
3 large eggs, lightly beaten
1½ cups fresh cranberries, coarsely
chopped
¾ cup coarsely chopped walnuts,
toasted

1. Preheat oven to 425°.
2. Roll dough into an 11-inch circle;
fit into a 9-inch pie plate coated
with cooking spray. Fold edges
under; flute. Line bottom of dough
with a piece of foil; arrange pie
weights or dried beans on foil. Bake
at 425° for 5 minutes. Remove pie
weights and foil; bake 1 minute.
Cool on a wire rack.
3. Reduce oven temperature to
350°.
4. Combine maple syrup and next
6 ingredients (through eggs) in a
medium bowl, stirring with a whisk.
Gently stir in cranberries and walnuts. Pour cranberry mixture into
prepared crust. Bake at 350° for 45
minutes or until filling is just set,
shielding edges of piecrust with foil
after 30 minutes. Cool on wire rack.
Serves 10 (serving size: 1 slice)

CALORIES 287; FAT 14.6g (sat 4.4g, mono 4g, poly 5.2g);
PROTEIN 4g; CARB 37g; FIBER 2g; CHOL 62mg;
IRON 1mg; SODIUM 210mg; CALC 32mg

Sautéed Green Beans with Spice-Glazed Pecans

Hands-on: 18 min. Total: 28 min.

2 tablespoons sugar
1 tablespoon water
¼ teaspoon ground cumin
¼ teaspoon ground red pepper
¾ cup coarsely chopped pecans
1 teaspoon minced fresh rosemary
½ teaspoon kosher salt, divided
2 pounds green beans, trimmed
2 tablespoons unsalted butter
¼ teaspoon freshly ground black
    pepper

1. Preheat oven to 350°. Line a jelly-roll pan with parchment paper.
2. Bring sugar, 1 tablespoon water, cumin, and red pepper to a boil in a small saucepan over medium heat, stirring constantly until sugar dissolves. Remove pan from heat; stir in pecans, rosemary, and ¼ teaspoon salt. Spread pecan mixture in an even layer on prepared pan. Bake at 350° for 12 minutes or until fragrant and browned. Cool in pan, stirring occasionally.
3. Place green beans in a large saucepan of boiling water; cook 4 minutes. Drain and plunge green beans into ice water; drain.
4. Melt butter in a large nonstick skillet over medium-high heat. Add beans; sauté 5 minutes or until thoroughly heated. Sprinkle ¼ teaspoon salt and black pepper over green beans; toss. Place beans on a serving platter; sprinkle with pecan mixture. Serve immediately. Serves 12 (serving size: about ¾ cup)

CALORIES 96; FAT 7g (sat 1.7g, mono 3.3g, poly 1.6g); PROTEIN 2g; CARB 8g; FIBER 3g; CHOL 5mg; IRON 1mg; SODIUM 85mg; CALC 34mg

Caramelized Onion and Garlic Mashed Potatoes

Hands-on: 15 min. Total: 30 min. You can respond to cries of "It's not Thanksgiving without mashed spuds!" by taking this classic to the next level: Think garlic-infused olive oil and sweet caramelized onions.

5 tablespoons extra-virgin olive oil,
    divided
2 medium onions, chopped
2½ pounds baking potatoes, peeled
    and cut into 1½-inch pieces
5 garlic cloves, crushed
1 cup 2% reduced-fat milk
¾ teaspoon kosher salt
¼ teaspoon black pepper

1. Heat a large skillet over medium heat. Add 1 tablespoon oil to pan; swirl to coat. Add onions; cook 16 minutes or until golden, stirring occasionally. Remove pan from heat.
2. Place potatoes in a large saucepan; cover with water to 2 inches above potatoes. Bring to a boil. Reduce heat, and simmer 14 minutes or until potatoes are tender. Drain. Return potatoes to pan; mash to desired consistency.
3. Combine 4 tablespoons oil and garlic in a small skillet; heat over medium-low heat 5 minutes or until garlic is lightly golden. Remove pan from heat; cool 3 minutes. Mash garlic into a paste with the back of a fork. Stir onion mixture, garlic mixture, milk, salt, and pepper into potato mixture. Return pan to medium heat; cook 3 minutes or until thoroughly heated. Serves 8 (serving size: about ½ cup)

CALORIES 216; FAT 9.2g (sat 1.6g, mono 6.3g, poly 1g); PROTEIN 4g; CARB 30g; FIBER 2g; CHOL 2mg; IRON 1mg; SODIUM 203mg; CALC 65mg

Rosemary Butter-Rubbed Turkey with Porcini Gravy

Hands-on: 60 min. Total: 2 hr. 50 min. Meaty shiitake and porcini mushrooms add incredible richness and depth to the gravy.

2 cups unsalted chicken stock
½ ounce dried porcini mushrooms
    (½ cup)
1 (12-pound) fresh or frozen turkey,
    thawed
5 tablespoons unsalted butter,
    softened and divided
1 tablespoon minced fresh garlic
1 tablespoon chopped fresh
    rosemary
1½ teaspoons kosher salt, divided
¾ teaspoon freshly ground black
    pepper, divided
10 garlic cloves
2 medium onions, chopped
2 celery stalks, chopped
2 carrots, chopped
Cooking spray
1 tablespoon olive oil
8 ounces shiitake mushroom caps,
    sliced
½ cup Madeira wine
3 tablespoons all-purpose flour

1. Preheat oven to 425°.
2. Bring stock to a boil in a small saucepan over medium-high heat; add porcini mushrooms. Remove pan from heat; let stand 15 minutes. Drain stock mixture in a colander over a bowl; reserve stock mixture. Chop porcini mushrooms; set aside.
3. Remove giblets and neck from turkey; discard liver. Pat turkey dry with paper towels; trim and discard excess fat. Starting at neck cavity, loosen skin from breast and drumsticks by inserting fingers, gently pushing between skin and meat. Combine 3 tablespoons butter, 1 tablespoon minced garlic, rosemary,

1 teaspoon salt, and ½ teaspoon pepper in a bowl. Rub butter mixture under loosened skin and over breasts and drumsticks. Lift wing tips up and over back; tuck under turkey. Tie legs together with kitchen string. Place reserved giblets, neck, 10 garlic cloves, onion, celery, and carrots in the bottom of a large roasting pan; add stock mixture to pan. Place roasting rack in pan; coat with cooking spray. Arrange turkey, breast side up, on roasting rack. Bake at 425° for 30 minutes. Cover turkey loosely with foil. Reduce oven temperature to 325° (do not remove turkey from oven). Bake 1 hour and 10 minutes or until a thermometer inserted into meaty part of thigh registers 165°. Remove pan from oven; place turkey on a cutting board. Let stand, covered, 20 minutes. Carve turkey.

4. Place a large zip-top plastic bag inside a 4-cup glass measure. Strain stock mixture through a sieve into bag; discard solids. Let stand 10 minutes. Seal bag; snip off 1 bottom corner of bag. Drain stock mixture into a bowl, stopping before fat reaches opening.

5. Heat a large nonstick skillet over medium-high heat. Add oil; swirl to coat. Add reserved porcini and shiitake mushrooms to pan; sauté 8 minutes. Add Madeira; cook 1 minute. Add stock mixture to pan; bring to a boil. Cook 3 minutes. Combine 2 tablespoons butter and flour in a small bowl. Gradually add butter mixture to stock mixture, stirring constantly with a whisk. Cook 2 minutes. Stir in ½ teaspoon salt and ¼ teaspoon pepper. Serve gravy with turkey. Serves 16 (serving size: 4 ounces turkey and about 2 tablespoons gravy)

CALORIES 297; FAT 10.9g (sat 4.3g, mono 3g, poly 2.2g); PROTEIN 39g; CARB 6g; FIBER 1g; CHOL 107mg; IRON 3mg; SODIUM 298mg; CALC 50mg

Make Ahead

Linguiça Sausage Stuffing with Mushrooms

Hands-on: 25 min. Total: 1 hr. 40 min.
This twist on a classic sausage and sourdough stuffing uses smoky Portuguese linguiça in place of crumbled pork sausage. Kielbasa or any smoked sausage would also work.

12 ounces sourdough bread, crusts removed and cubed
4 ounces linguiça sausage or kielbasa, halved lengthwise and cut into thin slices
1½ cups chopped onion
1 cup chopped celery
1 tablespoon thyme leaves
1 tablespoon minced fresh sage
½ teaspoon kosher salt, divided
½ cup chopped fresh flat-leaf parsley
1 tablespoon extra-virgin olive oil
½ pound cremini mushrooms, quartered
½ teaspoon freshly ground black pepper
2 cups unsalted chicken stock (such as Swanson)
2 large eggs, lightly beaten
Cooking spray

1. Preheat oven to 400°.
2. Arrange bread in a single layer on a baking sheet. Bake at 400° for 20 minutes or until toasted, stirring after 10 minutes. Place bread in a large bowl.
3. Reduce oven temperature to 350°.
4. Heat a large nonstick skillet over medium heat. Add sausage to pan; cook 2 minutes, turning to brown on all sides. Add sausage to bread. Return pan to medium-high heat. Add onion and celery to pan; sauté 5 minutes or until golden. Stir in thyme, sage, and ¼ teaspoon salt; sauté 1 minute. Add onion mixture and parsley to bread mixture; toss to combine.
5. Return pan to medium-high heat. Add oil; swirl to coat. Add mushrooms; sauté 5 minutes or until browned. Stir in ¼ teaspoon salt and pepper. Add mushroom mixture to bread mixture; toss to combine.
6. Combine stock and eggs in a bowl, stirring with a whisk. Add egg mixture to bread mixture; toss gently to combine. Let stand 5 minutes. Spoon bread mixture into an 11 x 7–inch glass or ceramic baking dish coated with cooking spray. Bake at 350° for 50 minutes or until browned. Serves 12 (serving size: about ¾ cup)

CALORIES 167; FAT 6.2g (sat 1.9g, mono 3g, poly 0.9g); PROTEIN 8g; CARB 20g; FIBER 1g; CHOL 39mg; IRON 2mg; SODIUM 386mg; CALC 38mg

QUICK & EASY

Here are time-saving shortcut recipes that free you up without compromising taste. The genius lies in the simplicity of every dish.

Kid Friendly • Quick & Easy
Gluten Free

Crispy Smashed Potatoes with Chive Sour Cream

Hands-on: 15 min. Total: 35 min. *These potatoes deliver the best of both worlds: creamy, starchy center and crisp, golden edges. To smash, place the back of a wide spatula over each potato, and then press with the heel of your hand.*

Cooking spray
2¹/₂ pounds small red potatoes
3 tablespoons extra-virgin olive oil, divided
³/₄ teaspoon kosher salt
¹/₄ teaspoon freshly ground black pepper
¹/₂ cup light sour cream
¹/₄ cup chopped fresh chives

1. Preheat oven to 500°. Place oven racks in upper and lower thirds of oven. Coat 2 jelly-roll pans with cooking spray.
2. Place potatoes on a microwave-safe plate; microwave at HIGH 8 minutes or until tender. Place potatoes in a bowl. Add 2 tablespoons oil, salt, and pepper; toss to coat. Divide potato mixture evenly between prepared pans. Using a spatula, flatten potatoes to about ½-inch thickness. Brush potatoes with 1 tablespoon oil. Bake at 500° for 10 minutes. Turn potatoes; rotate pans from front to back and top to bottom. Bake at 500° for 10 minutes or until browned and crisp. Place potatoes on a serving platter.
3. Combine sour cream and chopped chives in a small bowl, stirring with a whisk. Serve sour cream with potatoes. Serves 8 (serving size: ⅔ cup potatoes and about 1 tablespoon sour cream)

CALORIES 166; FAT 6.9g (sat 1.8g, mono 4.2g, poly 0.7g); PROTEIN 3g; CARB 24g; FIBER 2g; CHOL 5mg; IRON 1mg; SODIUM 217mg; CALC 38mg

Kid Friendly • Make Ahead
Vegetarian • Gluten Free

Honey-Roasted Butternut Squash

Hands-on: 12 min. Total: 1 hr. 12 min. *This side is simple and fabulous. The cooking is mostly hands-off, and the prep is easy. Serve the tender butternut squash in large pieces to catch every last bit of the honey butter drizzle.*

2 large butternut squash, halved lengthwise and seeded (about 4 pounds)
2 tablespoons honey
1¹/₂ tablespoons butter
¹/₂ teaspoon kosher salt
¹/₄ teaspoon freshly ground black pepper
2 tablespoons finely chopped toasted pecans
1 tablespoon minced fresh flat-leaf parsley

1. Preheat oven to 400°.
2. Place squash halves, cut sides up, on a foil-lined baking sheet. Place honey and butter in a microwave-safe bowl. Microwave at HIGH 30 seconds or until butter melts; stir to combine. Brush half of honey mixture over cut sides of squash; reserve remaining honey mixture. Sprinkle squash with salt and pepper. Bake at 400° for 1 hour or until tender.
3. Carefully place squash, cut sides up, on a cutting board. Halve squash lengthwise; cut each half crosswise into thirds. Place squash on a platter. Heat reserved butter mixture in microwave at HIGH 20 seconds. Drizzle remaining butter mixture over squash; sprinkle evenly with pecans and parsley. Serves 8 (serving size: 3 pieces)

CALORIES 133; FAT 3.6g (sat 1.5g, mono 1.3g, poly 0.5g); PROTEIN 2g; CARB 27g; FIBER 4g; CHOL 6mg; IRON 1mg; SODIUM 147mg; CALC 95mg

Kid Friendly • Quick & Easy
Make Ahead • Vegetarian
Gluten Free

Three-Ingredient Cranberry Sauce

Hands-on: 12 min. Total: 42 min. *You can "spike" your cranberry sauce by stirring in 1 to 2 tablespoons orange or black currant liqueur at the end. If you like it spiced, stir in ¹/₂ teaspoon ground cinnamon, ¹/₄ teaspoon ground nutmeg, and ¹/₄ teaspoon ground allspice.*

1 navel orange
1 cup sugar
¹/₄ cup water
1 (12-ounce) package fresh cranberries

1. Grate orange to yield 2 teaspoons rind. Cut orange in half; squeeze to yield ½ cup juice. Combine rind, juice, and remaining ingredients in a small saucepan; bring to a boil. Reduce heat to low, and simmer 7 minutes or until cranberries begin to pop. Remove from heat; cover and refrigerate at least 30 minutes. Serves 12 (serving size: about ¼ cup)

CALORIES 83; FAT 0.1g (sat 0g, mono 0g, poly 0g); PROTEIN 0g; CARB 21g; FIBER 1g; CHOL 0mg; IRON 0mg; SODIUM 1mg; CALC 4mg

Pecan-Pumpkin Drops

***Hands-on: 18 min. Total: 32 min.** Take canned pumpkin out of the pie shell realm and stir into tender drop biscuits. Serve them with a little honey butter.*

4.5 ounces all-purpose flour (about 1 cup)
4.75 ounces whole-wheat flour (about 1 cup)
2 tablespoons brown sugar
2 teaspoons baking powder
1/2 teaspoon baking soda
1/2 teaspoon salt
Dash of ground nutmeg
2 tablespoons cold butter, cut into small pieces
1 cup canned pumpkin
3/4 cup plus 1 tablespoon low-fat buttermilk
1/2 cup coarsely chopped pecans, toasted
Cooking spray

1. Preheat oven to 425°.
2. Weigh or lightly spoon flours into dry measuring cups; level with a knife. Combine flours, sugar, baking powder, baking soda, salt, and nutmeg in a bowl, stirring with a whisk; cut in butter with a pastry blender or 2 knives until mixture resembles coarse meal. Combine pumpkin and buttermilk in a bowl, stirring with a whisk. Add pumpkin mixture and chopped pecans to flour mixture, stirring just until combined.
3. Drop batter in mounds of about ⅓-cupfuls onto a baking sheet coated with cooking spray. Bake at 425° for 14 minutes or until golden. Remove from baking sheet; cool 5 minutes on a wire rack. Serve warm. Serves 12 (serving size: 1 biscuit)

CALORIES 148; **FAT** 5.9g (sat 1.7g, mono 2.4g, poly 1.2g); **PROTEIN** 4g; **CARB** 22g; **FIBER** 3g; **CHOL** 6mg; **IRON** 1mg; **SODIUM** 268mg; **CALC** 79mg

Sautéed Haricots Verts with Bacon Breadcrumbs

***Hands-on: 17 min. Total: 25 min.** Slender haricots verts get delightfully browned and crisp in the pan. A bacon breadcrumb topper makes them an instant crowd-pleaser.*

3 (12-ounce) packages haricots verts (French green beans), trimmed
1 (1-ounce) slice sourdough bread, torn into pieces
2 ounces thick-cut bacon, chopped
1 tablespoon olive oil
1/2 teaspoon kosher salt
1/2 teaspoon freshly ground black pepper

1. Place haricots verts in a saucepan of boiling water; cook 4 minutes. Drain and plunge into ice water; drain.
2. Place bread in a mini food processor; pulse until coarse crumbs form. Heat a large nonstick skillet over medium-high heat. Add bacon to pan; cook 5 minutes or until crisp, stirring occasionally. Remove bacon to a small bowl with a slotted spoon. Add breadcrumbs to pan; sauté 2 minutes. Add breadcrumb mixture to bacon. Add oil to pan; swirl to coat. Add haricots verts; cook 5 minutes or until lightly browned, stirring occasionally. Sprinkle with breadcrumb mixture, salt, and pepper. Serves 12 (serving size: about ¾ cup)

CALORIES 65; **FAT** 3.5g (sat 0.9g, mono 1.8g, poly 0.5g); **PROTEIN** 2g; **CARB** 7g; **FIBER** 2g; **CHOL** 3mg; **IRON** 1mg; **SODIUM** 137mg; **CALC** 33mg

Apple-Sage Stuffing Cups

***Hands-on: 20 min. Total: 45 min.** The muffin cups give you crispy edges and a tender interior in half the time, though the stuffing won't hold its shape like a traditional muffin. Presliced bread and prechopped onion and celery save time.*

12 ounces sourdough bread, cut into ½-inch cubes (about 8 cups)
1½ tablespoons butter
1½ cups diced apple
1¼ cups prechopped onion
2/3 cup prechopped celery
1½ tablespoons chopped fresh sage
1/2 teaspoon black pepper
1/4 teaspoon kosher salt
1/4 cup chopped fresh flat-leaf parsley
1¾ cups unsalted chicken stock
2 large eggs, lightly beaten
Cooking spray

1. Preheat oven to 375°.
2. Arrange bread in a single layer on a baking sheet. Bake at 375° for 15 minutes or until toasted, stirring after 8 minutes. Place bread in a large bowl.
3. Melt butter in a large skillet over medium heat. Add apple, onion, celery, sage, pepper, and salt; sauté 5 minutes or until tender. Add apple mixture to bread in large bowl; toss to combine. Stir in parsley.
4. Combine stock and eggs in a small bowl, stirring with a whisk. Add stock mixture to bread mixture, stirring gently to combine.
5. Divide bread mixture evenly among 12 muffin cups coated with cooking spray (about ½ cup each). Bake at 375° for 20 minutes or until lightly browned. Serves 12 (serving size: 1 muffin cup)

CALORIES 127; **FAT** 2.9g (sat 1.3g, mono 0.8g, poly 0.5g); **PROTEIN** 5g; **CARB** 20g; **FIBER** 1g; **CHOL** 35mg; **IRON** 1mg; **SODIUM** 235mg; **CALC** 31mg

Mocha Pie with Coffee Whipped Cream

Hands-on: 33 min. Total: 2 hr. This pie comes together quickly and won't hog oven space as it chills and sets in the fridge (a great make-ahead option). You can use decaf instant coffee granules instead of regular, or leave them out entirely for a silky-smooth chocolate pie with vanilla topping.

6.3 ounces chocolate wafers (about 30; such as Nabisco Famous Chocolate Wafers)
5 teaspoons instant coffee granules, divided
3 tablespoons butter, divided
1 tablespoon canola oil
1 large egg white, lightly beaten
Cooking spray
1/3 cup packed light brown sugar
3 tablespoons cornstarch
3 tablespoons unsweetened cocoa
1/8 teaspoon salt
1 (12-ounce) can fat-free evaporated milk
1/2 cup semisweet chocolate chips
1/3 cup heavy cream
1 tablespoon powdered sugar
1 teaspoon vanilla extract
2 tablespoons plain 2% reduced-fat Greek yogurt

1. Preheat oven to 350°.
2. Place chocolate wafers in the bowl of a food processor; process until finely ground. Place ground wafers in a bowl. Stir in 1 teaspoon instant coffee granules; 1 tablespoon butter, melted; oil; and 2 tablespoons egg white (discard remaining egg white). Press chocolate wafer mixture into bottom and up the sides of a 9-inch pie plate coated with cooking spray. Bake at 350° for 8 minutes. Cool crust 15 minutes on a wire rack.
3. Bring 1 tablespoon instant coffee granules, brown sugar, and next 4 ingredients to a simmer in a medium saucepan over medium heat, stirring constantly. Stir in 2 tablespoons butter, stirring until butter melts. Cook 18 minutes or until thickened. Remove pan from heat; add chocolate chips, stirring until smooth. Pour chocolate mixture into prepared crust. Refrigerate 1½ hours or until firm.
4. Place 1 teaspoon instant coffee granules, heavy cream, powdered sugar, and vanilla in a medium bowl; beat with an electric mixer at medium speed until soft peaks form. Add yogurt; beat just until smooth. Spoon cream mixture over center of pie. Serves 12 (serving size: 1 slice)

CALORIES 220; **FAT** 10.7g (sat 5.4g, mono 3.6g, poly 0.8g); **PROTEIN** 4g; **CARB** 29g; **FIBER** 1g; **CHOL** 19mg; **IRON** 1mg; **SODIUM** 189mg; **CALC** 85mg

Fennel and Cumin-Roasted Turkey Breast with Thyme Gravy

Hands-on: 25 min. Total: 2 hr. 10 min.

1 (5-pound) bone-in turkey breast
1 tablespoon extra-virgin olive oil
1 tablespoon ground cumin
1 teaspoon kosher salt, divided
1 teaspoon fennel seeds, crushed
5/8 teaspoon freshly ground black pepper, divided
2 garlic cloves, minced
1 medium onion, finely chopped
1 celery stalk, finely chopped
1 carrot, finely chopped
4 thyme sprigs
Cooking spray
2 cups unsalted chicken stock
2 tablespoons unsalted butter
1/2 teaspoon chopped fresh thyme
2 tablespoons all-purpose flour

1. Preheat oven to 400°.
2. Loosen skin from turkey breast by inserting fingers, gently pushing between skin and meat. Combine oil, cumin, ¾ teaspoon salt, fennel seeds, ½ teaspoon pepper, and garlic, stirring with a whisk. Rub spice mixture under loosened skin and over breast. Place onion, celery, carrot, and thyme sprigs in bottom of a large roasting pan coated with cooking spray. Arrange breast, skin side up, on vegetable mixture. Add stock to pan. Bake at 400° for 1 hour and 30 minutes or until a thermometer registers 165°. Remove from oven; place breast on a cutting board. Let stand, covered, 15 minutes. Remove meat from bones. Cut diagonally across grain into 16 slices; discard skin and bones.
3. Place a large zip-top plastic bag inside a 2-cup glass measure. Pour the stock mixture through a sieve into bag; discard solids. Let stand 10 minutes. Seal bag; snip off 1 bottom corner. Drain stock mixture into a bowl, stopping before fat layer reaches opening. Melt butter in a large saucepan over medium heat. Add ½ teaspoon chopped thyme; sauté 1 minute. Add flour; cook 3 minutes or until caramel-colored, whisking constantly. Stir in stock mixture. Increase heat to medium-high. Cook 5 minutes or until slightly thickened, stirring occasionally. Stir in ¼ teaspoon salt and ⅛ teaspoon pepper. Serve with turkey. Serves 10 (serving size: 4 ounces turkey and 1½ tablespoons gravy)

CALORIES 247; **FAT** 5g (sat 2g, mono 1.8g, poly 0.5g); **PROTEIN** 44g; **CARB** 4g; **FIBER** 1g; **CHOL** 124mg; **IRON** 3mg; **SODIUM** 301mg; **CALC** 40mg

PARTY TRICKS WITH HOLIDAY LEFTOVERS

From the turkey to the veggies to the pie, Thanksgiving has the building blocks for a "Friendsgiving" after-party that will save you time and gain you raves.

You'll want to make extra food for Thanksgiving just to have enough leftovers for the casual party menu that unfolds on the following pages. Invite your inner circle of food-loving friends who'll relish a post–Turkey Day veer from the traditional track. Serve up little plates to keep the whole gathering light and fun. Happy Friendsgiving!

Kid Friendly • Quick & Easy
Cranberry-Hoisin Turkey Buns

Hands-on: 30 min. Total: 30 min.
Look for frozen Chinese steamed buns at Asian specialty grocery stores. Or, if you'd rather, you can substitute mini pita breads for the buns.

1 cup rice vinegar
1 tablespoon sugar
2 teaspoons kosher salt
2 cups thinly sliced English cucumber
14 frozen Chinese steamed buns
2¹/₂ cups leftover shredded skinless white meat turkey (about 12¹/₂ ounces)
2¹/₂ tablespoons hoisin sauce
¹/₃ cup cranberry sauce
4 green onions, cut into (1-inch) pieces

1. Combine first 3 ingredients in a small saucepan over high heat, stirring until sugar dissolves. Pour vinegar mixture over cucumber. Let stand 20 minutes; drain.
2. Prepare buns according to package directions.
3. Combine turkey and hoisin in a bowl; toss to coat. Spread 1 teaspoon cranberry sauce on each bun. Top evenly with turkey mixture, cucumbers and onions. Serves 14 (serving size: 1 bun)

CALORIES 115; FAT 1.3g (sat 0.1g, mono 0.1g, poly 0.1g); PROTEIN 11g; CARB 5g; FIBER 0g; CHOL 21mg; IRON 1mg; SODIUM 200mg; CALC 10mg

> ## LEFTOVER:
>
> **TURKEY AND CRANBERRY SAUCE**
> With its zippy, tangy flavor, cranberry sauce makes a natural partner for sweetly spiced hoisin sauce. Add quick-pickled cukes and pillowy Chinese buns, and the bird takes a delicious detour East.

Quick & Easy • Make Ahead
Gluten Free
Cider Sangria

Hands-on: 15 min. Total: 35 min.

¹/₂ cup water
¹/₄ cup sugar
3 cinnamon sticks
³/₄ cup brandy
1 apple, cored and diced
1 pear, cored and diced
1 cup black seedless or Concord grapes
3¹/₂ cups leftover dry white wine, such as sauvignon blanc (a little more than 1 [750-milliliter] bottle)
1³/₄ cups sparkling apple-cranberry cider (such as Martinelli's)

1. Combine ½ cup water, sugar, and cinnamon sticks in a small saucepan over medium-high heat; cook until sugar dissolves, stirring as needed to dissolve sugar. Pour mixture into a large bowl; cool about 10 minutes. Stir in brandy. Add apple and pear; toss to coat. Cool completely.
2. Strain brandy mixture into a large pitcher, reserving apples and pears. Discard cinnamon sticks. Thread apples, pears, and grapes onto 10 short skewers or cocktail picks. Return any remaining fruit to the pitcher. Stir in wine and cider. Fill 10 glasses with ice. Divide punch evenly among glasses; garnish each glass with a fruit skewer. Serves 10 (serving size: ¾ cup and 1 skewer)

CALORIES 175; FAT 0.1g (sat 0g, mono 0g, poly 0g); PROTEIN 0g; CARB 22g; FIBER 2g; CHOL 0mg; IRON 4mg; SODIUM 5mg; CALC 13mg

> ## LEFTOVER:
>
> **WINE**
> Make the most of day-old wine by turning it into a lightly spiced, brandy-enhanced punch. Throw in some fresh fruit to soak up the flavors, and you have a happy, crowd-pleasing concoction.

Savory Harvest Vegetable Tart with Toasted Quinoa Crust

Hands-on: 25 min. Total: 35 min.

1 cup uncooked quinoa
½ cup almond meal
1 tablespoon cornstarch
¼ teaspoon kosher salt
2 tablespoons olive oil
1 large egg, beaten
Cooking spray
2 tablespoons chopped fresh parsley
1 tablespoon finely minced shallot
½ teaspoon coarsely ground black pepper
2 ounces ⅓-less-fat cream cheese, softened
2 ounces goat cheese, softened
2 cups chopped leftover roasted vegetables (such as carrots, acorn squash, Brussels sprouts, onions, and parsnips), at room temperature
2 tablespoons torn parsley leaves
1 tablespoon balsamic glaze

1. Preheat oven to 350°.
2. Place quinoa on a jelly-roll pan. Bake at 350° for 10 minutes or until golden brown; cool. Place half of quinoa in a food processor; pulse 30 seconds. Transfer to a large bowl. Add remaining toasted quinoa, almond meal, cornstarch, and salt to bowl; stir to combine. Add oil and egg; stir until mixture is crumbly but holds together when pressed. Press into bottom and up sides of a 4 x 13–inch removable-bottom tart pan coated with cooking spray. Bake at 350° for 15 minutes or until golden and crisp; cool completely on a wire rack.
3. While crust cools, combine chopped parsley, shallot, black pepper, cream cheese, and goat cheese, stirring until smooth; spread evenly in bottom of crust. Arrange vegetables evenly over cheese mixture; top with parsley leaves. Remove tart from pan; drizzle with balsamic glaze. Serves 12 (serving size: 1 [2-inch] tart wedge)

CALORIES 145; FAT 8.6g (sat 2.1g, mono 3g, poly 1g); PROTEIN 5g; CARB 13g; FIBER 2g; CHOL 21mg; IRON 1mg; SODIUM 115mg; CALC 26mg

LEFTOVER:

ROASTED VEGETABLES
The brilliant use of whole-grain quinoa for a press-in-the-pan tart shell hits all the right marks. Toasting the grain adds nutty crunch to the foolproof crust. Peppered goat cheese and a colorful crown of caramelized veggies make this dish simply spectacular.

Potato Pancakes with Salmon

Hands-on: 35 min. Total: 35 min.
Serve pancakes with a dollop of applesauce in place of the fish for a fast meat-free option.

½ cup reduced-fat sour cream
1 teaspoon freshly grated lemon rind
½ teaspoon freshly ground black pepper, divided
2 cups leftover mashed potatoes (about 15 ounces)
6 tablespoons all-purpose flour
½ teaspoon baking powder
⅛ teaspoon kosher salt
1 large egg
1 large egg white, beaten
½ small yellow onion, minced
2 tablespoons safflower oil, divided
¼ pound thinly sliced smoked salmon, torn into bite-sized pieces
1 to 2 tablespoons chopped fresh chives

1. Preheat oven to 200°. Place a wire rack on a baking sheet.
2. Combine sour cream, lemon rind, and ¼ teaspoon pepper in a small bowl. Cover and chill.
3. Combine potatoes, flour, baking powder, ¼ teaspoon pepper, salt, egg, egg white, and onion in a medium bowl. Heat a large nonstick skillet over medium heat. Add 1½ teaspoons oil; swirl to coat. Scoop about 1½ tablespoons potato batter per pancake onto hot pan, for a total of 8 pancakes; flatten each slightly. Cook pancakes 2 to 3 minutes on each side or until golden brown. Place pancakes on rack on baking sheet; place in oven to keep warm. Repeat procedure in 3 more batches with remaining oil and remaining potato batter. Top pancakes with sour cream mixture, salmon, and chives. Serves 16 (serving size: 2 pancakes, ¼ ounce salmon, and about 1¾ teaspoons sour cream mixture)

CALORIES 81; FAT 4g (sat 1.3g, mono 0.6g, poly 1.4g); PROTEIN 3g; CARB 8g; FIBER 1g; CHOL 21mg; IRON 0mg; SODIUM 187mg; CALC 33mg

LEFTOVER:

MASHED POTATOES
Little potato pancakes take almost no time to pat together, and they quickly sauté to golden-brown perfection. Topped with smoked salmon, sour cream, and chives, they're an elegant party nibble.

Spicy Turkey Lettuce Wraps

Hands-on: 25 min. Total: 25 min.

1 tablespoon safflower oil
1 medium yellow onion, finely
  chopped
2 garlic cloves, minced
½ cup water
3 tablespoons cranberry sauce
2 teaspoons adobo sauce
1 small chipotle chile (canned in
  adobo sauce), chopped
2 cups leftover shredded skinless
  turkey breast (about 9 ounces)
1 cup cooked brown rice
10 Bibb lettuce leaves
3 julienne-cut radishes
⅓ cup cilantro leaves
½ cup tomatillo salsa

1. Heat a large skillet over medium-high heat. Add 1 tablespoon oil to pan; swirl to coat. Add onion; cook 4 minutes or until soft. Add garlic; cook 30 seconds or until fragrant. Add ½ cup water, cranberry sauce, adobo sauce, and chipotle chile. Cook 4 minutes or until mixture thickens. Stir in turkey; cook 2 minutes or until thoroughly heated. Remove from heat; set aside.
2. Divide rice and turkey mixture evenly among lettuce leaves; top with radishes and cilantro. Serve wraps with salsa. Serves 10 (serving size: 1 wrap and about ¾ teaspoon salsa)

CALORIES 90; FAT 1.9g (sat 0.2g, mono 0.3g, poly 1.1g); PROTEIN 9g; CARB 9g; FIBER 1g; CHOL 21mg; IRON 1mg; SODIUM 96mg; CALC 18mg

LEFTOVER:

TURKEY BREAST AND CRANBERRY SAUCE
Here's a low-carb twist on a taco: shredded white-meat turkey dressed with cranberry sauce spiced with adobo and chipotle. Tuck it into tender lettuce leaves.

Crispy Green Beans with Sriracha Mayo

Hands-on: 15 min. Total: 30 min. No leftovers? Sub in a bag of microwaved steamed beans.

¼ cup canola mayonnaise
¼ cup low-fat buttermilk
2 teaspoons Sriracha
1 tablespoon fresh lime juice
2½ cups whole-wheat panko
  (Japanese breadcrumbs)
2 teaspoons thyme leaves
1 teaspoon garlic powder
½ teaspoon ground red pepper
⅛ teaspoon kosher salt
½ cup all-purpose flour
4 large egg whites, beaten
1 pound leftover steamed green beans

1. Preheat oven to 375°.
2. Combine mayonnaise, buttermilk, Sriracha, and lime juice in a small bowl; cover and chill.
3. Place panko in an even layer on a baking sheet. Bake at 375° for 4 minutes or until golden. Transfer panko to a shallow dish; cool completely. Add thyme, garlic powder, pepper, and salt; toss well. Place flour in a shallow dish. Place egg whites in another shallow dish. Dredge half of green beans in flour. Dip in egg whites; dredge in panko mixture. Place beans on a baking sheet. Repeat procedure with remaining beans, flour, egg whites, and panko mixture. Place remaining coated beans on another baking sheet. Bake green beans at 375° for 8 minutes or until crisp. Serve with Sriracha dip. Serves 8 (serving size: about ¾ cup beans and 1 tablespoon dip)

CALORIES 151; FAT 2.8g (sat 0.1g, mono 1.2g, poly 0.8g); PROTEIN 7g; CARB 24g; FIBER 3g; CHOL 0mg; IRON 1mg; SODIUM 198mg; CALC 38mg

LEFTOVER:

GREEN BEANS
Day-old veggies become irresistible crunchy munching sticks thanks to a coarse breadcrumb coating. Tangy chile dip takes flavors to the spicy edge.

Buttermilk-Pumpkin Pie Ice Cream

Hands-on: 20 min. Total: 3 hr. 50 min. Sandwich the ice cream between thin chocolate wafers for an easy ice-cream sandwich.

1 cup sugar, divided
6 large egg yolks
1½ cups half-and-half
1 cup evaporated fat-free milk
1 cup low-fat buttermilk
12 ounces leftover pumpkin pie
  (about [½] 9-inch pie), chilled and
  cut into small slices

1. Combine ½ cup sugar and egg yolks in a large bowl, stirring with a whisk until mixture is pale.
2. Combine half-and-half, evaporated milk, and ½ cup sugar in a medium saucepan; bring to a gentle boil over medium heat, stirring occasionally, until sugar is dissolved. Gradually add half of hot milk mixture to egg mixture, stirring constantly with a whisk; return milk-egg mixture to pan. Cook over medium-low heat 6 minutes or until mixture thickens and coats a rubber spatula, stirring constantly with spatula. Strain through a sieve into a large bowl set over a larger ice-filled bowl. Let stand until cool, stirring occasionally. Add buttermilk, stirring with a whisk. Pour into an airtight container; cover and chill 30 minutes. *continued*

3. Pour mixture into the freezer can of an ice-cream freezer; freeze according to manufacturer's instructions. Add pie just before removing ice cream and while machine is still churning. Remove ice cream to an airtight container; freeze 3 hours or until firm. Serves 12 (serving size: ¾ cup)

CALORIES 214; FAT 8.6g (sat 4g, mono 3.1g, poly 1g); PROTEIN 6g; CARB 29g; FIBER 0g; CHOL 117mg; IRON 1mg; SODIUM 126mg; CALC 115mg

LEFTOVER:

PUMPKIN PIE
This has to be the coolest way to serve pie "à la mode." Churn creamy spiced pumpkin pie into a rich custard for an all-in-one ice-cream treat. What a great way to stretch those last couple of slices into a festive new dessert.

Kid Friendly • Freezable
Make Ahead

Chocolate Pecan Pie Truffles

Hands-on: 20 min. Total: 1 hr. 20 min.

16 ounces pecan pie (about ½ pie), chilled and cut into 3-inch pieces
¼ cup unsweetened cocoa
1½ tablespoons bourbon
7½ ounces chopped dry-roasted, salted almonds, divided

1. Place pie in a food processor; pulse 30 seconds or until mixture resembles chunky peanut butter. Add cocoa, bourbon, and 4 ounces almonds; pulse 3 to 4 times or until combined. Remove mixture to a bowl; cover and chill 1 hour.
2. Line a baking sheet with parchment paper. Drop pecan pie mixture by 2 teaspoonfuls onto baking sheet to form 48 balls. Place in freezer 1 hour or until truffles are firm.

3. While truffles chill, very finely chop remaining almonds; place in a shallow dish. Remove truffles from freezer; gently shape each mound into a ball. Roll truffles in nuts to coat. Keep truffles chilled in an airtight container. Let stand 2 or 3 minutes at room temperature before serving. Serves 24 (serving size: 2 truffles)

CALORIES 119; FAT 7.9g (sat 1.2g, mono 4.1g, poly 1.7g); PROTEIN 3g; CARB 10g; FIBER 1g; CHOL 10mg; IRON 1mg; SODIUM 72mg; CALC 33mg

LEFTOVER:

PECAN PIE
This rich confection is a mash-up of cocoa and pecan pie, plus a little hooch for good measure. Rolling the truffles in dry-roasted almonds adds just the right amount of salty crunch along with each luscious bite.

A FEAST OF HOLIDAY SIDES

24 supersimple veggie, pasta, and grain side dishes to get your family through the season.

Quick & Easy • Make Ahead
Vegetarian
1. Carrot-Cilantro Bulgur
Combine ¾ cup uncooked bulgur and 2 cups water in a small saucepan; bring to a boil. Cover, reduce heat, and cook 12 minutes. Drain; rinse with cold water. Drain. Stir in ¾ cup shredded carrot, 2 tablespoons chopped fresh cilantro, 2 tablespoons fresh lime juice, 1½ tablespoons extra-virgin olive oil, ¾ teaspoon kosher salt, and ¼ teaspoon freshly ground black pepper. Serves 4 (serving size: about ⅔ cup)

CALORIES 145; FAT 5.5g (sat 0.8g); SODIUM 259mg

Kid Friendly • Quick & Easy
Vegetarian • Gluten Free
2. Mushroom Grits
Boil 3 cups water in a saucepan. Add ¾ cup uncooked quick-cooking grits and ¼ teaspoon kosher salt, stirring constantly. Bring to a boil; cover and reduce heat to low. Cook 7 minutes or until thick, stirring frequently. Melt 1 tablespoon butter in a nonstick skillet over medium heat. Add 8 ounces sliced mushrooms, 1 minced garlic clove, ⅛ teaspoon black pepper, and ⅛ teaspoon kosher salt; cook 8 minutes, stirring occasionally. Stir mushroom mixture into grits. Top with parsley. Serves 4 (serving size: about ¾ cup)

CALORIES 147; FAT 3.6g (sat 2g); SODIUM 209mg

Kid Friendly • Quick & Easy
Vegetarian
3. Pasta with Sugar Snap Peas and Ricotta Cheese
Cook 4 ounces uncooked trottole pasta according to package directions, omitting salt and fat; add 4 ounces sugar snap peas (1¼ cups) during last 3 minutes of cooking time. Drain. Combine pasta mixture, ½ cup part-skim ricotta cheese, 1 tablespoon chopped fresh chives, ¼ teaspoon kosher salt, and ⅛ teaspoon freshly ground black pepper. Serves 4 (serving size: about ¾ cup)

CALORIES 158; FAT 2.9g (sat 1.7g); SODIUM 160mg

Kid Friendly • Quick & Easy
Vegetarian
4. Baked Fennel Parmigiana
Preheat oven to 400°. Slice 1 trimmed fennel bulb lengthwise into ½-inch slices. Place in a microwave- and oven-safe dish; cover and microwave at HIGH 3 minutes. Top with ⅔ cup lower-sodium marinara, ½ cup shredded part-skim mozzarella, and 2 tablespoons grated fresh Parmesan cheese. Bake at 400° for 20 minutes or until golden. Serves 4 (serving size: about ½ cup)

CALORIES 98; FAT 5g (sat 2g); SODIUM 244mg

5. Wild Rice with Squash

Place 5 cups water and ⅔ cup un-cooked wild rice in a saucepan; bring to a boil. Cover, reduce heat, and simmer 30 minutes. Turn off heat; let stand, covered, 25 minutes. Drain. Heat a skillet over medium heat; add 1½ tablespoons olive oil. Add 1½ cups (½-inch) cubed peeled butternut squash, 1 chopped shallot, 1 teaspoon chopped fresh rosemary, and ⅛ teaspoon salt; cook 10 minutes. Add rice, ⅛ teaspoon freshly ground black pepper, and ¼ teaspoon salt to squash, stirring to combine. Serves 4 (serving size: about 1 cup)

CALORIES 169; FAT 5.4g (sat 0.8g); SODIUM 185mg

Kid Friendly • Quick & Easy
Gluten Free

6. Asparagus with Crispy Pancetta

Cut 1.5 ounces pancetta into matchsticks; cook in a nonstick skillet 3 minutes or until crisp. Drain on paper towels. Cook 1 pound trimmed asparagus spears in boiling water 2 minutes or until crisp-tender; drain. Sprinkle pancetta over asparagus. Season with ¼ teaspoon freshly ground black pepper and 1½ tablespoons fresh lemon juice. Serves 4 (serving size: about 3 ounces asparagus)

CALORIES 70; FAT 4.3g (sat 1.6g); SODIUM 158mg

Kid Friendly • Quick & Easy
Make Ahead • Vegetarian
Gluten Free

7. Garlic-Parmesan Rice

Heat a saucepan over medium heat. Add 1 tablespoon olive oil; swirl. Add 1 minced garlic clove; sauté 30 seconds. Add 1 cup uncooked basmati rice; cook 1 minute, stirring constantly. Add 2 cups water; bring to a boil. Cover, reduce heat, and simmer 12 minutes or until liquid is absorbed. Remove from heat. Let stand 5 minutes. Stir in 1 tablespoon

chopped fresh flat-leaf parsley, ¼ teaspoon kosher salt, ⅛ teaspoon black pepper, and 1 ounce grated fresh Parmesan cheese. Serves 4 (serving size: about ¾ cup)

CALORIES 242; FAT 5.4g (sat 1.7g); SODIUM 229mg

Kid Friendly • Quick & Easy
Make Ahead • Vegetarian
Gluten Free

8. Butternut Squash with Orange

Sauté 6 cups diced peeled butternut squash in 2½ teaspoons olive oil in a Dutch oven over medium-high heat 2 minutes; cover, reduce heat to low, and cook 12 to 15 minutes or just until tender when pierced with a knife. Toss with 2 teaspoons butter, 2 tablespoons finely grated orange rind, and ¼ cup fresh orange juice; puree with an immersion blender until smooth. Season with ¼ teaspoon salt and ½ teaspoon freshly ground black pepper. Serves 4 (serving size: about ¾ cup)

CALORIES 147; FAT 5g (sat 1.7g); SODIUM 173mg

Kid Friendly • Quick & Easy
Vegetarian • Gluten Free

9. Green Beans with Walnuts

Cook 1 pound trimmed green beans in boiling water 30 seconds; plunge into a bowl of ice water. Drain. Drizzle with 1 tablespoon walnut oil, ⅜ teaspoon fine sea salt, and ¼ teaspoon freshly ground black pepper. Top with 2 tablespoons chopped toasted walnuts. Serves 4 (serving size: about 3 ounces green beans)

CALORIES 89; FAT 6g (sat 0.6g); SODIUM 187mg

Kid Friendly • Quick & Easy
Vegetarian • Gluten Free

10. Roasted Rosemary Rutabaga Fries

Preheat oven to 425°. Peel and cut 2 medium rutabagas into ¼-inch slices; stack and cut into ¼-inch sticks. Toss with 2 tablespoons finely chopped fresh rosemary, 1½ table-

spoons olive oil, ⅜ teaspoon kosher salt, and ½ teaspoon freshly ground black pepper. Roast at 425° for 12 to 15 minutes, shaking pan often, until browned and tender. Serves 4 (serving size: about 4 ounces)

CALORIES 116; FAT 5.5g (sat 0.8g); SODIUM 219mg

Kid Friendly • Quick & Easy
Gluten Free

11. Quinoa with Broccoli and Bacon

Heat ¾ cup uncooked rinsed quinoa in a saucepan over medium-high heat; sauté 2 minutes. Add 1 cup water; bring to a boil. Cover, reduce heat, and simmer 13 minutes. Remove from heat; let stand 2 minutes. Heat 1 teaspoon olive oil in a saucepan over medium-high heat. Add 2 cups fresh broccoli florets; sauté 2 minutes. Add 2 tablespoons water; cover and reduce heat. Cook 2 minutes. Combine quinoa, broccoli, 2 teaspoons olive oil, ⅛ teaspoon salt, and 2 cooked and crumbled bacon slices. Serves 4 (serving size: about 1 cup)

CALORIES 170; FAT 6.4g (sat 1.2g); SODIUM 139mg

Kid Friendly • Quick & Easy
Vegetarian • Gluten Free

12. Sweet Potatoes with Spiced Yogurt and Honey

Pierce 4 small sweet potatoes with a knife; microwave at HIGH 8 to 10 minutes, turning halfway through. Combine ½ cup 2% reduced-fat Greek yogurt, 1 teaspoon pumpkin pie spice, 1 teaspoon grated orange rind, and ⅛ teaspoon ground red pepper. Halve potatoes lengthwise; sprinkle with ½ teaspoon kosher salt. Divide yogurt mixture among potatoes, spreading to cover. Drizzle with 1 teaspoon honey. Serves 4 (serving size: 1 potato, 2 tablespoons yogurt mixture, and ¼ teaspoon honey)

CALORIES 138; FAT 0.7g (sat 0.4g); SODIUM 321mg

Kid Friendly • Quick & Easy
Vegetarian

13. Sugar Snap Peas with Ginger and Soy

Steam 3 cups sugar snap peas 5 minutes or until crisp-tender. Combine 1½ tablespoons lower-sodium soy sauce, 2 teaspoons rice vinegar, ½ teaspoon grated peeled fresh ginger, and 1½ tablespoons olive oil in a lidded jar; shake to combine, and pour over peas. Serves 4 (serving size: about ¾ cup)

CALORIES 69; FAT 5.2g (sat 0.7g); SODIUM 218mg

Kid Friendly • Quick & Easy
Make Ahead

14. Louisiana Red Beans

Sauté 1 ounce diced andouille sausage in a skillet over medium heat 2 minutes. Add ½ cup sliced celery, ¼ cup diced onion, ¼ cup diced bell pepper, 1 teaspoon salt-free Creole seasoning, 1 bay leaf, 1 thyme sprig, and 2 minced garlic cloves; sauté 5 minutes. Add 2 (15-ounce) cans unsalted drained red kidney beans and 1 cup unsalted chicken stock. Bring to a boil; simmer 5 minutes. Stir in 1 tablespoon chopped parsley. Remove bay leaf and thyme sprig. Serves 4 (serving size: about ¾ cup)

CALORIES 120; FAT 1.3g (sat 0.5g); SODIUM 207mg

Kid Friendly • Quick & Easy
Vegetarian • Gluten Free

15. Rustic Garlic Mashed Potatoes

Place 2 pounds unpeeled baking potatoes, quartered lengthwise, and 1 peeled garlic head in a saucepan filled with water to cover; bring to a boil. Reduce heat, and simmer 15 minutes or until potatoes are tender. Drain and transfer to a bowl; mash with ¾ cup hot 1% low-fat milk, 1½ tablespoons melted butter, ½ teaspoon salt, and ¼ teaspoon black pepper. Serves 4 (serving size: about 1 cup)

CALORIES 254; FAT 5g (sat 3.1g); SODIUM 274mg

Quick & Easy • Vegetarian
Gluten Free

16. Steamed Spinach with Curry Butter

Heat 1 tablespoon unsalted butter and 1 tablespoon mild curry powder in a large Dutch oven; cook 2 minutes. Add 2 (16-ounce) containers fresh spinach in batches; cook 3 to 5 minutes or just until wilted. Remove from heat; stir in 1 tablespoon fresh orange juice, ⅛ teaspoon kosher salt, and ½ teaspoon ground red pepper. Serves 4 (serving size: about 1½ cups)

CALORIES 85; FAT 4g (sat 2g); SODIUM 240mg

Kid Friendly • Quick & Easy
Make Ahead • Vegetarian
Gluten Free

17. Carrots with Lemon and Thyme

Combine 1 pound carrots, cut diagonally into ¼-inch slices, and 5 (¼-inch-thick) slices lemon in a small saucepan; fill with water just to cover. Bring to a boil; simmer 20 minutes. Drain; discard lemon. Season with ¼ teaspoon kosher salt, ½ teaspoon freshly ground black pepper, and 1 tablespoon chopped fresh thyme. Serves 4 (serving size: about ½ cup)

CALORIES 52; FAT 0.3g (sat 0.1g); SODIUM 198mg

Kid Friendly • Quick & Easy
Vegetarian

18. Broccoli and Penne with Asiago

Cook 4 ounces penne pasta according to package directions, omitting salt and fat. Add 2 cups broccoli florets during last 3 minutes of cooking; drain. Add 1.5 ounces shredded Asiago cheese, 1 tablespoon extra-virgin olive oil, ⅛ teaspoon kosher salt, and ⅛ teaspoon freshly ground black pepper. Serves 4 (serving size: about ¾ cup)

CALORIES 185; FAT 7.3g (sat 2.5g); SODIUM 174mg

Quick & Easy • Vegetarian
Gluten Free

19. Wilted Kale with Golden Raisins and Pecans

Sauté 2 thinly sliced shallots in 1 tablespoon olive oil in a Dutch oven over medium-high heat 4 minutes; add ¼ cup loosely packed golden raisins and 2 tablespoons chopped pecans to pan, and cook 1 additional minute. Add 1 pound stemmed chopped Lacinato kale; cook 3 minutes or until kale wilts. Season with ¼ teaspoon kosher salt and ¼ teaspoon freshly ground black pepper. Serves 4 (serving size: about 1 cup)

CALORIES 148; FAT 6.7g (sat 0.8g); SODIUM 172mg

Kid Friendly • Make Ahead
Vegetarian

20. Lemon-Rosemary Barley

Combine ¾ cup uncooked pearl barley and 3 cups water in a saucepan; bring to a boil. Cover, reduce heat, and cook 50 minutes. Drain. Heat a skillet over medium heat. Add 2 teaspoons extra-virgin olive oil. Add ¾ cup chopped onion and 1 teaspoon chopped fresh rosemary; cook 5 minutes, stirring frequently until onion is lightly browned. Combine barley, onion mixture, 2 teaspoons extra-virgin olive oil, ½ teaspoon grated lemon rind, and ⅜ teaspoon kosher salt. Serves 4 (serving size: about ¾ cup)

CALORIES 184; FAT 5g (sat 0.7g); SODIUM 185mg

Kid Friendly • Quick & Easy
Vegetarian • Gluten Free

21. Goat Cheese and Basil Polenta

Bring 3 cups water to a boil in a medium saucepan. Gradually add 1 cup dry polenta, stirring constantly with a whisk. Reduce heat to low; cook 7 minutes, stirring occasionally. Remove from heat; stir in 3 ounces goat cheese, 1 tablespoon chopped fresh basil, ¼ teaspoon freshly ground black pepper, and ¼ teaspoon kosher salt. Serves 4 (serving size: ¾ cup)

CALORIES 204; FAT 4.5g (sat 3.1g); SODIUM 198mg

Quick & Easy • Make Ahead
Vegetarian • Gluten Free

22. Spicy Brown Rice

Combine 2 cups cooked brown rice, 1 teaspoon chile paste with garlic, 1 teaspoon sesame oil, ¼ cup chopped green onions, and ¼ teaspoon kosher salt. Serves 4 (serving size: about ½ cup)

CALORIES 120; **FAT** 2g (sat 0.3g); **SODIUM** 153mg

Kid Friendly • Quick & Easy
Vegetarian

23. Noodles with Carrot and Onion

Cook 4 ounces udon noodles according to directions, omitting salt and fat. Heat a skillet over medium-high heat. Add 1½ tablespoons canola oil. Add 1 small thinly sliced onion; sauté 3 minutes. Add 1 minced garlic clove; sauté 30 seconds. Remove from heat; stir in ½ cup shredded carrot, 1 tablespoon rice wine vinegar, and 1 tablespoon lower-sodium soy sauce. Add noodles; toss to coat. Serves 4 (serving size: ⅔ cup)

CALORIES 170; **FAT** 6.1g (sat 0.4g); **SODIUM** 150mg

Kid Friendly • Quick & Easy
Vegetarian

24. Cavatappi with Arugula and Cannellini Beans

Combine 2 cups hot cooked cavatappi pasta, 2 cups packed arugula, 1 cup rinsed and drained unsalted canned cannellini beans, 1½ tablespoons extra-virgin olive oil, 1 tablespoon fresh lemon juice, ⅛ teaspoon kosher salt, and ⅛ teaspoon freshly ground black pepper. Top with 1 ounce shaved Asiago cheese. Serves 4 (serving size: about 1 cup)

CALORIES 226; **FAT** 8.4g (sat 2g); **SODIUM** 151mg

LICENSE TO SPLURGE

BACON

Better by the dozen: 12 bacon bites under 150 calories

If bacon were rarer than caviar, it would be twice as expensive. No matter how trendy, it never fails to supercharge a dish. Bacon is the perfect way to make a small bite hugely gratifying.

Kid Friendly • Quick & Easy
Make Ahead

1. Banana-Bacon Sandwich Snack

Spread each of 4 (¾-ounce) slices whole-wheat bread with 1¼ teaspoons almond butter. Slice 1 banana into ½-inch-thick slices; arrange slices evenly over 2 bread slices. Cook 4 slices center-cut bacon in a nonstick skillet over medium heat until crisp. Remove bacon from pan; cut each slice in half, and divide evenly over bananas. Top with remaining 2 bread slices, almond butter side down. Add sandwiches to drippings in pan; cook over medium heat on each side 2 minutes or until lightly browned. Cut each sandwich in half diagonally. Sprinkle evenly with 1½ teaspoons powdered sugar. Serves 4 (serving size: ½ sandwich)

CALORIES 148; **FAT** 6.5g (sat 1.5g); **PROTEIN** 7g; **SODIUM** 250mg

Kid Friendly • Quick & Easy

2. Bacon S'mores

Break 2 whole-grain graham cracker sheets in half. Top each cracker half with 1 miniature dark chocolate bar (such as Hershey's). Microwave at HIGH 35 seconds or until chocolate is slightly melted; spread. Top chocolate with 1 large toasted marshmallow and ½ slice cooked center-cut bacon. Serves 4 (serving size: 1 s'more)

CALORIES 100; **FAT** 4.3g (sat 2g); **PROTEIN** 2g; **SODIUM** 112mg

Kid Friendly • Quick & Easy
Make Ahead • Gluten Free

3. Bacon-Peanut Popcorn Balls

Melt 2 teaspoons unsalted butter in a pan over low heat. Add 1 cup miniature marshmallows; cook 2 minutes. Remove from heat. Stir in 2 cups air-popped popcorn, 2 slices cooked and crumbled center-cut bacon, and 2 tablespoons chopped salted dry-roasted peanuts. Cool 2 minutes. Form into 4 (2-inch) balls. Serves 4 (serving size: 1 ball)

CALORIES 110; **FAT** 5.3g (sat 2g); **PROTEIN** 3g; **SODIUM** 107mg

Kid Friendly • Quick & Easy

4. Berry-Bacon Waffle Minis

Spread ¾ teaspoon chocolate-hazelnut spread on each of 8 toasted mini whole-wheat waffles. Top each waffle with ½ slice cooked and crumbled center-cut bacon and 1 strawberry quarter. Sprinkle with 2 teaspoons powdered sugar. Serves 4 (serving size: 2 mini waffles)

CALORIES 121; **FAT** 5.8g (sat 1.9g); **PROTEIN** 4g; **SODIUM** 171mg

Quick & Easy • Make Ahead
Gluten Free

5. Bacon Nigiri

Combine 1 (7.4-ounce) package Annie Chun's white sticky rice, 2 slices cooked and finely chopped center-cut bacon, 1½ tablespoons finely chopped green onions, 2 teaspoons toasted sesame seeds, 1½ tablespoons rice vinegar, and 1 teaspoon sugar. Shape rice mixture into 4 oblong portions. Refrigerate 20 minutes. Top each portion with 1 dot of Sriracha and ½ slice cooked center-cut bacon. Serves 4 (serving size: 1 piece)

CALORIES 113; **FAT** 2.6g (sat 1.1g); **PROTEIN** 4g; **SODIUM** 142mg

Kid Friendly • Quick & Easy
Gluten Free

6. Cheddar-Bacon-Chive Dip

Combine 5 tablespoons fat-free sour cream, 1 tablespoon canola mayo, ¾ ounce finely shredded cheddar cheese, 2 tablespoons finely chopped fresh chives, 2 slices cooked and crumbled center-cut bacon, and a dash of black pepper. Serve with 2 ounces reduced-fat kettle-cooked potato chips. Serves 4 (serving size: ½ ounce potato chips [about 10 chips] and about 2 tablespoons dip)

CALORIES 124; **FAT** 6.7g (sat 1.9g); **PROTEIN** 4g; **SODIUM** 236mg

Quick & Easy • Gluten Free

7. Oysters with Bacon Mignonette

Combine ⅓ cup champagne vinegar, 2 tablespoons minced shallots, 1½ teaspoons chopped fresh dill, 1½ teaspoons crushed black peppercorns, and 2 slices cooked and crumbled center-cut bacon in a small bowl. Spoon sauce evenly over 12 oysters on the half shell. Serves 4 (serving size: 3 oysters)

CALORIES 42; **FAT** 1.7g (sat 0.7g); **PROTEIN** 3g; **SODIUM** 143mg

Quick & Easy

8. Bacon Phyllo Cups

Combine 3 tablespoons apricot jam and 1 tablespoon cider vinegar in a small saucepan over medium heat. Cook 1 minute. Add 3 slices cooked and crumbled center-cut bacon; bring to a boil. Reduce heat; simmer 3 minutes. Place 1 teaspoon Brie into bottom of each of 8 frozen mini phyllo shells (such as Athenos), thawed. Top evenly with jam mixture. Bake at 350° for 10 minutes or until cheese is bubbly. Sprinkle evenly with 1 slice cooked and crumbled center-cut bacon and fresh thyme. Serves 4 (serving size: 2 filled phyllo cups)

CALORIES 117; **FAT** 5.7g (sat 2.1g); **PROTEIN** 3g; **SODIUM** 204mg

Kid Friendly • Gluten Free

9. Bacon-Roasted Pears

Combine 1 ounce goat cheese and 2 tablespoons plain nonfat Greek yogurt. Spread evenly into 4 ripe cored Bartlett pear halves. Wrap each pear half with 1 slice center-cut bacon, and place on foil-lined baking sheet. Place baking sheet in cold oven; bake at 375° for 40 minutes or until bacon is crisp. Turn broiler to high; broil 1 minute. Drizzle 1 teaspoon balsamic glaze over each pear. Serves 4 (serving size: 1 pear half)

CALORIES 106; **FAT** 3.6g (sat 2g); **PROTEIN** 4g; **SODIUM** 165mg

Make Ahead

10. Bacon and Ricotta-Stuffed Mushrooms

Cook 3 slices center-cut bacon in a nonstick skillet over medium heat until crisp. Remove bacon from pan, reserving drippings; crumble. Add 1½ teaspoons garlic to drippings in pan; sauté 3 minutes or until garlic begins to brown. Combine garlic, 3 tablespoons part-skim ricotta cheese, 1½ tablespoons grated fresh Parmesan cheese, ½ teaspoon coarsely chopped fresh thyme, and all but 2 tablespoons crumbled bacon in a bowl. Spoon ricotta mixture evenly into 12 small stemmed cremini mushrooms. Combine reserved 2 tablespoons bacon and 1 tablespoon whole-wheat panko. Sprinkle panko mixture evenly over ricotta mixture. Bake at 350° for 25 minutes or until tender. Serves 4 (serving size: 3 mushrooms)

CALORIES 62; **FAT** 3.1g (sat 1.7g); **PROTEIN** 5g; **SODIUM** 150mg

Kid Friendly • Quick & Easy
Make Ahead • Gluten Free

11. Microwave Bacon Brittle

Combine ½ cup sugar and ¼ cup light-colored corn syrup in a 2-quart microwave-safe glass bowl; cover with plastic wrap. Microwave at HIGH 2 minutes. Stir in ¼ cup coarsely chopped almonds. Microwave at HIGH 2 minutes or until edge of mixture is a light caramel color. Stir in 3 slices cooked and crumbled center-cut bacon, 1 teaspoon butter, ¼ teaspoon vanilla extract, and a dash of kosher salt. Add ½ teaspoon baking soda, and stir until foamy. Quickly pour mixture onto a jelly-roll pan lined with parchment paper; spread to ¼-inch thickness. Let stand 30 minutes. Break into pieces; store in an airtight container up to 1 week. Serves 6

CALORIES 147; **FAT** 3.6g (sat 1.1g); **PROTEIN** 2g; **SODIUM** 202mg

Gluten Free

12. Bacon-Stuffed Jalapeños

Combine 2 slices cooked and crumbled center-cut bacon, 1 ounce ⅓-less-fat cream cheese, ¼ cup plain nonfat Greek yogurt, 2 tablespoons shredded extra-sharp cheddar cheese, 2 tablespoons minced green onions, and 1 small minced garlic clove in a bowl, stirring well to combine. Divide cheese mixture evenly among 4 jalapeño peppers, halved lengthwise and seeded. Bake peppers on a foil-lined baking sheet at 375° for 25 minutes or until cheese is bubbly and browned. Top each jalapeño half with ¼ slice cooked center-cut bacon. Sprinkle with coarsely chopped fresh cilantro. Serves 4 (serving size: 2 halves)

CALORIES 71; **FAT** 4.8g (sat 2.7g); **PROTEIN** 5g; **SODIUM** 188mg

ENTERTAINING

Seductive flavors in a holiday plate for eight

From ultratender beef tenderloin with an indulgent cognac butter to a silky carrot mash, this meal can be the centerpiece for some brilliant holiday entertaining. For a sparkling start to the evening, try any of the cocktails beginning on page 329.

Kid Friendly • Make Ahead
Vegetarian • Gluten Free

Carrot Mash with Crème Fraîche

Hands-on: 12 min. Total: 48 min.
We like the smooth texture you get from pureeing in a food processor; if you prefer a chunkier texture, use a potato masher. Garnish with green onions for added color.

⅓ cup crème fraîche
1½ tablespoons finely chopped green
  onions
¾ teaspoon grated orange rind
½ teaspoon freshly ground black
  pepper
2 pounds carrots, peeled and cut
  crosswise into ½-inch slices
2 tablespoons fresh orange juice
1 tablespoon butter
½ teaspoon kosher salt

1. Combine first 4 ingredients; set aside.
2. Place carrots in a saucepan; cover with water. Bring to a boil; cover, reduce heat, and simmer 35 minutes or until tender. Drain; place in a food processor. Add juice, butter, and salt; process until smooth. Add crème fraîche mixture; pulse to combine. Serves 8 (serving size: about ⅔ cup)

CALORIES 96; **FAT** 5.2g (sat 3.1g, mono 1.5g, poly 0.3g);
PROTEIN 1g; **CARB** 12g; **FIBER** 3g; **CHOL** 13mg;
IRON 0mg; **SODIUM** 215mg; **CALC** 40mg

Roast Beef Tenderloin with Cognac Butter

Hands-on: 25 min. Total: 1 hr. 15 min.
You'll only use half of the cognac butter, but make all of it—cutting the amount in half doesn't work as well. Use the leftover butter within the week or freeze up to one month; bring to room temperature before serving.

1½ teaspoons butter
3 tablespoons minced shallots
3 tablespoons cognac
6½ tablespoons butter, softened
1 tablespoon thyme leaves
⅛ teaspoon black pepper
1 tablespoon Dijon mustard
2 teaspoons honey
1 teaspoon lower-sodium soy sauce
¾ teaspoon salt
½ teaspoon freshly ground black
  pepper
1 (2-pound) beef tenderloin, trimmed
2 tablespoons chopped fresh thyme
Cooking spray

1. Melt 1½ teaspoons butter in a small nonstick skillet over medium-low heat. Add shallots; cook 2 minutes or until tender, stirring shallots occasionally. Carefully stir in cognac; cook 1 minute or until liquid is reduced by about one-third. Remove from heat; cool.

2. Place 6½ tablespoons butter in a small bowl; stir in cooled cognac mixture, 1 tablespoon thyme leaves, and ⅛ teaspoon black pepper. Cover and chill 10 minutes. Divide butter mixture in half. Scrape each half of butter mixture onto a piece of plastic wrap; shape each portion into a 4-inch-long log. Wrap each butter log in plastic wrap; refrigerate or freeze 1 log for another use.
3. Preheat oven to 425°.
4. Combine mustard and next 4 ingredients (through ½ teaspoon pepper); stir with a whisk. Spread mustard mixture over all sides of tenderloin; sprinkle with 2 tablespoons thyme. Place tenderloin in a shallow roasting pan coated with cooking spray. Bake at 425° for 38 minutes or until a thermometer inserted in center of tenderloin registers 135° or until desired degree of doneness. Let stand 10 minutes.
5. Cut tenderloin crosswise into 16 slices. Arrange 2 slices on each of 8 plates. Cut 1 butter log into 8 slices; top each serving with 1 butter slice. Serves 8

CALORIES 202; **FAT** 10.9g (sat 5.4g, mono 3.6g, poly 0.4g);
PROTEIN 21g; **CARB** 2g; **FIBER** 0g; **CHOL** 73mg;
IRON 1mg; **SODIUM** 378mg; **CALC** 19mg

THE MENU

STARTERS
Crisp Autumn Serenade, page 329

Oysters with Bacon Mignonette, page 324

MAIN COURSE
Roast Beef Tenderloin with Cognac Butter, at left

Carrot Mash with Crème Fraîche, at left

Shredded Brussels Sprouts with Slow-Fried Shallots, page 326

DESSERT
Triple-Chocolate Cheesecake, page 328

Kid Friendly • Quick & Easy
Vegetarian • Gluten Free

Shredded Brussels Sprouts with Slow-Fried Shallots

***Hands-on: 12 min. Total: 28 min.** This recipe takes richness to a new level with the crunchy fried topping. Slow-frying allows the shallots to brown and crisp evenly without any burned pieces.*

½ cup plus 2 tablespoons canola oil, divided
1 cup thinly sliced shallots, separated into rings
¾ teaspoon kosher salt, divided
2 pounds Brussels sprouts, trimmed and thinly sliced (about 8 cups)
½ teaspoon freshly ground black pepper
2½ tablespoons fresh lemon juice

1. Heat a small, heavy skillet over medium heat. Add ½ cup oil; heat until oil is shimmering and oil bubbles around a shallot piece that's dropped into it. Add shallots to pan; slow-fry for 10 minutes or until browned and crispy, stirring occasionally. Remove shallots with a slotted spoon; drain on paper towels. Sprinkle shallots with ⅛ teaspoon salt.
2. Heat a large nonstick skillet over medium-high heat. Add 2 tablespoons oil; swirl to coat. Add Brussels sprouts; toss gently to coat. Sprinkle with pepper and ⅝ teaspoon salt; sauté 8 minutes or until lightly browned on edges. Reduce heat to low; cook 2 minutes or until tender. Stir in lemon juice; sprinkle with shallots. Serves 8 (serving size: about 1 cup sprouts and about 1½ tablespoons shallots)

CALORIES 142; FAT 9.1g (sat 0.7g, mono 5.6g, poly 2.7g); PROTEIN 4g; CARB 14g; FIBER 5g; CHOL 0mg; IRON 2mg; SODIUM 211mg; CALC 56mg

RELAX. INDULGE. BE HAPPY.

Splurg on the spirits and foods of the season, in a healthful way. We've perfected the recipes, right-sized the portions, and focused on foods that bring big joy in small bites and sips.

PERFECT BITES OF CHOCOLATE BLISS

That texture, that throat-catching, deep chocolate intensity: This treat is required by the Law of Holiday Indulgence. And we know the tricks to make a small amount eye-rollingly satisfying.

Kid Friendly • Freezable
Make Ahead

Double-Chocolate Cookies

***Hands-on: 16 min. Total: 1 hr. 15 min.** The secret to these cookies is not to over-bake them. For a gooey center, pull them out of the oven when they are still a bit glossy.*

6.75 ounces unbleached all-purpose flour (about 1½ cups)
6 tablespoons unsweetened cocoa
⅜ teaspoon salt
¾ cup sugar
¼ cup unsalted butter, softened
2 tablespoons canola oil
2 large eggs
¼ teaspoon vanilla extract
½ cup bittersweet chocolate chips

1. Weigh or lightly spoon flour into dry measuring cups; level with a knife. Combine flour, cocoa, and salt in a bowl, stirring with a whisk.
2. Place sugar, butter, and oil in a bowl; beat with a mixer at medium speed until well combined (about 5 minutes). Add eggs, 1 at a time, beating well after each addition. Add vanilla; beat 1 minute. Add flour mixture to butter mixture, beating at low speed just until combined. Add chocolate; beat at low speed just until combined. Cover with plastic wrap; chill 30 minutes.
3. Preheat oven to 350°.
4. Drop dough by 1½ tablespoonfuls 2 inches apart onto baking sheets lined with parchment paper. Bake at 350° for 8 minutes or until almost set. Cool on pan 2 minutes or until firm. Remove cookies from pan; cool on wire racks. Serves 26 (serving size: 1 cookie)

CALORIES 99; FAT 4.7g (sat 2.2g, mono 1.7g, poly 0.5g); PROTEIN 2g; CARB 14g; FIBER 1g; CHOL 19mg; IRON 1mg; SODIUM 40mg; CALC 7mg

Fudge Brownie Pops

Hands-on: 30 min. Total: 1 hr. 20 min.

3 ounces bittersweet chocolate, finely chopped and divided
¼ cup unsalted butter
1 cup sugar
1 teaspoon vanilla extract
1 large egg
1 large egg white
3.4 ounces all-purpose flour (about ¾ cup)
½ cup unsweetened cocoa
½ teaspoon baking powder
¼ teaspoon baking soda
¼ teaspoon salt
Cooking spray
1½ tablespoons dark corn syrup
16 lollipop sticks
¼ cup finely chopped roasted almonds

1. Preheat oven to 350°.
2. Combine 2 ounces chocolate and butter in a medium microwave-safe bowl. Microwave at HIGH 30 seconds or until mixture melts, stirring after 15 seconds. Add sugar, vanilla, egg, and egg white, stirring until well blended.
3. Weigh or lightly spoon flour into dry measuring cups; level with a knife. Combine flour and next 4 ingredients in a bowl, stirring with a whisk. Add flour mixture to chocolate mixture, stirring just until combined. Scrape batter into an 8-inch square glass or ceramic baking dish coated with cooking spray. Bake at 350° for 20 minutes or until a wooden pick inserted in center comes out clean. Cool completely in dish. Crumble brownies.
4. Place crumbled brownies in a food processor; process into fine crumbs. Add corn syrup; process until mixture forms a ball. Scoop about 2 tablespoons brownie mixture with a spoon; roll into a ball. Insert a lollipop stick into center of each ball.
5. Place 1 ounce chocolate in a microwave-safe bowl. Microwave at HIGH 30 seconds or until chocolate melts, stirring after 15 seconds. Dip balls into melted chocolate; dredge in nuts, pressing gently to adhere. Refrigerate until chocolate sets (about 20 minutes). Serves 16 (serving size: 1 pop)

CALORIES 155; **FAT** 6.8g (sat 3.5g, mono 1.7g, poly 0.5g); **PROTEIN** 3g; **CARB** 24g; **FIBER** 2g; **CHOL** 19mg; **IRON** 1mg; **SODIUM** 83mg; **CALC** 24mg

Five-Ingredient Chocolate Cakes

Hands-on: 35 min. Total: 1 hr. 30 min.

Cake:
Cooking spray
¾ cup sugar, divided
½ cup water
2 tablespoons unsalted butter, melted and cooled
3 large egg yolks
2 ounces cake flour (about ½ cup)
⅓ cup unsweetened cocoa
Dash of salt
3 large egg whites
Sauce:
¼ cup water
2 tablespoons sugar
2 tablespoons unsweetened cocoa
1 tablespoon unsalted butter
½ teaspoon cake flour
Topping:
2 large egg whites
2 tablespoons sugar
Mint leaves (optional)

1. Preheat oven to 350°.
2. To prepare cake, coat 6 (8-ounce) ramekins with cooking spray. Sprinkle ramekins evenly with 3 tablespoons sugar, tapping out excess.
3. Combine ¼ cup plus 1 tablespoon sugar, ½ cup water, 2 tablespoons butter, and egg yolks in a large bowl. Stir with a whisk until completely combined. Weigh or lightly spoon 2 ounces flour (½ cup) into a dry measuring cup, and level with a knife. Combine 2 ounces flour, ⅓ cup cocoa, and salt in a medium bowl, stirring with a whisk. Add flour mixture to yolk mixture, stirring until well combined (mixture will look a little grainy).
4. Place 3 egg whites in a large bowl; beat with a mixer at medium speed until foamy. Gradually add ¼ cup sugar, 1 tablespoon at a time, beating mixture at high speed until medium peaks form. Gently stir one-fourth of egg white mixture into batter; gently fold in remaining egg white mixture. Divide batter evenly among prepared ramekins; place on a baking sheet. Bake at 350° for 20 minutes or until a wooden pick inserted in center comes out clean. Cool completely on a wire rack. Run a knife around edge of ramekins; carefully invert cakes onto dessert plates.
5. To prepare sauce, combine ¼ cup water, 2 tablespoons sugar, 2 tablespoons cocoa, 1 tablespoon butter, and ½ teaspoon flour in a small saucepan over medium heat. Cook 2 minutes or until thick and bubbly, stirring constantly with a whisk. Remove from heat; keep sauce warm.
6. To prepare topping, combine 2 egg whites and 2 tablespoons sugar in the top of a double boiler, stirring with a whisk. Cook over simmering water until sugar dissolves (about 2 minutes), stirring constantly with a whisk. Pour mixture into a medium bowl. Beat with a mixer at high speed using clean, dry beaters until stiff peaks form (about 2 minutes). Top each cake with about 1½ tablespoons chocolate sauce and about ¼ cup meringue topping. Garnish with mint leaves, if desired. Serve immediately. Serves 6 (serving size: 1 cake)

CALORIES 274; **FAT** 9.3g (sat 5g, mono 2.7g, poly 0.8g); **PROTEIN** 6g; **CARB** 45g; **FIBER** 2g; **CHOL** 108mg; **IRON** 2mg; **SODIUM** 81mg; **CALC** 27mg

Milk Chocolate Crème Brûlée

Hands-on: 30 min. Total: 5 hr. 20 min.
A splash of nutty amaretto adds an extra layer of elegance to the milk chocolate in this decadently creamy dessert. If you don't own a kitchen blowtorch, simply sprinkle the chilled ramekins evenly with sugar and place on a baking sheet; broil close to heat source for 1 to 3 minutes or until sugar is melted and caramelized.

2 cups whole milk
¼ cup granulated sugar, divided
⅛ teaspoon salt
3 ounces milk chocolate, finely chopped
2 large eggs
2 large egg yolks
1 tablespoon amaretto (almond-flavored liqueur)
½ teaspoon vanilla extract
2 tablespoons superfine sugar

1. Preheat oven to 300°.
2. Bring milk, 2 tablespoons granulated sugar, and salt to a simmer in a medium, heavy saucepan (do not boil). Remove pan from heat; add chocolate, stirring until chocolate melts. Combine 2 tablespoons granulated sugar, eggs, and egg yolks in a medium bowl, stirring well with a whisk. Gradually add milk mixture to egg mixture, stirring constantly with a whisk. Stir in liqueur and vanilla. Divide mixture evenly among 6 (4-ounce) ramekins. Place ramekins in a 13 x 9–inch baking pan; add hot water to pan to a depth of 1 inch. Bake at 300° for 50 minutes or until center barely moves when ramekin is touched. Remove ramekins from pan; cool completely on a wire rack. Cover and chill at least 4 hours or overnight.
3. Sift 2 tablespoons superfine sugar evenly over custards. Holding a kitchen blowtorch about 2 inches from top of each custard, heat sugar, moving torch back and forth until sugar is completely melted and caramelized (about 1 minute). Serve immediately. Serves 6 (serving size: 1 crème brûlée)

CALORIES 226; **FAT** 9.9g (sat 5.2g, mono 3g, poly 0.9g); **PROTEIN** 7g; **CARB** 27g; **FIBER** 0g; **CHOL** 135mg; **IRON** 1mg; **SODIUM** 121mg; **CALC** 136mg

Triple-Chocolate Cheesecake

Hands-on: 25 min. Total: 14 hr. *This dessert gets well-rounded chocolate richness from three sources: chocolate graham crackers in the crust, plus intense cocoa powder and luscious milk chocolate in the filling.*

Crust:
⅔ cup old-fashioned rolled oats
8 chocolate graham cracker sheets
2 tablespoons dark brown sugar
⅛ teaspoon salt
1 tablespoon butter, melted
1 large egg white
Baking spray with flour
Filling:
1 cup granulated sugar
¼ cup unsweetened cocoa
2 tablespoons cake flour
¼ teaspoon salt
12 ounces fat-free cream cheese, softened
10 ounces ⅓-less-fat cream cheese, softened
4 large eggs, at room temperature
1 teaspoon vanilla extract
1 ounce milk chocolate, melted and cooled
2 cups frozen light whipped topping, thawed and divided
1 cup fresh or frozen blackberries

1. Preheat oven to 350°.
2. To prepare crust, spread oats on a baking sheet. Bake at 350° for 10 minutes or until lightly browned, stirring after 5 minutes. Cool. Place oats, crackers, brown sugar, and ⅛ teaspoon salt in a food processor; process until finely ground. Add butter and egg white; process until moist. Press mixture into bottom and 1½ inches up sides of a 9-inch springform pan coated with baking spray. Bake at 350° for 22 minutes. Cool completely on a wire rack.
3. Reduce oven temperature to 325°.
4. To prepare filling, sift together granulated sugar, cocoa, flour, and ¼ teaspoon salt.
5. Place cheeses in a large bowl; beat with a mixer at medium speed until smooth. Add eggs, 1 at a time, beating well after each addition. Add vanilla and chocolate, beating at low speed just until combined. Sprinkle sugar mixture over top of cheese mixture; beat at low speed until combined. Fold 1 cup whipped topping into mixture. Pour mixture into crust, smoothing top. Bake at 325° for 1 hour or until cheesecake center barely moves when pan is touched. Remove cheesecake from oven; run a knife around outside edge. Cool to room temperature. Cover and chill 8 hours or overnight. Slice cheesecake into 14 slices; top each serving with about 1 tablespoon whipped topping. Divide berries among servings. Serves 14 (serving size: 1 slice)

CALORIES 245; **FAT** 10.2g (sat 5.6g, mono 2.3g, poly 0.7g); **PROTEIN** 9g; **CARB** 32g; **FIBER** 2g; **CHOL** 74mg; **IRON** 1mg; **SODIUM** 381mg; **CALC** 168mg

BUBBLES

These sparkling cocktails will lift all spirits with their holiday flavors and winter-warming spices.

Gluten Free

Amaretto Cherry Fizz

Hands-on: 15 min. Total: 48 hr. 15 min. *The amaretto sour cocktail balances the sweetness of amaretto liqueur with the tartness of lemon and the cloudlike frothiness of shaken egg white. In this variation, the amaretto is infused with cherries and enlivened by a splash of prosecco (sparkling Italian wine).*

1 cup pitted fresh cherries
1 cup amaretto (almond-flavored liqueur)
1/2 cup fresh lemon juice (about 3 lemons)
1/2 cup pasteurized egg whites
2 cups chilled brut prosecco

1. Place fresh cherries in a glass container or jar; pour amaretto over cherries. Cover, shake gently, and let stand in a cool, dry place for at least 48 hours or up to 2 weeks.
2. Strain the cherries through a fine sieve over a bowl, reserving amaretto and cherries.
3. Pour amaretto into a large cocktail shaker or quart-sized mason jar. Add lemon juice and egg whites. Add as much ice as possible, cover, and shake vigorously for 15 seconds. Strain about ¼ cup into each of 8 chilled cocktail coupes or Champagne flutes; top each serving with ¼ cup prosecco. Garnish with amaretto-soaked cherries. Serve immediately. Serves 8 (serving size: ½ cup)

CALORIES 174; **FAT** 0.1g (sat 0g, mono 0g, poly 0.1g); **PROTEIN** 2g; **CARB** 22g; **FIBER** 0g; **CHOL** 0mg; **IRON** 0mg; **SODIUM** 25mg; **CALC** 4mg

Gluten Free

Spumante Molto Rosso

Hands-on: 10 min. Total: 48 hr. 10 min. *The Negroni is one of the great cocktails, and it's simple: equal parts gin, sweet vermouth, and the bittersweet Italian aperitivo Campari. This cocktail, a twist on that classic, aims to provide an easy introduction to Campari. Cranberry-infused gin complements Campari's bitter bite, which is smoothed out by the lime, sugar, and fruity prosecco. Roll the soaked cranberries in sugar and skewer on cocktail picks for a pretty garnish.*

1 cup fresh cranberries
1 cup London dry gin (such as Tanqueray or Beefeater)
1/2 cup Campari
1/2 cup fresh lime juice
1/2 cup simple syrup
2 cups chilled rosé brut prosecco
8 long pieces orange rind

1. Place cranberries in a glass container or jar; top with gin. Cover, shake gently, and let stand in a cool, dry place for at least 48 hours or up to 2 weeks.
2. Strain cranberries through a fine sieve over a bowl, reserving gin.
3. Pour gin into a large cocktail shaker or quart-sized mason jar. Add Campari, lime juice, and simple syrup. Add as much ice as possible, cover, and shake vigorously for 10 seconds. Strain about ¼ cup into each of 8 chilled cocktail coupes or Champagne flutes; top each serving with ¼ cup prosecco. Take an orange rind piece and, holding it by its sides, squeeze it, skin side down, over the drink to release the citrus oil. You should see the oil spray on the liquid's surface. Gently twist the peel to form a corkscrewlike curl, and drop it in as a garnish, if desired. Serve immediately. Serves 8 (serving size: ½ cup)

CALORIES 151; **FAT** 0g; **PROTEIN** 0g; **CARB** 9g; **FIBER** 0g; **CHOL** 0mg; **IRON** 0mg; **SODIUM** 2mg; **CALC** 2mg

Quick & Easy • Gluten Free

Crisp Autumn Serenade

Hands-on: 15 min. Total: 15 min. *This cocktail brings together the seasonal flavors of apples, pears, ginger, and maple. Bourbon gives it a bit of bite and backbone. (For a sweeter, richer version, you could use a dark rum, like Plantation Grande Reserve or El Dorado 5-year.) You'll make more of the tangy ginger-maple syrup than you need for the recipe; save the remaining syrup for other cocktails or to sweeten and spice up tea or mulled wine.*

1/2 cup maple syrup
1/4 cup diced peeled fresh ginger
1/4 cup boiling water
1 cup bourbon
1/2 cup pear brandy (such as Poire Williams) or pear-flavored vodka
1/2 teaspoon Angostura bitters
2 cups chilled brut-style hard sparkling apple cider (such as Foggy Ridge Serious Cider)
8 thin apple or pear slices (optional)

1. Place first 3 ingredients in a blender; process on HIGH 30 seconds or until ginger is almost liquefied. Cool 2 minutes; strain through a fine sieve into a bowl, pressing with the back of a spoon to extract liquid. Discard solids.
2. Combine 3 tablespoons maple mixture, bourbon, pear brandy, and bitters in a small pitcher. Add ice; stir at least 15 seconds or until well chilled. Strain about ¼ cup into each of 8 chilled cocktail coupes or Champagne flutes; top each serving with ¼ cup cider. Garnish with apple or pear slices, if desired. Serve immediately. Serves 8 (serving size: ½ cup)

CALORIES 146; **FAT** 0g; **PROTEIN** 0g; **CARB** 7g; **FIBER** 0g; **CHOL** 0mg; **IRON** 0mg; **SODIUM** 1mg; **CALC** 6mg

Sparkling Spanish Punch

Hands-on: 20 min. Total: 4 hr. *Today's cocktail is a descendent of punch. This one is based on the classic formula of the great recipes of the 17th and 18th centuries, most of which started with sugar soaked in lemon or orange oil. Here clementines are used instead, and all the spirits come from Spain.*

10 large clementines
Distilled water
1/2 cup sugar
1 1/2 cups Spanish brandy (Brandy de Jerez)
1 1/2 cups amontillado sherry
1 1/2 cups chilled cava (Spanish sparkling wine)
Whole nutmeg

1. Peel 2 clementines. Separate into segments. Make a decorative ice block by filling a Bundt pan or quart-sized container half full with distilled water; add segments. Freeze 4 hours or until solid.
2. Peel remaining clementines with a serrated vegetable peeler, being careful to avoid white pith. Combine clementine peels and sugar in a large bowl; muddle sugar and peels with a muddler or wooden spoon until the sugar is infused with the oils from the peels. Let stand at room temperature for at least 90 minutes.
3. Juice clementines to equal 1 cup. Add clementine juice to peels and sugar; stir until sugar dissolves. Strain through a sieve over a punch bowl; discard peels. Add brandy and sherry to punch bowl; stir well.
4. Unmold ice block; gently place in punch bowl. Add cava, and stir gently. Grate a small amount of nutmeg over the punch. Serves 12 (serving size: about 1/2 cup)

CALORIES 176; **FAT** 0.1g (sat 0g, mono 0g, poly 0.1g); **PROTEIN** 0g; **CARB** 13g; **FIBER** 1g; **CHOL** 0mg; **IRON** 0mg; **SODIUM** 1mg; **CALC** 10mg

A TRADITIONAL SOUP GETS A GOOEY UPGRADE

You won't miss the 28 grams of fat and the 540 calories of the original; a piping hot bowl of this soup is absolutely delicious and true to its oniony, cheesy nature.

French Onion Soup with Barley

Hands-on: 18 min. Total: 1 hr. 25 min. *We've updated the classic soup with whole-grain barley, whose hearty chew is a tasty addition. Pearl barley may be quick-cooking, but it's not whole grain; choose whole-grain barley here, sometimes labeled "hulled barley" and often found in the bulk foods section.*

6 cups water
1 cup hulled barley
2 tablespoons canola oil
1 1/2 pounds yellow onions, peeled and vertically sliced
1 pound sweet onions, peeled and vertically sliced
3/4 teaspoon kosher salt, divided
6 garlic cloves, thinly sliced
1/4 cup dry sherry
6 cups unsalted beef stock
1/2 teaspoon freshly ground black pepper
3 thyme sprigs
1 bay leaf
1 1/2 tablespoons thyme leaves
3 ounces French bread baguette, cut into 18 thin slices
3 ounces cave-aged Gruyère cheese, shredded (about 3/4 cup)
2 ounces part-skim mozzarella cheese, shredded (about 1/2 cup)

1. Bring 6 cups water and barley to a boil in a large saucepan; cover, reduce heat, and simmer 1 hour or until done. Drain.
2. While barley cooks, heat a Dutch oven over medium-high heat. Add oil to pan; swirl to coat. Add onions; cook 5 minutes, stirring frequently. Add 1/4 teaspoon salt and garlic; reduce heat to medium-low, and cook 45 minutes or until onions are caramelized and very tender, stirring occasionally.
3. Increase heat to medium-high. Add sherry; cook 2 minutes or until liquid almost evaporates. Stir in stock, pepper, thyme sprigs, and bay leaf; bring to a boil. Reduce heat, and simmer 30 minutes. Discard thyme sprigs and bay leaf. Stir in barley, thyme leaves, and 1/2 teaspoon salt.
4. Preheat broiler to high.
5. Arrange bread in a single layer on a baking sheet; broil 30 seconds on each side or until toasted. Ladle 1 1/3 cups soup into each of 6 ovenproof bowls. Arrange 3 toast pieces in each bowl; divide cheeses evenly over toasts. Place bowls on baking sheet. Broil 2 minutes or until cheese melts and begins to brown. Serves 6

CALORIES 380; **FAT** 11.7g (sat 4.2g, mono 4.9g, poly 2g); **PROTEIN** 16g; **CARB** 51g; **FIBER** 9g; **CHOL** 22mg; **IRON** 2mg; **SODIUM** 590mg; **CALC** 279mg

NEW TASTES IN MUSHROOM LAND

Beyond the buttons and the portobellos lies a world of amazing textures and flavors.

A brilliant specialty food store can excite a cook's mind like nothing else, whether the shop curates salt, cheese, chocolate, or, in the case of San Francisco's Far West Fungi shop in the Ferry Building, mushrooms. Our adventure was inspired by a traveling editor's casual iPhone snap of Far West's eye-popping, almost surreal mushroom assortment, ranging from lacy and delicate to ponderously dense, from bright orange to fawn brown to black. What could we do but order a variety box for our Test Kitchen? Soon more than a dozen exotic varieties saturated the kitchen with aromas of wood and loam. We marveled over the nubby texture of the lion's mane mushrooms, which felt exactly like the taut paw of a plush stuffed animal; the roasted-chicken fragrance of the maitake; the alarming sliminess (normal, it turns out) of the namekos.

The recipes here offer a taste of the fun we had. That gelatinous coating on the namekos? Perfect for giving body to a beautifully simple soup. Maitakes, with their meaty essence, make for meaty vegetarian tacos. If you don't have access to these exotics, each recipe here offers common-variety mushroom substitutions.

12 DELICIOUS EXOTICS

BLACK TRUMPET
Texture: Delicate
Taste: Nutty, piney

OYSTER
Texture: Velvety
Taste: Delicate, sweet

KING TRUMPET
Texture: Medium-firm
Taste: Buttery, sweet, meaty

MAITAKE
Texture: Snappy, springy
Taste: Notes of roasted chicken

LION'S MANE
Texture: Spongy
Taste: Intensely meaty

NAMEKO
Texture: Springy with sticky coating
Taste: Earthy-fruity

CHANTERELLE
Texture: Slightly chewy
Taste: Nutty sweetness

LOBSTER
Texture: Firm
Taste: Seafood-like sweetness

BLUE FOOT
Texture: Meaty, firm
Taste: Bright , strongly earthy

PIOPPINI
Texture: Firm
Taste: Peppery, intense

SHIITAKE
Texture: Chewy
Taste: Rich, bold, meaty

MOREL
Texture: Delicate and sponge-like
Taste: Deeply earthy-nutty

Quick & Easy • Vegetarian
Gluten Free

Sautéed Black Trumpets with Asparagus and Lemon

Hands-on: 17 min. Total: 17 min. *This is as simple—and delicious—as it gets: earthy mushrooms, crisp asparagus, and a wee hit of citrus to bring it all together. Because it's both robust and delicate, this side would go with pretty much any entrée.*

'Shroom subs: Chanterelle, morel, reconstituted dried wood ear mushrooms

8 cups water
2¼ teaspoons kosher salt, divided
1 pound asparagus, trimmed and cut diagonally into 1½-inch pieces
1 tablespoon extra-virgin olive oil
8 ounces black trumpet mushrooms
2 teaspoons butter
1½ teaspoons grated lemon rind
⅛ teaspoon freshly ground black pepper

1. Combine 8 cups water and 2 teaspoons salt in a Dutch oven; bring to a boil. Add asparagus; cook 2 minutes or until crisp-tender. Drain; plunge asparagus into ice water. Drain well.
2. Heat a large skillet over medium-high heat. Add oil; swirl to coat. Add mushrooms; sauté 4 minutes or until mushrooms release most of their liquid. Add asparagus; cook 1 minute or until thoroughly heated. Remove from heat; stir in ¼ teaspoon salt, butter, lemon rind, and pepper. Serve immediately. Serves 4 (serving size: about ¾ cup)

CALORIES 72; **FAT** 5.6g (sat 1.7g, mono 3g, poly 0.6g); **PROTEIN** 3g; **CARB** 4g; **FIBER** 2g; **CHOL** 5mg; **IRON** 2mg; **SODIUM** 237mg; **CALC** 18mg

BLACK TRUMPET

Texture: Delicate, with a bit of chew; cooks down to a soft texture
Taste: Bright and nutty, faintly eucalyptus-piney
Recipe ideas: Sauté and combine with firmer vegetables or scrambled eggs, or toss into pasta or risotto.

MAITAKE

Texture: Chewy, snappy, springy
Taste: Roasted dark-meat chicken, nutty essence
Recipe ideas: Sauté and toss in potpie, pasta, risotto, or tacos.

Vegetarian • Gluten Free

Mai-Tacos

Hands-on: 45 min. Total: 45 min. *The recipe title here is a playful pun, taking its cues from the pronunciation of the star ingredient. Mushrooms and chiles play surprisingly well together, and this peppy concoction highlights the maitake's robust, roast chicken–like flavor.*

'Shroom subs: Oyster, pioppini, portobello, shiitake, chanterelle

1 serrano chile, halved lengthwise
2 tablespoons olive oil, divided
12 ounces maitake mushrooms, coarsely chopped (about 6 cups)
3 green onions, thinly sliced
2 garlic cloves, minced
¼ cup organic vegetable broth
½ teaspoon kosher salt, divided
⅛ teaspoon ground red pepper
⅔ cup canned unsalted pinto beans, rinsed and drained
1 cup fresh corn kernels
½ poblano chile, seeded and julienned (about ½ cup)
8 (6-inch) corn tortillas
1 cup thinly sliced napa (Chinese) cabbage
3 ounces queso fresco, crumbled (about ¾ cup)
8 teaspoons Mexican hot sauce (such as Valentina)
8 lime wedges

1. Remove and discard seeds and membranes from half of serrano. Finely chop both chile halves.
2. Heat a large, heavy skillet over medium-high heat. Add 1 tablespoon oil to pan; swirl to coat. Add mushrooms; sauté 4 to 5 minutes or until mushrooms are browned, stirring occasionally. Add serrano, green onions, and garlic; sauté 30 seconds. Add broth, ¼ teaspoon salt, and red pepper; reduce heat, and cook 3 minutes or until mushrooms are tender. Stir in beans. Remove mushroom mixture from pan; wipe pan clean with a paper towel.
3. Increase heat to high. Add 1 tablespoon oil to pan; swirl to coat. Add corn and poblano; sauté 2 minutes or until slightly softened. Stir in ¼ teaspoon salt.
4. Heat tortillas according to package directions.
5. Place ⅓ cup mushroom mixture in each tortilla. Divide corn mixture evenly among tacos. Top each taco with 2 tablespoons cabbage, 1½ tablespoons cheese, and 1 teaspoon hot sauce. Serve with lime wedges. Serves 4 (serving size: 2 tacos and 2 lime wedges)

CALORIES 272; FAT 10.4g (sat 2.2g, mono 5.6g, poly 1.6g); PROTEIN 11g; CARB 39g; FIBER 7g; CHOL 7mg; IRON 1mg; SODIUM 540mg; CALC 120mg

NAMEKO

Texture: Springy, slightly crunchy, sticky gelatinous coating
Taste: Slightly fruity, foresty-earthy
Recipe ideas: Applications where the sticky coating aids in thickening, such as soups or sauces for pasta

LOBSTER

Texture: Firm, like an artichoke heart
Taste: Sweet hints of seafood
Recipe ideas: Versatile, great to toss into soups, sautés, or roasted dishes

Nameko and Lobster Mushroom Soup

Hands-on: 12 min. Total: 1 hr. 15 min. *This brothy soup was a home run at taste testing. Mushrooms and bacon have always been good friends, and here the nameko's sticky film gives depth and body to the smoky broth. You can make the broth in advance; it will keep in the refrigerator for several days.*

'Shroom subs: For the nameko: enoki, pioppini (though broth will have less body). For the lobster: maitake, fried chicken, shiitake

5 cups water
1 (3 x 6-inch) piece kombu (dried seaweed), rinsed
4 ounces uncooked bacon
3 cups nameko mushrooms (about 6 ounces)
1 cup chopped lobster mushrooms (about 1 ounce)
1 cup thinly sliced baby bok choy
1 tablespoon lower-sodium soy sauce
1 tablespoon rice wine vinegar
Cilantro leaves (optional)

1. Combine 5 cups water and kombu in a medium saucepan; bring to a boil. Remove from heat; let stand 20 minutes. Discard kombu. Add bacon to broth; bring to a boil. Reduce heat, and simmer 30 minutes. Strain broth through a cheesecloth-lined sieve into a bowl. Skim any fat from the surface; discard fat.
2. Return broth to saucepan; bring to a boil. Add mushrooms; reduce heat, and simmer 3 minutes. Stir in bok choy, soy sauce, and vinegar. Garnish with cilantro, if desired. Serve immediately. Serves 4 (serving size: about 1¼ cups)

CALORIES 51; FAT 3.4g (sat 1.1g, mono 1.4g, poly 0.4g); PROTEIN 3g; CARB 3g; FIBER 1g; CHOL 5mg; IRON 1mg; SODIUM 229mg; CALC 29mg

Texture: Spongy, sweetbread-like, absorbent
Taste: Concentrated chicken glacé or roast chicken skin flavor with a hint of crabmeat, intensely meaty, faintly livery
Recipe ideas: Roast with butter; sauté.

Quick & Easy • Vegetarian
Gluten Free

Roasted Lion's Mane Mushrooms with Sherried Shallots

Hands-on: 15 min. Total: 20 min.
Lion's mane mushrooms are an amazing discovery—incredibly meaty, with a faint, almost livery nuance—so this dish plays off the classic liver-and-onions combo with sweet and tangy shallots. Serve as a light entrée with a fall salad and crusty bread, or as a hearty side dish with robust meats such as lamb or beef.

'Shroom subs: Shiitake, cremini

2 tablespoons extra-virgin olive oil, divided
4 cups vertically sliced shallots (about 6 large)
1 tablespoon thyme leaves
1/2 teaspoon kosher salt, divided
1/3 cup dry sherry
1 tablespoon sherry vinegar
1/4 teaspoon freshly ground black pepper
12 silver dollar–sized lion's mane mushrooms (about 12 ounces)
1 tablespoon butter, cut into 12 pieces
1 tablespoon sliced fresh chives

1. Preheat oven to 425°.
2. Heat a medium saucepan over medium-high heat. Add 1 tablespoon oil to pan; swirl to coat. Add shallots, thyme, and 1/4 teaspoon salt; sauté 4 minutes, stirring frequently. Add sherry; cover, reduce heat, and simmer 10 minutes or until very tender. Stir in vinegar and black pepper. Remove from heat; keep warm.
3. Heat a large ovenproof skillet over medium-high heat. Add 1 tablespoon oil; swirl to coat. Add mushrooms, fuzzy side down; cook 4 minutes or until browned. Turn mushrooms over; top each with 1 butter piece. Place pan in oven; bake mushrooms at 425° for 5 minutes or until tender. Remove from oven; sprinkle with 1/4 teaspoon salt. Spoon about 1/2 cup shallot mixture onto each of 4 plates; top each serving with 3 mushrooms. Drizzle any pan juices over servings. Sprinkle evenly with chives. Serves 4

CALORIES 194; **FAT** 9.9g (sat 2.8g, mono 5.7g, poly 1g); **PROTEIN** 7g; **CARB** 22g; **FIBER** 1g; **CHOL** 8mg; **IRON** 2mg; **SODIUM** 270mg; **CALC** 7mg

CHANTERELLE

Texture: Chewy, slick
Taste: Musty, haylike, hazelnut sweetness
Recipe ideas: Golden color is lovely in sautés, stir-fries, or pickles.

KING TRUMPET

Texture: Scallop-like
Taste: Sweet and meaty, buttery, between steak and scallop
Recipe ideas: Sauté, stir-fry, pickle.

Make Ahead • Vegetarian
Gluten Free

Pickled Wild Mushrooms

Hands-on: 20 min. Total: 24 hr. 20 min. *These garlicky numbers are mouthwatering by themselves, and they can also take a salad, cheese board, or burger to another dimension. You can substitute most any mushroom; just trim them accordingly. The earthy pickles taste great after one day, but if you can wait three or more days, they get even better. Store in the refrigerator for up to one month.*

'Shroom subs: Pretty much any mushroom will work here; just trim or slice to fit the jar.

3 1/4 cups water
3/4 cup cider vinegar
1 1/2 tablespoons kosher salt
3 cups shiitake mushroom caps or blue foot mushrooms
3 cups king trumpet or French horn mushrooms, quartered lengthwise
3 cups chanterelle mushrooms, trimmed
2 teaspoons black peppercorns
8 Castelvetrano olives
6 garlic cloves, peeled
5 bay leaves
5 dried Indian chiles (such as Sanaam)
2 tablespoons olive oil

1. Bring 3 1/4 cups water, vinegar, and salt to a boil in a large saucepan, stirring until salt dissolves. Add mushrooms; reduce heat, and simmer 6 minutes. Remove from heat. Add peppercorns and next 4 ingredients; cool to room temperature. Place mushroom mixture in a 1-quart mason jar; top with olive oil. Seal tightly; refrigerate at least 24 hours before serving. Serves 16 (serving size: about 1/4 cup)

CALORIES 18; **FAT** 1.1g (sat 0.2g, mono 0.7g, poly 0.1g); **PROTEIN** 1g; **CARB** 1g; **FIBER** 0g; **CHOL** 0mg; **IRON** 0mg; **SODIUM** 194mg; **CALC** 1mg

GETTING STARTED WITH FINISHING SALT

A salt evangelist argues that the mineral is woefully underused by American cooks.

I n recent years, salt has started to strut its diverse true nature in the American food market. For decades there were really only two salts in most homes: superfine refined table salt and equally refined coarse kosher salt. But these lab-pure examples of sodium chloride are stripped of the character of salt as it occurs in nature. Natural salts sing of their origins: Crystals from the volcanoes of Hawaii are jet black. Those from the sea have briny complexity. In Maldon sea salt from the United Kingdom, traditional harvesting techniques produce delicate pyramid-shaped structures with perfect crunch. And then there are dozens of flavored varieties: smoked, jazzed up with chiles, even blended with tangy, ground-up mezcal worms.

No one works harder to raise salt's culinary stature than Mark Bitterman, who sells more than 120 artisanal salts at The Meadow (atthemeadow.com), with stores in Portland, Oregon, and New York. "You can't overemphasize the importance of salt," he says. "It's the most versatile and universal ingredient: Every culture has been making salt for at least 12,000 years. It's a nutritional necessity. And it's the most powerful food enhancer in cooking—more powerful than spice."

Bitterman doesn't buy the vilification of sodium by public health experts, and he'll e-mail you scholarly documents to support his arguments. Even the sodium-wary, though, will find that his approach to salt as a finishing agent makes sense. To him, salting early and often buries the virtues of salt in the dish: "You miss the fact that salt has its own voice, its own character," he says. A sprinkle at the end can be a game changer, raising flavor, adding melody, and delivering a playful crackle.

Bitterman recommends three finishing salts for every kitchen: sel gris, flake salt, and fleur de sel. Crunchy nuggets of sel gris cut through a rich steak and dissipate as you chew. The delicate shattering of flake salt echoes the crispness of lettuce while boosting its flavor. Fleur de sel is a workhorse in everything from baking to braising. Owning just three quality salts changes the conversation from "How much?" to "What works best here?" All are applied sparingly.

Learn how each works, Bitterman advises, and use them daily. "The worst news I can get from a customer is that they've had the same jar of salt for years."

Quinoa-Cilantro Tabbouleh with Flake Salt

Hands-on: 15 min. Total: 32 min. *The delicate crunch of flake salt is a beautiful finishing touch in this quinoa riff on tabbouleh; you can use easy-to-find Maldon flake salt or—for real drama—try black flake salt such as The Meadow's Black Diamond.*

- ³/₄ cup water
- ²/₃ cup uncooked quinoa, rinsed and drained
- ¹/₄ teaspoon fleur de sel
- 1 cup finely chopped plum tomato
- ¹/₂ cup finely chopped red onion
- ¹/₂ cup chopped fresh cilantro
- 2¹/₂ tablespoons fresh lemon juice
- 2 tablespoons extra-virgin olive oil
- 1 teaspoon lemon bitters
- ¹/₄ teaspoon freshly ground black pepper
- 6 tablespoons fresh flat-leaf parsley
- ⁵/₈ teaspoon flake salt

1. Bring ¾ cup water and quinoa to a boil in a small saucepan. Cover, reduce heat, and simmer 12 minutes or until quinoa is tender. Remove from heat; let stand 10 minutes. Fluff quinoa with a fork; stir in fleur de sel. Place quinoa in a medium bowl. Cool slightly.
2. Combine tomato and next 6 ingredients (through pepper) in a medium bowl, stirring to combine. Add quinoa mixture; toss to coat. Sprinkle with parsley; sprinkle flake salt evenly over parsley. Serves 6 (serving size: about ½ cup)

CALORIES 127; FAT 5.8g (sat 0.8g, mono 3.6g, poly 1.1g); PROTEIN 3g; CARB 16g; FIBER 2g; CHOL 0mg; IRON 1mg; SODIUM 323mg; CALC 21mg

Marcona-Rosemary Ice Cream Sandwiches

Hands-on: 35 min. Total: 3 hr. 20 min.
Salt is essential in desserts; here it enhances all the herby-nutty flavors. If you can't find Marcona almonds, use toasted blanched almonds.

- 2/3 cup Marcona almonds
- 1 tablespoon canola oil
- 1/3 cup granulated sugar
- 1/3 cup packed brown sugar
- 2 tablespoons butter, softened
- 1 teaspoon vanilla extract
- 1 large egg
- 3.4 ounces all-purpose flour (about 3/4 cup)
- 2 teaspoons finely chopped fresh rosemary
- 1/2 teaspoon baking soda
- 3/8 teaspoon fleur de sel, divided
- 1 pint pistachio ice cream, softened

1. Place nuts in a food processor; process until ground. With processor on, drizzle oil through food chute; process 30 seconds or until almost smooth. Combine almond mixture, sugars, and butter in a bowl; beat with a mixer at medium speed 1 minute or until well blended. Add vanilla and egg; beat to combine. Weigh or lightly spoon flour into a dry measuring cup; level with a knife. Combine flour, rosemary, baking soda, and 1/8 teaspoon fleur de sel. Add flour mixture to sugar mixture; beat at low speed just until combined. Chill 15 minutes.
2. Preheat oven to 375°.
3. Divide dough into 24 portions (2 teaspoons each); roll each into a ball. Arrange 12 balls on each of 2 baking sheets lined with parchment paper. Flatten each into a 1½-inch circle. Sprinkle 12 circles with ¼ teaspoon fleur de sel, pressing gently to adhere. Bake at 375° for 9 minutes or until lightly browned. Cool on wire racks.
4. Turn 12 unsalted cookies upside down; spread about 2½ tablespoons ice cream over each. Top with 12 salted cookies. Freeze 2 hours or until firm. Serves 12 (serving size: 1 sandwich)

CALORIES 253; **FAT** 14.5g (sat 5.4g, mono 6g, poly 1.9g); **PROTEIN** 5g; **CARB** 27g; **FIBER** 1g; **CHOL** 57mg; **IRON** 1mg; **SODIUM** 175mg; **CALC** 62mg

3 SALTS YOU NEED

FLEUR DE SEL
CRYSTAL: Medium-fine
FLAVOR: Rich. High mineral content, so it lingers on the tongue.
TRY ON: It's your all-purpose salt; especially good with butter.

SEL GRIS
CRYSTAL: Hefty, crunchy nuggets
FLAVOR: Briny intensity
TRY ON: Steaks, caramels. Cuts through rich, gamey meats or cloying sweets.

FLAKE SALT
CRYSTAL: Parchment-fine flakes
FLAVOR: Delicate. It flashes across the tongue and disappears.
TRY ON: Dressed salads

Strip Steak with Onions and Poblanos

Hands-on: 25 min. Total: 25 min. *The steak is very lightly salted before it's cooked. It's finished with coarse sel gris, which does all the heavy lifting, flavor-wise, with just a crystal or two popping with every bite.*

- 2 (10-ounce) New York strip steaks, trimmed
- 3/8 teaspoon smoked paprika
- 3/8 teaspoon fleur de sel, divided
- 3/8 teaspoon black pepper, divided
- 1½ tablespoons sesame oil, divided
- 1 (12-ounce) yellow onion, cut into 12 wedges
- 2 poblano peppers, seeded and cut into 1/2-inch strips
- 3/8 teaspoon sel gris
- 4 lime wedges

1. Heat a large cast-iron skillet over medium-high heat. Sprinkle steaks evenly with paprika, 1/8 teaspoon fleur de sel, and ¼ teaspoon black pepper. Add 1½ teaspoons oil to pan; swirl to coat. Add steaks to pan; cook 4 minutes on each side or until desired degree of doneness. Remove steaks from pan; let stand 10 minutes.
2. Add 1 tablespoon oil to pan; swirl. Add onion wedges; cook 2 minutes on each side. Add poblanos to pan; sauté 4 minutes, stirring occasionally. Remove from heat; cover and let stand 5 minutes. Stir in ¼ teaspoon fleur de sel and 1/8 teaspoon black pepper. Arrange onion mixture on a platter. Cut steak across the grain into thin slices. Arrange steak over onion mixture; sprinkle evenly with sel gris. Serve with lime wedges. Serves 4 (serving size: 3 ounces steak and ¾ cup onion mixture)

CALORIES 236; **FAT** 10.4g (sat 2.8g, mono 4.2g, poly 2.4g); **PROTEIN** 26g; **CARB** 9g; **FIBER** 2g; **CHOL** 67mg; **IRON** 2mg; **SODIUM** 449mg; **CALC** 42mg

SWISS CHARD

Growing the gorgeous stalks and sweeping leaves of this plant is definitely a bright idea.

Swiss chard is a gorgeous plant. It's highly nutritious and adaptable to year-round gardening. The leaves have a spinach-like quality and are less bitter than beet greens. And chard is rich in vitamins K, A, and C.

Like so many of the greens we have in the *Cooking Light* Garden, Swiss chard can be eaten in many stages of maturity. Sow the burr-like seeds every 4 to 5 inches and 1 inch deep, and then thin seedlings to 8 or 10 inches apart. Use tiny scissors to thin the seedlings (instead of pulling up) and enjoy as microgreens. As it grows, use 6-inch cuttings in salads, and stunning 18-inch leaves for sautés, stews, quiches, and more. The crunchy stems can be sliced into the sauté pan a bit before the greens, or pickled.

Swiss chard can be enjoyed nearly year-round in many climates, from spring to early winter. While spinach melts in summer and lettuce fizzles in frosts, Swiss chard stands tall and shines brightly. A late-summer planting will yield hearty production in fall, and the plants can overwinter in a protective cold frame. Using frost cloth stretched over hoops on raised beds keeps a cozy climate inside. This beauty is also highly ornamental in container plantings with flowers and throughout the garden.

Quick & Easy • Vegetarian
Make Ahead

Chopped Chard Salad with Apricot Vinaigrette

***Hands-on: 10 min. Total: 16 min.** This composed salad is a delicious mix of earthy, fruity, and tangy flavors. We love the trick of using apricot preserves to add sweetness and body to the dressing; you can also use orange marmalade for a bitter note.*

¼ cup thinly sliced shallots
2 tablespoons extra-virgin olive oil
2 tablespoons white wine vinegar
1½ tablespoons apricot preserves
1 teaspoon whole-grain Dijon mustard
6 cups chopped Swiss chard

1 (15.5-ounce) can chickpeas (garbanzo beans), rinsed and drained
2 tablespoons walnuts, toasted
1 tablespoon chopped green onions
1 teaspoon black pepper
½ ounce goat cheese, crumbled

1. Combine first 5 ingredients in a large bowl, stirring with a whisk. Let stand 10 minutes. Set aside half of shallot mixture. Add chard to bowl; toss to coat. Place chard mixture on a serving platter. Return reserved half of shallot mixture to bowl. Add chickpeas; toss to coat. Top chard mixture with chickpea mixture. Sprinkle evenly with walnuts and remaining ingredients. Serves 6 (serving size: about 1 cup)

CALORIES 147; FAT 8.6g (sat 2.1g, mono 3.7g, poly 2.1g); PROTEIN 5g; CARB 13g; FIBER 3g; CHOL 6mg; IRON 1mg; SODIUM 261mg; CALC 51mg

Quick & Easy • Vegetarian
Gluten Free

Sautéed Chard Agrodolce

Hands-on: 10 min. Total: 10 min.

2 teaspoons olive oil
½ cup thinly sliced shallots
4 garlic cloves, minced
6 cups chopped Swiss chard
½ cup dried sweet cherries
1 tablespoon water
½ teaspoon freshly ground black pepper
¼ teaspoon kosher salt
2 teaspoons balsamic vinegar

1. Heat a large skillet over medium-high heat. Add oil to pan; swirl to coat. Add shallots; sauté 2 minutes. Add garlic; sauté 1 minute. Add chard, cherries, 1 tablespoon water, pepper, and salt; toss to coat. Sauté 2 minutes or until chard begins to wilt. Stir in vinegar. Serves 4 (serving size: ½ cup)

CALORIES 122; FAT 2.4g (sat 0.3g, mono 1.7g, poly 0.3g); PROTEIN 2g; CARB 23g; FIBER 4g; CHOL 0mg; IRON 2mg; SODIUM 241mg; CALC 62mg

Make Ahead • Vegetarian

Rustic Chard, Potato, and Goat Cheese Tart

Hands-on: 60 min. Total: 2 hr.

7.25 ounces all-purpose flour (about 1⅔ cups)
¾ teaspoon kosher salt, divided
½ teaspoon baking powder
⅓ cup plus 1 tablespoon extra-virgin olive oil, divided
¼ cup water
1 bunch Swiss chard
1 cup vertically sliced red onion

1 cup thinly sliced Yukon gold potato
2 teaspoons chopped fresh thyme
1 teaspoon water
1 large egg white
½ teaspoon black pepper
2 ounces goat cheese, crumbled
   (about ½ cup)

1. Weigh or lightly spoon flour into dry measuring cups; level with a knife. Place flour, ½ teaspoon salt, and baking powder in a food processor; pulse 2 times to combine. Combine ⅓ cup oil and ¼ cup water in a small bowl. With processor on, slowly add oil mixture through food chute; process until dough is crumbly. Turn dough out onto a lightly floured surface. Knead 1 minute; add additional flour, if necessary, to prevent dough from sticking. Gently press dough into a 5-inch disk; wrap in plastic wrap, and chill 30 minutes. **2.** Remove stems from chard leaves; chop stems to equal 1 cup. Chop leaves to equal 4 cups. Heat a large skillet over medium-high heat. Add 1 tablespoon oil to pan; swirl to coat. Add chard stems and onion to pan; sauté 1½ minutes. Add chard leaves to pan; sauté 2½ minutes. Stir in ¼ teaspoon salt, potato, and thyme. Remove from heat; cool. **3.** Preheat oven to 375°. **4.** Unwrap dough, and roll into a 14-inch circle on a floured surface. Place dough on a baking sheet lined with parchment paper. Spread chard mixture over dough, leaving a 2-inch border. Fold edges of dough toward center, pressing gently to seal (dough will only partially cover chard). Combine 1 teaspoon water and egg white in a small bowl. Brush dough edges with egg white mixture. Sprinkle pepper and cheese over chard mixture. Bake at 375° for 40 minutes or until browned. Let stand 5 minutes; cut into 12 wedges. Serves 12 (serving size: 1 wedge)

CALORIES 168; **FAT** 8.3g (sat 1.7g, mono 5.4g, poly 0.9g); **PROTEIN** 4g; **CARB** 20g; **FIBER** 1g; **CHOL** 2mg; **IRON** 1mg; **SODIUM** 187mg; **CALC** 32mg

SLOW COOKER

SLOW-SIMMERED SQUASH SOUP

Thai flavors gently infuse sweet butternut for an oh-so-creamy bowl of comfort.

**Kid Friendly • Freezable
Make Ahead • Gluten Free**

Coconut-Red Curry Squash Soup

Hands-on: 20 min. Total: 8 hr. 20 min.

1 tablespoon olive oil
1 tablespoon butter
1½ cups chopped onion
1½ tablespoons minced peeled fresh
   ginger
1½ tablespoons minced fresh garlic
1 tablespoon red curry paste
8 cups chopped peeled butternut
   squash
3 cups unsalted chicken stock
1 cup chopped peeled baking potato
2 teaspoons brown sugar
1 teaspoon kosher salt
½ teaspoon black pepper
2 tablespoons fresh lime juice
1 (13.5-ounce) can light coconut milk
2 tablespoons coarsely chopped fresh
   cilantro

1. Heat oil and butter in a small skillet over medium heat. Add onion, ginger, garlic, and curry paste; cook 8 minutes or until onion is softened, stirring occasionally. Combine onion mixture, squash, and next 5 ingredients in a 6-quart electric slow cooker. Cover and cook on LOW for 6 to 8 hours or until squash is tender. **2.** Place half of squash mixture in a blender. Remove center piece of blender lid (to allow steam to escape); secure blender lid on blender.

Place a clean towel over opening in blender lid (to avoid splatters). Blend until smooth. Pour into a large bowl. Repeat procedure with remaining squash mixture. Stir in juice and coconut milk. Sprinkle with cilantro. Serves 8 (serving size: 1¼ cups)

CALORIES 182; **FAT** 4g (sat 1.8g, mono 1.6g, poly 0.3g); **PROTEIN** 5g; **CARB** 35g; **FIBER** 5g; **CHOL** 4mg; **IRON** 2mg; **SODIUM** 341mg; **CALC** 109mg

KID IN THE KITCHEN

FRESH, FAST PASTA

Our lemony linguine is an instant hit with Matisse and friends.

"Today I made pasta with spinach and tomatoes. I grated the lemon rind, juiced the lemon, and sliced the tomatoes and basil earlier, so I just had to cook the pasta at the last minute and throw in the final ingredients. Refrigerated fresh pasta doesn't take as long to cook as dry pasta, which makes this recipe even quicker. The blend of cream cheese and mascarpone makes the sauce really creamy, though it tastes light. The lemon and basil are so fresh tasting. This recipe was extremely popular with my family. I hope it is with yours, too!"

THE VERDICT

KEELEY (AGE 15)
She thought the pasta was restaurant quality. She loved the creaminess and freshness of the dish. **10/10**

MICA (AGE 12)
She just said, "Can I have more?" **10/10**

MATISSE (AGE 13)
I loved the spinach. The combination of the cheeses and lemon worked really well. **9/10**

continued

Mascarpone and Spinach Linguine

Hands-on: 12 min. Total: 21 min.

1 (9-ounce) package refrigerated fresh linguine
3 tablespoons ⅓-less-fat cream cheese
1½ tablespoons mascarpone cheese
½ teaspoon grated lemon rind
2 teaspoons fresh lemon juice
½ teaspoon salt
⅛ teaspoon freshly ground black pepper
⅛ teaspoon freshly grated nutmeg
4 cups baby spinach leaves
1 pint cherry tomatoes, halved
¼ cup sliced fresh basil
2 tablespoons grated Parmigiano-Reggiano cheese

1. Cook pasta according to package directions, omitting salt and fat. Drain pasta in a colander over a bowl, reserving 1 cup cooking liquid. **2.** Add cream cheese and mascarpone cheese to bowl, stirring with a whisk until smooth. Stir in lemon rind and next 4 ingredients. **3.** Heat a saucepan over medium-high heat. Add pasta and cream cheese mixture to pan; cook 1 minute, stirring constantly. Stir in spinach and tomatoes; cook 2 minutes or until spinach wilts, stirring frequently. Remove pan from heat; stir in basil. Sprinkle evenly with cheese; serve immediately. Serves 4 (serving size: about 2 cups pasta and 1½ teaspoons cheese)

CALORIES 292; FAT 10.2g (sat 5.6g, mono 2.7g, poly 1.5g); PROTEIN 12g; CARB 41g; FIBER 4g; CHOL 61mg; IRON 2mg; SODIUM 454mg; CALC 107mg

A NEW WAY TO LEARN TO COOK

This fall we publish *Mad Delicious*, a cookbook from *Cooking Light* columnist Keith Schroeder, with a unique recipe format that reveals the inner workings of Keith's healthy dishes: the techniques, the ingredients, the secrets, and the creative thinking that will transform your good cooking into great. Here, an excerpt.

My love of cooking started when I was a kid, and eventually it pushed me into professional kitchens. You'd think that was where the real cooking happened, in restaurant kitchens. What's hard for a chef to admit, though, is that cooking at home can be more satisfying. After all, cooking is an intimate, generous, and personal act, expressive of culture, place, community, and tradition.

I wanted to write this book because I'm a teacher at heart. I offered the team at *Cooking Light* some recipes with a format that mirrored the way I approach cooking, one that explained the purpose for using each and every ingredient in each and every recipe—in tabular format. Food. How Much. Why. It's a format I've long used when teaching people how to cook. Sometimes the why was fundamental to the recipe's success. Oftentimes, I offered up some science-meets-life experience reasons for tinkering with tradition. Good cooking's like that—attentive and purposeful—without being sterile or rote. I was told the format and the voice were "unique." Pause. Look at serious editor. Whew. It was "good" unique.

The intent of *Mad Delicious* is to make you a more purposeful cook, certainly to teach the "how," but most importantly to spotlight the critical "whys" of methods, ingredients, ingredient combinations, traditions, phenomena, et al. I want you to understand the recipe you are cooking, not just survive the process.

Yes, cooking involves applying heat to foods to make them edible, but it's an act of service to others, too. It is a dance. Enjoy the process. Shop reverently. Unpack deliberately. Activate sound track. Strategically position your cookbook. Read the whole recipe. Gather tools. Prep your ingredients. Clean as you go. Follow directions carefully. Enjoy your meal.

For great, stress-free meals to come together, an organized work space is key. Cooking requires you to move easily from ingredient to utensil to pan to stove to oven to sink to trashcan. Remove unnecessary clutter, keep yourself organized, and build in flow.

KEITH'S RECIPE BREAKDOWN

SORGHUM-ROASTED SALMON
Hands-on: 16 min. Total: 25 min.

INGREDIENT	AMOUNT	WHY
sorghum	3 tablespoons	It's an easy-to-work-with syrup, and its warm-toasty flavors go well with all things roasted or grilled.
hot water	1 tablespoon	To dilute the mustard.
dry mustard	1 teaspoon	For pungency and character.
freshly ground black pepper	1/4 teaspoon	Sorghum and black pepper. Sweet and piquant. Works. With. Everything.
lemon zest	2 tablespoons grated (about 2 lemons)	Perfume. The dish might be a little one-dimensional without it.
salmon	4 (6-ounce) fillets	A richer fish such as salmon takes to the oven better than a lean fish, and can stand up to the sorghum-mustard treatment.
cooking spray		To make your life easier.
fresh lemon juice	3 tablespoons (about 2 lemons)	It's essentially the sauce.
salt	1/2 teaspoon	It's added to finish so it sticks to the hot glaze, and so that none of the rationed sodium ends up in unusable browned bits in the pan.

SORGHUM SYRUP, MADE FROM
A VARIETY KNOWN AS SWEET SORGHUM,
HAS A LIGHT, MOLASSES-Y, TOASTY,
MINERALLY FLAVOR THAT TAKES WELL
TO SAVORY-SWEET APPLICATIONS.

Kid Friendly • Quick & Easy
Gluten Free

Sorghum-Roasted Salmon

Hands-on: 16 min. Total: 25 min.
Sorghum is essentially a grass, raised primarily as a feed grain in the heartland of the U.S. In the southeastern U.S., though, if you say sorghum, someone might exclaim "biscuit!"

• Preheat the oven to 450°.
• Combine the sorghum, 1 tablespoon of hot water, mustard, black pepper, and the lemon zest in a bowl.
• Brush the top sides of the salmon fillets evenly with the sorghum mixture.
• Spray a baking pan evenly with cooking spray.
• Lay the salmon fillets evenly spaced on the baking pan.
• Roast for 9 minutes, basting halfway through with the lemon juice, until the internal temperature reaches 110°. Remove the fillets from the oven.
• Preheat the broiler. Broil the fillets for 1 minute.
• Sprinkle the fillets evenly with salt.
• Serve hot. Serves 4 (serving size: 1 fillet)

CALORIES 330; FAT 13.9g (sat 3.1g, mono 5.8g, poly 3.2g); PROTEIN 36g; CARB 13g; FIBER 1g; CHOL 87mg; IRON 1mg; SODIUM 377mg; CALC 51mg

Thai Street Chicken

Hands-on: 20 min. Total: 1 hr. 30 min.
All over Thailand, especially in urban areas, street-food stalls are everywhere, their sights and smells delightfully overwhelming. Chicken offerings are abundant, varied, and almost universally Mad Delicious. Four condiments are showcased at restaurants and makeshift street-side dining areas: white sugar (sweet), Thai chiles in vinegar (sour-piquant), fish sauce (salty-savory), and intensely flavorful crushed dry chile (depth-heat). In this recipe, the dipping sauce that accompanies honors the Thai condiment caddy. And the marinade on this chicken is deeply savory, welcoming generous amounts of the sauce. Eat your veggies, too, with your fingers. We left them raw.

• Fire up a charcoal grill to low heat, creating a slow, even bed of coals. You can also use a grill pan heated to medium heat.
• Place the cilantro roots in a large zip-top plastic bag. Seal the bag. Use the side of a rolling pin to bruise.
• Add the sugar, the white pepper, the fish sauce, the oyster sauce, and the garlic to the bag, and combine. Add the chicken thighs. Massage until well incorporated.
• Seal and refrigerate for 30 minutes.
• Remove chicken from bag; discard marinade.
• Using flat and long stainless steel skewers, thread the chicken thighs so that they resemble a flat, Middle Eastern–style kebab.
• Using cooking spray, spray a clean grill rag and wipe down the grates of the grill very well. Use long tongs if proximity to fire makes you uncomfortable.

• Place the chicken skewers on the hot grill.
• Grill for 15 minutes, assuming the heat is between 275° and 300° and controlled; otherwise, you'll find yourself turning more frequently.
• Flip and grill for another 15 minutes, or until you can easily pull off a piece of cooked chicken as if it has been slow-cooked.
• Remove the chicken to a platter, and let rest 10 minutes.

• Slide the thighs off the skewers and onto the platter, arranging them to one side of the platter.
• On the other side of the platter, in rows, line up the carrots, cucumbers, cilantro, and lime wedges. Serve with the Dipping Sauce (page 341). Serves 6 (serving size: 1 chicken thigh, ⅔ cup vegetables, and about 2½ tablespoons sauce)

CALORIES 169; **FAT** 4.9g (sat 1.2g, mono 1.6g, poly 1.2g); **PROTEIN** 23g; **CARB** 7g; **FIBER** 1g; **CHOL** 94mg; **IRON** 2mg; **SODIUM** 356mg; **CALC** 38mg

KEITH'S RECIPE BREAKDOWN
THAI STREET CHICKEN
Hands-on: 20 min. Total: 1 hr. 30 min.

INGREDIENT	AMOUNT	WHY
cilantro roots	3 pieces	A staple ingredient in Thai cuisine. Substitute ½ cup cilantro stems and ½ cup parsley stems.
palm sugar or brown sugar	1 tablespoon	For depth of flavor and caramel-molasses notes.
white pepper	2 teaspoons	White pepper is an essential ingredient in Thai kitchens and food stalls.
fish sauce	2 tablespoons	Fermented, salty, and glutamate-rich, it seasons and heightens the meatiness of the dish.
oyster sauce	1 tablespoon	... so does this, but it adds some sweetness, too.
garlic cloves	4, grated	You're making a paste.
skinless, boneless chicken thighs	1½ pounds (6 thighs)	For grilling.
cooking spray		To season the grill grates.
carrots	1 cup, fine julienne	For enjoying some lively raw vegetables at will along with your chicken. The flavor is so robust, you can break it up with these veggies.
cucumbers	2, peeled, scored, and sliced	Again, for the solitary enjoyment of eating raw vegetables and grilled chicken.
fresh cilantro	12 whole sprigs	To eat. Whole.

KEITH'S RECIPE BREAKDOWN

DIPPING SAUCE FOR THAI STREET CHICKEN
Hands-on: 10 min. Total: 10 min.

INGREDIENT	AMOUNT	WHY
white vinegar	6 tablespoons	For neutral acidity. You want the chicken flavor to shine.
palm sugar or brown sugar	6 tablespoons	For real-deal Southeast Asian sweetness.
shallots	¼ cup, shaved	For some pungency.
fresh lime juice	4 tablespoons	Thais use a lot of lime juice. This is a preferred acidic ingredient.
fish sauce	1 teaspoon	For "meatiness" and some salt.
Thai bird chiles	2, minced	Floral and crazy-intense.
garlic clove	1, crushed	Harmonizes acid and umami.
white pepper	½ teaspoon	Layers perfectly into the fish sauce. Fermented on fermented.

Dipping Sauce For Thai Street Chicken

Hands-on: 10 min. Total: 10 min. *You're hitting the sweet, sour, salty, spicy flavors in perfect harmony, albeit at fortissimo. Embrace the bird chile! Recipe adapted from* Mad Delicious.

- Bring first 3 ingredients to a boil; simmer 10 minutes. Puree with an immersion blender. Cool.
- Stir in juice and remaining ingredients. Serve with Thai Street Chicken or other grilled meats. Serves 6 (serving size: about 2½ tablespoons)

CALORIES 62; **FAT** 0g; **PROTEIN** 0g; **CARB** 16g; **FIBER** 0g; **CHOL** 0mg; **IRON** 0mg; **SODIUM** 84mg; **CALC** 17mg

ONE THING TO REMEMBER IS THAT **THE PAN IS NOT GLUED TO THE STOVE.** IN ADDITION TO REGULATING THE HEAT, YOU CAN LIFT THE PAN FROM THE BURNER WHEN COOKING, LIGHTLY AGITATING IT IN THE AIR TO ALLOW THINGS TO COOL OFF. YOU DON'T HAVE TO STAND THERE AND WATCH THINGS BURN.

KEITH'S RECIPE BREAKDOWN

LEMON SAUCE FOR EVERYTHING
Hands-on: 20 min. Total: 20 min.

INGREDIENT	AMOUNT	WHY
unsalted chicken stock	2 cups	Stock picks up natural gelatin from the bones of the chicken and provides a tad more body than broth.
large eggs	3	Whole eggs are essential to the viscosity of the sauce.
lemon zest	2 tablespoons grated	Aroma.
fresh lemon juice	2½ tablespoons	Acidity and brightness.
kosher salt	½ teaspoon	Requirement, particularly against acid.
olive oil	1 tablespoon	To enrich and provide a silkier mouthfeel.

Kid Friendly • Quick & Easy
Gluten Free

Lemon Sauce For Everything

Hands-on: 20 min. Total: 20 min.
OK, it's true: This is essentially the classic Greek lemon-egg soup, avgolemono. Every time I encountered a bowl of this creamy, rich, perfectly balanced soup, I thought to myself, "This is a sauce." And then I remembered my very first culinary instructor telling us that the only difference between a sauce and a soup was presentation. I agree, and this is a sauce. Put it on everything.

• Heat the chicken stock over medium-high heat in a heavy, medium saucepan to 180° or until tiny bubbles form around the edge. Do not boil.

• Combine the eggs, lemon zest, lemon juice, and salt in a medium bowl. Whisk until the eggs are frothy and lighter in color. (Alternatively, you can use a blender.)
• Ladle about a cup of the hot chicken stock into the egg mixture ¼ cup at a time, while stirring constantly (but not too vigorously) with a whisk.
• Lower the heat on the remaining chicken stock to as low as possible. Wait for 2 minutes, and then add the egg, lemon, and stock mixture back to the pot, stirring to combine.
• Warm the sauce gently until it reaches 180° and coats a spoon. Turn off the heat.
• Whisk in the olive oil to finish.
• Serve warm. Serves 10 (serving size: ¼ cup)

CALORIES 39; FAT 2.8g (sat 0.7g, mono 1.5g, poly 0.4g); PROTEIN 3g; CARB 1g; FIBER 0g; CHOL 56mg; IRON 0mg; SODIUM 169mg; CALC 10mg

10 SMART DIABETIC SWAPS

The holiday season has everyone munching and mingling around tables loaded with treats. Here are 10 simple carb-smart swaps to help make snacking easier when apps and sweets beckon.

1. Choose Pumpkin Pie over pecan.
Pecan pie gets a double-sugar boost from corn syrup and brown sugar. Choose a slice of pumpkin pie instead to save 10g carbohydrates. Eat it slowly, and savor just a few bites.

2. Choose Dark Chocolate over Brownies.
Just 1 satisfying ounce of dark chocolate has half the carbohydrates of a sugar-loaded brownie. Bonus: The flavonoids in dark chocolate can offer heart-healthy benefits.

3. Choose Shortbread over a Frosted Sugar Cookie.
A buttery shortbread square has only 9g carbohydrates—that's 75% less than a frosted sugar cookie. Even better: Go for the shortbread with nuts to add a little protein and fiber.

4. Choose Salsa over Creamy Spinach Dip.
Add zip to your chip by choosing naturally low-carb salsa (just 4g per ¼ cup) over mayo and sour cream–filled dip. You'll also save 120 calories and 14g fat per ¼ cup.

5. Choose fresh Raw Veggies as Dippers over Crackers.
An ounce of wheat crackers has the same amount of carbohydrates found in about 2½ cups fresh veggies. You'll also save on sodium and fat and get a vitamin and mineral boost, too.

6. Choose Bean-Based Spreads over Cream Cheese Spreads.
Opt for fiber-packed bean spreads like black bean dip or hummus. Fiber helps control blood sugar and will help you feel full longer so you're less tempted to overeat.

7. Choose Mixed Nuts over Snack Mix.
Go for plain mixed nuts instead of a snack mix with cereal, dried fruit, and candy—which can have more than 24g carbohydrates per ½ cup. Nuts are packed with protein, fiber, and heart-healthy fats and contain only 7g carbohydrates per ounce.

8. Choose a Lemon Sparkler over a Soda.
A 12-ounce can of soda contains 40g carbohydrates—all from sugar. That's nearly 3 tablespoons! Instead, mix 4 ounces fresh lemonade with 8 ounces sparkling water for a drink that cuts carbs and sugar by two–thirds. Garnish with a lemon slice.

9. Choose Oil and Vinegar over Bottled Creamy Dressing.
Bottled dressings, especially light and fat-free versions, are often filled with sugar and added salt. Vinegar and heart-healthy oils don't have any effect on blood sugar.

10. Choose Boiled Shrimp over Fried.
Ten large boiled shrimp have less than 1g carbohydrates and only 60 calories. You'll save 12g carbohydrates, 170 calories, and 14g fat over fried. A tablespoon of spicy cocktail sauce adds only 3g carbohydrates.

SMARTER CARB HABITS

DIABETES-FRIENDLY HOLIDAY DISHES

Simple swaps that help you in a carb-crazy season

The current approach to dietary management of diabetes is to tailor the meal plan for each individual. But in general, a healthy diabetic diet involves controlling total carbohydrates (particularly refined carbohydrates), reducing calories and sodium, increasing fiber, and replacing saturated fats and trans fats with more heart-healthy mono- and polyunsaturated fats. This approach, of course, is healthy for anyone who wants to eat better.

Here, you'll find three recipes for when you're in charge of Thanksgiving cooking. Our 10 easy swaps for dining at a restaurant or at a friend's home begin on page 342.

CHOOSE SEASONAL HERBS, FRUIT, AND FIBER-PACKED VEGGIES FOR HIGH-IMPACT FLAVOR.

Kid Friendly • Make Ahead

Multigrain Pilaf with Sunflower Seeds

Hands-on: 11 min. Total: 67 min. Grace your holiday table with this delicious pilaf featuring the low-glycemic, high-fiber grains barley, brown rice, and bulgur. It's a better choice for people with diabetes than white-bread stuffing or corn bread dressing.

4 teaspoons canola oil, divided
⅓ cup sunflower seed kernels
½ teaspoon salt, divided
2 teaspoons butter
1 cup thinly sliced leek (about 1 large)
2½ cups water
1½ cups fat-free, lower-sodium chicken broth
½ cup uncooked pearl barley
½ cup brown rice blend (such as Lundberg) or brown rice
½ cup dried currants
¼ cup uncooked bulgur
¼ cup chopped fresh parsley
¼ teaspoon freshly ground black pepper

1. Heat a Dutch oven over medium-high heat. Add 2 teaspoons oil, sunflower seeds, and ¼ teaspoon salt; sauté 2 minutes. Remove from pan.
2. Heat pan over medium heat; add 2 teaspoons oil and butter. Add leek; cook 4 minutes or until tender, stirring frequently. Add 2½ cups water and next 3 ingredients (through rice); bring to a boil. Cover, reduce heat, and simmer 35 minutes. Stir in currants and bulgur; cover and simmer 10 minutes or until grains are tender. Remove from heat; stir in remaining ¼ teaspoon salt, sunflower seeds, parsley, and pepper. Serve warm. Serves 8 (serving size: ½ cup)

CALORIES 198; **FAT** 6.6g (sat 1.1g, mono 2.2g, poly 2.6g); **PROTEIN** 5g; **CARB** 33g; **FIBER** 5g; **CHOL** 3mg; **IRON** 2mg; **SODIUM** 266mg; **CALC** 26mg

Kid Friendly • Quick & Easy
Vegetarian

Rosemary Mashed Sweet Potatoes with Shallots

Hands-on: 20 min. Total: 39 min.
*Replace sugar-packed sweet potato cas-
serole (often topped with marshmallows or
sugar-heavy streusel) with these mashers
that include only a hint of brown sugar. The
potatoes are already naturally sweet, so
there's no need for lots of added sweetener.*

**5½ teaspoons extra-virgin olive oil,
   divided**
**½ cup thinly sliced shallots (about 2
   medium)**
1½ teaspoons brown sugar
**1⅓ pounds sweet potatoes, peeled
   and diced**
**2 teaspoons finely chopped fresh
   rosemary**
¼ teaspoon coarse sea salt
**¼ teaspoon freshly ground black
   pepper**

1. Heat a medium skillet over low
heat. Add 4 teaspoons oil to pan;
swirl to coat. Add shallots to pan;
cook 5 minutes, stirring occasionally.
Sprinkle with sugar; cook 20 minutes
or until shallots are golden, stirring
occasionally.
2. Place potatoes in a medium saucepan; cover with water. Bring to a boil;
cook 8 minutes or until tender. Drain.
Place potatoes in a large bowl; beat
with a mixer at medium speed until
smooth. Add rosemary, salt, and pepper; beat until blended. Spoon into
a bowl; top with shallots, and drizzle
with 1½ teaspoons oil. Serves 4
(serving size: about ½ cup)

CALORIES 202; FAT 6.3g (sat 0.9g, mono 4.5g, poly 0.9g);
PROTEIN 3g; CARB 35g; FIBER 5g; CHOL 0mg;
IRON 1mg; SODIUM 278mg; CALC 55mg

Kid Friendly • Make Ahead
Vegetarian • Gluten Free

Fresh Cranberry-Orange Relish

Hands-on: 8 min. Total: 24 hr. 8 min.
*Canned cranberry sauce contains about
22g carbohydrates per slice, and homemade fresh cranberry sauce often uses a
cup of sugar (or more). This fresh relish contains just 10g carbohydrates per generous
¼-cup serving and has double the fiber of
canned. It does include some added sugar,
which is needed to offset the tartness of the
cranberries. Be sure to make it a day ahead
so the flavors have time to marry.*

1 large orange
¼ cup plus 2 tablespoons sugar
**2 (10-ounce) packages fresh
   cranberries**

1. Grate orange rind; place rind in
a food processor. Peel and section
orange over bowl of food processor. Add orange sections, sugar, and
cranberries to processor; process
until coarsely chopped. Cover relish,
and refrigerate at least 1 day. Serves
16 (serving size: ¼ cup)

CALORIES 40; FAT 0.1g (sat 0g, mono 0g, poly 0g);
PROTEIN 0g; CARB 10g; FIBER 2g; CHOL 0mg;
IRON 0mg; SODIUM 1mg; CALC 7mg

NUTRITION MADE EASY

A LOWER-FAT, LOWER-CARB MASH

Creamy, comfort-filled potatoes with
half the calories. Here's how.

One thing—as certain as turkey
and cranberry and groans from
couch-bound overeaters—is de-
manded of this holiday season:
heaping bowls of fluffy mashed
potatoes. It's a rich dish: As any cook
knows, the secret to smooth texture
is a knob of butter and a serious glug
of cream. A serving of potatoes is
about 250 calories, with 8g of sat
fat. But we found a secret ingredient
that lends sweet, comforting flavor
and cuts back on the need for fat:
cauliflower.

Compared to potatoes, cauliflower
has one-third the calories and 50%
more fiber per pound. Swap it in for
half the spuds, and you'll end up with
a starchy base that has 67 fewer calories, 17g fewer carbs, and 0.5g more
fiber per cup. For deeper flavor, roast
the cauliflower first, and then puree
until creamy. Fold into your potatoes,
and round it out with milk, a touch
of butter, and a sprinkle of seasonings. Voilà—a twist on tradition.

Kid Friendly • Quick & Easy
Make Ahead • Vegetarian
Gluten Free

Roasted Cauliflower Mashed Potaotes

Preheat oven to 400°. Boil 1 pound
chopped peeled baking potato 15
minutes or until tender. Drain; mash.
Coat 1 pound cauliflower florets
with cooking spray; roast at 400° for
15 minutes or until browned. Place
cauliflower in a food processor; process until smooth. Fold cauliflower
into potatoes. Add ½ cup warm
2% milk, 2 tablespoons butter, ½
teaspoon salt, and ¼ teaspoon freshly
ground black pepper; stir well. Serves
6 (serving size: ⅔ cup)

CALORIES 122; FAT 4.7g (sat 2.8g); SODIUM 185mg

BE PORTION-SMART

Use holiday feasting season to practice some healthy new habits of mind.

This time of year, more than any other, it's far easier to be happy about the foods we eat than the amount we eat. How much healthier would it be to skate from Thanksgiving to New Year's without having to make midnight resolutions on December 31 about "eating better" that mostly reflect weeks' worth of overindulging?

Resolutions often spring from guilt about failure of willpower, when the focus can be on developing new portion awareness and habits that will work throughout the year. The goal isn't to shun foods but to be mindful of the portions we're eating while we're eating them.

"Some people think eating less means restricting foods they love," says Jim Painter, PhD, this month's Healthy Habits hero and a food psychology and nutrition professor at Eastern Illinois University. "That just doesn't work. As soon as you restrict a food, the cravings build until you finally give in and eat the entire thing."

One area of Painter's research looks at the visual cues that can help people understand what they're consuming. "If you're eating chocolate candies, let the wrappers pile up on the side," he advises. "We've found that people eat less because they can see how many chocolates they've eaten. You're not restricting your consumption; you're just making yourself more aware."

Simple techniques like reducing plate size help to shift perception about what a healthy portion is. And then there's the important matter of speed: The longer you take to eat, the less likely it is that you will reach for

seconds. It takes time for the body to begin signaling satiety.

"We just bypass those cues by eating so much so fast that the body doesn't have time to react," Painter says. This can be particularly problematic during the holidays.

Kid Friendly • Freezable Make Ahead

Individual White Lasagnas

Hands-on: 30 min. Total: 1 hr. 15 min.

8 uncooked lasagna noodles
1 ounce prosciutto, thinly sliced
1 teaspoon extra-virgin olive oil
1 shallot, chopped
1 (12-ounce) package presliced mushrooms
1 (9-ounce) package fresh spinach
2 cups part-skim ricotta cheese
2 ounces Parmesan cheese, grated
2 tablespoons chopped fresh thyme, divided
½ teaspoon kosher salt
½ teaspoon black pepper
1 ounce fontina cheese, shredded
Cooking spray
2 ounces part-skim mozzarella cheese, shredded (about ½ cup)

1. Preheat oven to 350°.
2. Cook pasta according to directions until al dente, omitting salt and fat; drain. Cut each noodle crosswise into 4 pieces, forming 32 squares.
3. Cook prosciutto in a large skillet over medium-high heat until crisp. Remove prosciutto from pan, and crumble. Return pan to medium-high heat. Add oil; swirl. Add shallot; sauté 2 minutes. Add mushrooms; cook 8 minutes, stirring occasionally. Stir in spinach; cook 2 minutes or until spinach wilts. Remove from heat. Drain.
4. Combine ricotta cheese, Parmesan, 1½ tablespoons thyme, and next 3 ingredients. Add spinach mixture and prosciutto, stirring to combine.

5. Coat 8 (6-ounce) ramekins with cooking spray. Place ramekins on a jelly-roll pan. Arrange 1 pasta square in bottom of each ramekin. Spoon one-third of filling evenly over pasta squares; top filling with 1 pasta square. Repeat layers twice, ending with pasta. Combine 1½ teaspoons thyme and mozzarella cheese. Sprinkle evenly over lasagnas.
6. Cover pan loosely with foil coated with cooking spray. Bake at 350° for 20 minutes. Uncover and bake an additional 15 minutes or until bubbly and browned. Let stand 10 minutes before serving. Serves 8 (serving size: 1 lasagna)

CALORIES 276; FAT 11.3g (sat 6g, mono 3.1g, poly 0.5g); PROTEIN 19g; CARB 26g; FIBER 2g; CHOL 35mg; IRON 2mg; SODIUM 503mg; CALC 356mg

DR. PAINTER'S PORTION SMART STRATEGIES

1. DON'T GRAZE AT THE PARTY.
Distracted eating quickly leads to overeating. Standing by the buffet makes it very hard to know how much you're eating. Instead, take a healthy portion (on a small plate), sit down, and eat slowly.

2. GIVE YOURSELF CUT-OFF CUES.
"When we choose something like a candy bar, we eat the entire thing, and then we don't want any more," Painter says. "That's because the food packaging tells us when we're done much more than internal cues of satiety. Almost never does someone eat a candy bar, and then pick up another one." Single-serving foods, like Individual White Lasagnas (at left) or Five-Ingredient Chocolate Cakes (page 327), give those cues, too.

3. MAKE A PLATE CHANGE.
"Plate size has real power to make people feel full and at the same time eat less," Painter says. "You can fill up a smaller plate and eat the whole thing, and you will have still eaten less than you would have had you eaten on a larger plate." People are more satisfied with smaller plates because they feel like they've eaten more."

RED, WHITE, AND BLUE SCONES

Tender, whole-grain treats in honor of Veterans Day

Make one batch at a time when doubling up on these Stars and Stripes–inspired breakfast beauts so that the dough doesn't get overworked. A light kneading is all you need. Old-fashioned oats contribute a delightful hearty texture to these patriotic goodies; toasting them before mixing into the batter provides a robust flavor boost. With their golden crust, scones happen to be great travelers. Just pack them in an airtight container, and deliver some to your own special hero.

Kid Friendly • Make Ahead Vegetarian

Red, White, and Blue Toasted Oat Scones

Hands-on: 34 min. Total: 60 min.

1 cup old-fashioned rolled oats
4.5 ounces all-purpose flour (about 1 cup)
1/3 cup granulated sugar
2 teaspoons baking powder
1/2 teaspoon baking soda
1/2 teaspoon salt
1/4 cup cold unsalted butter, cut into 1/4-inch cubes
1/4 cup white chocolate chips
1/4 cup dried cherries
1/4 cup dried blueberries
1/2 cup low-fat buttermilk
1 large egg white, lightly beaten
1 teaspoon water
2 teaspoons turbinado sugar

1. Preheat oven to 375°.
2. Spread oats on a baking sheet; bake at 375° for 10 minutes. Cool 5 minutes.
3. Weigh or lightly spoon flour into a dry measuring cup; level with a knife. Combine oats, flour, and next 4 ingredients in a bowl; cut cold butter into flour mixture with a pastry blender or 2 knives until mixture resembles coarse meal. Add chocolate chips, cherries, and blueberries, tossing to combine. Add buttermilk, stirring just until moist (dough will be sticky).
4. Turn dough out onto a lightly floured surface; knead lightly 4 to 5 times with floured hands. Pat dough into a 7-inch circle on a baking sheet lined with parchment paper. Cut dough into 8 wedges, cutting into but not through the dough.
5. Combine egg white and 1 teaspoon water in a small bowl, stirring with a whisk. Lightly brush egg white mixture over surface of dough; sprinkle evenly with turbinado sugar. Bake at 375° for 25 to 28 minutes or until golden. Serves 8 (serving size: 1 scone)

CALORIES 254; **FAT** 8.6g (sat 4.9g, mono 2.3g, poly 0.6g); **PROTEIN** 4g; **CARB** 39g; **FIBER** 3g; **CHOL** 18mg; **IRON** 1mg; **SODIUM** 377mg; **CALC** 106mg

FRESH RIGHT NOW

CIPOLLINI

These plump onions are one of autumn's sweetest delights.

First cultivated in Italy, cipollini are most often served there as agrodolce (the Italian word for "sweet and sour"), a condiment that pairs beautifully with cheese or roasted meat. Try our version of this vinegar and sugar–braised dish. It's ready in only 20 minutes.

These squat, silver dollar–sized onions, at their peak from fall through midwinter, have an unusually high sugar content, which helps them caramelize quickly to a gorgeous brown. You can put them in the oven with carrots and potatoes alongside your favorite roast for a hearty fall feast.

Quick & Easy • Make Ahead Vegetarian • Gluten Free

Sweet and Sour Cipollini

Hands-on: 20 min. Total: 20 min.
Just a few ingredients make for a complex condiment that dresses up simple roast chicken or pork. To add a floral note, replace the brown sugar with clover honey.

20 ounces cipollini onions
4 teaspoons extra-virgin olive oil, divided
3 tablespoons red wine vinegar
1 1/2 tablespoons light brown sugar
1/2 teaspoon kosher salt
1/4 teaspoon freshly ground black pepper

1. Soak cipollini in a bowl of boiling water 1 minute. Drain. Trim top and root ends from onions; peel. Cut each onion in half crosswise.
2. Heat a large nonstick skillet over medium-high heat. Add 2 teaspoons olive oil; swirl to coat. Place half of onions, cut sides down, in pan, and cook 2 minutes on each side or until browned. Remove from pan. Repeat procedure with 2 teaspoons oil and remaining onions. Return onions to pan, and sprinkle with vinegar and brown sugar. Swirl to melt sugar and coat onions with syrupy mixture. Stir in salt and pepper. Serve cipollini hot or at room temperature. Serves 6 (serving size: about 3 cipollini halves)

CALORIES 114; **FAT** 3.1g (sat 0.5g, mono 2.2g, poly 0.3g); **PROTEIN** 1g; **CARB** 21g; **FIBER** 2g; **CHOL** 0mg; **IRON** 0mg; **SODIUM** 168mg; **CALC** 33mg

LAMB WITH SHAVED FALL VEGETABLES

One of Nevada's top toques finds the parsnip's sweet spot.

If you think of parsnips as a sweeter, more complexly flavored carrot, you'll understand why it's an integral part of any root veggie medley. Of course, most folks don't think of parsnips at all. "It's one of the most underrated vegetables, maybe in part because it looks like a carrot that went funny," says Mark Estee, chef-owner of Campo, a modern Italian mecca in Reno, Nevada, that has earned raves nationwide. "They have an earthy sugariness and carry flavors really well."

Raw, shaved root veggies make this recipe shine: You expect them to be roasted in this context, but the uncooked ribbons lend toothy textural contrast to the tender, succulent lamb. Try Estee's original version of the dish this month at Campo.

Gluten Free

Leg of Lamb with Shaved Fall Vegetables

Hands-on: 1 hr. 30 min. Total: 27 hr. 45 min.

3 tablespoons garlic powder
2 tablespoons freshly ground black pepper
2 tablespoons cumin seeds, toasted
1 tablespoon coriander seeds, toasted
1 tablespoon sweet paprika
1 tablespoon ground cinnamon
2 tablespoons harissa or hot chile sauce

2 teaspoons fennel seeds, toasted
2 teaspoons kosher salt, divided
1 (5-pound) boneless leg of lamb, trimmed
4 cups water
½ cup finely diced sweet onion
½ cup chopped mint leaves
3 tablespoons extra-virgin olive oil
2 tablespoons red wine vinegar
2 teaspoons minced fresh garlic
½ teaspoon freshly ground black pepper
2 cups shaved peeled parsnips
2 cups shaved peeled carrots
2 cups shaved peeled butternut squash
1 cup shaved peeled turnips
2 tablespoons extra-virgin olive oil
2 tablespoons fresh lemon juice

1. Combine first 8 ingredients in a bowl. Add 1 teaspoon salt to spice mixture. Rub spice mixture over lamb. Reroll roast; secure at 1-inch intervals with twine. Wrap in plastic wrap; refrigerate 6 to 24 hours.
2. Preheat oven to 375°.
3. Remove lamb from refrigerator; let stand at room temperature 30 minutes. Place lamb on a wire rack; place rack in a roasting pan. Pour 4 cups water into pan. Roast lamb at 375° for 1 hour and 45 minutes or until thermometer registers 130°. Remove from oven. Let stand at room temperature 20 minutes; cut across grain into thin slices.
4. Place drippings from pan in a small saucepan over high heat; bring to a boil. Cook until reduced to 1 cup.
5. Combine onion and next 5 ingredients in a small bowl. Stir in ½ teaspoon salt.
6. Combine ½ teaspoon salt, parsnips, and remaining ingredients; toss to coat. Serve with lamb. Top lamb with herb mixture; drizzle with jus. Serves 16 (serving size: about 3 ounces lamb, ⅓ cup vegetables, 2 teaspoons herb mixture, and 1 tablespoon jus)

CALORIES 311; FAT 16.8g (sat 5.5g, mono 8.4g, poly 1.4g); PROTEIN 30g; CARB 9g; FIBER 3g; CHOL 96mg; IRON 3mg; SODIUM 329mg; CALC 57mg

FRAGRANT CARDAMOM

By Naomi Duguid

A touch of this spice makes sweet and savory dishes unforgettable.

Cardamom, the intensely aromatic sweet spice native to India, is a precious asset to cooks all over the world. You'll see it sold preground or as green pods with small seeds packed inside. Buy the pods, if possible; the spice loses aroma and flavor quickly once ground. Crack open the pods, remove the seeds, and grind to a powder in a coffee grinder or a small mortar.

Whole pods work beautifully in savory dishes from the Indian repertoire, such as curries and pilafs, where they add complexity. The spice comes into its own, though, in ground form in sweet baking dishes, from the Finnish cake-bread called pulla to the rice-flour shortbread cookies in the recipe on page 348. I also love it in rice pudding and to flavor whipped cream.

Cardamom also gives a great lift to hot tea and coffee. No need to grind—just crack pods before using them. Make a warming chai by tossing several cardamom pods into the teapot, along with tea, minced ginger, and/or black pepper. In Arab cultures and in Ethiopia, coffee is often flavored with cardamom. To make, crack two pods and add them to your French press along with the ground coffee before you pour in the hot water. The water will draw flavor and aroma from the cardamom as the coffee steeps.

continued

Cardamom Cookies

Hands-on: 20 min. Total: 12 hr. 40 min.
These cookies are a special gluten-free version of shortbread—just be sure to use powdered sugar that doesn't include a starch with gluten.

1 cup powdered sugar
6 tablespoons unsalted butter, barely melted
5 tablespoons sunflower oil
¾ to 1 teaspoon ground cardamom
1 large egg yolk
6.88 ounces brown rice flour (about 1½ cups)
¼ teaspoon salt
3 tablespoons finely chopped pistachios

1. Combine sugar, butter, and oil in the bowl of a stand mixer; beat at medium speed 1½ minutes or until well combined and pale. Add cardamom and egg yolk, beating until combined. Weigh or lightly spoon flour into dry measuring cups; level with a knife. Gradually add flour and salt to butter mixture, beating just until combined. Divide dough into 2 equal portions. Shape each portion into a 6-inch log. Wrap logs individually in plastic wrap; refrigerate 12 to 24 hours.
2. Preheat oven to 350°.
3. Cover 2 baking sheets with parchment paper. Remove dough logs from refrigerator. Cut each log into 20 slices; place slices 1 inch apart on baking sheets. (Pat slices together if they crumble.) Sprinkle with pistachios. Bake at 350° for 17 minutes or until edges begin to brown, rotating pans halfway through. Let stand 5 minutes; place cookies on a wire rack. Cool completely. Serves 40 (serving size: 1 cookie)

CALORIES 71; FAT 4.3g (sat 1.4g, mono 1.1g, poly 1.6g); PROTEIN 1g; CARB 8g; FIBER 0g; CHOL 9mg; IRON 0mg; SODIUM 18mg; CALC 3mg

MARINATED GRAINS AND GREENS

Crispy baked tofu sits atop savory barley and fresh chard in this hearty dinner bowl.

Make Ahead • Vegetarian

Sesame Barley with Greens and Teriyaki Tofu

Hands-on: 30 min. Total: 2 hr. Don't skip the chilling step: It gives flavors time to soak into the barley.

3 cups water
½ cup uncooked pearl barley
¼ cup rice wine vinegar
3 tablespoons brown sugar, divided
3 tablespoons lower-sodium soy sauce, divided
4 teaspoons dark sesame oil, divided
2 teaspoons finely grated peeled fresh ginger, divided
2 garlic cloves, minced and divided
6 cups thinly sliced Swiss chard (about 1 bunch)
1 (14-ounce) package organic extra-firm tofu, drained
¼ teaspoon crushed red pepper
Cooking spray
4 teaspoons toasted sesame seeds
2 green onions, thinly sliced

1. Bring 3 cups water to a boil in a medium, heavy saucepan. Add barley; reduce heat, and simmer 30 minutes or until barley is tender. Drain and cool slightly.
2. Combine vinegar, 1 tablespoon brown sugar, 1 tablespoon soy sauce, 1 tablespoon oil, 1 teaspoon ginger, and 1 garlic clove in a large bowl, stirring well with a whisk. Add chard and barley, and toss well to coat. Cover and chill 1 hour.
3. Preheat oven to 375°.
4. Cut tofu crosswise into 5 (1-inch-thick) slices. Place tofu slices on several layers of paper towels; cover with additional paper towels. Let stand 20 minutes, pressing down occasionally.
5. Cut each tofu slice into ½-inch cubes. Combine 1 teaspoon sesame oil, 2 tablespoons brown sugar, 2 tablespoons soy sauce, 1 teaspoon ginger, garlic clove, and pepper in a medium bowl, stirring well with a whisk. Add tofu; toss to combine. Let stand 10 minutes.
6. Arrange tofu in a single layer on a foil-lined baking sheet coated with cooking spray. Bake at 375° for 30 minutes or until tofu is browned on all sides, stirring three times.
7. Divide barley mixture evenly among 4 plates, and top evenly with tofu. Sprinkle evenly with sesame seeds and onions. Serves 4 (serving size: 1 cup barley mixture and ½ cup tofu)

CALORIES 299; FAT 12.5g (sat 1.5g, mono 6.7g, poly 3.3g); PROTEIN 15g; CARB 37g; FIBER 6g; CHOL 0mg; IRON 4mg; SODIUM 530mg; CALC 257mg

BAKE IT!

In the oven, tofu gets a crisp crust and stays creamy in the middle. If you make the dish ahead, the tofu gets wonderfully chewy.

FEED 4 FOR LESS THAN $10

Corn, chile, and cumin give potpies a Mexican kick. Plus: pork, farro, and escarole.

Kid Friendly

Tamale Chicken Potpies

$2.49 PER SERVING

Hands-on: 28 min. Total: 43 min.
Serve these individual potpies with a side of spicy black beans: Heat 2 teaspoons canola oil in a medium saucepan over medium heat. Add ½ cup diced green bell pepper and 2 minced garlic cloves; sauté until soft. Stir in 1 (15-ounce) can rinsed and drained black beans, 1 tablespoon fresh lime juice, and ½ teaspoon grated lime rind; cook until thoroughly heated (about 5 minutes).

2 teaspoons canola oil
1 cup chopped onion
12 ounces ground chicken
1 tablespoon ground cumin
½ teaspoon chili powder
½ teaspoon salt, divided
1 cup chopped zucchini
¾ cup fresh corn kernels
1 (10-ounce) can diced tomatoes and green chiles, undrained
1 (8-ounce) can unsalted tomato sauce
Cooking spray
½ cup coarsely ground yellow cornmeal
1½ cups water, divided
3 ounces Monterey Jack cheese, shredded and divided (about ¾ cup)

1. Preheat oven to 400°.
2. Heat a large skillet over medium-high heat. Add oil to pan; swirl to coat. Add onion; sauté 3 minutes. Add chicken; cook 3 minutes, stirring to crumble. Stir in cumin, chili powder, and ¼ teaspoon salt; cook 1 minute. Add zucchini, corn, tomatoes, and tomato sauce; bring to a boil. Reduce heat; simmer 8 minutes, stirring occasionally. Divide chicken mixture evenly among 4 (10-ounce) ramekins coated with cooking spray. Place ramekins on a jelly-roll pan.
3. Place ¼ teaspoon salt, cornmeal, and ½ cup water in a medium bowl, stirring to combine. Bring 1 cup water to a boil in a medium saucepan. Gradually add cornmeal mixture to pan; cook 3 minutes or until thickened, stirring frequently. Stir in 2 ounces cheese. Divide cornmeal mixture evenly among ramekins. Sprinkle evenly with 1 ounce cheese. Bake at 400° for 15 minutes or until light golden brown. Serves 4

CALORIES 355; FAT 16.8g (sat 6.4g, mono 6.6g, poly 2.5g); PROTEIN 24g; CARB 28g; FIBER 3g; CHOL 92mg; IRON 3mg; SODIUM 493mg; CALC 194mg

Kid Friendly • Quick & Easy

Grilled Pork Medallions with Farro and Escarole

$2.41 PER SERVING

Hands-on: 30 min. Total: 40 min. *This dish is both incredibly simple and versatile. Try swapping the escarole for a healthy green that happens to be on sale, such as kale, Swiss chard, collard greens, or even spinach. You could also switch things up by substituting bulgur, brown rice, or whatever whole grain you have on hand for the farro.*

5 teaspoons olive oil, divided
1 cup sliced onion
¾ cup uncooked farro
4 teaspoons minced fresh garlic, divided
2 cups unsalted chicken stock
½ teaspoon salt, divided
4 cups chopped escarole
¼ teaspoon freshly ground black pepper
1 (1-pound) pork tenderloin, cut crosswise into 8 pieces

1. Heat a large skillet over medium-high heat. Add 1 tablespoon oil to pan; swirl to coat. Add onion; cook 3 minutes, stirring frequently. Add farro and 1 tablespoon garlic to pan; cook 3 minutes or until farro begins to toast, stirring frequently. Stir in stock and ¼ teaspoon salt; bring to a boil. Reduce heat to low; cover and simmer 20 minutes or until farro is almost tender. Uncover and cook 5 minutes. Stir in escarole; cook 3 minutes or until wilted.
2. Combine 2 teaspoons oil, 1 teaspoon garlic, ¼ teaspoon salt, pepper, and pork. Using the palm of your hand, gently flatten the pork into ½-inch-thick pieces. Heat a grill pan over medium-high heat. Add 4 pork pieces to pan; cook 4 minutes on each side or until desired degree of doneness. Remove from pan. Repeat procedure with remaining pork pieces. Serve with farro mixture. Serves 4 (serving size: ¾ cup farro mixture and 2 pieces pork)

CALORIES 348; FAT 9.1g (sat 1.6g, mono 5g, poly 1.1g); PROTEIN 33g; CARB 35g; FIBER 8g; CHOL 74mg; IRON 4mg; SODIUM 640mg; CALC 99mg

SUPERFAST 20-MINUTE COOKING

Chicken and Rice Soup with Lemon and Ginger

1 tablespoon olive oil
½ cup chopped onion
1½ tablespoons finely minced peeled fresh ginger
1 tablespoon white miso
1 (8-ounce) package presliced cremini mushrooms
4½ cups unsalted chicken stock
1½ cups shredded skinless rotisserie chicken breast
3 cups chopped bok choy
1 (8.5-ounce) pouch precooked brown rice
1 tablespoon lower-sodium soy sauce
½ teaspoon kosher salt
½ teaspoon freshly ground black pepper
1 tablespoon grated lemon rind
2 tablespoons fresh lemon juice

1. Heat a Dutch oven over medium-high heat. Add oil to pan; swirl to coat. Add onion, ginger, and miso; sauté 4 minutes. Add mushrooms; sauté 2 minutes. Add stock, chicken, and bok choy; bring to a boil. Reduce heat, and simmer 8 minutes.
2. While soup simmers, prepare rice according to package directions. Stir rice, soy sauce, salt, and pepper into soup; cook 4 minutes or until bok choy is tender. Remove from heat; stir in lemon rind and juice. Serves 6 (serving size: 1½ cups)

CALORIES 185; FAT 5g (sat 0.8g, mono 2.2g, poly 0.6g); PROTEIN 18g; CARB 18g; FIBER 2g; CHOL 33mg; IRON 1mg; SODIUM 607mg; CALC 71mg

Thai Green Curry with Shrimp and Kale

Lacinato kale provides a delightful textural contrast to the tender rice noodles.

6 ounces dried rice noodles
2 teaspoons olive oil
⅓ cup chopped green onions
1 tablespoon chopped fresh garlic
1 tablespoon chopped peeled fresh ginger
2 tablespoons Thai green curry paste
1¼ cups matchstick-cut carrots
½ cup unsalted chicken stock
1 (13.5-ounce) can light coconut milk
6 cups packed chopped Lacinato kale (about ½ bunch)
¼ teaspoon kosher salt
1 pound peeled and deveined medium shrimp
¼ cup chopped fresh cilantro
1 teaspoon grated lime rind
1½ teaspoons fresh lime juice

1. Prepare rice noodles according to package directions. Drain and rinse with cold water. Drain and set aside.
2. Heat oil in a large skillet over medium-high heat. Add oil to pan; swirl to coat. Add green onions, garlic, and ginger; sauté 1 minute. Stir in curry paste; sauté 30 seconds. Add carrots, chicken stock, and coconut milk, stirring well to combine; bring to a simmer, and cook 5 minutes.
3. Fold in kale; sprinkle with salt. Cook 3 minutes or until kale is wilted and tender. Add shrimp; cook 3 minutes or until shrimp are done. Remove from heat; top with cilantro, lime rind, and juice. Serve over rice noodles. Serves 4 (serving size: ¾ cup noodles and 1½ cups curry)

CALORIES 398; FAT 9.7g (sat 4.3g, mono 1.8g, poly 0.8g); PROTEIN 20g; CARB 60g; FIBER 4g; CHOL 143mg; IRON 3mg; SODIUM 608mg; CALC 230mg

Pork Cutlets with Butternut Squash, Apple, and Cranberry Sauté

Steaming squash tenderizes it before you pan-sear it to a caramelized finish.

3 cups precut peeled butternut squash
1 cup dried cranberries
1 (1-pound) pork tenderloin, trimmed and cut into 12 thin medallions
¾ teaspoon kosher salt, divided
¼ teaspoon freshly ground black pepper
2 tablespoons all-purpose flour
1 tablespoon olive oil, divided
1 cup unsalted chicken stock
1 tablespoon unsalted butter
1 cup chopped onion
1 cup chopped peeled Granny Smith apple
2 teaspoons sugar
¼ teaspoon ground red pepper
2 tablespoons chopped fresh parsley

1. Place squash and cranberries in a microwave-safe dish. Add water to a depth of ¼ inch; cover with plastic wrap. Microwave at HIGH 7 minutes; drain.
2. While squash cooks, heat a nonstick skillet over medium-high heat. Sprinkle pork with ½ teaspoon salt and black pepper. Place flour in a shallow dish; dredge pork in flour. Add 1½ teaspoons oil to pan; swirl to coat. Add half of pork; cook 2 minutes per side. Transfer cooked pork to a platter. Repeat with remaining oil and pork.
3. Add chicken stock to pan; cook until liquid is reduced by half, stirring occasionally.
4. Melt butter in a skillet over medium-high heat. Add onion, apple, sugar, and red pepper to pan,

and toss to coat; sauté 4 minutes. Add squash, cranberries, and ¼ teaspoon salt; toss and remove from heat. Pour pan sauce over pork, and serve with squash mixture; garnish with chopped parsley. Serves 4 (serving size: 3 pork medallions, 2 tablespoons sauce, and 1 cup squash mixture)

CALORIES 379; FAT 9.4g (sat 3.2g, mono 4.2g, poly 1.2g); PROTEIN 27g; CARB 50g; FIBER 5g; CHOL 81mg; IRON 3mg; SODIUM 461mg; CALC 80mg

Kid Friendly • Quick & Easy

Chicken Cutlets with Sesame Broccoli Slaw

Toasted sesame oil and seeds release a huge depth of nutty flavor into this easy entrée.

3 tablespoons rice vinegar
2 tablespoons lower-sodium soy sauce
2 tablespoons toasted sesame oil
1 tablespoon grated peeled fresh ginger
1 teaspoon sugar
½ teaspoon crushed red pepper
3 medium garlic cloves, minced
1 tablespoon olive oil
4 (4-ounce) chicken breast cutlets
¼ teaspoon kosher salt
¼ teaspoon freshly ground black pepper
4 ounces presliced cremini mushrooms
1 red bell pepper, seeded and sliced
1 cup matchstick-cut carrots
1 (12-ounce) bag broccoli slaw mix
2 teaspoons toasted sesame seeds
2 green onions, sliced

1. Combine first 7 ingredients in a bowl, stirring with a whisk.
2. Heat a large skillet over high heat. Add oil to pan; swirl to coat. Sprinkle chicken with salt and pepper. Add chicken to pan; cook

3 minutes, turning once. Remove from pan. Add mushrooms and bell pepper to pan; stir-fry 2 minutes. Add carrots and slaw to pan; stir-fry 90 seconds. Add soy sauce mixture; toss to coat. Remove from heat. Divide slaw among 4 plates; top each serving with 1 chicken cutlet. Sprinkle evenly with sesame seeds and onions. Serves 4 (serving size: 1 chicken cutlet and 1¼ cups broccoli slaw)

CALORIES 317; FAT 14.3g (sat 2.2g, mono 6.3g, poly 4.1g); PROTEIN 29g; CARB 17g; FIBER 6g; CHOL 73mg; IRON 2mg; SODIUM 577mg; CALC 73mg

Quick & Easy

Cauliflower with Anchovy Breadcrumbs

6 cups cauliflower florets
1½ ounces torn French bread pieces
2 teaspoons chopped fresh sage
¼ teaspoon freshly ground black pepper
¼ teaspoon salt
3 anchovy fillets, rinsed and drained
3 garlic cloves
1½ tablespoons butter

1. Bring a large saucepan of water to a boil; add cauliflower. Boil 6 minutes; drain.
2. Place bread and next 5 ingredients (through garlic) in a mini food processor; process until finely chopped. Melt butter in a medium skillet over medium heat. Add crumb mixture; cook 4 minutes. Toss crumbs with cauliflower. Serves 6 (serving size: 1 cup)

CALORIES 76; FAT 3.5g (sat 1.9g, mono 0.8g, poly 0.1g); PROTEIN 3g; CARB 9g; FIBER 2g; CHOL 9mg; IRON 1mg; SODIUM 222mg; CALC 33mg

Kid Friendly • Quick & Easy
Vegetarian • Gluten Free
Cauliflower with Sesame Toasted Cashews

Bring a saucepan of water to a boil; add 6 cups cauliflower florets. Boil 6 minutes; drain. Heat 2 tablespoons sesame oil in a skillet over medium heat. Add ⅓ cup unsalted cashew halves, 1 teaspoon grated peeled fresh ginger, ½ teaspoon salt, and ¼ teaspoon pepper; cook 4 minutes. Toss cauliflower with nut mixture; top with 2 tablespoons sliced green onions. Serves 6 (serving size: 1 cup)

CALORIES 112; FAT 8.5g (sat 1.4g); SODIUM 194mg

Quick & Easy • Vegetarian
Gluten Free
Cauliflower with Garlic-Thyme Vinaigrette

Bring a saucepan of water to a boil; add 6 cups cauliflower florets and 2 tablespoons sliced shallots. Boil 6 minutes; drain. Combine 2½ tablespoons olive oil, 1½ tablespoons sherry vinegar, 1 tablespoon minced fresh garlic, 2 teaspoons fresh thyme leaves, ½ teaspoon salt, and ¼ teaspoon black pepper. Toss cauliflower and shallots with vinaigrette. Serves 6 (serving size: 1 cup)

CALORIES 89; FAT 6.4g (sat 0.9g); SODIUM 226mg

Quick & Easy • Vegetarian
Cauliflower with Coconut Curry Sauce

Combine ¾ cup light coconut milk, ⅓ cup water, 2¼ teaspoons red curry paste, 2¼ teaspoons lower-sodium soy sauce, 1 tablespoon rice vinegar, and ¼ teaspoon salt in a saucepan; bring to a boil. Add 1 head cauliflower, stem side down, to pan. Reduce heat; cover and steam 13 minutes. Cut cauliflower into florets; drizzle with coconut mixture. Sprinkle with 2 tablespoons chopped fresh cilantro. Serves 6 (serving size: 1 cup)

CALORIES 55; FAT 1.9g (sat 1.5g); SODIUM 250mg

Butternut Squash Pizza with White Sauce, Spinach, and Goat Cheese

Try swapping out the goat cheese for feta or Gorgonzola to switch up the flavor profile.

2 cups precut peeled butternut squash (about 12 ounces)
1/4 teaspoon kosher salt, divided
1 (8-ounce) prebaked thin pizza crust (such as Mama Mary's)
5 tablespoons refrigerated light alfredo sauce
1 teaspoon extra-virgin olive oil
6 cups fresh baby spinach
1 ounce goat cheese, crumbled (about 1/4 cup)
1/4 teaspoon freshly ground black pepper

1. Preheat oven to 450°.
2. Place squash in a large microwave-safe dish; add water to a depth of 1/2 inch. Cover with plastic wrap; microwave at HIGH 5 minutes. Drain and toss squash with 1/8 teaspoon kosher salt.
3. While squash cooks, place pizza crust on a baking sheet; spread alfredo sauce over crust.
4. Heat a nonstick skillet. Add oil to pan; swirl to coat. Add spinach; sauté 1 minute. Stir in 1/8 teaspoon salt. Arrange wilted spinach over sauce. Top with squash and goat cheese; sprinkle with pepper.
5. Bake pizza in bottom third of oven at 450° for 6 minutes. Turn oven to broil; cook pizza 1 additional minute or until crust is crispy. Cut pizza into 8 wedges, and serve immediately. Serves 4 (serving size: 2 wedges)

CALORIES 284; FAT 10.1g (sat 3.2g, mono 2.2g, poly 3.6g); PROTEIN 9g; CARB 41g; FIBER 4g; CHOL 10mg; IRON 4mg; SODIUM 504mg; CALC 149mg

Ham and Veggie Fried Rice

Tossing in frozen green peas at the end of cooking keeps them bright and lively.

2 (8.5-ounce) pouches precooked brown rice (such as Uncle Ben's)
2 teaspoons lower-sodium soy sauce
2 teaspoons chili garlic sauce
1 teaspoon toasted sesame oil
2 tablespoons canola oil, divided
1 cup cubed reduced-sodium ham
1 large egg, lightly beaten
1 cup sliced cremini mushrooms
1/2 cup chopped red bell pepper
1/2 cup bean sprouts
1/3 cup sliced green onions
2 large garlic cloves, peeled and sliced
1 (1/2-inch) piece fresh ginger, peeled and thinly sliced
1/2 cup frozen green peas

1. Prepare rice according to package directions; set aside.
2. Combine soy sauce, chili garlic sauce, and sesame oil in a bowl. Heat a wok over high heat. Add 1 tablespoon canola oil. Add ham; cook 2 minutes, stirring frequently. Transfer ham to soy sauce mixture.
3. Add egg to pan; cook 30 seconds. Remove from pan; chop.
4. Add remaining 1 tablespoon oil to pan. Add mushrooms and next 5 ingredients (through ginger); stir-fry 2 minutes. Add rice; stir-fry 2 minutes. Add ham mixture and peas; cook 2 minutes. Stir in egg. Serves 4 (serving size: 1 1/2 cups)

CALORIES 364; FAT 13.9g (sat 1.5g, mono 5.5g, poly 2.8g); PROTEIN 17g; CARB 43g; FIBER 3g; CHOL 69mg; IRON 2mg; SODIUM 575mg; CALC 19mg

Cuban Pork Sliders

As with traditional Cuban sandwiches, pressing these sliders as they cook yields a thin and crisp bite.

1 1/2 teaspoons yellow mustard
2 teaspoons minced fresh garlic
1 teaspoon olive oil
1 (7-ounce) loaf Cuban bread
2 1/2 ounces kosher dill pickle slices
3 ounces thinly sliced lower-sodium deli ham
2 ounces sliced Swiss cheese
1 cup baby spinach leaves
Cooking spray

1. Combine first 3 ingredients (through olive oil) in a small bowl, stirring with a whisk.
2. Cut bread in half lengthwise; cut each half into 8 (2 1/2-inch-thick) slices. Spread mustard mixture evenly over bottom halves. Slice pickles into 2-inch pieces. Divide pickles, ham, cheese, and spinach evenly among bottom halves of bread; top with remaining bread halves. Lightly coat sandwiches with cooking spray.
3. Heat a large skillet over medium heat. Add 4 sandwiches to pan; place a cast-iron or other heavy skillet on top of sandwiches. Press gently, and cook 2 minutes on each side or until sandwiches are golden brown and cheese is melted. Repeat procedure with remaining sandwiches. Serves 4 (serving size: 2 sandwiches)

CALORIES 244; FAT 7.6g (sat 3.4g, mono 2.7g, poly 0.5g); PROTEIN 13g; CARB 29g; FIBER 2g; CHOL 22mg; IRON 2mg; SODIUM 801mg; CALC 183mg

DINNER TONIGHT

Kid Friendly • Quick & Easy
Make Ahead • Vegetarian

Farfalle with Butternut Squash and Sage

with Browned Butter and Lemon Brussels Sprouts

3 cups cubed peeled butternut squash (about 1 pound)
2 tablespoons olive oil, divided
¼ teaspoon kosher salt
¼ teaspoon black pepper
½ cup walnut halves
8 ounces uncooked farfalle
1½ cups organic vegetable stock
1½ tablespoons white balsamic vinegar
1 garlic clove, minced
¼ cup flat-leaf parsley leaves
1 tablespoon minced fresh sage
2 ounces vegetarian Parmesan cheese, shaved (about ½ cup)

1. Preheat oven to 400°.
2. Combine squash, 1 tablespoon oil, salt, and pepper on a baking sheet; arrange in a single layer. Bake at 400° for 15 minutes or until tender. Add walnuts to baking sheet; bake at 400° for 5 minutes or until toasted. Cool slightly; coarsely chop walnuts.
3. Cook pasta according to package directions, omitting salt and fat. Drain.
4. Combine 1 tablespoon oil, stock, vinegar, and garlic in a skillet over medium-high heat; simmer until reduced to ½ cup. Combine pasta, squash mixture, walnuts, stock mixture, parsley, and sage. Sprinkle with cheese. Serves 6 (serving size: about 1 cup)

CALORIES 317; **FAT** 13.3g (sat 2.9g, mono 4.8g, poly 4.6g); **PROTEIN** 11g; **CARB** 41g; **FIBER** 3g; **CHOL** 8mg; **IRON** 2mg; **SODIUM** 292mg; **CALC** 164mg

---

Kid Friendly • Quick & Easy
Make Ahead • Vegetarian
Gluten Free

Browned Butter and Lemon Brussels Sprouts

Heat a large skillet over medium-high heat. Add ¼ cup water and 1½ pounds trimmed, halved Brussels sprouts to pan; cover and cook 5 minutes. Add 2 tablespoons unsalted butter, ¼ teaspoon kosher salt, and ¼ teaspoon freshly ground black pepper to pan; cook, uncovered, 2 minutes. Increase heat to high, and cook 1 minute, stirring frequently. Stir in 1 teaspoon grated lemon rind and 1 tablespoon fresh lemon juice. Serves 6 (serving size: about ⅔ cup)

CALORIES 84; **FAT** 4.2g (sat 2.5g); **SODIUM** 109mg

READY IN 35 MINUTES

SHOPPING LIST

Farfalle with Butternut Squash and Sage
Fresh parsley
Fresh sage
Butternut squash (1 pound)
Garlic
Extra-virgin olive oil
White balsamic vinegar
Organic vegetable stock
Farfalle (bow tie pasta)
Walnut halves
Vegetarian Parmesan cheese

Browned Butter and Lemon Brussels Sprouts
Lemon
Brussels sprouts (1½ pounds)
Unsalted butter

GAME PLAN

While oven preheats:
- Prepare squash mixture.
- Trim and halve Brussels sprouts.
While squash roasts:
- Cook pasta.
- Cook Brussels sprouts.

Kid Friendly • Quick & Easy

Chicken Stir-Fry with Peanut Sauce

with Coconut-Cilantro Rice

2 teaspoons dark sesame oil, divided
1 pound chicken cutlets, trimmed
2 cups broccoli florets
1 large red bell pepper, sliced
¼ cup light coconut milk
2 tablespoons lower-sodium soy sauce
2 tablespoons creamy peanut butter
1 tablespoon Sriracha
2 teaspoons grated lime rind
1 tablespoon fresh lime juice
¼ teaspoon ground ginger
¼ teaspoon ground cumin
¼ cup unsalted cashews

1. Heat a wok or large skillet over high heat. Add 1 teaspoon oil; swirl to coat. Add chicken; cook 1 minute on each side. Remove chicken from pan; cut into thin slices. Add broccoli and bell pepper to pan; stir-fry 4 minutes or until vegetables are lightly browned.
2. Reduce heat to medium-high. Combine 1 teaspoon oil, coconut milk, and next 7 ingredients (through cumin) in a small bowl, stirring with a whisk. Add chicken and coconut milk mixture to pan; cook 30 seconds. Sprinkle evenly with cashews. Serves 4 (serving size: about 1 cup)

CALORIES 283; **FAT** 14.2g (sat 3.3g, mono 6.1g, poly 3.3g); **PROTEIN** 29g; **CARB** 10g; **FIBER** 3g; **CHOL** 73mg; **IRON** 2mg; **SODIUM** 526mg; **CALC** 35mg

continued

Quick & Easy • Vegetarian
Gluten Free
Coconut-Cilantro Rice

Combine 1 cup light coconut milk and ¼ cup water in a medium saucepan over medium-high heat; bring to a boil. Stir in 1 cup uncooked long-grain white rice. Reduce heat to low; cover and simmer 17 minutes or until liquid is absorbed. Let stand 5 minutes. Stir in ¼ cup chopped cilantro. Serves 4 (serving size: about ½ cup)

CALORIES 203; FAT 3.3g (sat 2.9g); SODIUM 18mg

SHOPPING LIST

Chicken Stir-Fry with Peanut Sauce

Lime
Broccoli florets
Red bell pepper
Ground ginger
Ground cumin
Dark sesame oil
Lower-sodium soy sauce
Sriracha
15-ounce can light coconut milk
Creamy peanut butter
Unsalted cashews
Chicken cutlets (1 pound)

Coconut-Cilantro Rice

Fresh cilantro
15-ounce can light coconut milk
Long-grain white rice

GAME PLAN

While rice cooks:
- Cook chicken, broccoli, and bell pepper.
- Prepare coconut milk mixture.
While rice stands:
- Finish stir-fry.

Kid Freindly • Quick & Easy
Gluten Free

Smoky Steak Fajitas

with Avocado and Tomato Salad

2 teaspoons smoked paprika
2 teaspoons dried oregano
1½ teaspoons garlic powder
1½ teaspoons ground cumin
1 teaspoon brown sugar
¼ teaspoon kosher salt
¼ teaspoon black pepper
⅛ teaspoon ground red pepper
1 (1-pound) flank steak, trimmed
Cooking spray
1 small red onion, cut into ¼-inch slices
1 small red bell pepper, cut into ½-inch slices
1 small yellow bell pepper, cut into ½-inch slices
8 corn tortillas
¼ cup chopped fresh cilantro
8 lime wedges (optional)

1. Combine first 8 ingredients in a small bowl. Rub 2 tablespoons spice mixture evenly over steak.
2. Heat a grill pan over medium-high heat. Coat pan with cooking spray. Add steak to pan; grill 5 minutes on each side or until desired degree of doneness. Place steak on a cutting board; let stand 10 minutes. Cut across the grain into thin slices.
3. Combine 2½ teaspoons spice mixture, onion, and bell peppers in a bowl; toss to coat. Arrange onions and peppers on pan; grill 5 minutes on each side or until lightly charred. Remove vegetables from pan. Add tortillas to pan; grill 30 seconds on each side or until lightly browned.
4. Divide steak and bell pepper mixture among tortillas. Top with chopped cilantro. Serve with lime wedges, if desired. Serves 4 (serving size: 2 fajitas)

CALORIES 305; FAT 8.2g (sat 2.7g, mono 2.6g, poly 1g); PROTEIN 28g; CARB 30g; FIBER 6g; CHOL 70mg; IRON 3mg; SODIUM 209mg; CALC 91mg

---

Kid Friendly • Vegetarian
Gluten Free
Avocado and Tomato Salad

Combine 2 cups halved red and yellow cherry tomatoes, ½ cup chopped white onion, 2 tablespoons fresh lime juice, 2 tablespoons extra-virgin olive oil, ¼ teaspoon kosher salt, ¼ teaspoon ground cumin, a dash of ground red pepper, and 1 large avocado, cubed; toss. Serves 4 (serving size: 1 cup)

CALORIES 140; FAT 12.2g (sat 1.7g); SODIUM 128mg

SHOPPING LIST

Smoky Steak Fajitas

Lime (optional)
Red bell pepper (small)
Red onion (small)
Yellow bell pepper (small)
Fresh cilantro
Brown sugar
Smoked paprika
Dried oregano
Garlic powder
Ground cumin
Ground red pepper
Corn tortillas
Flank steak (1 pound)

Avocado and Tomato Salad

Lime
Avocado
Cherry tomatoes
Onion
Ground cumin
Ground red pepper
Extra-virgin olive oil

GAME PLAN

While steak grills:
- Prepare avocado salad.
While steak rests:
- Grill onion and peppers.

Baked Cod with Feta and Tomatoes

with Lemon-Orange Orzo

1 tablespoon extra-virgin olive oil
1½ cups chopped onion
3 cups chopped tomato
¼ cup dry white wine
2 teaspoons coarsely chopped fresh oregano, divided
1 teaspoon red wine vinegar
⅜ teaspoon kosher salt, divided
¼ teaspoon freshly ground black pepper
Dash of crushed red pepper
4 (6-ounce) cod fillets
1 tablespoon chopped fresh flat-leaf parsley
2 ounces feta cheese, crumbled (about ½ cup)

1. Preheat oven to 400°.
2. Heat a large ovenproof skillet over medium heat. Add oil; swirl to coat. Add onion; sauté 5 minutes or until tender. Stir in tomato, wine, 1 teaspoon oregano, vinegar, ⅛ teaspoon salt, black pepper, and crushed red pepper; bring to a simmer. Cook 3 minutes, stirring occasionally. Sprinkle fish evenly with ¼ teaspoon salt. Nestle fish in tomato mixture. Bake at 400° for 18 minutes or until fish flakes easily when tested with a fork. Sprinkle with 1 teaspoon oregano, parsley, and feta. Serves 4 (serving size: 1 fillet, about ½ cup tomato mixture, and 2 tablespoons feta)

CALORIES 247; **FAT** 7.5g (sat 2.8g, mono 3.3g, poly 0.8g); **PROTEIN** 30g; **CARB** 12g; **FIBER** 3g; **CHOL** 93mg; **IRON** 1mg; **SODIUM** 470mg; **CALC** 117mg

Lemon-Orange Orzo

Melt 1 tablespoon butter in a medium saucepan over medium heat. Add ¾ cup uncooked whole-wheat orzo; toss to coat. Add 1½ cups unsalted chicken stock (such as Swanson) to pan; bring to a simmer. Cover, reduce heat, and simmer 17 minutes or until liquid is absorbed. Stir in 2 tablespoons chopped fresh flat-leaf parsley, ½ teaspoon grated lemon rind, ½ teaspoon grated orange rind, and ¼ teaspoon kosher salt. Serves 4 (serving size: about ½ cup)

CALORIES 147; **FAT** 3.5g (sat 1.8g); **SODIUM** 195mg

READY IN 35 MINUTES

SHOPPING LIST

Baked Cod with Feta and Tomatoes
Tomatoes
Fresh parsley
Fresh oregano
Onion
Crushed red pepper
Extra-virgin olive oil
Red wine vinegar
Dry white wine
Feta cheese
Cod fillets (1½ pounds)

Lemon-Orange Orzo
Lemon
Orange
Fresh parsley
Unsalted chicken stock
Whole-wheat orzo
Butter

GAME PLAN

While oven preheats:
■ Prepare fish.
While fish bakes:
■ Prepare orzo.

Bruschetta Burgers

with Spiced Oven Fries

1 pound 90% lean ground sirloin
½ teaspoon kosher salt, divided
½ teaspoon black pepper, divided
1 tablespoon extra-virgin olive oil, divided
1 ounce part-skim mozzarella cheese, shredded (about ¼ cup)
8 (1-ounce) slices Italian bread
Cooking spray
2 garlic cloves, divided
1 cup diced tomato
¼ cup chopped fresh basil

1. Divide beef into 4 equal portions; shape into patties. Flatten each patty to a ¼-inch thickness. Sprinkle evenly with ¼ teaspoon salt and ¼ teaspoon pepper.
2. Heat a large cast-iron skillet over medium-high heat. Add 2 teaspoons oil to pan; swirl. Add patties; cook 2 minutes. Turn patties; top with mozzarella cheese. Cook 2 minutes or until cheese melts. Remove patties from pan. Coat bread slices with cooking spray. Add 4 bread slices to pan; cook 30 seconds on each side or until toasted. Repeat procedure with remaining bread slices and cooking spray. Cut 1 garlic clove in half; rub cut sides of garlic on both sides of bread slices.
3. Mince remaining garlic clove. Combine minced garlic, ¼ teaspoon salt, ¼ teaspoon pepper, 1 teaspoon oil, tomato, and basil in a bowl; toss to coat. Top each of 4 bread slices with 1 patty. Divide tomato mixture evenly among patties. Top with remaining 4 bread slices. Serves 4 (serving size: 1 burger)

CALORIES 395; **FAT** 16.6g (sat 5.5g, mono 7.3g, poly 1.6g); **PROTEIN** 29g; **CARB** 31g; **FIBER** 2g; **CHOL** 73mg; **IRON** 4mg; **SODIUM** 676mg; **CALC** 120mg

continued

Kid Friendly • Quick & Easy
Vegetarian • Gluten Free
Spiced Oven Fries

Preheat oven to 450° (place baking sheet in oven as it preheats). Cut each of 3 (8-ounce) baking potatoes lengthwise into 8 wedges. Combine potatoes, 1 tablespoon canola oil, ½ teaspoon paprika, ½ teaspoon dried oregano, ¼ teaspoon kosher salt, ¼ teaspoon ground cumin, and a dash of ground red pepper; toss to coat. Arrange potatoes on preheated pan in a single layer. Bake at 450° for 30 minutes or until browned, stirring after 15 minutes. Serves 4 (serving size: 6 wedges)

CALORIES 167; **FAT** 3.7g (sat 0.3g); **SODIUM** 129mg

READY IN
35
MINUTES

SHOPPING LIST

Bruschetta Burgers
Tomato
Fresh basil
Garlic
Extra-virgin olive oil
Italian bread (8 ounces)
Part-skim mozzarella cheese
90% lean ground sirloin (1 pound)

Spiced Oven Fries
Baking potatoes (1½ pounds)
Paprika
Dried oregano
Ground cumin
Ground red pepper
Canola oil

GAME PLAN

While oven preheats:
■ Prepare potatoes.
■ Prepare beef patties.
While potatoes cook:
■ Cook patties.
■ Prepare tomato mixture.

QUICK TRICKS

9 STANDOUT COOKIE STIR-INS

One simple dough provides the base for an array of sweet holiday-season treats.

Cookie Dough

Preheat oven to 350°. Combine 1¼ cups granulated sugar, ½ cup brown sugar, ½ cup softened unsalted butter, and 1 teaspoon vanilla extract in a large bowl; beat with a mixer at medium speed until fluffy. Add 1 large egg to mixture; beat just until blended. Beat in 7.9 ounces (about 1¾ cups) all-purpose flour, 1 teaspoon baking soda, and ¼ teaspoon salt. Mix in one of these flavor combos to customize your cookies.

Kid Friendly • Freezable
Strawberry, Black Pepper, and Pistachio

Beat 1 teaspoon black pepper into cookie dough with a mixer at medium speed. Stir in ½ cup chopped dried strawberries and ¼ cup finely chopped pistachios. Drop dough by tablespoonfuls 2 inches apart on parchment paper–lined baking sheets. Bake 10 to 12 minutes or until lightly browned. Serves 36 (serving size: 1 cookie)

CALORIES 101; **FAT** 3.2g (sat 1.7g); **SODIUM** 55mg

Freezable • Make Ahead
Bourbon, Cranberry, and Walnut

Combine ¾ cup dried cranberries and ¼ cup bourbon in a saucepan over medium heat. Bring to a simmer; cover and remove from heat. Let stand 15 minutes. Stir plumped cranberries and ½ cup toasted walnut pieces into cookie dough. Drop dough by tablespoonfuls 2 inches

---

apart on parchment paper–lined baking sheets. Bake 10 to 12 minutes or until cookies are lightly browned. Serves 36 (serving size: 1 cookie)

CALORIES 114; **FAT** 3.9g (sat 1.8g); **SODIUM** 55mg

Freezable • Make Ahead
Lemon, Lavender, and Poppy Seed

Beat 2 teaspoons grated lemon rind, 2 tablespoons lemon curd, 1 tablespoon poppy seeds, and 1 teaspoon dried lavender buds into cookie dough with a mixer at medium speed. Drop dough by tablespoonfuls 2 inches apart on parchment paper–lined baking sheets. Bake 10 to 12 minutes or until lightly browned. Serves 36 (serving size: 1 cookie)

CALORIES 97; **FAT** 3g (sat 1.7g); **SODIUM** 55mg

Kid Friendly • Freezable
Make Ahead
Rocky Road

Stir ⅓ cup mini marshmallows, ¾ ounce coarsely chopped dark chocolate, and ⅓ cup chopped toasted pecans into cookie dough. Drop dough by tablespoonfuls 2 inches apart on parchment paper–lined baking sheets. Bake 10 to 12 minutes or until lightly browned. Combine 1 ounce chopped dark chocolate and ¼ teaspoon canola oil in a small microwave-safe bowl. Microwave at HIGH 1 minute or until melted, stirring every 20 seconds. Drizzle chocolate over cooled cookies. Serves 40 (serving size: 1 cookie)

CALORIES 98; **FAT** 3.6g (sat 1.8g); **SODIUM** 50mg

Kid Friendly • Freezable
Make Ahead
Caramel Popcorn

Stir ⅓ cup finely crushed hard caramel candies (such as Werther's Original; about 12 candies) and ⅛ teaspoon salt into cookie dough. Prepare 1 mini bag plain microwave popcorn according to package directions. Stir 3 cups prepared popcorn into cookie dough with a rubber spatula. Drop dough by tablespoonfuls 2 inches apart on parchment paper–lined baking sheets. Bake 10 to 12 minutes or until lightly browned. Serves 50 (serving size: 1 cookie)

CALORIES 71; FAT 2.2g (sat 1.3g); SODIUM 52mg

Kid Friendly • Freezable
Make Ahead
Orange, Sesame, and Honey

Beat ⅓ cup toasted sesame seeds, 2 tablespoons honey, and 2 teaspoons grated orange rind into cookie dough with a mixer at medium speed. Place ⅓ cup toasted sesame seeds in a bowl; scoop dough by tablespoonfuls, and roll in sesame seeds. Arrange cookies 2 inches apart on parchment paper–lined baking sheets. Bake 10 to 12 minutes. Combine 1 tablespoon fresh orange juice and 1 tablespoon honey in a bowl; drizzle mixture over cooled cookies. Serves 36 (serving size: 1 cookie)

CALORIES 116; FAT 4g (sat 1.7g); SODIUM 55mg

Kid Friendly • Freezable
Make Ahead
Peanut Butter Crunch

Beat ⅓ cup creamy peanut butter into cookie dough with a mixer at medium speed. Stir in ½ cup lightly crushed peanut butter–flavored cereal (such as Barbara's Peanut Butter Puffins) and ¼ cup unsalted, dry-roasted peanuts. Drop dough by tablespoonfuls 2 inches apart on parchment paper–lined baking sheets. Bake 10 to 12 minutes or until cookies are lightly browned. Drizzle 3 tablespoons melted creamy peanut butter over cooled cookies. Serves 36 (serving size: 1 cookie)

CALORIES 122; FAT 5.2g (sat 2.1g); SODIUM 76mg

Kid Friendly • Freezable
Make Ahead
Chocolate and Peppermint

Beat ½ teaspoon peppermint extract into cookie dough with a mixer at medium speed. Stir in 1½ ounces crushed hard peppermint candies (such as

Starlight) and ⅓ cup semisweet chocolate chips. Drop dough by tablespoonfuls 2 inches apart on parchment paper–lined baking sheets. Bake 10 to 12 minutes or until lightly browned. Serves 36 (serving size: 1 cookie)

CALORIES 103; FAT 3.2g (sat 2g); SODIUM 55mg

Kid Friendly • Freezable
Make Ahead
Coconut, Lime, and Macadamia

Lightly toast ¾ cup shredded coconut on a parchment paper–lined baking sheet in preheated oven. Beat 2 tablespoons fresh lime juice and 1 tablespoon grated lime rind into dough with a mixer at medium speed. Stir in toasted coconut and ¼ cup chopped macadamia nuts. Drop dough by tablespoonfuls 2 inches apart on parchment paper–lined baking sheets. Bake 10 to 12 minutes or until lightly browned. Serves 36 (serving size: 1 cookie)

CALORIES 107; FAT 4g (sat 2.3g); SODIUM 60mg

RECIPE MAKEOVER

5-INGREDIENT SAUSAGE BALLS

The classic comfort-food appetizer gets healthy with a whole-grain add.

We tweak a lot of things to make over a recipe, but one thing is for sure: We don't like to mess with simplicity. Maintaining a short ingredient list and 30-minute-or-less time frame was a must for this appetizer. Traditional sausage balls use a premixed boxed baking product—a combination of flour, leavening, salt, and shortening, a known source of trans fats. We turned to trusty whole-grain quinoa. When cooked, this gluten-free, salt-free grain binds our reduced-fat sausage and cheese beautifully and keeps this party app

light and fluffy. A little cornstarch helps lock in the melty cheese for extra moisture. A five-ingredient make-ahead sausage and cheese–filled bite with half the calories, fat, and salt makes for a happy hostess and a healthier gathering. Party on.

OURS SAVES
37 calories, 1.5g sat fat, and 90mg sodium per ball over traditional cheesy sausage balls

Kid Friendly • Freezable
Make Ahead • Gluten Free
Cheesy Sausage Balls

Hands-on: 10 min. Total: 30 min. To make ahead, cover and refrigerate unbaked balls up to 24 hours; or place in a heavy-duty zip-top plastic bag and freeze unbaked balls up to 1 month. Bake frozen balls at 375° for 22 to 25 minutes or until done.

1 cup cooked quinoa, chilled
1 tablespoon cornstarch
¼ teaspoon black pepper
4 ounces reduced-fat sharp cheddar cheese, shredded (about 1 cup)
1 pound reduced-fat pork sausage (such as Jimmy Dean)
Cooking spray

1. Preheat oven to 375°.
2. Combine first 5 ingredients in a bowl. Shape mixture into 40 (1½-inch) balls. Place balls on a foil-lined baking sheet coated with cooking spray. Bake at 375° for 18 minutes or until lightly browned and done. Serves 20 (serving size: 2 sausage balls)

CALORIES 85; FAT 5.3g (sat 2.1g, mono 2.1g, poly 0.5g); PROTEIN 6g; CARB 3g; FIBER 0g; CHOL 17mg; IRON 0mg; SODIUM 175mg; CALC 53mg

THE COMFORT FOOD SMACKDOWN

Our favorite heavyweights go head-to-head in the ultimate comfort food contest—six recipes, three rounds each. See which kitchen tools take the title for chili, risotto, beef stew, and more.

The methodology for our little experiment was straightforward: six recipes for braises, stews, and the like, each tested three ways—in the slow cooker, the pressure cooker, and the Dutch oven. The results were sometimes expected, sometimes startling. Somehow we knew deep down that the ever-reliable Dutch oven was the best way to get to a rich, hearty, old-fashioned chicken soup. But we were shocked to find that the pressure cooker makes some of the creamiest, most intensely flavored risotto we've had, without stirring your way to a repetitive stress injury. Here we feature the recipe with the vessel that worked best for each dish, along with tips for converting to other vessels that also worked well.

Slow Cooker
What It Does: Provides low, steady, even heat for hours at a time. Depending on make, model, and heat setting, food generally cooks between 200° and 300°. A tight, heavy lid seals in heat and moisture and minimizes evaporation.
Price Range: $30 to $250 and up for high-tech, bells-and-whistles models

Pressure Cooker
What It Does: Creates an airtight cooking environment. Because steam can't escape, it creates extreme pressure that raises the boiling point of water from 212° to 250°, which causes food to cook much faster.
Price Range: $50 to $150 for many six-quart models

Dutch Oven
What It Does: This is up to you, really: It can cook on the stovetop or in the oven. Traditionally made of cast iron (though the term also loosely covers stainless steel models), the thick pot provides even heat when braising, stewing, or browning.
Price Range: $40 to $300 and up

Make Ahead
The Winner: Slow Cooker

Beef Marsala Stew

Hands-on: 30 min. Total: 8 hr. This is an ideal recipe for the slow cooker, where gentle prolonged cooking transforms tough beef into tender bites. A splash of Marsala wine cooks down at the beginning and flavors the beef over the long cook time; a little Marsala goes in at the end, too, for more pronounced wine flavor. Serve over Fluffy Mashed Potatoes.

2 tablespoons canola oil, divided
2 pounds boneless chuck roast, trimmed and cut into 2-inch cubes, divided
1 teaspoon kosher salt, divided
12 ounces cipollini onions
4 garlic cloves, minced
2 tablespoons unsalted tomato paste
$\frac{1}{2}$ cup plus 2 tablespoons sweet Marsala wine, divided
1$\frac{1}{2}$ cups unsalted beef stock
1 teaspoon freshly ground black pepper
3 thyme sprigs
8 ounces small button mushrooms
4 large carrots, cut into 1-inch pieces
2 tablespoons all-purpose flour
Thyme sprigs

1. Heat a large, heavy skillet over medium-high heat. Add 1 tablespoon oil to pan; swirl to coat. Add half of beef; cook 8 minutes or until well browned, turning to brown on all sides. Place browned beef in a 6-quart electric slow cooker; sprinkle with ⅛ teaspoon salt. Repeat procedure with 1 tablespoon oil, remaining beef, and ⅛ teaspoon salt.
2. Add onions to pan; cook 1 minute on each side or until browned. Add onions to slow cooker. Add garlic to pan; sauté 1 minute. Add tomato paste; cook 1 minute, stirring constantly. Add ½ cup wine, scraping pan to loosen browned bits; cook 2 minutes or until half of liquid

evaporates. Add stock and pepper; bring to a simmer. Pour stock mixture into slow cooker; nestle thyme sprigs into liquid. Top beef mixture with mushrooms; scatter carrots over top.

3. Cover and cook on LOW 7½ hours.

4. Strain mixture through a colander over a Dutch oven or large skillet; discard thyme sprigs. Bring cooking liquid to a boil; cook 6 minutes or until liquid reduces to 2 cups. Stir in ¾ teaspoon salt. Combine 2 tablespoons wine and flour, stirring with a whisk to form a slurry. Stir into cooking liquid; cook 1 minute or until bubbly and thickened, stirring constantly. Pour over beef mixture; toss gently to combine. Garnish with thyme sprigs. Serves 8 (serving size: about ¾ cup)

CALORIES 271; FAT 12.2g (sat 3.5g, mono 6g, poly 1.4g); PROTEIN 24g; CARB 13g; FIBER 2g; CHOL 74mg; IRON 3mg; SODIUM 382mg; CALC 40mg

Pressure Cooker:

Using a 6- or 7-quart pressure cooker, follow instructions through step 2. Close lid securely; bring to high pressure over high heat (about 4 minutes). Adjust heat to medium-high or level needed to maintain high pressure; cook 25 to 30 minutes. Remove from heat. Place cooker under cold running water to release pressure. Remove lid. Proceed with step 4.

Dutch Oven:

Using a large Dutch oven, follow instructions through step 2. Cover and bake at 300° for 2½ hours or until beef is tender. Proceed with step 4.

Kid Friendly • Quick & Easy Vegetarian
Fluffy Mashed Potatoes

Place 3 pounds peeled baking potatoes in a large saucepan; cover with water. Bring to a boil; reduce heat, and simmer 15 minutes or until very tender. Drain. Press potatoes through a ricer or food mill back into pan. Add 1¾ cups warm whole milk, 1½ tablespoons butter, and 1

teaspoon kosher salt; stir vigorously with a whisk until butter melts. Serves 8 (serving size: about ¾ cup)

CALORIES 198; FAT 4.1g (sat 2.4g); SODIUM 290mg

Kid Friendly • Gluten Free
The Winner: Pressure Cooker

Mushroom and Roasted Butternut Squash Risotto

Hands-on: 25 min. Total: 45 min.
While old-school stovetop-stirred risotto is undeniably delicious, the pressure cooker delivers astonishingly good results: perfectly creamy al dente risotto without constant stirring. Make the dish vegetarian by swapping vegetable stock for chicken stock.

2 cups (³/₄-inch) cubed peeled butternut squash
3 tablespoons extra-virgin olive oil, divided
Cooking spray
1 cup boiling water
½ ounce dried porcini mushrooms
1 (12-ounce) package sliced button mushrooms
½ cup chopped shallots
4 garlic cloves, minced
1 cup uncooked Arborio rice or other medium-grain rice
⅓ cup Madeira wine or dry sherry
2½ cups unsalted chicken stock (such as Swanson)
1.5 ounces pecorino Romano cheese, grated (about ⅓ cup)
½ teaspoon salt
⅛ teaspoon freshly ground black pepper

1. Preheat oven to 450°.

2. Combine squash and 1 tablespoon oil in a bowl; toss to coat. Arrange squash in a single layer on a baking sheet coated with cooking spray; bake at 450° for 20 minutes or until lightly browned and tender, stirring after 10 minutes. Set aside.

3. Combine 1 cup boiling water and porcini mushrooms in a small bowl; let stand 20 minutes. Strain through a cheesecloth-lined colander over a bowl. Reserve soaking liquid; chop mushrooms.

4. Heat 2 tablespoons oil in a pressure cooker over medium-high heat. Add sliced mushrooms; sauté 12 minutes or until liquid evaporates and mushrooms brown. Add porcini mushrooms, shallots, and garlic; sauté 2 minutes. Add rice; cook 30 seconds, stirring constantly. Add reserved soaking liquid and wine; cook 3 minutes or until liquid almost evaporates, stirring constantly.

5. Stir in stock. Close lid securely; bring to high pressure over high heat (about 4 minutes). Adjust heat to medium-high or level needed to maintain high pressure; cook 7 minutes. Remove from heat; let stand 10 minutes. Place cooker under cold running water to release pressure. Remove lid; stir in reserved butternut squash, cheese, salt, and pepper. Serve immediately. Serves 4 (serving size: about 1½ cups)

CALORIES 426; FAT 13.9g (sat 3.8g, mono 7.4g, poly 1.1g); PROTEIN 13g; CARB 59g; FIBER 5g; CHOL 10mg; IRON 2mg; SODIUM 576mg; CALC 150mg

Dutch Oven:

Keep stock hot in a small pan over low heat. Using a large Dutch oven, follow instructions through step 4. Ladle in 1 cup stock; cook 2 minutes or until liquid is nearly absorbed, stirring constantly. Continue adding stock, ½ cup at a time, stirring constantly until each portion of stock is absorbed before adding more (about 26 minutes total). Stir in reserved squash, cheese, and remaining ingredients.

Slow Cooker:

Not recommended for this dish.

Kid Friendly • Freezable
Make Ahead
The Winner: Dutch Oven

Beefy Bolognese over Penne Pasta

Hands-on: 25 min. Total: 1 hr. 30 min.

3 center-cut bacon slices, chopped
8 ounces 90% lean ground beef
4 ounces ground bison or lean ground pork
1½ cups finely chopped onion
½ cup finely chopped carrot
⅓ cup finely chopped celery
1 tablespoon minced fresh garlic
¼ cup unsalted tomato paste
½ cup unsalted chicken stock
⅓ cup dry red wine
1 (14.5-ounce) can unsalted diced tomatoes, undrained
½ teaspoon black pepper
¼ teaspoon salt
8 ounces uncooked penne pasta
Chopped fresh flat-leaf parsley (optional)

1. Place bacon in a large Dutch oven over medium-high heat; sauté 5 minutes or until bacon begins to crisp. Add beef and bison to pan; cook 6 minutes or until partly browned, stirring to crumble. Remove beef mixture from pan. Add onion, carrot, celery, and garlic; sauté 4 minutes. Add tomato paste; sauté 1 minute. Add stock and wine; bring to a boil. Cook 1 minute, scraping pan to loosen browned bits. Return beef mixture to pan; stir in tomatoes, pepper, and salt.
2. Cover; reduce heat to low, and cook 1 hour, stirring 3 times to prevent sticking.
3. Cook pasta according to package directions. Serve pasta with Bolognese; garnish with parsley, if desired. Serves 4 (serving size: 1 cup Bolognese and ½ cup pasta)

CALORIES 434; FAT 10.4g (sat 3.9g, mono 3.3g, poly 0.4g); PROTEIN 28g; CARB 54g; FIBER 4g; CHOL 58mg; IRON 4mg; SODIUM 393mg; CALC 59mg

Pressure Cooker:
Using a 6- or 7-quart pressure cooker, follow instructions through step 1. Close lid securely; bring to high pressure over high heat (about 4 minutes). Adjust heat to medium-high or level needed to maintain high pressure; cook 30 minutes. Remove from heat. Place cooker under cold running water to release pressure. Remove lid. Proceed with step 3.

Slow Cooker:
Using a large skillet, follow instructions through step 1. Place mixture in a slow cooker. Cover and cook on LOW 6 hours. Proceed with step 3.

Freezable • Make Ahead
The Winner: Pressure Cooker

Chili Con Carne

Hands-on: 30 min. Total: 1 hr. 10 min.

2 (6-inch) corn tortillas
4 teaspoons olive oil, divided
1 (2½-pound) bottom round roast, trimmed and cut into 1-inch cubes
¾ teaspoon salt, divided
2 medium onions, chopped
6 garlic cloves, minced
3 tablespoons chili powder
2 tablespoons ground ancho chile pepper
1 tablespoon ground cumin
3 tablespoons unsalted tomato paste
1 tablespoon finely chopped chipotle chile, canned in adobo sauce
1 teaspoon dried oregano
1 teaspoon lower-sodium soy sauce
¼ teaspoon ground cinnamon
2 (14.5-ounce) cans unsalted fire-roasted diced tomatoes
½ ounce semisweet chocolate, chopped
Chopped green onions (optional)
Sliced radish (optional)

1. Place tortillas in the bowl of a food processor; process to form fine crumbs.
2. Heat a 6-quart pressure cooker over medium-high heat. Add 1 teaspoon oil to pan; swirl to coat. Sprinkle beef with ½ teaspoon salt. Add one-third of beef to pan; sauté 3 minutes or until browned on all sides. Remove beef from pan. Repeat procedure twice more with 2 teaspoons oil and remaining beef.
3. Add remaining oil to pan; swirl to coat. Add onions and garlic; sauté 3 minutes. Add tortilla crumbs, chili powder, and next 8 ingredients; stir well. Stir in beef.
4. Close lid securely; bring to high pressure over high heat (about 4 minutes). Adjust heat to medium-high or level needed to maintain high pressure; cook 25 minutes. Remove from heat; let stand 20 minutes. Place cooker under cold running water to release pressure. Remove lid; stir in chocolate and ¼ teaspoon salt, stirring until chocolate melts. Top with green onions and radish, if desired. Serves 8 (serving size: about 1 cup)

CALORIES 384; FAT 14.8g (sat 4.7g, mono 6.5g, poly 0.9g); PROTEIN 45g; CARB 16g; FIBER 3g; CHOL 121mg; IRON 4mg; SODIUM 433mg; CALC 35mg

Dutch Oven:
Using a large Dutch oven, follow instructions through step 3. Bring mixture to a boil; cover and bake at 300° for 2½ hours, stirring two or three times to prevent sticking. Stir in chocolate and remaining salt to finish.

Slow Cooker:
Using a large skillet, follow instructions through step 3. Transfer to a 6- or 7-quart slow cooker. Cover and cook on LOW 8 hours. Stir in chocolate and remaining salt to finish.

The Winner: Slow Cooker

Pulled Pork Sandwiches with Sriracha BBQ Sauce

Hands-on: 20 min. Total: 8 hr. 20 min.

3 tablespoons brown sugar
1 tablespoon ground coriander
1 teaspoon garlic powder
1 teaspoon chili powder
3/4 teaspoon salt
1 (3 1/2-pound) boneless pork shoulder (Boston butt), trimmed and cut into 4 pieces
1/2 cup ketchup
1/3 cup seasoned rice vinegar
2/3 cup water
3 tablespoons Sriracha (hot chile sauce, such as Huy Fong), divided
1 tablespoon minced peeled fresh ginger
12 (1 1/2-ounce) whole-wheat hamburger buns

1. Combine first 5 ingredients in a small bowl. Rub pork with sugar mixture.
2. Combine ketchup, vinegar, 2/3 cup water, 2 tablespoons Sriracha, and ginger in a slow cooker, stirring well. Add pork; toss to coat.
3. Cover and cook on LOW for 8 hours or until pork is very tender.
4. Skim fat from surface of cooking liquid. Stir in 1 tablespoon Sriracha. Shred pork; return to Sriracha mixture. Place about 3 ounces meat mixture on each of 12 bottom bun halves; top with top halves. Serves 12

CALORIES 231; FAT 6.5g (sat 2g, mono 1.9g, poly 1.5g); PROTEIN 20g; CARB 28g; FIBER 5g; CHOL 46mg; IRON 4mg; SODIUM 619mg; CALC 269mg

Pressure Cooker:
Using a 6- or 7-quart pressure cooker, follow instructions through step 2. Close lid securely; bring to high pressure over high heat (about 4 minutes). Adjust heat to medium-high or level needed to maintain high pressure; cook 55 minutes. Remove from heat; let stand 20 minutes. Place cooker under cold running water to release pressure. Remove lid. Place pork in a bowl; keep warm. Skim fat from cooking liquid. Bring to a boil over medium-high heat; cook 10 minutes or until mixture thickens slightly. Stir in 1 tablespoon Sriracha. Shred pork; return to Sriracha mixture.

Dutch Oven
Using a large Dutch oven, follow instructions through step 2. Cover and cook over medium-low heat 3 hours and 15 minutes or until pork is tender. Proceed with step 4.

The Winner: Dutch Oven

Hearty Chicken Soup

Hands-on: 25 min. Total: 45 min.

2 tablespoons olive oil
1 1/2 cups vertically sliced onion
1 1/2 cups diagonally sliced carrot
3/4 cup diagonally sliced parsnip
3 garlic cloves, crushed
7 cups unsalted chicken stock
5 flat-leaf parsley sprigs
3 thyme sprigs
2 (6-ounce) bone-in chicken thighs, skinned
2 bay leaves
1 (1-pound) bone-in chicken breast, skinned
4 ounces medium egg noodles
4 cups baby spinach
1/4 cup flat-leaf parsley leaves
3/4 teaspoon salt
1/2 teaspoon black pepper

1. Heat a large Dutch oven over medium-high heat. Add oil to pan; swirl to coat. Add onion, carrot, parsnip, and garlic to pan; sauté 5 minutes. Add stock and next 5 ingredients.
2. Bring mixture to a boil. Reduce heat, and simmer 20 minutes or until chicken is done.
3. Remove chicken and vegetables from pan; let chicken stand 10 minutes. Shred chicken into bite-sized pieces. Discard parsley sprigs, thyme, and bay leaves. Increase heat to medium-high. Stir in noodles; cook 6 minutes or until done. Return chicken and vegetables to pan; stir in spinach and remaining ingredients. Serves 6 (serving size: 1 1/3 cups)

CALORIES 314; FAT 10g (sat 2.1g, mono 4.9g, poly 1.3g); PROTEIN 31g; CARB 25g; FIBER 4g; CHOL 104mg; IRON 3mg; SODIUM 606mg; CALC 80mg

Pressure Cooker:
Using a 6- or 7-quart pressure cooker, follow instructions through step 1. Close lid securely; bring to high pressure over high heat (about 4 minutes). Adjust heat to medium-high or level needed to maintain high pressure; cook 20 minutes. Remove from heat. Place cooker under cold running water to release pressure. Remove lid. Proceed with step 3.

Slow Cooker:
Replace chicken breast with 2 additional chicken thighs (calories stay about the same; fat goes up by 1g and sat fat by 0.4g per serving). Place oil, onion, carrot, parsnip, garlic, stock, herb sprigs, bay leaves, and chicken in slow cooker. Cover and cook on LOW 5 hours. Shred chicken as instructed, and discard aromatics. Cook noodles separately, and add to cooker with spinach and remaining ingredients.

A FAREWELL IN SIX SIMPLE RECIPES

As Editor Scott Mowbray prepared to say goodbye, he got cooking.

Very late in my career at this magazine—in fact, the day after I decided to write a farewell-to-readers article in the form of six simple recipes of my own devising—I discovered what a pain in the ass it is to actually develop recipes for this magazine. This is ironic, if not imbecilic—to not have fully grasped, as the editor, the complexity of annotating the act of cooking. I came to *Cooking Light* five years ago knowing (if you will pardon the boast) that this magazine sets the gold standard for healthy recipes. I went on to taste hundreds of dishes in the *Cooking Light* Test Kitchen and offer my share of sharp comments. I knew my way around a fair number of cuisines, from French to Indian to Chinese. And I was an ardent cook. But I was a magazine-maker, not a recipe-maker, and it hadn't occurred to me that the trick of developing recipes is that you have to take notes while you're doing a complex physical activity in which flow is crucial. Imagine taking notes while dancing.

From Day One here, I've been delighted by the wisdom and passion of those readers who are confident cooks and email me with their stories. But there's another group out there, a cohort of excited newbies who are daunted by kitchenwork. These latter often take up serious cooking in their thirties or forties because they're concerned about the health of kid or spouse or self. For them, a reliable recipe is a lifeline, a successful dish a victory.

The recipes here represent everyday cooking, nothing fancy. There's only one tricky bit—getting pizza dough gossamer-thin so that the crust crackles. It's worth playing with dough until you get the hang of it, because it's a nifty dinner-party trick that yields naturally small, healthy portions. There's also a way of making pasta in the style of risotto, which I prefer to the rice dish it imitates. And with a tweak on garlicky, lemony gremolata, you'll turn chicken skin—this year's fat of choice among hip chefs, by the way—into a crunchy topping for tender chicken thighs.

Hope you enjoy. Find me on Instagram: @scottmowb.

Cracker-Thin Pizza with Super-Garlicky Tomato Sauce

Hands-on: 28 min. Total: 2 hr. 28 min.
This emerged from my obsession with getting store-made pizza dough to be ultrathin and yield a crackerlike crust, perfect for a healthy-portion appetizer. I bake the dough until done, and then add a room-temperature garlicky tomato sauce and fresh basil. To get the dough cracker thin, you have to abandon the rolling pin and tease the dough by hand. It takes some practice, but it's fun. The cutting-away of excess dough in step 4 helps preserve the round shape: Start with a circle, end with a circle. You'll have leftover dough, which you can use to make breadsticks.

1 (1½-pound) piece fresh pizza dough
   (such as Whole Foods)
Cooking spray
1 tablespoon olive oil
4 garlic cloves, finely chopped
1 cup lower-sodium marinara sauce
   (such as Dell'Amore)
Basil leaves

1. Place dough on a lightly floured wood surface; lightly coat with cooking spray, and cover with plastic wrap, making sure there's no air getting in. Let stand 2 hours. You want the dough to be at room temperature when you stretch it; it will likely start to bubble a bit. It should feel a bit loose and flabby.
2. While dough stands, make sauce. Heat a medium nonstick skillet over medium-low heat. Add oil; swirl to coat. Add garlic; cook 30 seconds or until garlic softens but doesn't brown. Add marinara; simmer until slightly thickened (about 6 minutes). Cool to room temperature.
3. Place a 15-inch pizza stone or heavy pizza pan in oven. Preheat

oven to 500° (leave pan in oven as it preheats).

4. Place dough on a work surface dusted with flour. (Keep a bit of extra flour on hand.) Dough will be about 8 inches across. With a pizza cutter, cut an inner circle of dough by cutting away an outer ring of dough that's about 2½ inches wide. This will leave a round of dough that weighs about 8 ounces. Reserve cutaway dough for another use.

5. Sprinkle dough circle with a bit of flour if it is damp, and begin to tease the dough out with your fingers, working it in all directions. It will persist in bouncing back. When it is flat and wide as a dinner plate, pick it up with hands close together, and begin working it by holding the edge and rotating along the edge as the circle dangles, like you're quickly turning a steering wheel. As you rotate the dough, holding the edges, it will stretch downward by its own weight. If it's stretching too fast, you can also put the dough over both of your hands and gently stretch and rotate. Watch for areas that are getting too thin—most of the available dough for stretching is at the edges. Continue working the dough until it reaches a diameter of about 12½ inches.

6. Carefully remove hot pizza stone from oven, and place on a heat-resistant surface. Carefully transfer dough to the stone. Pierce dough all over liberally with a fork.

7. Bake at 500° for 7 to 8 minutes, watching closely. If it's baking too much on one side, rotate the dough. Bake until very brown but not burned, and remove. Slide pizza to a wood or stone surface. Spread evenly with sauce; top with basil. Serve immediately. Serves 6

CALORIES 145; **FAT** 4.3g (sat 0.3g, mono 3.1g, poly 0.5g); **PROTEIN** 4g; **CARB** 22g; **FIBER** 3g; **CHOL** 0mg; **IRON** 1mg; **SODIUM** 246mg; **CALC** 14mg

---

Kid Friendly • Gluten Free

Braised Chicken Thighs with Chicken Skin Gremolata

Hands-on: 35 min. Total: 1 hr. 15 min. *At Cooking Light we sometimes remove the skin from rich chicken thighs to reduce the saturated fat, but I realized last February that I could roast that very same skin till it's crisp, rendering out much of the fat and capturing lots of chickeny goodness for a wintery braised main dish. The gremolata idea came from my love of flat-leaf parsley: I never use the regular stuff anymore. Start checking the skins after 30 minutes in 5-minute intervals; they can quickly go from perfectly crisp to burned.*

1 cup boiling water
⅓ cup dried sour cherries
4 skin-on, bone-in chicken thighs (about 2 pounds)
Dash of kosher salt
Dash of freshly ground black pepper
1 tablespoon olive oil
½ teaspoon kosher salt, divided
½ teaspoon freshly ground black pepper, divided
⅔ cup finely chopped onion
2 garlic cloves, thinly sliced
¼ cup Madeira wine or oloroso sherry
1½ cups unsalted chicken stock
2 teaspoons chopped fresh thyme
1 teaspoon red wine vinegar
1 tablespoon grated lemon rind
¼ cup finely chopped fresh flat-leaf parsley
1 garlic clove, minced

1. Pour 1 cup boiling water over dried cherries in a bowl; let stand 30 minutes. Drain.

2. Preheat oven to 375°.

3. Remove skin from chicken thighs. Place skin flat on a parchment paper–lined jelly-roll pan. Bake at 375° for 40 minutes, making sure skin gets brown and thoroughly crisp but not burned. Drain on paper towels. Sprinkle with dash of salt and dash of pepper. Finely chop chicken skin; set aside.

4. Heat a large, heavy skillet over medium-high heat. Add oil to pan; swirl to coat. Sprinkle chicken with ¼ teaspoon salt and ¼ teaspoon pepper. Add chicken to pan, meaty side down; cook 4 minutes on each side or until browned. Remove chicken from pan. Reduce heat to medium. Add onion and sliced garlic; sauté 3 minutes, stirring frequently. Add wine; cook 1 minute or until reduced by half. Return chicken to pan; add cherries, ¼ teaspoon salt, ¼ teaspoon pepper, stock, thyme, and vinegar. Bring to a boil; cover, reduce heat, and simmer 15 minutes or until chicken is tender. Remove chicken from pan; keep warm. Increase heat to medium-high; cook sauce 2 minutes or until slightly thickened (about 1 cup).

5. Combine chicken skin, lemon rind, parsley, and minced garlic in a small bowl. Serve chicken with sauce; top with gremolata. Serves 4 (serving size: 1 chicken thigh, about ¼ cup sauce, and about 3 tablespoons gremolata)

CALORIES 343; **FAT** 15.7g (sat 3.9g, mono 7.5g, poly 2.8g); **PROTEIN** 30g; **CARB** 15g; **FIBER** 4g; **CHOL** 151mg; **IRON** 2mg; **SODIUM** 422mg; **CALC** 46mg

Beet Ribbon Salad with Lemon and Pickled Shallots

Hands-on: 15 min. Total: 6 hr. 15 min.
I never ate raw beets until I learned the trick of shaving them ribbon-thin. I now prefer them this way to cooked. You can make the pickled shallots first thing in the morning or up to a day ahead.

²/₃ cup water
¹/₃ cup cider vinegar
2 tablespoons sugar
1 teaspoon maple syrup
¹/₂ teaspoon black peppercorns
¹/₂ teaspoon whole allspice
3 whole cloves
2 bay leaves
5 ounces shallots, peeled and sliced into very thin rings
1 pound small white and golden beets, peeled
1 tablespoon grated lemon rind
2 tablespoons fresh lemon juice
1 tablespoon extra-virgin olive oil
¹/₂ cup coarsely chopped fresh flat-leaf parsley
¹/₄ teaspoon flake salt (such as Maldon)

1. Combine first 8 ingredients in a saucepan; bring to a boil. Pour hot vinegar mixture over shallots; cool to room temperature. Cover and refrigerate 6 hours or overnight. Drain; discard spices.
2. Shave beets into thin ribbons using a mandoline or vegetable peeler.
3. Combine rind, juice, and oil in a large bowl, stirring with a whisk. Add ¹/₂ cup drained shallots (reserve remaining shallots for another use), beets, and parsley; toss gently to coat. Sprinkle with salt. Serves 4 (serving size: about ³/₄ cup)

CALORIES 111; **FAT** 3.7g (sat 0.5g, mono 2.5g, poly 0.5g); **PROTEIN** 3g; **CARB** 18g; **FIBER** 5g; **CHOL** 0mg; **IRON** 2mg; **SODIUM** 217mg; **CALC** 45mg

---

Risotto-Style Pasta with Caramelized Onions

Hands-on: 25 min. Total: 25 min.
When I discovered tiny, rice-sized acini di pepe pasta, I immediately plotted a risotto strategy: gradually adding liquid until the pasta plumps. This year I learned from Keith Schroeder, our Cooking Class columnist, to toast the pasta for extra flavor (it almost tastes malted). The sweetness of the caramelized onions is balanced by the salt of the blue cheese.

2 tablespoons olive oil, divided
1¹/₂ cups minced white onion
1¹/₄ cups uncooked acini di pepe pasta (about 8.4 ounces)
3 cups unsalted chicken stock, divided
¹/₂ cup unoaked white wine
¹/₂ teaspoon kosher salt
¹/₄ teaspoon freshly ground black pepper
2 ounces Gorgonzola piccante or other hard, salty blue cheese, crumbled (about ¹/₂ cup)
1 teaspoon thyme leaves

1. Heat a medium skillet over medium heat. Add 1 tablespoon oil to pan; swirl to coat. Add onion; reduce heat to low, and cook 20 minutes or until onion is light brown, creamy, and caramelized, stirring occasionally. (The longer the cooking, the sweeter the caramelization, but watch for hot spots and burning. If liquid cooks off too quickly, add a bit of water.) Remove pan from heat; set aside.
2. Heat a heavy saucepan over medium heat. Add 1 tablespoon oil; swirl to coat. Add dry pasta; cook 5 minutes or until the pasta is a nice toasty color, stirring constantly. Add onion and 1 cup stock, stirring frequently until stock is absorbed.

As the pasta absorbs the stock and liquid bubbles away, add wine and then more stock, ¹/₂ cup at a time, stirring frequently until each portion of stock is absorbed before adding the next. You want the pasta to be al dente and "together" but not mushy. When it's done, stir in salt and pepper. Remove from heat, and add cheese; stir gently to mostly melt the cheese, but you still want chunks. Transfer to serving plates, and garnish with thyme. Serve immediately. Serves 4 (serving size: about 1¹/₄ cups)

CALORIES 394; **FAT** 11.7g (sat 3.9g, mono 6g, poly 0.8g); **PROTEIN** 16g; **CARB** 52g; **FIBER** 3g; **CHOL** 11mg; **IRON** 2mg; **SODIUM** 541mg; **CALC** 117mg

---

Farro with Honey-Garlic Roasted Tomatoes

Hands-on: 15 min. Total: 60 min. *This hearty side was inspired by the simple recipe for roasted tomatoes in the River Cottage Veg cookbook, by Hugh Fearnley-Whittingstall. Since gaining my whole-grain enthusiasm at Cooking Light, I've settled upon farro as my number-one favorite, but the trick is not to overcook it: It's best chewy, with the grains intact and not "blown out" into starchy, wet puffs. Combining the farro with the sweet, garlicky tomatoes makes for a dish that's delicious year-round—cherry and grape tomatoes are the only sweet ones in the winter. You can serve as soon as the tomatoes and farro are cool and combined, but I find the dish benefits from a couple of hours in the fridge.*

1¹/₂ tablespoons olive oil
1 tablespoon honey
3 garlic cloves, minced
1 pound cherry or grape tomatoes, halved lengthwise
³/₄ cup uncooked farro
1¹/₂ teaspoons sherry vinegar

⅝ teaspoon kosher salt
3 tablespoons toasted walnuts, coarsely chopped
2 ounces feta cheese, crumbled (about ½ cup)
2 teaspoons chopped fresh thyme

1. Preheat oven to 375°.
2. Combine oil, honey, and garlic in a large bowl. Add tomatoes; gently, with your hands, toss until thoroughly coated. Pour tomatoes onto a foil-lined jelly-roll pan; turn tomatoes until they're all cut-side down. Draw tomatoes together until they're cozy and touching. If there's any honey mixture left in bowl, drizzle over tomatoes. Bake at 375° for 20 to 25 minutes or until wrinkled and soft but not mushy (do not brown). (Grape tomatoes may take less time.) Remove from oven; cool to room temperature.
3. While tomatoes cook, place farro in a medium saucepan; cover with water to 2 inches above farro. Bring to a boil. Cover, reduce heat, and simmer 15 minutes or until nicely chewy and not puffed open and starchy. Drain and rinse with cold water; drain.
4. Combine farro, tomato mixture, vinegar, and salt in a large bowl; toss gently to combine. Top with walnuts and feta; garnish with thyme. Serve immediately, or let the flavors marry in the fridge for an hour or 2. Serves 6 (serving size: about ½ cup)

CALORIES 191; FAT 8.4g (sat 2.1g, mono 3.3g, poly 2.2g); PROTEIN 6g; CARB 25g; FIBER 4g; CHOL 8mg; IRON 2mg; SODIUM 310mg; CALC 73mg

Kid Friendly • Gluten Free

Smashed Bacony Potatoes with Kale and Roasted Salmon

Hands-on: 39 min. Total: 59 min.
Since falling in love with very smoky Tennessee bacon (Benton's), I've moved to using it as a flavor agent; I almost never eat it on its own. Any very smoky bacon will do. This is a hearty winter dish, layering potatoes with kale and crisp-skinned roasted salmon.

12 ounces new or fingerling potatoes
1 teaspoon sherry vinegar
¾ teaspoon kosher salt, divided
2 smoked bacon slices, thinly sliced crosswise into matchstick pieces
½ cup finely chopped shallots
1 tablespoon olive oil, divided
5 cups packed coarsely chopped kale, large stems removed
½ cup unsalted chicken stock, divided
1 teaspoon finely chopped fresh rosemary
½ teaspoon freshly ground black pepper, divided
4 (6-ounce) skin-on salmon fillets
¼ cup half-and-half
4 fresh flat-leaf parsley sprigs

1. Preheat oven to 425°.
2. Place potatoes in a large saucepan; cover with cool water to 2 inches above potatoes. Bring to a boil. Reduce heat, and simmer 20 minutes or until almost tender; drain. Put potatoes in a bowl, and crush potatoes with a thick, sturdy glass; you want the potatoes broken open but still fairly intact. Sprinkle with vinegar and ⅛ teaspoon salt.
3. Heat a large heavy skillet over medium heat. Add bacon; cook 3 minutes or until almost crisp. Add shallots to pan; cook 2 to 3 minutes or until bacon is crisp and shallots are browned, stirring occasionally. Remove bacon and shallots from pan with a slotted spoon, reserving any drippings. Add 2 teaspoons oil to drippings in pan. Increase heat to medium-high. Add potatoes in an even layer; cook 2 minutes or until potatoes begin to lightly brown on bottom. Add kale, ¼ cup stock, and rosemary. Reduce heat to medium. Cover and cook 2 minutes or until kale is almost tender (you want it still chewy). Uncover and drizzle with ¼ cup stock if too dry; it should be a bit moist. Stir in reserved bacon mixture, ¼ teaspoon salt, and ¼ teaspoon pepper. Keep warm.
4. Sprinkle tops of salmon fillets with ⅜ teaspoon salt and ¼ teaspoon pepper. Heat a large cast-iron skillet over medium-high heat until a drop of water evaporates quickly when dropped on it. Add 1 teaspoon oil to pan; swirl to coat. Add salmon fillets, skin side down; cook, without turning, for 3 minutes. Place pan in oven (salmon should still be skin-side down); bake at 425° for 7 minutes or until a thermometer registers 130° and salmon is still medium-rare within.
5. Just before serving, add half-and-half to kale-potato mixture; stir gently just to incorporate. Immediately place 1 cup potato-kale mixture on each of 4 plates; top each serving with 1 salmon fillet, skin side up. Garnish each serving with a parsley sprig. Serves 4

CALORIES 472; FAT 21.7g (sat 5.1g, mono 7.4g, poly 3.5g); PROTEIN 43g; CARB 26g; FIBER 5g; CHOL 104mg; IRON 3mg; SODIUM 635mg; CALC 159mg

5-INGREDIENT HOLIDAY APPETIZERS

Small effort, big flavor: Our easy party nibbles get you in and out of the kitchen in a flash.

Quick & Easy • Vegetarian
Gluten Free

Endive Boats with Pears, Blue Cheese, and Walnuts

Hands-on: 18 min. Total: 18 min.

1 tablespoon olive oil
1½ cups finely chopped red Bartlett
  or Anjou pear
1 tablespoon honey
⅛ teaspoon kosher salt
⅛ teaspoon black pepper
2 ounces Gorgonzola cheese,
  crumbled (about ½ cup)
16 Belgian endive leaves
¼ cup chopped walnuts, toasted

1. Heat a medium skillet over medium heat. Add oil to pan; swirl to coat. Add pear; cook 2 minutes or until softened, stirring occasionally. Remove from heat; stir in honey. Cool 3 minutes; stir in salt, pepper, and cheese. Spoon about 2 teaspoons pear mixture into each endive leaf. Sprinkle evenly with walnuts. Serves 8 (serving size: 2 stuffed leaves)

CALORIES 90; FAT 6.2g (sat 1.8g, mono 2.1g, poly 2g); PROTEIN 2g; CARB 8g; FIBER 2g; CHOL 5mg; IRON 0mg; SODIUM 130mg; CALC 47mg

Kid Friendly • Quick & Easy
Make Ahead • Gluten Free

Gingery Shrimp Salad Bites

Hands-on: 16 min. Total: 20 min.

2 teaspoons dark sesame oil, divided
8 ounces peeled and deveined
  medium shrimp
2 teaspoons minced peeled fresh
  ginger
⅛ teaspoon kosher salt
2 tablespoons canola mayonnaise
1 teaspoon Sriracha
32 (1½-inch) pieces fresh chives
  (optional)

1. Heat a medium skillet over medium-high heat. Add 1½ teaspoons oil to pan; swirl to coat. Add shrimp; sauté 2 minutes. Add ginger and salt; sauté 2 minutes or until shrimp are done. Cool slightly. Coarsely chop shrimp.
2. Combine mayonnaise, Sriracha, and ½ teaspoon oil in a bowl. Add shrimp; toss to coat. Spoon about 1 tablespoon shrimp mixture into each of 16 Chinese soup spoons; top each with 2 chive pieces, if desired. Serves 8 (serving size: 2 spoons)

CALORIES 40; FAT 2.4g (sat 0.2g, mono 1.1g, poly 0.9g); PROTEIN 4g; CARB 0g; FIBER 0g; CHOL 36mg; IRON 0mg; SODIUM 111mg; CALC 15mg

Kid Friendly • Quick & Easy
Make Ahead • Vegetarian
Gluten Free

Marinated Feta Skewers

Hands-on: 10 min. Total: 30 min.

1 medium lemon
1 tablespoon chopped fresh oregano
3 tablespoons extra-virgin olive oil
½ teaspoon black pepper
4 ounces feta cheese, cut into 16 cubes
16 small cherry or grape tomatoes

1. Grate rind from lemon; squeeze juice to equal 2 tablespoons. Combine rind, juice, oregano, oil, and pepper in a shallow dish. Add cheese; marinate at room temperature 20 minutes, turning cheese after 10 minutes. Drain. Arrange 1 tomato and 1 feta cube on each of 16 small skewers or party picks. Serves 8 (serving size: 2 skewers)

CALORIES 50; FAT 4g (sat 2.3g, mono 1.4g, poly 0.2g); PROTEIN 2g; CARB 1g; FIBER 0g; CHOL 13mg; IRON 0mg; SODIUM 159mg; CALC 74mg

Kid Friendly • Quick & Easy

Mini Crab Cakes

Hands-on: 25 min. Total: 40 min.

1 ounce French bread, torn into pieces
1 large lemon
1 tablespoon chopped fresh tarragon
¼ teaspoon kosher salt
¼ teaspoon black pepper
1 large egg, lightly beaten
8 ounces lump crabmeat, drained
  and shell pieces removed
2 tablespoons canola oil

1. Place bread in a mini food processor; pulse until fine crumbs form.
2. Finely shred lemon rind; set aside. Squeeze juice to equal 1 tablespoon. Combine juice, tarragon, salt, pepper, and egg, stirring with a whisk. Add

bread; toss to combine. Add crab-meat; toss. Shape crab mixture into 16 equal patties (about 1½ tablespoons each). Chill 15 minutes.
3. Heat a large nonstick skillet over medium-high heat. Add oil; swirl. Add crab cakes; cook 2 minutes on each side or until browned. Arrange crab cakes on a platter; sprinkle evenly with rind. Serves 8 (serving size: 2 cakes)

CALORIES 74; **FAT** 4.4g (sat 0.5g, mono 2.5g, poly 1.2g); **PROTEIN** 6g; **CARB** 2g; **FIBER** 0g; **CHOL** 51mg; **IRON** 0mg; **SODIUM** 199mg; **CALC** 33mg

Kid Friendly • Quick & Easy
Make Ahead • Vegetarian

Pesto Pastries

Hands-on: 20 min. Total: 40 min.

2 tablespoons pine nuts, toasted
1 garlic clove, chopped
3 tablespoons grated Parmigiano-Reggiano cheese
2 (1-ounce) packages fresh basil
1 sheet frozen puff pastry dough, thawed
³/₈ teaspoon kosher salt

1. Preheat oven to 400°.
2. Place nuts and garlic in a mini food processor; pulse until finely chopped. Add cheese; pulse to combine. Remove large stems from basil. Tear leaves, and add to processor; process until very finely chopped and almost paste-like.
3. Unfold dough; roll dough into a 10 x 9–inch rectangle. Spread pesto over dough to edges. Sprinkle with salt. Roll up both long sides of dough, jelly-roll fashion, until they meet in the middle. Place in freezer 10 minutes.
4. Cut dough roll crosswise into 20 slices. Arrange slices in a single layer on a baking sheet lined with parchment paper. Bake at 400° for 16 minutes or until lightly browned. Serves 10 (serving size: 2 pastries)

CALORIES 156; **FAT** 11.1g (sat 1.7g, mono 2.6g, poly 6.1g); **PROTEIN** 3g; **CARB** 12g; **FIBER** 1g; **CHOL** 1mg; **IRON** 1mg; **SODIUM** 157mg; **CALC** 30mg

WINE & DINE MIGHTY FINE

Elevate your menu with smart wines. Here, a few easy lessons—and good bottles—for pulling off a spectacular pairings party.

Sip a beautiful wine that's perfectly matched with good food, and you'll find it's an eye-opening pleasure. We hear you, though: As food lovers, we need to strip the concept of wine pairing from the usual pretensions and dive deeper into the joy and fun. We called in help from local experts who have shaped the wine culture in our hometown of Birmingham, Alabama, (see more about them on page 368). These guys are the opposite of snobs. They are retailers and wholesalers who love food and share a real passion for connecting people with wines—at all price points—that make them happy. You don't need, and they don't use, pretentious language to discuss the subject. "Wine is a condiment. It's there to help you enjoy your meal," says Scott Atkinson, wine director at Western Supermarkets in Mountain Brook, Alabama, which has one of the largest wine selections in the state. Matched nicely, wine can go beyond helping you enjoy your meal; it can *make* the meal.

How to Throw a Great Wine Dinner Party
It's easy, fun, and low-stress if you follow our simple plan.

1. Create a menu that's broken into at least three courses so you can try at least three wines. Try to keep the dinner to six people total, as each 750-milliliter bottle will provide six nice-sized pours. (Hint: Our menu here works beautifully.)
2. Take your menu to the wine shop, and get some recommendations in different price ranges and for different styles: sparkling, white, rosé, red, fortified. Decide how many wines you'd like to try per course, knowing that more than two per course may prove overwhelming.
3. Invite guests. Assign each couple one of the wines on the list to bring.

4. Get plenty of basic wineglasses for the table. If you like, you can provide a different glass for each wine, or just one per person per course—even if you're tasting two wines at that course. Look to party supply stores, where you can rent glasses at a reasonable price (bonus: you usually just have to rinse the glasses before returning), or purchase a box of glasses at a discount store.

Rule-of-Thumb Wine Pairing
These easy principles from our experts go a long way in making great matches.

1. Try to match the geographical origin of the dish to that of the wine. There's a reason why the food and the wine should come from the same place; there's harmony there.

continued

2. Compare the structure of the wine to the structure of the dish. If the food is delicate, go with a delicate wine. If you have a big, charred, robust meat dish, you'll need a robust wine to go with it.

3. Look on the back of each wine bottle and see if the importer is reputable. Our experts highly recommend Terry Theise, Kermit Lynch, Neal Rosenthal, and Vineyard Brands.

4. Always be willing to try new things. Many towns offer free wine tastings at wine shops—go, explore, and find some new favorites.

5. Find a wine expert you like and trust. Jonathan, Scott, and Alex are passionate about this point. The wine folks are there to help you, so you should not be intimidated. Be realistic about what price range you're comfortable with: A good wine expert will find you a wine that fits your needs and will not judge you for your tastes. Alex points out, "A customer might say, 'I like cabernet. Is it wrong to drink that with my salad?' And I say, and any good wine person will do the same, 'Not if it's what you like.'" That's the type of relationship and respect you should expect.

Meet the Experts

Scott Atkinson is wine director at Western Supermarkets in Mountain Brook, Alabama.

Alex Floyd ran the wine programs at some of Birmingham's top restaurants. He is now a sales representative with Grassroots Wine Wholesalers in Birmingham.

Jonathan Thomas is sales manager at Grassroots Wine Wholesalers in Birmingham.

THE WINES

Appetizer:
Chicken-Phyllo Turnovers

Bargain wine: *Anne Amie Vineyards Cuvée A "Amrita" White Blend, 2013, $14*
"The wine has bright, juicy fruit but no sugar, which makes it go well with a hint of sweetness in the dish." —Scott Atkinson

Mid-priced wine: *Dönnhoff Estate Riesling, 2012, $24*
"This dish screamed good riesling to me—one with sugar qualities but a balance of acid to keep the sweetness in check." —Jonathan Thomas

Wild card wine: *A. Margaine Demi-Sec NV Champagne, $44*
"Crispy food goes great with sparkling wine. This dish is complex, savory with a bit of sweet. The Champagne is not overly sweet or dry; it's all about balance." —Alex Floyd

First Course:
Golden Beet Soup
with Toasted Grains

Bargain wine: *Le Paradou Viognier, 2013, $10*
"This has a bit of floral and soapy qualities, but it's very dry—which all plays off the flavor of the beets." –JT

Mid-priced wine: *Schloss Gobelsburg Grüner Veltliner "Gobelsburger," 2013, $16*
"This is a higher acid, drier style of wine, a little bit slate-y; its minerality works with the earthiness of the beets." –AF

Wild card wine: *Domaine FL "Chamboureau" Savennieres-Chenin, 2008, $25*
"The chenin blanc grape can be very sweet, but this wine is on the dry side and has a lot of weight. A little bit of sweetness lifts everything up and picks up the spice notes from the soup." –SA

Main Course:
Lamb, Carrots, Eggplant

Bargain wine: *Esporão Alandra Tinto, 2013 (Portuguese Red Blend), $9*
"This is a great, widely distributed Portuguese wine using a blend of port grapes. It has enough deep tannins to go beautifully with the lamb and counterbalance the sweetness in the sauce." –JT

Mid-priced wine: *Sattler Zweigelt, 2011, $16*
"This has a zinfandel-like quality but doesn't repeat the zin in the sauce. It's one of the most diverse reds out there—not quite a zin, merlot, or cabernet, with a little more pinot noir quality, a little spice." –AF

Wild card wine: *Melville Estate Syrah "Verna's," 2011, $30*
"Rich spice and great acidity complement without conflicting."–SA

Dessert:
Pomegranate-Orange Tart
with Pistachio Shortbread Crust

The unanimous choice: *Dolin Rouge vermouth, $11, on the rocks with a splash of soda and orange rind twist.*

"The components of the drink mirror the components of the dish. You have the bitter and the sweet—they're sisters, but not the same exact flavors. They elevate each other." —JT

"The orange in the filling matches the bit of rind in the cocktail. The spice of the vermouth goes with the crumbly crust." —SA

Chicken-Phyllo Turnovers

Hands-on: 40 min. Total: 60 min.
These traditional Moroccan pastries are a delightful mix of savory, spiced meat and flaky phyllo made sweet with a dusting of cinnamon and powdered sugar. It's traditionally made with pigeon; we opt for rich chicken thighs. To make ahead: Freeze unbaked pastries up to 1 month ahead; bake frozen pastries (do not thaw) 5 additional minutes or until browned.

Cooking spray
1 cup chopped onion
1 teaspoon grated peeled fresh ginger
3 garlic cloves, minced
¼ teaspoon kosher salt
¼ teaspoon ground turmeric
¼ teaspoon freshly ground black pepper
1½ cups water
6 ounces skinless, boneless chicken thighs
1 cinnamon stick
1 large egg, lightly beaten
¼ cup chopped fresh flat-leaf parsley
⅓ cup sliced almonds, toasted
2 tablespoons powdered sugar, divided
24 (14 x 9-inch) sheets frozen phyllo dough, thawed
¼ teaspoon ground cinnamon

1. Heat a medium skillet over medium heat. Coat pan with cooking spray. Add onion, ginger, and garlic; reduce heat to medium-low, and cook 8 minutes or until tender, stirring occasionally. Stir in salt, turmeric, and pepper; cook 30 seconds, stirring constantly. Add 1½ cups water, scraping pan to loosen browned bits. Add chicken and cinnamon stick. Bring to a boil; cover, reduce heat, and simmer 25 minutes or until chicken is tender,
turning chicken occasionally. Remove chicken from pan.
2. Increase heat to medium-high; cook onion mixture 15 minutes or until mixture is reduced to about ¾ cup. Reduce heat to medium-low. Add egg to pan, stirring with a whisk. Cook 1 minute or until thick, stirring constantly (mixture will be curdled). Remove from heat. Stir in parsley. Finely chop chicken; stir into egg mixture.
3. Combine almonds and 1 tablespoon sugar.
4. Preheat oven to 400°.
5. Place 1 phyllo sheet on a large cutting board or work surface (cover remaining phyllo to keep from drying); coat phyllo with cooking spray. Arrange another phyllo sheet over coated phyllo sheet; coat with cooking spray. Repeat once more for a total of 3 phyllo sheets. Gently press layers together. Cut phyllo stack lengthwise into 3 (3-inch-wide) strips. Spoon about 1 tablespoon chicken mixture onto 1 end of each strip; sprinkle with about 1 teaspoon almond mixture. Fold 1 corner of phyllo dough over mixture, forming a triangle; keep folding back and forth into a triangle to end of strip. Place triangle, seam side down, on a baking sheet lined with parchment paper; cover to prevent drying. Repeat procedure with remaining phyllo, cooking spray, chicken mixture, and almond mixture. Lightly coat triangles with cooking spray. Bake at 400° for 20 minutes or until lightly browned. Combine 1 tablespoon sugar and cinnamon; dust over pastries. Serve warm. Serves 12 (serving size: 2 pastries)

CALORIES 114; FAT 2.7g (sat 0.4g, mono 1.2g, poly 0.5g); PROTEIN 6g; CARB 16g; FIBER 1g; CHOL 29mg; IRON 1mg; SODIUM 132mg; CALC 33mg

Golden Beet Soup with Toasted Grains

Hands-on: 20 min. Total: 1 hr. 30 min.
We love the look of striped Chioggia beets atop the golden soup; if you can't find them, use red beets instead. Popped amaranth, a whole grain, adds loads of toasty flavor that's truly unique and delicious. You can make the soup up to 2 days ahead; reheat gently over medium-low heat before serving. Take care when popping the amaranth, and be sure to use a large pan.

1½ tablespoons unsalted butter
1 large fennel bulb, vertically sliced (about 3 cups)
4 garlic cloves
½ teaspoon kosher salt, divided
½ teaspoon turmeric
¼ cup dry white wine
2 pounds golden beets, peeled and cut into wedges
6 cups water
¾ cup very thinly julienne-cut peeled Chioggia or red beet
2 teaspoons fresh lemon juice
1 teaspoon sugar
3 tablespoons chopped fresh cilantro
¼ cup uncooked amaranth or sesame seeds
⅛ teaspoon ground red pepper

1. Melt butter in a large Dutch oven over medium-low heat. Add fennel, garlic, and ¼ teaspoon salt; cover and cook 20 minutes or until fennel is very tender, stirring occasionally (do not brown). Increase heat to medium-high. Add turmeric; cook 30 seconds. Add wine; cook 1 minute or until liquid is reduced by half. Add golden beets and 6 cups water. Bring to a boil; cover, reduce heat, and simmer 1 hour or until beets are very tender.

continued

2. While soup simmers, combine Chioggia beets, juice, sugar, and cilantro; let stand 30 minutes. Drain. **3.** Heat a large heavy saucepan over medium heat. Add amaranth; cook until amaranth pops, shaking pan frequently. Remove amaranth from pan. **4.** Place half of soup mixture in a blender. Remove center piece of blender lid (to allow steam to escape); secure blender lid on blender. Place a clean towel over opening in blender lid (to avoid splatters). Blend until smooth. Pour into a large bowl. Repeat procedure with remaining soup mixture. Stir in ¼ teaspoon salt and red pepper. Spoon mixture into shallow bowls. Top with pickled Chioggias; sprinkle with amaranth. Serves 6 (serving size: about ¾ cup soup, 2 tablespoons pickled beets, and about 2 teaspoons amaranth)

CALORIES 129; **FAT** 3.8g (sat 2g, mono 1g, poly 0.4g); **PROTEIN** 4g; **CARB** 21g; **FIBER** 5g; **CHOL** 8mg; **IRON** 2mg; **SODIUM** 274mg; **CALC** 56mg

Leg of Lamb with Olive-Wine Sauce

Hands-on: 15 min. Total: 1 hr. 15 min.

¾ teaspoon garlic powder
¾ teaspoon ground cumin
¾ teaspoon ground coriander
¾ teaspoon black pepper
½ teaspoon kosher salt
½ teaspoon ground cinnamon
1 (1½-pound) boneless leg of lamb roast, trussed
1½ tablespoons olive oil
1 tablespoon chopped fresh thyme
2 Medjool dates, pitted and finely chopped
1 shallot, minced
¾ cup fruity red wine (such as zinfandel)
1½ cups unsalted beef stock

¼ cup chopped pitted kalamata olives
1½ tablespoons fresh lime juice
1 tablespoon honey
¼ cup cilantro leaves

1. Preheat oven to 425°.
2. Combine first 6 ingredients. Rub spice mixture over all surfaces of lamb.
3. Heat a large ovenproof skillet over medium-high heat. Add oil; swirl. Add lamb; cook 10 minutes, turning to brown on all sides. Place pan in oven. Roast at 425° for 20 minutes or until a thermometer inserted in center registers 130°. Remove lamb from pan; let stand at room temperature 20 minutes. Cut across the grain into thin slices.
4. While lamb rests, heat skillet over medium-high heat. Add thyme, dates, and shallot to pan; sauté 2 minutes or until softened, scraping pan to loosen browned bits. Add wine to pan; cook 2 minutes or until slightly syrupy. Add stock; cook 5 minutes or until reduced to ½ cup. Stir in olives, juice, and honey. Cook 3 minutes or until slightly thickened. Serve sauce with lamb. Sprinkle with cilantro. Serves 6 (serving size: 3 ounces lamb and about 2 tablespoons sauce)

CALORIES 252; **FAT** 10.4g (sat 2.5g, mono 6g, poly 1g); **PROTEIN** 24g; **CARB** 12g; **FIBER** 1g; **CHOL** 73mg; **IRON** 2mg; **SODIUM** 370mg; **CALC** 25mg

Harissa-Roasted Carrots

Hands-on: 10 min. Total: 40 min.

2 tablespoons extra-virgin olive oil
1½ pounds peeled baby carrots
4 bay leaves
1 lime, sliced
1 teaspoon ground cumin
1 teaspoon ground harissa spice mix
¼ teaspoon kosher salt

1. Preheat oven to 450°.
2. Combine first 4 ingredients in a bowl. Sprinkle with cumin and harissa spice mix. Arrange carrot mixture in a single layer on a foil-lined jelly-roll pan. Cover pan with foil. Bake at 450° for 13 minutes. Uncover pan; bake an additional 10 minutes or until tender. Sprinkle with salt. Serves 6 (serving size: about ¾ cup)

CALORIES 94; **FAT** 5g (sat 0.7g, mono 3.6g, poly 0.6g); **PROTEIN** 1g; **CARB** 12g; **FIBER** 4g; **CHOL** 0mg; **IRON** 1mg; **SODIUM** 159mg; **CALC** 44mg

Sesame Steamed Eggplant

Hands-on: 15 min. Total: 1 hr. 15 min.

2 pounds eggplant, peeled and halved vertically
1½ tablespoons lower-sodium soy sauce
1 tablespoon toasted sesame oil
2 teaspoons sherry vinegar
1 teaspoon Worcestershire sauce
½ teaspoon freshly ground black pepper
½ teaspoon sugar
2 tablespoons chopped fresh mint
1 tablespoon toasted sesame seeds

1. Arrange eggplant in a vegetable or bamboo steamer; steam 40 minutes or until tender. Cool slightly. When eggplant is cool enough to handle, tear into long, thin strips and place in a colander. Let stand 20 minutes. Press lightly to extract any moisture without mashing eggplant.
2. Combine soy sauce and next 5 ingredients in a large bowl, stirring with a whisk. Add eggplant; toss gently to coat. Sprinkle with mint and sesame seeds. Serves 6 (serving size: about ¾ cup)

CALORIES 69; **FAT** 3.3g (sat 0.5g, mono 1.3g, poly 1.4g); **PROTEIN** 2g; **CARB** 10g; **FIBER** 5g; **CHOL** 0mg; **IRON** 1mg; **SODIUM** 157mg; **CALC** 16mg

Pomegranate-Orange Tart with Pistachio Shortbread Crust

Kid Friendly • Make Ahead

Hands-on: 25 min. Total: 3 hr. 35 min.

¼ cup finely chopped dry-roasted, unsalted pistachios
4.5 ounces all-purpose flour (about 1 cup)
¼ cup powdered sugar
¼ teaspoon salt
5 tablespoons chilled butter, cut into small pieces
2 tablespoons canola oil
Baking spray with flour
½ cup fresh or frozen (thawed) blueberries
2 cups pomegranate juice
⅓ cup granulated sugar
3 tablespoons cornstarch
2 large egg yolks
1 teaspoon grated orange rind
3 large egg whites
½ teaspoon vanilla extract
¼ teaspoon cream of tartar
⅛ teaspoon salt
¾ cup granulated sugar
⅓ cup water

1. Preheat oven to 350°.
2. Place pistachios in a food processor; process until almost ground. Weigh or lightly spoon flour into a dry measuring cup; level with a knife. Add flour, powdered sugar, and ¼ teaspoon salt to food processor; pulse to combine. Add butter to flour mixture; drizzle with oil. Pulse just until mixture resembles coarse meal. (Mixture will be dry and slightly sandy. It will not form a proper dough but comes together as you press it into pan.) Press mixture into bottom and up sides of a 9-inch removable-bottom tart pan coated with baking spray. Bake at 350° for 25 to 30 minutes or until golden. Cool completely on a wire rack.
3. Place blueberries in a saucepan; mash with a potato masher. Add juice, ⅓ cup sugar, and cornstarch, stirring with a whisk. Bring mixture to a low boil over medium-high heat, stirring frequently. Reduce heat; simmer 1 minute or until thickened, stirring constantly. Place egg yolks in a bowl; add ½ cup hot juice mixture to yolks, stirring with a whisk. Pour egg mixture into pan; bring to a boil over medium-low heat. Cook 1 minute or until bubbly and thick, stirring constantly. Remove from heat. Strain through a sieve into a bowl; stir in rind. Place bowl in a larger ice-filled bowl 20 minutes or until cooled, stirring occasionally. Pour mixture into crust. Cover and chill 3 hours or until completely set.
4. Place egg whites in a large bowl. Add vanilla, cream of tartar, and ⅛ teaspoon salt; beat with a mixer at high speed until soft peaks form. Combine ¾ cup sugar and ⅓ cup water in a saucepan; bring to a boil. Cook, without stirring, until a candy thermometer registers 250°. Gradually pour hot sugar syrup in a thin stream over egg whites, beating at medium-low speed, then at high speed until stiff peaks form. Spread meringue over tart. Serves 12 (serving size: 1 slice)

CALORIES 243; FAT 9.2g (sat 3.6g, mono 3.7g, poly 1.4g); PROTEIN 3g; CARB 38g; FIBER 1g; CHOL 43mg; IRON 1mg; SODIUM 137mg; CALC 17mg

THE ART OF SIMPLE, TASTEFUL GIVING

A couple bottles of fruity red wine and a DIY mulling spice blend make for a thoughtful and thoroughly enjoyable gift.

Some of the simplest homemade gifts, like a hand-packed mulling sachet plus the wine to steep it in, can make a big impression. What's more, it takes little time and almost no effort to prepare and enjoy this aromatic gift. For an alcohol-free alternative, give the mulling spices with apple cider or pomegranate juice.

Make Ahead • Gluten Free

Warm Spiced Zinfandel

Hands-on: 15 min. Total: 3 hr. 45 min.
If you are making, rather than giving, this recipe, you can skip dehydrating the orange slices in step 2.

1 large orange, cut crosswise into ⅛-inch-thick slices
Cooking spray
10 black peppercorns
5 whole cloves
4 cardamom pods, lightly crushed
3 whole allspice
2 (3-inch) cinnamon sticks
½ vanilla bean, split lengthwise
⅓ cup sugar
⅓ cup fresh orange juice
2 (750-milliliter) bottles zinfandel or other fruity dry red wine

1. Preheat oven to 200°.
2. Arrange orange slices on a wire rack coated with cooking spray; place rack on a baking sheet. Bake at 200° for 3 hours or until dried.
3. Combine peppercorns and next 5 ingredients on a double layer of cheesecloth. Gather edges of cheesecloth together; tie securely.
4. Combine orange slices, spice sachet, sugar, orange juice, and wine in a medium saucepan over medium heat. Heat just to a simmer and tiny bubbles begin to form (do not boil). Reduce heat to low, and simmer 30 minutes. Discard sachet. Serves 10 (serving size: ½ cup)

CALORIES 172; FAT 0.1g (sat 0g, mono 0g, poly 0g); PROTEIN 0g; CARB 15g; FIBER 1g; CHOL 0mg; IRON 3mg; SODIUM 1mg; CALC 10mg

BAKE IT FORWARD

This holiday, join the movement and bake a second batch for charity, friends, or family.

Kid Friendly • Freezable
Make Ahead • Vegetarian

Linzer Muffins

Hands-on: 20 min. Total: 60 min.
There is no problem doubling the muffin batter as long as you have 2 (12-cup) muffin tins so that all the muffins can be baked on the middle and top racks at once. Rotate the pans halfway during baking, and you might need to let the muffins bake a minute or two longer. Pack a batch of these muffins by dividing the cooled muffins in half and placing them in zip-top plastic bags to help keep them still. Then place the bags in a box with tissue paper to cushion the sides. These muffins can be shipped overnight without worry.

Cooking spray
6.75 ounces all-purpose flour (about 1¹/₂ cups)
¹/₂ cup almond flour
2 teaspoons baking powder
¹/₂ teaspoon salt
¹/₄ teaspoon baking soda
2 ounces almond paste
¹/₂ cup sugar
¹/₄ cup butter, softened
¹/₂ teaspoon vanilla extract
2 large eggs
²/₃ cup 2% reduced-fat milk
¹/₄ cup raspberry jam
¹/₄ cup sliced almonds

1. Preheat oven to 425°. Place 12 muffin-cup liners in muffin cups; coat liners lightly with cooking spray.
2. Weigh or lightly spoon all-purpose flour into dry measuring cups; level with a knife. Combine flour and next 4 ingredients in a bowl, stirring with a whisk.
3. Place almond paste and sugar in a bowl; beat with a mixer at medium-low speed until mixture resembles sand (about 3 minutes). Add butter and vanilla; beat 2 minutes or until well combined. Add eggs, 1 at a time, beating well after each addition. Add flour mixture and milk alternately to butter mixture, beginning and ending with flour mixture; mix after each addition.
4. Spoon half of batter into prepared pan, filling muffin cups one-third full. Top each with about 1 teaspoon jam; divide remaining batter evenly over jam. Sprinkle nuts evenly over muffins. Bake at 425° for 5 minutes. Reduce oven temperature to 375°. Bake at 375° an additional 10 minutes or until muffins spring back when touched lightly in center. Immediately remove muffins from pan, and place on a wire rack. Serves 12 (serving size: 1 muffin)

CALORIES 219; **FAT** 9.6g (sat 3.3g, mono 2.8g, poly 0.9g); **PROTEIN** 5g; **CARB** 29g; **FIBER** 1g; **CHOL** 42mg; **IRON** 1mg; **SODIUM** 224mg; **CALC** 93mg

Kid Friendly • Freezable
Make Ahead

Molasses Cookies

Hands-on: 15 min. Total: 60 min.
Double the dough and bake these cookies without a hitch. To mail, wrap small stacks together using plastic wrap and nestle them in a box with plenty of padding.

8 ounces all-purpose flour (about 1³/₄ cups)
1 teaspoon ground cinnamon
¹/₂ teaspoon baking soda
¹/₂ teaspoon ground ginger
¹/₂ teaspoon ground cloves
¹/₄ teaspoon baking powder
¹/₄ teaspoon salt
6 tablespoons butter
8 tablespoons granulated sugar, divided
¹/₄ cup dark brown sugar
1 large egg
¹/₄ cup molasses

1. Weigh or lightly spoon flour into dry measuring cups; level with a knife. Combine flour and next 6 ingredients in a bowl, stirring with a whisk.
2. Place butter, 5 tablespoons granulated sugar, and brown sugar in a large bowl; beat with a mixer at medium speed 5 minutes or until fluffy. Add egg; beat 30 seconds or until well combined Add molasses; beat just until combined. Add flour mixture to butter mixture; beat at low speed or just until combined. Cover and chill 30 minutes.
3. Preheat oven to 350°.
4. Shape dough into 24 balls, about 1½ tablespoons each. Roll balls in 3 tablespoons sugar; place 2 inches apart on baking sheets covered with parchment paper. Bake at 350° for 12 minutes or just until set. Cool 3 minutes on pan; remove to wire rack and cool. Serves 24 (serving size: 1 cookie)

CALORIES 96; **FAT** 3.2g (sat 1.9g, mono 0.8g, poly 0.2g); **PROTEIN** 1g; **CARB** 16g; **FIBER** 0g; **CHOL** 15mg; **IRON** 1mg; **SODIUM** 85mg; **CALC** 15mg

Chocolate Zucchini Loaf Cake

Hands-on: 25 min. Total: 1 hr. 50 min.
Double up on this batter and bake two loaves with no problems. To pack up this cake, wrap it whole and unglazed in plastic wrap and pack it securely in a box. The cake is sturdy enough to ship overnight. Either way, because the icing stays moist, mix up the glaze, pour into a small zip-top bag, and send with instructions to snip the corner and squeeze over top.

2 cups shredded zucchini (about ½ pound)
8 ounces all-purpose flour (about 1³/₄ cups)
7 tablespoons unsweetened cocoa, divided
1 teaspoon baking powder
½ teaspoon baking soda
¼ teaspoon salt
⅓ cup granulated sugar
¼ cup packed brown sugar
¼ cup unsalted butter, at room temperature
¼ cup canola oil
1 teaspoon vanilla extract
2 large eggs
½ cup semisweet chocolate chips
Baking spray with flour
½ cup powdered sugar
1 tablespoon 2% reduced-fat milk
Dash of salt

1. Preheat oven to 350°.
2. Press zucchini on several layers of paper towels; cover with additional paper towels. Let stand 10 minutes, pressing down occasionally.
3. Weigh or lightly spoon flour into dry measuring cups; level with a knife. Combine flour, 6 tablespoons cocoa, and next 3 ingredients in a medium bowl, stirring with a whisk.
4. Place granulated sugar and next 4 ingredients in a large bowl; beat with a mixer at medium speed until lemon-colored (about 5 minutes). Add eggs, 1 at a time, beating well after each addition. Add flour mixture to sugar mixture; beat at low speed 1 minute or just until combined. Add zucchini and chocolate chips; beat at low speed 1 minute or just until combined. Spoon batter into a 9 x 5–inch metal loaf pan coated with baking spray. Bake at 350° for 38 minutes or until a wooden pick inserted in center comes out clean. Cool in pan 10 minutes on a wire rack. Loosen edges from sides using a narrow spatula. Remove from pan and cool completely on wire rack.
5. Combine powdered sugar, 1 tablespoon cocoa, milk, and dash of salt; stir until smooth. Drizzle over loaf. Serves 12 (serving size: 1 slice)

CALORIES 260; **FAT** 12.1g (sat 4.6g, mono 5.1g, poly 1.8g); **PROTEIN** 4g; **CARB** 37g; **FIBER** 2g; **CHOL** 41mg; **IRON** 2mg; **SODIUM** 171mg; **CALC** 46mg

Semolina Almond Orange Cake

Hands-on: 20 min. Total: 2 hr. *You need to have three things to double this cake batter: a stand mixer, two Bundt pans, and an oven wide enough to fit both pans on the same (middle) shelf. Without those you should make the cakes one at a time. The leavening agents in the batter begin to do their work as soon as the liquid is mixed in, so the batter should not sit. Wait until the first cake is out of the oven before starting the batter for the second cake. Transport the cake or ship it overnight by wrapping it whole to a cardboard cake circle or plate using plastic wrap to help keep it in place before placing it in a box that has little wiggle room.*

1 cup almond flour
8 ounces all-purpose flour (about 1³/₄ cups)
1 cup semolina flour
2 teaspoons baking powder
½ teaspoon baking soda
¼ teaspoon salt
½ cup unsalted butter
1½ cups sugar, divided
2 tablespoons grated orange rind, divided
1³/₄ teaspoons vanilla extract, divided
4 large eggs
1 cup plain whole-milk yogurt
Baking spray with flour
³/₄ cup fresh orange juice
¼ cup orange liqueur (such as Grand Marnier), optional

1. Preheat oven to 350°.
2. Spread almond flour on a baking sheet. Bake at 350° for 5 minutes or until fragrant, stirring after 3 minutes. Cool completely on pan.
3. Weigh or lightly spoon all-purpose flour into measuring cups; level with a knife. Combine flours, baking powder, baking soda, and salt in a bowl.
4. Place butter and 1¼ cups sugar in a large bowl; beat with a mixer at medium speed 5 minutes or until well combined. Add 1 tablespoon rind and 1½ teaspoons vanilla; beat 1 minute. Add eggs, 1 at a time, beating well after each addition. Add flour mixture; beat at low speed 1 minute or just until combined. Add yogurt; beat 1 minute or just until combined. Scrape batter into a 10-cup Bundt pan coated with baking spray. Bake at 350° for 45 minutes or until a wooden pick inserted in center comes out completely dry.
5. Combine ¼ cup sugar, 1 tablespoon rind, and orange juice in a small saucepan; bring to a boil. Remove pan from heat; stir in ¼ teaspoon vanilla and liqueur, if desired. Pierce entire surface of cake in pan liberally with a skewer; drizzle half of glaze over cake. Let stand 15 minutes. Loosen cake from sides of pan using a narrow metal spatula. Invert onto a plate. Pierce top of warm cake liberally with a skewer; drizzle remaining glaze over cake. Serve cake at room temperature. Serves 16 (serving size: 1 wedge)

CALORIES 290; **FAT** 10.6g (sat 4.6g, mono 4g, poly 1.3g); **PROTEIN** 6g; **CARB** 41g; **FIBER** 2g; **CHOL** 64mg; **IRON** 2mg; **SODIUM** 147mg; **CALC** 92mg

Gingersnap and Lemon Cheesecake Bars

Hands-on: 25 min. Total: 9 hr. 25 min.
It's safe to simply double the ingredients and bake two pans of these bars at once. Bake the bars on the same (middle) shelf of the oven. To give these bars, pack them in a single layer in a box that doesn't allow them to slide around. Place that box in a slightly larger box with chill packs and packing materials to cushion the smaller box and prevent it from moving. Because these custardy bars are not very firm, they should not be shipped.

Crust:
25 gingersnaps (about 6½ ounces)
2 teaspoons cornstarch
2 tablespoons butter, melted
1 teaspoon grated peeled fresh ginger
Baking spray with flour
Filling:
8 ounces ⅓-less-fat cream cheese, softened
4 ounces fat-free cream cheese
½ cup sugar
½ teaspoon vanilla extract
¼ teaspoon baking powder
⅛ teaspoon salt
2 large eggs
¼ cup light sour cream
½ teaspoon grated lemon rind
1 tablespoon fresh lemon juice
Topping:
⅓ cup sugar
½ teaspoon grated lemon rind
⅓ cup fresh lemon juice
2 teaspoons cornstarch
2 large egg yolks
1 teaspoon butter

1. Preheat oven to 350°.
2. To prepare crust, place cookies and 2 teaspoons cornstarch in a food processor; process until finely ground. Add 2 tablespoons butter and ginger; process until moist crumbs form. Lightly press mixture into bottom of a 9-inch square metal baking pan coated with baking spray. Bake at 350° for 14 minutes or until set. Cool on a wire rack.
3. Reduce oven temperature to 325°.
4. To prepare filling, place cream cheeses in a medium bowl; beat with a mixer at medium speed until smooth. Add ½ cup sugar, vanilla, baking powder, and salt; beat at low speed until well combined. Add eggs, 1 at a time, beating well after each addition. Add sour cream, ½ teaspoon rind, and 1 tablespoon juice; beat until combined. Pour cheese mixture into prepared pan. Bake at 325° for 30 minutes or until almost set in the center. Remove pan from oven; place on a wire rack.
5. To prepare topping, combine ⅓ cup sugar, ½ teaspoon rind, ⅓ cup juice, 2 teaspoons cornstarch, and yolks in a small saucepan, stirring with a whisk until smooth. Place pan over medium-low heat; cook 5 minutes or until mixture bubbles and thickens, stirring constantly with a whisk. Remove pan from heat; add 1 teaspoon butter, stirring until butter melts. Spread topping over warm cheesecake. Cool completely on a wire rack. Cover and refrigerate overnight. Serves 16 (serving size: 1 bar)

CALORIES 170; FAT 7.6g (sat 3.9g, mono 2.5g, poly 0.6g); PROTEIN 4g; CARB 21g; FIBER 0g; CHOL 63mg; IRON 1mg; SODIUM 212mg; CALC 67mg

Whole-Grain Breakfast Bars

Hands-on: 20 min. Total: 45 min. *Make a double batch of these bars all in one bowl, and bake them on the same (middle) shelf in the oven. Because the bars have a tendency to be a little bit crumbly, wrap them well to transport or ship overnight. There are two*
options: You can release them from the pan onto a clean cardboard cake board and securely wrap them, uncut, to the board, or the bars can be cut and individually wrapped. Either method will work well for mailing as long as the bars are securely packed with plenty of padding to keep them still.

4.75 ounces whole-wheat flour (about 1 cup)
2 tablespoons flaxseed meal (optional)
2 cups old-fashioned rolled oats
1 teaspoon ground cinnamon
½ teaspoon baking powder
½ teaspoon baking soda
½ teaspoon salt
2 ripe bananas
¾ cup brown sugar
¼ cup 2% reduced-fat milk
2 tablespoons canola oil
1 teaspoon vanilla extract
1 large egg
1 large egg white
¾ cup chopped walnuts
¾ cup dried cranberries
Cooking spray

1. Preheat oven to 375°.
2. Weigh or lightly spoon flour into a dry measuring cup; level with a knife. Combine flour, flaxseed meal (if desired), and next 5 ingredients in a medium bowl.
3. Place bananas in a large bowl; mash with a fork until smooth. Add sugar and next 5 ingredients; stir until well combined. Add flour mixture, stirring until combined. Stir in nuts and cranberries.
4. Spread dough into a 13 x 9–inch metal baking pan coated with cooking spray. Bake at 375° for 22 minutes or until a wooden pick inserted in center comes out clean. Cool completely in pan on a wire rack. Cut into 16 bars. Serves 16 (serving size: 1 bar)

CALORIES 198; FAT 7.1g (sat 0.8g, mono 2.1g, poly 3.8g); PROTEIN 4g; CARB 32g; FIBER 3g; CHOL 12mg; IRON 1mg; SODIUM 141mg; CALC 37mg

LIGHTER, NATURALLY-RED VELVET CAKE

No red dye here: Read on for the secret to our three-layer holiday classic.

Just the name red velvet cake suggests something elegant and rich—those dramatically red, supermoist layers of tinted chocolate cake coated in a dense, creamy white frosting. 'Tis the season to treat yourself, right? Though it may be the time of year to splurge, it's hard to justify an 880-calorie, 57-gram-of-fat piece of cake. Ho-ho-holy cow! We simply had to find a way to bake this favorite holiday cake and feel better about eating it, too.

Our secret weapon: red beets. Yep, this vibrant-red, naturally sweet veggie transforms into a rich, luscious cream when cooked and pureed with nonfat buttermilk and a hint of vanilla. It adds a moist, velvety texture to the cake that allows us to use less oil and butter—a savings of 255 calories and 22g fat. Double bonus: Its rich color eliminates the need for artificial dye. Rather than weigh down the entire cake with a cream cheese and butter icing, we create two frosting elements. Between the layers, we spread a light cream cheese and Greek yogurt filling, sweetened with a touch of sugar and whipped until fluffy with a splash of cream. The entire cake is then covered in a fluffy, cloudlike meringue—a decadent white icing combo that saves 344 calories and 16g sat fat over cream-cheese buttercream. It's the dramatic splurge you'd expect: tender, moist cake with rich, creamy frosting—for only 284 calories per slice. You simply can't "beet" it.

OURS SAVES
596 calories, 48g total fat, and 16g saturated fat over traditional red velvet cake

Kid Friendly • Make Ahead

New Classic Red Velvet Cake

Hands-on: 48 min. Total: 2 hr. 7 min.

1 (10-ounce) beet, peeled and cut into 8 wedges
³/₄ cup nonfat buttermilk
1¹/₂ teaspoons vanilla extract
8 ounces cake flour (about 2 cups)
3 tablespoons unsweetened cocoa
1¹/₄ teaspoons baking powder
¹/₂ teaspoon salt
1¹/₂ cups granulated sugar
¹/₄ cup butter, softened
¹/₄ cup canola oil
2 large eggs
1 large egg white
Baking spray with flour
4 ounces ¹/₃-less-fat cream cheese, softened
2 tablespoons heavy whipping cream
2 tablespoons 2% reduced-fat Greek yogurt
¹/₂ teaspoon vanilla extract
Dash of salt
¹/₂ cup powdered sugar
²/₃ cup granulated sugar
4 large egg whites
¹/₄ teaspoon cream of tartar
Dash of salt

1. Preheat oven to 350°.
2. Place beet in a small saucepan; cover with water. Bring to a boil. Cook 10 minutes or until tender. Drain and cool slightly.
3. Place beet in a food processor; process until very finely chopped. Remove 1 packed cup beet from processor; reserve remaining beet for another use. Place 1 cup beet, buttermilk, and 1½ teaspoons vanilla in food processor. Process until very smooth, scraping sides of bowl as necessary.
4. Weigh or lightly spoon flour into dry measuring cups; level with a knife. Combine flour, cocoa, baking powder, and ½ teaspoon salt in a bowl, stirring well with a whisk.
5. Place 1½ cups granulated sugar, butter, and oil in a large bowl; beat with a mixer at medium speed until light and fluffy (about 5 minutes). Add eggs and 1 egg white, 1 at a time, beating until incorporated. Add flour mixture and beet mixture alternately to butter mixture, beginning and ending with flour mixture. Divide batter among 3 (8-inch) round metal cake pans coated with baking spray. Bake at 350° for 23 to 24 minutes or until a wooden pick inserted in center comes out clean. Cool 15 minutes in pans on a wire rack. Remove cake from pans; cool completely on wire rack.
6. Place cream cheese, cream, yogurt, ½ teaspoon vanilla, and dash of salt in a bowl; beat with a mixer at high speed until smooth. Add powdered sugar; beat at low speed 1 minute or until well combined (do not overbeat).
7. Combine ⅔ cup granulated sugar and remaining ingredients in the top of a double boiler. Cook over simmering water 2 to 3 minutes or until a candy thermometer registers 160°, stirring constantly with a whisk. Remove from heat. Beat egg mixture with a mixer at medium speed until soft peaks form; beat at high speed until stiff peaks form (do not overbeat).
8. Place 1 cake layer on a plate, and spread half of filling over top; top with another cake layer. Spread remaining filling over top; top with remaining cake layer. Spread meringue frosting over top and sides of cake. Serves 16 (serving size: 1 slice)

CALORIES 284; **FAT** 9.6g (sat 3.7g, mono 3.9g, poly 1.4g); **PROTEIN** 5g; **CARB** 46g; **FIBER** 1g; **CHOL** 39mg; **IRON** 1mg; **SODIUM** 199mg; **CALC** 55mg

SILKY PUREED SOUPS

Old-school French chefs are serious about sweating vegetables for soups, and you should be, too.

Slowly cooking fresh produce such as celery root, onions, and garlic in the right fat (aka butter) can yield a gloriously creamy pureed soup—a potage—with nothing but water and stock, no cream, to adjust viscosity. We take sweating a touch further here, rounding out the almost citrusy aroma of celery root with chicken stock and fresh thyme. You must be patient and cook slowly over relatively low heat. You're not looking to sauté the vegetables here; that would leave them with some crunch, and you want them meltingly tender for the silkiest soup.

KEITH'S RECIPE BREAKDOWN

CREAMY CELERY ROOT AND SWEET ONION SOUP

Hands-on: 20 min. Total: 1 hr. 20 min.

INGREDIENT	AMOUNT	WHY
unsalted butter	1 tablespoon	Potages (creamy pureed soups) need beurre.
celery root	4 cups, peeled and cubed (1 pound)	It has the subtle perfume of celery, the typical sweetness of a root vegetable, and an almost lemony tinge.
sweet onion	3 cups, vertically sliced (1 pound)	They collapse and render to a silken puree.
fresh thyme leaves	2 tablespoons	A crucial herb in French cuisine, its flavor absolutely bursts when warmed with butter.
garlic	8 cloves, peeled, trimmed, halved, and germ removed	Slowly cooked, it transforms into an almost dairy-like cream. It's textural magic. Remove any green germs, the sprouts that grow inside the bulb; they're pungent.
unsalted chicken stock	4 cups	For comfort.
water	2 cups	For thinning to the best texture without added salt or fat.
kosher salt	½ teaspoon	Because a little elevates the flavor.
lemon rind	1 (2-inch) strip	It perfumes the soup.
French bread, stale or oven-dried	1 (1-ounce) slice, cubed	This is your thickening agent. Flavors of yeast and toast are wonderful against sweet onions.
buttermilk	¼ cup	The lactic acid from buttermilk perks up flavors.
crème fraîche	2 tablespoons	The luxe finish. It's both rich and bright at the same time.
fresh chives	2 tablespoons, minced	Most of the flavors are deep and rich. Chives provide a fresh, grassy finish.

Follow These Steps:

• Melt butter in a large Dutch oven over low heat. Add celery root, onion, thyme, and garlic; toss to coat. Cover; increase heat to medium-low, and sweat the vegetables for 25 minutes, stirring occasionally.

• Add stock, 2 cups water, salt, and rind. Bring to a steady simmer; cover, reduce heat, and cook 20 minutes or until all vegetables are very tender. Carefully remove rind with tongs.

• Add bread to soup. Stir with a wooden spoon, being sure to "hit bottom," scraping purposefully as you stir.

• Pour half of soup into a blender. Remove center piece of blender lid (to allow steam to escape); secure blender lid on blender. Drape a clean towel over opening in blender lid (to avoid splatters). Blend until smooth, and pour into a large bowl. Repeat procedure with remaining soup. Return pureed soup to pan.

• Stir in buttermilk; heat soup over medium-high heat until very hot (do not boil). Ladle soup into bowls; top with crème fraîche and chives. Serves 8 (serving size: 1 cup soup,

¾ teaspoon crème fraîche, and ¾ teaspoon chives)

CALORIES 108; FAT 3.4g (sat 2g, mono 0.5g, poly 0.2g); PROTEIN 5g; CARB 15g; FIBER 2g; CHOL 8mg; IRON 1mg; SODIUM 293mg; CALC 73mg

Make Ahead
Variation: Creamy Garlic Soup
Substitute 4 cups garlic cloves for celery root; omit 8 cloves in original recipe. Reduce onion to 2 cups; add 1 cup cubed peeled baking potato. Increase salt to ¾ teaspoon. Stir in 1½ tablespoons dry sherry with buttermilk. Omit crème fraîche and chives. Combine ⅓ cup toasted bread crumbs, 2 tablespoons grated pecorino Romano cheese, 1 tablespoon chopped fresh parsley, 2 teaspoons grated lemon rind; sprinkle over soup. Serves 12 (serving size: about ¾ cup soup and about 2 teaspoons topping)

CALORIES 105; FAT 1.8g (sat 1.1g); SODIUM 219mg

KID IN THE KITCHEN

EAT YOUR VEGETABLES

Parents, take note: Our carrot soup is a real hit with the kids!

"Today I made carrot soup with Parmesan crisps. When I first heard about this dish, I have to admit I was not too sure. Lesson to myself: Don't underestimate the humble carrot soup! This soup is now at the top of my list. It's packed with flavor. The white wine vinegar adds a hint of sweet and sour flavor at the end without overpowering your taste buds. The crème fraîche, kind of like a rich sour cream, gives it a nice creamy balance. Leeks add a nice onion flavor. They can be really sandy on the inside, so make sure to rinse them well before slicing for the soup.

"The Parmesan crisps are as divine as they sound—a salty, cheesy crunch against the creaminess of the soup. You could pile the cheese inside a cookie cutter on the baking sheet so that the crisps have the same round shape. These are meant to be thin, so don't use too much cheese for each one. This soup was easy to make and a real hit with my family. You'll love it."

Kid Friendly • Make Ahead
Gluten Free

Carrot Soup with Parmesan Crisps

Hands-on: 37 min. Total: 1 hr. 13 min.
This appetizer soup is deceptively lush, without any butter or cream. Chive crème fraîche adds an herbaceous touch, while the accompanying Parmesan crisp lends a contrasting salty crunch.

1 ounce Parmigiano-Reggiano cheese, grated (about ¼ cup)
3⅔ cups coarsely chopped carrot
2½ cups unsalted chicken stock (such as Swanson)
2 cups plus 1 teaspoon water, divided
2 cups coarsely chopped leek, white and light green parts only (about 2 large)
1 tablespoon white wine vinegar
¼ teaspoon kosher salt
¼ teaspoon black pepper
⅛ teaspoon ground nutmeg
3 tablespoons crème fraîche or sour cream
1 tablespoon finely chopped fresh chives

1. Preheat oven to 350°.
2. Line a baking sheet with parchment paper. Spread 2 teaspoons cheese evenly into a 2-inch circle on a baking sheet. Repeat procedure with remaining cheese, leaving 1 inch between circles, to form 6 cheese

rounds. Bake at 350° for 8 minutes or until golden. Remove pan from oven; carefully lift crisps from pan with a spatula, and place on a wire rack. Cool cheese crisps completely.
3. Combine carrot, stock, 2 cups water, and leek in a large Dutch oven; bring to a boil. Partially cover, reduce heat, and simmer 30 minutes or until vegetables are tender. Remove pan from heat; let stand 10 minutes.
4. Place half of carrot mixture in a blender. Remove center piece of blender lid (to allow steam to escape); secure blender lid on blender. Place a clean towel over opening in blender lid (to avoid splatters). Blend until smooth. Strain mixture through a sieve over a large bowl; discard solids. Repeat procedure with remaining carrot mixture. Stir in vinegar, salt, pepper, and nutmeg.
5. Combine 1 teaspoon water, crème fraîche, and chives in a small bowl, stirring with a whisk. Place about 1 cup soup in each of 6 bowls. Top each serving with about 1 teaspoon crème fraîche mixture and 1 crisp. Serves 6

CALORIES 107; FAT 4.2g (sat 2.5g, mono 0.4g, poly 0.2g); PROTEIN 5g; CARB 12g; FIBER 3g; CHOL 10mg; IRON 1mg; SODIUM 277mg; CALC 112mg

THE VERDICT

FRAANZ (AGE 9)
He loved the Parmesan cheese crisps, especially when he dunked them in the soup. **10/10**

KALANI (AGE 16)
He said, "The soup was way creamier than I imagined and really full of flavor. **10/10**

MATISSE (AGE 13)
The soup was incredibly smooth and light. The Parmesan crisps were a magical addition. **10/10**

FEED 4 FOR LESS THAN $10

Kid Friendly

Chili-Orange Glazed Pork Tenderloin

$2.46 PER SERVING

Hands-on: 10 min. Total: 45 min.

3 small sweet potatoes, cut into
   1-inch wedges (about 1½ pounds)
2 teaspoons olive oil
¼ teaspoon kosher salt
¼ teaspoon black pepper
Cooking spray
1 (1-pound) pork tenderloin, trimmed
2 tablespoons all-fruit orange
   marmalade
2 teaspoons cider vinegar
2 teaspoons adobo sauce from 1 can
   chipotle chiles in adobo sauce

1. Adjust two oven racks to middle of oven. Preheat oven to 450°.
2. Combine sweet potatoes, oil, salt, and pepper in a medium bowl; toss to coat. Arrange sweet potatoes on a foil-lined baking sheet coated with cooking spray. Bake at 450° on bottom rack 10 minutes. Stir potatoes; roast an additional 20 minutes or until golden brown.
3. Place tenderloin on a foil-lined baking sheet coated with cooking spray. Combine marmalade, vinegar, and adobo sauce in a small bowl. Roast tenderloin at 450° on top rack of oven 20 minutes. Turn broiler to high. Brush pork with half of marmalade mixture. Broil 5 minutes or until a thermometer registers 145°; remove from oven. Let stand 5 minutes.

4. Slice pork crosswise into (½-inch-thick) slices. Serve with sweet potatoes and remaining marmalade mixture. Serves 4 (serving size: 3 ounces pork, 2 teaspoons sauce, and 1 cup potato wedges)

CALORIES 305; **FAT** 4.9g (sat 1.1g, mono 2.5g, poly 0.7g); **PROTEIN** 26g; **CARB** 38g; **FIBER** 5g; **CHOL** 74mg; **IRON** 2mg; **SODIUM** 301mg; **CALC** 58mg

Kid Friendly • Vegetarian
Gluten Free

Spinach and Feta Quiche with Quinoa Crust

$2.09 PER SERVING

Hands-on: 15 min. Total: 1 hr. 10 min.

2 cups cooked quinoa, chilled
⅛ teaspoon black pepper
1 large egg, beaten
Cooking spray
1 teaspoon canola oil
½ onion, thinly sliced
1 (5-ounce) bag baby spinach
½ cup 1% low-fat milk
½ teaspoon kosher salt
¼ teaspoon black pepper
¼ teaspoon crushed red pepper
4 large eggs
2 large egg whites
1.5 ounces feta cheese, crumbled
   (about ⅓ cup)

1. Preheat oven to 375°.
2. Combine quinoa, ⅛ teaspoon pepper, and 1 egg in a bowl, stirring well to coat. Press mixture into bottom and up sides of a 9-inch pie plate coated with cooking spray. Bake at 375° for 20 minutes; cool.
3. Heat a nonstick skillet over medium heat. Add oil to pan; swirl to coat. Add onion; sauté 3 minutes. Add spinach; sauté 3 minutes or until liquid evaporates. Remove from heat; cool slightly.

4. Combine milk and next 5 ingredients in a large bowl; stir with a whisk. Arrange spinach mixture in crust; pour egg mixture over spinach. Sprinkle with feta. Bake at 375° for 35 minutes or until set. Let stand 5 minutes; cut into 4 wedges. Serves 4 (serving size: 1 wedge)

CALORIES 282; **FAT** 11.6g (sat 3.8g, mono 3.6g, poly 1.6g); **PROTEIN** 17g; **CARB** 28g; **FIBER** 5g; **CHOL** 243mg; **IRON** 4mg; **SODIUM** 552mg; **CALC** 172mg

VEGETARIAN COOKING FOR EVERYONE

Quick & Easy • Make Ahead
Vegetarian • Gluten Free

Hominy with Winter Squash and Cilantro-Avocado Salsa

Hands-on: 24 min. Total: 35 min.

1 tablespoon olive oil
2 cups (½-inch) cubed peeled
   butternut squash
1 cup diced onion
1 teaspoon dried oregano
1 dried red New Mexican or guajillo
   chile, seeded and crumbled
1 teaspoon smoked paprika
¼ teaspoon kosher salt
¼ teaspoon ground red pepper
   (optional)
2 (15.5-ounce) cans hominy,
   undrained
⅔ cup diced avocado
½ cup minced fresh cilantro
4 teaspoons diced jalapeño pepper

1 teaspoon olive oil
1½ teaspoons grated lime rind
1½ tablespoons fresh lime juice
1 ounce Monterey Jack cheese, shredded (about ¼ cup)
¼ cup 2% reduced-fat Greek yogurt

1. Heat a 3-quart saucepan over medium-high heat. Add 1 tablespoon oil to pan; swirl to coat. Add squash, onion, oregano, and chile; cook 10 minutes or until onion and squash begin to brown, stirring frequently. Add paprika, salt, red pepper, and hominy; bring to a boil. Cover, reduce heat, and simmer 10 minutes or until squash is tender.
2. Combine avocado, cilantro, jalapeño, and 1 teaspoon oil in a small bowl; toss to combine. Stir in rind and juice. Divide hominy mixture evenly among 4 bowls; top evenly with salsa, cheese, and yogurt. Serves 4 (serving size: about 1¼ cups stew, about ¼ cup salsa, 1 tablespoon cheese, and 1 tablespoon yogurt)

CALORIES 351; **FAT** 12.8g (sat 3g, mono 6.9g, poly 2g); **PROTEIN** 9g; **CARB** 51g; **FIBER** 10g; **CHOL** 7mg; **IRON** 3mg; **SODIUM** 634mg; **CALC** 146mg

LET'S GET COOKING

ROASTED CAULIFLOWER WITH DIJON VINAIGRETTE

One of Boston's best chefs shares his take on the trendy crucifer.

Dismissed for generations as bland, boiled, and gassy, cauliflower has recently blossomed into the "it" veggie at restaurants around the country. Michael Leviton, chef-owner of Lumière, one of the Boston area's most esteemed restaurants, recalls how enterprising chefs some years

back started featuring cauliflower puree on their menus instead of mashed potatoes, introducing the public to its versatility. "Then roasted cauliflower became all the rage," he says.

Leviton's dazzling résumé includes time training under legendary chef Daniel Boulud at Le Cirque, where the menu 25 years ago featured a roasted cauliflower grenobloise, which inspired Leviton's own roasted cauliflower dish below. "I love the idea of using one ingredient in different ways in a dish to show its different personalities," he says.

Leviton roasts cauliflower florets to caramelize them and develop complex flavor. He also blends the meaty stems into a silky puree for textural contrast. A tangy Dijon vinaigrette brightens flavors, and briny capers complete the Grenoble homage. Try Leviton's original dish at Lumière in West Newton this month.

Vegetarian

Roasted Cauliflower with Dijon Vinaigrette

Hands-on: 35 min. Total: 65 min. This dish showcases two of cauliflower's most desirable traits: the golden-brown caramelized crust it forms when roasted, and the silky texture it provides when pureed.

1 (1-ounce) slice sourdough bread
1 head cauliflower
7 teaspoons extra-virgin olive oil, divided
¼ teaspoon salt, divided
¼ teaspoon freshly ground black pepper
2 cups water
⅛ teaspoon fresh lemon juice
3 tablespoons parsley leaves
1 tablespoon minced fresh garlic
2 teaspoons grated lemon rind
2 teaspoons Dijon mustard
4 teaspoons rice vinegar

4 teaspoons canola oil
Cooking spray
2 teaspoons capers, rinsed, drained, and chopped

1. Preheat oven to 350°.
2. Remove crust from bread. Tear into very small pieces. Place on a baking sheet; bake at 350° for 13 minutes or until toasted and golden brown, stirring occasionally. Remove from oven. Increase oven temperature to 450°.
3. Cut cauliflower into 2-inch florets, reserving stems. Place florets on a foil-lined baking sheet. Drizzle with 1 tablespoon olive oil; toss well. Bake florets at 450° for 25 minutes or until dark golden brown in spots and almost tender. Sprinkle florets with ⅛ teaspoon salt and pepper.
4. Combine reserved cauliflower stems and 2 cups water in a small saucepan over medium heat; bring to a boil. Cover, reduce heat, and simmer 10 minutes or until very tender. Drain well. Place stems, ⅛ teaspoon salt, and juice in a food processor; process until smooth.
5. Combine parsley, garlic, and rind in a small bowl. Combine mustard and vinegar in a small bowl; mix well. Gradually add 4 teaspoons extra-virgin olive oil and canola oil to mustard mixture, stirring constantly with a whisk.
6. Heat a large skillet over medium-high heat. Coat pan with cooking spray. Add cauliflower florets; sauté 1 minute or until thoroughly heated. Stir in capers and parsley mixture. Sprinkle with breadcrumbs. Place 2 tablespoons cauliflower puree on each of 6 plates. Top each with ¾ cup floret mixture; drizzle with 2 teaspoons vinaigrette. Serves 6

CALORIES 117; **FAT** 8.8g (sat 1.1g, mono 5.8g, poly 1.5g); **PROTEIN** 3g; **CARB** 9g; **FIBER** 2g; **CHOL** 0mg; **IRON** 1mg; **SODIUM** 222mg; **CALC** 31mg

5 TANTALIZING BRUSCHETTA TOPPERS

Start Here: Slice 1 (4-ounce) whole-wheat French baguette into 8 thin slices; arrange on a baking sheet coated with cooking spray. Toast bread under broiler 3 minutes or until golden brown, turning bread slices halfway through. Remove from oven, and pile on one of these toppers.

Kid Friendly • Quick & Easy Vegetarian
Chocolate-Tangerine
Spread each warm toast with 1 tablespoon chocolate-hazelnut spread (such as Nutella). Top each with 3 tangerine segments. Sprinkle toasts evenly with ¼ teaspoon smoked sea salt. Serves 8 (serving size: 1 toast)

CALORIES 136; FAT 5.8g (sat 1.8g); SODIUM 137mg

Kid Friendly • Quick & Easy Vegetarian
Lemony Herbed Ricotta and Roasted Tomato
Preheat oven to 450°. Toss 1 pint cherry tomatoes with 1 tablespoon olive oil, ¼ teaspoon kosher salt, ¼ teaspoon black pepper, and ¼ teaspoon granulated sugar; bake at 450° on a jelly-roll pan 20 minutes or until blistered. Using a rubber spatula, fold 2 tablespoons chopped fresh basil, 1 tablespoon fresh thyme leaves, 1 tablespoon chopped fresh oregano, 1 teaspoon grated lemon rind, and 1 tablespoon fresh lemon juice into ¾ cup part-skim ricotta cheese. Spread 1½ tablespoons ricotta mixture over each toast; top with roasted tomatoes. Sprinkle toasts evenly with ⅛ teaspoon kosher salt. Serves 8 (serving size: 1 toast)

CALORIES 85; FAT 3.9g (sat 1.4g); SODIUM 193mg

Quick & Easy
Black-Eyed Pea, Bacon, and Pickled Okra
Place 1 drained (15-ounce) can unsalted black-eyed peas, 2 tablespoons olive oil, 1 tablespoon water, 2 teaspoons fresh lemon juice, 1 peeled garlic clove, ⅛ teaspoon kosher salt, and ¼ teaspoon crushed red pepper in the bowl of a food processor; process until smooth. Divide puree evenly over toasts; spread to coat. Top each toast with ½ slice cooked and crumbled bacon and 1 pod drained pickled okra, sliced into ¼-inch-thick rounds. Serves 8 (serving size: 1 toast)

CALORIES 100; FAT 4.9g (sat 1g); SODIUM 177mg

Quick & Easy
Smoked Trout and Horseradish Dill Cream
Combine ¼ cup crème fraîche, ¼ cup nonfat plain Greek yogurt, 1½ tablespoons prepared horseradish, 1 tablespoon chopped fresh dill, and ⅛ teaspoon kosher salt in a small bowl, stirring with a whisk. Spread 1 tablespoon cream over each toast; top each with ¼ ounce smoked trout, skinned. Serves 8 (serving size: 1 toast)

CALORIES 74; FAT 3.5g (sat 1.9g); SODIUM 190mg

Kid Friendly • Quick & Easy
Pear, Brie, and Balsamic
Preheat oven to 400°. Divide 3 ounces Brie cheese evenly over toasts; arrange on a jelly-roll pan. Bake at 400° for 3 minutes or until cheese melts. Slice 1 ripe Bartlett pear into thin slices; fan 3 to 4 slices over each toast. Combine 2 teaspoons honey and 2 teaspoons balsamic vinegar in a small bowl, stirring with a whisk. Drizzle ½ teaspoon honey-balsamic mixture over each toast. Serves 8 (serving size: 1 toast)

CALORIES 84; FAT 3.2g (sat 1.9g); SODIUM 140mg

20-MINUTE COOKING

Kid Friendly • Quick & Easy
Sausage and Kale Skillet with Polenta

Any leftovers from this dish can make for a delightful breakfast the following morning—simply reheat and top with an over-easy egg.

1 tablespoon olive oil
4 ounces sweet pork Italian sausage, casings removed
8 ounces prepared polenta, cut into 8 (½-inch-thick) slices
6 ounces prechopped kale (about 6 cups)
1 tablespoon water
½ teaspoon freshly ground black pepper
1½ cups lower-sodium marinara sauce (such as Dell'Amore)
2 ounces fresh mozzarella cheese, torn into small pieces

1. Preheat broiler to high.
2. Heat a large skillet over medium-high heat. Add oil to pan; swirl. Add sausage; cook 3 minutes or until browned, stirring to crumble. Remove sausage from pan. Add polenta; cook 5 minutes or until browned on 1 side (do not stir or turn). Remove polenta from pan. Add kale, 1 tablespoon water, and pepper to pan. Cover and cook 2 minutes. Uncover and stir in sausage and marinara. Nestle polenta, browned side up, into sausage mixture; sprinkle with cheese. Broil 2 minutes or until cheese browns. Serves 4 (serving size: 2 polenta slices and about ¾ cup sausage mixture)

CALORIES 260; FAT 16.6g (sat 5.7g, mono 6.6g, poly 1.6g); PROTEIN 10g; CARB 18g; FIBER 3g; CHOL 33mg; IRON 3mg; SODIUM 408mg; CALC 79mg

Spinach, Egg, and Prosciutto Flatbreads

Cooking eggs in a separate pan, rather than directly on each flatbread, helps get these personal pizzas on the table in record time.

4 (2-ounce) rectangular multigrain
  flatbreads (such as Joseph's)
Cooking spray
1 tablespoon olive oil, divided
1 cup finely chopped sweet onion
$1/4$ teaspoon salt
$1/4$ teaspoon crushed red pepper
10 cups baby spinach
4 large eggs
3 ounces shredded part-skim
  mozzarella cheese (about $3/4$ cup)
2 ($1/2$-ounce) slices prosciutto,
  chopped
$1/4$ teaspoon freshly ground black
  pepper

1. Preheat broiler to high.
2. Place flatbreads on a large baking sheet lightly coated with cooking spray; lightly coat tops of bread with cooking spray. Broil 1 minute. Remove pan from oven; turn breads over. Lightly coat breads with cooking spray. Broil 1 minute or until browned. Remove pan from oven.
3. Heat a large skillet over medium heat. Add 1 teaspoon oil to pan; swirl to coat. Add onion, salt, and red pepper; cook 3 minutes or until onion begins to soften. Add spinach; cook 1 minute or until spinach begins to wilt. Remove mixture from pan; keep warm.
4. Wipe pan clean with a paper towel. Heat pan over medium heat. Add 2 teaspoons oil to pan; swirl to coat. Crack eggs into pan; cook 1 minute on each side or until desired degree of doneness.
5. Divide spinach mixture evenly among flatbreads. Top evenly with cheese and chopped prosciutto. Broil 1 minute or until cheese melts. Top each flatbread with 1 egg; sprinkle black pepper over eggs. Serve immediately. Serves 4 (serving size: 1 flatbread pizza)

CALORIES 343; FAT 12.6g (sat 4.5g, mono 5.6g, poly 1.7g); PROTEIN 20g; CARB 36g; FIBER 3g; CHOL 204mg; IRON 4mg; SODIUM 655mg; CALC 279mg

Pan-Roasted Fingerling Potatoes with Cilantro Mojo and Sour Cream

4 teaspoons olive oil, divided
1 pound fingerling potatoes, halved
  lengthwise
1 cup unsalted chicken stock
$3/8$ teaspoon salt
$1/4$ teaspoon freshly ground black
  pepper
$2/3$ cup tightly packed cilantro leaves
  and tender stems
1 teaspoon fresh lime juice
1 teaspoon water
1 teaspoon white wine vinegar
$1/8$ teaspoon honey
1 large garlic clove, chopped
$1/4$ cup low-fat sour cream

1. Heat a large skillet over medium-high heat. Add 1 tablespoon oil to pan; swirl to coat. Add potatoes to pan, cut sides down. Cook 6 minutes or until golden brown. Add stock, salt, and pepper to pan; cover and cook on medium-high 6 minutes or until potatoes are tender. Uncover; cook 2 minutes or until liquid evaporates.
2. While potatoes cook, place 1 teaspoon oil, cilantro, and next 5 ingredients in a mini food processor. Process until finely chopped.
Add cilantro mixture to pan, and gently stir to coat. Divide potatoes evenly among 4 plates; top with sour cream. Serves 4 (serving size: $1/4$ of potato mixture and 1 tablespoon sour cream)

CALORIES 151; FAT 6.5g (sat 1.8g, mono 3.3g, poly 0.5g); PROTEIN 4g; CARB 20g; FIBER 2g; CHOL 8mg; IRON 1mg; SODIUM 280mg; CALC 44mg

Blue Cheese Sauce and Walnuts
Cut 1 pound fingerling potatoes in half lengthwise. Heat 1 tablespoon olive oil in a skillet over medium-high heat. Cook potatoes, cut sides down, 6 minutes. Cover, reduce heat to medium, and cook 6 minutes; sprinkle with $1/4$ teaspoon salt. Combine $1/2$ cup 2% milk and $1 1/2$ teaspoons all-purpose flour in a saucepan, stirring with a whisk; bring to a boil, stirring constantly. Cook 1 minute. Add 1 ounce crumbled blue cheese and $1/8$ teaspoon black pepper. Cook 1 minute or until mixture is smooth. Top potatoes with cheese sauce, 2 tablespoons toasted chopped walnuts, and 2 teaspoons chopped fresh parsley. Serves 4 (serving size: $1/4$ of potatoes, 2 tablespoons sauce, $1 1/2$ teaspoons chopped walnuts, and $1/2$ teaspoon chopped parsley)

CALORIES 178; FAT 8.7g (sat 2.4g); SODIUM 279mg

continued

Spinach and Garlic

Cut 1 pound fingerling potatoes in half lengthwise. Heat 1 tablespoon olive oil in a skillet over medium-high heat. Cook potatoes, cut sides down, 6 minutes. Cover, reduce heat to medium, and cook 6 minutes; sprinkle with ¼ teaspoon salt. Add 2 tablespoons minced fresh garlic; cook 30 seconds. Add 4 cups baby spinach leaves; cook 1 minute. Top with 2 tablespoons toasted pine nuts and ½ ounce grated Asiago cheese. Serves 4 (serving size: ¼ of potatoes, 1½ teaspoons pine nuts, and about 1 tablespoon cheese)

CALORIES 184; **FAT** 8.3g (sat 1.4g); **SODIUM** 239mg

Quick & Easy • Vegetarian
Gluten Free
Quick Pickled Red Onions

Cut 1 pound fingerling potatoes in half lengthwise. Heat 1 tablespoon olive oil in a skillet over medium-high heat. Cook potatoes, cut sides down, 6 minutes. Cover, reduce heat to medium, and cook 6 minutes; sprinkle with ¼ teaspoon salt. Combine ½ cup white wine vinegar, 1 tablespoon yellow mustard seeds, 1 tablespoon sugar, and ¼ teaspoon salt in a small saucepan; bring to a boil. Remove from heat; stir in 1 cup thinly sliced red onion. Let stand 5 minutes. Drain; discard liquid. Add onion to pan; toss to combine. Top with 2 teaspoons chopped parsley. Serves 4 (serving size: ¼ of potatoes)

CALORIES 144; **FAT** 4.2g (sat 0.5g); **SODIUM** 313mg

TO PREVENT THE FLOUNDER FROM FLAKING APART BEFORE SERVING, USE A FISH SPATULA TO GENTLY REMOVE EACH FILLET FROM THE GINGER-INFUSED BROTH.

Quick & Easy • Gluten Free

Flounder Poached in Ginger-Sesame Broth with Edamame and Bok Choy

2 teaspoons sesame oil
12 shiitake mushroom caps, thinly sliced
2 cups seafood stock (such as Kitchen Basics)
1 cup water
2 tablespoons mirin (sweet rice wine)
1½ tablespoons white miso (soybean paste)
2 teaspoons rice vinegar
3 garlic cloves, thinly sliced
1 (2-inch) piece peeled fresh ginger, thinly sliced
4 (6-ounce) flounder fillets
2 cups chopped baby bok choy
1 cup frozen shelled edamame (green soybeans), thawed
2 green onions, thinly diagonally sliced
1 red bell pepper, thinly sliced
2 teaspoons black or white sesame seeds

1. Heat a large saucepan over medium-high heat. Add oil to pan; swirl to coat. Add mushrooms; cook 2 minutes, stirring occasionally. Add stock and next 6 ingredients (through ginger); bring to a boil. Reduce heat and simmer 5 minutes. **2.** Gently add fish to pan. Top with bok choy and edamame. Cover and simmer 6 to 8 minutes or until fish flakes easily when tested with a fork. **3.** Carefully remove fish from pan; divide evenly among 4 bowls. Divide broth and vegetables evenly among bowls. Top with green onions, red pepper, and sesame seeds. Serves 4 (serving size: 1 fish filet and 1 cup broth-vegetable mixture)

CALORIES 258; **FAT** 8.6g (sat 1.3g, mono 2.2g, poly 2.2g); **PROTEIN** 30g; **CARB** 15g; **FIBER** 5g; **CHOL** 77mg; **IRON** 2mg; **SODIUM** 653mg; **CALC** 174mg

Two-Cheese Penne with Chicken and Spinach

8 ounces uncooked quick-cooking penne (such as Ronzoni)
Cooking spray
12 ounces skinless, boneless chicken cutlets
¼ teaspoon kosher salt
¼ teaspoon freshly ground black pepper
1 tablespoon extra-virgin olive oil
7 ounces fresh spinach
¼ teaspoon crushed red pepper
2 garlic cloves, minced
1 tablespoon fresh lemon juice
2 ounces fresh pecorino Romano cheese, shredded (about ½ cup)
2 ounces ⅓-less-fat cream cheese (about ¼ cup)

1. Cook pasta according to package directions, omitting salt and fat. Drain in a colander over a bowl, reserving ¼ cup pasta cooking water.
2. Heat a large skillet over medium-high heat. Coat pan with cooking spray. Sprinkle chicken breasts with salt and pepper. Add chicken to pan; cook 3 minutes on each side or just until done. Remove chicken from pan; thinly slice across grain.
3. Return pan to medium heat. Add oil; swirl to coat. Add spinach, red pepper, and garlic to pan; cook 3 minutes or until spinach wilts. Add cooked pasta, reserved pasta cooking water, chicken, lemon juice, and cheeses to pan; toss to coat. Cook 1 minute or until cheeses melt. Serve immediately. Serves 4 (serving size: about 1¼ cups)

CALORIES 436; FAT 13.5g (sat 5.1g, mono 3.9g, poly 0.9g); PROTEIN 33g; CARB 46g; FIBER 3g; CHOL 75mg; IRON 4mg; SODIUM 526mg; CALC 236mg

Roast Beef, Broccoli Rabe, and Provolone Sandwiches

Transform a simple sandwich to a dinner-worthy entrée with the addition of a garlicky, peppery broccoli rabe sauté.

8 cups water
8 ounces broccoli rabe, stem ends removed
1 tablespoon extra-virgin olive oil
4 garlic cloves, divided
¼ teaspoon black pepper
⅛ teaspoon kosher salt
8 (1-ounce) slices rustic whole-grain bread
8 ounces thinly sliced low-sodium roast beef (such as Boar's Head)
3 ounces thinly sliced provolone cheese

1. Preheat broiler to high.
2. Bring 8 cups of water to a boil in a large saucepan. Cut broccoli rabe into 2-inch pieces. Add to pan; boil 1½ minutes. Drain. Pat dry with paper towels.
3. Heat a large nonstick skillet over medium heat. Add oil; swirl to coat. Mince 3 garlic cloves; add to pan. Cook 30 seconds or until golden, stirring constantly. Add broccoli rabe to pan; cook 2 minutes. Stir in pepper and salt.
4. Place bread slices on a baking sheet; broil 2 minutes or until toasted. Cut remaining garlic clove in half; rub bread slices with cut side of garlic. Top 4 bread slices evenly with roast beef, broccoli rabe, and provolone cheese. Broil 30 seconds or until cheese melts. Top with remaining bread slices. Serves 4 (serving size: 1 sandwich)

CALORIES 357; FAT 14.1g (sat 5.6g, mono 4.5g, poly 1.6g); PROTEIN 30g; CARB 29g; FIBER 4g; CHOL 45mg; IRON 4mg; SODIUM 583mg; CALC 252mg

Cabbage Soup with Andouille Sausage

Smoked Andouille gives this hearty and comforting soup a wealth of deep flavor, while chopped coleslaw mix allows it to come together in a flash.

2 cups unsalted beef stock
1 cup water
2 medium Yukon gold potatoes, peeled and cut into ½-inch pieces (about 8 ounces)
2 thyme sprigs
4 ounces smoked Andouille sausage, diced
1 cup chopped onion
3 garlic cloves, minced
1 (14-ounce) package coleslaw
¼ cup dry white wine
1 (14.5-ounce) can stewed tomatoes, undrained
1 tablespoon red wine vinegar
¼ teaspoon freshly ground black pepper

1. Place stock, 1 cup water, potatoes, and thyme in a large saucepan; bring to a boil. Reduce heat and simmer 10 minutes or until potatoes are tender.
2. Heat a large nonstick skillet over medium heat. Add sausage; cook 3 minutes or until lightly browned, stirring frequently. Add onion; cook 3 minutes. Stir in garlic; cook 30 seconds. Add coleslaw and wine; cook 3 minutes or until tender, stirring frequently.
3. Remove thyme from potato mixture. Coarsely mash potatoes in pan with a potato masher. Add sausage mixture to potato mixture; stir in tomatoes, vinegar, and pepper; simmer 3 minutes. Serves 4 (serving size: about 1¾ cups)

CALORIES 215; FAT 5.4g (sat 2.1g, mono 2.3g, poly 0.7g); PROTEIN 10g; CARB 30g; FIBER 5g; CHOL 20mg; IRON 3mg; SODIUM 564mg; CALC 103mg

DINNER TONIGHT

READY IN 40 MINUTES

SHOPPING LIST

Swiss Chard and White Bean Soup

Lemon (1)
Cherry tomatoes
Swiss chard
Fresh rosemary
Yellow onion (1)
Yukon gold potatoes (8 ounces)
Crushed red pepper
Olive oil
15-ounce can unsalted cannellini beans (1)
White vinegar
Unsalted vegetable stock (such as Kitchen Basics)
Eggs (4)

Garlic-Parmesan Toasts

Garlic
Olive oil
Whole-grain bread (4 ounces)
Vegetarian Parmesan cheese

GAME PLAN

While soup simmers:
- Poach eggs.
While broiler preheats:
- Prepare toasts.

Quick & Easy • Make Ahead
Vegetarian • Gluten Free

Swiss Chard and White Bean Soup

with Garlic-Parmesan Toasts

1 tablespoon olive oil
1 cup chopped yellow onion
1 teaspoon grated lemon rind
1 teaspoon minced fresh rosemary
$1/2$ teaspoon kosher salt
$3/8$ teaspoon crushed red pepper, divided
2 cups unsalted vegetable stock
2 cups water
8 ounces Yukon gold potatoes, diced (about $1^1/2$ cups)
4 cups chopped Swiss chard
1 (15-ounce) can unsalted cannellini beans, rinsed and drained
$1/2$ cup quartered cherry tomatoes
2 teaspoons white vinegar
4 large eggs

1. Heat a large Dutch oven over medium-high heat. Add oil; swirl to coat. Add onion; sauté 6 minutes. Stir in rind, rosemary, salt, and ¼ teaspoon pepper; cook 1 minute. Stir in stock, 2 cups water, and potatoes; bring to a boil. Reduce heat to low; cover and simmer 10 minutes. Stir in chard and beans; simmer 10 minutes. Stir in tomatoes.
2. Fill a skillet two-thirds full with water; bring to a boil. Reduce heat; simmer. Add vinegar. Break each egg into a custard cup, and pour each gently into pan; cook 3 minutes or until desired degree of doneness. Carefully remove eggs from pan using a slotted spoon. Ladle 1½ cups soup into each of 4 bowls; top with a poached egg. Sprinkle with ⅛ teaspoon pepper. Serves 4

CALORIES 224; FAT 8.8g (sat 2.1g, mono 4.3g, poly 1.4g); PROTEIN 12g; CARB 25g; FIBER 5g; CHOL 186mg; IRON 3mg; SODIUM 532mg; CALC 83mg

---

Kid Friendly • Quick & Easy
Vegetarian

Garlic-Parmesan Toasts
Preheat broiler to high. Combine 1 teaspoon minced fresh garlic, 1 teaspoon olive oil, ¼ teaspoon freshly ground black pepper, and ⅛ teaspoon kosher salt in a bowl. Arrange 4 (1-ounce) whole-grain bread slices on a baking sheet. Brush bread slices evenly with oil mixture; top with 1 ounce grated vegetarian Parmesan cheese. Broil 30 seconds or until cheese melts. Serves 4 (serving size: 1 bread slice)

CALORIES 117; FAT 4.4g (sat 1.6g); SODIUM 288mg

READY IN 40 MINUTES

SHOPPING LIST

Steak and Herbed Tomatoes with Roast Potatoes

Tomatoes (2 medium)
Fresh oregano
Shallot (1)
Garlic
Fingerling potatoes (1 pound)
Olive oil
Balsamic vinegar
Sugar
Flank steak (1 pound)

Balsamic Broccoli Rabe
Broccoli rabe (1 pound)
Extra-virgin olive oil
Balsamic vinegar
Vegetarian Parmesan cheese

GAME PLAN

While oven preheats:
- Bring water for broccoli rabe to a boil.
- Prepare potatoes.
While potatoes bake:
- Cook steak.
- Finish broccoli rabe.

Steak and Herbed Tomatoes with Roast Potatoes

with Balsamic Broccoli Rabe

1 pound fingerling potatoes, halved
2 tablespoons olive oil, divided
½ teaspoon kosher salt, divided
½ teaspoon freshly ground black
  pepper, divided
5 teaspoons chopped fresh oregano,
  divided
1 (1-pound) flank steak, trimmed
2 tablespoons finely chopped shallot
1 teaspoon minced fresh garlic
2 cups chopped tomato
½ teaspoon sugar
1 teaspoon balsamic vinegar

1. Preheat oven to 425°.
2. Combine potatoes, 1 tablespoon oil, ¼ teaspoon salt, and ¼ teaspoon pepper on a baking sheet. Bake at 425° for 25 minutes or until tender, stirring after 10 minutes. Add 2 teaspoons oregano to pan; toss to coat.
3. Heat a large skillet over medium-high heat. Rub steak with 1 teaspoon oil; sprinkle with ¼ teaspoon salt and ¼ teaspoon pepper. Add steak to pan; cook 4 minutes on each side or until desired degree of doneness. Place steak on a cutting board; let stand 5 minutes. Cut across the grain into thin slices.
4. Return pan to medium-high heat. Add 2 teaspoons oil to pan; swirl to coat. Add shallot and garlic to pan; sauté 30 seconds. Stir in 1 tablespoon oregano, tomato, and sugar; cook 1 minute. Stir in vinegar. Spoon tomato mixture evenly over steak. Serve with potato mixture. Serves 4 (serving size: 3 ounces steak, ⅓ cup tomato mixture, and about ¾ cup potatoes)

CALORIES 326; **FAT** 13.4g (sat 3.3g, mono 7.2g, poly 1.1g); **PROTEIN** 28g; **CARB** 24g; **FIBER** 3g; **CHOL** 70mg; **IRON** 3mg; **SODIUM** 329mg; **CALC** 60mg

Balsamic Broccoli Rabe
Bring a large saucepan of water to a boil. Add 1 pound broccoli rabe, cut into 1-inch pieces; boil 3 minutes or until crisp-tender. Drain. Combine broccoli rabe, 2 teaspoons extra-virgin olive oil, 2 teaspoons balsamic vinegar, ¼ teaspoon kosher salt, and ¼ teaspoon freshly ground black pepper in a large bowl; toss to coat. Sprinkle with 1 tablespoon shaved vegetarian Parmesan cheese. Serves 4 (serving size: about ⅔ cup)

CALORIES 62; **FAT** 2.6g (sat 0.5g); **SODIUM** 173mg

READY IN
35
MINUTES

SHOPPING LIST

Mustard-Glazed Salmon with Roasted Cauliflower
Lemon (1)
Fresh dill
Cauliflower (1 large head)
Olive oil
Dijon mustard
Honey
Salmon fillets (1½ pounds)

Buttery Lentils with Shallots
Fresh parsley
Fresh thyme
Shallots (2 large)
Dried petite green lentils
Butter

GAME PLAN

While oven preheats:
■ Prepare cauliflower.
While cauliflower roasts:
■ Cook lentils.
■ Cook salmon.

Mustard-Glazed Salmon with Roasted Cauliflower

with Buttery Lentils with Shallots

6 cups cauliflower florets
2 tablespoons olive oil
½ teaspoon freshly ground black
  pepper, divided
¼ teaspoon kosher salt, divided
3 tablespoons Dijon mustard
1 tablespoon honey
2 teaspoons chopped fresh dill
2 teaspoons fresh lemon juice
4 (6-ounce) sustainable salmon fillets
Cooking spray

1. Preheat oven to 400°.
2. Combine cauliflower, oil, ¼ teaspoon pepper, and ⅛ teaspoon salt on a baking sheet; toss to coat. Bake at 400° for 25 minutes or until lightly browned, stirring after 10 minutes.
3. Combine mustard, honey, dill, and juice in a small bowl. Arrange fillets, skin sides down, on a foil-lined baking sheet coated with cooking spray; sprinkle with ¼ teaspoon pepper and ⅛ teaspoon salt. Spread mustard mixture evenly over fillets. Bake at 400° for 17 minutes or until desired degree of doneness. Serve fillets with cauliflower. Serves 4 (serving size: 1 fillet and about ¼ cup cauliflower)

CALORIES 371; **FAT** 16.9g (sat 3.1g, mono 8.1g, poly 4g); **PROTEIN** 39g; **CARB** 15g; **FIBER** 3g; **CHOL** 90mg; **IRON** 1mg; **SODIUM** 519mg; **CALC** 54mg

continued

Kid Friendly • Quick & Easy
Make Ahead • Gluten Free
Buttery Lentils with Shallots
Place ⅔ cup dried petite green lentils
in a medium saucepan. Cover with
water to 3 inches above lentils; bring
to a boil. Reduce heat, and simmer
20 minutes or until lentils are tender.
Drain. Heat a large skillet over medium heat. Add 1 tablespoon butter;
swirl until butter melts. Add ½ cup
chopped shallots; sauté 2 minutes.
Add lentils, 2 tablespoons chopped
fresh flat-leaf parsley, 1 teaspoon
chopped fresh thyme, ¼ teaspoon
kosher salt, and ¼ teaspoon freshly
ground black pepper; toss. Serves 4
(serving size: about ½ cup)

CALORIES 154; FAT 3.3g (sat 1.9g); SODIUM 151mg

Kid Friendly • Quick & Easy
Make Ahead • Gluten Free

Chicken with Citrus Sauce and Quinoa

with Coriander Carrots

**1¾ cups unsalted chicken stock (such
as Swanson), divided**
**¾ cup uncooked quinoa, rinsed and
drained**
⅓ cup chopped fresh cilantro
1 teaspoon grated lime rind, divided
⅜ teaspoon kosher salt, divided
1 tablespoon olive oil
**4 (6-ounce) skinless, boneless
chicken breast halves**
**¼ teaspoon freshly ground black
pepper**
¼ cup fresh orange juice
2 tablespoons fresh lime juice
2 teaspoons honey
1 tablespoon butter

1. Combine 1¼ cups stock and
quinoa in a medium saucepan; bring
to a boil. Reduce heat; cover and
simmer 15 minutes or until quinoa
is tender and liquid is absorbed. Stir
in cilantro, ½ teaspoon rind, and ⅛
teaspoon salt.
2. Heat a large skillet over medium-
high heat. Add oil to pan; swirl to
coat. Sprinkle chicken with ¼ teaspoon salt and pepper. Add chicken
to pan; cook 5 minutes on each side
or until done. Remove chicken from
pan. Add ½ cup stock to pan; cook
1 minute, scraping pan to loosen
browned bits. Stir in ½ teaspoon rind,
orange juice, lime juice, and honey;
simmer 2 minutes or until thickened
slightly. Stir in butter. Return chicken
to pan; turn to coat. Serve chicken
with quinoa. Serves 4 (serving size:
1 chicken breast half, about 2 tablespoons sauce, and ½ cup quinoa)

CALORIES 398; FAT 12.6g (sat 3.5g, mono 5g, poly 2.2g);
PROTEIN 43g; CARB 26g; FIBER 2g; CHOL 116mg;
IRON 2mg; SODIUM 462mg; CALC 37mg

Kid Friendly • Quick & Easy
Make Ahead • Gluten Free
Coriander Carrots
Crush 1 teaspoon whole coriander
seeds with a heavy skillet. Heat a
large skillet over medium heat. Add
coriander; cook 30 seconds or until
toasted. Add 1 pound diagonally cut
carrots (about 3 cups), ¼ cup water,
and 1 tablespoon butter to pan.
Reduce heat to medium-low; cover
and cook 10 minutes or until carrots
are crisp-tender. Sprinkle with ¼
teaspoon kosher salt and ¼ teaspoon
freshly ground black pepper. Cook,
uncovered, 3 minutes or until liquid
evaporates. Serves 4 (serving size:
about ⅔ cup)

CALORIES 74; FAT 3.2g (sat 1.9g); SODIUM 224mg

FLAVOR HIT

Whole coriander seeds have a floral,
citrusy flavor. Crush and toast the seeds
to bring out their nutty earthiness.

LEFTOVER LUNCH

Make a tasty wrap with leftover quinoa:
Spread hummus over a whole-grain flatbread. Top with spinach, sliced bell pepper, quinoa, and feta; roll up.

READY IN
35
MINUTES

SHOPPING LIST

**Chicken with Citrus Sauce and
Quinoa**

Lime (1)
Orange (1)
Fresh cilantro
Olive oil
Honey
Unsalted chicken stock (such as
Swanson)
Quinoa
Skinless, boneless chicken breast halves
(1½ pounds)
Butter

Coriander Carrots

Carrots (1 pound)
Whole coriander seeds
Butter

GAME PLAN

While quinoa cooks:
■ Prepare carrots.
While carrots cook:
■ Cook chicken.

Ginger-Soy Pork Loin Sandwiches

with Radish and Carrot Slaw

2 tablespoons lower-sodium soy sauce
1 tablespoon rice vinegar
1 teaspoon brown sugar
1 teaspoon minced fresh garlic
1 teaspoon grated peeled fresh ginger
1 pound boneless center-cut pork loin, cut into ¼-inch-thick slices
Cooking spray
1 (12-ounce) French bread loaf, halved lengthwise and cut into fourths
¼ cup canola mayonnaise
2 teaspoons hoisin sauce
4 romaine lettuce leaves
24 slices English cucumber
1 small jalapeño pepper, seeded and thinly sliced

1. Combine first 5 ingredients in a medium bowl, stirring with a whisk. Add pork, turning to coat. Let stand 10 minutes.
2. Heat a grill pan over high heat. Coat pan with cooking spray. Arrange half of pork on pan; grill 1½ minutes on each side or until done. Remove pork from pan. Repeat procedure with remaining pork. Hollow out top and bottom halves of bread, leaving a 1-inch-thick shell; reserve torn bread for another use. Combine mayonnaise and hoisin in a small bowl. Spread mayonnaise mixture evenly over top halves of bread. Arrange lettuce over bottom halves of bread; top evenly with pork, cucumber, and jalapeño. Top with top halves of bread. Serves 4 (serving size: 1 sandwich)

CALORIES 372; **FAT** 11.3g (sat 2.1g, mono 4.6g, poly 2.5g); **PROTEIN** 29g; **CARB** 37g; **FIBER** 2g; **CHOL** 66mg; **IRON** 3mg; **SODIUM** 748mg; **CALC** 56mg

---

Gluten Free
Radish and Carrot Slaw

Combine 2 tablespoons fresh lime juice, 2 teaspoons fish sauce, and 1½ teaspoons sugar in a large bowl, stirring with a whisk. Add 2 cups matchstick-cut carrots, 1 cup shredded radishes, and ¼ cup chopped fresh cilantro; toss to coat. Serves 4 (serving size: about ½ cup)

CALORIES 38; **FAT** 0.2g (sat 0g); **SODIUM** 244mg

READY IN
30
MINUTES

SHOPPING LIST

Ginger-Soy Pork Loin Sandwiches

Romaine lettuce
English cucumber (1 medium)
Jalapeño (1)
Ginger
Garlic
Lower-sodium soy sauce
Rice vinegar
Hoisin sauce
Canola mayonnaise
Brown sugar
French bread loaf (12 ounces)
Boneless center-cut pork loin (1 pound)

Radish and Carrot Slaw

Lime (1)
Matchstick-cut carrots (2 cups)
Radishes
Fresh cilantro
Fish sauce
Sugar

GAME PLAN

While pork mixture stands:
■ Prepare radish and carrot slaw.
While pork grills:
■ Prepare hoisin mixture.

NUTRITION MADE EASY

LIGHTER CHOCOLATE GANACHE

No butter, no cream. Just pure-form silky-smooth chocolate.

Elegant and indulgently delicious, chocolate ganache wears many hats this time of year—as a decadent glaze over fluffy cake layers, a silky coating for fresh berries, or chilled and rolled into truffles. It's a simple combo of chocolate and heavy cream—but hefty, too: 80 calories and 3.8g sat fat per tablespoon.

What we've recently learned from a few of our chocolate aficionados is that all that cream (and sometimes butter!) actually alters the taste of the chocolate in pure form. Replace it with water, and you'll end up with a more intense chocolate flavor, a glossy-smooth texture, and a ganache with 40% less sat fat than one made with heavy cream. For tastiest results, use high-quality chocolate, and sprinkle with a dash of sea salt for a more complex chocolate experience.

The Recipe

Combine 8 ounces high-quality bittersweet chocolate and 4 fluid ounces water in the top of a double boiler. Cook over simmering water until smooth (about 10 minutes), stirring frequently with a whisk. Remove from heat; let stand 15 minutes. For a thicker glaze, add less water. Serves 22 (serving size: 1 tablespoon)

CALORIES 60; **FAT** 4g (sat 2.3g); **SODIUM** 6mg

NUTRITIONAL INFORMATION

What the Numbers Mean For You

Glance at the end of any *Cooking Light* recipe, and you'll see how committed we are to helping you make the best of today's light cooking. With chefs, registered dietitians, home economists, and a computer system that analyzes every ingredient we use, *Cooking Light* gives you authoritative dietary detail like no other magazine. We go to such lengths so you can see how our recipes fit into your healthful eating plan. If you're trying to lose weight, the calorie and fat figures will probably help most. But if you're keeping a close eye on the sodium, cholesterol, and saturated fat in your diet, we provide those numbers, too. And because many women don't get enough iron or calcium, we can help there, as well. Finally, there's a fiber analysis for those of us who don't get enough roughage.

Here's a helpful guide to put our nutritional analysis numbers into perspective. Remember, one size doesn't fit all, so take your lifestyle, age, and circumstances into consideration when determining your nutrition needs. For example, pregnant or breast-feeding women need more protein, calories, and calcium. And women older than 50 need 1,200mg of calcium daily, 200mg more than the amount recommended for younger women.

IN OUR NUTRITIONAL ANALYSIS, WE USE THESE ABBREVIATIONS

sat	saturated fat	**CHOL**	cholesterol
mono	monounsaturated fat	**CALC**	calcium
poly	polyunsaturated fat	**g**	gram
CARB	carbohydrates	**mg**	milligram

Daily Nutrition Guide

	WOMEN ages 25 to 50	WOMEN over 50	MEN ages 25 to 50	MEN over 50
CALORIES	2,000	2,000*	2,700	2,500
PROTEIN	50g	50g	63g	60g
FAT	65g*	65g*	88g*	83g*
SATURATED FAT	20g*	20g*	27g*	25g*
CARBOHYDRATES	304g	304g	410g	375g
FIBER	25g to 35g	25g to 35g	25g to 35g	25g to 35g
CHOLESTEROL	300mg*	300mg*	300mg*	300mg*
IRON	18mg	8mg	8mg	8mg
SODIUM	2,300mg*	1,500mg*	2,300mg*	1,500mg*
CALCIUM	1,000mg	1,200mg	1,000mg	1,000mg

NUTRITIONAL VALUES USED IN OUR CALCULATIONS EITHER COME FROM THE FOOD PROCESSOR, VERSION 10.4 (ESHA RESEARCH) OR ARE PROVIDED BY FOOD MANUFACTURERS. *Or less, for optimum health.

METRIC EQUIVALENTS

The information in the following charts is provided to help cooks outside the United States successfully use the recipes in this book. All equivalents are approximate.

Cooking/Oven Temperatures

	Fahrenheit	Celsius	Gas Mark
Freeze Water	32° F	0° C	
Room Temp.	68° F	20° C	
Boil Water	212° F	100° C	
Bake	325° F	160° C	3
	350° F	180° C	4
	375° F	190° C	5
	400° F	200° C	6
	425° F	220° C	7
	450° F	230° C	8
Broil			Grill

Liquid Ingredients by Volume

¼ tsp	=						1 ml
½ tsp	=						2 ml
1 tsp	=						5 ml
3 tsp	=	1 tbl	=	½ fl oz	=		15 ml
2 tbls	=	⅛ cup	=	1 fl oz	=		30 ml
4 tbls	=	¼ cup	=	2 fl oz	=		60 ml
5⅓ tbls	=	⅓ cup	=	3 fl oz	=		80 ml
8 tbls	=	½ cup	=	4 fl oz	=		120 ml
10⅔ tbls	=	⅔ cup	=	5 fl oz	=		160 ml
12 tbls	=	¾ cup	=	6 fl oz	=		180 ml
16 tbls	=	1 cup	=	8 fl oz	=		240 ml
1 pt	=	2 cups	=	16 fl oz	=		480 ml
1 qt	=	4 cups	=	32 fl oz	=		960 ml
				33 fl oz	=	1000 ml	= 1 l

Dry Ingredients by Weight

(To convert ounces to grams, multiply the number of ounces by 30.)

1 oz	=	¹⁄₁₆ lb	=		30g
4 oz	=	¼ lb	=		120g
8 oz	=	½ lb	=		240g
12 oz	=	¾ lb	=		360g
16 oz	=	1 lb	=		480g

Length

(To convert inches to centimeters, multiply the number of inches by 2.5.)

1 in	=					2.5 cm
6 in	=	½ ft			=	15 cm
12 in	=	1 ft			=	30 cm
36 in	=	3 ft	=	1 yd	=	90 cm
40 in	=					100 cm = 1 m

Equivalents for Different Types of Ingredients

Standard Cup	Fine Powder (ex. flour)	Grain (ex. rice)	Granular (ex. sugar)	Liquid Solids (ex. butter)	Liquid (ex. milk)
1	140g	150g	190g	200g	240 ml
¾	105g	113g	143g	150g	180 ml
⅔	93g	100g	125g	133g	160 ml
½	70g	75g	95g	100g	120 ml
⅓	47g	50g	63g	67g	80 ml
¼	35g	38g	48g	50g	60 ml
⅛	18g	19g	24g	25g	30 ml

MENU INDEX

A topical guide to all the menus that appear in *Cooking Light Annual Recipes 2015.*

DINNER TONIGHT

25-Minute Dinners

FISH & SHELLFISH

Shrimp Marinara Soup with Crumbled Feta and Simple Salad (page 131) *serves 4*

Glazed Salmon with Couscous and Haricots Verts (page 131) *serves 4*

Grilled Shrimp with Miso-Ginger Sauce and Cucumber and Shaved Carrot Salad (page 160) *serves 4*

Coconut-Curry Salmon with Brown Basmati Rice and Sautéed Sesame Snow Peas (page 298) *serves 4*

PORK

Cheesy Skillet Gnocchi with Grape and Hazelnut Salad (page 300) *serves 4*

POULTRY

Greek-Style Chicken Breasts with Herbed Gold Potatoes (page 130) *serves 4*

Moroccan Chicken Salad Pitas with Orange-Carrot Salad (page 133) *serves 4*

30-Minute Dinners

BEEF

Smoky Steak Fajitas with Avocado and Tomato Salad (page 354) *serves 4*

FISH & SHELLFISH

Seared Salmon Filets with Orzo Pilaf and Garlic Broccolini (page 66) *serves 4*

PORK

Pork Tenderloin with Cannellini Beans and Arugula Salad (page 100) *serves 4*

Spinach and Ham Stuffed Baked Potatoes with Apple and Almond Salad (page 271) *serves 4*

Ginger-Soy Pork Loin Sandwiches with Radish and Carrot Slaw (page 387) *serves 4*

POULTRY

Peach-Glazed Chicken and Peach–Studded Bulgur with Arugula, Tomato, and Almond Salad (page 161) *serves 4*

Chicken and Bell Pepper Sauté with Lemony Kale Quinoa (page 299) *serves 4*

VEGETARIAN

Caprese Mac and Cheese with Chopped Tricolor Salad (page 268) *serves 4*

35-Minute Dinners

BEEF

Picadillo Sloppy Joes with Spinach and Parmesan Salad (page 41) *serves 6*

Charred Flank Steak with Grilled Tomato Bruschetta with Tarragon Green Beans (page 158) *serves 4*

London Broil with Chimichurri with Grilled Pepper, Onion, and Blue Cheese Salad (page 187) *serves 4*

Ginger Steak with Sesame Brown Rice and Chili-Basil Slaw (page 269) *serves 4*

Bruschetta Burgers with Spiced Oven Fries (page 355) *serves 4*

FISH & SHELLFISH

Browned Butter Flounder with Snap Peas and Brown Rice Pilaf (page 40) *serves 4*

Crab Cakes with Buttermilk Ranch Dressing and Orzo Salad (page 100) *serves 4*

Shrimp-Mango Stir-Fry with Rice Noodles and Cucumber Salad (page 101) *serves 4*

Tortellini with Snap Peas and Pesto with Radiccio Caesar Salad (page 133) *serves 4*

Seared Tilapia with Pineapple Salsa and Tomato-Avocado Salad with Black Bean–Cilantro Rice (page 159) *serves 4*

Catfish with Corn Hash with Heirloom Tomato and Zucchini Salad (page 186) *serves 4*

Olive and Pesto–Crusted Cod with Summer Bread Salad (page 245) *serves 4*

Baked Cod with Feta and Tomatoes with Lemon-Orange Orzo (page 355) *serves 4*

Mustard-Glazed Salmon Fillets with Roasted Cauliflower and Buttery Lentils with Shallots (page 385) *serves 4*

LAMB

Lamb and Butternut Squash Stew with Roasted Cauliflower with Pine Nuts (page 299) *serves 6*

PORK

Pork Tenderloin Paprikash with Egg Noodles and Apple Salad (page 37) *serves 4*

POULTRY

Coconut Chicken Strips with Basmati Rice and Broccolini (page 102) *serves 4*

Turkey Pitas with Tahini-Yogurt Sauce and Chopped Romaine Salad (page 184) *serves 4*

Chicken Stir-Fry with Peanut Sauce with Coconut-Cilantro Rice (page 353) *serves 4*

Chicken with Citrus Sauce and Lime-Cilantro Quinoa with Coriander Carrots (page 386) *serves 4*

VEGETARIAN

Farfalle with Butternut Squash and Sage with Browned Butter and Lemon Brussels Sprouts (page 353) *serves 6*

40-Minute Dinners

BEEF

Hearty Beef and Stout Stew with Kale Mashed Potatoes (page 39) *serves 4*

Flank Steak Tacos with Slaw and Sweet Potato–Black Bean Salad (page 66) *serves 4*

Beef and Bell Pepper Kebabs with Mushroom-Ginger Noodles (page 245) *serves 4*

Steak Pizzaiola with Herb-Roasted Potatoes with Balsamic Broccoli Rabe (page 385) *serves 4*

FISH & SHELLFISH

Tilapia and Fennel-Yogurt Sauce with Red Pepper Couscous and Shaved Carrot Salad (page 270) *serves 4*

PORK

Paprika Pork Chops with Zucchini and Grilled Corn with Lime (page 186) *serves 4*

Honey-Glazed Pork Chops with Tomato Salad and Corn Cakes (page 246) *serves 4*

POULTRY

Stuffed Chicken & Herb Gravy with Polenta and Green Beans (page 38) *serves 4*

Chicken Kebabs with Cucumber Noodles and Sesame-Carrot Salad (page 67) *serves 4*

Hazelnut Chicken with Roasted Squash and Wilted Spinach (page 68) *serves 4*

Turkey Meatball Subs with Skillet-Blistered Green Beans (page 69) *serves 4*

Chicken Posole with Corn Bread Muffins and Avocado Salad (page 99) *serves 4*

Chipotle Chicken with Coriander Rice and Simple Salad with Parmesan (page 185) *serves 4*

Chicken Schnitzel with Smashed Mustard Potatoes and Apple, Fennel, and Celery Slaw (page 247) *serves 4*

Dijon-Herb Chicken Thighs with Tomato-Basil Bread Salad (page 269) *serves 4*

VEGETARIAN

Summer Veggie Salad with Green Onion and Dill Quinoa (page 160) *serves 4*

Vegetable Hash and Poached Eggs with Multigrain Toast and Red Red Pepper Tapenade (page 244) *serves 4*

Eggplant and Zucchini Parmesan with Lemon-Parsley Pasta (page 297) *serves 4*

Swiss Chard and White Bean Soup with Poached Eggs with Garlic-Parmesan Toasts (page 384) *serves 4*

ONE COOLER, ONE WEEKEND

Orange, Pumpkin Seed, and Smoked Almond Granola (page 178) *serves 4*

Multipurpose Vinaigrette (page 179) *serves 8*

Mojito Cooler (page 179) *serves 4*

Pancetta-Wrapped Pork Tenderloin (page 179) *serves 4*

Cantaloupe-Red Pepper Salsa (page 179) *serves 4*

Shaved Zucchini and Parsley Salad (page 179) *serves 4*

Orange, Pumpkin Seed, and Smoked Almond Granola with Greek Yogurt (page 180) *serves 4*

Figgy Pork Tenderloin Sandwiches (page 180) *serves 4*

Yogurt "Romesco" Dip (page 180) *serves 4*

Grilled Romaine Hearts with Pepper (page 181) *serves 4*

Grilled Vegetable Pizzas with Anchovies (page 181) *serves 4*

Cantaloupe Granita (page 181) *serves 4*

Farro Salad with Cherry Tomato, Onion, and Almonds (page 182) *serves 4*

FRIDAY NIGHTS LIGHT!

THE CHILI BAR

Five-Bean Chili (page 259) *serves 8*

Cheese Corn Bread Croutons (page 259) *serves 12*

Toasted Corn and Tomato Chili Topping (page 260) *serves 6*

THE STUFFED POTATO BAR

Perfect Roasted Sweet Potatoes (page 260) *serves 6*

Cheddar, Broccoli, and Barley Sweet Potatoes (page 260) *serves 6*

Sweet Potatoes with Cinnamon Chicken and Cashews (page 260) *serves 6*

THE TACO BAR

Lemon-Pepper Flank Steak Tacos (page 261) *serves 6*

Cabbage and Mango Slaw (page 261) *serves 6*

Smoky Tilapia Tacos (page 261) *serves 6*

Simmered Pinto Beans with Chipotle Sour Cream (page 262) *serves 6*

WINE & DINE DINNER MENU

Chicken-Phyllo Turnovers (page 369) *serves 12*

Golden Beet Soup with Toasted Grains (page 369) *serves 6*

Leg of Lamb with Olive-Wine Sauce (page 370) *serves 6*

Harissa-Roasted Carrots (page 370) *serves 6*

Sesame-Steamed Eggplant (page 370) *serves 6*

Pomegranate-Orange Tart with Pistachio Shortbread Crust (page 371) *serves 12*

RECIPE TITLE INDEX

An alphabetical listing of every recipe title that appeared in the magazine in 2014.
See page 394 for the General Recipe Index.

GENERAL RECIPE INDEX

A listing by major ingredient and food category for every recipe that appeared in the magazine in 2014.